FENG SHUI

FENG SHUI

MIND & BODY & SPIRIT & HOME

CONTROL AND ENHANCE THE ENERGIES OF YOUR HOUSE, GARDEN, AND
INNER SELF BY UNDERSTANDING AND USING PROVEN ANCIENT TECHNIQUES

Gill Hale and Mark Evans

HERMES HOUSE

This edition is published by Hermes House

Hermes House is an imprint of Anness Publishing Ltd
Hermes House, 88–89 Blackfriars Road, London SE1 8HA
tel. 020 7401 2077; fax 020 7633 9499; info@anness.com

A CIP catalogue record for this book is available from the British Library.

Publisher: Joanna Lorenz
Editorial Director: Helen Sudell
Executive Editor: Joanne Rippin
Project Editor: Emma Gray
Photographs: John Freeman, Michelle Garrett, Alistair Hughes,
    Don Last, Lucy Mason and Debbie Patterson
Designers: Nigel Partridge, Balley Design Associates
Jacket Design: Peter Ridley
Production Controller: Pedro Nelson
Editorial Reader: Lindsay Zamponi

Previously published as two separate volumes: *The Complete Guide to Feng Shui* by Gill Hale
and *Mind, Body, Spirit*, contributing Editor Mark Evans

10 9 8 7 6 5 4 3 2 1

CONTENTS

INTRODUCTION 6

THE PRINCIPLES OF FENG SHUI 12

Feng Shui in the Home 36
The Outside World 38
Inside the Home 52
Putting the Principles into
    Practice 88

THE FENG SHUI GARDEN 134

Feng Shui Principles in the
    Garden 136
Garden Features 160
Creating the Garden 174

THE FENG SHUI OFFICE 198

External Factors 200
The Working Office 214
Office Energies and
    Personalities 242

NATURAL HEALING 258

Herbalism 260
Homeopathy 280
Ayurveda 306

THE POWER OF TOUCH 334

Massage 336
Aromatherapy 358
Shiatsu 378
Reflexology 400

THE PATH TO INNER HARMONY 424

Alexander Technique 426
T'ai Chi 444
Yoga Stretches 472
Meditation 488

USEFUL ADDRESSES 500

GLOSSARY 504

INDEX 506

PICTURE ACKNOWLEDGEMENTS 512

INTRODUCTION

Life in the modern Western world, for all its comfort, sophistication and prosperity, does not guarantee happiness, health or fulfilment. Our frantic existence often leaves too little time to relate to each other or to the natural world, and we cannot thrive in such isolation. We may even be too busy to listen to the needs of our own bodies, as we struggle with rising stress levels and chronic illness. When we recognize the problem and begin to search for the sense of integration lacking in modern life, the wisdom of previous generations can often help us towards it.

The philosophical traditions of the East particularly emphasize humanity's interdependence with the rest of the universe. In Taoist theory everything is seen as an integral part of the same system. So while everything that happens in the universe affects us, everything we do has an effect, however slight, on the system as a whole: nothing is separate. In recent years we have come to understand the need for a holistic approach to our own health – that physical, mental and spiritual health are all interdependent. The origins of the word "health" are linked

▲ *Use the principles of Feng Shui to turn your home into a tranquil sanctuary to restore your soul.*

with those of wholeness and healing, and it is that complete sense of harmony, of being whole, that brings true health. By extending this understanding to embrace the world in which we live, we can seek to achieve a similar sense of harmony with our environment.Feng Shui is an environmental science that follows the principles of Taoism, and its origins are simple. It is based on an interpretation of the natural world that enabled the Chinese to create efficient agricultural systems, though over centuries it grew more complex and was removed from its original purpose. As its exponents spread out from China across the world, they adapted their theories to fit into local beliefs and customs.

In essence, all societies retain the knowledge contained in Feng Shui, but it has become absorbed into different disciplines. In China it underlies all aspects of life, from nutrition and medicine to exercise and the arts. By understanding its basic concepts, we can choose designs, images and symbols from our own culture to bring harmony into our lives.

As practised today, Feng Shui gives us advice on how to create environments in which we feel comfortable and supported. Some of this is common sense, while other aspects may not make sense until we understand that by recognizing problem areas in our lives and taking positive steps to improve them, we can connect to the energy of the spaces around us and bring about the changes we desire.

There is much discussion about the correct way to practise Feng Shui in the West. Should we stick strictly to what is now called Traditional Chinese Feng Shui or should we allow for other interpretations? Have we adapted the term

▶ *Spiky orange tapers set against soft, rounded shapes help to balance yin/yang energy in a room.*

to mean something else for us? This book aims to set what we have come to understand as Feng Shui in context and, by using modern examples alongside ancient ones, explore its basic principles.

In the present age, concern for our environment and an awareness of the damage we inflict on it must form part of Feng Shui. We have reached a stage where the human race has become capable of the most amazing feats on the one hand and the most amazing follies on the other. Modern lifestyles leave little

▶ Gentle aromatherapy treatments such as this hot compress can calm minor ailments and aid relaxation.

time to stop and consider the effect our surroundings have on us. There is increasing awareness that some aspects of modern technology, the materials we use and the substances we release into the atmosphere can create lasting damage to our health and to the planet. We have the capacity to cure hereditary diseases, but also to let genetically engineered organisms loose into the environment in the most dangerous form of

warfare humankind has ever known. We send people into space to collect information never dreamed of half a century ago, yet at the same time we allow the planet we inhabit to become increasingly polluted

◀ Colour in the home can have a profound influence on mood: yellow is optimistic and stimulates the brain.

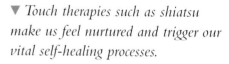

▼ Touch therapies such as shiatsu make us feel nurtured and trigger our vital self-healing processes.

◀ *Mirrors make small spaces seem larger and lighter, and are used to "cure" many problems in Feng Shui.*

▲ *Displays of fresh flowers and fruit energize your home with the vibrancy of the natural world.*

and less able to sustain the life forms on which we depend for our survival. These anomalies of modern living are becoming increasingly destructive, and more and more people are turning to different approaches to living in order to attempt to redress the balance. Feng Shui offers us the opportunity to achieve health, happiness and well-being through living in harmony with our environment.

The first section of this book aims to interpret the principles of Feng Shui for modern times. While it cannot teach the interpretative skills

◄ *The harmonious sounds of wind chimes are soothing and refreshing, and they are often used in Feng Shui to slow down fast-moving energy.*

and the unwelcome side-effects of allopathic medicine. At the same time, traditional Western forms of treatment such as herbalism and massage have become increasingly popular. Therapies involving touch – a primal requirement that is sadly neglected in today's world – have a vital role to play in banishing the feelings of separation and isolation that beset us. Daily meditation practice refreshes the spirit and fosters a sense of integration with the universe, as well as aiding relaxation.

The holistic approach to health seeks to embrace life rather than dissect illness, and one of the strengths

▼ *Traditional herbal remedies have a gentle action, and preparing them helps us to connect with the natural world.*

and understanding that professional practitioners acquire with many years of study and practice, it can give an insight into ways in which we can create nurturing and life-enhancing spaces in our homes, gardens and offices.

The second part of the book turns to our search for inner harmony, introducing a wide range of natural therapies and energy work that can help to reduce stress, calm the mind and strengthen the body. All these systems of natural healing adopt a holistic view, rather than the reductionist perspective that prevails in

much of conventional modern medicine, which seeks to cure diseases by treating the physical symptoms they give rise to in isolation from the system as a whole.

Eastern cultures such as those of China and India have retained a strong tradition of therapies aimed at balancing energy. They regard all parts of the body as interconnected and infused with vital energy. In recent years there has been a surge of interest in these therapies in the West, both in recognition of their effectiveness and as a move away from the rather impersonal approach

▲ *The bedroom is one of the most important rooms in the home, and should be a haven of relaxation.*

▲ *The beneficial effects of massage extend beyond the physical relief it brings. While its caring touch helps to release tense muscles, it also promotes relaxation and increases well-being by stimulating the body's release of endorphins.*

of natural therapies is their role in preventing the onset of ill-health, rather than waiting until illness occurs and then treating it, though there are many ways in which natural therapies can be used as self-help remedies for a variety of common complaints.

It is recognized that one of the major factors affecting our health these days is stress, and nearly everyone has felt its grasp at some time. Our systems are always striving to achieve a state of equilibrium, but the body's balancing, adaptive energy is constantly challenged by the stresses and strains we all face. If you

▶ *Use essential oils singly or in simple combinations to create mood-changing massage oils or bath essences.*

are under pressure for a long time its cumulative impact may mean that eventually you cannot go on coping, and illness may result as your body takes the strain. By reducing the impact of stress on your system,

natural treatments work to restore your vital energy. The therapies outlined in this book will help you to create havens of calm and harmony to help you cope with all the demands of daily life.

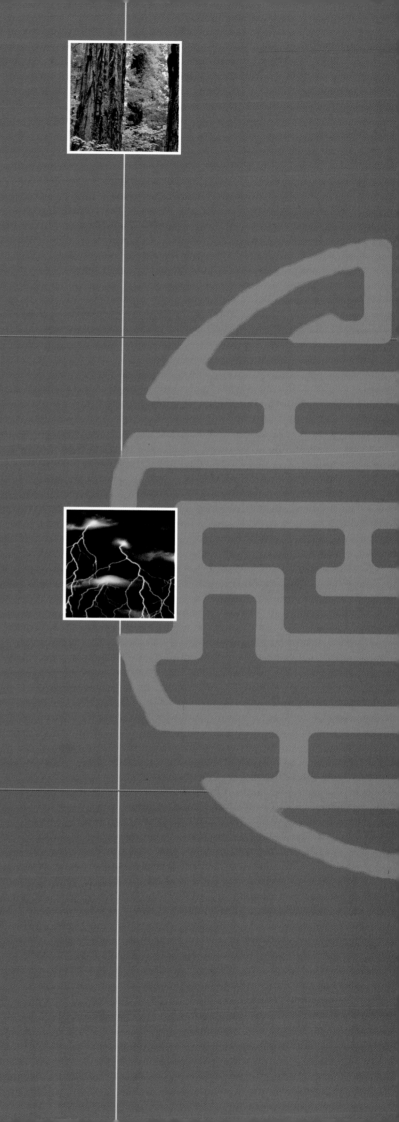
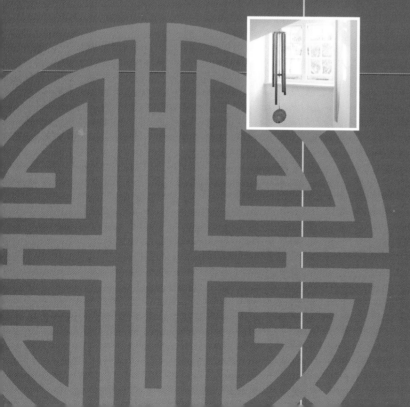

THE PRINCIPLES OF FENG SHUI

BEFORE YOU BEGIN TO APPLY FENG SHUI, IT IS
IMPORTANT TO HAVE SOME UNDERSTANDING
OF THE THEORY AND PRINCIPLES THAT LIE
BEHIND IT. THIS SECTION OF THE BOOK
EXPLAINS CLEARLY AND SIMPLY THE PHILOSOPHY
OF THIS ANCIENT ART.

WHAT IS FENG SHUI?

The Chinese have a saying, "First, luck; second, destiny; third, Feng Shui; fourth, virtues; fifth, education": although Feng Shui can be a powerful force in shaping our lives, it is not a cure for all ills. Luck plays a major role, and personality, or karma, is almost as important. What we do with our lives and how we behave towards others will play a part, and education gives us the tools to make sense of the world. Feng Shui is just one part of the complete package.

▲ *In China the dragon symbolizes good fortune. Its presence is felt in landforms and watercourses.*

▲ *The Dragon Hills which protect Hong Kong are believed to be responsible for its prosperity.*

The single factor which sets Feng Shui apart from other philosophical systems is that it has the capacity for change built into it. Most systems evolved from similar principles; understanding the natural world played a major role and natural phenomena were believed to be imbued with a spirit or deity, recognition of which would give people some benefit in their lives. Where these systems became established as religions, the deities were worshipped, but Feng Shui has remained a philosophy and can be used in any culture and alongside any belief system.

▶ *Much of the symbolic imagery in Feng Shui is taken from landscapes such as this in Guilin, southern China.*

Feng Shui uses formulae which determine the rising and falling energy in a given time span of an individual or a house. Other formulae indicate a person's best location within a home or office, and can suggest the best placing of beds and desks. Many Chinese people consult astrologers annually to further refine this, so that every activity within the year can be pinpointed accurately and undertaken at an auspicious time. This can be as precise as the best time to conceive or even when to wash your hair.

The philosophy of Feng Shui is embraced by people who are aware of the impact their surroundings have on them and feel the need to take action to improve their lives, but using Feng Shui correctly is a skill and its principles cannot be adapted simply to suit the circumstances of a place or an individual.

▼ *Our surroundings affect us. Fresh air, natural products and a healthy environment enhance our mental and physical well-being.*

Feng Shui enables us to position ourselves within our environment to our best advantage. The positioning of our houses and offices as well as their internal design affects each of us positively or negatively. Feng Shui helps us to determine the most favourable positions for us and the layouts, colours and designs which will support us. In the garden we can determine the best locations for the different activities we intend to pursue there, but we also have to take account of the plants in the garden and their needs, which are equally important if the environment is to thrive.

▲ *Water energy plays a significant role in Feng Shui. Here a fountain brings life to an office courtyard.*

The following chapters provide information on those aspects of this complex and fascinating subject that can be utilized by everyone in their own space. When we introduce Feng Shui into our lives we can only benefit, even where we only touch the surface. As we become more aware of our surroundings, and actively begin to change those factors with which we feel uncomfortable, we begin to gain a deeper insight into ourselves and our part in the wider picture.

▼ *The T'ung Shui almanac, produced for centuries, details the best times to move house, conceive and even wash your hair.*

APPROACHES TO FENG SHUI

Feng Shui is about interpreting environments. Practitioners use a number of different approaches to connect with the energy or "feel" of a place, and fine-tune it to make it work for those living or working there. Provided the principles are understood, the different approaches will be effective. More often than not, practitioners use a mixture of methods to create the effects they want.

THE ENVIRONMENTAL APPROACH

In ancient times, people lived by their wits and knowledge of local conditions. Their needs were basic: food and shelter. Observation would tell them from which direction the prevailing winds were coming and they would build their homes in protective sites. They needed water in order to grow and transport their crops so rivers were important, and the direction of the flow and the orientation of the banks would determine the type of crops which could be grown. This branch of Feng Shui is known as the Form or Landform School and was the earliest approach to the subject.

▼ *The Form School regards this as the ideal spot on which to build. The Black Tortoise hill at the rear offers support while the White Tiger and Green Dragon give protection from the wind, with the all-powerful dragon slightly higher than the Tiger. The Red Phoenix marks the front boundary, and the river irrigates the site and enables crops to be transported for trade.*

▲ *These "Karst" limestone hills in China symbolically protect an area of rich agricultural land.*

▶ *A luo pan or compass, used by geomancers in ancient China. Much of the information it records is regularly used by Feng Shui consultants.*

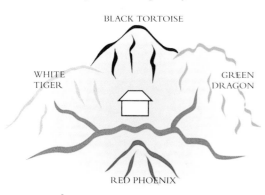

BLACK TORTOISE

WHITE TIGER

GREEN DRAGON

RED PHOENIX

THE COMPASS APPROACH

In ancient China, geomancers investigated earth formations and watercourses while astronomers charted the skies. Those who understood the power of the information they possessed recorded their knowledge on an instrument called a luo pan, or compass. The luo pan illustrates not only direction, but also investigates the energy of each direction, depending on the landform or heavenly body to be found there. Interpreting these energies suggests suitable sites for human beings. Feng Shui is based on the *I Ching*, a philosophical book which interprets the energies of the universe. Its 64 images from the yearly nature cycle form the outer ring of the luo pan. With the wisdom of ancient sages added to it over the centuries, the *I Ching* offers us a means to connect to the natural flow of the universe. Its built-in time factor allows individuals to connect to it in different ways at different times in their lives.

THE INTUITIVE APPROACH

Ancient texts illustrate every shape of mountain and watercourse. The names illustrate concepts significant to the Chinese psyche. "Tiger in Waiting" suggests a negative place, where residents will never be able to relax, whereas "Baby Dragon Looking at its Mother" indicates a much more restful environment.

The ancient text of the *Water Dragon Classic* provides more information on the best places to build, showing flow direction and position within the tributaries, with the names again indicating the type of environment. The sensibilities of people living and working on the land were finely tuned and their knowledge of the natural world endowed them with an instinct for suitable sites to grow crops.

▶ *Mountain sites (1 & 2) and river sites (3 & 4); the dots represent buildings. All except for "Tiger in Waiting" are auspicious positions to build a new home.*

▼ *This prime site is protected by mountains, with healthy watercourses.*

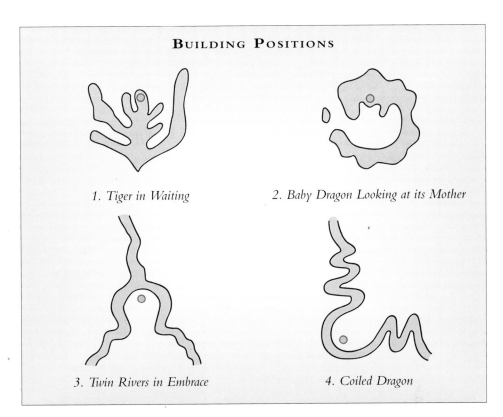

BUILDING POSITIONS

1. Tiger in Waiting

2. Baby Dragon Looking at its Mother

3. Twin Rivers in Embrace

4. Coiled Dragon

THE THEORY OF FENG SHUI

Ancient peoples regarded the heavens, the earth and themselves as part of one system. This holistic view of life persists in many cultures, where health and medicine, food and lifestyle, and the route to salvation are all interconnected in one ecological system.

THE WAY

The Tao, or the Way, the philosophy of which underlies Feng Shui, shows how to order our lives to live in harmony with ourselves, each other and the natural world. We can use Feng Shui to help us work towards achieving this.

▼ *"The Dragon Breathing on the Lake"* *– the lake is a powerful Chinese image, symbolizing a light-reflective surface harbouring a dark and deep interior.*

YIN AND YANG

Positive and negative forces act together in order to create energy – in electricity, for instance. Yin and yang represent these two forces which are in constant movement, each attempting to gain dominance. Where one achieves dominance, an imbalance occurs, so when one

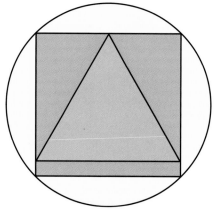

force becomes too strong its influence subsides and the other takes over. Still water, for example, is yin; a raging torrent is yang. Imagine a slow-moving yin river. When it hits rocks and descends, turbulence occurs, it speeds up and becomes yang. When it flows into a lake, it slows down and becomes yin once more. Yin and yang are opposing but interdependent concepts – without the idea of cold we would not be able to describe heat. At their extremes they

▲ *The T'ai Chi symbol illustrates the concept of yin and yang, the opposite yet interdependent forces that drive the world.*

◀ *Circle, Square, Triangle – signifying Heaven, Earth, human beings – the universal cosmological symbol.*

YIN	YANG
Moon	Sun
Winter	Summer
Dark	Light
Feminine	Masculine
Interior	Exterior
Low	High
Stillness	Movement
Passive	Active
Odd numbers	Even numbers
Earth	Heaven
Cold	Heat
Soft	Hard
Valleys	Hills
Still water	Mountains
Gardens	Houses
Sleep	Wakefulness

change into each other; ice can burn and sunstroke sufferers shiver. The aim is to achieve a balance between them. There are examples throughout the book of how we can achieve this in our own environments. Some of the more common associations are listed left.

CHI

Chi is a concept unknown in Western philosophy but figures repeatedly in the philosophies of the East. It is the life force of all animate things, the quality of environments, the power of the sun, the moon and weather systems, and the driving force in human beings. In China, the movements in T'ai Chi encourage chi to move through the body. Acupuncture needles are used to unblock its flow when stuck. Chinese herbal medicine uses the special energetic qualities of herbs to correct chi when it becomes unbalanced. Meditation helps to establish a healthy mind: every brush stroke of the Chinese artist or sweep of the calligrapher's pen is the result of trained mental processes and the correct breathing

▼ *An acupuncturist at work. The needles unblock the energy channels and enable chi to flow round the body.*

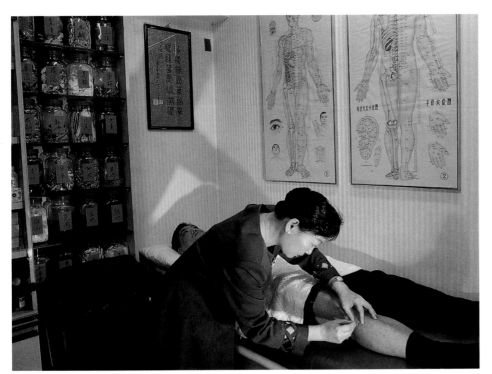

▲ *Chinese people practising T'ai Chi. The exercises are designed to aid the flow of chi in the body.*

techniques, which ensure that each carefully composed painting or document is infused with chi.

The purpose of Feng Shui is to create environments in which chi flows smoothly to achieve physical and mental health. Where chi flows gently through a house, the occupants will be positive and will have an easy passage through life. Where chi moves sluggishly or becomes stuck, then the chances are that problems will occur in the day-to-day life or long-term prospects of those living there.

Where chi flows smoothly in the garden, the plants will be healthy and the wildlife there will flourish. Animals, birds, insects and the myriad of unseen micro-organisms that live there will regulate themselves and create a balanced and supportive environment. Where chi cannot flow unimpeded and becomes sluggish or stuck, an area may become dank or there may be an imbalance which creates, say, a plague of aphids.

In an office where chi flows freely, employees will be happy and supportive, projects will be completed on time and stress levels will be low. Where the chi is stuck, there will be disharmony and the business will not flourish.

FIVE TYPES OF ENERGY

Some of the latest scientific theories enable us to make sense of the ancient formulae on which Feng Shui is based. It is accepted that everything in the universe vibrates. All our senses and everything we encounter are attuned to certain frequencies, which react with us in a positive or negative way. We are all familiar with sound waves, which bring us radio, and electromagnetic waves, which bring us television. Colours, shapes, food, weather conditions – everything in our lives affects us on a vibrational level for good or ill and, in turn, we react in various yet predictable ways, depending on our individual traits.

The concept of elements exists throughout the world. The Chinese recognize five which arise out of the interplay of yin and yang and represent different manifestations of chi. They represent a classification system for everything in the universe, including people, some of these are shown in the "Relationships of the Five Elements" table.

Ideally, there should be a balance of all the elements. Where one dominates or is lacking, then difficulties occur. Interpreting and balancing the elements plays a major part in the practice of Feng Shui. The elements move in a predetermined way, illustrated as a cycle in which they all support each other. A useful way of remembering this is by looking at the cycle in the following way. Water enables Wood to grow, Wood enables Fire to burn resulting in ashes or Earth, in which forms Metal, which in liquid

form resembles Water. Another cycle indicates how the elements control each other and can be memorized as follows: Water extinguishes Fire, and in turn is soaked up by the Earth, which is depleted of energy by Wood in the form of trees, which can be destroyed by Metal tools. the "Relationships of the Five Elements" table introduces another aspect – how in supporting another element, an element can itself be weakened. The applications of the five elements are illustrated throughout this book.

▲ *Storms are nature's way of restoring a balance. They replenish negative ions in the atmosphere, which improves air quality.*

▼ *The heavenly bodies are essential to our lives and their movements lie at the heart of Feng Shui.*

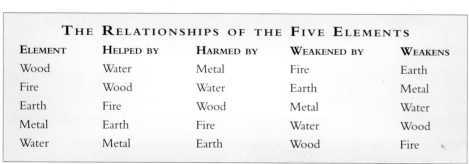

THE RELATIONSHIPS OF THE FIVE ELEMENTS				
ELEMENT	HELPED BY	HARMED BY	WEAKENED BY	WEAKENS
Wood	Water	Metal	Fire	Earth
Fire	Wood	Water	Earth	Metal
Earth	Fire	Wood	Metal	Water
Metal	Earth	Fire	Water	Wood
Water	Metal	Earth	Wood	Fire

THE FIVE ELEMENTS

ELEMENT	CHARACTERISTICS	PERSONALITIES	ASSOCIATIONS
WOOD 	Symbolizes spring, growth and plant life. In its yin form, it is supple and pliable, in its yang form as sturdy as an oak. Positively used, it is a walking stick; negatively used, a spear. Bamboo is cherished in China for its ability to sway in the wind yet be used as scaffolding. Viewed as a tree, Wood energy is expansive, nurturing and versatile.	Wood people are public-spirited and energetic. Ideas people, their outgoing personalities win them support. They visualize rather than committing themselves to plans. *Positively* – they are artistic and undertake tasks with enthusiasm. *Negatively* – they become impatient and angry and often fail to finish the tasks they have begun.	Trees and plants Wooden furniture Paper Green Columns Decking Landscape pictures
FIRE	Symbolizes summer, fire and heat. It can bring light, warmth and happiness or it can erupt, explode and destroy with great violence. Positively, it stands for honour and fairness. Negatively, it stands for aggression and war.	Fire people are leaders and crave action. They inspire others to follow, often into trouble, as they dislike rules and fail to see consequences. *Positively* – they are innovative, humorous and passionate people. *Negatively* – they are impatient, exploit others and have little thought for their feelings.	Sun symbols Candles, lights and lamps Triangles Red Man-made materials Sun or fire pictures
EARTH 	Symbolizes the nurturing environment that enables seeds to grow, which all living things emanate from and return to. It nurtures, supports and interacts with each of the other elements. Positively, it denotes fairness, wisdom and instinct. Negatively, it can smother or represent the nervous anticipation of non-existent problems.	Earth people are supportive and loyal. Practical and persevering, they are a tower of strength in a crisis. They do not rush anything, but their support is enduring. Patient and steady, they possess inner strength. *Positively* – earth people are loyal, dependable and patient. *Negatively* – they are obsessional and prone to nit-picking.	Clay, brick and terracotta Cement and stone Squares Yellow, orange and brown
METAL 	Symbolizes autumn and strength. Its nature represents solidity and the ability to contain objects. On the other hand, metal is also a conductor. Positively, it represents communication, brilliant ideas and justice. Negatively, it can suggest destruction, danger and sadness. Metal can be a beautiful and precious commodity, or the blade of a weapon.	Metal people are dogmatic and resolute. They pursue their ambitious aims single-mindedly. Good organizers, they are independent and happy in their own company. Faith in their own abilities inclines them towards inflexibility although they thrive on change. They are serious and do not accept help easily. *Positively* – they are strong, intuitive and interesting people. *Negatively* – they are inflexible, melancholic and serious.	All metals Round shapes Domes Metal objects Door furniture and doorsteps Kitchenware White, grey, silver and gold Coins Clocks
WATER 	Symbolizes winter and water itself, gentle rain or a storm. It suggests the inner self, art and beauty. It touches everything. Positively, it nurtures and supports with understanding. Negatively, it can wear down and exhaust. Associated with the emotions, it can suggest fear, nervousness and stress.	Water people communicate well. They are diplomatic and persuasive. Sensitive to the moods of others, they will lend an ear. They are intuitive and make excellent negotiators. Flexible and adaptable, they view things holistically. *Positively* – water people are artistic, sociable and sympathetic. *Negatively* – water people are sensitive, fickle and intrusive.	Rivers, streams and lakes Blue and black Mirrors and glass Meandering patterns Fountains and ponds Fish tanks Water pictures

CHINESE ASTROLOGY

An analysis of an environment using a luo pan compass looks at the energetic qualities of the various compass points. The Earthly Branches on the compass represent 12 of these points and also correspond to the 12 animals which relate to Chinese astrology. We often find ourselves in situations at home, or at work, when we canot understand how another person can view the same situation so differently from us, or can make us feel uncomfortable, or find different things irritating or amusing. Looking at the animals enables us to explore these differences by allowing us an insight into the make-up of our natures and personalities.

With this knowledge, we can come to know ourselves better and to accept the personalities of others. At home, it may encourage us to think twice, for instance, before launching into a tirade on tidiness or punctuality. It also has an important use in the workplace in keeping warring factions apart and ensuring a harmonious balance between productive output and socializing.

THE CYCLES

The Chinese calendar is based on the cycle of the moon, which determines that each month is approximately 29½ days long, beginning with a new moon. The years progress in cycles of 12 and it is helpful to appreciate the subtleties of Chinese symbology since each year is represented by an animal and the characteristics of each animal and its way of life are used to identify different types of people. Cultural differences are apt to get in the way if we attempt this identification ourselves; whereas Westerners would describe the Rat's character, for example, as sly and crafty, the Chinese respect its quick mind and native cunning.

◄ In the Chinese calendar each year is represented by an animal and each animal is governed by an element.

Each animal is governed by an element which determines its intrinsic nature. The cycle of 12 is repeated five times to form a larger cycle of 60 years and in each of these cycles, the animals are ascribed an element with either a yin or yang characteristic, which determines their characters. Thus in 60 years, no two animals are the same. We begin by investigating the basic animal characteristics.

THE NATURE OF THE ANIMALS

Rat	Water
Ox	Earth
Tiger	Wood
Rabbit	Wood
Dragon	Earth
Snake	Fire
Horse	Fire
Goat	Earth
Monkey	Metal
Rooster	Metal
Dog	Earth
Pig	Water

If we do not get on with someone, it may be that the animals associated with us in the Chinese calendar are not compatible. Alternatively, it may be that the elements that represent the time of our birth are not in harmony with the elements of the other person.

FINDING YOUR ANIMAL

The Chinese year does not begin on 1st January but on a date which corresponds with the second new moon after the winter equinox, so it varies from year to year. Thus someone born on 25th January 1960 according to the Western calendar would actually be born in 1959 according to the Chinese calendar. The "Chinese Animals Table" opposite gives the exact dates when each year begins and ends, as well as its ruling animal and element. Their outer characteristics are identified by the element of the year they were born, as shown in "The Nature of the Animals" box (left). The ways in which the elements affect an animal's personality are described in "The Five Elements" table.

ANIMAL CYCLES

One of the 12 animals represents each lunar month, each with its own element governing its intrinsic nature. Over 60 years, the Five Elements cycle spins so that each animal can be Wood, Fire, Earth, Metal or Water, which determines its character.

In a full analysis by an experienced Feng Shui consultant, each of us will have a collection of eight elements that together make up not only our character, but also our destiny.

CHINESE ANIMALS TABLE

YEAR	YEAR BEGINS	YEAR ENDS	ANIMAL	ELEMENT	YEAR	YEAR BEGINS	YEAR ENDS	ANIMAL	ELEMENT
1920	20 February 1920	7 February 1921	Monkey	Metal +	1967	9 February 1967	29 January 1968	Goat	Fire −
1921	8 February 1921	27 January 1922	Rooster	Metal −	1968	30 January 1968	16 February 1969	Monkey	Earth +
1922	28 January 1922	15 February 1923	Dog	Water +	1969	17 February 1969	5 February 1970	Rooster	Earth +
1923	16 February 1923	4 February 1924	Pig	Water −	1970	6 February 1970	26 January 1971	Dog	Metal +
1924	5 February 1924	24 January 1925	Rat	Wood +	1971	27 January 1971	15 February 1972	Pig	Metal −
1925	25 January 1925	12 February 1926	Ox	Wood −	1972	16 February 1972	2 February 1973	Rat	Water +
1926	13 February 1926	1 February 1927	Tiger	Fire +	1973	3 February 1973	22 January 1974	Ox	Water −
1927	2 February 1927	22 January 1928	Rabbit	Fire −	1974	23 January 1974	10 February 1975	Tiger	Wood +
1928	23 January 1928	9 February 1929	Dragon	Earth +	1975	11 February 1975	30 January 1976	Rabbit	Wood −
1929	10 February 1929	29 January 1930	Snake	Earth −	1976	31 January 1976	17 February 1977	Dragon	Fire +
1930	30 January 1930	16 February 1931	Horse	Metal +	1977	18 February 1977	6 February 1978	Snake	Fire −
1931	17 February 1931	5 February 1932	Goat	Metal −	1978	7 February 1978	27 January 1979	Horse	Earth +
1932	6 February 1932	25 January 1933	Monkey	Water +	1979	28 January 1979	15 February 1980	Goat	Earth −
1933	26 January 1933	13 February 1934	Rooster	Water −	1980	16 February 1980	4 February 1981	Monkey	Metal +
1934	14 February 1934	3 February 1935	Dog	Wood +	1981	5 February 1981	24 January 1982	Rooster	Metal −
1935	4 February 1935	23 January 1936	Pig	Wood −	1982	25 January 1982	12 February 1983	Dog	Water +
1936	24 January 1936	10 February 1937	Rat	Fire +	1983	13 February 1983	1 February 1984	Pig	Water −
1937	11 February 1937	30 January 1938	Ox	Fire −	1984	2 February 1984	19 February 1985	Rat	Wood +
1938	31 January 1938	18 February 1939	Tiger	Earth +	1985	20 February 1985	8 February 1986	Ox	Wood −
1939	19 February 1939	7 February 1940	Rabbit	Earth −	1986	9 February 1986	28 January 1987	Tiger	Fire +
1940	8 February 1940	26 January 1941	Dragon	Metal +	1987	29 January 1987	16 February 1988	Rabbit	Fire −
1941	27 January 1941	14 February 1942	Snake	Metal −	1988	17 February 1988	5 February 1989	Dragon	Earth +
1942	15 February 1942	4 February 1943	Horse	Water +	1989	6 February 1989	26 January 1990	Snake	Earth −
1943	5 February 1943	24 January 1944	Goat	Water −	1990	27 January 1990	14 February 1991	Horse	Metal +
1944	25 January 1944	12 February 1945	Monkey	Wood +	1991	15 February 1991	3 February 1992	Goat	Metal −
1945	13 February 1945	1 February 1946	Rooster	Wood −	1992	4 February 1992	22 January 1993	Monkey	Water +
1946	2 February 1946	21 January 1947	Dog	Fire +	1993	23 January 1993	9 February 1994	Rooster	Water −
1947	22 January 1947	9 February 1948	Pig	Fire −	1994	10 February 1994	30 January 1995	Dog	Wood +
1948	10 February 1948	28 January 1949	Rat	Earth +	1995	31 January 1995	18 February 1996	Pig	Wood −
1949	29 January 1949	16 February 1950	Ox	Earth −	1996	19 February 1996	6 February 1997	Rat	Fire +
1950	17 February 1950	5 February 1951	Tiger	Metal +	1997	7 February 1997	27 January 1998	Ox	Fire −
1951	6 February 1951	26 January 1952	Rabbit	Metal −	1998	28 January 1998	15 February 1999	Tiger	Earth +
1952	27 January 1952	13 February 1953	Dragon	Water +	1999	16 February 1999	4 February 2000	Rabbit	Earth −
1953	14 February 1953	2 February 1954	Snake	Water −	2000	5 February 2000	23 January 2001	Dragon	Metal +
1954	3 February 1954	23 January 1955	Horse	Wood +	2001	24 January 2001	11 February 2002	Snake	Metal −
1955	24 January 1955	11 February 1956	Goat	Wood −	2002	12 February 2002	31 January 2003	Horse	Water +
1956	12 February 1956	30 January 1957	Monkey	Fire +	2003	1 February 2003	21 January 2004	Goat	Water −
1957	31 January 1957	17 February 1958	Rooster	Fire −	2004	22 January 2004	8 February 2005	Monkey	Wood +
1958	18 February 1958	7 February 1959	Dog	Earth +	2005	9 February 2005	28 January 2006	Rooster	Wood −
1959	8 February 1959	27 January 1960	Pig	Earth −	2006	29 January 2006	17 February 2007	Dog	Fire +
1960	28 January 1960	14 February 1961	Rat	Metal +	2007	18 February 2007	6 February 2008	Pig	Fire −
1961	15 February 1961	4 February 1962	Ox	Metal −	2008	7 February 2008	25 January 2009	Rat	Earth +
1962	5 February 1962	24 January 1963	Tiger	Water +	2009	26 January 2009	13 February 2010	Ox	Earth −
1963	25 January 1963	12 February 1964	Rabbit	Water −	2010	14 February 2010	2 February 2011	Tiger	Metal +
1964	13 February 1964	1 February 1965	Dragon	Wood +	2011	3 February 2011	22 January 2012	Rabbit	Metal −
1965	2 February 1965	20 January 1966	Snake	Wood −	2012	23 January 2012	9 February 2013	Dragon	Water +
1966	21 January 1966	8 February 1967	Horse	Fire +	2013	10 February 2013	30 January 2014	Snake	Water −

THE ANIMAL SIGNS

Using characteristics that are perceived to be an inherent part of the natures of the 12 animals, Chinese astrology attributes certain aspects of these to the characteristics and behaviour of people born at specific times. This system operates in much the same way as Western astrology.

THE RAT

The Rat is an opportunist with an eye for a bargain. Rats tend to collect and hoard, but are unwilling to pay too much for anything. They are devoted to their families, particularly their children. On the surface, Rats are sociable and gregarious yet underneath they can be miserly and petty. Quick-witted and passionate, they are capable of deep emotions despite their cool exteriors. Their nervous energy and ambition may lead Rats to attempt more tasks than they are able to complete successfully. Rats will stand by their friends as long as they receive their support in return. However, they are not above using information given to them in confidence in order to advance their own cause.

▼ *Sociable and family-minded, rats are quick witted and opportunistic.*

▼ *Dependable and loyal, the Ox displays endless patience until pushed too far.*

THE OX

The Ox is solid and dependable. Oxen are excellent organizers and systematic in their approach to every task they undertake. They are not easily influenced by others' ideas. Loyalty is part of their make-up, but if crossed or deceived they will never forget. Oxen do not appear to be imaginative though they are capable of good ideas. Although not demonstrative or the most exciting people romantically, they are entirely dependable

▲ *Dynamic and generous, Tigers are warm-hearted unless they are crossed.*

and make devoted parents. They are people of few words but fine understated gestures. Oxen are renowned for their patience, but it has its limits – once roused, their temper is a sight to behold.

THE TIGER

The Tiger is dynamic, impulsive and lives life to the full. Tigers often leap into projects without planning, but their natural exuberance will carry them through successfully unless boredom creeps in and they do not complete the task. Tigers do not like failure and need to be admired. If their spirits fall, they require a patient ear to listen until they bounce back again. They like excitement in their relationships and static situations leave them cold. Tigers are egotistic. They can be generous and warm, but will also sometimes show their claws.

THE RABBIT

The Rabbit is a born diplomat and cannot bear conflict. Rabbits can be evasive and will often give the answer they think someone wishes to hear rather than enter into a discussion. This is not to say they give in easily: the docile cover hides a strong will and self-assurance. It is difficult to gauge what Rabbits are thinking and they can often appear to be constantly daydreaming, though in reality they may be planning their next strategy. The calmest of the animal signs, Rabbits are social creatures up to the point when their space is invaded. Good communication skills enable Rabbits to enjoy the company of others and they are good counsellors. They prefer to keep away from the limelight where possible and to enjoy the finer things of life.

▲ *Good counsellors and communicators, Rabbits also need their own space.*

THE DRAGON

The Dragon will launch straight into projects or conversations with a pioneering spirit. Dragons often fail to notice others trying to keep up or indeed those plotting behind their backs. Authority figures, they make their own laws and cannot bear restriction. They prefer to get on with a job themselves and are good at motivating others into action.

▲ *Powerful leaders, Dragons prefer to follow their own path in life.*

They are always available to help others, but their pride makes it difficult for them to accept help in return. Although they are always at the centre of things, they tend to be loners and are prone to stress when life becomes difficult. Hard-working and generous, Dragons are entirely trustworthy and are loyal friends. They enjoy excitement and new situations. When upset, they can be explosive, but all is soon forgotten.

THE SNAKE

The Snake is a connoisseur of the good things in life. Inward-looking and self-reliant, Snakes tend to keep their own counsel and dislike relying on others. They can be ruthless in pursuing their goals. Although very kind and generous, Snakes can be demanding in relationships. They find it hard to forgive and will never forget a slight. Never underestimate the patience of a snake, who will wait in the wings until the time is right to strike. They are elegant and sophisticated and although they are good at making money, they never spend it on trifles. Only the best is good enough for them. Very intuitive, Snakes can sense the motives of others and can sum up situations accurately. If crossed, Snakes will bite back with deadly accuracy. They exude an air of mystery, ooze charm and can be deeply passionate.

▼ *Mysterious and passionate, Snakes have endless patience.*

▲ *Active and excitable, the Horse's nervous energy often runs away with them.*

THE HORSE

The Horse is ever-active. Horses will work tirelessly until a project is completed, but only if the deadline is their own. Horses have lightning minds and can sum up people and situations in an instant, sometimes too quickly, and they will move on before seeing the whole picture. Capable of undertaking several tasks at once, Horses are constantly on the move and fond of exercise. They may exhaust themselves physically and mentally. Horses are ambitious and confident in their own abilities. They are not interested in the opinions of others and are adept at side-stepping issues. They can be impatient and have explosive tempers although they rarely bear grudges.

THE GOAT

The Goat is emotional and compassionate. Peace-lovers, Goats always behave correctly and they are extremely accommodating to others. They tend to be shy and vulnerable to criticism. They worry a lot and appear to be easily put upon, but when they feel strongly about something they will dig their heels in and sulk until they achieve their objectives. Goats are generally popular and are usually well cared for by others. They appreciate the finer things in life and are usually lucky. They find it difficult to deal with difficulties and deprivation. Ardent romantics, Goats can obtain their own way by wearing their partners down and turning every occasion to their advantage. They will do anything to avoid conflict and hate making decisions.

▼ *Peace-loving Goats are kind and popular, they hate conflict and will try to avoid it.*

THE MONKEY

The Monkey is intelligent and capable of using its wits to solve problems. Monkeys often wriggle out of difficult situations and are not above trickery if it will further their own ends. Monkeys tend to be oblivious of other people and of the effect their own actions may have on them. In spite of this, they are usually popular and are able to motivate others by their sheer enthusiasm for new projects. Monkeys are constantly on the look out for new challenges and their innovative approach and excellent memories generally make them successful. They are full of energy and are always active. They have little sympathy for those who are unable to keep up with them, but will soon forget any difficulties.

▼ *Energetic Monkeys use their intelligence to push their own ideas forward.*

not all that interested in accumulating wealth for themselves. They like to spend time relaxing. Dogs take time to get to know people but have a tendency to pigeon-hole them. When they want something badly they can be persistent. If roused they can be obstinate and occasionally they lash out, although their temper is usually short-lived. Some Dogs can be rather nervous and they may be prone to pessimism.

▲ *The flamboyant Rooster can be easily won over by flattery and admiration.*

THE ROOSTER

The Rooster is a very sociable creature. Roosters shine in situations where they are able to be the centre of attention. If a Rooster is present, everyone will be aware of the fact because no Rooster can ever take a back seat at a social gathering. They are dignified, confident and extremely strong-willed, yet they may have a negative streak. They excel in arguments and debates. Incapable of underhandedness, Roosters lay all their cards on the table and do not spare others' feelings in their quest to do the right thing. They never weary of getting to the bottom of a problem and are perfectionists in all that they do. Roosters can usually be won over by flattery. Full of energy, Roosters are brave, but they hate criticism and can be puritanical in their approach to life.

THE DOG

The Dog is entirely dependable and has an inherent sense of justice. Intelligent, Dogs are loyal to their friends and they always listen to the problems of others, although they can be critical. In a crisis, Dogs will always help and they will never betray a friend. They can be hard workers, but are

▼ *Dogs are loyal and hard-working, but enjoy relaxing too.*

▲ *Peace-loving Pigs are sociable and popular and are able to organize others well.*

THE PIG

The Pig is everybody's friend. Honest and generous, Pigs are always available to bail others out of difficulties. Pigs love the social scene and are popular. They rarely argue and if they do fly off the handle, they bear no grudges afterwards. They abhor conflict and very often will not notice when others are attempting to upset them. They prefer to think well of people. Over-indulgence is their greatest weakness and Pigs will spend heavily in pursuit of pleasure. They always share with their friends and trust that, in return, their friends will make allowances for their own little weaknesses. Great organizers, Pigs like to have a cause and will often rally others to it as well.

COMPATIBILITY OF SIGNS

The saying, "You can choose your friends but not your family", is often heard from those who do not have harmonious family relationships, and we all find that we are drawn more to some people than to others. Chinese astrology uses the year, month, day and time of birth (each of which is represented by an animal and the yin or yang attributes of its accompanying element) to analyse characters and predict fortunes. Analyses of relationships depend upon the interaction of the elements on each person's chart. We can gain some insight into our

▼ *We are drawn to people for a variety of reasons. Compatibility of animal signs and elements can certainly help.*

own characters and those of our family and colleagues by using the "Chinese Animals Table" and then looking at the associated elements with their yang (+) (positive characteristics) or yin (−) (negative characteristics) in "The Five Elements" table.

▲ *We function well at work when we are compatible with our colleagues. The man on the right looks uncomfortable.*

▼ *This table shows which of our family, friends and colleagues we relate to best according to Chinese astrology.*

COMPATIBILITY TABLE

	Rat	Ox	Tiger	Rabbit	Dragon	Snake	Horse	Goat	Monkey	Rooster	Dog	Pig
Rat	+	=	+	−	★	=	−	−	★	−	+	+
Ox	=	+	−	=	+	★	−	−	+	★	−	+
Tiger	+	−	+	−	+	−	★	+	−	=	★	=
Rabbit	+	+	−	+	=	+	−	★	−	−	=	★
Dragon	★	−	+	=	−	+	−	+	★	+	−	=
Snake	+	★	−	+	=	+	−	=	−	★	+	−
Horse	−	−	★	−	=	+	+	=	+	+	★	+
Goat	−	−	=	★	+	+	=	+	+	−	−	★
Monkey	★	+	−	−	★	−	−	+	=	+	+	=
Rooster	−	★	+	−	=	★	+	=	−	−	+	+
Dog	+	−	★	=	−	+	★	−	+	−	=	+
Pig	=	+	=	★	+	−	−	★	−	+	+	−

KEY: ★ Excellent   = Good   + Workable   − Difficult

THE ANIMAL YEARS

As we have seen, each year is ruled by an animal and its character is said to denote the energetic quality of the year.

The animal which rules each year and the date of the Chinese New Year for around a hundred-year period are shown on the "Chinese Animals Table". For ease of reference, 1999–2010 are shown below. Our fortunes in each year are indicated by whether or not we are compatible with the animal ruling that year, which can be checked by referring back to the "Compatibility Table".

1999	Rabbit	2005	Rooster
2000	Dragon	2006	Dog
2001	Snake	2007	Pig
2002	Horse	2008	Rat
2003	Goat	2009	Ox
2004	Monkey	2010	Tiger

YEAR OF THE RABBIT
A respite from the past year and a breather before the next, rest is indicated here. This is a time for negotiations and settlements, but not for new ventures. Women's and family concerns are considered important.

YEAR OF THE DRAGON
The time for new business ventures and projects. Euphoric and unpredictable, this is the year for outlandish schemes and taking risks. Dragon babies are considered lucky.

YEAR OF THE SNAKE
Peace returns and allows time to reflect. Care should be taken in business matters as treachery and underhand dealings are indicated. Money is made and communication is good. A fertile year, in which morality becomes an issue.

YEAR OF THE HORSE
An energetic and volatile year in which money will be spent and borrowed. Some impulsive behaviour will bring rewards, while some will fail. A year for marriage and divorce.

YEAR OF THE GOAT
A quiet year in which family matters are to the fore. A year for consolidating and for diplomatic negotiations, rather than launching new projects.

YEAR OF THE MONKEY
An unpredictable year when nothing goes according to plan. Only the quick-witted will prosper. New ideas abound and communication will flourish.

YEAR OF THE ROOSTER
A year for making feelings known and letting grievances out. This may cause disharmony in families so tact is required.

YEAR OF THE DOG
Worthy causes abound – human and animal rights and environmental issues are in the public eye. Security should be

▼ *Family relationships are usually harmonious if the animal signs are compatible and the elements do not clash.*

checked, by governments and at home. A year for marriage and the family.

YEAR OF THE PIG
The last year of the cycle and unfinished business should be concluded. Optimism abounds and the pursuit of leisure is indicated. Family concerns will go well.

YEAR OF THE RAT
This is a lucky year, a good time to start a new venture. The rewards will not come without hard work, but with careful planning they will arrive.

YEAR OF THE OX
Harvest is the symbol for this year so we will reap what we have sown. Decisions should be made now and contracts signed. This is a conservative year so grand or outrageous schemes are not considered appropriate.

YEAR OF THE TIGER
Sudden conflicts and crises arise in this year and will have an impact for some time. The year for grand schemes for the courageous, but underhand activities may suffer from repercussions.

THE BAGUA AND THE MAGIC SQUARE

The compass directions and their associations are fundamental to the practice of Feng Shui. Astronomical and geomantic calculations and the place of human beings within them are plotted on a luo pan, an instrument so powerful that it has been likened to a computer. The luo pan can indicate, to those who know how to interpret it, which illness someone in a certain location might be suffering from, or the fortunes of a person living in a certain room in a house.

This vast amount of information has been reduced to a shorthand form incorporated in a "Magic Square". In cultures worldwide, this was used as a talisman. Many formulae based on the magic square are used to discover whether a place is auspicious, in itself and for the people living there, and the simplest of these are introduced in this book. The diagram on the right shows how the energies represented by the Magic Square always move in a fixed pattern. These patterns are repeated over time and can indicate the fortunes of a person or building in a certain year.

THE BAGUA

The information contained in the luo pan is condensed into the Magic Square, which forms the basis of the Bagua, or Pa Kua, a tool we can use to investigate our homes and offices. The Bagua below holds some of the images which describe the energies of the eight directions and the central position. The Bagua represents the journey of life, the Tao, and we can use it to create comfortable living, working and leisure spaces.

When applying Feng Shui principles to your house, garden or office you will need a tracing of the Bagua with the colours, compass points and directions all added on.

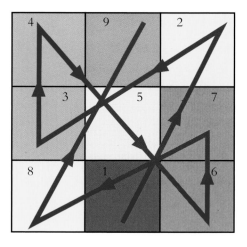

▲ *The Magic Square: the "magic" lies in the fact that every line adds up to 15. Magic squares exist all over the world. In ancient cultures, such symbols were a source of power to their initiates. In Hebrew culture, the pattern formed by the movement of energies is known as the seal of Saturn and is used in Western magic. In Islamic cultures, intricate patterns are based on complex magic squares.*

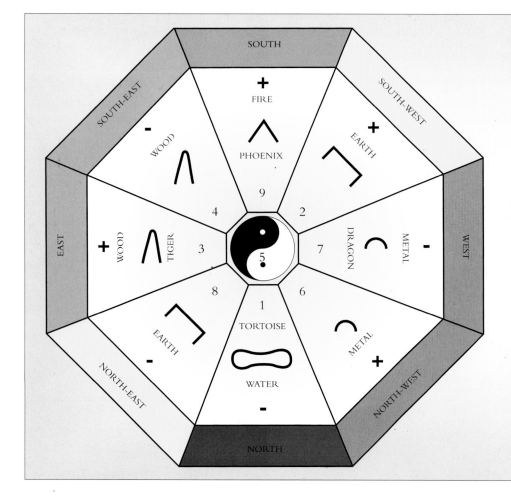

THE BAGUA, OR PA KUA

This diagram shows the energies associated with each of the eight directions. The outer bar shows the colours and directions associated with the five elements. The symbols indicate the yin (-) or yang (+) quality of the element associated with each direction. Also shown are the shapes associated with each element. The four symbolic animals which represent the energy of each of the four cardinal directions – north, south, east, west – are indicated, and the numbers of the Magic Square are shown in their associated directions. We take on the characteristics of a number and the energies associated with it, which are thought to shape who we are, where we feel comfortable, and our fortunes. The Chinese compass is always drawn facing south since this is the favoured direction for houses to face in parts of China. This does not affect the actual magnetic north-south directions.

FINDING YOUR MAGIC NUMBER

To complete the picture, it is necessary to discover how human beings fit into the scheme. Each person is allocated a "magic" number that enables them to position themselves to their best advantage. Before finding our number from the tables opposite, we must check the date of the Chinese New Year from the "Chinese Animals Table". The previous year is used if our birthday falls before the start of the new year.

▼ *Each of the magic numbers represents a particular type of energy suggested by the annual nature cycle. Find your number on the table and discover your energy below.*

ENERGY OF NUMBERS

1: Water. Winter. Independent. Intuitive

2: Earth. Late Summer. Methodical.

3: Thunder. Spring. Progressive

4: Wind. Late Spring. Adaptable.

5: Earth. Central Force. Assertive.

6: Heaven. Late Autumn. Unyielding.

7: Lake. Autumn. Flexible. Nervous.

8: Mountain. Late Winter. Obstinate. Energetic.

9. Fire. Summer. Impulsive. Intelligent.

USING THE MAGIC NUMBERS

Some Feng Shui consultants use only the male, or yang, numbers in their calculations, some use both male and female, or yin, numbers. Others regard the yin (female) numbers as depicting the inner self, while the yang (male) numbers represent the image a person presents to the world. Traditional male and female stereotypes are no longer the norm. Modern men and women, with more interchangeable roles, tend to have both yin and yang characteristics.

EAST-WEST DIRECTIONS

People tend to fare better in some directions than in others. They fall into two groups, the east group or the west group. Those who fall into the east group should live in a house facing an east group direction, those in the west group a west group direction. If this is not possible, your bed and/or your chair should face an appropriate direction.

▼ *Once you have found your magic number, you can identify which group you are in, east or west, which directions suit you. and whether your house is compatible.*

GROUP	NUMBERS	DIRECTIONS
East	1, 3, 4, 9	N, E, SE, S
West	2, 5, 6, 7, 8	SW, NW, W, NE, CENTRE

THE MAGIC NUMBERS

YEAR	M	F	YEAR	M	F	YEAR	M	F	YEAR	M	F
1920	8	7	1952	3	3	1984	7	8	2002	7	8
1921	7	8	1953	2	4	1985	6	9	2003	6	9
1922	6	9	1954	1	5	1986	5	1	2004	5	1
1923	5	1	1955	9	6	1987	4	2	2005	4	2
1924	4	2	1956	8	7	1988	3	3	2006	3	3
1925	3	3	1957	7	8	1989	2	4	2007	2	4
1926	2	4	1958	6	9	1990	1	5	2008	1	5
1927	1	5	1959	5	1	1991	9	6	2009	9	6
1928	9	6	1960	4	2	1992	8	7	2010	8	7
1929	8	7	1961	3	3	1993	7	8	2011	7	8
1930	7	8	1962	2	4	1994	6	9	2012	6	9
1931	6	9	1963	1	5	1995	5	1	2013	5	1
1932	5	1	1964	9	6	1996	4	2	2014	4	2
1933	4	2	1965	8	7	1997	3	3	2015	3	3
1934	3	3	1966	7	8	1998	2	4	2016	2	4
1935	2	4	1967	6	9	1999	1	5	2017	1	5
1936	1	5	1968	5	1	2000	9	6	2018	9	6
1937	9	6	1969	4	2	2001	8	7	2019	8	7
1938	8	7	1970	3	3						
1939	7	8	1971	2	4						
1940	6	9	1972	1	5						
1941	5	1	1973	9	6						
1942	4	2	1974	8	7						
1943	3	3	1975	7	8						
1944	2	4	1976	6	9						
1945	1	5	1977	5	1						
1946	9	6	1978	4	2						
1947	8	7	1979	3	3						
1948	7	8	1980	2	4						
1949	6	9	1981	1	5						
1950	5	1	1982	9	6						
1951	4	2	1983	8	7						

Key: M = male F = female

▼ *A Chinese Feng Shui expert studies the luo pan (compass).*

PERCEPTION AND THE SYMBOLIC BAGUA

Much of the skill in undertaking a Feng Shui survey of our immediate environment is in reading the signals there. If we are healthy and happy, this may prove to be a comparatively easy process. If we are not, our perception may be coloured by our emotional or physical state and we may not be able to see things clearly.

The Chinese phrase "First, luck; second, destiny; third, Feng Shui; fourth, virtues; fifth, education" is worth repeating, as it shows that to some extent our fortunes and personalities are out of our hands. If we embrace Feng Shui, think and act positively, and make use of the knowledge the universe has to offer, then

we can begin to take charge of the parts of our lives that we can control and make the best of them.

Part of the process of Feng Shui is to awaken our senses and sensibilities to our environment. Among other things, each of the Five Elements governs different senses, and our aim is to create a balanced environment in which all our senses are satisfied and none is allowed to predominate over the rest to create an imbalance.

We can heighten our perception of the world if we introduce ourselves to different experiences. Take an objective look at your weekly routine and decide on a new experience or activity which will add something different to your life.

A MAGICAL TEMPLATE

When Feng Shui began to take off in the West several years ago, the workings of the compass were known only to a handful of scholars. Those early days were distinguished by the creation of, and endless discussions on, the workings of the Bagua. It was used then, as it is now, by the Tibetan Black Hat practitioners, as a magical template that is aligned with a front door, the entrance to a room, the front of a desk or even a face.

This template is then used to supply information which can enable us to understand our energy and make corrections to create balance and harmony. Some Chinese practitioners have since

A HEALTHY LIFESTYLE AND A HEALTHY MIND

Stuck energy in our homes is often a reflection of our lifestyle and state of mind. A healthy daily regime will make us receptive to the powers of Feng Shui.

Ideally, we should take time out each day to meditate – or just to escape from stress. Often a short walk, gardening or a few minutes sitting quietly will help us to relax. Holidays and new experiences can help our mental energy.

Chi Kung and T'ai Chi are part of the same system. Their exercise programmes help to keep the energy channels in the body unblocked, while also releasing the mind.

Eating a healthy balanced diet of food-stuffs, produced without chemical interference, is another way of ensuring that harmful energies, or toxins, do not upset our bodily balance.

If we do become ill, acupuncture and acupressure and Chinese herbal medicine can balance the energies in our bodies and help to keep us fit.

◄ *Meditation (left), hiking in the mountains (bottom left) or a daily session of T'ai Chi (bottom right) will all benefit our mental energy and help to heighten our perceptions.*

sought to use the Bagua alongside the compass method. They place it over the plan of a home so that it is positioned with the Career area in the north, irrespective of where the front door lies.

Other traditional Chinese approaches concentrate on interpreting the energies indicated by the Five Elements and by the rings of the luo pan. Such is the "magic" of Feng Shui that, in the right hands, all approaches appear to work.

Newcomers to Feng Shui may find it difficult to connect to a compass. Hopefully, they will use either method to experience for themselves the magic of the early days of discovery, and will be drawn deeper into this amazing philosophy, gaining an insight into its power.

THE SYMBOLIC BAGUA

Throughout this book we will see how various images are connected to each of the eight points of the Magic Square or the Bagua, which is based on it. The symbolic Bagua uses the energies of each direction to relate to the journey of life. The journey begins at the entrance to our home – the mouth of chi – and moves in a predetermined way through the home until it reaches its conclusion. By focusing on an aspect of our lives which we want to stimulate or change, we can use the energies of the universe and make them work for us. Psychologically, focusing on an area enables us to create the circumstances to bring about change.

So far, a traditional compass approach has been used, but the diagram to the left allows us to use either approach. From now on readers should feel free to connect with the Bagua as they wish, and through it to the intangible forces which make this such a fascinating subject. Most people who have used Feng Shui have experienced changes in their circumstances. These often correspond to the actual energy around a relationship or situation rather than our desires. The results will ultimately serve our best interests, but the outcome is often unexpected.

▲ *Mountains afford protection to the rear and sides of this village, while a lake in front accumulates chi – all that remains is to arrange the inside of the house to create a supportive environment.*

▼ *The Three Gates Bagua. This may be entered through "Career" (back), "Knowledge" (bottom left) or "Helpful People" (bottom right). The compass Bagua with associated colours is shown inside to help you balance the elements of your home.*

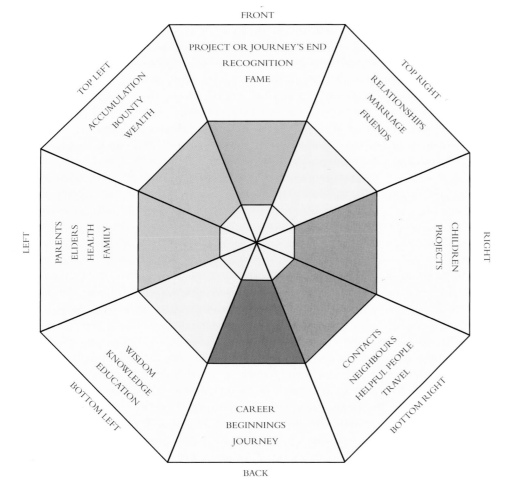

FRONT

PROJECT OR JOURNEY'S END
RECOGNITION
FAME

TOP LEFT

ACCUMULATION
BOUNTY
WEALTH

TOP RIGHT

RELATIONSHIPS
MARRIAGE
FRIENDS

LEFT

PARENTS
ELDERS
HEALTH
FAMILY

RIGHT

CHILDREN
PROJECTS

WISDOM
KNOWLEDGE
EDUCATION

BOTTOM LEFT

CAREER
BEGINNINGS
JOURNEY

CONTACTS
NEIGHBOURS
HELPFUL PEOPLE
TRAVEL

BOTTOM RIGHT

BACK

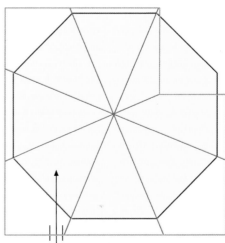

▲ *The Three Gates Bagua is flexible. If a home has an irregular shape, the corresponding area of the Bagua is also considered to be missing. In this house, the front entrance is in the "Knowledge" area and the "Relationships" part of the house is missing.*

FENG SHUI IN THE MODERN WORLD

Modern lifestyles are far removed from those of our ancestors. For them, charting the progress of the moon and sun, and interpreting the different weather conditions and other activities occurring in the natural world in relation to the movement of the stars and planets,

▲ *Night-time in Mexico City. The 23 million inhabitants are denied a view of the stars because of neon lighting and pollution.*

▶ *The rice harvest in traditional regions of China has used many of the same processes for the past thousand years.*

▼ *There are still thriving cultures in which ancient skills and lifestyles remain such as this village in Chad.*

was essential. These peoples depended on the land to provide them with the means to survive. The modern city-dweller may never see food growing naturally and may not even be able to view the night sky because of pollution and neon lighting. However, we still depend on the natural world for our well-being. We can be at the mercy of hurricanes, or bask on sun-drenched beaches; mountains may erupt, or provide sustenance for livestock; human beings can pollute the air and contaminate the land, or create sanctuaries for wildlife species.

Ancient peoples, through necessity, regarded the heavens, the earth and themselves as part of one system. This holistic view of life has persisted in many cultures, where health and medicine, food and lifestyle are all interconnected. In the West, scientific development created different disciplines which advanced in isolation from each other. Through recent movements in health and food production, we are seeking to correct the imbalances caused by this approach. The Tao, or the Way, the philosophy which underlies Feng Shui, shows how it is possible to order our lives to exist in harmony with each other and the natural world. We can use Feng Shui to help us work towards achieving this.

The traditional concept of Gaia, the Greek earth goddess, was used by James Lovelock and Lynne Margulis in the 1970s to encourage us to perceive the world as a biosphere in which each constituent part has a role to play. In order to understand Feng Shui we need to expand this concept of ecosystems further to include human beings and the impact of

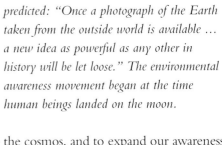

▲ *In 1948 science writer Fred Hoyle predicted: "Once a photograph of the Earth taken from the outside world is available … a new idea as powerful as any other in history will be let loose." The environmental awareness movement began at the time human beings landed on the moon.*

WORKING WITH THE NATURAL WORLD

A good example of working with the natural world is provided by an apparently admirable scheme to plant 300 oak forests in Britain to celebrate the millennium. But in the natural world oak trees grow singly and not in rows in large groups, and recent research has indicated that where many oaks grow together there is a higher incidence of Lyme disease, a debilitating illness which attacks the nervous system. The reason for this is that mice and deer feed on acorns and also carry the ticks which transmit the disease. Thus, where there are many oaks, there is also a high

incidence of Lyme disease. Mixed planting, which mirrors the natural world, would be preferable.

In order to save money, one forest was planted with Polish oak trees that came into bud two weeks later than the native trees. This meant there were no caterpillars feeding on the buds to provide food for newly-hatched fledglings. These mistakes might have been avoided if Taoistic principles had been applied to the scheme.

▼ *Native trees act as the Tortoise, Dragon, Tiger formation to protect these buildings.*

the cosmos, and to expand our awareness so that we can predict the consequences of our actions.

As we investigate the ideas behind Feng Shui and consider practical ways of introducing them into our lives, we also need to shift our perception. Feng Shui in the modern world incorporates intuition. Maori warriors navigate hundreds of miles by the feel of a place and by observing signs. The Inuit language incorporates many words to describe the complexities of different types of snow. Similarly, we can heighten our awareness of our environment by adopting the principles of Feng Shui.

Until recently navigators used the stars to steer by, and in some parts of the world those who work with the land still use the stars to determine planting times for their crops. These people recognize patterns in the interrelationship between different parts of the natural world, noticing which plants are in flower or when birds return from migration and comparing them to the weather. Many customs are firmly based in natural wisdom.

FENG SHUI
IN THE
HOME

WHEREVER WE LIVE, IN THE TOWN OR THE
COUNTRY, WE CAN ARRANGE OUR IMMEDIATE
ENVIRONMENT SO THAT WE RECEIVE MAXIMUM
SUPPORT. SOME HOUSES INSTINCTIVELY "FEEL"
RIGHT AND A LUO PAN READING WILL USUALLY
CONFIRM THIS. OTHER HOMES MAY NOT, AND
SOMETIMES EXTERNAL INFLUENCES CAN
ADVERSELY AFFECT BENEFICIAL ENERGY.
THIS SECTION OF THE BOOK OFFERS SOLUTIONS
TO HELP US TO BE NOURISHED BY OUR HOMES.

THE OUTSIDE WORLD

We need to feel comfortable inside our homes but sometimes the external environment impinges upon us. Perhaps the view from the windows is unattractive or the traffic is noisy. We are aware of such things but there may also be other influences that affect us psychologically over a period of time. Our physical health can also be harmed by more subtle forces that we cannot see. Feng Shui can identify these influences and forces for us, and can help us to take precautionary measures. When we move house, we can use the information we have gained to show us what to look for.

CHOOSING A LOCATION

Whether we own our own home or apartment or live in rented accommodation, we can use the principles which follow to create a living space in which we feel comfortable. If we are on the verge of moving, or are in the fortunate position of having acquired a piece of land to design and build our own home upon, there are some important considerations to make. You will probably already have a location in mind, but within the area there will be choices you can make which will affect your well-being in your new home.

When choosing a property we normally investigate the immediate environment. We use certain criteria to judge it according to our individual requirements – the appearance of neighbouring properties, proximity to schools, efficient transport for travel to work, green spaces, sports facilities and so on.

Some moves are dictated by new jobs in different areas, some when people give up their hectic urban lifestyles and relocate to rural areas. Many older people retire to the coast. Young people leaving home for the first time might be

▲ *The modern city of Durban in South Africa is full of young energy.*

▶ *A seaside location is very attractive in summer but can be inhospitable in winter.*

attracted by the hurly-burly of city living. The decline of heavy industry in many countries has seen a rise in the regeneration of dockland and riverside areas with large warehouses being developed as spacious apartments for these new city dwellers. Whatever the reason for the move, few people remain where they were born, or retain the extended support networks which prevailed only a generation or two ago. Our choice of home as a nurturing space is therefore important. With a little foresight and a knowledge of Feng Shui principles, we can select prime positions for our homes.

THINK BEFORE YOU MOVE

There are certain things to consider when selecting an area to which to move before we even consider choosing a house. Ideally we should know the area well. An idyllic bay in summer may be cold and windswept in winter, and a woodland glade at the end of an unmade track may be inaccessible after heavy winter snows.

Neighbours can prove to be a problem. They may resent a new house which spoils a view, or may erect screens that maintain their privacy but deprive you of

▼ *Living on a remote farm will suit some people perfectly, but not others.*

ASSESSING A LOCATION

NATURAL PHENOMENA	IMMEDIATE ENVIRONMENT	POSITIVE ASPECTS	NEGATIVE ASPECTS
Wind direction	Proposed road developments	Local amenities	Factories
Sun direction	Proposed building developments	Trees	Petrol stations
Rainfall	Land use plans	Street lighting	All-night cafés
Flood areas	Previous land use	Good street maintenance	Pubs and discos
Geological faults	Tree preservation orders	Good schools	Police stations
Soil type	Local architecture	Community spirit	Fire stations
Height above sea level	Neighbours, predecessors	Local shops	Airports
		Clubs and classes	Cemeteries and crematoriums
		Playgroups and nurseries	Motorways and highways
			Electricity sub-stations and pylons

◄ *This sheltered village is a delightful location to return home to after a day in the bustling city.*

► *High-rise flats in Hong Kong – financially the sky is the limit and young people are attracted there, but few of them stay to put down roots.*

light. It is important to determine the ownership of boundaries. Previous owners are another consideration. Earlier occupants may have tipped chemicals just where you want to grow strawberries, or you may learn that all the previous owners got divorced or mysteriously contracted a similar illness. Feng Shui may be able to offer an explanation. The box above indicates some things to check before moving to a new area.

The modern world has problems that

▼ *Pavement cafés are part of metropolitan life in many cities around the world.*

did not exist in the ancient world and these must be taken into consideration when we apply Feng Shui today. It is no use selecting a site with the classic Tortoise, Dragon, Tiger formation if the Tortoise is an electricity pylon, which may be linked to childhood leukemia, the Dragon is a chemical factory leaking its waste into the river, and the Tiger is a poorly managed petrol station. In modern times we have to apply the formulae to contemporary life and the ancient sages were wise enough to allow us the leeway to do this by building in formulae for change.

Our environment makes a psychological impact on us: whatever we see, hear or smell will make an impression. We also have to look at ourselves and what type of people we are in order to understand our needs in terms of living spaces. There is no point moving to a remote country area if you enjoy street life and love shopping because you will never feel comfortable. A Rabbit who retires to the

seaside will, at best, be tired and drained and, at worst, become ill. With a new insight into our own natures and increased awareness of the effect our environment has on us, we can use Feng Shui principles to find harmonious spaces for ourselves and our families.

When you are ready to sell your home and move on, Feng Shui can help to speed up this often lengthy and stressful process. The tip below combines the energy of the Five Elements to give a powerful boost to the sale.

FENG SHUI TIP FOR SPEEDING UP A HOUSE SALE

Take a red envelope and place in it:

♦ A piece of metal from the kitchen
♦ Some earth from the garden
♦ Some wood from a skirting board

Throw the envelope into a fast-moving river.

UNSEEN ENERGIES

Before finally deciding on a location, it is wise to check if there are any underground water sources, geological faults or other earth disturbances. These all create unseen energies which could affect your well-being.

GEOPATHIC STRESS

The word "geopathic" comes from the Greek *geo*, meaning "Earth", and *pathos*, meaning "disease". It covers naturally occurring phenomena that cause problems for us and our homes. The Earth and living organisms vibrate at complementary frequencies, which are negatively affected by geopathic faults. Dowsers are able to detect these problems, which a property surveyor may miss.

UNDERGROUND STREAMS

Just as water erodes rocks on the coast, underground streams have had the same effect beneath the Earth's surface. This process alters the electromagnetic frequency of the Earth so that it is out of our frequency range. Fast-moving and polluted underground water produces the same effect.

Underground streams produce energy spirals, the effects of which are felt inside

 If trees lean for no reason, they may be situated on a geopathic stress line.

any buildings directly overhead. Where a clockwise spiral meets an anti-clockwise spiral, ill health may be experienced by people situated above them. Where spirals meet other forces, such as leys, the problems are accentuated.

LEYS

Leys, or ley lines, are a network of surface energy lines running across the countryside. Our distant ancestors may have built their churches and standing stones on these lines, performing an "acupuncture of the Earth" as they tapped into its energy. It is believed the leys also provided routes for travellers.

▲ *Underground water creates magical places, but it is not desirable near a house as it can undermine the foundations.*

◀ *Stone circles are extremely powerful places. They harness the Earth's energies and respond to those of the Cosmos.*

▲ *The Chinese believe that quarrying damages the Dragon – the spirit of a place.*

▲ *Nearby railway lines can cause land disturbance and create instability.*

earth is covered by a series of force lines which are activated by the interaction of the Earth's magnetic field and the gravitational pull of the sun and moon. It is thought that these lines shift as a result of their interaction with the movement of charged particles trapped in the atmosphere as the sun blasts the Earth with radiation. The point where these lines cross may adversely affect the human body.

HUMAN ACTIVITY

Human beings can also disturb the Earth's energies. Quarries, tunnels, mines, polluted water and railways have all been found to contribute negative effects. Before erecting or buying a house, check for any mining or tunnelling that may have taken place in the area.

RADON

We are exposed to radiation throughout our lives, mainly from the sun. Exposure over long periods to higher than normal levels may make us ill. Leukemia and birth defects have been linked to exposure to radon, which occurs naturally in uranium in the Earth. As the uranium breaks down, it forms radioactive ions which attach themselves to air particles that become trapped inside houses. Some regions in the world have recorded

levels of radioactivity in excess of those recorded after the Chernobyl disaster. Pockets of high incidence have been found in Sweden and the United States as well as in Derbyshire and Cornwall in Great Britain. Local authorities are aware of the problem and assistance is available to eradicate it from buildings.

EARTH GRIDS

Two German doctors, Hartmann and Curry, have advanced the theory that the

---

STRESS INDICATORS

Leaning trees
Cankers on tree trunks
Elder trees
Illness shortly after moving
Uneasy atmosphere
Tunnelling activity
Cold, damp rooms

CLEARING THE ENERGIES

If there is no apparent reason for feeling unwell for a long period of time, then geopathic stress is a possible cause. Experienced dowsers are able to detect Earth energies and, in some instances, divert negative energies, albeit often only on a temporary basis. Many people can detect water with rods or pendulums, but experience is needed to deal with Earth energies and protection is needed to minimize ill effects. It is best, if possible, to move away from such energies, and it may be a question of simply moving a bed 60 cm–1 m (2–3 ft). The effect of clearing energies can be dramatic and can even cause shock. When dealing with heart patients, for example, the work should be done slowly.

▲ *Dowsing rods are part of a Feng Shui consultant's tools. Metal coat hangers also work for dowsing.*

▲ *Dowsing rods cross when they detect underground water. They are used to locate landmines and to find pipes.*

THE URBAN ENVIRONMENT

An enticing night scene in Villefranche, Cote d'Azur, France. Summer in the city can be invigorating and exciting.

U rban environments are very diverse. Living in an apartment above a shop in a city centre throbbing with night-life is quite different to the tranquillity of a house in a leafy suburb or the vast buildings in a redeveloped docklands area.

CITY AND TOWN CENTRES

The centres of large cities, where clubs and restaurants are open through the night, are full of yang energy and lifestyles will reflect this. City centres attract younger people with no roots, who can move about freely. Homes tend to be apartments and inside we should aim for some yin energy – muted colours, nat-ural flooring and a large plant or two to create a quiet haven. Smaller town cen-tres, particularly where there are shopping precincts, tend to close down at night and the atmosphere is yin and rather spooky. If you live here, make sure you have plenty of lights on the perimeter of your property and bright colours inside to prevent feeling closed in.

PARKS AND SPACES

These green oases are somehow apart from the bustling city centre. Homes are usually expensive and sought after, since they provide tranquil spaces and fresh air while still connected to the life of the city. People residing here will have more stable lifestyles as they have the yin-yang

Suburban living at its best in Sag Harbour, New York; wide streets, mature trees and no parked cars.

balance. Their homes should reflect this with a mixture of stimulating shapes, colours and materials, plus restful spaces.

DOCKLANDS

The energy of docklands is interesting. The yang energy of the large converted warehouses contrasts with the daytime yin energy when the occupants, usually young executives, are at work. At week-ends this changes as café life and boating activities take over. Docklands are usual-ly on main traffic routes, so on weekdays there is often stuck energy. Large trees should be planted to help cope with the pollution, and also to bring yin energy into the area. Rooms tend to be huge and it is difficult to ground the energy. Cosy yin spaces need to be created within the vast expanse to offer support. Large plants will also help the yin-yang balance.

SUBURBS

The energy in the suburbs is mainly yin, with little nightlife. People tend to hide and become insular in suburbs, and often a yang balance is required. Imaginative use of colour is often all that is required to raise the energy of suburban homes.

ROADS

Roads conduct chi through an environment and transport patterns can affect the nature of a neighbourhood. Living close to urban highways is an obvious health risk, but so too is living on narrow suburban "rat runs". Chi travels fast on straight urban roads and thus residents will not relax easily. In the United States, where suburban roads are built on a grid system, large gardens compensate and help to maintain a balance. Check the transport patterns before purchasing a new home and visit at different times of the day. Well-designed cul-de-sacs have excellent chi, but those where car movement has not been well planned create stuck energy and danger for children playing there.

The visual impact of a flyover in a residential area can be devastating. The fast-moving traffic conducts chi away from the area and will greatly affect the fortunes of those living at eye level or underneath the flyover.

RAILWAYS

The effect of a railway is similar to a motorway in that trains carry chi away from an area, particularly if they are at the end of the garden. Trains also create slight unease in the expectation of their arrival. Underground trains are destabilizing if they pass immediately below houses. If systems are old and poorly maintained the Chinese saying "Angry Dragons waiting to erupt" applies.

▼ *Parks and green areas are an important part of city life. This park is located in Adelaide, Australia.*

ROADS AND CHI

Today roads serve as conductors of chi. Steadily moving traffic on curving roads near our homes is beneficial. Fast traffic and roads pointing at us are not.

THE CURVING ROAD The road gently curves and appears to "hug" this house. This is a very auspicious Feng Shui position for a dwelling.

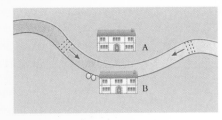

THE BENDING ROAD House B is in an inauspicious position. Traffic from both directions may break suddenly at the bend and could hit the house. At night, car beams will illuminate the rooms. There will always be a negative air of expectancy here. Convex mirrors on the outer bend would be the usual solution, but they would deflect and deplete the energy of the auspicious house A. Instead, a better solution would be to have traffic-calming measures in place as shown.

THE FAST ROAD This creates a visual and psychological barrier. Waist-high shrubs and plants on the boundary of the garden and plants on the windowsill inside the houses will slow down the chi. Those living at the junction of such roads are likely to be jumpy. Screeching brakes and even crashes are common at such points.

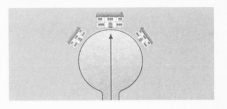

THE DEAD-END ROAD The house facing the entrance is at risk since the chi seems to hurtle towards it, as at a T-junction. Deflection is needed, and a hedge would help. An alternative would be to build a porch with the door at the side. Mirrors are often used to return the harmful influence back on itself. If the path to the door faces the road, it would be better to move and curve it. The effect is the same where a bridge points at a house. Residents will feel exhausted in such a location.

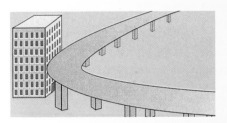

THE KNIFE The road appears to cut into the apartments like a knife. The constant flow past the window will leave residents tetchy. A mirror outside will symbolically deflect the problem. Coloured glass in the windows facing the road would block the unattractive view whilst allowing light in.

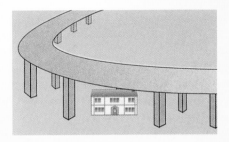

THE FLYOVER Residents here will feel overwhelmed and apprehensive. Lights on the corners of the house will symbolically lift the flyover, but this is not a good house to live in. Residents will feel oppressed and have no energy.

RURAL LOCATIONS

The energies found in the country-side are quite different to those of urban areas, but just as powerful. By carefully positioning our homes within the natural features of the landscape we can draw on their protection to nourish us.

COUNTRY LIVING

A sheltered position contained by trees or hills is ideal, especially in remote areas where protection from the elements is very important in winter. The classical arrangement of the four animals is the perfect site but if there are no woods or mountains where you wish to live, large trees and buildings can also act as protectors. Road access is vital in rural areas but, as in towns, it is preferable not to live close to major roads or through routes.

BENEFICIAL LOCATIONS

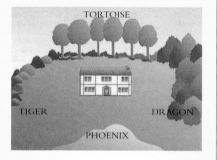

A tree belt behind acts as the Tortoise, and hedges represent the Dragon and Tiger. The Dragon is higher to keep the unpredictable Tiger in its place. A small hill in the foreground acts as the Phoenix.

A stream feeding a healthy pond is auspicious. Shrubs hide the water's exit from the property.

▲ *This lovely Mediterranean-style house is positioned in a supportive rural setting.*

Even if you live out in the wild, it is important to have a social centre within reach. Out-of-town superstores have knocked the heart out of many country towns and villages, and have made an impact on the chi of these places, but those that continue to thrive usually have an excellent yin-yang balance. They provide sport and leisure facilities for young people and a good community life, which are the yang activities in the yin setting of the countryside.

In the fields and woods, chi is good and there are many opportunities to restore the balance in our busy modern lives. Intensive farming methods can be harmful, however, so look out for telltale signs such as few songbirds or no hedges before purchasing a property.

POSITIVE ASPECTS	POSSIBLE NEGATIVE ASPECTS
Natural smells	Agrochemicals
Leisurely pace of life	Isolation
Walks	Flooding
Trees	Travel distances & access
Wildlife	Limited public transport
Fresh food	Landfill
Air quality	Military training areas
Relaxed lifestyle	Bad weather
Outdoor life	Effluent pipes
Happy people	Amenities closed in winter

RIVERS AND LAKES

Energy is usually very good near water, especially near slow-flowing rivers that meander through the countryside. Proportion is important, so if the water is balanced by an undulating landscape and plenty of green vegetation it will feel comfortable. A stream feeding into a healthy pond is ideal as it will accumulate chi and also attract wildlife to visit your garden. The energy near lakes is different, reflecting the breathless movement of the wind across the water and the sudden appearance and disappearance of water sports activities at weekends.

If you decide to live in a flood plain you will need to make enquiries about the likelihood of floods in the area, especially following those of recent years.

COASTAL AREAS

Being beside the sea gives most of us a sense of well-being. This is partly due to the beneficial effects of negative ions in the air, which create an invigorating atmosphere. Waves can, however, adversely affect some people, depending on their animal sign – Rabbits, for example, tend to feel uneasy near the sea.

▲ *A house situated next to a slow-moving river will benefit from good chi flow.*

In the summer, the teeming beaches full of holiday-makers are yang. In winter the towering seas are also yang, but the deserted seaside towns and isolated bays are yin. It is a good idea to visit the area in both seasons as they are so different. The elements of wind and water are never so much in evidence as when the storms lash the sea against the rocks. A peninsula is difficult to live on because the chi there dissipates in the winter when it is hammered by the elements.

► *A tranquil bay in summer looks very different in winter.*

ROADS TO HOME

Living in rural areas may mean that you have to commute to work and spend quite some time in the car. The daily journey you make, and the roads on which you travel, will have a considerable impact on your life, so check both when considering your new home.

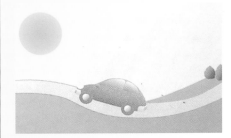

Travelling to work in an easterly direction in the morning and returning in a westerly direction with the sun glaring on the windscreen could affect our moods considerably. This can be particularly dangerous on narrow roads.

Wonderful views can make us feel euphoric and energized, although care must be taken not to lose concentration when driving. Scenic roads can be tricky in adverse weather conditions.

Where trees overhang a road they can afford a welcome relief from the glaring sun. However, long stretches may cause nausea and headaches brought on by the flickering, dappled light.

Narrow country lanes with high banks or hedges funnel chi and afford no relief for the driver. Where they twist and turn, the driver's vision is extremely limited. Regular use will become a strain.

HOUSE STYLES

The position of our homes within their environment and how they fit in with the surrounding buildings can affect how comfortable we are living there. At a simple level, if our home is a big detached house in a road of smaller terraced houses, then we will be set apart from the rest of the community. Similarly, if the house is very different in style from its neighbours it will not fit into its environment. Strict planning laws in some

▼ *This painted house is not in sympathy with its neighbours.*

▲ *A balance of Metal, suggested by the circular lawn, and Water in the curved path.*

areas have preserved the "spirit" or chi of towns and villages, and such places tend to have a sense of community. On the other hand, where building has been unrestricted and tall blocks spring up between two-storey houses with no regard for the character of the environment, then the area's chi dissipates and its sense of community is lost.

When we make alterations to our houses or decorate them, we should be mindful of the impact on the neighbourhood. If ours is the only stucco house in a row of brick houses, we isolate ourselves and change the chi of the area. If all the houses in the neighbourhood are of a certain era and we decide

BALANCING THE ELEMENTS

ELEMENT	HELPED BY	HARMED BY	WEAKENED BY	WEAKENS
Wood	Water	Metal	Fire	Earth
Fire	Wood	Water	Earth	Metal
Earth	Fire	Wood	Metal	Water
Metal	Earth	Fire	Water	Wood
Water	Metal	Earth	Wood	Fire

▲ *The intrusive tower blocks have completely changed the nature of this area.*

to change the style of the windows or substantially alter the architectural detail, we again damage the energy of the environment. Doors, chimney stacks and porches all add to the character and overall proportion not only of our house, but of the neighbourhood.

HOUSE SHAPES

The best-shaped house is square. It is well proportioned and is the symbolic shape for Earth, which gathers, supports and nourishes. Rectangular buildings are also well regarded. An L-shaped building is considered inauspicious since it is said to resemble a meat cleaver and the worst position to have a room is in the "blade". If a teenager has a room in this position, they may feel isolated and may get up to all sorts of things undetected. An older

FIVE ELEMENT CURES FOR CORRECTING IMBALANCES

WOOD: Posts, pillars, tower-shaped plant supports, green walls, trees
FIRE: Pyramid-shaped finials, wigwam-shaped plant supports, garden buildings with Fire-shaped roofs, red walls, lights
EARTH: Straight hedges, rectangular garden buildings, flat-topped trellis, terracotta troughs, or terracotta walls
METAL: Round finials, round weather vanes, metal balls, white walls
WATER: Wavy hedges, water features, black or blue walls

BUILDINGS AND THE FIVE ELEMENTS

WOOD: Tall thin apartment blocks and offices are often Wood-shaped.

EARTH: Earth-shaped buildings are long and low such as bungalows.

FIRE: Fire buildings have pyramid-shaped or pointed roofs.

FIRE: Wood-shaped windows and Earth-shaped lines give balance.

METAL: Metal buildings have domed roofs; the shape of these African homes is mirrored in Western churches.

WATER: Water buildings are those which have had sections added to them over the years in a random pattern.

relative with such a room may feel unwanted. Where houses are not a uniform shape, we need to make them more regular, as we will investigate later.

ORIENTATION

The direction in which a building faces will also affect its chi. North-facing buildings with the main windows at the front will feel cheerless since they will not receive any sun. The energy can become stagnant and it is important to warm the house with colour. Houses with the main windows facing south and south-west will receive strong yang energy and will need cool colours to compensate. Houses facing east receive early morning sun and vibrant energy. In the west, the energy is falling. Directions determine room placement within the house.

ENTRANCES, PATHS AND FRONT DOORS

The entrance to our home is very important. It represents the image we present to the world and can indicate the view we have of ourselves. When we return to our home, we need to be drawn into our own nurturing space through a pleasant environment, however small. If we live in an apartment, we need to distinguish our own special part of the block and make it unique, by using a colourful doormat, introducing plants or by other means.

ENTRANCES

Front gardens can fill up with an accumulation of stagnant energy unless we are careful. In house conversions where the grounds are not managed, the situation can be difficult since no-one is in overall charge of the garden. As a result, packaging, old furniture, chunks of wood and other assorted rubbish can pile up. Often, dustbins are sited in the front garden and can seriously affect how we feel when we return home. Bins should be placed away

▲ *Tree guardians mark the entrance to this attractive house. The effect that is created is very welcoming.*

from the front entrance, preferably behind a hedge or fencing. If one resident clears up, others may follow suit.

PATHS

These should gently meander through the garden to enable us to unwind at the end of a long day, or to welcome us back from a trip. Straight paths from the street to the front door carry chi too quickly and we do not have time to change gear. Ideally there should be an open space in front of the entrance where the chi can gather, but often these are filled with parked cars and there is no distinction

▼ *A meandering path enables us to shed the cares of the day before arriving home.*

ENTRANCES

◀ This tree is overpowering the house. A convex mirror on the front door or a polished door knob will disperse its energy. Gateposts symbolically reverse the flow and send it back to the tree.

▼ This tree blocks the gap between the two opposite houses. Such gaps symbolically represent money escaping.

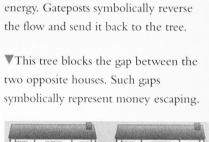

▼ This house illustrates a situation known as "long eye", which can cause health problems.

▼ Counteract "long eye" by ensuring both eyes have the same focal length. Placing trees as shown is one way.

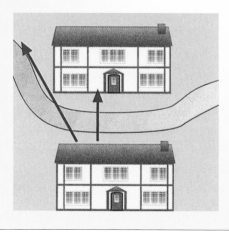

PATHS

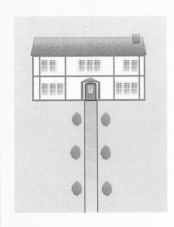

▲ Straight paths to the front door funnel chi too quickly to and from the house.

▲ Ideally, garden paths should meander to the front door to slow down the energy.

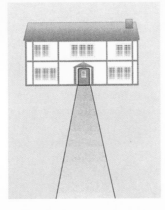

▲ Narrowing paths of this shape funnel chi too quickly into our homes.

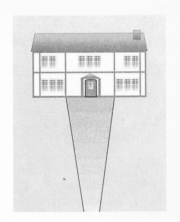

▲ Paths this shape resemble a jug pouring away from the house and disperse chi.

between home and work. Squeezing past a car to enter the house is claustrophobic, as are very small enclosed porches, creating restriction which may be mirrored in our approach to life.

FRONT DOORS

These should be well-maintained and clean. A tub of plants on either side is welcoming but they should not restrict the space. House numbers should be visible by day and night and doorbells should be in working order to maintain

◄ *Plants either side of the poles would improve these well-maintained apartments.*

harmonious relationships with callers. The chi of an area can be severely depleted if visitors whistle, shout or use their car horns. Door colours should reflect the compass direction they face and be balanced according to the Five Elements.

DEPARTING

What we see when we leave our homes can also colour our day. Large objects like telegraph poles and trees directly in line with the front door send "poison arrows" of chi at the house, as do the corners of other buildings. If tall hedges or fences restrict our vision from the house we may become insular or feel depressed.

▼ *A balance of the Five Elements, but taller plants would improve the proportion.*

▼ *A plant pot on the left would help to balance this front entrance.*

▼ *The Metal-shaped pot plants on either side of this door are full of energy.*

INSIDE THE HOME

—

Once you have found a suitable location, make sure that your house is facing a supportive direction and then turn your attention to the interior. Even if the external environment is less than perfect, you can still maximize the potential of your home by choosing suitable rooms for different activities and decorating them appropriately. Using Feng Shui, you can enhance specific areas of your home and thus improve certain aspects of your life that you are not satisfied with.

BENEFICIAL POSITIONS

Having selected a protected site in which to live, it is desirable that the house is orientated in what is considered in Feng Shui to be an auspicious direction which will support its occupants. Those who fall into the east category should face their houses toward the east directions; west group people should face the west directions. It is very likely that there will be a mixture of east and west group people within a family or others sharing a house. The people who are compatible with the house will feel most comfortable in it. Others should ensure that principle rooms fall into their favoured directions or at least that beds, desks and chairs are positioned correctly.

POSITIONING YOURSELF

Once you know your "magic" numbers, it is possible to design the interior of your house so that you position yourself in directions which are beneficial to you. Beds should be orientated so that the top of your head when lying down faces one of the four beneficial locations. In the same way chairs that you sit in should also face one of your beneficial locations.

▶ *We need to relax at the end of the day. A room with windows facing west is good, or a position favoured by our "magic" number.*

▼ *We aim to locate our rooms in good directions and decorate to suit the elements.*

▲ *The compass direction your house faces is dependent on where the main entrance is, and is the starting point for positioning yourself inside the house.*

FIND YOUR BEST AND WORST DIRECTIONS

1. Check your magic number on "The Magic Numbers" table.
2. Check the "Best and Worst Directions" table to determine prime places for you to sit, sleep and work.

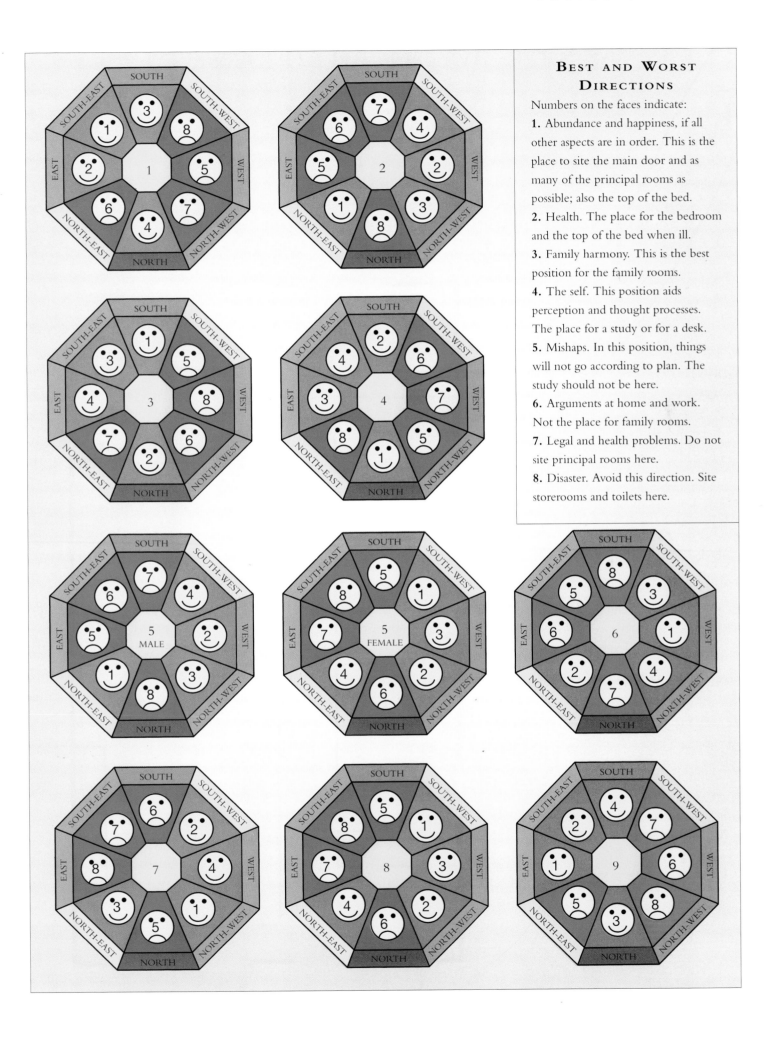

BEST AND WORST DIRECTIONS

Numbers on the faces indicate:

1. Abundance and happiness, if all other aspects are in order. This is the place to site the main door and as many of the principal rooms as possible; also the top of the bed.

2. Health. The place for the bedroom and the top of the bed when ill.

3. Family harmony. This is the best position for the family rooms.

4. The self. This position aids perception and thought processes. The place for a study or for a desk.

5. Mishaps. In this position, things will not go according to plan. The study should not be here.

6. Arguments at home and work. Not the place for family rooms.

7. Legal and health problems. Do not site principal rooms here.

8. Disaster. Avoid this direction. Site storerooms and toilets here.

DRAWING THE PLAN

It is now possible to begin to apply the principles we have learned. In order to position ourselves to our best advantage, we need to determine the compass readings for our homes.

YOU WILL NEED

◆ A compass with the eight directions clearly marked

◆ A protractor – a circular one is best

◆ A scale plan of your home. If you own your home you will already have one. If not, it will be necessary to draw one, in which case you will also need a tape measure and graph paper

◆ A ruler

◆ A lead pencil and five coloured pencils – green, red, yellow, grey, dark blue

◆ A tracing of the Bagua with the suggested information marked on

TO DRAW A PLAN

Using graph paper, take measurements for each floor, marking external walls, internal walls, alcoves, staircases, doors, windows and permanent fixtures such as baths, toilets, kitchen units and equipment, and fireplaces.

TAKE A COMPASS READING

1. Remove watches, jewellery and metal objects and stand clear of cars and metal fixtures.

2. Stand with your back parallel to the front door and note the exact compass reading in degrees.

3. Note the direction, eg 125° SE, on to your plan as shown in the diagram. You are now ready to transfer the compass readings on to your Bagua drawing.

▶ *Use this table to double check that your heading in degrees corresponds with the direction your front door faces, since it is possible to misread the protractor.*

DIRECTIONS AND DEGREES	
North	337.5–22.5°
North-east	22.5–67.5°
East	67.5–112.5°
South-east	112.5–157.5°
South	157.5–202.5°
South-west	202.5–247.5°
West	247.5–292.5°
North-west	292.5–337.5°

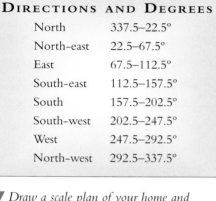

▼ *Draw a scale plan of your home and mark on it the positions of windows, doors, alcoves and all internal fixtures and fittings as well as bed and desk positions.*
A compass, protractor, ruler, coloured pencils and a tracing of the Bagua diagram will allow you to survey your home.

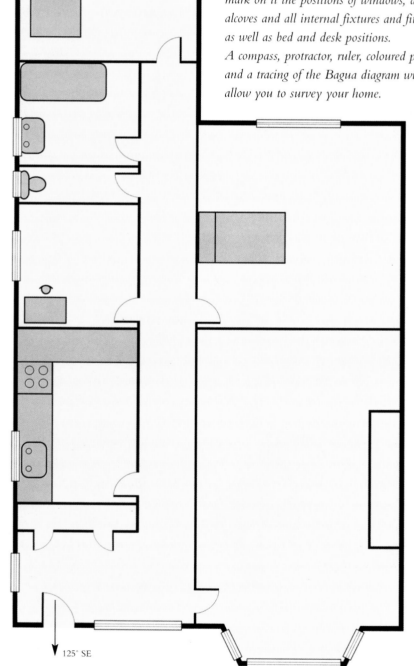

125° SE

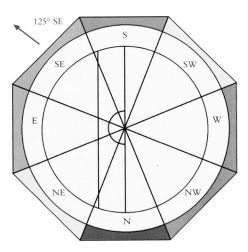

TRANSFER THE COMPASS READING TO THE BAGUA

1. Place the protractor on the Bagua diagram so that 0° is at the bottom at the north position and mark the eight directions.

2. Having found the compass reading for your home, ie the direction faced by your front door, check it matches the direction; if not you may be reading the wrong ring. Mark the position of your front door.

3. Double-check the direction by looking at the "Directions and Degrees" table. When you have done this you will end up with a Bagua diagram such as the one above, with the front door position marked. You are now almost ready to place this template on to your home plan.

EAST WEST DIRECTIONS

Just as people fit into east or west categories, so too do houses. Determine whether your house belongs to the east or west group of directions by checking the direction in which the front door faces.

EASTERN DIRECTIONS: north-east, south-east, south

WESTERN DIRECTIONS: south-west, north-west, west, north-east

East group people should preferably live in east group houses and west group people in west group houses.

TRANSFER THE DIRECTIONS TO THE PLAN

1. Find the centre of the plan. Match the main walls across the length of the plan and crease the paper lengthways.

2. Match the main walls across the width and crease the paper widthways. Where the folds cross is the centre of your home. If your home is not a perfect square or rectangle, treat a protrusion of less than 50% of the width as an extension to the direction. If the protrusion is more than 50% of the width, treat the remainder as a missing part of the direction.

3. Place the centre of the Bagua on the centre point of the plan and line up the front door position.

4. Mark the eight directions on the plan and draw in the sectors.

5. Transfer the colour markings.

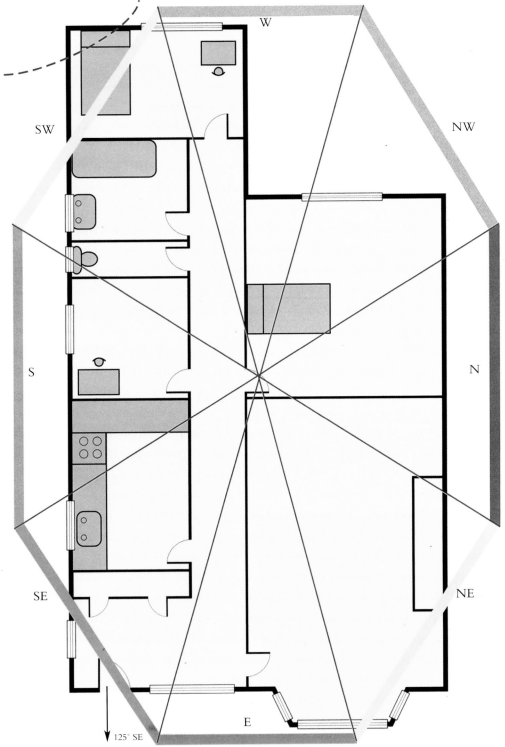

EDGES, CORNERS AND SLANTING WALLS

Certain structural details are problematic in Feng Shui. Often the result of conversions, they affect chi and can cause discomfort for the occupants of the house.

EDGES

Wherever the chi flow in a room is disrupted, difficulties occur. Anyone who has ever walked down a windy street flanked by high buildings will know that the gusts are always worse at the corners of buildings where the wind whips up into a spiral. Where major structural work has been undertaken and walls have been knocked down, a room is often left with supporting pillars. These are not conducive to the free flow of chi because they are usually square and have four corners which point, knife-like, into the room, and they can also interfere with vision.

If there are edges we should aim to soften them. Plants are one solution and fabrics are another. Wherever possible, make columns rounded as this creates an entirely different feel.

Having the edges of furniture pointing at us can make us feel uncomfortable, as can the edges of shelves and fireplaces. Keeping books in cupboards is a solution, but the pleasure of plucking a book from a shelf would be lost and the cupboards would become harbingers of tired energy. Instead, we can use plants to soften shelf edges near where we sit.

▲ *Round pillars are less obtrusive than square ones. The plant softens the effect.*

CORNERS

The corners of rooms are often dark, so it is a good idea to place something colourful there, like a vase of silk flowers for example. Alternatively, you can use something that moves such as a lava lamp or a water feature. Putting plants in dark corners where stagnant chi accumulates will help the chi to move on. Spiky plants are particularly good provided they are away from chairs where they could direct "poison arrows" towards the occupants. Uplighters or round tables with lamps on them are other options for dark corners.

Alcoves on either side of a fireplace are often filled with shelves, which help to prevent stagnant areas provided they are not crammed full and some gaps are left.

▲ *A plant will enliven an awkward corner and move the chi on.*

◄ *Plants can be used to soften shelf edges near to where we sit.*

▲ *Here, in one place, we have several methods of introducing movement into a dark corner – an octagonal table, a plant, a corner cupboard and a little shelf.*

▼ *This slanting wall will not adversely affect anyone sleeping in this room as there is plenty of headroom.*

THE FLOW OF CHI IN A LIVING ROOM

1. These chairs need to be repositioned as the corners of the fireplace will shoot "poison arrows" at people sitting in them.
2. The edges of these built-in shelves will affect anyone sitting here unless the offending edges are softened with plants.
3. A round table with a plant or lamp will move the chi on in this dark corner.
4. The corner of this pillar will send a "poison arrow" at the occupant of the chair; the chair can be moved or the edge of the pillar softened in some way.
5. Anybody who chooses to sit in this seat will be unaffected by this pillar as it is a safe distance away.
6. Uplighters in these corners of the room will lift the energy.

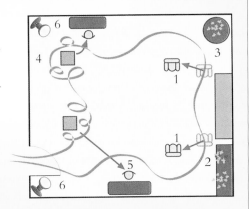

SLANTING WALLS

These are becoming increasingly common as expanding families in small houses convert attic space into rooms. Attic rooms with sloping ceilings are often turned into children's bedrooms or home offices. Sleeping or working under a slope depresses personal chi and these areas do nothing to aid the regenerative process of sleep nor creative processes during the day. Sloping ceilings also create a visual imbalance in a room. Mirrors and lights may help to create the illusion of lifting the slope and paint can achieve the same effect. Such rooms are far better used as hobby or play rooms or for any activity of a temporary nature.

If possible, it is preferable to have a smaller room of a conventional shape created instead of a room with sloping walls. A good solution is to fill the sloping walls in with built-in cupboards for storage. Where roof windows are installed to let light into attic conversions, make sure it is possible to see more out of them than just a patch of sky.

▼ *Placing storage cupboards under the eaves gives an attic room a more regular shape.*

BEAMS

Beams are not recommended in Feng Shui because they can be oppressive when positioned over a bed, stove or desk and suppress the chi of the people living beneath them. Proportion, however, is everything. In a barn conversion or in some of the eco-houses now being built, the ceilings are high and often vaulted so the beams do not seem to press down on the occupants. The reverse problem occurs when people and small-scale furniture rattle around in vast spaces and are unable to gather chi around them. However, beams in normally proportioned houses do tend to upset the flow of chi in a room, especially if we

▼ The oppressive effect of these beams is reduced by painting them a light colour.

position ourselves in unsuitable places under them. Simply by moving the dining table, desk or bed, we can often overcome any difficulties.

Many people dream of owning a country cottage, complete with roses round the door, log fires and beams. Traditionally it has been the custom to paint beams black so that they stand out, but when these cottages were built it is highly unlikely that this was their original colour. In the same way that pollution and time turn pale sandstone buildings in cities to a tobacco brown, so cooking and fires down the ages have transformed pale oak beams into charcoal-coloured wood. Interior fashions change, however, and it is now more common for beams to be painted the same colour as the ceiling,

▲ These beams are unobtrusive because the roof is so high. Avoid sitting under the low crossbeam running across the room.

a welcome trend which makes all the difference to low-ceilinged rooms.

Another way of reducing the effect of beams is to use uplighters underneath them, which give the illusion of "lifting" the beam. Small, light-coloured hanging objects will lighten a beam. Do not hang large, dark or heavy objects below a beam, or anything that collects dust. False ceilings can be attached to beams, either

▼ Sloping walls and a beam across the bed make this an inauspicious bedroom. The insecurity of the window behind the bed adds to the effect.

the conventional type or translucent ones with light behind. In larger spaces, such as restaurants, beams have been successfully mirrored, but this would not look good in most homes. Muslin or other fabrics will hide them, but these will harbour dust and create stagnant chi unless washed regularly. Traditionally, bamboo flutes tied with red ribbon were hung from the beam to create an auspicious octagon shape. Beams over a bed are believed to cause illnesses to occupants at

◀ *This modern living room is made inauspicious by the sloping walls and the dark beam running down the centre of the room.*

▲ *Imagine this room with dark beams – the light beams create quite a different effect.*

the points where they cross. A beam that runs along the length of the bed can cause a rift between the couple that shares it. When beams are situated over the stove or dining room table, they are thought to hamper the fortunes of the family. If they are over a desk, they may hinder the creative flow of the person who works there, and may even be a cause of depression. It is certainly better not to sleep under a beam, and sitting in a chair under a beam or under a gallery is not a comfortable experience either.

DOORS AND WINDOWS

Doors represent our freedom and our access to the outside world; they are also a barrier, acting as protection, supplying support and comfort. Windows act as our eyes on the world. Both play an important role in Feng Shui and if our access or vision through them is impeded in any way we may suffer problems as a consequence.

DOORS

Open doors allow us access to a room or to the outside world. Closed doors shut off a room or our entire home. If either of these functions is impeded, then the

▶ *The uplifting view from this window has not been restricted by curtains or blinds.*

chi flow around the house will suffer. Doors which squeak, stick, have broken latches, or handles too close to the edge so we scrape our knuckles whenever we open them, should all be repaired. Keep a wedge close to doors that might slam irritatingly in the breeze.

Ideally, a door should not open to a

▼ *Stained glass panels in doors permit light and lift the energy in dark spaces.*

CURES FOR PROBLEM DOORS

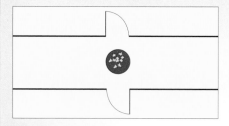

▲ If doors are located opposite each other, place an obstruction such as a table or a bookcase to slow down the chi.

▲ Where there are three or more doors in a row, break up the perspective by hanging low lights or positioning semi-circular tables to slow down the chi.

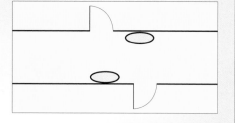

▲ Where doors are out of alignment, create a balance by positioning mirrors or pictures on each side.

▲ Where an opened door restricts the view into a room, position a mirror to correct this. Doors were traditionally hung in this way to prevent draughts. This practice may also have arisen because of the desire to preserve modesty in Victorian times.

restricted view of the whole room on entering, but doors in old houses used to be hung in this way to prevent draughts or, some speculate, to preserve modesty during the decorous Victorian era.

WINDOWS

Sash windows which only open halfway restrict the amount of chi that can enter a room. Some double-glazed units only open halfway, with the same result. Ideally, all windows should open fully, and outwards. Beware of windows which have fixed double-glazed panels with only a small opening section at the top. These can cause fatal accidents if fire breaks out; they are usually fitted with safety glass, so it is virtually impossible to smash them.

▲ *Adding an attractive stained-glass hanging can offer some privacy while creating a lively energy in the room.*

▼ *This stencilled decoration allows privacy in a bathroom, while at the same time letting in as much daylight as possible.*

▲ *Tied-back curtains are ideal here as they do not restrict the pleasant view.*

If these have been fitted in your home, it is advisable to remove them as soon as possible, particularly in children's rooms.

Safety is, of course, paramount in children's rooms and measures should be taken to ensure that they cannot fall out of windows.

The top of a window should be as tall as the tallest person in the house. Everyone should have a view of the sky through the seasons or they will lose their connection with the natural world. Drooping blinds which prevent this view lower the chi of a room considerably, and slatted blinds send cutting chi into the room.

If you keep your curtains closed during the day, the chances are that you are depressed and feel vulnerable. Net curtains, although necessary in some areas, blur the view out of the window. Experiment with other solutions, such as large plants, coloured glass or window stickers to prevent the outside world looking in. The aim should be to see out as much as possible. South-west-facing windows will, however, need some screening in summer, particularly in a study or kitchen.

Too many windows can create excessive yang since they blast the house with chi, while too few windows restrict its flow and are yin. Windows too near the

▲ *The seating in this room impedes access to the window, and can be easily rearranged.*

floor in attic rooms feel unstable and a solid object or low table should be placed in front. It is preferable for bathrooms to have windows with an air flow. If this is not available, a water feature containing aromatic oils should be used and an extraction unit installed.

Too many windows in the dining room are considered to be especially inauspicious since the aim is to gather chi around the dining table and the food prepared for friends and family.

▼ *This lovely etched bathroom window allows the occupants privacy, but still permits the maximum amount of light.*

MATERIALS

The materials with which we surround ourselves affect us on a physical level by how they feel and what they look like. They also affect us on a psychological level through their energy. Like everything else, materials have

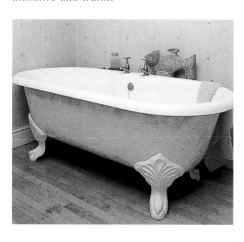

▼ *A wooden floor makes the room look attractive and warm.*

▲ *Natural materials such as wood, wicker and cotton fabrics look fresh and inviting.*

elemental qualities which affect the chi of the part of the home in which they are used, and they can also have a profound effect on our health and well-being.

Hard, reflective surfaces such as those used in the kitchen have a yang energy and chi moves across them quickly. Soft materials and those with depth of colour or texture are yin and tend to slow chi movement down.

MATERIALS AND HEALTH

Our choice of materials for fabrics and soft furnishings, furniture, decorating materials, and cleaning and washing

HARMFUL CHEMICALS ARE FOUND IN

◆ *Wood preservation treatments:* use safe alternatives
◆ *Cavity wall foam*
◆ *Paint:* use natural pigments
◆ *Vinyl wallpaper and paints:* use untreated papers and paints
◆ *Synthetic carpets and treated woollen carpets:* use natural untreated materials
◆ *Plastic floor tiles and coverings:* use linoleum or rubber
◆ *Adhesives:* use non-chemical and acrylic alternatives
◆ *Upholstery foam:* use natural fibres
◆ *Processed wood products:* use solid or recycled wood
◆ *Cleaning materials:* use natural alternatives
◆ *Food:* Select organic food
◆ *Fuels:* keep consumption to a minimum
◆ *Water supply:* dispose of hazardous chemicals safely

PLANTS WHICH CLEAN THE AIR

Lady Palm – *Rhapis excelsa*
Anthurium – *Anthurium andraeanum* (below right)
Rubber Plant – *Ficus robusta*
Dwarf Banana – *Musa cavendishii*
Peace Lily – *Spathiphyllum*
Ivy – *Hedera helix*
Heart Leaf Philodendron
Croton – *Codiaeum variegatum pictum*
Kalanchoe – *Kalanchoe blossfeldiana* (below left)
Golden Pothos – *Epipremnum aureum*
Ficus alii
Boston Fern – *Nephrolepis exaltata* 'Bostoniensis'

agents can play a part in our health and well-being. Each of us takes responsibility for our own health and that of our families whenever we choose materials for use inside our homes. Many substances present in the products we select can cause life-threatening illnesses over time and many are known to be responsible for allergies.

While investigating the air quality inside spacecraft, scientists at NASA discovered that some plants are useful in extracting harmful substances from the atmosphere. This is a very good reason for introducing plants into our homes, in addition to their other virtues. The list above shows plants which have been found useful in cleaning the air.

◀ *Wicker furniture is strong and comfortable, and it is also biodegradable.*

MATERIALS AND THE FIVE ELEMENTS

Materials and their colours and shapes can be used to enhance, weaken or support the energy of an area according to the relationships of the elements.

WOOD

Wood plays a crucial role in most houses. Its strength can support the structure of a house, yet its grain suggests fluidity and movement. Highly polished woods conduct chi quickly but stripped pine seems to absorb it. Wood is ideal for use on floors as it is easy to clean and does not harbour dust and mites, which can cause allergies.

BAMBOO, WICKER AND RATTAN

These natural products fall into the Wood element category. In contrast to the yang characteristics of highly polished wood, these materials tend to be yin and thus slow down chi.

COIR, SISAL, SEA GRASS AND RUSH MATTING

These are popular because they are natural products. They make attractive floor coverings but are difficult to clean; this must be done regularly or they will harbour dirt and insects.

FABRICS

These can be made of natural fibres, like cotton and linen which belong to the Wood element, or from man-made fibres. Provided they are not treated with chemicals for fire or stain resistance, natural fibres are preferred since man-made fibres create static electricity and deplete the beneficial negative ions in the home. Fabrics can encourage stagnant chi if they become faded and dirty.

PLASTICS

Plastics and other man-made materials generally fall into the Fire element category as they have usually been produced using heat processes. They can block chi and produce harmful vapours and chemicals which may affect health, so they should be kept to a minimum.

METAL

Metal objects – steel, chrome and other metals – speed up chi flow. The reflective surfaces suggest efficiency and action, and metal is therefore useful in the kitchen and in stagnant areas such as bathrooms. Being smooth and reflective, glass is often classified in the Metal element and some of its qualities are similar.

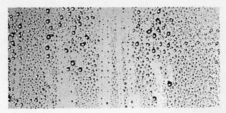

GLASS

Glass is often classified as the Metal element and shares some of its qualities. However, glass has depth, and light reflecting on it suggests patterns which flow like Water. Sand is used in the production of glass, so sometimes it also suggests Earth. It depends on the energetic quality of the particular glass and the use to which it is put.

CLAY AND CERAMICS

These two related materials fall into the Earth element category. They can be yin or yang in nature, depending on whether or not their surfaces are shiny. Glazed surfaces such as china and vases are more yang and they conduct chi quickly.

STONE AND MARBLE

Stone floors and walls fall into the Earth element category. They tend to be yin since their surfaces are non-reflective and the natural patterning on them gives them depth. Stone floors are stable and are particularly useful in kitchens. Marble, on the other hand, is yang because it is smooth, hard and polished. The natural patterns in marble also suggest the flow of the Water element.

MIRRORS

Mirrors have been described as "the aspirin" of Feng Shui and they have many curative uses. They should always reflect something pleasant, such as an attractive view or a landscape, which will bring the vibrant energy of a garden or scene into the house. When placing a mirror to enhance a space or "cure" an area, be aware of what is reflected in it or a problem may be created elsewhere. Mirrors should never distort or cut into the image of a person as this symbolically distorts or cuts their chi. They should always have frames to contain the chi of the image.

Mirrors are useful in small spaces where they apparently double the size of the area. Don't hang them opposite a door or a window since they merely reflect the chi back at itself and do not allow it to flow around the home. Mirrors opposite each other indicate restlessness and are not recommended. Other reflective objects can be used in the same way as mirrors; for example, highly polished door furniture, metal pots, glass bowls and shiny surfaces.

▲ *This hallway is already light but the mirror makes it positively sparkle. Mirrors create an illusion of space and depth.*

▼ *A mirror will make a small space seem much larger. Do not position it directly opposite a door or window.*

IRREGULAR SPACES

Where part of a house is "missing", in other words irregularly shaped, mirrors can be used to effectively recreate the missing space and make a regular shape.

STAGNANT AREAS

Use mirrors in dark corners and at bends in passages to help the chi to circulate around these awkward places.

LONG CORRIDORS

In long corridors the chi moves too fast. Mirrors offer one method of slowing the chi down. Position several mirrors in a staggered manner to reflect pleasant images placed on the opposite wall.

MIRRORS TO DEFLECT

Convex mirrors are used in Feng Shui to deflect fast-moving chi or the influences

THE DO'S AND DON'TS OF MIRRORS

Do
- ✔ Have frames around mirrors
- ✔ Keep them clean
- ✔ Replace broken ones
- ✔ Reflect your whole image

DON'T
- ✘ Have joins or mirror tiles
- ✘ Hang mirrors opposite each other
- ✘ Place them opposite the bed
- ✘ Place them opposite doors
- ✘ Place them directly opposite windows
- ✘ Hang Bagua mirrors indoors

THE BAGUA MIRROR

The markings on the Bagua mirror are a kind of shorthand, representing the energies of the Cosmos.

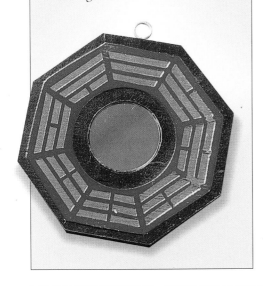

of uncomfortable features outside the house, for example, corners of buildings, telegraph poles and trees which overpower the front of the house. They will also deflect unwanted influences indoors, but because they distort images position them where they will not reflect people.

BAGUA MIRRORS

Bagua mirrors are used to protect a house from malign energies which may attack the occupants. They can often be seen outside Chinese homes and shops. They are used on front doors to deflect the influences of negative energy sources – harsh corners, tall objects and other features. Bagua mirrors represent a yin energy cycle and, as such, should never be hung inside the house or they will affect the energies of the occupants.

▲ *If a house is not of a perfect shape, a mirror hung inside will symbolically reflect the missing area.*

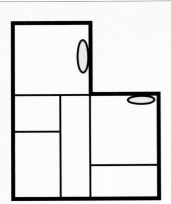

The Wealth area of this house is missing. Place mirrors to symbolically repair the shape and energize the missing space.

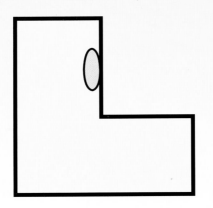

Use a mirror to repair the shape of an L-shaped room by symbolically drawing in the missing area.

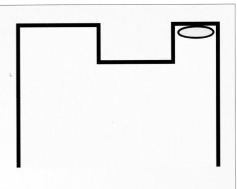

A mirror placed in this gloomy corner, reflecting a view or plant, will enliven a dark space and prevent energy stagnating.

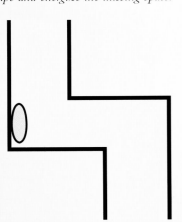

Place a mirror to reflect a bright picture on the opposite wall and thus bring energy to this dark area.

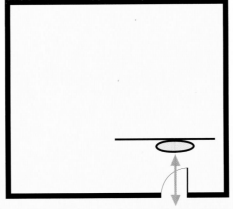

A mirror in this position will not allow the chi into the house or room and will reflect it back through the door.

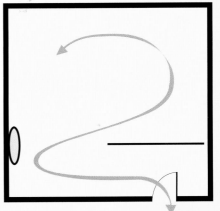

This is a better position as it draws the chi into and through the living area and does not act as a barrier.

PLANTS

Plants play an important role in Feng Shui because they bring a life force into the home and help to keep the air fresh. Depending on their shape, plants create different types of energy. Upright plants with pointed leaves are yang, and are useful in the south and in corners to move energy. Round-leaved and drooping plants are more yin and calming, and best placed in the north. Plants should be healthy – sick plants and those which shed leaves and flowers profusely will create stagnant energy.

COLOUR AND SHAPE

Plants with shapes and colours that correspond to the Five Elements are ideal. Care should be taken when siting spiky plants to ensure that they are not directing harmful energy towards a chair where someone may sit.

INDOOR BULBS

SPRING: Dwarf tulip, Dwarf narcissus, Crocus, Hyacinth (above)

SUMMER: *Scilla peruviana, Albuca humulis, Calochortus subalpinus, Rocoea humeana*

AUTUMN: Nerine, Autumn crocus, Cyclamen, *Liriope muscari*

WINTER: *Iris reticulata, Chionodoxa luciliae,* Muscari, Cymbidium

▲ *Colourful plants will brighten any area and increase Wood energy. Plants in these colours will benefit an Earth area.*

▲ *The money plant has been adopted as the Feng Shui plant. Its leaves resemble coins and Metal energy.*

▶ *This trained ivy plant brings a lively energy to a room. It would look best in the west or north-west.*

PLANTS THAT REPRESENT THE FIVE ELEMENTS

▲ *Geraniums are easy to grow on a sunny windowsill and represent Fire.*

FIRE: Geranium, Cordyline, Begonia, Bromeliad, Poinsettia, Aspidistra.
EARTH: Slipper flower, Marigolds, Sunflowers and other yellow plants.
METAL: Money plant, Jasmine, Fittonia, Oleander, Calathea.

▲ *All the elements are here, captured in both the colours and the shapes of this attractive pot of lillies.*

▲ *Summer jasmine is often grown in an arch shape. Its delicate white flowers have a beautiful scent.*

WATER: The Water element can be introduced by standing plant pots on blue or clear glass nuggets.
WOOD: All plants are representative of the Wood element.

FLOWERS

Flowers look beautiful in a vase but, once cut, they are technically dead and often stand forgotten in stagnant water. The cut-flower industry uses vast amounts of energy in heating greenhouses, transportation and the manufacture of chemicals to feed their products and keep them pest-free. Choose potted plants

▼ *Use a pretty flowering plant in the house like this Cymbidium, instead of cut flowers.*

instead. You could grow pots of bulbs through the seasons and plant them afterwards in the garden.

Dried flowers are also technically dead and have a stagnant energy, particularly when their colours fade and they gather dust. As an alternative, pictures of flowers, brightly painted wooden replicas and silk flowers are all acceptable to symbolize growth and stimulate energy in the house.

THE FENG SHUI PLANT

The money plant (*Crassula ovata*) has been adopted as the Feng Shui plant. The name helps, but the round succulent leaves are representative of Metal energy. Use them in the west and north-west. If used in the south-east (the Wealth area), their Metal energy will be in conflict with the Wood energy of that direction.

▶ *This bright arrangement would do well in the south-west – an Earth area.*

USE PLANTS TO:

- ◆ Hide a jutting corner
- ◆ Move energy in a recessed corner
- ◆ Harmonize Fire and Water energy in kitchens
- ◆ Slow down chi in corridors
- ◆ Drain excess Water energy in the bathroom
- ◆ Bring life into the house
- ◆ Enhance the east and south-east, and support the south

LIGHTING

Life on Earth depends directly or indirectly on the sun. Our bodies are attuned to its cycles and in every culture the daily rhythms of light and dark are built into the mythology. In China, the yin-yang or T'ai Chi symbol reflects the daily and annual cycles of the sun: the white yang side representing daytime and

▼ Stained glass is very decorative and provides privacy in a room which is overlooked.

▲ Our bodies need plenty of sunlight in order to stay healthy.

▶ Muslin filters the light in rooms where the sun's glare is too strong, or offers privacy.

the dark yin side night-time. In the modern world, many of us spend a lot of time inside buildings and our rhythms become out-of-tune with the natural cycle of the sun. In northern countries, which have little sunlight, a condition known as SAD (Seasonal Affective Disorder) is prevalent. It is treated with light that imitates the ultraviolet and infra-red rays of the sun.

The correct type and level of light are very important to our general health and well-being. In our homes, natural light is important but its quality varies throughout the day according to the way our houses face. Natural light can cause glare or create shadows and we often have to subdue it or enhance it by artificial means. Light can be reflected off shiny

surfaces or filtered by net or muslin curtains, blinds or frosted or tinted glass. Being aware of how natural light comes into our homes enables us to position our furniture and arrange our activities to make the best use of it.

ARTIFICIAL LIGHTING

In rooms where we are active, such as kitchens, offices and workrooms, and where safety is important, for example on staircases, direct lighting is necessary. In rooms we relax in – living rooms and bedrooms – we can use softer lighting which can be reflected or diffused. To highlight particular areas, such as a picture, chopping board or desk, task lighting can be used.

The position of lighting has a profound effect on the occupants of a house. If shadows are cast where we read or prepare food, or the lights flicker, or light glares on to the computer or TV screen, we will constantly be irritated. Harsh lighting can also affect our moods.

The quality of light is important. Ordinary light bulbs produce light which veers towards the red end of the spectrum, with little blue or green light. Fluorescent light is the opposite; it emits higher electromagnetic fields than other sources and its flicker can cause headaches. Full spectrum lighting was designed to copy natural daylight as much as possible, but unfortunately contains slightly higher levels of ultraviolet radiation than ordinary light sources.

Energy production is a drain on the world's natural resources. Recent developments designed to reduce this include CFL (compact fluorescent lamp) bulbs, which not only last longer but also use

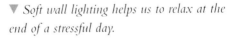

▼ *Soft wall lighting helps us to relax at the end of a stressful day.*

▲ *Glass bricks have been used here instead of a solid wall. They can be very useful if you want to open up dark areas.*

► *Use uplighters to transform dark corners. Placed under heavy beams, they serve to lighten their negative effect.*

less electricity. Tungsten-halogen lamps give a bright, white light that is close to daylight. The high-voltage varieties are too bright for task lighting but are useful as uplighters; the low-voltage varieties can be used for spotlights. These bulbs are also energy-efficient.

ELECTROSTRESS

We are becoming increasingly aware of the negative effects of electromagnetic radiation on the human body. The effects of exposure to ionizing radiation in X-rays and ultraviolet rays in sunlight are now well-known. The low-frequency radiation which surrounds power lines has also been linked to childhood illness. Such radiation also exists around electrical appliances. Non-ionizing radiation emitted by household appliances can be equally harmful over time. Cathode ray tubes in televisions and computer monitors are particularly harmful because both adults and children now spend so much time in front of them. It is wise to sit as far away as possible from the screen. Lap-top computers should not be used on our laps as we would then be connected to an electric circuit. The electromagnetic field around ionizers has a particularly large range so it is not a good idea to place them in bedrooms.

▲ *Placing a Boston fern next to the television screen has been shown to absorb some of the radiation it emits.*

◀ *Round-the-clock working and satellite links to the rest of the world have resulted in Hong Kong having higher-than-average electromagnetic activity.*

▼ *Mobile phones are convenient and allow us to conduct business outside, but pose a health risk if used constantly. A laptop computer should not be used on our laps.*

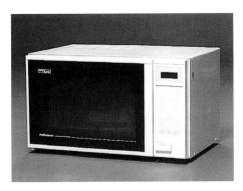

◀ Microwave ovens can damage your health if they leak. Have them checked annually as you would other household fixtures. They are not well regarded in Feng Shui.

▶ A gadget-free bedroom is essential for a healthy body and peace of mind. While we sleep, our body cells can regenerate naturally, a process which works best if unimpeded by any harmful external influences.

We live in an electrical "soup". Radio, TV and microwave emissions pass around and through us wherever we live. There are few places left on Earth where this is not the case. Satellites connect continents instantly and we can communicate with people across the world, but at a price. Recent research into the use of mobile telephones indicates that frequent use can affect us. The radiation from the appliances we use every day of our lives has been linked to various cancers, allergies, Parkinson's disease, Alzheimer's disease, cataracts, ME and even the total breakdown of the immune system.

Despite our awareness of the effects of radiation, we are so dependent on appliances and communication technology that we are unwilling, or unable, to live without them. We should therefore take precautions. At night, electric blankets should never be left on when we are in bed; if we must use them, they should be unplugged from the mains before we get into bed. Water beds are connected to the electricity supply, so in Feng Shui terms they display the conflict of Fire (electricity) and Water. We need to feel secure when we sleep and the constant motion of a water bed is not a natural way for us to rest.

Microwave ovens are potentially the most dangerous of all household appliances and should be used with care. They have been found to emit low-frequency radiation far in excess of that known to cause lymphatic cancer in children.

Apartments that have under-floor or overhead heating systems should be avoided as they can create the effect of living in an electromagnetic box.

PRECAUTIONS

- Use mobile phones as little as possible
- Make lengthy social calls from a conventional telephone
- Fit screen filters to VDUs
- Sit, and make sure children sit, at least 2 m (6 ft) away from the television
- Sit as far away from the computer as possible when not working
- Limit children's use of the computer
- Do not use the computer and television as substitute babysitters
- Do not stand near a microwave when it is on
- Dry your hair naturally instead of using electrical appliances
- Choose gas or wood-burning stoves and heaters rather than electric
- Keep all electrical appliances away from the bed
- Do not have wiring under the bed
- Do not use storage heaters in bedrooms

▼ Storing electrical equipment out of sight will help us to relax.

▲ Children sleep better if they are not surrounded by stimulating equipment.

▼ A wood-burning stove lends an attractive focus to a room.

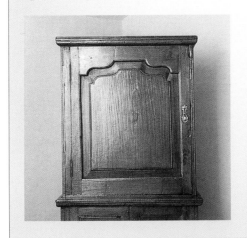

THE SENSES: SIGHT

What we see affects us positively or negatively, or even subconsciously so we may not even be aware of the effect. If we surround ourselves with wonderful views, bright colours, interesting food and a clean and clear environment we are more likely to lead full and happy lives, because our surroundings will reflect a positive attitude to life. The reverse is equally true.

Most homes have problem areas – dark corners which would benefit from light, rooms with columns or L-shaped rooms where the corners point at us – but we can disguise them with plants and materials to soften the edges. There may be things outside which affect us and we may want to keep their influence out.

▲ *Skyscapes are so beautiful that we should make sure we can capture a view of them in our homes.*

We can attempt to deflect the problem with mirrors and other reflective objects, or create a barrier, such as a hedge or shrub, to keep it at bay. There is a difference between this type of positive, or yang, barrier designed to keep the negative exterior forces out and a yin barrier which we sometimes create to keep our own negative energies in – tall hedges and walls and drawn curtains. Wherever the ancient Chinese had a wall, there would be a window, or "Moon Gate", in it through which to see the world beyond and open up future possibilities.

◄ *"Moon Gates" were built into ancient walls in China to afford a glimpse of the world outside.*

▲ *This intricately decorated window can be found in a temple in China.*

▼ *Crystals are used to bring a sparkle to stuck energy. Suspend one in a window and the light will shine through it, creating a rainbow effect on a wall or ceiling.*

CRYSTALS

Colour resonates with us on both a conscious and a subconscious level, and can affect our moods. The combination of crystal and light gives a lively dancing pattern which will enliven a dark room if the crystal is hung in a window. Where energy is stuck, crystals can help to move it on.

Crystals should be used with care. They have many facets which break light up into tiny segments and can do the same to other energies. If the energy of an area is not working, do not hang up a crystal to repair it – or the problem will be exacerbated. A small crystal is adequate for the average home, but larger ones would be needed for a large area.

▶ *Coloured glass panels in a window add life to a colourless room. They also provide privacy and so are ideal for a bathroom or for ground floor rooms.*

▼ *This lovely room has been transformed by the balanced pairs of stained glass windows. Little extra decoration is needed.*

COLOURED GLASS

Coloured glass makes a bolder statement than crystal and its effects can be stunning. Many urban houses have side doors which look out on to a wall and there is a temptation, if they are overlooked by a window from a neighbouring house, to keep a blind permanently down. Replacing the plain glass in a door or window with bold coloured glass which supports the elements of the area will bring a wonderful energy into a dark room and transform it. Stained glass is especially decorative and suitable for most rooms in the home.

THE SENSES: SOUND

Each of the Five Elements governs a different musical quality and sound. We all connect to a particular sound and in Chinese medicine the tone of our voice is categorized according to the elements and used in diagnosis. We each have our own favourite sounds. Gentle background music, the rustle of leaves, bird songs – all have a therapeutic effect. Where noise is rhythmic – a dripping tap, music from a neighbour's party, even someone sneezing at regular intervals – it can grate on our nerves.

Pleasant sounds in the right place and at the right time can soothe and refresh. Bubbling water will create a peaceful ambience and slow us down. If we want to bring life to a place, honky-tonk music, drums and cymbals will fulfil the purpose. Background sounds are comforting and the sound of passing traffic or a ticking clock can be reassuring.

WIND CHIMES

Wind chimes feature in Feng Shui as an enhancer and it is interesting to note how people respond differently to their

▼ *The vibrations from Tibetan bells will energize a room.*

various tones. Take care when using wind chimes near fences since your neighbours may not enjoy their sound as much as you do.

Wind chimes are used to slow energy down, for example, where a staircase faces the front door, but only if they are activated as the door opens. Chimes are also used in the kitchen where people stand at the sink or stove with their backs to the door, because it is comforting to know that the chimes will sound if anyone enters.

Chimes should be hollow to allow the chi in. They can be used to enhance the Metal area of a building, particularly if placed outside the door of a west-facing house, until 2003, when they should be removed. Do not use them in a Wood area (east or south-east) because in that position they are detrimental to the energy of the area.

▼ *The deep-toned, soothing ticking of a grandfather clock is a reassuring sound.*

▲ *Here wind chimes help to balance the negative effect of a sloping ceiling.*

WATER

The sound of gently bubbling water can be relaxing and there are many delightful indoor water features available. Water should be placed in the north, the east, where it is particularly auspicious until 2003, and in the south-east. From 2004 until 2023, the south-west is auspicious. Fish tanks are recommended, but must be clean, and contain living plants and natural features. Neglected tanks and unhealthy fish will have a negative effect. The preferred number of fish is nine, one being black to absorb negative chi.

SOUND ENHANCERS

Wind chimes, Moving water, Music, Clocks, Rustling leaves

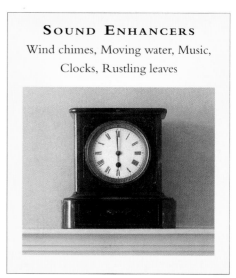

THE SENSES: TOUCH

Too often disregarded, touch is as vital as the other senses and is linked to our primeval desire to be in contact with the Earth. No mother can forget her first contact with a new baby – skin on skin is the most basic yet the most magical feeling there is. The tactile sensations in our homes affect our feelings of comfort and security. A scratchy plant that brushes our ankles as we return home will colour our evening, and a cold or harsh feel underfoot as we step out of bed affects the start of our day.

People who have impaired vision develop their other senses and touch becomes much more important. Guide dogs provide physical contact as well as being their owner's eyes. Isolated elderly people are said to live longer if they have pets to stroke.

When we are depressed, physical contact such as a hug from a relative or partner plays an important part in the healing process. Those who are deprived of physical affection as children often have difficulty making relationships.

▲ *No mother ever forgets her first skin-to-skin contact with her new baby.*

The materials with which we surround ourselves in our homes make a considerable impact on us. Few people can resist the urge to stroke a beautiful wooden bowl, although they might pass by a steel sculpture without touching it. Visitors to stately homes are asked to refrain from stroking fabrics and priceless furniture, but it is an irresistible urge, especially if the furnishings are particularly sumptuous. If we clothe ourselves and cover our furniture in fabrics which feel soft and luxurious, it will positively affect the way we feel. The yin-yang balance in our homes is revealed in the sense of touch. Yang rooms like the kitchen and study are full of yang metal objects which are utilitarian, we would never dream of connecting with these except on a working basis. In yin rooms (bedrooms and other rooms for relaxation) we put on warm and comfortable clothing and snuggle into soft beds and sofas.

▲ *Velvet furnishings and accessories feel wonderfully luxurious.*

◄ *Different textures provide sensual appeal and give a room character.*

TOUCH ENHANCERS
Plants, Wooden objects, Fabrics, Pets, People, Fruit, Smooth objects

THE SENSES: TASTE

This is not as easy as the other senses to describe in terms of Feng Shui yet it forms as great a part of our well-being as any sense. The Chinese see the tastes affiliated to the Five Elements as an integral part of life. If we are to change our perceptions and lifestyles, part of the process includes how we treat our bodies. If the chi is to flow unblocked, then we need to live in a holistic way in every aspect of our lives.

"We are what we eat" expresses the view that our diet directly affects our health. The frantic lifestyles that many of us lead mean that we often grab what we can to eat without taking balance into account. Modern medicine may come up with the cures, but if we eat healthy balanced diets then we are less likely to become ill in the first place.

Using yin and yang and the Five Elements in the kitchen is a science in itself. Chinese herbal medicine balances the constitution using the same techniques as Feng Shui does to balance an environment. (Chaucer's red-faced, lecherous Summoner in *The Canterbury Tales*, a lover of onions and leeks, is a classic case of an excess of the Fire element.) Being aware of the balance of elements in our food, and of the nutritional value

◄ *Using fresh natural ingredients keeps us healthy — and tastes wonderful.*

▲ *Spend time preparing home-cooked meals rather than resorting to store-bought foods.*

of the man-made fast food products which we now consume, enables us to take charge of all aspects of our lives. The benefits and disadvantages of genetically engineered food products are currently being debated, but we do not need scientific reports to tell us that we should make time in our lives to use natural ingredients and not rely on packaged food when we do not know the effects of the chemicals they contain.

SUPPORTIVE FOODS

Once we have consulted the "Chinese Animals" Table and discovered which element governs our sign, we can see below which food types support us. Using "The Relationships of the Five Elements" table, we will then be able to see which of the elements are beneficial to us and which are not, and adjust our eating habits accordingly.

Wood	sour
Fire	bitter
Earth	sweet
Metal	pungent
Water	salt

THE SENSES: SMELL

Large stores know only too well the power of the sense of smell. Who can fail to be tempted by the aroma of freshly baked bread at the supermarket entrance, pumped through grills to lure us into the store where the bakery is almost always in the farthest corner?

Animals excrete pheromones to attract their mates and to mark their territory. Our homes also have a unique smell and most of us, if blindfolded, could tell which of our friends' homes we were entering. First impressions make an

▲ *A herb path by the back door will smell wonderful and give us pleasure.*

▲ *The smell of freshly-baked bread and natural foods heighten our senses.*

▼ *Scented oils give pleasant aromas and can make a colour statement too.*

impact and if our homes smell less than fresh, this can affect how comfortable we and our visitors feel there.

There is something very different about the subtle smell of lavender as we brush past it in the garden on a warm evening after rain and the artificial lavender-scented air-fresheners sold commercially. Natural smells affect us in a way that manufactured scents never can, with the added advantage of not causing us respiratory problems or polluting the atmosphere. There is nothing to beat the flower-perfumed fresh air which wafts through an open window from a garden, balcony or window box. Many cultures use incense to sweeten the air, and we are now beginning to rediscover the long-lost knowledge of the benefits to health of certain aromatic oils.

SMELL ENHANCERS

Fresh air, Aromatic oils, Plants, Fresh potpourri, Fruit

COLOUR

The Tao teaches that out of the interplay of yin and yang all things come. Yin is the blackness which absorbs all colours and yang the whiteness which reflects them. They give rise to the Five Elements and their associated colour representations, from which arise the whole spectrum of colours. Colour is vibration and we each respond to it on many levels, consciously and unconsciously. Colour affects how comfortable we are in different environments and can affect our moods. Our use of colour also affects how others perceive us. Colour is used to cure physical ailments and can be used symbolically to enhance spaces or evoke emotions.

When we use colour we are also working with light since light contains all colours, each with its own frequency. Every situation is different – each home

▼ *African colours – browns, beiges and terracottas – predominate here.*

BEWARE PEACH

Using the colour peach in your bedroom is asking for trouble if you are married. "Peach-Blossom Luck" is a well-known concept in China, meaning a husband or wife with a roving eye. A married person may be drawn into adultery. A single person, however, will have an active social life but will probably be unable to find a life partner.

▲ *This room works wonderfully well. All the elements are there but not contrived.*

and each room within it. The light quality depends on the aspect, the size of the windows and how they are decorated, artificial light sources and the size of the rooms. The materials we use on floors and in decorations and furnishings have the ability to reflect and transmit light or to absorb it. We can use colour to create illusions – of size (dark colours absorb more light than lighter ones); of depth (natural pigments draw light in or reflect it according to the time of day and the season); and of movement (spots of colour around a room create movement and energy there).

Light quality varies around the world. In Africa, pigments, fabrics and skins in browns, beiges and terracottas are used where the sun beats down under a bright blue sky. In Britain, where the climate suggests an indoor life and the light is much less vibrant, the same colours signify closing in and, used to excess, can

lead to withdrawal and depression. Similarly, the intense colours of Indian silks and the warm colours of the Mediterranean palette have to be used with care when introduced in countries where light quality differs. However, they can play a useful role in moving the energy and, with thought, can be effective.

▼ *Mediterranean colours make us think of sunshine and holidays.*

◄ In this conservatory, the Metal and Wood elements are in conflict.

▶ The colours green (Wood), red (Fire) and yellow (Earth) balance the Five Elements.

THE FIVE ELEMENTS

The five colours associated with the elements evoke the quality of the energy of each one. We use them to highlight areas of our lives we wish to concentrate on, and the Bagua diagram gives us the associated colours for each direction. In Feng Shui balance and harmony are essential. We should decorate our homes according to our tastes or we will never be comfortable there. We should remember the purpose of the room and the element associated with the direction it is in. Then we can achieve true balance and harmony. It would be treating the subject superficially to ensure that a room has, say, a cushion in each of the Five Elemental colours, but a single green-stemmed red artificial tulip in a glass vase in the south of an all-white room would bring in the Wood element in the green stem, and the Fire element in the red flower. The Metal element is represented by the white room, the Water element by the light moving through the glass vase and the Earth element in the sand used to make the glass and as the medium which gave rise to the flower.

THE COLOURS

White represents a fresh canvas and black symbolizes a clean slate upon which we can create a picture with the colours below, as well as the many shades and hues which evolve from them.

RED: Red is stimulating and dominant, it reduces the size of rooms and increases the size of objects. It is useful as an accent colour. It is not suitable for dining rooms, children's bedrooms, kitchens or workshops. It is associated with warmth, prosperity and stimulation, but also anger, shame and hatred.

YELLOW: Yellow is associated with enlightenment and intellect, it stimulates the brain and aids digestion. Its positive qualities are optimism, reason and decisiveness, while its negative are craftiness, exaggeration and rigidity. Suitable for hallways and kitchens, but not for meditation rooms or bathrooms.

GREEN: Green symbolizes growth, fertility and harmony; it is restful and refreshing. Its positive associations are optimism, freedom and balance, and its negatives envy and deceit. Good in therapy rooms, conservatories and bathrooms but not in family rooms, playrooms or studies.

BLUE: Blue is peaceful and soothing and is linked with spirituality, contemplation, mystery and patience. Its positive associations are trust, faithfulness and stability. Negatives are suspicion and melancholia. Blue can be used in meditation rooms, bedrooms, therapy rooms and as a means of enlarging spaces, but not in family rooms, dining rooms and studies.

PURPLE: Encouraging vitality, purple is impressive, dignified and spiritual. Positive associations are excitement, passion and motivation, negatives are mournfulness and force. Use in bedrooms and meditation rooms but not bathrooms or kitchens.

PINK: Pink is linked with purity of thought and has the positive association of happiness and romance with no negatives. Suitable for bedrooms but not kitchens or bathrooms.

ORANGE: A powerful and cheerful colour, orange encourages communication. Its positive qualities are happiness, concentration and intellect, and its negative is rebelliousness. Use in living or dining rooms and hallways, but not in small rooms or bedrooms.

BROWN: Brown suggests stability and weight. Its positives are safety and elegance, while its negatives are dinginess, depression and aging. Good for studies but not for bedrooms.

WHITE: White symbolizes new beginnings, purity and innocence. its positive qualities are cleanliness and freshness, its negatives cold, lifelessness, starkness. Use for bathrooms and kitchens, not suitable for children's rooms and dining rooms.

BLACK: Black is mysterious and independent. Its positive qualities are intrigue, strength and allure, while its negatives are death, darkness and evil. Often used in teenagers' rooms and in bedrooms, it should not be used in young children's rooms, therapy rooms, studies or living rooms.

CLUTTER

lutter is a state of mind. It can be the things we haven't done which prey on our minds, like unreturned telephone calls and appointments not made, or the ideas and perceptions we hoard which prevent us from doing the things we really want to do. Everything we do not use or wear, or which we are keeping in case it comes in handy one day, constitutes clutter. Inherited objects, and those given to us as presents which we do not like but feel guilty about parting with, are also clutter.

For one reason or another, perhaps due to our upbringing or past experiences, or because we doubt our own abilities, we hang on to situations and ideas which do not let us move on. We may stay in a job thinking we are indis-

▲ *This low-beamed cottage room looks oppressive with fussy decoration and too many ornaments.*

▼ *A similar room but less cluttered gives a lighter, more airy feel.*

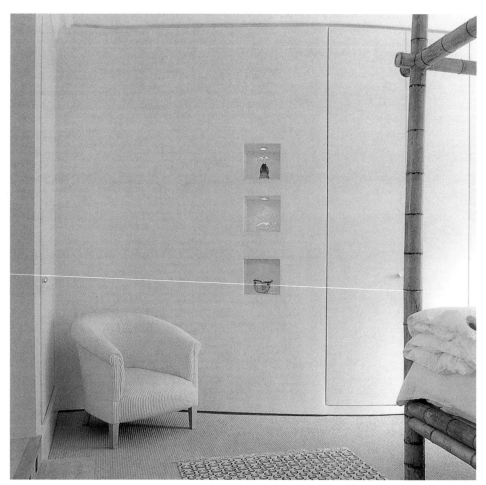

▲ *Any extraneous objects would look out of place in this cool, clutter-free bedroom, a perfect place to unwind.*

pensable or we are doing it out of a sense of loyalty, but often it is because we are afraid to take the leap and change direction. We may stay in a relationship through fear of emotional upheaval, or not accept a job away from a familiar area through fear of the unknown. All these attitudes clutter our thought processes but by clearing out our physical clutter we see the benefits of "letting go", which will help us to clear out the mental clutter restricting our development.

CLEARING OUT

"Things" constitute a major problem in most homes. Useless kitchen gadgets, empty gift boxes to recycle, presents we hate or have outgrown, inherited objects which fear of embarrassment or guilt will not let us part with, and an endless list of other items. We do not need these things in our lives if we are to open up and let

new experiences in. Give them to charity shops or sell them at car-boot sales and buy something you really want.

Most of us hold on to clothes "in case" we might need them, grow back into them or our children might like them one day. It is far better to live for today and create space for something new which we will enjoy wearing now.

Books are difficult to get rid of as many people believe it is a sacrilege to throw them out. If books sit and gather dust for years on end, unread and not referred to, they too constitute clutter and stuck energy and we should move them on. The world is changing fast and information becomes out of date almost before it is in print. Should we require a

▲ *If these overladen shelves are thinned out, there will be room for new books.*

fact in ten years' time, the information will always be available elsewhere. Magazines and newspapers also constitute clutter. We are unlikely to read last week's, or even yesterday's, paper and we can always extract any information we require from magazines provided we file it immediately in a place where we are likely to find it again.

Clutter represents stagnant energy and the list is endless – blown light bulbs we keep forgetting to replace, dead wasps and dropped leaves on the window ledge, scum marks round the bath, the unfilled vinegar shaker, the squeaking door. Each of these requires only one minute's attention, but their accumulated effect can make years of difference to the pace and quality of our lives.

Do not attempt to rid the whole house of clutter in one go. Start in a small way with a drawer, and complete the whole task of clearing out, tidying and getting rid of unwanted items before moving on to the next.

▲ *There is no clutter here but enough objects and colours to make the space interesting.*

ENERGIZING OUR HOMES

When we move into a new house, or have had an unpleasant experience in our home, the energy there can become stuck and feel heavy. We can lighten it to some extent by clearing out all the clutter and by cleaning everywhere thoroughly.

Vibrations are important and we resonate at a level which is in harmony with the natural vibrations of the Earth. The senses also work at a vibrational level and if we can improve their quality in our homes we will feel the benefit. Often the vibrations which have caused

▼ *Candles represent Fire. Use with care in the South and to support the West.*

▲ *Burning aromatic oils or incense raises the energy in a room.*

the previous owner to behave in a certain way or adopt a certain way of life will have the same effect on us and we should take note of any problems which have befallen them before moving to a new home.

There are various methods we can use to improve the vibrations in our homes. Having cleaned and rid the house of clutter, open the windows and make a noise in

every room (check first that the neighbours are out). Bells, gongs and clapping are all useful in raising the vibrational level. Take particular care to go into the corners, where energy is likely to have become stuck. Natural light should be present in the form of sunlight and candles, placed in the four corners of the room and in the centre. Smell can be introduced in the form of incense or aromatic oils. Spring water, charged by the vibrations of the moon, can be sprayed around to introduce negative ions back into the air.

▼ *Candles in the corners and centre of a room will help move any stuck energy.*

USING THE SYMBOLIC BAGUA

We all wish at certain times in our lives that some aspect was working better. By focusing on a particular aspect of our lives, we can often stimulate the energy to make things work well for us. Used as a template that we can place on the plans of our home, the Symbolic Bagua gives us a tool for focus with its division into eight life sections. The eight life sections of the Bagua are: Career, Relationships, Family, Wealth, Helpful People, Children, Knowledge and Fame and each area has its own enhancers. By using some of the methods described on the following pages we can hopefully harness some of the "magic" of Feng Shui for ourselves.

The enhancements used in Feng Shui are designed to focus the mind. For example, we can create the belief that it is possible to stabilize something in our lives by using heavy objects such as stones or pictures of mountains. We can move on a "stuck" situation by creating or alluding to movement, for instance, using water or wind-blown items. Whatever image we use must have meaning for us in that we can see it physically and relate to its symbolism. Thus we should use images from our own cultures and experiences. Whatever we use, it should not clash with the element of the direction but if possible should strengthen it.

CAREER

This concerns itself with where we are going in life, either in our jobs or in our journeys through life. It can also mark the beginning of a project. ENHANCERS INCLUDE: moving images, a photograph of an aspiration such as a university, or a company brochure if applying for a job.

RELATIONSHIPS

These play an important part in our lives. Getting on well with people and having the support of partners, family or friends play a major role in a happy life.

▲ *A perfect arrangement for a table in the Relationships area of a room.*

ENHANCERS INCLUDE: double images for romance, two vases or candlesticks, a photograph of yourself with your partner or group images of friends, a poster or photograph, or a collection of something. Plants are useful to improve the chi, and ribbons or wind-activated objects will energize it as they move, provided there is a breeze. Do not use them if there is no breeze.

FAMILY

Our families, past as well as present, will have coloured who we are, how we relate to the world around us and will have

▼ *Framed photographs can be placed in the Family area of a room.*

contributed to our health and well-being. ENHANCERS INCLUDE: Family photographs and documents, and heirlooms.

WEALTH

This is often taken to be monetary wealth, but it also covers the richness of our lives, fulfilment and the accumulation of beneficial energies around us. ENHANCERS INCLUDE: coins, plants, empty bowls and movement, for example, an indoor water feature.

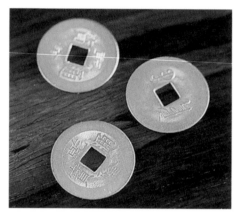

▲ *Chinese coins for the Wealth area – the circle symbolizes Heaven, the square Earth.*

HELPFUL PEOPLE

Interaction with others is an essential part of life, and this area is a very important one. "What goes round, comes round" and "You reap what you sow" are Eastern and Western ways of saying the same thing. If you are willing to help others and need some help in return, this is the area to focus on. ENHANCERS INCLUDE: telephones and telephone directories, and business cards.

CHILDREN

Not quite the same as family, since children are the future rather than part of the past. This area also covers personal projects – the tasks and jobs you nurture from their conception to their conclusion. ENHANCERS INCLUDE: photographs of children, project details, and your artistic and other achievements.

▲ *Family photographs of children are placed in the Children area.*

KNOWLEDGE

This is the area for wisdom and education, not of the enforced variety, but that which is sought after and which can enrich our lives. ENHANCERS INCLUDE: books, framed words of wisdom and pictures of mentors.

FAME

This does not mean notoriety for its own sake, but recognition of an undertaking well done and a sense of fulfilment.

HOME ENHANCER

An enhancer for any space that will nurture the supportive energy in any home is a feature which represents all five elements. Fill a glass or crystal bowl (Earth) with blue glass nuggets (Earth and Water), top up with water and a floating candle (Fire) and some flowers or petals (Wood). Add coins (Metal) to complete the cycle.

THE POWER OF FENG SHUI

Feng Shui works in mysterious ways and the results of any action taken may not be quite as expected. Our actions trigger the energy required to achieve the outcomes we seek. This may not correspond to what we think we need or offer a quick fix. A consultant will offer solutions having ensured that everything is balanced. If we decide to undertake some of the recommendations and not others there will be no balance. Proceed carefully. Instigate one change at a time and give it several days before introducing the next.

The following case study illustrates the unpredictable nature of Feng Shui. Richard and Anne had lived in their house for ten years and had never settled. Through lethargy they had let it run down and now could not sell it. The electric lights blew regularly and there was evidence of a water leak outside the house. The only decorating they had done was to paint the living room walls a deep pink which, together with the red carpet laid throughout the house, resulted in an overload of Fire energy.

Richard and Anne did not want to spend money on a new carpet, so they were advised to paint the walls white to drain the Fire. They had already installed a large fish tank in the Wealth area since they wanted their money to move. They put several recommendations into practice, but not the major one – the walls. The result was that the energies took over. Within a week, the washing machine flooded the ground floor, ruining the carpet and forcing out the Fire energy, the overloaded electrical system finally blew and the fish in the tank died. The Chinese use fish as a sacrifice to human bad luck, believing they soak it up on behalf of the people.

Thus Feng Shui achieved its objectives and moved the energy on. Richard and Anne were left with no choice but to fix the electrics and change the carpet, and this time they chose wisely. The changes made the house sellable and they were able to move. Never underestimate the power of Feng Shui, be prepared for the unexpected.

ENHANCERS INCLUDE: certificates, newspaper cuttings, products of achievement.

Feng Shui cannot help you to win the lottery but if you have worked hard and followed an honest and ethical path towards self-fulfilment, then the magic may work for you. If this happens, you will probably not want to win the lottery anyway and other, more rewarding bounty may come your way.

THE CENTRE OF THE BAGUA

The centre is a special place. In a house it is where the occupants meet and where the energies accumulate and flow on. It should be treated well, be bright and welcoming, and not be cluttered. Do not introduce a light fitting with five bulbs here; glass and crystal light fittings will stimulate the area far better. A round rug often works well.

THE RIGHT TIME

Most of us will have heard or read of people who have used Feng Shui and received rewards – a job, a long-awaited child, or a partner. We may be tempted to take Feng Shui on board and tweak every area of our homes in order to achieve perfection. Life is not perfect, however, and it is constantly changing. Essentially, the energies of the various directions change over time. Thus if we activate a particular area when the energies are good, things will be fine. If we leave whatever we have done when the energies are inauspicious, then we will create problems.

The adage, "If it ain't broke, don't fix it" applies. Remember when using these symbolic measures that the compass directions and their related elements are still important.

INVESTIGATING YOUR HOME

The following Feng Shui case study can only offer a glimpse into the kind of analysis which takes place when investigating a home.

William and Julia and their son Steven moved into their apartment a year ago. Julia feels comfortable there but William and Steven do not, and Steven has gradually become very run down and cannot concentrate on his schoolwork. William does some freelance work at home to supplement his income, but has not been getting many clients lately. There is tension and the couple's relationship is suffering. A Feng Shui consultant investigates the birthday of each person, their animal, the corresponding element and the compatibility of the animals.

William is a Fire – Rooster, Julia is a Metal + Rat and Steven a Water – Pig. This indicates that while William and Julia have a workable relationship with Steven, William and Julia's relationship can be difficult. According to the Five Elements relationships, Fire (William) is weakened by Metal (Julia), who in turn is weakened by Water (Steven). Being a Metal Rat with yang characteristics, Julia is quite strong and domineering so can hold her own. As a Fire Rooster, William can be inflexible and is not easily swayed by others' emotions so may not be sym-

▼ *This bed is well balanced by the matching tables and lamps on either side.*

▲ *The position of the bed is crucial. It should be protected behind and face an auspicious direction for the occupants.*

pathetic to Steven. Fortunately, as a Water Pig, Steven accepts that things are difficult and is perceptive enough to steer clear when necessary.

Next, the consultant looked at the magic numbers, the corresponding east and west directions, each person's favourable and unfavourable directions, and the compass direction of the house.

William is a 7 and belongs to the west group. Julia, a 4, belongs to the east group and Steven, an 8, belongs to the west group. The house faces south-east, an east group direction, and is therefore most supportive of Julia. William's best direction is north-west, which is missing from the house. His office falls between the south and south-west sectors. The south-west is his second-best direction and the south his sixth. Steven's room has geopathic stress by the head of his bed. His best direction is south-west and his second is north-west. Julia's best direction is north and the second south. The consultant then looked at the shape of the house, Steven's room, William's desk position and William and Julia's bed. He made recommendations listed below.

KEY TO DIAGRAM

1. A mirror here symbolically completes the house shape and seemingly draws in the energy of the missing section. A metal frame is used which represents the element of the area.

2. The head of the bed was re-positioned to face south-west, Steven's best direction, and to remove him from the stressed area.

3. Steven's desk now faces north-west, his second-best direction. This also enables him to see the door and protects him from the fast-moving chi along the long passage. The bookcase, aided by the plant on top, also protects him from the chi in the passage.

4. Semi-circular tables with silk flowers slow the chi further. The passage was too dark for live plants.

5. William's desk now faces north-west, his best position. A plant behind him prevents stagnant energy from building up in the corner. A plant on the desk

deflects fast-moving chi through the door and hides the point which would symbolically stab him as he enters.

6. The "mouth of chi" to the stove, the point of entry of the energy source and symbolic of wealth, comes from the south, Julia's second-best position.

7. In this room the bed is best in Julia's best position, north. A mirror should not reflect the bed, so a small mirror has been used here (see 1).

8. Two square tables, signifying containment, are placed on either side of the bed.

9. A picture of a couple is placed here to symbolize togetherness in the symbolic Relationships area.

10. In the compass Relationships area, which is Earth, stones have been placed on the bathroom and toilet windowsills.

11. A plant is placed on the windowsill here to support William's personal Fire element.

▼ *A floor plan of William and Julia's room after the changes were made. The numbers correspond with the captions in the box, left.*

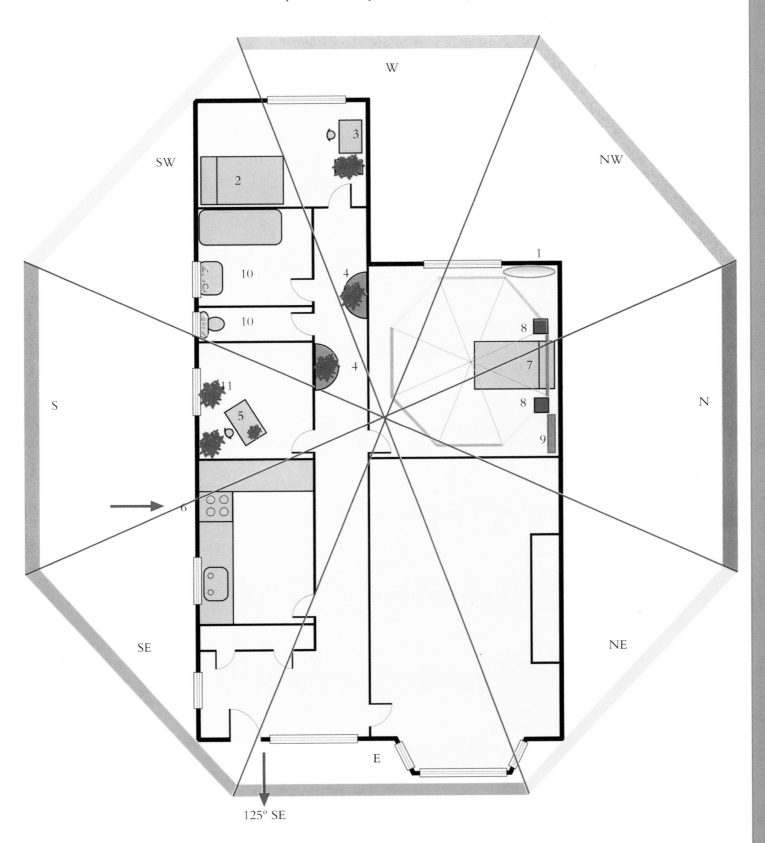

W

SW

NW

3

2

1

10

4

8

S

10

7

N

4

8

11

9

5

SE

NE

6

E

125° SE

PUTTING THE PRINCIPLES INTO PRACTICE

———

Now that we are familiar with the basic principles of
Feng Shui, it is time to look at our homes room by room
and see if we can arrange them differently to create spaces
that will nourish us. When we move energy about there
may be unexpected consequences, so it is important to
proceed slowly and discover what will work for us.
Allow children to create spaces that are meaningful
for them at each stage of their development.

HALLS, LOBBIES AND STAIRCASES

When we step though the front door, the first impression we have of a house is the hall. If it is light and spacious with a pleasant, fresh smell, and is clean and tidy, then our spirits will rise. A long dark corridor, the smell of last night's cooking and a stack of newspapers in the corner will set the tone for the whole house. If the energy channels of the house are restricted or blocked, this can have a knock-on effect. Those who live with narrow, dark hallways may suffer restriction mentally or as a blockage in one of their body channels. Psychologically such a place is depressing. It is possible to deal with this by using bright colours and mirrors. Coat hooks at levels to accommodate even the smallest family members and shoe cupboards or racks can all make our

▼ In this spacious hall, natural finishes, and a variety of shapes, colours and textures create an energetic space.

homecoming easier. The last thing we need to see on returning is a mess; we will not look forward to returning home.

THE VIEW FROM THE DOOR

If a door opens immediately on to a wall, people will feel overwhelmed and they will feel life is a struggle. A landscape picture which attracts the eye will give the illusion of drawing us on into the main part of the home. An entrance opposite

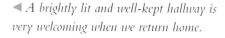

◀ A brightly lit and well-kept hallway is very welcoming when we return home.

▼ Plenty of coat hooks and storage space prevent the hall from becoming cluttered.

the back door or window will funnel chi straight out and it will not have the opportunity to circulate. Keep doors closed, place plants on windowsills or install coloured glass into the back door window to reflect chi back into the room. If the first room seen from the door is the kitchen, it will be the first port of call on returning home. Food will be on our minds before we do anything else. Children will tumble in on returning from school with outdoor clothes and school bags to raid the fridge. An office opposite the door will encourage us to rush in to check the answerphone. Work will be on our minds and we will not be able to relax. Toilet doors should be kept closed at all times, according to Chinese wisdom, so that we do not watch our wealth being flushed away, and a closed lid is an extra precaution.

> ### HALL CLUTTER
> Coats, Shoes, Bags, Junk mail,
> Free papers, Laundry, Items to
> take upstairs

COMMUNAL LOBBIES

In buildings which were once large houses but are now small flats, or in badly managed apartment blocks, the communal entrance lobby is often a problem. There are two ways of approaching a dirty, messy, badly decorated lobby: negatively, by blaming others, or by taking positive action. Stuck personal chi is often a contributory factor to stuck energy in a house so it is in the interests of all the occupants to move it.

▼ *Plants either side of the entrance welcome the residents of this apartment block.*

▲ *The front door of this house opens directly on to the stairs. There is no barrier against the chi, which enters through the door and rushes through the house too quickly.*

▲ *A large plant placed in this position makes all the difference. It masks the corner of the stairs from view of the front door and slows down the chi.*

CASE STUDY
Nancy lived in a house that had been converted into four flats, with a communal hallway and staircase. The turnover of residents was high and the communal areas were a mess. Approaches to the landlord and other tenants failed, so Nancy painted the hall herself and put up a shelf with a box for each flat into which she sorted the mail and free papers. A bright poster and a plant completed the project. Almost immediately, the neighbours became more friendly and began to stop for a chat. The turnover of tenants slowed down and within two years Nancy and her neighbours bought the freehold of the property and set about renovating it. As a result the house was transformed and has become a very desirable place to live.

STAIRCASES
Often the front door of a house or apartment opens straight on to the staircase. Again the chi will be funnelled without having the chance to circulate so it is a good idea to block the view of the stairs by using a plant, a bookcase or other piece of furniture. If this is not possible, a round rug or a crystal chandelier will gather the chi in the hall. A wind chime which sounds as the door opens will also help to slow down the chi.

Some attention should be paid to how staircases and hallways are lit and decorated. Low ceilings can feel restricting and make the moving of furniture difficult, and a steep stairwell causes problems when decorating, but overcoming these difficulties and making the best of your hall and staircase will pay off.

The staircase should be in proportion to the dimensions of the rest of the house. Steep stairs conduct chi too quickly. Modern conversions often have spiral staircases leading to the bedroom area. These are considered inauspicious in Feng Shui because they resemble a corkscrew through the home. Wrap some ivy or green silk around the staircase and make sure a light shines from top to bottom. Stairs with open treads allow the chi to escape. Place plants, real or symbolic, representing Wood energy underneath.

CHI FLOW IMPROVEMENT IN A HALLWAY
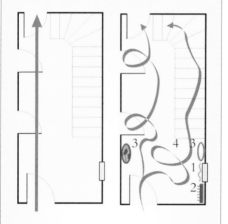
BEFORE   AFTER

1. Muslin curtains create a pause between the outside and the house.
2. Children and guests leave coats, shoes and umbrellas neatly on hooks and racks. These also block the view of the stairs from the door and hide outer garments from the inside.
3. At the foot of the stairs a mirror reflects a plaster plate with a painted landscape, which has the effect of drawing visitors deeper into the house.
4. The children can go up to their rooms at this point and may not even enter the kitchen until suppertime. If the chi flow upstairs works, they may even have washed their hands first!

LIVING ROOMS

Aliving room is used for a number of activities – for relaxation, as a family room where games are played, and an entertainment room for watching television and playing music. In some homes, particularly in apartments, the living room may have a dining area attached, or part of it may be used as a study or office space. The arrangement of the room is therefore important if these diverse functions are to be supported successfully.

▼ *Natural materials, lots of colour and a pleasant view give this living room an energetic feeling.*

Living areas should be welcoming, and the colour scheme can help this. Proportion is also important. In barn or warehouse conversions with large open-plan spaces and high ceilings, it is preferable to create small groupings of furniture rather than attempt to create a single room within the space. In small rooms, try to keep bookcases and built-in wall units low, otherwise the room will feel top-heavy and appear to close in. It is especially important to be able to screen off study or office areas so that work is not constantly preying on the mind when we are trying to relax.

SEATING

Living rooms are yin spaces full of comfortable, fabric-covered seats which are also yin. Chairs and sofas with high backs and arms are protective and represent the Tortoise, Dragon, Tiger formation offering support to those who sit in them. A footstool nearby marks the Phoenix position.

Those sitting in the room should, where possible, not sit with their backs to the door. Guests should feel welcome when they come, so offer them the prime positions facing the door. In rooms where chairs and sofas are not backed by

▶ *All these chairs are supportive to the occupants, adding to the peaceful energy of this elegant room.*

a wall, create stability behind the seating by placing a table or bookcase there. Furniture is always best if it has rounded edges. If the bedroom leads off the main living area, make sure that the furniture is not sending a "poison arrow" into the room from a corner. Keep doors from the living room closed.

BACKS TO THE DOOR

If you have a visitor who does more than their fair share of the talking, position them with their back to the door to reduce their dominance in the group. In addition, uninvited guests who you would like to leave as soon as possible should also be placed outside the main group.

▲ *The Earth colour on the walls and lamps is welcoming, but the blue Water energy drains it.*

▼ *Plenty of Earth colours on the walls and in the furnishing fabrics make this a nurturing and cosy room.*

SEATING ARRANGEMENTS

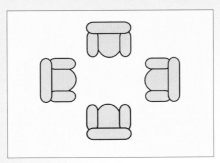

▲ This seating arrangement is suitable for a harmonious family or social gathering. The "circle" is used in all cultures for community gatherings.

▶ In this arrangement the table is sending a "poison arrow" into the bedroom. Re-position the furniture to prevent this.

▼ The television arrangement spells death to social chat and family unity.

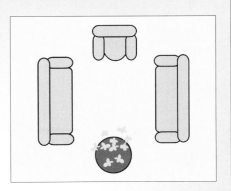

▲ This arrangement is useful for a meeting as it focuses people on whatever is taking place, but also has space to allow the energy in.

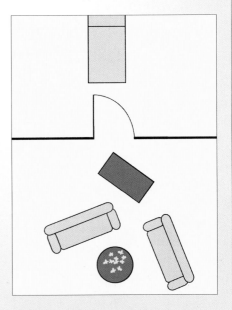

FIREPLACES

In previous centuries fires were used for cooking, warmth and protection, and were carefully tended. The communal fire was the focal point of family life. These days a real fire is less common, and when it is present it is often a secondary heat source, lit only at festival times or at weekends, rather than a vital source of life. A coal or wood fire, however, always makes a room feel welcoming and draws family and friends toward it.

Since a fireplace is an opening into the room, a mirror above it is beneficial to symbolically prevent the chi from escaping. A fireguard will be necessary, especially where there are children. Plants positioned on either side of the fireplace represent Wood energy, which will symbolically feed the fire and enhance its gathering qualities.

The chimney wall often juts into the living room, creating alcoves on either side. Be aware of this when placing chairs as people sitting in them may be the recipients of harmful chi from the corners. Soften any jutting angles on the mantelpiece with hanging plants.

LIGHTING

A variety of lighting is necessary, particularly if the room is used for a number of purposes. Bright lighting is required for family activities and for children playing, and also in north-facing rooms which get

▼ *A larger sofa would give more support in this well-proportioned room.*

▲ *A cosy living area has been created in the middle of this vast space.*

little natural light. In addition, there should be softer lights; uplighters in the corners or wall lights, and task lighting if there is a desk in the room.

SCREENS

Ideally, kitchens and dining rooms should be separate from the main living room. Where they are attached or adjoining, screen them off in some way or food will become too important and grazing habits will be encouraged.

A BALANCE OF LIGHT

▲ Here the blue (Water) energy is overpowering the green (Wood) energy and the red (Fire) energy.

▲ The red lamp makes an enormous difference, restoring the balance of the various energies in the room.

▲ *The additional colours and the mixture of whites turn this into a warm room.*

TELEVISIONS AND STEREOS

Always arrange the seating so that it does not allow the television to be the main focus of the room. Where the TV is the focal point, instead of a warm, gathering fire, the family will sit in rows and communication will be negligible. (However, this is better than each child having a television in their bedroom, which can result in a total breakdown of the social aspects of family life.) Position stereos as far away from seating as possible to avoid electromagnetic radiation.

FURNISHINGS

If the living room is painted in a single colour, small areas of stimulation are necessary to keep the energy moving. Too much fabric can harbour dust and fade, creating stagnant energy, but in a room where people gather curtains help to create a cosy feeling. Undressed windows

◀ *A small television set is far better than a large set that will dominate the room.*

▶ *Natural materials and fresh colour give this room a good feel.*

and ones with blinds can be harsh and, being rectangular, add to the Earth energy of the room. In rooms that have many rectangular features and are also decorated in Earth colours – magnolia, brown, mustard – the energy will feel sluggish and can make the occupants feel depressed. Keep family rooms well-ventilated and allow in as much natural light as possible.

PAINTINGS AND OBJECTS

We should always be aware of the effect of the images with which we surround ourselves, since they reflect our inner selves. Gruesome images and spiky objects can reflect inner turmoil, whereas bells, rainbows and pictures of the seasons will reflect inner peace. If we live alone our living rooms will reflect our desire for a peaceful haven or our need for companionship and we can use the space to create positive atmospheres.

Images and artwork displayed in family spaces should be cheerful and reflect pleasant and harmonious themes. Ideally, photographs of the family should be displayed in this room. If one child is more artistically talented than the others, in the interests of family harmony, his/her achievements should not be spread all round the room or the other children will feel that they are failures by comparison. Guns, swords and other weapons have no place in the living room.

It is important that the contents of the home, especially the communal areas, should be balanced and reflect the lives of all the occupants. If our working lives are hectic, our living rooms will reflect our desire for a peaceful haven. Lonely people should, however, use this room to reflect their need for companionship and remove all single images – such as pictures of lone figures; ornaments should

▼ *This oval urn prevents stagnation in an otherwise gloomy corner.*

▲ *This is a room designed for sitting and chatting. The round table ensures the conversation will not get too serious.*

▼ *We should surround ourselves with positive images. The clean lines of this carved wooden bird make the energy soar.*

LIVING ROOM CLUTTER
Newspapers and magazines
Full ashtrays
Used cups
Children's toys after bedtime
Fallen plant leaves
Unpaid bills and unanswered letters
on the mantelpiece

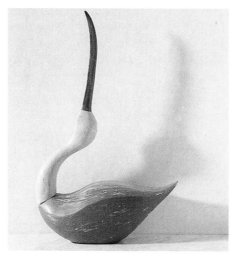

be grouped in pairs, and the room should be used to create a positive energy.

Where we share our homes with friends, with a partner, or as part of a family, we need to create personal spaces within which we feel comfortable and where we can express ourselves. Relationships with those whose horoscopes or numbers conflict with our own are common and we will be familiar with the phrase "opposites attract". Formulae may suggest, however, that one partner should live in an east group house and the other a west group house. We have to be practical. Where the energies of a house favour one occupant more than the other, it is important to take this into account and enable the other to express themselves within the house and to position themselves in favourable directions in bed and when working and relaxing.

▶ *We should position ourselves in favourable directions surrounded by supportive images.*

CASE STUDY

When David and Sarah retired to the coast from their family house in the country, they left behind a large garden which Sarah had lovingly tended for 20 years. David, a keen angler, purchased a share in a boat and joined the local fishing club, and soon had a full and active social life. Photographs of his activities, pictures of boats and his prize catch preserved in a glass case along with accompanying trophies appeared around the house. Having decorated the house and finished arranging the tiny garden, Sarah became bored and felt unfulfilled in her new life, but since David was so happy she kept to herself the fact that she preferred life in the country.

As David had an office and a workshop, it was agreed that Sarah should have part of the house designated as her own space and the living room was chosen as her personal area.

1. Sarah, a Water Rooster, was being overwhelmed by too much water in her new environment. A large plant in the North symbolically drained some of the Water energy.

2. Born in 1934, Sarah's magic number is 3, making her best direction south, so the seating was arranged accordingly.

3. David's fishing trophies and photographs were placed in his study and, since she did not want to hurt his feelings but did not like having dead animals in the house, Sarah compromised and suggested that the prize fish could go into the bathroom and not be banished to the workshop. Sarah framed some watercolours she had painted at their former home and hung them on the wall instead.

4. To dispel the idea that this lifestyle was to be Sarah's lot for the rest of her retirement, and particularly since the windows faced west and the setting sun, the rising growth energy of the east was stimulated with a picture of the rising sun.

5. A mirror placed in the south-east, also representing Wood, reflected the garden

and drew it into the house to support Sarah's love of the countryside.

6. After reading a Feng Shui book, Sarah decided to try to activate the Relationships area to see if she could find new friends. Using the Symbolic Bagua, she put up a poster of a group of people chatting, which was also reflected in the mirror, thus doubling the effect.

When the changes had been made, a neighbour visited and admired Sarah's watercolours and suggested she should display them at the local garden show. Someone admired and purchased them, and with the money Sarah bought a greenhouse where she now grows exotic plants which she paints portraits of and sells. Interestingly, the picture of the rising sun is, according to the Symbolic Bagua, in Sarah's Offspring or Projects area. She is now an active member of a gardening group, where she has made lots of friends and is busy all the time.

DINING ROOMS

The dining room is a social area where family and friends can meet, talk and enjoy good food together. As snacking and "grazing" typify modern eating habits, the dining room has diminished in importance. For the Chinese it is a centre of wealth, where a full table, often mirrored to apparently double the quantity, is indicative of the financial standing of the family.

Dining room colours should be bright

▶ If there is a window behind the dining table, it is important that the chairs have backs to them for support.

▲ This wonderful dining room has a lovely view of the garden. Small shelves would protect diners from the axe-like glass overhead.

and stimulating to whet the appetite. Dull, lifeless colours should be avoided as they suppress the appetite. Lighting should be chosen with care to complement the food and not cast shadows over the table. Candles can be romantic, but may get in the way when people are serving themselves or become irritating if they are too tall or flicker. Beware of pictures and ornaments that conjure up inappropriate images – hunting scenes or

▲ *A lovely setting for a meal. The candles are low enough not to get in the way or prevent people seeing each other properly.*

▼ *An excellent dining room – the chairs are backed by a wall and the mirror reflects the table, doubling its apparent size.*

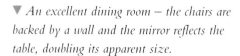

▲ *Kitchen diners make a good setting for an informal meal, and round tables are ideal as they encourage lively conversation.*

▶ *Low candles such as these pretty shell candles are safer than tall ones at the table.*

a china pig collection are not suitable if you have vegetarian friends. The best images to display are ones of fruit, the fresh, clean outdoors, or of friends dining. If mirrors are used, position them so that diners will not feel uncomfortable.

High-backed solid chairs, preferably with arms, represent the supportive Tortoise, Tiger, Dragon formation. Sitting positions are considered to be very important. The prime positions in the room should have a solid wall behind them and a view of the door. The most vulnerable positions are those with a door behind them, followed by seats with their backs to a window.

Table shapes are also important and can affect the quality of the meal. Round tables tend to make your guests leave early because the chi spins round them, while square tables allow more stability. Rectangular tables are difficult as those at either end tend to feel left out. The best shaped tables are octagonal, which not only enable guests to interact with everyone else on the table, but also represent the Cosmos as reflected in the Bagua.

BALANCED EATING

Much has been made of balanced eating recently but this is not a new concept. Since ancient times, diet has formed part of the same philosophy as Feng Shui. Meals are planned to create a yin-yang balance and with the nature of the Five Elements in mind. Some foods are regarded as having yin qualities and some yang, and different tastes are associated with the Five Elements.

We should learn to recognize the signals that our bodies and our state of mind give out and recognize whether we are becoming yin (feeling tired and slowing down) or yang (unable to relax and stressed). We can balance our diets by ensuring we eat the same proportion of

▲ *Conservatory dining rooms are becoming popular and can create light, spacious areas for eating in all the year round.*

◄ *In such a large area as this your guests might feel slightly ill-at-ease. High-backed chairs would help dispel any nervousness. A round table is a good shape for this room.*

yin foods – such as alcohol, chocolate, citrus fruits, coffee and sugar – and yang foods – such as cheese, eggs, meat, pulses and salt.

Yin and yang attributes are attached to each of the Five Elements, and in Chinese medicine herbs and other remedies, including food, are recommended in order to maintain a healthy and balanced body. In northern countries (yin) there is a tendency and need to consume more cooked foods (yang) while in southerly areas (yang) more raw foods are consumed. Eating native products in season is highly recommended.

TASTES AND THE ELEMENTS				
Wood	**Fire**	**Earth**	**Metal**	**Water**
spring	summer	late summer	autumn	winter
sour	bitter	sweet	pungent	salt
yin	yang	yin	yin	yang

THE BAGUA AND FAMILY SEATING

We have seen that each sector of the Bagua can represent several things. The sectors are associated with particular manifestations of the energy of one of the Five Elements – in its yin or yang form. Each also represents a certain type of energy reflecting a direction, season or time period. The Symbolic Bagua suggests the journey of life, with each sector representing a particular aspect – career, wealth, relationships and so on.

Here we look at the energies of each sector in terms of the family. In the past the Bagua may have been used to allocate rooms in a house, but great fun can be had using the Bagua in seating plans at the dining table. The diagram (right) shows the arrangement of family members around the Bagua. Each represents the energy of the direction they fall within, and this can add further insight into the qualities of the energy in that location. Bear in mind that we are looking at centuries-old imagery; house-husbands and executive mothers should appreciate that this is an energetic quality, not stereotyping.

FATHER: Representative of solidity, the leader and the head of the household. Sometimes called the Creative energy.

MOTHER: Complements the Father. A

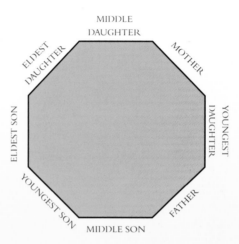

nurturing, supporting energy. Also known as Receptive energy.

ELDEST SON: Also known as the energy of Thunder and the Dragon, whose energy erupts from below and soars upwards.

ELDEST DAUGHTER: Called the Gentle energy, this energy is perceptive and supportive and represents growth.

MIDDLE SON: Sometimes called the Abysmal energy, which suggests hard work without much reward.

MIDDLE DAUGHTER: A Clinging energy, representing a fire, bright and impenetrable outside but burning-out and weakness within.

YOUNGEST SON: Also called the Mountain energy, suggesting a firm stillness and waiting.

YOUNGEST DAUGHTER: Also known as the Joyful, or the Lake, which suggests a deep inward energy or stubbornness and a weak, excitable exterior.

THE DINNER PARTY

The Bagua can be used for all sorts of social occasions. Imagine that an executive is retiring from your company and you and a rival are in the running for the job. You arrange a dinner party and invite your boss, your rival and a young employee who reminds you of yourself when younger and whom you have taken under your wing. You can use the Bagua to seat your colleagues and their partners to ensure that you will get the job.

Out of respect, the boss and his/her partner are in the prime positions. When the boss is not giving any attention to the vivacious spouse of your protégé (with his back thus turned to your rival) and is concentrating on eating, the first people he/she will see when he/she looks up are you and your partner, and also your protégé. Your rival, seated in the worst position, representing hard toil for no reward, and his partner are too far apart to be able to support each other. The attention of the boss's spouse is taken up by the bubbly person chatting to the boss, and your partner opposite. After several attempts at conversation, with no support, your rival's spouse gives up. The result is that you get the job, and your protégé moves into your shoes.

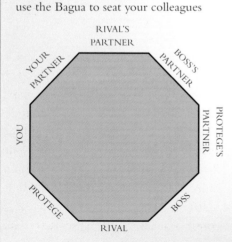

◀ *Manipulate situations by using ancient interpretations of the energies of the Bagua.*

▶ *Whatever the occasion or intention a decorated table with well-presented, nourishing food will be supportive.*

KITCHENS

The kitchen is probably the most important room in the house and, being multi-functional, often the most difficult room to deal with. Apart from its primary purpose for storing, preparing and consuming food, it is a meeting place for family and friends, a children's play area and occasionally even an office. More than any other room, the kitchen holds clues to a person's lifestyle. It is the health centre of our lives and it is important that it functions well and supports us.

The direction a kitchen faces has a powerful effect on its function. In ancient China, kitchens were open to the southeast to catch the breezes that would help ignite the cooking stove. This practical application of Feng Shui reflects the principle of living in harmony with nature. When we have discovered in which direction our kitchen lies, we can use "The Relationships of the Five Elements" table to help us create balance.

A red kitchen facing south will be overloaded with yang Fire energy which needs to be drained. "The Relationships of the Five Elements" table shows that Earth drains Fire, so incorporating a stone floor or some stone pots would be appropriate. As the Fire element is far too dominant, representation of the Water element in the form of a picture of water or a blue blind or tablecloth would also considerably lessen the effect. Plants would not be advisable here since they belong to the Wood element,

▲ *Task lighting is ideal in kitchens. Here it gives focus in a high-ceilinged room, where other lights would cast shadows.*

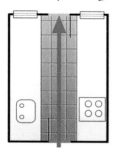 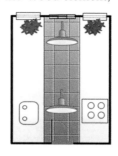

▲ *Left: Chi rushes through this kitchen, creating a feeling of discomfort.*
Right: Ceiling lights and plants by the window slow down the chi and contain it.

which feeds Fire and makes it stronger. In the case of all kitchens, the Fire element, represented by the cooker and electrical cooking appliances, is in conflict with Water, represented by actual water and the fridge. A delicate balance has to be maintained.

Some modern kitchens are so streamlined that nothing is on display. Since the major features consist of only one or two colours or materials, the kitchen can appear lifeless. Sometimes a dash of red, or a green plant can bring a room to life. Ideally, kitchens should contain something from each of the elements.

THE STOVE

The stove is considered to be of great importance. Where possible, the energy source which flows into it, the electric

socket or the gas pipe, should be in your most auspicious location. It is important not to feel vulnerable while standing at the stove. The reasoning behind this is that, since food is the prime source of nourishment and health for the family, it is important that the cook should not feel jumpy or the food will be spoiled through lack of concentration.

A reflective surface positioned behind the cooker, or a chrome cake tin or toaster nearby, will enable the cook to be aware of anyone entering the room. A wind chime or other sound device activated by the door opening will also serve the same purpose.

▲ *The kitchen stove is the heart of the home and should face in an auspicious direction.*

CHI FLOW IN THE KITCHEN

As elsewhere in the house, chi should be able to circulate freely round the kitchen. It cannot do this if the kitchen door is in direct line with the outside doors and windows since it is channelled straight through. If this is the case, you should aim to slow it down by physical or psychological barriers. The simplest method

▲ *If you cook with your back to the door, shiny objects can reflect the space behind you.*

is to keep the door closed. Barriers could include furniture, vegetable trolleys or large plants. More subtle methods such as mobiles, lampshades and colour can be used to create visual and psychological barriers. Barriers can be detrimental, however, and a tall fridge or cupboard by the door will block the natural flow of chi into the room.

Fast-moving chi is not the only problem. Stagnant chi is particularly harmful in a kitchen. It can occur in a room with

▲ *Keep your cooking area as clutter-free as possible.*

▲ *Smooth, rounded lines allow the chi to move gently around this lovely kitchen.*

◄ *In a kitchen where the chi flows straight out of the window, place some red glass, plants or another barrier on the windowsill to slow it down.*

▼ *Eye-level cupboards over the cooking area are oppressive; open shelves would be better.*

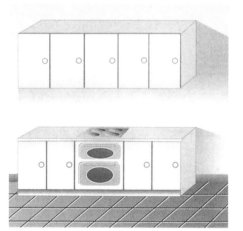

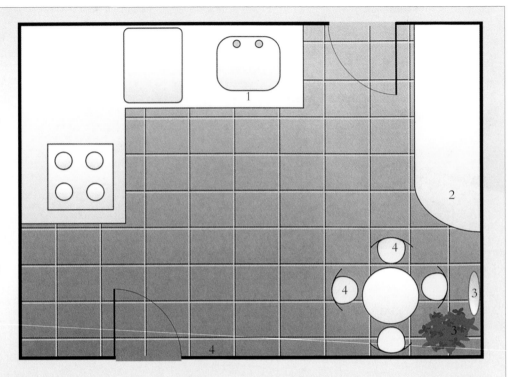

CASE STUDY

This typical modern kitchen has both good and bad points.

1 The cooker, sink and fridge are in an excellent triangle formation.

2 The corner of this work surface has been rounded off so there are no "poison arrows" which otherwise would have pointed at the chairs.

3 The energy is not moving in this corner. A plant or mirror here will help to move the chi along.

4 The chairs have their backs to the door and are vulnerable. A large plant or vegetable basket would act as a barrier. Alternatively, the table and chairs could move out of the corner so the door is visible from each chair.

no window and poor circulation, or in a room with dark inaccessible corners. One cause of this is simply having too much furniture in the room, which impedes movement. If we catch our hip on the corner of a table each time we need to

KITCHEN CLUTTER

Rotting fruit and vegetables
Out-of-date packets and jars
Unlabelled boxes in the freezer
Unused gadgets
Rarely used electrical appliances
Over-full waste bins
Odd pieces of crockery
Plastic bags
Bits of string
Laundry
Crumbs
Fallen plant leaves
Things which "might come in handy"

get to the fridge our body chi will not flow as it should because we are forever twisting to avoid it. At the end of a long day, a ready-made meal may seem an easier option than dodging the furniture to obtain fresh ingredients from the fridge. Rather than put things away, we may be

tempted to leave out milk bottles and food, which can have health risks as well as cluttering up the kitchen.

Piles of newspapers, overflowing rubbish bins, crumbs and stains on work surfaces all represent stagnant chi. Another undesirable feature of many apartment kitchens is the cat-litter tray. Bathrooms and toilets are not desirable near a kitchen because of the antipathy of the Water element to the Fire element of the kitchen, as well as for more obvious reasons. If we take trouble with the location of our own toilets and bathrooms, we should also give serious thought to those of our pets.

Pointed corners are a feature of most kitchens – the edges of appliances, the corners of work surfaces, knives, shelf edges and the edges of slatted blinds all send out chi that makes us feel uncomfortable. Knives should be kept out of sight in a drawer and work surfaces should have rounded edges, if possible. Among the worst sources of this inauspicious chi, known as "poison arrows", are wall cupboards. Most of us have banged our heads on an open door, but even when shut the cupboards can be oppressive. There is a tendency to store far too

much in the kitchen – out-of-date jars, gadgets we never use, a dinner service we only bring out on special occasions or when the person who gave it to us visits. If we examine the contents of the kitchen, we will probably be able to throw away or relocate many items to give us more space and enable the chi to flow. There are many useful storage systems available which will enable us to make optimum use of the space.

▼ *Efficient storage systems reduce kitchen clutter; review the contents regularly.*

▲ *Waist-high cupboards by a work surface are preferable to overhead ones, which can be oppressive, especially in a small kitchen. Keep any frequently used equipment to hand and store cooking equipment, rather than crockery or food, inside cupboards that are adjacent to an oven.*

THE HEALTHY KITCHEN

Kitchens appeal to all our senses. Magazine pictures tantalizingly portray them as rooms featuring bowls of fresh fruit and views over lawns and flower beds. Healthy, freshly prepared meals can be seen on tables where friends and family gather to socialize. Delicious smells, tastes, merry sounds, abundance and happiness radiate from these pages but the reality is often different. Modern kitchens, far from supporting and stimulating us, can unbalance and affect us negatively. The noise from kitchen gadgets, the contamination of food by substances used in packaging, dangers posed by the cleaning agents we use on our work surfaces, the chemicals used in food production, all serve to assault our senses and diminish our well-being.

▲*There is plenty of Wood in this country-style kitchen, which provides excellent levels of energy.*

CASE STUDY

Mary's kitchen was dark and oppressive. The small area in front was a particular problem because the staircase formed a deep slope, and the space on the left was too narrow for conventional units. The main area felt claustrophobic, with work surfaces and wall cupboards sending out chi in the form of "poison arrows". The cooker could not be moved to face Mary's best direction but this was considered secondary to getting the chi flow right.

1. Red, yellow and green opaque glass was used in the south-facing door and window overlooking a brick wall to stimulate the south Fire element. The light coming through the glass sent a rainbow effect into the room which stimulated the chi there.

2. The plants on the windowsill were placed to stimulate the Wood element of the East.

3. The work triangle is in place. Care was taken not to place the fridge opposite the cooker, so there is no conflict between the Fire and Water elements.

4. Pale yellow cupboards and a terracotta

container in the north-east introduced the Earth element.

5. Stainless steel pans hung in the north-west stimulate the Metal area.

6. These oddly sized and shaped walls were made into cupboards to make the shape

regular. The one on the right was built over and around the washing machine and drier. Glass doors were put in front of the window to enable the coloured light to shine in. Mary placed her china collection on glass shelves here.

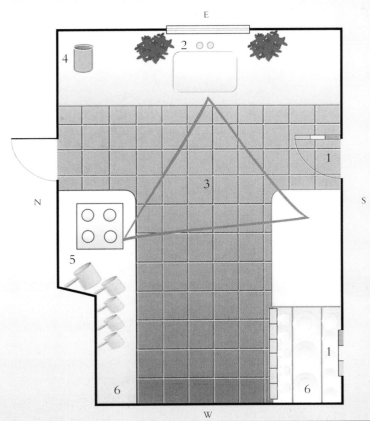

BEDROOMS

The bedroom is considered to be one of the most important rooms of the house in Feng Shui. Adults spend a third of their lives in bed, while children and teenagers often spend even more than this. We must therefore be certain that these rooms are suitable for relaxing and regenerating us, as well as for encouraging romance in our lives.

BEDS

A bed should face in one of our auspicious directions, which means that the top of our heads should point that way when we are lying down. Where partners have different auspicious directions, there has to be a compromise; for example, if the house is a West group house and favours one partner, then the bed direction should favour the other.

The best bed position is diagonally opposite the door. The element of surprise is never recommended in the bedroom. If the occupants of the bed do not have a reasonable view of the door, a mirror should be placed to reflect anyone entering. Having the foot of the bed in direct line with the door is known as the "mortuary position" in China because coffins are placed in that position when awaiting collection.

Doors and windows situated opposite each other are not considered auspicious. If a line of chi between two windows – or a door and window – crosses the bed, this is thought to cause illness.

▲ *Four-poster beds can be claustrophobic if they have heavy wood and elaborate fabric canopies, but this elegant bamboo bed without any excess curtaining gives a very light effect.*

▼ *The symmetry of the tables and lamps at each side of this bed is perfect. Each side of the bed should have identical furnishings.*

▼ *Here the view of the garden is auspicious, but less spiky ornaments behind the bed would be better for relaxation.*

▼ *This soft, dreamy room is very restful. Do not have too many books in the bedroom as they are mentally stimulating.*

FURNISHINGS

Images in the bedroom should be in pairs, particularly in the Relationships corner of the room. Images of a solitary figure in a single person's bedroom indicate loneliness, as does a single bed. It is possible to feel isolated and insecure within a marriage. If this is the case, hang a picture of a couple on the wall and display pairs of objects. Photographs of parents, children or friends have no place in a couple's bedroom.

Mirrors in the bedroom should not face the bed. The Chinese believe that the soul leaves the body as we sleep and will be disconcerted to come across itself in the mirror. A modern interpretation

Ideally, beds should be raised off the floor with enough space for air to circulate underneath. Storage drawers full of old clothes and crates of old magazines and other items stored beneath them create a stagnant chi which is not desirable.

Beds should be made of natural materials which can breathe. Wood is the usual choice although bamboo is also used. People belonging to the Metal element often favour metal beds. Since metal conducts heat and electricity, be very careful to keep electrical equipment and heaters away from the bed. Water beds are not recommended because they cause conflict between Fire, the electrical heating source, and Water, as well as creating instability while we sleep.

Headboards offer support but should always be tightly secured. They represent the Tortoise position, and as such, should be higher than the Phoenix, or the footboard. Beds should be backed by a wall, not a window, which feels insecure and can let in draughts.

Where a double bed is in a confined space and one occupant has to climb over the other to get in or out, harmony will not prevail. The best position for a bed is with a wall behind and enough room on either side for a small table or cupboard. These should always be balanced at either side; one will not do.

▲ *Headboards offer support and this magnificent carved wooden headboard is a particularly fine example.*

▼ *This is an attractive bedroom but the mirror should not reflect the bed. En suite bathrooms are not recommended either.*

CASE STUDY

Although Joe and Amy had a comfortable house, lovely children and were blessed in all aspects of their lives, they revealed separately that they felt lonely and isolated. A look at the bedroom revealed all. On a shelf opposite the bed sat a TV, video and stereo system. Joe enjoyed watching videos in bed and waking up to his favourite rock bands. Amy disliked Joe's

choice of videos and her collection of self-improvement books on relationships and stress sat on the next shelf. On the top shelf were photographs of the children, and a box of toys to keep them amused when they came in early in the morning was on the bottom shelf. On the walls to either side of Joe and Amy's bed an image of a solitary man and woman gazed wistfully at each other across the room.

Following the Feng Shui consultation, the toys were removed to the children's rooms, where they were encouraged to play on waking. The two pictures were placed side by side, where the wistful gaze could turn into a lustful glance, and the TV, video and stereo were relocated. Joe is no longer worried that Amy is miserable and unfulfilled as she no longer has need of her books.

▲ *A dressing room is ideal as it frees the bedroom for rest and romance.*

might be that most of us are not at our best in the mornings and would not want our tousled image to be the first thing we see on waking. It would be much better to see a picture of the sun rising or a fresh green landscape. Street lights outside the room can also create reflective images in a mirror, which may disturb us when we are half-asleep. In contrast, strategically placed mirrors facing a wonderful view will draw it into the room.

The bedroom should not become a storage area or an office, nor serve any function other than romance and sleep. If you have space in your house, dressing

rooms are ideal since they remove most extraneous things from the bedroom. Most bedrooms, however, contain wardrobes and drawer space. Keeping these clear of clutter means we can close them easily and make sure we have plenty of room to hang up our clothes. Garments strewn over chairs for days on end constitute clutter and worry us psychologically since we know we will have to deal with them eventually. The worst form of storage is the overhead cupboard linking wardrobes on either side of the bed. This acts in the same way as a beam and can leave those sleeping under it feeling vulnerable. The same applies to anything else hanging over the bed.

ELECTRICAL EQUIPMENT

Electrical equipment in the bedroom is not desirable for two reasons. First, it detracts from the main functions of the

▼ *The beam over this double bed symbolically divides the couple occupying the bed.*

room. Secondly, the harmful electro-magnetic waves that are generated can have an adverse effect on those sleeping there. Ionizers positioned close to a bed present the most serious threat, but even clock radios send out waves over a considerable distance.

Electric blankets are a real problem because they encase the bed in an electromagnetic field. They should be unplugged from the wall before anyone gets into bed.

All electrical items should be on the opposite side of the room from the bed, and this includes electrical clocks. One advantage of this is that it makes the snooze button redundant. People find

▼ *Cramped spaces under slanting walls are not recommended in Feng Shui as they restrict the flow of chi.*

more time to eat a proper breakfast in the morning and are more punctual for work when they have to get out of bed to turn off the alarm.

It is surprising how many people have telephones sitting on bed-side tables. They have no place in a bedroom as they prevent relaxation, especially if late night social calls are common. The best place for mobile phones outside office hours is in a briefcase, switched off; everyone is entitled to some time for themselves.

▶ *A harp has been placed in the Wealth corner of this room to lift the energy of the sloping wall.*

BED POSITIONS

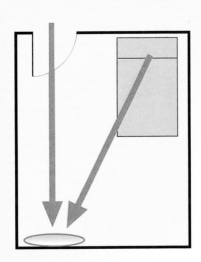

1. If the bed is positioned so that the occupant cannot see who is entering, place a mirror opposite the door.

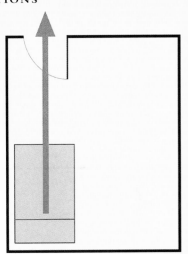

2. When the foot of the bed is in direct line with the door, this is known in China as the "mortuary position".

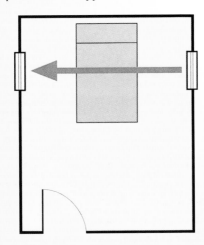

3. A line of harmful chi crosses this bed from two facing windows.

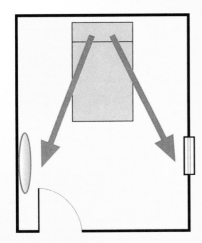

4. A mirror opposite a window can draw in wonderful views.

THE NURSERY

Medical research has shown that pollutants in decorating materials and furniture may be responsible for breathing difficulties and cot deaths in susceptible babies. Decorate the room for a new baby as long as possible before it is due and air the room thoroughly. If this cannot be done, put the baby in the parents' room until the smell of fresh paint has disappeared. Decorating materials should be manufactured from natural products and cot bedding preferably made from natural untreated fibres.

STIMULATING THE SENSES

We can help small children to distinguish colours and shapes by providing them with suitable stimulation. A mobile hung above the foot of a baby's cot will keep it fascinated for a long time and provide comfort before it falls asleep. Do not place one directly over the head of the baby as this can be threatening.

Very small children could be suffocated if furry toy animals fall on their faces so keep these out of the cot but place

▶ *This is a bright, cheerful room with plenty of stimulation for a baby.*

▼ *Bright colours and shapes give lots of visual appeal during the day.*

▼ *A chalkboard gives a child scope for freedom of expression.*

▼ *This large chest will take many toys and keep the room free from clutter.*

▲ *This first bed for a young child has a canopy to keep it cosy.*

them where the baby can see them, perhaps on a nearby shelf. A bright wall frieze can also occupy a baby's attention, as can a large colourful poster.

Sound can be introduced in a number of ways. Fractious babies who do not sleep well may be soothed by taped music, and the sound of voices from a radio may help the insecure to fall asleep. Musical mobiles can be useful in lulling a baby to sleep, but they might be disturbed if you have to keep rewinding the mobile. Babies soon learn to do things themselves and the look of wonder on its face as a child discovers it can make something happen is magical. By tying bells and rattles to the bars of the cot we help the child on its way to independence, but these are best not left in the cot at night or they will disturb its sleep.

The sense of touch is stimulated by numerous textures – furry, soft, hard and smooth. Allow your child access to a variety of experiences but secure playthings to the cot or you will be forever picking them up from the floor. Do not be tempted to introduce manufactured smells to small children as they are too strong. The familiar smell of a mother or well-loved teddy is far better. At teething time, ensure that all materials which can be put into the mouth conform to safety standards and that cot paint is lead-free.

POSSIBLE HAZARDS

Pets can be a problem if they snuggle up to the baby for warmth or become jealous of the attention it receives. Suitable

safety precautions should be taken inside the home. As children begin to crawl, and later to walk and climb, ensure that all fires and electrical sockets are securely covered, that windows are secure and stairs have barriers at the top and bottom.

▲ *Brightly decorated furnishings in this bedroom lift the energy in a dark corner.*

▼ *Wood energy, symbolized by the frieze of trees, suits the growing child, who needs to be allowed freedom of expression.*

CHILDREN'S ROOMS

Children's rooms can be a challenge as they often need to fulfil two opposing functions – sleep and play. Although parents aim to ensure that sleep takes place at night and play during the day, a look at some children's rooms indicates why they do not always get it the right way round as there is no division between the two. Children's rooms should also support them and their needs as they grow. Where a room is shared, each child should have a private space within it that they feel is their own.

The energy of the east with the rising sun in the morning is ideal for children. The west with the setting sun at night is good for hyperactive children who cannot settle, although this direction is normal-

▲ *A stark, but restful child's room. The bed would be better backed by the wall.*

ly better for elderly people to sleep in.

The heads of beds should face their supportive directions, although this is not always possible when there is more than one child in the room. It is more important that they should feel safe, and a view of the door is essential for children. Rooms with dark corners which house strange shapes and cast shadows on the walls can prove disturbing for young children with vivid imaginations.

BEDS

Wooden beds are preferable because they do not pick up electromagnetic radiation. Bunk beds are not considered suitable since they depress the chi, both of the child on top who is close to the ceiling and the one underneath who has a body above, often a fidgety one. Canopies over the bed have the same effect and can also

harbour dust. Cupboards and beams can also have a debilitating effect. Children's beds should have a headboard and should not back on to a window or a door.

DECORATION

As children grow, mentally as well as physically, part of the learning process is to be able to make choices. Children instinctively know the type of energy

▼ *Plenty of storage space means that toys can be neatly stacked away.*

CLUTTER IN CHILDREN'S ROOMS
Broken, irreparable toys
Outgrown toys
Books they never look at
Outgrown clothes
Dry felt-tip pens
Games and jigsaw puzzles with pieces missing

▲ A reassuring first bed for a young child, as the canopy offers protection.

they require to support them and should be allowed to design their own bedrooms and have a major say in the decoration and colours, even if it is not to the parents' taste. We can always shut the door and we should respect it when it is shut. Children need their privacy as we do and if we set an example by knocking and asking permission to enter, then we can expect the same in return.

If there is a family room or playroom elsewhere, then excessive stimulation in the form of toys should not be a problem in the bedroom. Where the room serves a dual purpose, create a separate sleeping area and provide storage for toys to be put away out of sight at night.

FURNISHINGS

If the floor is hard, a soft rug by the bed is welcoming in the morning and will give a gentle start to the day. Furniture with curved corners helps to prevent minor accidents. If your child has chosen

the colours, you can select shades and hues to suit the child's personality – cooler ones to balance an active child and brighter ones to stimulate a more reticent personality.

It is disturbing how many very small children have their own television sets in

▼ A child's room should give her or him the space and facility to read and be creative.

their rooms as this must inevitably isolate them from their families and hamper their social interaction outside. Apart from this consideration, the electromagnetic radiation from TVs and computers in children's bedrooms is a cause for concern, particularly as these rooms are often small and confine the electro-pollution. Where possible, remove all electrical items from children's rooms and relocate them in other areas of the house.

▼ Low windows can create a fear of falling, the puppet theatre here acts as a screen.

TEENAGERS' ROOMS

▲ *The high, sloping ceilings do not impinge on this modern room.*

▼ *This is a pretty room for a young teenage girl beginning to move away from childhood.*

Teenagers' rooms are evolving places where children who are growing into adults can express themselves – their happiness, their loves, their hurts and their anger. The latter may be directed against us if we attempt to curb their individuality and try to impose our personalities and values on the private space that will nurture them through to adulthood. The needs and the tastes of a thirteen-year-old are very different from those of a seventeen- or eighteen-year-old, and the room may be changed on almost an annual basis. Some principles will remain constant, however. We can encourage our child to place their beds in an auspicious position and introduce them to Feng Shui, which they may come to regard as a help when they encounter some of the usual trials of growing up.

Older teenagers' rooms are multifunctional and usually act as bedroom, study, sitting room and entertainment area for their friends. It is no wonder that their occupants sometimes become

TEENAGE CLUTTER
Sweet wrappings and crisp packets
Unwashed clothes
Over-flowing wastebins
Do not touch anything else
in a teenager's private space

▲ *Black and white – a bold colour choice – is popular with teenagers.*

confused. Teenagers need our support when they ask for it, even though they do not welcome unsolicited advice. They require their own space, physically and intellectually, but they also need positive affirmation from adults. Hold out against a television in the bedroom and encourage the use of family rooms. A computer in the study will draw teenagers out of their bedrooms and preserve this space for sleep and relaxation.

▼ *The bright decor and pretty feel of this room might not suit an older teenager.*

CASE STUDY

Marie, aged sixteen, was going through an "awkward" phase. Her mother, Ella, was at her wits' end trying to get her out of bed in the mornings to catch the one bus guaranteed to get her to school on time. Every morning was a battle, and the resentment festered throughout the day and affected family harmony in the evening. Homework was left undone and Marie's studies were suffering.

A Metal Ox, Marie could be stubborn and, although a girl of few words, she occasionally exploded. Her arrogant manner irritated her father, a Fire Ox, who didn't take kindly to being opposed or to Marie's surliness. He became impatient with his wife, an Earth Goat, who knew Marie needed support and was torn between them in arguments.

Ella decided to take action and offered to redecorate Marie's bedroom and let her choose the decor. Out to shock, Marie chose purple for her room and was surprised when her mother, who knew purple to be stimulating for the mind and good for raising self-esteem, acquiesced.

1. Ella took Marie to a fashionable store and invited her to choose something for her room. As she had hoped, Marie chose a multi-coloured bead curtain for the window.

2. Ella suggested that Marie should turn her bed around so that she could see the curtain.

3. Ella removed the old square bedside table, since the square shape symbolizes containment, and ordered a round one.

4. The alarm clock was placed on Marie's desk so she no longer had access to the snooze button and had to get up to turn it off.

5. To go on the new round table Ella gave Marie a framed photograph showing the family boarding a plane to go on holiday; this energized the "Family" area of the Bagua.

6. Taking a chance, Ella purchased two huge silk sunflowers and suggested they would look lovely in the top right-hand corner of the room – the Earth "Relationships" area of the Bagua represented by the magic number 2.

Now when Ella calls Marie in the morning, she opens the window slightly so the bead curtain moves and tinkles, stimulating the chi. When the alarm rings later Marie has to get out of bed to turn it off, but she is already awake. Family harmony has been restored and they meet on friendly terms more often. Feng Shui is a mixture of common sense and psychology as well as harnessing unseen forces of the universe.

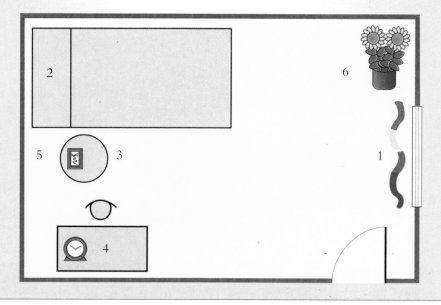

BATHROOMS

The position of the bathroom is considered to be important in Feng Shui because water is synonymous with wealth, and thus the disposal of waste water symbolizes the dispersal of the family fortune. Changing climatic conditions have highlighted how precious a commodity water is, and that measures should be taken not to waste it. Conservationists recommend saving water from baths and sinks to water gardens. Dripping taps are symbolic of wealth running away. When we consider that a dripping tap, leaking at a rate of one drip per second, wastes 1,000 litres (264 gallons) per year, we can see the sense in applying ancient rules to modern problems. Baths and sinks which are clogged, apart from being a constant

source of irritation, can also be a health risk so it is important that we fix them as soon as possible.

▼ *No need for morning queues in this large and airy bathroom.*

▲ *This spacious and opulent bathroom provides room to relax in.*

POSITION

Bathrooms should be positioned well away from the front door as this is not an image we want visitors to our homes to subconsciously take away. It is most important not to have bathrooms close to kitchens for health reasons, but they should also be away from dining and sitting areas so that guests won't be embarrassed to use them.

TOILETS

It is not desirable to see the toilet on entering the bathroom and, if possible, it should be situated where it is hidden from view. Screens can be utilized or the toilet positioned behind the door. Toilet doors should be closed and the seat cover closed at all times.

Bathrooms are considered to be linked to the body's plumbing system so a large bathroom using too much water can lead to health problems concerned with evacuation, while cramped bathrooms are connected with restriction in bodily functions. Large bathrooms are also associated with vanity and an excessive

obsession with cleanliness, whereas small bathrooms are restricting and can cause accidents as people manoeuvre round.

MIRRORS AND CABINETS

The use of mirrors can give the illusion of more space. Generally, mirrors opposite each other are not considered to be auspicious in Feng Shui because they conjure up an image of constant movement away from the self, with no grounding influences. However, unless

▼ *Use plants and coloured towels to balance the Water element in a bathroom.*

▲ *Screens can be used to hide the bathroom from an entrance or en suite bedroom.*

▶ *The reflective materials in this bathroom help to counteract its heavy ceiling. A large plant or dash of colour would also help.*

▼ *Curvy, watery lines and Metal shapes work well in this unusual bathroom.*

we spend a vast amount of time in front of the bathroom mirror, this is acceptable if it improves the suggestion of space. Mirror tiles are not recommended, or those which in any way cut the image. Fixed mirrors are preferred to those which jut out from walls and normal mirrors are preferred to magnifying mirrors that distort the image.

Bathroom cabinets are places where stagnant chi can easily accumulate. Most cosmetics have a limited shelf life and many cabinets contain items dating back years. There is a limit to the number of eye baths, tweezers and combs which are required in a lifetime.

En Suite Bathrooms

The growing trend to have en suite bathrooms is not in accordance with Feng Shui rules. Where possible, create a separate room for the toilet or else make sure the bathroom area in the bedroom has a well-maintained ventilation system. En suite bathrooms that have been built into the bedroom often create an L-shape with a corner jutting into the room, so action needs to be taken to ensure that this does not point at the bed.

Clutter in the Bathroom

Full waste bins
Empty bottles and toothpaste tubes
Unnecessary soap dishes
Unpolished mirrors
Out-of-date medication
Untried cosmetic samples
Bath oils and perfumes which are never used

▲ *A good balance of colours, elements, plants and natural materials raises the energy in this bathroom.*

▶ *Keep any clutter in the bathroom down to its absolute minimum and keep any soap dishes or holders clean and unclogged.*

Relaxation

Very few of us find the time to relax sufficiently and this often affects our health, both physical and mental. The bathroom is one of the few places where we can escape from the world and be alone. Bathrooms should be decorated so as to enable us to wind down at the end of a busy day, or allow us some peaceful moments in the morning.

▲ *An ideal bathroom – it would be difficult to resist rushing home to relax in this at the end of a hard day.*

▶ *The huge mirror doubles the space in this elegant bathroom. A frame to the top and bottom would contain the chi.*

The colours we use to decorate the bathroom affect how we feel there. Blue is a soothing colour, associated with serenity and contemplation. Colour therapists believe that it lowers the blood pressure, promotes deeper exhalation and induces sleep. Green, on the other hand, rests the eyes and calms the nerves. Whatever colours we choose, we can create a space to relax and soothe ourselves by playing gentle music and by adding a few drops of essential oils to the bathwater. Bergamot, lavender and geranium alleviate stress and anxiety, while camomile, rose, lemon balm and ylang ylang are used to alleviate irritability and to create a peaceful mood. The bath is an ideal place for self-massage while taking a bath or having just had one. Try stroking one of these oils towards the heart to stimulate the circulation.

Taoists consider that the nutrition we receive from the air when we breathe is more valuable to us than food and water. As we inhale we draw in energy, which provides energy; when we exhale, we cleanse and detoxify our bodies. The art of breathing properly has been part of the Chinese health regime for centuries, and is based on balancing yin and yang and creating the correct chi flow around the body. It is thought that illness occurs when the correct chi flow is not maintained. Use your time in the bathroom to practise controlled breathing.

Meditation is another relaxation technique. The Chinese call it "sitting still and doing nothing", which is a deceptively simple description of an art that can take years to perfect. Whether our aim is to reflect on the day or to let our minds wander freely and wind down, the bathroom is the ideal place.

CONSERVATORIES

Conservatories are a popular way of extending our homes and they act as a mediating space between the garden and the house. Ancient Chinese architects designed homes and gardens to interconnect and regarded each as being essential to balance the other. Glimpses through windows and latticed grilles gave views over lakes and vistas, and gardens were planted right up to the house.

Some conservatories are used for plants or as garden rooms, and are places to sit in to relax. Others have become an integral part of the home, taking on the role of dining room, sitting room and in some cases kitchen. Depending on its purpose and aspect, the conservatory can be decorated in various ways.

THE CONSERVATORY KITCHEN

The conservatory kitchen can become very warm in the summer and adequate ventilation will be necessary. It is not considered auspicious to have a glass roof in the kitchen because the symbolic wealth, the food, will evaporate away. Practically speaking, it is not comfortable to work with the sun, or with the rain, beating down above, and a blind or

▼ *This conservatory opens into the kitchen, enabling the cook to join in the conversation.*

▲ *A conservatory is a glorious place to relax in all weathers.*

▶ *An indoor garden which opens into a family kitchen, the conservatory provides an ideal outlook when eating or preparing meals.*

fabric should be put up to block the sky. Choose fabrics that are easy to clean and ensure that they do not hang too low and are not highly flammable. The same conditions apply to conservatory kitchens as to conventional ones. If working with the door behind you, place a sheet of metal or a large shiny object so that you can see anyone entering the room.

THE CONSERVATORY DINING ROOM

The conservatory dining room should be treated in the same way as a conventional diner, but there are difficulties. The

conservatory room often opens directly into the kitchen and occasionally also into the main living area. There will be doors to the garden and two or three of the walls will be glass. This makes it very difficult to sit with support from behind, so it is important that chairs have high backs, and preferably arms, to provide this.

Depending on the aspect, the evening sun may cause glare so protective measures, such as blinds, should be available. Conservatories can be very warm until quite late in the evening and fans can help to move the air around.

Any water features in the conservatory are not conducive to good digestion and should be turned off during meals.

THE CONSERVATORY LIVING ROOM

Whether it is used as a living room or simply for enjoying an apéritif at the end of a long day, the conservatory will be a tranquil spot so long as adequate shade and ventilation are provided.

A water feature will cool the air and be soothing, providing it is placed in an auspicious spot according to the Five

◀ *What a healthy way to dine – absorbing energy from the landscape as much as the food and company.*

▼ *Curtains are not really necessary when you have a wonderful view like this.*

▲ *A wide variety of different foliage plants adds interest to this small conservatory area.*

Elements. North is auspicious as it is the Water position. If the conservatory sits in the east or south-west, then this is the spot for a water feature, which will symbolize present and future prosperity.

BALCONIES AND WINDOW-BOXES

Many apartments have balconies which are purely cosmetic and act as barriers between neighbouring apartments when the doors are opened. Others are larger but do not really enable outdoor living as such, having no room for tables and seating. Some apartments have neither but may have an external windowsill on which to put plants or window-boxes. All these small spaces bring the natural world inside our homes.

The outlook in many urban apartments is bleak. The most auspicious sites overlook a park or a river, but most overlook a busy road or even a brick wall.

▶ *Flowers in a window-box are guaranteed to lift the spirits.*

▼ *Even in a small space there is usually room for a windowsill display.*

CASE STUDY

A flower-lover who lived on the seventh floor was so troubled by pigeons nibbling his plants that he decided to give up trying to grow them. Yet his balcony still looked wonderful from below. He had purchased lots of green silk plants and ivy strands, and a collection of flowers to represent the seasons. Set in oasis and weighted with gravel, these saw him through several years and few people could tell the difference.

▶ *Silk plants are very effective in awkward sites and don't need watering.*

WINDOWSILLS

A kitchen windowsill, inside or outside, is a useful place to have a herb collection and bring not only the sight of the natural world into your home but also the smell and the taste.

The window box on the far left contains nasturtiums, pansies and marigolds, all of which are edible and can be used for flavour and garnishes. The window box in the picture on the near left contains chervil, coriander, fennel, garlic, purple sage, French tarragon, savory, oregano and basil – an entire herb garden in a box.

Many apartments overlook the windows of other apartments and we can be overlooked by dozens of eyes as we wash up or stand on our balconies. The Four Animals formation suggests that we need to define our space. By placing a window-box on our windowsill we not only define the Phoenix position, we also fill our homes with the Wood energy of growing plants. Recent studies have shown that hospital patients who overlook a garden recover more quickly than patients who do not have such a view. A healthy display of green plants to greet us in the morning will spur us on for the day ahead and welcome us home in the evening.

Growing plants on a balcony can be problematic. Compost (soil mix) is heavy and can be difficult to transport to the

▲ *This green oasis in a bustling city is shaded by an awning which, with the well-maintained plants, creates a protected space.*

◄ *Even a small outdoor space such as this will provide plenty of energy.*

apartment and also to dispose of later. Cosmetic balconies may not be able to cope with heavy weights and we must be mindful of this when choosing containers and plants. Bulbs can be a useful solution since they require a comparatively small amount of compost. A succession of bulbs throughout the year will connect us to the seasons, which is auspicious in Feng Shui. Providing we keep them watered until the foliage has died down, we can lift the bulbs and store them for the following year. Depending on the direction in which the balcony faces, the colours of the bulbs may be chosen to correspond to the direction or to focus on a life aspiration, using the Bagua. Of course this is not essential; other plants may be used. It is preferable to plant shrubs and miniature trees and to use annual plants as spots of colour, rather than attempting to uproot plants and dispose of them several times a year.

SWIMMING POOLS

Large volumes of water exude power-ful energies and great care should be taken in siting pools with regard to the effect they will have on the area and the house, and on the elemental cycle of the location.

Large areas of still water are yin and in theory accumulate chi to balance the yang energy of the home. Where they are situated too close to the house, they can deplete the yang energy and cause problems. Auspicious shapes are those

▲ *This swimming pool is the correct size for the house and the points are hidden by the large bushy plants.*

with rounded edges and kidney-shaped pools which appear to hug the house.

POOL SHAPES

This kidney-shaped pool has no harmful points. It appears to hug the house and its shape is auspicious.

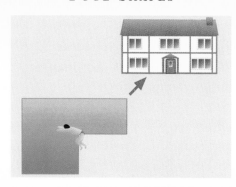

The corners of this L-shaped pool are sending "poison arrows" at the house and the swimmers.

Without the planting to obscure part of its view from the house, the energy of this pool would be overwhelming.

▲ *The flowing, natural lines of this swimming pool are in harmony with the surrounding garden.*

Where straight-sided pools are at an angle to the house, the edges of the pool can send "poison arrows" of chi to the detriment of the inhabitants.

Although a body of water in theory accumulates chi, there are other factors to be taken into consideration. The surrounding landscape, symbolically the Dragon, may have been excavated to create the pool and will probably have been damaged, or the appearance and energy of the place may have been damaged.

▲ *Here large rocks add stability to this lovely pool, while the vegetation brings life and vitality.*

▼ *Flowing curves and gentle planting make this swimming pool very inviting. The entrance to the house is well-balanced.*

Another factor is the direction of the swimming pool. A large body of water in the south will destroy the Fire energy there. The east and south-east are good locations since the water will feed growth and at the same time its energy will be kept under control by the Wood.

The colour of the pool tiles is important and care should be taken to retain a balance of the elements in and around the pool. Pale blue is a favourite colour, but again will not suit all locations. Refer back to "The Relationships of the Five Elements" table to ensure a balance has been maintained.

The size of the pool must be in proportion to the house and the surrounding landscape. An enormous pool in a small back garden can symbolically "drown" the occupants. Consider also the direction of the sun at various times of the day when you are choosing a site.

INDOOR POOLS

These are not recommended in Feng Shui and need to be well secured if they are part of the house. If you already have one, it should be kept separate from the house by closed doors. Pools in basements are considered a destabilizing influence, and rooftop pools are thought to symbolically "drown" residents and weigh them down.

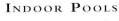

THE HOME OFFICE

Home offices differ from studies in that they are more yang because they have more contact with the outside world. For this reason, they are better placed close to the entrance so that work does not impinge on the whole house and visitors do not have to walk through the living accommodation. Home offices can be difficult places, particularly when situated in the main body of the house. There is always a temptation to take time out to do household tasks, or for the family to drop in. Although home working allows flexibility, it demands a high level of self-discipline in order to work for long enough but not too long, to

▼ A garden studio or office, removed from the main house, is an excellent idea.

▲ This luxurious office space is obviously designed for meetings with clients.

▶ If the chair and desk positions in this study were to be reversed it would open up a view of the outside world.

allow time for social activities. A balance has to be maintained. Ideally, home offices should be placed where visitors have access via a separate door and apart from the main house, in a wing or even in a separate building in the garden.

OFFICE POSITION

The ideal position for the office is in your best direction or in one of the other three favoured positions. The south-west is not favoured for office locations since the energy levels are falling there. Wherever it is situated, some care in the north will be advantageous.

Any "poison arrows" should be deflected or hidden, using mirrors or screens. Metal supports Water so hollow metal wind chimes or a metal object would be helpful. Water is also auspicious here but do not use the area to display plants as they will drain the energy.

DESK POSITIONS

Desk locations are the same as those for the study but if there is a secretary or another person working in the home office the desks should not face each other. The secretary should sit nearer to the door to protect the employer from having to deal with mundane matters. Both desks should have the support of a wall behind and both should have suitably supportive chairs which follow the favourable Four Animals formation. If a desk is close to a door, a plant on the edge will protect the occupant from unfavourable chi.

When visiting clients are received in the office, the owner's chair should always be backed by the wall facing the door and the clients should be seated in the

THE BAGUA AND DESKS

Use the Bagua to arrange your desk according to Feng Shui principles.

1. This represents Career or the start of the day and should be clear to open up possibilities for the day ahead.

2. The Relationships area is suitable for brochures and details of people with whom you will come into contact in the course of your present project.

3. A plant here in the Elders area will help to freshen the air and symbolize longevity and stability.

4. Accounts and paying-in books should be placed here in the Wealth area, but not cheque books, which represent money going out.

5. Use this central area for the task in hand and then clear it away. Do not leave things to pile up here.

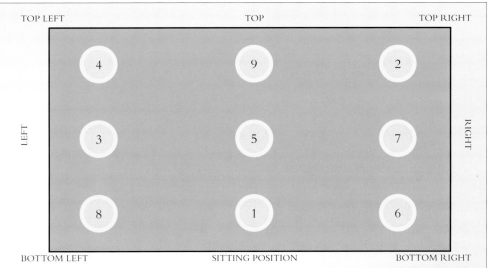

TOP LEFT — TOP — TOP RIGHT

4   9   2

LEFT   3   5   7   RIGHT

8   1   6

BOTTOM LEFT — SITTING POSITION — BOTTOM RIGHT

6. The Helpful People area is the place for the telephone and address book.

7. The Children or Projects position is ideal for putting the current project files.

8. Knowledge and Wisdom – the place to store reference books.

9. The Fame area and the Phoenix position. A crystal paperweight here will denote the boundary of your desk, and of the current project. An uplifting image or landscape hung on the wall in front will represent future possibilities.

▲ *This studio's view would be improved if the foliage outside wasn't so dense.*

subordinate position in a smaller chair, with their backs to the door.

Having sorted out the best location for the furniture, focus on the contents of the desk, either using compass directions or symbolically. Take care that any measures taken are not in conflict with the element of the area. Task lighting should always be diagonally opposite the writing hand to prevent shadows.

THE OFFICE ENVIRONMENT

Be aware of the approach to the office from outside and check for dustbins and other obstacles, overhanging branches and anything which will detract from your entrance. Inside the house, the same attention is necessary. Clients who come to visit you will not want to clamber over toys or other paraphernalia, which present an unprofessional approach.

It is important, particularly when the office is a section of a room that is used at other times for another purpose, to mark the boundaries – by a screen, piece of furniture or even a rug. Inside the space, aspirational images, landscapes,

▼ *This uncluttered desk is arranged following Feng Shui principles.*

good lighting and bright colours all make a psychological contribution to success.

A clutter-free office environment is essential and work spaces should be clear of everything but the task in hand. Do not have stacked filing trays which, symbolically and literally, allow the work to mount up. Deal with letters and telephone calls the same day and note conversations and dates meticulously. Discard catalogues as new ones arrive as well as all out-of-date paperwork.

HOME STUDY OR STUDIO

The home study may be used by one or more members of the family to study for school or college examinations, for continuing education later in life or for pursuing a hobby or interest. It should be situated in a quiet part of the home, if possible. If study areas form part of another room – the bedroom, sitting room or even the kitchen – care should be taken to ensure that the activities of the two areas are kept quite separate, for example, by screening. It is not a good idea to use a bedroom as a home study, because it will no longer be a place to relax in.

▶ *Screens can be used to conceal work equipment in bedrooms and living rooms.*

DESK LOCATIONS

The three desk positions below have the support of a wall. You can also see the door and anyone entering. The desk on the right is directly opposite the door. The three desks below right are vulnerable from behind and anyone working in these positions would feel nervous.

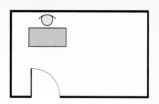

Good: facing the door

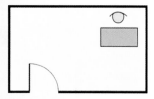

Good: diagonally opposite the door

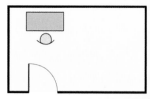

Bad: back to the door

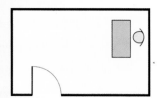

Good: with a view of the door

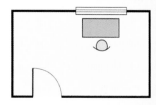

Bad: facing a window

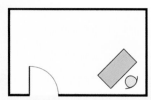

Good: here you can see who is entering

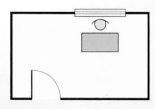

Bad: back to a window

DESK POSITIONS

The position of the desk is crucial if maximum benefits are to be gained from studying and it should be placed to avoid any areas of damaging chi.

The view from a study window should be pleasant but not detract from work. A view of the neighbours' swimming pool and barbecue area will not be conducive to work. Sitting opposite the windows of a neighbouring house is not recommended since it can cause discomfort, as can facing telephone wires or having roof points aimed at the office. If

▼ *An ideal solution – the folding doors allow light and air in during the day, and you can close down the office at night.*

there are distractions outside, the window should be covered by muslin, or something similar, to admit light but keep distractions out. Plants placed on the windowsill might serve the same purpose. Studies should have a good supply of fresh air in order to prevent tiredness.

When a considerable amount of time is spent in one position, the furniture should be ergonomically correct. Chairs should fit comfortably under desks and the seat should be at the correct height for writing and using a keyboard. If a conventional computer is used, it should be placed as far away as possible from the chair to reduce the radiation from the screen. Where possible, use a laptop computer. Trailing wires are dangerous and cause irritation, so tie them together

CLUTTER IN THE STUDY
Piles of used paper
Piles of unread journals
Out-of-date books
Cluttered hard drive
Noticeboards with out-of-date
information
More than two adhesive notes
Broken equipment
Run-down batteries

▲ *It would be difficult to work in this room. The stacked bookshelves are also reflected in the mirror and are overwhelming.*

◀ *A Mayan chime ball hung in the window deflects the "poison arrow" created by the roof of one of the buildings outside.*

and tape them out of the way. Printers should be positioned to ensure the paper can eject easily. Plants in the study help to improve the air quality and also add some yin balance to the yang machines.

ORDER IN THE STUDY
The study should be as streamlined as possible and there should be a place for everything. Cupboards, shelves and bookcases will keep books and equipment off the desk surface. Coloured files and filing boxes store information and prevent paper mountains appearing on the desk and floor. Coloured adhesive bookmarkers avoid piles of open books and journals stacking up on the desk, but the marked items should be read in a day or two otherwise the stickers will be a constant reminder of things left undone.

Journals can pile up. You should try to read them immediately and discard them if they contain nothing of interest. If it is necessary to keep them, a small card index in subject order with the journal title, date, article title and page number will help you to quickly locate the items you want.

Once a piece of work has been completed and recognition received for it, it is unlikely that it will ever be referred to again. Consider whether a paper copy is really necessary. If not, store all completed work on floppy disks, which take up considerably less space. Remove past work from the computer hard drive to free up space and improve performance.

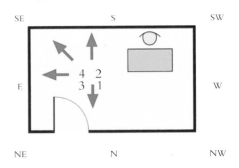

▲ *Ensure you face your best direction (or one of your other three favoured directions).*

FENG SHUI AND YOUR CAR

▲ *Our cars, just like ourselves, need to be kept healthy and in good condition.*

Many people spend hours at a time in their cars which become like mini-homes. Like our homes, they become a reflection and extension of ourselves. Negative chi in cars has the power to create lasting damage and destruction to their owners and to others. Cars are extensions of ourselves. With the right treatment they serve us well. Some people talk to their cars, others give them names and personalize them. In some parts of the world they are blessed. Negative energy breeds negative response, so we should aim to build up a caring relationship with our cars.

Generally, cars follow the classic Four Animals formation, being taller at the back than the front, and having support on either side. Car seats should also follow this formation. Cars which slope away to the back and those which open at the back can leave us feeling insecure, as anyone who has driven off as a rear

▼ *Yellow, an Earth colour, representing stability, is auspicious.*

door or boot (trunk) lid has flown open can testify. Small pick-up trucks are vulnerable from behind since their cargoes can fall off or may be stolen.

The rear lights act as our Tortoise, warning those behind to brake. It is therefore essential to ensure they are clean and in working order, and that spent bulbs are replaced immediately. Cars with reclining seats, such as expensive sports models, also suggest vulnerability behind since the Tortoise position is weak. Their "laid-back" effect is often reflected in the driving habits of the owners of such cars.

CAR ORNAMENTS

Stickers on the rear window can strengthen the Tortoise position, particularly those which say "Please Keep Your Distance" or "Baby on Board" and other, polite, warning signs. Jokes and stickers which are difficult to read have the opposite effect in that they encourage the car behind to come closer. Stickers should not obstruct the window.

Any ornaments that act as a distraction behind should be avoided. The windscreen can act as the Phoenix and moving objects, like hanging ornaments, can create instability and affect concentration. Do not allow loose items to collect in the

▲ *The white Metal energy drains the flamboyant red on this quirky car.*

back of the car as sudden braking will send them cannoning around.

Even people who would not admit to being superstitious carry talismen when they travel. In the West, a small St Christopher symbol is believed to be protective because he was the patron saint of travellers. Other cultures have their own protection symbols. Attitudes to numbers on registration plates also indicate cultural differences. The Chinese avoid 4 because it resembles the word for death, while Westerners prefer not to use 13 and treble 6 for superstitious reasons.

▼ *Our cars reflect our personalities. An untidy car is as revealing as an untidy home. Secure anything that rattles.*

THE CAR AND THE SENSES

Fresh air is necessary in cars, in order to link the occupants with the world outside and to cleanse the air within the confined space. If the air is not fresh, the driver can become tired and lose concentration. To freshen the air we can introduce natural oils, which also affect our moods. Rosemary, neroli and lemon oils are helpful for calming anger and promoting clear thinking.

Vision is important in the car and a clean screen and headlights enable us to see and be seen clearly on a foggy day and at night.

If we regard the car engine in the same way that we do our bodies, then we

Element	Helped by	Harmed by	Weakened by	Weakens
Wood	Water	Metal	Fire	Earth
Fire	Wood	Water	Earth	Metal
Earth	Fire	Wood	Metal	Water
Metal	Earth	Fire	Water	Wood
Water	Metal	Earth	Wood	Fire

can appreciate that for the car to be healthy and function well its tubes have to be unblocked and its components well maintained. Regular servicing is therefore important.

PERSONALITY AND THE CAR

Our cars reflect our personalities in the same way as our homes do. A neat, clean car generates a different impression of its owner to a dirty one. The colours we choose also affect our attitude to a car and the perception other drivers have of us. How many of us give red cars driven by very young men a wide berth? When choosing cars we would do well to bear the Five Elements relationships in mind.

CHOOSING THE COLOURS

We should ensure the colours of our cars do not conflict with the colour of the element associated with our Chinese animal. For example, a young and rather macho male, particularly a Fire Horse,

▼ *Young male energy is excessively yang. Black, a yin Water energy, will drain it.*

▲ *Red sports cars show too much yang. Black accessories will reduce the impact.*

should not choose red because this colour will intensify the fire. A dark blue or black to cool the Fire, and Metal – white or grey – to weaken it is preferable, and safer. On the other hand, a driver who cannot concentrate and who is a Water Pig will need some Wood (green) to draw them on and some Metal, white or silver, as support.

CAR CLUTTER

Rattles left unfixed

A worn spare tyre

Spent lamps

Confectionery wrappers

Fast-food cartons

Car park tickets

Rubbish in the boot (trunk)

CAR NUMBERS

Number associations vary between different cultures. In China, they often depend on sound. The number 4 sounds like the Chinese word for 'death' and is therefore considered unlucky. The number 8 on the other hand sounds like the Chinese word for "happiness" and is well-regarded. 88 is therefore doubly auspicious, meaning "double happiness". Car number plates containing the number 888 are very sought-after and command high prices.

PETS

F eng Shui is about environments and people and originally pets would not have played any part in the design of homes at all. Animals were domesticated as long as 8000 years ago but until quite recent times they were mainly used to work for their owners, and regarded as property rather than as best friends to human beings. Today, pets play a

▲▼ Today pets – in particular cats and dogs – are an important part of a family unit and need to be considered in Feng Shui.

very important role in the lives of their owners and their presence has to be taken into account when applying Feng Shui principles to the home.

DOGS AND CATS

Whether we or our pets choose their sleeping places it is possible to ensure that the colour and pattern of their beds and bedding are in harmony with the elemental energy of the position. The table opposite shows the colours associated with each direction. Should a cat choose to sleep somewhere other than its basket, then there may be some geopathic stress which they are attracted to, or they may just enjoy snuggling up.

FROGS AND WEALTH

A china frog, carrying a coin in its mouth and placed inside the front door (particularly if it is the west or north-west, the Metal areas which signify money), supposedly attracts wealth to the house.

COLOUR OF BEDDING	
DIRECTION	COLOUR
East	Green
South-east	Green
South	Red
South-west	Yellow, brown
West	Grey
North-west	Grey
North	Blue/Black
North-east	Yellow, brown

PETS AND HEALTH

Although we get pleasure from our pets and studies have shown that stroking animals can actually relieve signs of stress, we should not be blind to the fact that they can cause health risks in the home. More than once clients have wondered why people do not stay long when they visit and the answer is so obvious. A litter tray in full view in the kitchen is the greatest turn-off for a guest, particularly when they have come to eat. Likewise, caged animals in children's bedrooms can create an unhealthy energy unless the cage is well maintained, and they are best located elsewhere. It might also be prudent to consider the health of the animals and we need to provide conditions which mirror their natural habitats and lifestyles as far as possible if our pets are to remain healthy. Just as human beings enjoy better health with good food and exercise, so pets will remain healthier if they are not imprisoned in confined spaces and fed on poor diets for the duration of their lives. The mental health of our animals is also important and problems often occur where pets are locked in a house or flat alone all day and often through the evening as well.

▲ *Fish are considered to be very auspicious in China where they are kept to attract wealth to the household.*

FISH

Fish symbolize success and wealth in China and an aquarium by the entrance or in the sitting room is thought to encourage this. Eight gold fish and one black one in a tank are believed to be an auspicious combination. When fish die it is not regarded as a sad occasion since it is thought that they are absorbing the bad luck of the family and the fish are replaced immediately. In the West, where animal welfare issues are considered, unless the tank can be large enough to provide a reasonable environment for the fish, a picture or image may be more acceptable. An indoor water feature in the south-east will serve as well. Outdoor pools, provided they are large enough and well maintained, provide a more natural environment. When in a front garden place them to the left of the front door, never to the right.

ANIMALS AND SYMBOLOGY

The use of animals as luck symbols is widespread in China and their symbolism lies deep within the culture of the country and does not necessarily translate into other cultures with their own symbols. Where a symbolic quality is desired, an ornament or picture will suffice to invoke the desired energy to an area.

▼ *An alert, intelligent dog such as this collie makes an ideal family pet.*

SYMBOLIC CHINESE ANIMALS	
Bat	luck
Bear	protection
Crane	health and longevity
Deer	luck and wealth
Elephant	wisdom
Fish	success
Horse	recognition
Leopard	protection
Lion	authority and protection
Stork	longevity
Tortoise	longevity

▼ *Animals need healthy diets as well as humans and our pets will be happier if they are fed regular, balanced meals.*

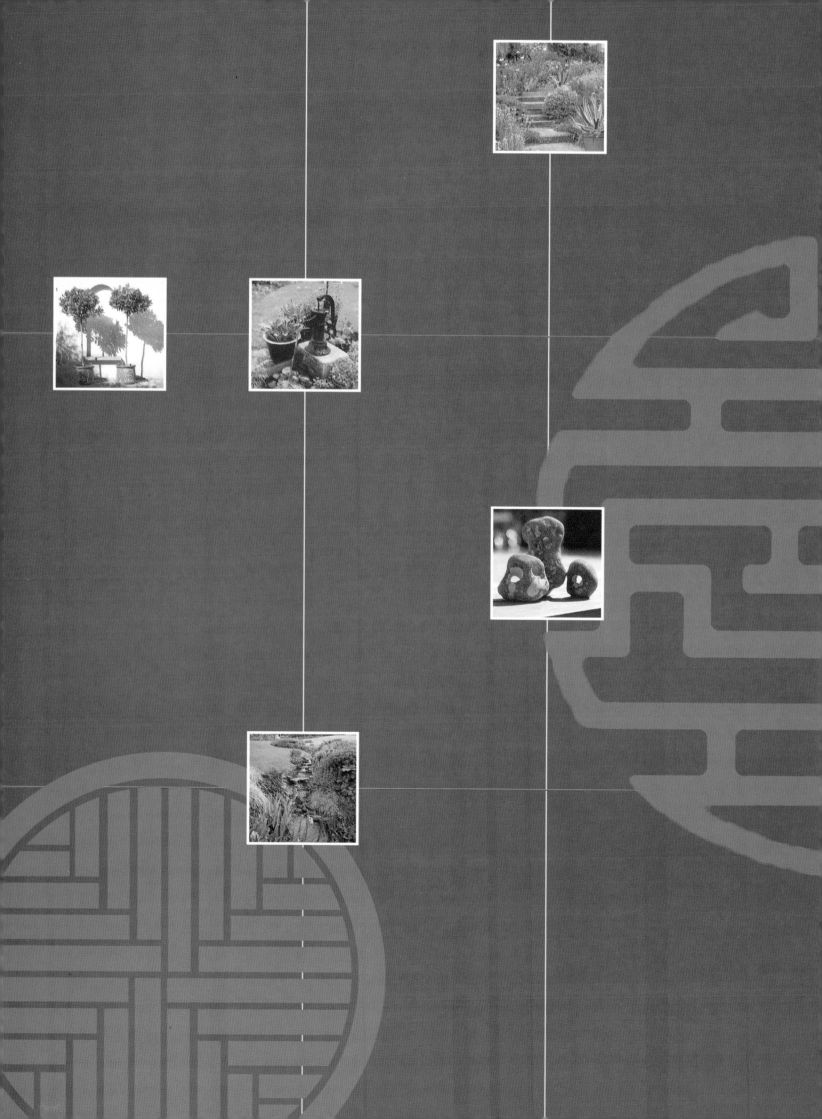

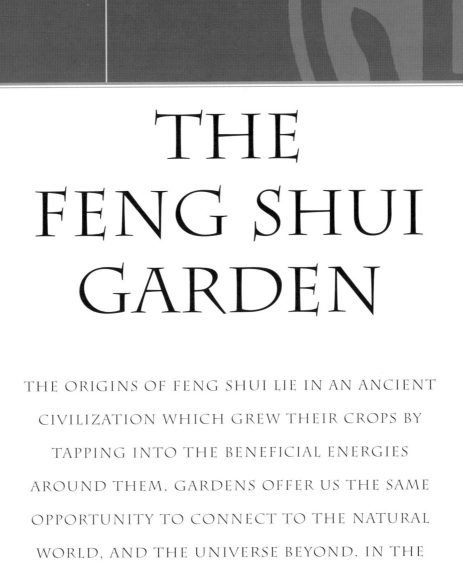

THE FENG SHUI GARDEN

THE ORIGINS OF FENG SHUI LIE IN AN ANCIENT
CIVILIZATION WHICH GREW THEIR CROPS BY
TAPPING INTO THE BENEFICIAL ENERGIES
AROUND THEM. GARDENS OFFER US THE SAME
OPPORTUNITY TO CONNECT TO THE NATURAL
WORLD, AND THE UNIVERSE BEYOND. IN THE
GARDEN WE ARE IN PARTNERSHIP WITH OTHER
LIVING THINGS. IF WE WORK WITH THEM,
BALANCE AND HARMONY WILL FOLLOW.

FENG SHUI PRINCIPLES IN THE GARDEN

—

Taoist principles lie at the heart of Chinese garden design and can be seen in the ancient gardens in the province of Suzhou today. Many of the principles are echoed in what is considered to be good garden design around the world. Other principles stem from the culture and mythology of China and are not included here, since every culture has its own beliefs and practices which are part of its heritage and should be preserved. Feng Shui allows for these differences. Hopefully, with an adaptation of the principles we will be able to develop our own gardens in a way which will enhance our lives.

QUIET HAVENS

When we purchase a house or move into an apartment our first concerns are likely to be the number of bedrooms, the size of the kitchen and the condition of the roof. Rarely do we choose a home on the basis of its garden, even though it can play an important role in correcting the imbalance created by the frantic pace of modern living. We are driven in pursuit of work and its rewards, bombarded with stimulating experiences via the media, and we can even shop 24 hours a day if we want to. These yang activities take their toll on our mental and physical health. An excellent way to redress the balance is to create quiet havens for ourselves in our gardens.

When we recall the books we read as children, many of our favourite stories were set in the countryside. There can be few of us who have not, at some point in our lives, peered into a hole in search of Brer Rabbit or walked by a river hoping to see Ratty and Mole or Mr Toad sweeping by in his magnificent car. The magic of raindrops on a spider's web, the first ladybird to land on a small pudgy finger, a beautiful mahogany-coloured

▲ *However small, a garden can offer us a retreat from the hurly-burly of modern life.*

▶ *Studying details such as a spider's web enables us to make links with nature.*

▼ *Green spaces in the inner city give the inhabitants a relief from stress.*

chestnut and the swish of autumn leaves as we wade through in shiny boots, these are all early experiences which link us to the natural world.

Until quite recently, gardens for contemplation were the preserve of the rich. Poorer people cultivated the soil for their survival, but their hard work did keep them in touch with the land. There are many children now who have never seen fruit or vegetables growing or experienced the magic of watching a tiny seed develop into a plant. Our gardens are furnished like our homes with everything bought off-the-peg from garden centres. But the mood is changing. In big cities like London and New York there are moves to create community gardens on derelict sites between inner-city buildings and skyscrapers. More and more schools are creating gardens to teach children about the natural world. The demand for food uncontaminated by chemicals is growing as we begin to realize the folly of some of the current trends in industrial food production. It seems that there is a latent longing to reconnect with the natural world.

In the Feng Shui garden the design principles of the ancient Chinese landscapers are used to create, not Chinese gardens, but indigenous ones which relate to our own psyche as well as to the spirit of the place where we live. By using local plants and natural methods to grow them we can make a garden in which we can distance ourselves from the hurly-burly of modern living and gain repose. Even if we live in an apartment block, we can take the initiative by tending the ill-

▲ *Choose plants to suit the soil and situation for a healthy, harmonious garden.*

▼ *With some pots, seeds and imagination, we can create tranquil and beautiful spaces.*

kept communal spaces which provide our window to the outside world. We need to have restful yet energizing green spaces when we return to the nurturing space of our home.

The following pages reveal how the ancient principles of Feng Shui can be employed in our gardens today to create supportive and nurturing environments. We will see how centuries-old formulae can be translated into modern-day garden design techniques and discover how yin and yang and the Five Elements can be interpreted outside.

Feng Shui is the art of directing the energy of an environment to move in ways with which we feel comfortable. The plants, furnishings and other objects we surround ourselves with have an impact on how we feel about the garden and how we use it. The ever-present unseen energies of the earth and the universe can be exploited to our advantage.

CHINESE GARDENS

Chinese gardens originated in the centres of power, the homes of the wealthy and around religious sites, and they represent an attempt to recreate the perfection of nature and the unity of human beings, Heaven and Earth. In China, garden design conforms to the same philosophical principles as the other arts. It grew out of the fusion of the Confucian concept of art, as something created by human beings but modelled on nature, and the Taoist belief in the superiority of the natural world as an art form. It produced some of the most dramatic yet tranquil places in the world.

In China, the garden and home are considered to be a single entity. The garden is drawn into the house through windows and latticed panels, while the walls serve as backdrops to carefully chosen plants. Chinese gardens are designed to accommodate human beings and their activities so buildings are a major feature, whether for recreation, as viewing platforms, or as observatories. In the same way that European landscape architects like "Capability" Brown and Humphrey Repton used the natural scenery as a backdrop to their gardens, ancient Chinese

▼ *Mountains and water – shan shui – are essential features of the gardens of China.*

designers incorporated mountains, natural water features and trees into theirs. If such natural features were absent they created them, building hills and importing large rocks to emulate mountains. It was said that the Sung Dynasty fell because the Emperor became obsessed with transporting huge rocks for his garden from a remote province and bankrupted the state.

Chinese domestic architecture determined a key concept of garden design. Houses were built around three sides of a central courtyard, and the empty centre is an important feature of Feng Shui. Whereas Western designers might fill the

▲ *Large gnarled rocks are used in Chinese gardens to symbolize mountains, and are often subjects of meditation.*

▼ *This garden in England shows natural planting typical of Chinese-style gardens.*

▲ *Open, enclosed and covered spaces all feature in the design of the Chinese garden.*

▶ *Openings in walls and windows offer inviting glimpses of pleasures to come.*

PLANTS AND THEIR MEANINGS

Aspidistra: Fortitude
Chrysanthemum: Resolution
Cypress: Nobility
Gardenia: Strength
Hydrangea: Achievement
Kerria: Individualism
Orchid: Endurance
Peony: Wealth
Pine: Longevity
Pomegranate: Fertility
Rhododendron: Delicacy
Virginia Creeper: Tenacity

▲ *According to Taoist principles, the interest of these stones lies in their holes, since it is they that bring the stones to life.*

▶ *The design of this garden is based on natural plant forms, rocks and water.*

allowed to develop naturally. Thus the clipped trees and hedges which can be seen in Western gardens do not occur in a Chinese garden where the natural forms of trees are allowed to develop. Whatever alterations are carried out in a Chinese garden, the result must look natural. Ponds, lakes and hills all resemble their natural counterparts.

The aesthetic principles behind all Chinese art forms, as well as the moral and ethical principles on which society is built, are all based on observations and interpretations of the natural world. Human characteristics are compared with natural phenomena, such as stone, bamboo and blossoms. Mountains and water, which play an integral part in the study of Feng Shui, feature largely in Chinese gardens and paintings.

centres of enclosed spaces with geometrically aligned beds, the Taoist view of a space lies in its potential. It is not a lifeless void, but an energetic area brimming with possibilities. Walls are given meaning by inserting windows which look to the world beyond; rocks are brought to life by the hollows and crevices which give them character.

According to the Tao, human activity should never dictate the shape of the natural world, since all things should be

THE FENG SHUI GARDEN

The "Magic Square" on which Feng Shui is based represents a picture of the universe. Its arrangement lies at the heart of Feng Shui and represents the dynamic interaction of all natural phenomena and life forms. Much of the art of applying Feng Shui lies in interpreting the natural imagery associated with each section of the Magic Square.

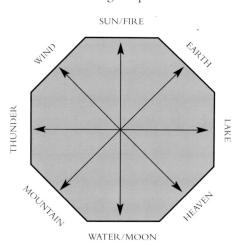

SUN/FIRE

WIND   EARTH

THUNDER   LAKE

MOUNTAIN   HEAVEN

WATER/MOON

We can interpret these natural phenomena at their face value or can read into them ancient concepts describing the workings of the universe. For example, scientists investigating the beginnings of life on Earth believe that huge storms were a catalyst which sparked life into action in the waters. This can be read into the interaction of the opposites Thunder and Lake on the diagram. In the same vein, the interaction of Sun and Water brings about photosynthesis in plants which enable the planet to breathe and on which all living things depend. The Wind, the Sun's rays and rain from

◀ *This arrangement shows how the dynamic forces of the universe interact to create life.*

▶ *Rice terraces in China follow the contours of the mountains, showing how human beings can work in harmony with Nature.*

▲ *Observations of the natural world and an understanding of the laws of nature led to the creation of the formulae on which Feng Shui is based.*

the skies (Heaven) bring this about, while the Earth and Mountain create a stable and nourishing environment in which life forms can thrive.

In ancient China, garden designers were inspired by the wonderful mountain formations and the water-filled valleys. Poets wrote about mountains, seen from near and far, from above and below, and rocks were placed in gardens so that they could be seen from different vantage points. Scenes were designed to change with the seasons and the weather, and garden buildings and walkways were designed to take in these different views. Rocks and buildings were placed high on hills or mounds where they could be seen from a distance, or low in valleys, by lakes and pools. All the garden features were contained in large open spaces, within which smaller vistas opened up.

▲ *Zigzag walkways are designed to offer different views of the garden as they twist and turn through it.*

◀ *The Moon Gate invites us to move beyond our immediate space, symbolically opening up our vision.*

THE FOUR ANIMALS

The classic Four Animal formation governs the placement of each building and each vista in a garden. The backdrop, in the Tortoise position, is something solid, like a clump of pine trees or a rock, with trees and shrubs or more rocks to the east in the Dragon position. To the west, the area should be lower and flatter to keep the unpredictable energy of the Tiger under control, and in front, in the Phoenix position, should be a small clump of trees or a small rock to mark the boundary of the garden space.

YIN AND YANG

Nowhere is the duality of the two opposing yet complementary forces of yin and yang more pronounced than in the garden. The strong, solid mountains, or the rocks which represent them, contrast with the still, deep waters in the lakes and ponds. The image portrayed by each would not be so effective if they were not set in contrast to each other. The beauty of a single flower is more pronounced when set against a dark, rocky surface, as are the twisted branches of an ancient tree when seen against the sky.

There is a feeling of serenity in a Chinese garden, but not because it is lifeless and still. There is movement and also sound – the rustle of the wind through the trees and the call of birds and animals. Movement is suggested by the shapes of the rocks, which may be given evocative names like Crouching Tiger and Flying Dragon, as well as in the patterns within the weathered rock faces. The bent trunks and twisted stems of carefully positioned

▲ *An example of yin and yang – solidity and emptiness. The path tempts us forward.*

◀ *Solid rocks set off delicate plants and a tiny spray of water that wets the pebbles.*

▼ *The twisted stems of* Corylus avellana *'Contorta' would be lost against foliage but stand out against a white wall.*

Yin Plants	Yang Plants
Apricot	Bamboo (below)
Jasmine	Cherry
Magnolia	Chrysanthemum
Pear	Orchid
Rhododendron	Peony
Rose (below)	Willow

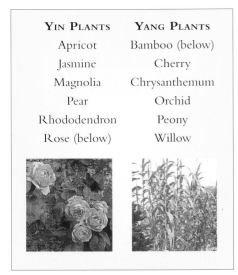

▲ *A small rock and a pool can take on the characteristics of a mountain and a lake.*

trees and shrubs contrast with pale walls or the sky. Ancient Chinese gardens provided the backdrop for social life in wealthy circles. Operas, dancing and music filled the gardens with sound. They were lit by lanterns which created their own tableaux.

Everything in a Chinese garden is strategically placed to highlight its beauty and impact and is seen in relation to everything else around it. An English cottage garden, filled with a rich variety of flowers, is lovely in a completely different way to one in which a beautiful stone or a single bloom is all that is needed to create a powerful visual impact. Every plant is endowed with yin or yang

▼ *A wooden arch acts as a Moon Gate to beckon us to a different part of the garden.*

Yang	Yin
People	Nature
Narrow	Broad
Hard	Soft
Dominant	Supportive
Straight	Curved
Solidity	Emptiness
Movement	Stillness
High	Low
Visible	Concealed
Exterior	Interior

depending on its qualities or the symbolism of the character which represents it in the Chinese language.

Perspective is used in an interesting way in the Chinese garden. Vistas like those created by the great Western landscape designers are an integral part of Chinese design, but there is an additional emphasis. Sizes are seen to be relative. A vast mountain viewed from a distance can appear small, but a small stone close

at hand can be given great importance. The notion of the "garden room", which has been part of Western design for a number of years, is also a traditional feature of Chinese gardens. Small gardens are created within larger spaces and larger vistas are opened up within quite small areas by using "windows" to give glimpses of the world beyond.

The Island of the Immortals

Ponds and lakes often contain an island in imitation of the sacred dwelling place of the Eight Immortals far off in the eastern seas. It is designed to lure them into the garden to reveal the secrets of eternal life. Trees are never planted on islands since this would symbolize isolation.

CHI – THE UNIVERSAL ENERGY

Chi is the life force present in all animate beings and is also the subtle energy expressed by seemingly inanimate objects. Gardens reflect the human quest for longevity, which in China means the maintenance of youth, rather than the Western concept of being long-lived. Every feature in a garden is placed there to achieve this aim; rocks and lakes represent permanence, and long-lived trees, shrubs and perennial plants are preferred to annuals or biennials. This makes the chi, the life force of the environment, strong and stable.

ROCKS

Rocks are symbolic of the mountains which are the dominant features of many parts of China. Three types of rock were incorporated into the design of large classical gardens – huge rocks big enough to walk through, delicate upright rocks and those which had complex patterns or shapes. Rockeries were built in the north and west of gardens to provide shelter and to act as a contrast to pools, which were situated in the south and east to capture the beneficial energies believed to emanate from those directions.

Rocks may appear to be inanimate, but the Chinese perceive them to be powerful and to speak volumes in the veining on their surfaces and the symbolic expressions suggested by their shapes. Small stones, known as dreamstones, are set into the backs of chairs and hung on walls in garden pavilions. As objects for contemplation, they can lead us, via the energy channels in their markings, to pursue the Tao in our quest to be at one with the universe.

WATER

Water brings energy to a garden. A still pond reflects the ever-changing heavens, and brings in the energy of the universe and the sun, the moon, the stars and the clouds that are reflected on the surface.

Moving water brings sound and movement as it tumbles over pebbles and creates small whirlpools and eddies. Fountains did not feature in ancient Chinese gardens, but modern technology enables us to bring the energy of water into even the tiniest space.

Water symbolizes wealth and is believed to be a good collector and conductor of chi. Gently flowing water, entering a healthy pool from the east, is very auspicious, particularly when it meanders slowly away and cannot be seen

▲ *Water is an integral part of a Chinese garden, with a variety of paths and walkways to provide different vistas over it.*

leaving. Gold and silver coloured fish symbolize money and are therefore found in abundance in China. Although pools may be square, the planting should create a kidney-shaped arrangement which appears to hug a building protectively. Symmetrical arrangements do not exist in large Chinese gardens but are acceptable in smaller ones.

▶ *Bridges with semi-circular arches are common in China. Reflected in the water, the arch creates a circle symbolizing Heaven.*

PATHS AND BRIDGES

Paths meander through Chinese gardens, in the open or under covered walkways, gently curving from the east to bring in the auspicious rising energy, or more curved if coming from the west, to slow down the falling, depleted energy associated with that direction. Arched bridges span waterways, creating perfect circles with their reflections in the water, symbolizing Heaven. Others zigzag, an odd number of twists being yang and offering a soft yin vista of still water and plants. An even number of twists is yin, offering a yang view of rocks or buildings. Pagodas are often placed in the north-east and the south-west, sometimes referred to as "Doors of the Devil", to keep evil influences at bay, as these are the directions of the prevailing winds.

TREES AND PLANTS

The planting in Chinese gardens is permanent so that the trees and plants build up an energetic relationship with their

▼ *The walkway at Jiangling Museum, China, links the building to its surroundings and offers different vistas as it zigzags.*

▼ *An unobscured outside window such as this links the inner world of the house with the outer world beyond.*

▼ *The same window seen from the inside shows how the link is maintained and the garden beckons us outside.*

environment. We may find it strange that colour is not given special consideration, except when it reflects the passing of the seasons, but it is incidental to the main purpose of the Chinese garden.

BUILDINGS AND STRUCTURES

Since people are an integral part of the garden, pavilions and decks are important features, encouraging them to congregate and pursue leisure interests. Bridges, paths and covered walkways give access to vistas and secluded places and enable people to enjoy gentle exercise. Walls and doorways link the inner world of the house with the outer world beyond.

FURNITURE AND OTHER OBJECTS

Seats and pots feature in the Chinese garden, but the main focus is on the rocks and the plants. In public gardens, amusing objects like huge colourful dragons appear at festival times. In parks, vivid beds of brightly coloured plants, often with swirling designs incorporated, reflect the public, or yang, space as opposed to the yin space of the private garden.

THE FIVE ELEMENTS

The Five Elements of Wood, Fire, Earth, Metal and Water are the agents of chi and they represent shapes, colours, and the senses. The aim in the Feng Shui garden is to create a space where no one element is dominant and in which there is a balance of yin and yang. The feel of a garden is very different when a balance exists, and we can achieve this in our planting schemes and by careful placement of garden buildings and ornaments. This is not to say that a garden must have something of every colour, or of every shape. There is an old

▼ *Any plant, regardless of its shape or size, represents the Wood element. Tall, upright trees symbolize the Wood element shape.*

Chinese saying, "Too many colours blind the eye", and we have all seen gardens that are full of brightly coloured plants, ornaments and features. They make an incredible visual show and grab the attention of passers-by, but are not conducive to relaxation or harmony.

The Feng Shui garden follows the example of the natural world in striving for a balance between shape and colour. It gives us the scope to experiment and introduce our favourite exotic plants or outlandish sculptures as well as intriguing garden buildings or brightly coloured walls – provided the perspective, proportions and balance are right. See "The Relationships of the Five Elements" table for details of the balancing elements.

▲ *These three examples of Fire shapes – the cordyline, the potted conifers and the clipped bay – each have a different energy.*

WOOD

All plants represent the Wood element which obviously dominates the planting in any garden, yet the shapes and colours of the plants and the settings in which we place them can suggest other elements. To introduce the Wood element specifically, we can use columnar trees and trellis with upright wooden supports.

FIRE

Fire is suggested in plants with pointed leaves and the introduction of even a single specimen can transform a lifeless bed.

▼ *The rounded domes on this hedge suggest Metal but the meandering shape is Water, which follows Metal in the elemental cycle.*

FIVE ELEMENT FEATURES IN THE GARDEN

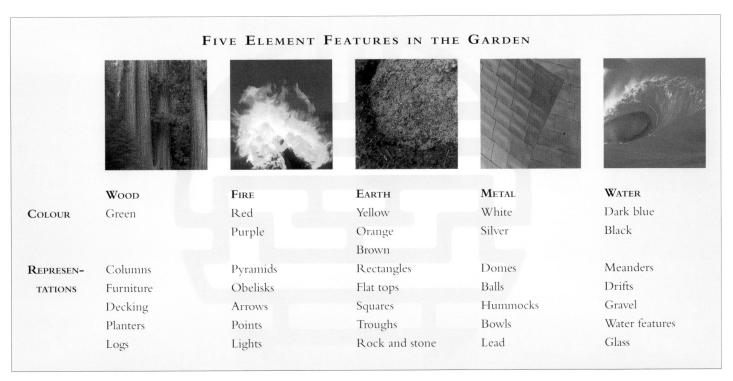

	WOOD	FIRE	EARTH	METAL	WATER
COLOUR	Green	Red	Yellow	White	Dark blue
		Purple	Orange	Silver	Black
			Brown		
REPRESEN-TATIONS	Columns	Pyramids	Rectangles	Domes	Meanders
	Furniture	Obelisks	Flat tops	Balls	Drifts
	Decking	Arrows	Squares	Hummocks	Gravel
	Planters	Points	Troughs	Bowls	Water features
	Logs	Lights	Rock and stone	Lead	Glass

Triangles and pyramid shapes are also representative of Fire and many supports for climbing plants are available in this shape. When siting them, be careful that they are not out of proportion to the structures and plants surrounding them. The Fire element is powerful. A splash of red which represents this element is enough to make a definite statement.

EARTH

Earth is suggested in paving and pathway materials. The real thing – the garden soil – is not on show in the Feng Shui garden

▼ The metal shapes of these trees appear to dance, bringing a lively energy to the garden.

since it will be covered with plants. Flat-topped fences, trellises and walkways suggest the Earth element. Too much of this shape can depress the chi of a place and it can easily dominate a garden surrounded by walls and fences. Introduce different shapes in garden buildings and structures and attempt to alter the shape of the view.

METAL

Round shapes and domes represent the Metal element. The yin and yang aspects of this in the garden can be very different. Tall, closely packed oval conifers can be menacing to walk through. On the other hand, a series of small coniferous balls spread around the garden introduce an element of fun. All-white gardens can have a lifeless feel about them but in a small conservatory they have a pleasantly cooling effect.

WATER

Apart from the real thing, the Water element is suggested by meandering shapes, both in paths and in planting. Gravel and heather gardens are an example of Water-shaped planting and similar effects can be achieved by low planting or by introducing drifts of the same plant or colours.

▲ Low, meandering planting suggests the Water element, as it resembles a stream.

THE TRANSFORMATION OF THE ELEMENTS

Just as yin and yang each transform into the other when their energy reaches its peak, so can the Elements transform into their opposites. The best example of this in the garden is where the Wood element transforms into Earth. In a predominantly green garden, with Earth-shaped boundaries and brown, wooden, rectangular furniture, the Wood is transformed into the Earth element and the result is a low-energy garden. The remedy is to introduce other shapes and splashes of colour to bring the garden to life.

THE UNSEEN ENERGIES

There are many unseen energies at work in the garden. Some manifest themselves in physical conditions which we can observe. Others, if we are unaware of them, can create difficulties when we are sitting and working in the garden. Many, however, work for our benefit and we must take care to create a safe haven for them.

UNDERGROUND WATER

There may be some areas in the garden which are situated over underground water sources. We need to be aware of this in order to choose plants which will survive in such conditions – it is no use putting in plants which prefer dry conditions here. Such areas will have a bearing on how we design the garden and we should mark them on any plan we make.

Underground streams can create a disturbance in the earth which may affect plants growing above them and could have an adverse effect on us if we are sitting or working above them for any length of time. Dowsing is the best way to find these and it may be worth engaging a dowser to check an area before you

▲ *Underground water can create difficulties in gardens in terms of geopathic stress and waterlogged areas.*

▶ *Trees have a relationship with their environment and provide a home to thousands of different species of animals and plants.*

▼ *If you respect the garden's natural ecological system you will be rewarded with a garden full of healthy, beautiful plants.*

build a garden office or workshop. Distressed plants – trees which lean for no apparent reason, shrubs which develop cankers or plants which look sickly and die for no obvious reason – reveal that something is amiss.

THE SOIL

Our greatest ally in the garden is healthy soil. Before we plant anything we need to ensure that the soil is right for the plants we want to grow. Nurseries sell soil-testing kits and gardening books provide advice on the suitability of plants for

▶ *Ancient peoples ran their lives by the movement of the stars and watched the skies for signs to plant and harvest crops.*

specific conditions. Acid-loving plants will never thrive in alkaline soil and vice versa. A Feng Shui garden should go with the flow. It is virtually impossible to alter the soil permanently in order to grow your favourite plants, so before buying a new house it is worth looking in neighbouring gardens to see which plants do well in the area.

The soil is a living entity teeming with millions of micro-organisms, each with its own role to play in the ecology of the garden. In the Feng Shui garden these microbes are valued and we should provide them with the conditions in which to thrive, in terms of sun, rain and air, as well as food made from composting our garden and kitchen waste. The folly of planting through plastic or microporous sheeting, which prevents weeds but also suffocates the micro-organisms and causes the soil to become stagnant and lifeless, is now understood.

SPIRIT OF THE PLACE

Some people believe that trees and plants are imbued with spirits. Others respect the relationship that long-lived trees have built up with the Earth and the support and nourishment that they provide for

▼ *The new moon – time to plant annual flower seeds, leafy vegetables and cereals.*

micro-organisms, other plants and animals, including human beings. Every garden has its support team of mammals, birds and insects, and even snails, which have a role. The slightest tinkering in terms of chemicals or soil disturbance can have an unsettling effect on the ecological chain. In the Feng Shui garden we respect our fellow workers.

▶ *The numbered days correspond to the days of the moon's cycle. It is advisable not to plant close to the equinoxes and the solstices.*

COSMIC ENERGIES

Ancient peoples around the world respected the part played by the sun, the moon and the weather in their lives and the growth of their crops, and many festivals reflect this. The cosmos affects who we are and determines our characters. This also applies in the plant world although plants cannot take charge and manipulate circumstances as we can. We must determine the best conditions for them. By planting according to the movements of the moon, we can greatly improve the conditions for our plants. Planting by the moon's phases is an ancient skill and requires only watching the sky or consulting a diary giving the dates of the new and full moons.

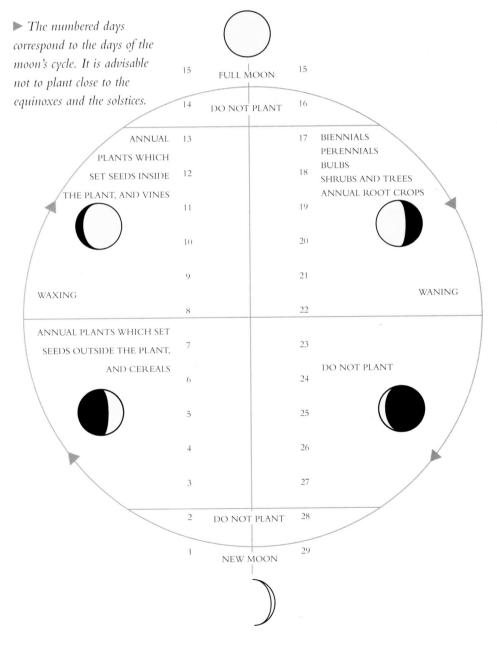

THE SHAPE OF THE GARDEN

The shape of the plot of land on which we build, or on which our existing home is sited, is important in Feng Shui. Regular shapes are best, so that there are no missing areas. We can use various means to make a plot appear more regular in shape than it already is. Fences and trellis can divide awkwardly-shaped plots into separate areas which are easier to deal with individually. The use of different materials as edging can create boundaries and, of course, plants can open up or conceal the most difficult spaces. Creative planting can create virtually any illusion we desire.

▼ *Trellis can be used to divide up gardens which have difficult shapes.*

▼ *This house sits well in its plot. The back gardens of houses built in Britain over the past century tend to be larger than the front but in most of Europe and in the United States, the reverse is true. Trees and shrubs protect the rear and sides and a fence shields the front, in line with the classic Four Animals formation.*

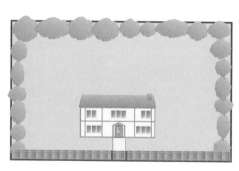

▲ *This picket fence defines the space and acts as a boundary without shutting out the world to a garden full of energy. The whole effect would be improved by taking out the dead tree on the right.*

▼ *This house sits too far to the back of its plot. The tall trees here will be overwhelming to the occupants of the house and from a more practical point of view could even be dangerous in high winds. Local preservation orders should be checked before taking steps to reduce the height of the trees.*

▲ *By changing the shape of the plot within the garden and with careful planting, the harsh lines of a triangular plot are lessened.*

▲ *Trellis or other features, preferably rounded, will serve to reduce the effect of the triangle's points. Mirrors in the positions indicated (A and B) reflect interesting planting, not each other, and will give the illusion of pushing the boundaries out.*

THE RECTANGULAR PLOT

A rectangular plot is regarded as the ideal shape. The house should be sited on the centre of the plot so that the garden is in proportion around the house.

THE TRIANGULAR PLOT

Triangular plots are not considered desirable in Feng Shui because the sharp points are felt to resemble knives. They are also difficult to deal with because they create three areas of stagnant energy. However, with careful planting and the erection of screens, it is possible to create the illusion of a regular shaped plot. An alternative is to plant heavily on the boundaries and use meandering paths within the garden.

ROUND AND L-SHAPED PLOTS

Round plots are difficult. Although the chi is able to flow freely round, it is difficult to contain it and it is advisable to create other, more stable shapes within the circle for seating areas. L-shaped and other irregularly shaped plots are best divided into regular shaped sections to make them simpler to deal with.

THE BRIGHT HALL

The Bright Hall was originally a pool of water in front of a house. Its function was to gather energy and to preserve an open space there. It could take the form of a sunken garden or simply an open, gathering space. These days it is the space in front of the front door. It should be in proportion to the front of the house, and be well maintained and uncluttered.

▲ *The chi flows quickly around this circular plot. Contain it with a shrub hedge and create inner areas for seating.*

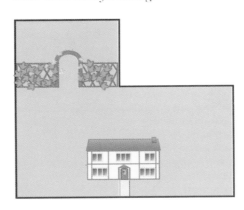

▲ *A trellis or fence positioned as shown will regularize this L-shaped plot.*

CASE STUDY

Care has to be taken when designing a Bright Hall, as Tom and Rhoda discovered. They created a wonderful Bright Hall in front of their house. Made of mellow stone and edged with red brick, which blended with the house, it was welcoming and greatly enhanced the front entrance. However, a Chinese Feng Shui consultant pronounced it inauspicious and suggested they have a straight step instead. They were flabbergasted but the reason was that on coming out of the house, the round edge turned into the lip of a jug, symbolically pouring money away down the sloping drive and into the road.

Some people have a greater level of perception than others but the skill can be acquired with practice. Before building or planting we should mark out our ideas and view them from all angles.

▲ *Viewed from the front this well-built Bright Hall appears to create a welcoming space in front of the house.*

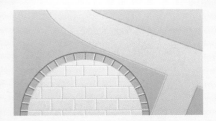

▲ *However, seen from this angle, it resembles the lip of a jug, symbolically pouring money away.*

DRAWING THE PLAN

Before creating a Feng Shui garden it is first necessary to investigate the compass directions around the site to determine the direction of the prevailing winds and to site the plants according to their preferences. When we are sitting or working in the garden it is useful to place ourselves in auspicious directions. We also need to investigate the positions of the Five Elements of the site to create a balance between them and with the features which we place in the garden.

DRAW A PLAN

Using graph paper to a suitable scale, take measurements for the length and breadth of the garden and mark

◆ House and garage
◆ Walls and fences
◆ Large trees and shrubs
◆ Garden buildings

◆ Semi-permanent features such as ponds, rockeries and patios.
◆ Features in the surrounding environment such as trees, other buildings, lampposts and so on.

TAKE A COMPASS READING

1. Remove watches, jewellery and metal objects and stand clear of cars and other metal fixtures.
2. Stand with your back parallel to the front door and note the exact compass reading in degrees.
3. Note the direction, e.g. 349° North, and mark it on to the plan of the garden as shown in the diagram. You are now ready to transfer the compass readings on

▼ *The Bagua should be superimposed on the plan to line up the main entrance with its corresponding direction and element.*

to your Bagua drawing.
4. Place the protractor on the Bagua diagram so that 0° is at the bottom at the North position.
5. Find the compass reading for your home and check you have the corresponding direction – if not you may be reading the wrong ring.
6. Mark the position of your house.
7. Look at the "Directions" table on the opposite page to double check the compass direction.

TRANSFER THE DIRECTIONS TO THE PLAN

1. To find the centre of the plan, match the main boundaries across the length of the plan and crease the paper lengthways.
2. Match the main boundaries across the width and crease the paper widthways.
3. Where the folds of the creases cross

YOU WILL NEED

◆ A scale plan of your home. If you own your home you will already have one. If not, it will be necessary to draw one, in which case you will also need a tape measure and graph paper
◆ A compass with the eight directions clearly marked
◆ A ruler
◆ A lead pencil and five coloured pencils – green, red, yellow, grey, dark blue
◆ A tracing of the Bagua with the suggested information marked on
◆ A protractor

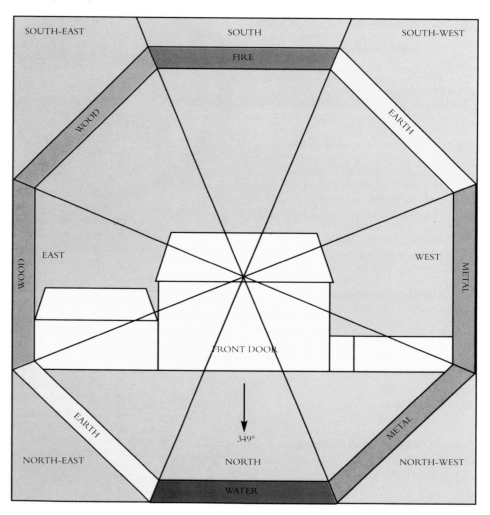

DIRECTIONS

North	337.5 – 22.5°
North-east	22.5 – 67.5°
East	67.5 – 112.5°
South-east	112.5 – 157.5°
South	157.5 – 202.5°
South-west	202.5 – 247.5°
West	247.5 – 292.5°
North-west	292.5 – 337.5°

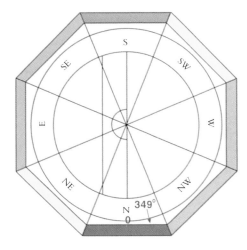

▲ *A circular protractor will help you line up the compass direction and the Bagua.*

▶ *Semi-permanent features like this pond, and all buildings and boundaries, should be marked on the plan.*

marks the centre of your garden.

4. If your garden is not a perfect square or rectangular shape, treat a protrusion less than 50% of the width as an extension to the direction.

5. If the protrusion is more than 50% of the width, treat the remainder as a missing part of the direction.

6. Place the centre of the Bagua on the centre point of the plan and line up the front door position.

7. Mark the eight directions on the plan and draw in the sectors.

8. Transfer the Bagua's colour markings on to the plan.

▶ *Once you have marked on the exisitng main features of your plot you will be ready to investigate the Feng Shui potential of your garden.*

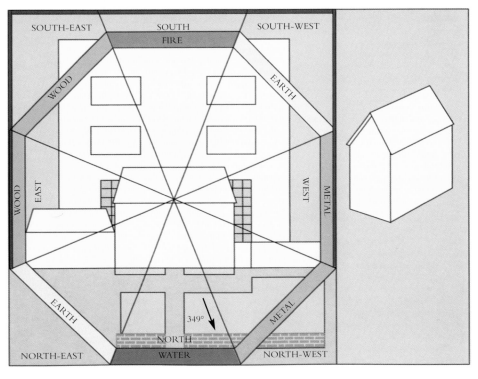

CASE STUDY

Mike and Sarah wanted a more interesting garden which required as little maintenance as possible. The neighbours on their left complained that the four-year-old *Cupressocyparis leylandii* trees were blocking their light and those on the right that they were killing near-by plants. Mike came to realize that they were a high-maintenance feature as they grew so fast. With three sons under the age of 12, they required a large space for ball games. Sarah wanted to grow some fruit and a few summer salad vegetables.

▼ *Once you know your magic number you can determine which directions are beneficial and will support you. Whether you are relaxing in the garden or enjoying a meal with family or friends you can choose to place your chair to face your best direction.*

Where to Sit	
1	SE or N
2	NE or SW
3	S or E
4	N or SE
5(m)	NE or SW
5(f)	SW or NE
6	W or NW
7	NW or W
8	E or S
9	E or S

▼ *We can bring water into the garden even in the smallest space, as illustrated by this Japanese-style water feature.*

▲ *While not exactly looking after themselves, interesting gardens like this require reasonably low maintenance.*

▼ *Water features come in many shapes and sizes and, placed in auspicious positions, can bring good luck and focus thought.*

The family wanted a low-maintenance pond to attract wildlife. Sarah also wanted a water feature on the patio.

Much to everyone's relief, the *leylandii* were removed and the soil was improved with organic matter and compost.

1. The four "cornerstones" were addressed first. In the south-west, an ivy-covered trellis was erected to filter the wind. A solid hedge would have set up wind turbulence.

2. A blossom tree was placed on the lawn to filter the north-east wind and to encourage the vibrant energy of the east on to the site.

3. A closed-back arbour was placed in the south-east to hide the compost bins, ideally placed in the Wealth area to provide sustenance for the garden, and to stabilize the area. The Fire-shaped roof moves the energy forward.

4. In the north-west a rounded metal plate was positioned showing the number of the house.

5. A light is placed in the north-east.

6. A rockery is sited in the Phoenix position in the front garden.

7. The path meanders to a spacious step, and pots with round-shaped plants as guardians sit on either side of the door.

8. A shrub is grown on the wall between the garage and house to help reduce the impact of a north-east wind.

9. A shrub here balances the one on the other side.

10. A yellow-berried pyracantha is placed here to stimulate the Metal energy and to give some prickly protection against unwelcome intruders.

11. A meandering stepping-stone path leads from the garage and the side gate, giving a balanced formality to the garden but affording different vistas as it curves.

12. The large back lawn area is surrounded by trees and shrubs – staggered, like fielders, to catch the children's stray balls and also to provide a pleasant walk around the garden.

13. The pond is backed by evergreen plants and shrubs to prevent leaves from

falling into it. Situated in the south-west it signifies future prosperity and should be kept healthy with oxygenating plants.

14. On a square wooden table stands a round metal sundial with an arrow pointing upwards. Every one of the Five Elements is used here to stimulate the Fame and Future Possibilities area of the symbolic Bagua.

15. Sarah places perennial plants and bulbs in an urn in front of the arbour – silver and gold to represent money in the summer months and red berries in the winter months to stimulate the Wealth area of the Symbolic Bagua.

16. A medium-height evergreen tree is planted here which will eventually block the point of the roof of a neighbouring house. Meanwhile, a concave mirror is

placed on the side of the house to symbolically absorb the "poison arrow".

17. Trellis is erected around the edge of a paved area to protect the house from any thrown balls and to enable Sarah to grow espalier-trained fruit. Herbs are grown in the flower beds as companion plants and salad vegetables are grown in the gaps.

18. A small water feature in the east stimulates the area of current prosperity.

19. Sarah's small greenhouse enables her to overwinter her perennial pot plants.

20. The patio chairs are positioned so that Sarah and Mike are backed by the garage wall, facing favourable positions. The protective Four Animal arrangement corresponds to the back, front and side aspects of the house and not to actual compass directions.

USING THE BAGUA IN THE GARDEN

The symbolic Bagua is generally discussed in terms of the house, yet we can use its magic in the garden too. If there is a certain aspect of our lives on which we need to focus, the symbolic Bagua gives us a tool to stimulate the energy associated with it, particularly when we look out on the area through the kitchen or sitting room windows. As in the house, we can divide the garden into rooms when applying the Bagua since it is not usual to be able to see the whole garden from one vantage point.

The enhancements used are designed to focus the mind and to create a stabilizing effect by using or alluding to

▲ *A garden full of energy – different shapes, colours and levels, and a variety of materials, add to the interest.*

heavy objects such as stones or mountains, or to shift something in our lives by creating or alluding to movement, water, or wind-blown items. Empty pots and

▲ *A herb garden directly outside a window is a good area to apply the Bagua.*

◄ *Use pots of plants in a group as a focus point in the garden.*

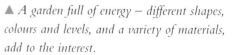

SUGGESTIONS FOR ENHANCEMENTS:

◆ Rocks, stones and large pots for added stability

◆ Wind objects to stir up the energy and create movement

◆ Fountains and water features for abundance

◆ Empty urns and dishes to accept the gifts of the universe

◆ Lights to illuminate paths or particular features in the garden

◆ Collections and art works for achievement

◆ Pot plants for focus

Paul and Claire both work from home. Paul is a writer who has had two novels published. He would like a more settled life, with a regular contract with a publisher, and would like to branch out and write for TV. Claire runs an aromatherapy practice and is planning to develop an idea and sell products by mail order. They both adore gardening and, when they are not in their respective study or workrooms, they spend much of their leisure time there. They have enhanced the appropriate areas of the Bagua in their home and would like to do the same in the garden.

1. Paul placed a bird table in the Helpful People area of the small side garden outside his office window in order to encourage the calls from publishers and TV companies to roll in. As organic gardeners, Paul and Claire do not like spraying insect pests, so small birds are very welcome in the garden. Paul greased the pole of the table to keep the birds safe from cats and prevent squirrels from taking the food. He takes care to observe which plants the birds are attracted to naturally and uses seeds from those plants to feed them, since he feels that bread and commercially produced bird food may harm them. He also places a dish of clean water there every day.

2. In the Fame area, Paul placed a large terracotta sun which smiles at him when he looks up from his work and will hopefully help him to fulfil his ambitions.

3. In the small garden outside Claire's therapy room, she placed a dish containing her rock plant collection in the Offspring area in order to focus on her business plans.

4. On the trellis separating Claire's garden from the main garden, the couple planted a *Trachelospermum jasminoides* – an evergreen climbing plant with fragrant white flowers which will last for most of the summer. This is in the Offspring area of the main garden.

5. Opposite the climber, Paul and Claire created a pond with a fountain, in the Family area of the main garden, having first checked that the water was not in an inauspicious position with regard to the Five Elements.

urns can suggest an empty space waiting for something to happen – this is particularly helpful in the Wealth area, for example. Whatever image we use must have meaning for us in that we can see it physically and relate to its illusion and symbolism. Thus we should use images from our own culture and experience. Whatever we use should not clash with the element of the direction, but if possible should strengthen it. A pot of plants suggesting the colour of the element can always be used, or an enhancement suggested on the facing page.

Since the enhancements are meant to trigger an emotion or action, we should place them where we can see them. If we have a large front garden, gardens to the side and at the back of the house, the chances are that there will be areas which we rarely look at. Those areas which are more useful to us in placing the Bagua are those which we constantly look at. For example, if we have a herb garden outside the kitchen window, or if our study faces the side garden, then these are the areas to concentrate on.

GARDEN FEATURES

—

For the most part we cannot determine the natural phenomena in our gardens or in the wider environment. We are, however, responsible for the plants and features we install there. With an understanding of the principles which govern Feng Shui, we can choose furniture, buildings, plants and colours which work in harmony with each other and the surrounding area and which create a balanced and supportive environment for us. We can also deliberately introduce features which clash in order to create a more vibrant energy in the garden.

PATHS

Paths carry chi through the garden and their size, shape and the materials they are made of can affect the movement of the energy. This will affect the way we feel about and perceive the space.

FRONT GARDENS

Generally speaking, paths lead to entrances, doors or gates. When they are straight, they channel energy quickly so we tend not to notice the garden and instead simply move between our homes and the outside world. In the Feng Shui garden, the aim is to use the front garden

▼ *There are points of interest all along this gently curving path.*

▲ *Winding paths slow us down and allow us to observe the garden. Note how the spiky potted plants bring this garden to life.*

as a space between home and the outside world where we can gather energy in the morning and slow down at the end of a hard day.

To enable us to slow down, paths should gently curve or meander, presenting us with different angles and views as we move along them. If we have no control over the shape of the path,

then placing pots along them or planting so that the lines of a straight path are broken up by overhanging plants are possible alternatives. Another option is to make breaks every so often, either with beds containing plants or some kind of ornamental feature, or by creating a visual barrier using different materials.

BACK GARDENS

Paths should also meander around the back garden so that we constantly happen upon different views. Ideally, we

▲ *This straight path channels chi to and from the door far too quickly.*

▲ *This curving path slows down the chi and offers us different views.*

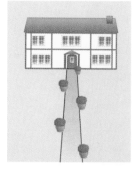

▲ *Pots spaced along a straight path will help to slow down the chi.*

▲ *Straight paths broken up in this way help to slow the energy down.*

▲ *The use of different materials also helps to slow down the energy.*

The materials we use will depend on local architectural style and we should aim to harmonize with it. Coloured concrete might blend into a modern urban garden but would look out of place in a rural garden, as would mellow weathered stone in an urban basement. Although the materials chosen must blend with the surroundings, we can make our paths individual by blending different materials into the design. Brick edging for concrete paths or the use of two different coloured bricks are just two of many ideas we can use.

Crazy paving is rarely used in the Feng Shui garden since its broken appearance symbolizes instability. However, it does feature in ancient Chinese gardens. Where crazy paving is well-laid, on a stable concrete foundation, the joints do not crack and the paving does not lift, it can be safely used.

▲ *This meandering path gives the right impression but is a little too narrow.*

need to get in a hurry. A straight path is acceptable here, but in the case of the home office, an alternative, meandering route would be ideal.

should not be able to take in the whole area in one glance. Where gardens are large, paths can tantalizingly draw us through gaps in trees, walls and trellises into other garden rooms beyond. Offices and sheds are places to which we often

▲ *Although straight, this wide pathway is practical in the herb and vegetable garden – and the plants hang over to slow down the flow of energy.*

▼ *Hidden pathways in different materials – which one should we take?*

MATERIALS FOR PATHS
Stone blocks (below), Brick, Gravel, Cobbles, Tiles, Bark, Wood, Concrete slabs, Grass

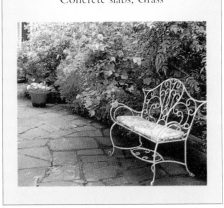

MATERIALS
Paths need to be stable and suited to their purpose. In a large garden they may need to carry heavy barrows, and therefore deep gravel would not be suitable. Cobble stones are not suitable path materials in the homes of elderly or disabled people since stability is especially important. Materials can vary in suitability between different areas – for instance in a wooded area bark paths with log edgings are fine, but grass paths and smooth surfaces are not a good idea in such damp places as they become slippery.

BOUNDARIES

We all need boundaries in order to feel protected and safe. As children, our boundaries are formed by the family unit and, as we get older, they expand to include school, our work and the organizations we join. When we become adults we continue to live within the boundaries of our social, recreational and professional groups. Our most important space is our home where we go to be ourselves and for support and rest. Boundaries are important in our relationships with our neighbours and with the world at large, as demarcation lines which give us a sense of security.

FRONT GARDENS

In China, the ideal is to have an open view in front of a building, with a small barrier to mark the boundary and, of course, to be facing south. In the West, the reverse is often the case and in temperate climates most people prefer a south-facing back garden. In Feng Shui it is recommended that a front barrier should never exceed the height of the downstairs windowsill, or waist height. To maintain a balance in life, it is important to be able to connect, not only with the immediate outside world but also with the universe, and we should all have

A front garden divides the home from the outside world but maintains a connection.

a view of the sky and the changing seasons. People who shut themselves off from the world will be at best disenchanted or, at worst, suffer from a depressive illness. Privacy is important but we should not become disconnected from the world or the people in it.

BACK GARDENS

The boundaries we choose for our garden perimeters can act as a backdrop for our plants as well as providing protection. In order for us to feel secure they should be well maintained. Good maintenance helps our relationships with our neighbours, as quarrels over boundaries frequently feature in neighbourly disputes. Thoughtless planting of unsuitable hedging plants, like the fast-growing *Cupressocyparis leylandii*, has been known to result in neighbours ending up in court. Whether we build walls, erect fences or use trees and hedges as our boundaries we need to keep a sense of proportion and plant things which will not outgrow their space or interfere with buildings, other plants or the well-being of our neighbours. If there are insecure

areas in the garden perimeter we need to create barriers which will repel intruders. Plants such as holly and pyracantha serve this purpose admirably, but do not place prickly plants where you might brush up against them accidentally.

Smaller boundaries within the garden divide it up into different areas. These can take the form of hedges, fences or trellis, or even a change from grass to flower bed or from path to lawn. We can use a single shrub or a pot to create the illusion of a barrier. Like the Moon Gates in ancient Chinese gardens, gaps in

Boundaries protect us and our homes, but should not cut us off from the world outside.

A gate such as this gives protection without isolating the home from outside.

hedges, doors in walls and paths through trellis and arbours allow us a glimpse of an area beyond our immediate space. In small gardens the same effect can be achieved by using mirrors and *trompe-l'oeil* designs on walls to draw the eye.

MATERIALS

Boundaries can be created from a variety of materials, or grown, using suitable plants. In either case, skill is required to

▲ Cupressocyparis leylandii *is a good hedge but needs to be kept under control.*

▶ *A pyracantha hedge makes an effective, if prickly, barrier.*

MATERIALS FOR BOUNDARIES
Brick, Pre-cast blocks, Close board wooden panels, Woven wooden panels, Chain link, Post and rail, Wattle hurdles, Split bamboo, Trellis, Chestnut

HEDGING PLANTS FOR THE SIDE GARDEN
(1.5–3m/5–10ft)
Cotoneaster simonsii, Berberis stenophylla, Escallonia macrantha, Aucuba japonica

create a visually pleasing and lasting effect. If a plot curves, then placing a straight wall along the boundary will spoil the look. If a hedge is built using mixed planting, incorrect weaving and supports will create a problem for the future. When positioning fences and hedges it is important to remember that windy conditions can affect plants as well as people sitting on the other side of a solid structure. In such places a permeable structure is often preferable. Fencing materials and the finials used on the posts can suggest the shapes of the Five Elements and this needs to be taken into consideration when balancing the elements.

▼ *Old brick walls are a perfect garden backdrop. Complementing materials should be chosen with care, as in this garden.*

BOUNDARIES AND THE FIVE ELEMENTS

Fencing materials and shapes can introduce the elements in to your garden. Make sure you balance them with care.

▲ *This is the Destructive Cycle.*

▲ *The first illustration shows the harmful cycle of Wood and Earth. In the second, Fire has been added for balance.*

▲ *The first illustration shows the weakening cycle of the elements. In the second Fire has been added as a balance.*

▲ *All the elements are suggested here, but the result is over-elaborate.*

▲ *The Five Element cycle.*

WATER IN THE GARDEN

Water is of great importance in Feng Shui. In China it symbolizes the accumulation of chi, which is synonymous with wealth.

GARDEN PONDS

Any water feature situated near the home should be in proportion to the size of the house. Bigger is not better in this case, since large expanses of water will symbolically drown us. A pond which is too large will dampen our career prospects, and if a fountain is out of proportion we will find it exhausting. Everything in the garden should blend in with existing features and with the landscape. The materials we use are as important as the siting of the feature. Sharp angles could direct "poison arrows" at the house or outdoor seating area.

Whether we live in towns or in the country, our ponds will attract wildlife. Small animals that jump or fall into a pond may not be able to get out again, unless we provide them with some means to do so. If a pond has steep sides, we should make sure that there are rocks or ledges to allow creatures an escape route.

▼ *If you have a stream through the garden slow it down with overhanging plants.*

If there are small children in the household it is important to ensure that ponds are completely safe. It may be better to install another type of water feature until children are old enough to take care.

The ideal shape for ponds is irregular, imitating natural ones. The more irregular the shape, the more plants and wildlife will thrive in and around it.

▲ *Ponds should fit naturally into a garden; irregular shapes with planting work best.*

Round ponds tend to carry the chi away too quickly and square ponds create "poison arrows". Regular shapes are easier to construct, however, and can be softened and shaped into a more natural form by careful planting round the edges.

ROCKERIES

To balance the yin of a still pond we can introduce the yang energy of a rockery. This combination reflects the mountain and lake formations so important in Chinese philosophy and art and can represent the Tortoise, Dragon and Tiger formation, with the pond in front. The rules for rockery building are:

◆ Use an odd number of stones
◆ Bury the stones by at least a third in the soil
◆ Place stones the correct way up as indicated by the graining
◆ Use a flat stone next to an upright one on its concave side
◆ Line the other stone up with the "toe" of the first
◆ Do not place a round stone by a jagged stone
◆ Choose the most weathered, front

"face" of the rock to face forwards
◆ Use the yin and yang theory to create a complementary arrangement

▼ *Rockeries should mirror the natural world and reflect the shape of mountains.*

WATER PLACEMENT

Ancient Chinese writings set great store by the patterns on the surface of the water, probably as a way of determining the direction of the wind. The Water Dragon Classic, an ancient text, gives details of beneficial places to build amid various shapes of water courses. The direction of the flow determines the best places to plant certain types of crops.

The direction from which water enters or leaves a property is deemed to

▲ *A water feature in the south-west of the garden can symbolize future prosperity.*

▶ *Water trickling towards the house symbolizes wealth rolling in.*

▲ *The straight sides of this formal garden pond are softened with overhanging plants.*

be crucial, but theories vary. One theory suggests that it should correspond to our auspicious directions. Another suggests that in houses facing north, south, east or west, the water should enter from the east or from left to right in front of the property. Conversely, if a house faces north-east, south-east, north-west or south-west, the water should enter from the west. Another theory favours east since this is the direction of growth.

Since few of us have a river running in front of our homes or are in a position to do anything about the flow, we should look at more relevant reasons for siting water features in our gardens.

The major, common-sense rule for water placement is that it should not flow quickly towards you from a point higher than your house because of the danger of flooding. A house built on a flood plain or below sea level might well experience problems, particularly as the effects of global warming cause water levels to continue to rise. It is deemed to be auspicious if the water is gently trickling towards the house, symbolizing wealth rolling in. Trickling from the east and towards our beneficial direction is also auspicious.

We are at present in a period when it is considered auspicious to place a water feature in the east to signify good luck and wealth until 2003. From 2004 until 2023, the south-west will be considered auspicious.

There are many types of water feature available commercially and many more which could be created by an imaginative gardener. Whichever feature we choose should be in harmony with the surroundings in terms of design and materials and the elements around it should be balanced.

GARDEN FURNITURE AND STRUCTURES

As we expand our living space outside, the furnishings we choose should reflect the intended functions of the garden – play, entertainment, relaxation – as well as personal preferences. We should employ the same principles in our gardens as we do in our homes and carefully select furnishings that meet the purpose, reflect our tastes and support us.

CHAIRS AND TABLES

Garden chairs should follow the classic Four Animals formation and provide firm support for our backs as well as having arm rests. The colours chosen can be dictated by our individual preferences, but only if the Five Elements are taken into

▼ *A perfect seat, circles and squares, with the four protective animal positions in place.*

▲ *An octagonal table is auspicious and allows everyone to communicate.*

▶ *A supportive shape, this chair looks like a very inviting place to sit and dream.*

account. Chairs should be comfortable but as they are usually made of wood or metal they tend to be hard, which is acceptable if the design is right but uncomfortable if they are not ergonomically correct.

Tables should be chosen according to their function. Square tables are containing and a small square table by our favourite chair in a quiet spot may tend to keep us there and prevent us from

▼ *A comfortable chair in which to spend a leisurely afternoon in the garden.*

searching for things to do. Round tables make for lively discussion but do not contain people for long. Rectangular tables with rounded ends are a common shape for garden furniture and are useful for summer lunch parties, although those seated at either end may sometimes feel left out. Octagonal tables are excellent because they are an auspicious shape and each person can communicate with everyone else around the table.

BARBECUES

Choosing a good location for a barbecue is mainly a matter of common sense. The north-west of the garden, next to a neighbour's fence where the south-west wind blows the smoke straight towards their kitchen window, is not a sensible choice. Barbecues are often positioned near a wall, but it is far better to position the cooking grid where the cook faces into the patio or terrace and is able to join in the party. Green is the best colour for a portable barbecue as black and blue represent the Water element and red might just add too much fuel to the flames.

GARDEN BUILDINGS AND STRUCTURES

Our gardens can also be furnished with buildings. Where we position these will affect their use and make a great impact on the overall structure and harmony of the garden. The materials used should blend with the surrounding buildings and the shapes and colours are important if we aim to keep a balance of yin and yang with the Five Elements.

▼ *A wonderful children's tree house that also blends well with its environment.*

▲ *The structures we build should blend in with the character of the garden.*

It is important that the house sits well in its environment and that we create stability at the four "cornerstones" of the garden – south-east, south-west, north-west and north-east. Garden buildings and decorative structures are a useful way of achieving this, provided they follow the Five Elements balance.

Where we use garden buildings for a specific purpose, such as our work, for growing seeds, or craft activities, the work bench should face one of our best directions, as determined earlier. We should arrange the layout to ensure that we face the entrance when standing at the bench. If this is not possible, then we should take measures to ensure we are not surprised from behind. A wind chime will alert us to someone entering and something reflective on the bench will enable us to see behind us. Mirrors are not recommended because the combination of mirror and sun can start a fire.

Some garden buildings are purely for decoration. Gazebos, although attractive to look at, are not comfortable to sit in as they are open to the wind. Structures with open sides offer no support when sitting and are therefore not ideal places in which to relax. Carefully positioned, however, they can provide excellent private spaces where we can escape and enjoy the solitude. Facing east, a gazebo can be a good place to eat an early breakfast and enjoy the energizing impact of the rising sun. Facing west, a gazebo will provide a restful spot to relax and unwind at the end of the day.

When siting garden features, take care that the edges and corners do not shoot "poison arrows" at the house or seating areas. Where points exist, climbing plants will soften or conceal them.

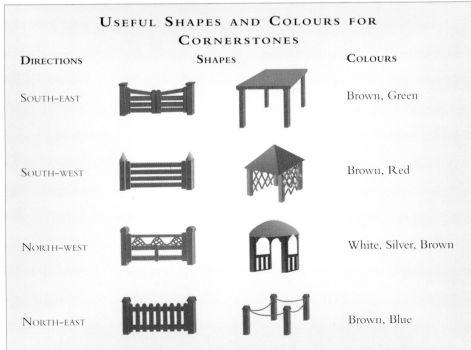

USEFUL SHAPES AND COLOURS FOR CORNERSTONES

DIRECTIONS	SHAPES		COLOURS
SOUTH-EAST			Brown, Green
SOUTH-WEST			Brown, Red
NORTH-WEST			White, Silver, Brown
NORTH-EAST			Brown, Blue

POTS AND ORNAMENTS

Containers of every conceivable size, colour and pattern are now available commercially, and they can be used to hold plants or as features on their own. Clay is the traditional material for pots and certainly plants look their best in them. Some pots are brightly coloured, which makes a welcome change and can look attractive, but they may clash with the natural colours in a garden. Consult the Five Elements table to check if the colours of the pots are compatible with the plants which will go in them. Shapes are also important and again the elements should be balanced.

Pots are imported from around the world, including many countries where frost is not a problem, so it is worth making sure that pots are frost-resistant if they are to stay outside during winter in colder climates. Frost may not be a problem when the pots are empty as it is the freezing and swelling of the water in the soil which causes pots to fracture. If plants are to remain outside in pots during the winter an extra-deep layer of drainage materials should be placed in the bottom at planting time and, when in position, the pots should be raised off the ground.

▲ *Pots of bulbs are useful throughout the year for a statement of colour. This one enlivens a dark corner.*

Be aware of the impact the pots make. Highly decorative pots are generally suitable for formal gardens where they can be viewed from a distance but they may look out of place, or be an unnecessary expense, in a smaller garden, where they might be screened by other pots or where we will be looking down at them. We rarely notice pots at ground level and tend only to see the plants. Pots which are raised up are more noticeable.

ORNAMENTS

Ornaments in the garden can be fun, particularly if they have been made by the owner. A garden can be a place in which to display our creativity and provides a wonderful backdrop for arts and crafts. Willow figures and wire sculptures are very popular and they have flowing

▶ *Fire planting – use these colours to make a statement in the south or focus on Wealth in the south-east.*

◀ *Muscari never fail to please and are a welcome sight in Spring.*

▲ *There is nothing dull about these pots of auriculas. They should be placed in a corner that needs bringing to life.*

lines which can bring a garden to life. Mosaics may be used as decorative features on pots and set into patios, pools and walls to bring vibrant colours into the garden. Stained glass is being increasingly used in windows and walls. Sundials are popular in gardens and can provide a useful learning aid for children.

▲ *A lovely corner in which to enjoy the fruits of our labours. Even a small town garden can have a similar restful space.*

▼ *Place animal ornaments with care so that they are in natural positions and with a background of the correct scale.*

PLACING POTS AND ORNAMENTS

EAST: Wooden objects. Avoid metal, including wind chimes, and any pointed objects.

◆ Green and blue pots.

SOUTH: Wooden objects. Sundials.

◆ Green and red pots. Terracotta is included because of its reddish colour.

WEST: Terracotta or metal pots and ornaments.

◆ White or terracotta pots.

NORTH: Metal ornaments. Avoid terracotta and wood.

◆ White or blue pots.

▲ *A spotless cherub in a beautifully maintained garden.*

▼ *Use discarded items from the home to make unusual garden features*

Think about how an ornament will look in its garden setting: is it reassuring or will its shape cause you to jump as it looms out of a mist or at dusk? Only choose images you like.

Objects placed in the garden should blend in with the overall design. We should be able to observe them one at a time rather than all at once, which can confuse the eye. A single object at the end of a path will have a completely different effect to one which we happen to notice at a turn in the path. We should choose objects for the former position very carefully if we are not to be disappointed at the end of our journey.

▲ *With some imagination you can create unusual and original garden ornaments.*

▼ *Be sure to position sundials where they will receive the sun all day long.*

STATUES

Garden suppliers offer an excellent array of statuary, making it possible to create anything from an historical garden to a Japanese garden or even a fantasy garden full of fairies. The same design principles apply to statues as to any other aspect of Feng Shui. It is a question of proportion, style and materials and whether they blend with their surroundings. Another consideration is the impact they make on us subconsciously in a positive or negative sense.

Statues usually take the form of people or animals and we need to feel comfortable with the images we have in our gardens: we need to like the faces of the people they portray. Statues of small children can be pleasing, but may make us feel sad if our own children have grown up and left home, or if we are unable to have children. Statues of animals may be fun so long as they do not become a constant reminder of pets that have died, or resemble species we dislike. Be aware of a statue's energy, whether it

▲ *A beautiful delicate statue that is perfectly framed by the well-balanced planting.*

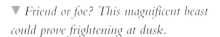

▼ *Friend or foe? This magnificent beast could prove frightening at dusk.*

▶ *New garden statuary may take time to become weathered and antique-looking.*

is grim and dour or pert and lively, it will affect how we feel in the garden.

Statues are made from a variety of materials and they should blend in with and not stand out from their surroundings. Unblemished grey concrete is not aesthetically pleasant until it has aged and weathered. Fake verdigris on modern metal statues clashes with the natural greens of the plants in the garden. Brilliantly white statues have a harsh appearance and do not age well.

The placement of statues is important and ideally we should happen upon them as we take a meandering route around the garden, but they should not appear to leap out at us as we round a bend. It is not a good idea to place the life-size statue of a person in an open space as the effect can be disconcerting at night. Proportion is also important and bigger is not always better. A huge, ornately carved fountain sits well in Versailles but not in a small urban garden.

GARDEN LIGHTING

There are two types of lighting in the garden. The first is practical, to enable us to make use of our gardens after dark, and the second is for special effects.

LIGHTING THE WAY

Particularly where there is no street lighting, it is important for occupants and visitors to gain safe access to the house.

▲ *Candlelight and the floodlights under this tree create a romantic setting.*

Lights which line a path and those which are set into stair risers can make a homecoming much more welcoming than if we have to carefully pick our way through obstacles in the dark. One neglected area is the house name and number. How much more sociable for guests to be able to locate the house, the doorbell and, in the case of apartment buildings, the person's name. Floodlights are widely used, but ensure they are correctly positioned so that they are not triggered by every passing cat.

Garden lighting can extend the day. The key rule for lighting the garden is to keep it simple by accenting certain

◀ *Simple but effective – this lantern can prolong the time spent outdoors.*

▶ *The lights in this modern town garden also make interesting shapes by day.*

features to create a calm, yin atmosphere. Lighting placed below or nearby can light up a statue or rock and give it an entirely different night-time appearance.

LIGHTING UP PLANTS

We normally view plants from above, but placing lights behind and under them enables us to view them from a different perspective and the results can be stunning. Trees lit from below, particularly blossom trees and those with interestingly shaped branches, can make wonderful features. Placing low-voltage lights in trees creates dancing shadows below as the light is filtered through the branches. Tiny bulbs in a tree produce an energetic party feel.

Garden lighting is best placed below eye level to reduce dazzle and to avoid creating shadows which can be disconcerting at night. We should aim to create pools of light that lead us through the garden rather than attempt to light up the whole area. Careful attention should be paid to siting the lights or we may experience feelings of unease as we peer into the dark spaces beyond.

Safety is paramount when we use electricity in the garden. Ponds should not contain lights, though perimeter lights can be stunning.

CREATING THE GARDEN

With some knowledge of the principles behind
Feng Shui, we will approach the creation of our gardens
with a keener eye for detail. The plants we use –
their colour, form, textures and smells – can feed our
senses and create life-enhancing environments in which
we can relax, entertain and indulge in our hobbies.
Whether we have a minute basement or a rambling
country garden, we can design our surroundings to
support and nourish our senses.

THE HEALTHY GARDEN

A healthy garden is a place where we, the plants, and any food that we grow will thrive. Some plants are poisonous while others can adversely affect our health. Some gardening methods do not benefit us or the plants in the long term. There are alternatives to using chemicals in the garden, and our health and that of the wildlife will benefit if we turn to them where possible. If we follow the natural order then we, the plants, and the wildlife in the garden can live in harmony and support each other.

POISONOUS PLANTS

Many well-known garden plants are poisonous and some wild ones may also find their way in. While adults are comparatively safe with these plants, children may be attracted by their colourful berries and seeds, and we need to take preventative measures to exclude dangerous plants from the garden at least when young children are part of the household.

POISONOUS GARDEN PLANTS

Laburnum, Lupins, Yew, Daphne

COMMON POISONOUS WILD PLANTS

Lords and ladies, Deadly nightshade, Black nightshade, Buckthorn

---

PLANTS AND ALLERGIES

In recent years there has been an increase in the number of people suffering from allergies. We regard the garden as a healthy place, but some of the plants we love best can cause a great deal of distress for asthma and hay fever sufferers and a number of plants can cause dermatitis when handled. Some popular plants which cause allergic reactions are shown in the box (right). Common names have been used as these plants are familiar to most people, even if they are not gardeners.

COMMON ALLERGENS

THE POLLEN OF: Grasses, Yarrow, Marigold

THE LEAVES OF: Chamomile, Ivy, Rue

THE SAP OF: Spurge, Christmas rose, Burning bush

THE SCENT OF: Pelargonium, Carnation (below), Evening primrose

▲ *With careful planting we can obviate the need to use chemicals in the garden since nature can do the job just as well if we let it.*

MUTUAL SUPPORT

In nature there are few devastating plant diseases, nor are many plants wiped out by insect damage. This is because plants regulate themselves and a variety of plants grow together in a mutually supportive way. Some species secrete chemicals that are required by neighbouring plants, or which repel predators. Others provide shade for their neighbours. By far the most natural way to plant a garden is to grow trees, shrubs and perennial plants which will build up a relationship with each other and the earth. Annual plants and vegetables can fill the gaps. The soil is fed with compost made from prunings,

▲ *Grow herbs in containers, with other herbs, or in the herbaceous border.*

PEST DETERRENTS

APHIDS: Fennel, nasturtiums, dill

FLEA BEETLES: Catnip, hyssop, tomatoes

COLORADO BEETLES: Coriander, onion, dandelion

NEMATODES: African and French marigolds (below), chrysanthemums

SACRIFICIAL PLANTS

We can also use plants to attract pests away from those we want to protect.

MUSTARD: Wireworms

TOBACCO PLANT: Whitefly

BROAD BEANS: Red spider mites

NASTURTIUMS: Blackfly

PLANTS TO ATTRACT BENEFICIAL PREDATORS

WASPS: Celery, chamomile, sunflowers

HOVERFLIES: Fennel, solidago, ivy

LADYBIRDS: Stinging nettles, tansy, yarrow

HERB COMPANIONS

HERB	SUPPORTS
Basil	Tomatoes
Borage	Strawberries
Chives	Apples
Garlic	Roses
Parsley	Asparagus
Tansy	Raspberries

leaves and kitchen waste, so it is in effect recycled from the garden itself. By bringing in outside composts (soil mix) and chemicals we create an imbalance and potential problems. If we follow the example of nature we will not dig the soil because this damages its structure and disturbs the creatures which work there for us, breaking down the organic matter. Some plants are known to be particularly beneficial to other plants growing close by. Many herbs fall into this category.

PLANTS TO DETER PESTS

In a healthy garden chemical-based formulas should not used to control insect pests because in doing so we may kill beneficial insects as well as the birds and small mammals which feed on them. Plants that are grown monoculturally are more vulnerable to insect damage than they would be if they were grown together with plants of other species. We can help this natural process further by introducing plants which secrete substances to repel certain types of pest.

PLANTS TO ATTRACT PREDATORS

There are some insects which we should positively encourage into the garden, since they are predators of common garden pests. Certain plants act as hosts to these beneficial insects.

CHOOSING PLANTS

taken into consideration in terms of soil type, aspect, temperature and spacing. There is no point attempting to nurture a plant which needs alkaline soil and a southerly aspect in a space that has acid soil, facing north. There will be less difficulty and disappointment in the garden

◄ *Native plants flourish in a medieval-style English garden. Indigenous species will always grow better than imported plants in the right conditions.*

▲ *Plants need the correct soil and growing conditions in which to thrive.*

▼ *Summer in the garden – roses and lavender make good companion plants.*

The rules for planting in the Feng Shui garden are simple. Each plant should be chosen carefully with regard to the specific features we wish to introduce. You need to think in terms of the colour, size and form of each individual plant, and how they will look side by side.

The planting should also blend in with the topography of the surrounding area – unless we want to make a definite statement to the contrary. You might live in an area that has identical houses in gardens which have evolved a particular look. You may feel happiest following the established style of your area, but since change is a key feature of Taoism, in which Feng Shui has its roots, individual expression in garden design is to be welcomed or we will not develop. When planting, the needs of plants should be

FAVOURITE SEASONAL PLANTS IN CHINA

SPRING: Magnolia and Peony
SUMMER: Myrtle and Locust
AUTUMN: Maple and Chrysanthemum
WINTER: Bamboo (below) and
Wintersweet

if plants are chosen wisely. Plants which are indigenous to an area will always grow best, since all the conditions will be right for them.

THE SEASONS

Gardens should have all-year-round interest and, more importantly, we should be able to see the changes brought about by the seasons through windows from inside the house and also from various vantage points in the garden.

Within each season it is considered desirable that each stage of a plant's development should be represented – flowers, leaves, fruits and seed.

TREES

Trees are used to enhance a space, to obscure unwelcome features and to balance other features in the garden. In ancient China, trees were regarded as

▲ *Spruce trees should be planted alone.*

having special powers. We are more aware now of the importance to our ecological system of trees and the way in which they act as the lungs of the planet.

Trees need to be planted meticulously to reflect a number of philosophical principles as follows:

◆ Trees should grow naturally, since their beauty is in their true shape.

◆ A single tree can be admired for its shape, bark, leaves and blossom.

◆ Groups of trees should be in odd numbers; threes or fives.

◆ Trees with branches growing horizontally, such as cedar or spruce, should be planted alone.

◆ Upright trees, such as bamboo or cypress, should not be planted alongside trees with horizontal branches.

◆ Weeping and pendulous trees, like

willow or birch, do not mix with those bearing horizontal branches.

◆ Only trees with a canopy, such as oak or elm, are suitable for mass planting.

◆ Trees with distinctive shapes, such as yew and plane, should be planted alone.

▼ *The deeply furrowed trunk of the Dawn redwood. The bark of a tree can be as beautiful and remarkable as any flower.*

GARDENING FOR THE SENSES

We respond to our gardens through our emotions and senses. The scent of a favourite plant can bring on a feeling of euphoria, while stroking the hairy leaves of *Stachys lanata*, or lambs' ears, can be soothing.

SIGHT

When we think of sight it is usually in terms of the immediate visual impression made by a tree or a flower bed and whether or not we like what we see. In the Feng Shui garden, seeing is rather more than that. When we look at a tree we should see the shape of its trunk, observe the way the branches spread out and the intricate criss-crossing of the canopy. We should also perceive the veining on the leaves and the patterning on the bark and notice the small creatures busying themselves on it. We may think that it resembles an old man, slightly stooped, as it is highlighted against the glowing red of the evening sky. If we let our imagination run riot, he may appear to be wearing Aunt Hilda's sun hat with the large bunch of cherries on the side and if we were then to call the scene "Grandfather wearing Aunt Hilda's hat", we would be coming close to the way the Chinese perceive the world in their art and philosophy.

▼ *The magnificent show of colour provided by this Cotinus obovatus will encourage anyone to plant it for seasonal interest.*

▲ *There is immediate visual interest in this busy garden, but a single flower could make just as powerful a statement.*

Observing the seasons is important in the Feng Shui garden, and we should plant carefully to ensure that we maintain some interest all the year round. We can achieve this by:
◆ Arranging plants which have different flowering times in tiers.
◆ Positioning flowers of the same colour but with different flowering periods in successive tiers.
◆ Mixing plants which have different flowering times.
◆ Planting varieties with long flowering times and vivid colours.
◆ Planting trees first and filling the gaps with perennials.

What we see when we look out into our gardens is of the utmost importance, not only for the pleasure it gives us, but because of the subconscious impression it makes on us, which can affect us psychologically. Clutter around the garden, just as it is inside the house, will become a constant source of irritation.

WINTER INTEREST IN THE GARDEN

FOLIAGE PLANTS
Cornus alba, Vitis vinifera 'Purpurea', *Liquidambar styraciflua*

FLOWERING PLANTS
Hamamelis x *intermedia* 'Pallida', *Jasminum nudiflorum, Viburnum* x *bodnantense, Choisya ternata*

BERRIES
Cotoneaster horizontalis, Skimmia, Pyracantha (below), Holly

BARK
Acer capillipes, Pinus pinea, Prunus serrula

▲ *We can rely on wildlife or create our own sounds in the garden. This bamboo wind chime will resound gently in the breeze.*

SOUND

It is rare in the modern world to be able to escape from the noise of machinery or traffic, even in the garden, although by planting trees and dense hedges we can cushion ourselves to a certain extent. The garden itself is not really silent, and we would wish to encourage the sounds of nature there. Birdsong is always welcome, except perhaps for the harsh cawing of crows or the repetitive cooing of pigeons. Through careful planting, we can encourage the small songbirds into the garden, by tempting them with berries, seeds and the small insects which will be there if we do not spray with chemicals. The buzzing of bees while they work is another welcome noise which we can

CLUTTER

Unwashed flower pots

Leaves in corners

Plants which catch on our clothes

Plants which catch our ankles

Dead branches

Dead plants

Overgrown hedges

Any jobs left undone

CASE STUDY

Even a garden in a perfect setting requires careful planning. Harry and Ann had a back garden with a beautiful view but when they hired a garden designer they did not feel comfortable with the result. A Feng Shui consultant came up with the following solution.

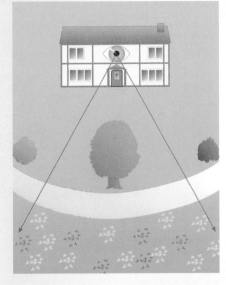

This beautiful open garden has a river meandering along the bottom and hugging the house. In the Phoenix position is a large oak tree marking the boundary of the property and beyond that a wonderful meadow with wild flowers, where horses graze.

The designer incorporated a row of conifers from the river to the door, blocking the wide view and creating a "poison arrow" of harmful chi from the gnarled trunk of the oak, which had become a threat to the house. This was likely to make the people living in the house feel irritable and restricted. At worst, this could result in mental instability and put a strain on their marriage. Removing the conifers from the design enabled Harry and Ann to have the full benefit of the wonderful view from their house once more.

foster by adding their favourite plants.

The sound of gurgling water is relaxing, and bamboo plants, willow trees and tall grasses all make gentle swishing noises in the breeze. Placing Aeolian harps and wooden or shell wind chimes near where we sit is a good idea, provided we keep them near the house so they do not interfere with the finely tuned hearing of the wildlife. In the early autumn we should not be in too much of a hurry to sweep up since children like nothing more than the simple pleasure of crunching through leaves.

▶ *Bamboo is an integral part of Chinese gardens, art and culture and grows well in a Western gravel garden.*

TOUCH

Touch is a sense which is often neglected in the garden. We tend to venture
forth with caution, wearing gardening
gloves and alerted to the perils lurking in
the soil, the chemicals we have sprayed
on the leaves, and even the plants themselves. Certainly we should be aware of
the dangers, but to forgo the pleasure of
feeling the soil running through our fingers as we plant a precious seedling, of
burying our faces in a conifer after rain
to smell its heady resinous scent, or to
run our hands over rosemary and lavender as we pass, is to lose our connection
with the earth.

The leaves of plants provide a range of
sensations – stroking the woolly leaves of
verbascum, the cold smooth leaves of
mesembryanthemums or the rough carpet of dwarf thyme each gives its own
form of tactile pleasure. The texture of
bark on trees ranges from perfectly
smooth to the peeling bark of the paper
birch. We can get pleasure from stroking
the soft petals of an iris or lily, or the face
of a sunflower, or running our hands over
the surface of the grass.

TASTE

Nothing tastes better than home-grown
fruit and vegetables, and it is possible to

▲ *When harvesting your own fruit and
vegetables remember to enjoy the feel of
the earth and its produce.*

▲ *No shop-bought produce can beat the
taste of home-grown vegetables freshly dug
from the garden.*

◄ *Rosemary delights in many ways – the
colour of the flowers, the bees it attracts and
the feel and smell of its leathery foliage.*

► *Fruit does not have to take up a lot of
space: cordons or espaliers grown on walls
and fences can be very productive.*

▲ *Roses, particularly the old-fashioned varieties, provide a heady perfume.*

SCENTED PLANTS

SPRING
Daphne odora, Viburnum fragrans, Osmanthus burkwoodii, Ribes odoratum

SUMMER
Deutzia, Philadelphus, *Cytisus battandieri, Lupinus aboreus*

AUTUMN
Lonicera fragrantissima, Rosemary, Lavender, Sage

WINTER
Chimonanthus praecox, Sarcococca hookeriana digyna, Hamamelis mollis, Acacia dealbata

▼ *The herb garden below will be full of wonderful aromas.*

of tomatoes plucked from the vine in passing takes some beating. Herb beds close to the house also offer tempting flavours and lemon balm, sorrel, chervil, basil and parsley can give us a wide range of taste experiences.

SMELL

No manufactured perfume surpasses the smell of a damask rose or of wild honeysuckle. The joy of scent in the garden is its subtlety. When the smell of elderflowers fills the house on a damp evening we crave more, but that would mask the other smells which drift in from the garden. The scents of *Lilium regale* and wintersweet are pervasive. Others will need to

▼ *Some lilies are very fragrant and a pot by the back door will scent the kitchen.*

be placed near paths where we can brush against them to release the fragrance of plants like *Choisya ternata* and eucalyptus. Some plants do not object to being trodden on occasionally, and the Treneague chamomile and most thymes are suitable for planting on or near to paths.

grow them in the smallest of spaces. Salad vegetables sown in succession in a border will feed us through the summer months. Fruit trees grown on dwarfing rootstocks take up little space. Those grown on a single upright stem can be grown in pots near where we sit, to give us pleasure and remind us of earth's bounty. The taste of a freshly-picked sun-warmed apple or

▼ *A traditional wattle fence provides the backdrop for this mixed herb bed.*

COLOUR

We all respond to colour in different ways, as is evident in the way we dress and decorate our homes. Our response is emotional and psychological and sometimes colours which we do not like can even bring about a physical response. In the Feng Shui garden, colour is part of the way in which the planting fits in with the garden's immediate environment, and with the natural contours of the landscape. In the natural world, colour blends into the background hue of the place – green in woodland, sand and pebble colours on the coast, purple

▲ *Our response to colour in the garden is emotional and psychological.*

shades on mountain slopes. If we look at poppies in a field they appear to shimmer on the surface, whereas a formal planting of marigolds or salvias in a park forms a solid mass of colour.

The way in which we group plants is a matter of taste but all too often it is a hit-or-miss affair. If we examine an artist's use of colour, it can give us clues as to the harmonies which exist between different colours.

When any two of the three basic colours, red, blue and yellow, are mixed they give rise to a secondary colour – orange, violet, or green. These six colours make up the basic colour wheel as adapted by Gertrude Jekyll, whose harmonious planting ideas have influenced

◄ *Observe the impact of the poppies which appear to shimmer across the field behind.*

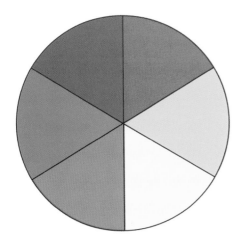

▲ *Use this simple diagrammatic colour wheel as a guide to basic colour harmonies and contrasts.*

gardeners all over the world. Three adjacent colours are known as harmonies. The others are contrasts. Those which sit diagonally opposite are complementary. Most of us respond positively to colours which are in harmony, and either complement or contrast with one another. In places where these rules cannot be applied, conflicting colours should be separated by neutral ones – white, grey or dark green.

In recent years research has been conducted into the use of colour in healing. Feng Shui practitioners believe that it is possible to determine a person's health or mood by the colours they use in their

▲ *White breaks up the vivid pink and orange plants in this bed.*

environment and that it is possible to alter perceptions by changing colours or by combining them in a variety of ways. It is fun to experiment and create gardens in which the colours are supportive and inspirational. Colours affect our mood, and it is worth remembering this when planning a garden in any climate.

Colour is affected by the quality of the light. In Morocco and the Mediterranean countries bright colours look magnificent: brilliant red pelargoniums in Spanish courtyards are a sight to behold. Larger civic gardens and parks in these countries use green and abundant foliage to create cool shade, and a feeling of oasis-like sanctuary from the heat.

◀ *A stunning colour for a Mediterranean garden. The tone would need to be adjusted for it to work in a cooler climate.*

▼ *Vivid colours work well in hot countries because of the quality of the sunlight.*

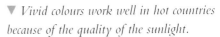

PLANTING WITH A COLOUR THEME

We have seen that colour alters our emotions and moods, but we can also use colour to focus on areas of the Bagua, depending on the elemental qualities of the area.

RED

Red plants will dominate a garden when planted in large patches and are not restful to sit near. They make excellent spot plants to draw the eye to a certain area.

▲ *Red plants like this* Euonymus alatus *'Compactus' make an impact at a distance.*

RED TREES AND SHRUBS: *Acer rubrum, Berberis thunbergii* 'Atropurpurea', *Cotinus coggygria, Euonymus alatus* 'Compactus'.
RED HERBACEOUS PLANTS: *Ajuga reptans, Bergenia cordifolia, Paeonia lactiflora.*

WHITE AND SILVER

All-white gardens appear fresh and clean and, in the evening light, luminous. Although calming, there may be a deadness to a large all-white garden unless it is carefully planned with many different shades and shapes of green to vary it.
WHITE TREES AND SHRUBS: *Pyrus salicifolia, Drimys winteri, Skimmia japonica* 'Fructu Albo'.
WHITE HERBACEOUS PLANTS: *Eremurus himalaicus, Aruncus dioicus, Astilbe* 'Irrlicht'.

YELLOW

Yellow is usually associated with spring and late summer. It is a rich and cheerful colour, but, in its paler forms or when combined with white, it can feel uncomfortable and demoralizing.

◄ *White in a garden can soothe but also be strangely lifeless with no other colours near.*

▲ *Yellow works well in this understated mixed planting.*

▼ *A collection of hostas showing just how many shades of green there are.*

YELLOW TREES AND SHRUBS: *Laburnum x watereri* 'Vossii', *Acer japonicum* 'Aureum', *Hypericum* 'Hidcote'.
YELLOW HERBACEOUS PLANTS: *Phlomis russeliana, Rudbeckia fulgida* 'Goldsturm', *Achillea filipendulina* 'Gold Plate'.

GREEN

Spot planting, using pots of coloured plants and bulbs, is very effective against the backdrop of a green garden. In itself, the green garden, containing various shades and shapes of foliage, can be a

▲ *Muscari brings this gravel garden to life.*

restful, tranquil place. Green is the predominant colour in the Chinese garden.
GREEN TREES AND SHRUBS: *Juniperus chinensis, Chamaecyparis lawsoniana, Thuja occidentalis.*
GREEN HERBACEOUS PLANTS: Hostas, *Phyllostachys nigra,* Euphorbia.

BLUE
Blue borders have a sedative effect but unrelieved blue can be gloomy. Blue plants can be mixed with white and silver foliage and with soft pink flowers.
BLUE TREES AND SHRUBS: *Picea glauca* 'Coerulea', *Ceanothus impressus, Abies concolor* 'Glauca Campacta'.
BLUE HERBACEOUS PLANTS: *Echinops bannaticus, Gentiana asclepiadea, Salvia patens.*

PURPLE
A purple border can be sumptuous and restful at the same time. Mix purple with blues, whites and soft pinks for calm.
PURPLE TREES AND SHRUBS: *Jacaranda mimosifolia,* Syringa, *Hydrangea macrophylla.*

▼ *Purple and red make a powerful combination in this tub.*

▲ *Pink is a warm colour. This pink works remarkably well with the black pansies.*

PURPLE HERBACEOUS PLANTS: *Verbena patagonica,* Iris, *Salvia nemorosa* 'May Night'.

PINK
Pink is a warm colour and draws people to it. The gentler shades are preferable.
PINK TREES AND SHRUBS: *Magnolia campbellii,* Prunus, Spiraea.
PINK HERBACEOUS PLANTS: Lavatera, Peony, Geranium.

ORANGE
Orange is a rich, warm, happy colour, but difficult to place. It is probably best against a dark green background.
ORANGE TREES AND SHRUBS: *Spathodea campanulata,* Berberis, *Leonotis leonurus.*
ORANGE HERBACEOUS PLANTS: Rudbeckia, *Lychnis chalcedonica,* Chrysanthemum.

▼ *The colours work well together here since the shades are subtle and not harsh.*

THE COURTYARD GARDEN

Depending on the style of the property, courtyard gardens can be formal or great fun, giving expression to the artistic talent latent in everyone. With walls or fences to paint, floor surfaces to experiment with and only a tiny space to fill, courtyards can allow us unlimited scope for expression.

Often the difficulty in designing a small garden is in deciding what not to include. Gardens packed full of plants, using several different materials and textures, can appear fussy and make the space look even smaller than it is. On the

▲ *Careful planting at a variety of levels creates a haven of peace and beauty in a tiny courtyard.*

▶ *A restrained use of colour stops a small space from looking too fussy.*

other hand, the impact of one architectural plant with some pebbles and moss can look stunning in a tiny space, although gardens which are too minimal emphasize their small size.

A wide variety of materials is available now and, cleverly combined, they can become a work of art in themselves. Beware of surfaces which are likely to become slippery in damp areas: decking can look stunning when sun-baked by a pool, but in a dark shady area it can become stained and unpleasant. Often

such spaces create their own microclimate where we can grow plants which will not normally grow outside. If a courtyard is overlooked, overhead wires supporting a vine will afford privacy while letting in light, creating an exotic Mediterranean feeling in the middle of a town.

Every feature in a small garden needs to earn its keep and it is self-defeating to hold on to a plant which has outgrown

◀ *Wall-mounted pelargoniums are common in Mediterranean courtyards.*

ARCHITECTURAL PLANTS FOR IMPACT

Cordyline australis, Acer, *Fatsia japonica*, Fatshedera, *Juniperus scopulorum*, Box (below)

PLANTS FOR SHADE

Euonymus fortunei 'Silver Queen', *Choisya ternata*, Philadelphus, Skimmia

PLANTS TO HIDE WALLS

Campsis radicans, *Actinidia kolomikta*, Ivy, Jasmine, Roses (below)

its space or is past its prime. It constitutes clutter if it is a problem. We need to make the best use of trees and interesting features outside our own gardens and borrow them for our own design. Those we do not want – ugly walls, unsightly pipes and other features – we can blot

▼ *Climbers and baskets can be useful where ground space is limited.*

COMBINATIONS OF MATERIALS

Wooden decking and pebbles
Shingle and granite slabs
Stone and moss
Coloured concrete and mosaics
Paving slabs and brick

---

out. Coloured trellis can work wonders on an unsightly wall. The plants we choose should be those which will fill the space when they reach maturity. They may take longer to grow than fast-growing species, but will ultimately be more rewarding since they will not cause maintenance problems later.

Some houses have enclosed spaces, with access only from a window, but if we design with care, we can use the colour and textures of different materials to create interesting and energetic spaces there. Some plants thrive in the most unlikely places. With just a chink of light in the darkest cave, a fern will usually grow, and the ivy family is invaluable in awkward corners. In small spaces, plants

may even be incidental if we use materials, water and illusion to design what is essentially another room. Ornaments, sculptures and pots, strategically placed mirrors and brightly coloured walls can create stunning environments which will energize and stimulate us.

▼ *Strategically placed pots can enliven any space and are useful in paved courtyards.*

CASE STUDY

Moira and her family had just finished renovating an old house. Moira loved the spaciousness of their new home and the feeling that the family were doing things together, but she craved a space for herself where she could pursue her hobby – watercolour painting. The renovations had left a small courtyard at the back of the house.

1. The lean-to greenhouse was renovated to enable Moira to store her art materials and overwinter some plants.

2. The basement staircase was made safe by installing a gate. A trellis (Earth shape in the north-east) gave some height to the planting. A blue *Clematis alpina* scrambles over it.

3. Planting has been kept to a minimum so that watering does not become a chore, and because the space is small. Single plants, if they are large, can give a

feeling of lusciousness and so a *Prunus stiloba simplex* was positioned here.

4. A cordyline was placed in this corner to liven it up and in front, a small pebble water feature was also added.

5. A terracotta wall feature of an upright jug was placed here to raise the view above the staircase and lifts the energy of the north-east.

6. Moira's chair and easel are here. A

canopy above the window shields them when it is hot. Since the window leads into the house it was not felt to be a problem behind the chair.

7. This table and storage unit for Moira's painting equipment can be wheeled into the greenhouse.

8. An ivy covered ball brings a playful energy to this corner

9. Moira plans to have a mosaic wall here with a blank space above the table for her still life arrangements. The space opens up ideas from the rising energy of the east, which Moira can draw on from her position opposite.

10. Moira hopes to sell her paintings one day. Taking her chair as the mouth of chi, and aligning the symbolic Bagua with it, this wall is the Offspring area. Moira plans to paint murals on this wall, which she can change over the years.

ROOFS AND BASEMENTS

A light gravel layer on top of the pots will help to conserve moisture. Light free-draining compost (soil mix) in the pots and containers is preferable to heavy garden soil. Feeding will be necessary.

Temperatures may be higher than average in big cities. Pergolas can be used for shading, but great care should be taken that the structures are secure. Overhead wires are another option.

In such an unnatural environment plants will eventually outgrow their space and the only option will be to replace them. Sickly plants create stagnant chi and should be renewed quickly. It is possible to grow vegetables and fruit on roofs, either in pots or in growing bags.

▲ *On this secluded roof you would never dream you were in the city.*

I n urban areas where space is at a premium, living areas extend upwards and downwards. For people living in the centre of a city, a roof garden is a haven from the bustling life below. For those who live below street level in basements, sometimes their only view is of walls and of feet passing overhead. Both these spaces are difficult when planning a garden. The roof garden is totally exposed

▲ *Wooden decking creates an indoor feel to this well designed outdoor space.*

and unsupported, with little chance of capturing chi unless some structural alterations are made. In the basement garden chi becomes trapped and stagnant since it cannot circulate, so careful planning and planting are needed.

ROOF GARDENS

Roof gardens are unique in that they encompass a number of problems which are not found all in one place in a conventional garden. Structure and load-bearing capacity are the first priorities, followed by drainage.

High winds will be a problem. Open trellis is preferable to a solid screen which creates wind turbulence. Winds cause damage to young shoots and causes soil to dry out quickly so maintenance is high, watering systems are an advantage.

▼ *This country cottage-style garden is actually on an urban roof.*

▼ *Quarry tiles can be a hard-wearing and practical surface for a roof garden.*

Lighting is a consideration on the roof since there may not be sufficient light generated from within the building. Uplighters are useful since they show off the plants but avoid causing glare which could disturb neighbours.

BASEMENTS

At the other end of the scale, basements can be confined places with restricted amounts of natural light available. However, these conditions can be alleviated. If the outlook from the windows is bleak and the basement area is damp and fills up with wind-blown rubbish and leaves it is important to summon up the energy and initiative to clear up and take control of the space. Living without much natural light can drain personal energy so, in the basement garden, the object is to raise the chi of the space and the spirits of the occupants.

▲ *This* trompe l'oeil *effect seems to double the perceived size of the basement area.*

▼ *This could have been a dismal basement area but it has been transformed by the addition of scores of potted plants.*

Light-coloured walls are essential in a basement, and dark walls should be painted white. If the walls are high use a trellis to support climbing plants, rooted in the ground, if possible, or in large pots. As the plants grow and climb upwards they will raise the energy. Choose plants which are evergreen or have fairly large leaves, or clearing up will be a problem. Lush simplicity is preferable to fussy planting where space is restricted.

If there are stairs which are wide enough, pots of colourful plants can be placed at intervals to light the way. Avoid trailing plants, like ivy, which will have a depressing effect. Gertrude Jekyll suggested that even in the smallest space there should be a distinctive feature – an ornament, fountain or raised bed to create an interesting focal point.

Lighting is important in basements, and uplighters, shining through climbing plants, can improve the energy. Visual illusion can be used to good effect with murals or *trompe l'oeil*, or even strategically placed mirrors, and the area can be cheered by a bright floor surface – tiles and mosaics can be used if they blend in with the surrounding architecture.

TERRACES AND PATIOS

Terraces, or patio areas, feature in both urban and rural gardens. They can be as simple as a few rows of paving outside the back door, or elaborate balustraded affairs running the length of grand country houses. Whatever their size, they enable a range of activities to take place and the emphasis will change over time as children arrive, grow up and eventually leave home, when parents can return to a more leisurely lifestyle. With careful planning, paddling pools and sand pits can be transformed into flower beds.

The size of the terrace will be determined by the size of the garden and should be in proportion. Those less than 2m (6ft) wide do not really allow enough

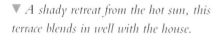
▼ *A shady retreat from the hot sun, this terrace blends in well with the house.*

▲ *A dream terrace in an idyllic situation where the planting complements the view.*

room for much activity to happen there. Privacy may be a problem. Depending on the direction the terrace faces, some protection from the wind may be needed. Overhead shading may be required in the form of a plant-covered pergola, giving a dappled light effect, or a canopy to give more complete cover.

Patios can become extremely yang places in the height of summer, with the sun blazing overhead, the hard surfaces giving off heat, pools and metal objects

▼ *Tomatoes grow well in pots and are ideally close for picking if grown on a terrace.*

and tables reflecting the glare. By introducing some height in the form of shading, and with plants around the edges as well as in containers, we can create a balance and make a cool and relaxing place to sit.

Terraces need easy access from the kitchen if eating or entertaining is to take place there. In north-facing gardens it is advisable to place terraces at a distance from the house, where they will have some sun and can be reached via a hard path so that trolleys can be wheeled along

▲ *A delightful terrace with the view framed like a picture between the planting.*

▶ *Many fruit varieties are now grown on dwarf rootstocks suitable for growing in pots.*

PLANTS FOR THE TERRACE

CLIMBERS

Clematis, *Lathyrus grandiflorus*, Vitis, Gourds, Wisteria

SMALL TREES FOR SHADE

Catalpa bignoniodes, Corylus alternifolia 'Argentea', Acer, Prunus, Magnolia

PLANTS TO TRAIN ON WALLS

Malus, Ceanothus, Pyracantha, Jasmine, Chaenomeles

HERBS FOR THE BARBECUE

Rosemary, Sage (below bottom), Thyme, Oregano (below top)

FRUIT AND VEGETABLES FOR POTS

Tomatoes, Peppers, Aubergines Strawberries (below), Apples

---

and people can carry dishes safely. On small terraces, built-in seating will save space and can look attractive if the materials used blend into the overall plan and with the house. On the other hand, built-in seating with raised beds behind it can be uncomfortable if insects are attracted to the area by the plants. Often on terraces, chairs are not backed by a wall, so if we want to keep our guests there for any length of time, we should provide them with high-backed chairs.

If the terrace is used for reading or quiet reflection we should place our chairs to face one of our auspicious directions. We can also align sun-loungers in the same way, depending on which way the terrace faces.

A paved area or deck may be a large space that is required for a variety of different family activities. Young children may like to have a sand pit and paddling pool there, though if you do have both, it is a good idea to keep the two well apart. Be mindful of the Five Elements when positioning the paddling pool. It is advisable to cover both the sand pit and the pool when not in use, especially if

you have cats that are fond of using the former as a litter tray. Covering the pool will ensure that the water remains clean and hygienic.

Small children may want to ride trikes in the garden, so the patio or deck should be level with the adjoining grass area to prevent accidents. Where the area is raised and there are steps, secure barriers should be erected. Swings should never be placed on hard surfaces; if they are not on grass, bark chippings or another soft surface should be placed underneath.

The area near the house may also need to accommodate a number of items such as dustbins (trash cans), wood piles, sheds and washing lines. Keep these separate from any seating, hidden behind plant-covered screens or fences if possible.

RURAL GARDENS

out an ugly view. Rather than planting at the edge, a tree in the lawn with space to move behind will add depth and more interest to the garden.

Within the plot we can create special areas: places to be alone, to entertain, for the children to play and so on, always bearing in mind that the elements need to be balanced with regard to colour and shapes and that we need to maintain a balance of yin and yang, combining hard landscaping with soft planting, and in the height of plants or the shapes of their leaves.

Paths should meander through the garden, opening up new vistas at each turn and allowing us to happen upon things such as statues, rocks, pots or prize plants. A path can take us directly to the shed or greenhouse, which should ideally be situated fairly near to the house for

◀ *The "rooms" in this medieval-style garden mimic field divisions in the landscape beyond and are in harmony with it.*

▲ *A few pots at the base of the tree act as a stop before the eye moves on to travel around the garden.*

◀ *A variety of heights, shapes, forms and colours in planting schemes will ensure that the yin-yang balance is maintained.*

Ⅰn the rural garden the possibilities for design would appear to be greater than in the urban garden. Yet, in many ways, the design is more restricted by convention and the need to blend in with the natural landscape. In the Feng Shui garden, we capture the landscape and draw it into our gardens while, at the same time, ensuring that the garden is an extension of the house, linked physically but also by style.

Boundaries in the rural garden can be hidden by planting linked into a hill or group of trees beyond, which we can frame and use as our own. We can create boundaries within the garden using trellis, gateways and gaps in hedges to lead our eyes on and suggest new experiences beyond. Even a closed door in a wall will

suggest possibilities, and adds an air of mystery. Proportion is important and can make all the difference to the feel of a garden. Tall narrow openings are far less inviting than wide ones. Since rural gardens are often larger than their city counterparts, it will not always be necessary to disguise the boundary or block

be attracted to it. If you are not willing to share your terrace with hundreds of baby frogs, a fox, mice and the odd visiting rat, site the pond away from the house and, if you stock it with fish, be prepared for herons.

We should allow plants to breathe by enabling the wind to blow through them; spacing them well will mean less disease. We should extend this principle, by opening up the centres of each area and enabling the chi to circulate and move on. Above all we should respect the spirit of the place and choose plants and materials which are at home there, remembering that there are many things which human beings have to learn about the natural world and that the less we tamper with it and poison it, the better it will be for us, our families and the generations to come.

▲ *Produce which is harvested once a year can be positioned at the end of the garden.*

◄ *The plants in this garden have built up a relationship with their environment.*

convenience, and from there to the vegetable patch or fruit-growing area. We may like to consider the possibility of cultivating crops which take longer to grow and take up a lot of space, or are harvested infrequently – such as potatoes, asparagus and rhubarb – at the bottom of the garden, and those which we need on a daily basis – like herbs and salad vegetables – near to the house. A path, or even stepping stones in the lawn to the vegetable garden, will enable us to pick produce even on the wettest day. Picking a lettuce is less fun if you need to find boots and wet weather gear first.

Water makes a difference in any garden, but remember that all the creatures in the garden and surrounding area will

RURAL GARDEN PLANTS

PLANTS FOR HEDGES
Aucuba, Berberis, Euonymus, Ribes, Ilex, Mahonia

PLANTS FOR SHADY PLACES
Arundinaria, *Aucuba japonica*, *Fatsia japonica*, Eleagnus, Mahonia, Skimmia

SHRUBS FOR INTEREST
Chaenomeles, Cotoneaster, Hebe, Philadelphus, Pyracantha, Viburnum

GROUND COVER PLANTS
Ajuga reptans, Bergenia, *Euphorbia amygdaloides*, Helleborus, Hosta, *Hypericum calycinum*

TREES FOR SMALL GARDENS
Acer, Betula, Eucalyptus, Malus, Prunus, Sorbus

PLANTS FOR POOL SIDES
Astilbe, Hosta, Iris, Ranunculus, Rheum, Trollius

SCENTED PLANTS
Oenothera (below left), Lavender (below right), Jasmine, Honeysuckle

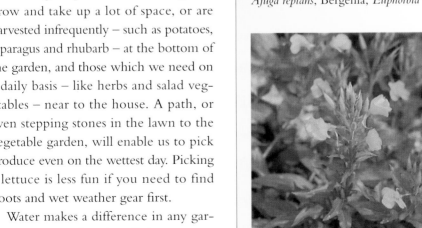

WATERSIDE GARDENS

Water, in the form of pools, waterfalls and streams, is an important element in the Feng Shui garden. When the garden is situated beside a large river or lake, or by the sea, its design needs some special consideration.

COASTAL GARDENS

Coastal gardens are among the most difficult to cultivate. The effects of the salt-laden winds can spread as far as 8km (5 miles) inland, bending plants and trees double and scorching the leaves. However, given some shelter, these can also be the most rewarding gardens since they are virtually frost-free and rarely have snow. The climate lends itself to growing many plants which will not grow elsewhere.

The quality of the light in coastal locations is more vibrant than it is inland and planting can be brighter, although very colourful planting can seem harsh on dull days. Seaside resorts in temperate northern climes can come alive in summer when brilliant pelargoniums grow against whitewashed walls and give a Mediterranean feel. In winter it is often

▼ *Bright Mediterranean colours – of plants and paint – look good in a seaside garden.*

▲ *Low planting is less likely to suffer wind damage than taller plants.*

a matter of battening down the hatches, and hanging baskets and pots have to be secured against the elements. There is no better illustration of yin and yang than the vibrant yang bustle of a summertime resort in contrast with the yin stillness of the calm sea in the bay. When the holidaymakers have departed in the winter, the resort becomes quiet and yin while the sea is churned up and becomes yang.

Beach gardens can be fun and look attractive adorned with driftwood and other items washed up by the sea. Few plants flourish in such locations, but some grasses and plants which grow naturally there, such as horned poppies and thrift, do well. Windbreaks should fit in with the look of the area and bamboo or rush permeable fencing will help to fend off the wind. There are a number of shrubs that are useful as hedging in such areas. Higher up are the cliff-side gardens

▲ *Many tropical plants will also grow in temperate conditions in protected locations.*

▼ *The results of beachcombing make a natural seaside garden.*

which fringe many coastal towns. Planted on the cliff face and linked by meandering paths, they escape the worst of the weather and can reveal some gems of plants, more suited to tropical climates.

RIVERSIDE GARDENS

Riverside locations can be idyllic, particularly in summer. Homes bordering a river tend to be orientated towards it and occasionally the mouth of chi, the entrance, becomes the rear of the house. Fast-moving water is felt to dissipate energy and certainly the banks of fast-moving rivers are not home to the variety of plants which thrive by those which meander gently through the garden. Waterside gardens can incorporate a range of plants which do not thrive in other conditions: lush green carpets of bay arums provide a perfect foil for the dancing swards of sweet flag and the narrow stems of irises and rushes. Equally magnificent, delicate weeping willows vie

▼ *A slow-moving river at the bottom of the garden can be auspicious.*

▲ *This garden has incorporated the river as part of its design.*

for attention with the massive leaves of gunnera. It is not advisable to block the view of the river but to set a small shrub or rock as the boundary in the Phoenix position, and frame the river with some planting to block its coming and going at the boundaries – symbolic in China of wealth coming in then running away.

In urban and inner city areas, where heavy industry has moved out, housing developments often spring up around rivers and in dockland areas. Huge buildings dwarf most planting schemes and where possible, large trees should be introduced to create some yin energy.

THE FENG SHUI OFFICE

MANY OF US SPEND A LARGE PART OF OUR LIVES AT WORK AND OUR SURROUNDINGS THERE ARE AS IMPORTANT AS THOSE IN OUR HOMES. WE USUALLY HAVE LITTLE CONTROL OVER THE BUILDINGS WE WORK IN, BUT AWARENESS OF PROBLEMS THAT CAN AFFECT US WILL ENABLE US TO TAKE COUNTER-MEASURES AND MAY ENCOURAGE THE CREATION OF STIMULATING AND NURTURING ENVIRONMENTS.

EXTERNAL FACTORS

—

The buildings we inhabit are part of a wider environment that can have a profound effect on how we operate within them. Their location, what they are surrounded with and even their shape can make us feel comfortable, or it can jar and can have a great impact on our clients. The energy emanating from different directions suits some businesses more than others and we can design our office space in order to encourage these different energies. When we move to a new building, or travel, the timing is crucial to the success of the venture.

OFFICE ENERGIES

T he Feng Shui principles are "First, luck; second, destiny; third, Feng Shui; fourth, virtues; fifth, education". While we have no control over our luck or our destiny, we can have an impact on the quality of our lives by applying ourselves to the other three areas. Education in childhood may vary in quality but as we get older we are able to take more responsibility for it. We are privileged if our early education is of a high standard and enables us to acquire the knowledge and skills needed to enhance our careers,

▼ *The energy of an office is dependent on the people who work there, and the relationships they form with each other.*

▲ *In this clutter-free and airy office, there is room for personal space and a central meeting point.*

▶ *In this modern office, meeting areas again combine with individual spaces to give a harmonious working environment.*

but we should also take steps to improve our knowledge and expertise when we are adults. The term "virtues" applies to the way we relate to people and situations. How we relate to people is, to some extent, written in our horoscopes, but our own personal energy also plays a large part. We can also apply Feng Shui to create an environment which will support us and enable us to make progress.

The energy of any office can be dramatically improved if its occupants respond to each other in a positive way and co-operate with one another. If the office environment is unsatisfactory, it is possible to offer to paint it and to move in plants and images which will improve it and make it a better place to work. If the management is considered to be unreasonable and deadlines are unrealis-

tic, there should be a way of approaching a situation positively to avoid conflict. Negativity breeds negativity so forward planning and planning work programmes holistically, rather than on a day-to-day basis, will reduce stress.

Our relationships with our colleagues will influence our happiness and performance at work. Astrology plays a part in determining our characteristics and those of the people we have positive and negative relationships with. Understanding this will benefit us and help us to create harmony in the office or workspace.

The location of the office is not normally something over which we have control but its internal layout can make a great difference to the way people feel and behave. It is now thought that some buildings are "sick" and an awareness of the causes can improve the lot of those who work there. When we employ Feng Shui in an office environment we can assist the movement of the energies and at the very least we can take positive steps to keep our personal workspace clear of an accumulation of clutter which will affect our performance.

It is accepted that the energies of home and workplace are not independent of each other and if something is not working well in one, it will affect the other. If relationships at home are not happy, it could be because of a problem in the office, which could be caused by a lack of harmonious relationships there, or the problem could simply be a blockage of chi resulting from the position of a desk or workstation.

Feng Shui can help in the office environment in two ways. It can help to make the business function efficiently and prosper; to gain an advantage over competitors, as it is widely used in the East; and to give individuals the edge over rivals in career development – all yang aspects. The second, yin, application is to improve job satisfaction, foster harmonious working relationships, and provide a stress-free environment in which personal careers can develop and the company can thrive.

FENG SHUI IN PRACTICE

The plans for the famous Hong Kong and Shanghai Bank in Hong Kong, designed by British architect Sir Norman Foster, required modification before it was considered suitable by a local Feng Shui consultant. Detail on the outside of the building was altered so that the symbolic arrows point up and not down as on the original plan. The escalators

▲ *The Hong Kong and Shanghai Bank stands in a prime position facing Victoria harbour and is protected behind by the Peak, one of the Dragon Hills that protect Hong Kong.*

were realigned to draw chi into the building from an auspicious direction and the large stone lions which protect the entrance were placed in position at an auspicious time.

The bank's main rival, the Bank of China, erected a new building soon afterwards and started a Feng Shui war. The new building's design was such that its corners directed "poison arrows" of negative energy at its rival, who had to ward it off by installing mirrored glass to symbolically direct it back again.

Another aggressive measure in the East is to point cannons at rivals, who respond by installing larger ones to point back.

LOCATION

When you are searching for suitable business premises there are important questions to ask even before finding out about access and other practical matters. A walk around the area will indicate if it is thriving or not and what type of activities are located there. The fortunes of the previous occupants can provide a clue to how successful the new undertaking will be, and it is worth making enquiries as to their activities and how they fared before committing yourself to a building or area.

The maxim, "Location is everything" applies to offices as well as houses. A prestigious address may be taken as a sign of success by clients who may not realize that your office is little more than a cupboard on a floor shared by three other companies, but a company operating in such a space would not thrive for long unless other factors were right. Some areas are traditionally associated with certain types of business – for example, lawyers. Support networks spring up,

▲ *The varied skyline of downtown San Francisco indicates a thriving and successful city, full of business opportunities.*

contacts are made in cafés during lunch breaks and in bars after office hours, and other enterprises which are not associated will feel isolated. One question which needs to be asked by organizations on the move, or those setting up, is whether or not the area really needs the

services it is offering. There are only so many solicitors, estate agents or expensive boutiques that one area can support, and in many cases the success of a business is down to market research and is not something that Feng Shui can cure.

Sometimes we have an impractical dream of setting up a business or opening a shop offering a service or products which the area does not need. For example, a sushi bar in a district predominantly

▼ *The water and greenery around this building, appropriately home of a building design company, help to energize its environment.*

populated by low-income families with small children will not thrive since the food tends to be expensive, such families have to budget carefully and young children are notoriously unadventurous when it comes to diet. A themed diner-type establishment offering burgers and fries and catering for children's parties would probably thrive in such an area. Similarly, a shop selling modern craftwork and ethnic jewellery is unlikely to do well in an area where the population is elderly. Market research is well worth doing before establishing a business and a little research initially may prevent problems later.

It is true that the fortunes of locations run in cycles but, even so, an area which is run down, where vegetation does not thrive, and where there are many empty or vandalized buildings is best avoided. It is often possible to read patterns into the energy of an environment or a particular building. If a building has had a fire, then it pays to be wary. If the previous occupants of a building were in a similar line

of business and went bankrupt, or had to reduce their activities drastically, warning bells should ring. It may have been due to poor management, but it could also be associated with the building and its environment. In either case, potential clients may associate the two businesses so it

▲ *Water is good for communications, but some Wood and Fire energy is also needed for this book-supplying company. At present the Earth element dominates.*

would be better to steer clear. It is recognized in Feng Shui that certain types of business thrive in certain types of building and location. Choosing the correct ones for a business is the first step on the road to success.

▼ *This restaurant will thrive – the colours and seating are designed for a quick turnover of people in a bustling city location.*

THE FIVE ELEMENTS AND BUILDINGS

Buildings and environments associated with each of the Five Elements support different types of business activity.

ELEMENT	TYPE OF BUILDING, ENVIRONMENT AND ENERGY	SUITABLE BUSINESSES
WOOD	Wood buildings are tall and narrow in shape, or are made of wood. Wood environments are ones where there are trees and vegetation. The energy suggests new ideas and new beginnings.	Woodcrafts, Garden centres, Artists, New businesses, Products
FIRE	Fire buildings have pointed roofs and spires. Fire environments may have chimneys. The energy suggests production and dynamism.	Manufacturing, PR and marketing, Sales
EARTH	Earth buildings are rectangular and have flat roofs. Earth environments tend to be flat and fenced. The energy suggests stability, nourishment and nurture.	Storage and warehousing, Agriculture, Housing
METAL	Metal buildings tend to be round or domed. Metal environments are those where fuels, minerals and gases are extracted from the earth. The energy suggests consolidation and profit.	Metal crafts, Jewellery, Mining, Finance
WATER	Water buildings are those which have irregular shapes. Water environments are ones suggesting flow and making links. The energy is that of communication.	Communications, Electrical systems, Liquids, Healing

THE OFFICE SITUATION

Where offices are situated and the support they receive from other buildings are crucial. Open communication channels and access are also very important to the success of a business.

THE FOUR DIRECTIONS
The first consideration when choosing an office location is support and we can apply the Four Animals arrangement here. Although it is not considered good Feng Shui for an office to be dwarfed by surrounding buildings, it is useful if there is a taller building to the rear to act as the Tortoise, with supportive buildings on either side: the Dragon, to the right when facing the building, should be higher than the Tiger on the left. Alternatively, trees or (for lower buildings) walls and fences, can fulfil these roles.

In the Phoenix position, at the front of the building, it is important to mark the front boundary of the business in

▲ *In Feng Shui terms, round-edged buildings are more sociable than square-edged buildings.*

▼ *This building would benefit from having railings right across the front and lowering the wall to give an even view.*

some way, with a low wall or fence, or with a sign carrying the company name. If a tall barrier is needed for security reasons, choose railings rather than a solid wall or fence. This allows a view from the building whereas a solid barrier would be restricting. Since it enables others to see in, it will also offer more security against break-ins.

Having found a good position to locate your business, it is important to check for any threatening features in the environment. The corners of adjacent or opposing buildings, glare from glass buildings and satellite dishes, and flag poles or decorative features pointing at the office are all of concern since they appear to attack us.

ACCESS
In ancient times, rivers were the main routes of access. Today roads and other transport links serve the same purpose

▲ *Hong Kong harbour accumulates chi for the island and helps to create prosperity for the many businesses located there.*

Businesses situated on urban freeways will suffer if they have frequent visitors and deliveries but do not have adequate parking facilities. Those situated by roundabouts rarely do well since traffic, or chi, is constantly passing by, unable to stop or collect there. Buildings located at crossroads, on the other hand, are considered to have good Feng Shui, since traffic approaches them from two directions. However, this is diminished if there are other buildings pointing at them from the diagonally opposite corner. A mirror, or other reflective surface, will direct the negative energy back at itself.

Buildings at the end of a T-junction, with traffic travelling straight towards them, are seen to be under threat and

▲ *The Johannesburg Stock Exchange depends entirely on efficient communication channels and can only thrive if these are working well.*

and their importance in the siting of business premises will depend on the nature of the business, the numbers of visitors, deliveries and so on. A company which uses technology as its main communication channel will not be so dependent on roads. Whatever the nature of the business, it is important that its communication channels are kept open. Poor service from network providers and computer engineers to such a business is the equivalent of unreliable rail links and road systems to others.

▲ *Stunning foliage helps to provide a vibrant energy for an international western company in this Malaysian suburb.*

▼ *The green area around these office buildings provides some protection from the Lyndon Johnson Freeway in Dallas, USA.*

those in a peninsula position are considered to be unstable. A cul-de-sac location is not generally considered to be good Feng Shui, since parking will almost certainly be restricted and the energy will become stuck.

Wherever possible, attempt to create a well-maintained garden or green area around the building, which will be attractive to workers and visitors alike and will provide a barrier between the office and the road.

WHICH DIRECTION?

Feng Shui considers that different types of energies emanate from each direction. Since it is based on the cycles of nature, it is easy to understand that, for example, the energy of the east is represented by the rising sun and by spring and fresh young growth. If we employ this imagery we can see that the rising energy of the east would suit new companies; the south, dynamic activities such as marketing; the west, consolidation and financial activities; and the more static northern energy, activities indicating stillness such as storage or counselling.

The energy of your business is primarily determined by the direction in which the entrance faces.

▲ *This designer's home and studio symbolize the Wood element – it even looks as if a tree is growing through the centre.*

◀ *Libraries and archives are ideal in the north, which symbolizes storage and communication activities.*

YIN AND YANG

We can utilize the principles of Feng Shui to help us determine the types of activities which will be suitable in each direction. The Bagua diagram indicates the elements associated with the directions, and which of them are considered to have yin qualities and which have yang attributes.

 **WOOD:** Often known as "The Arousing" in its yang form, Wood signifies growth and movement. In its yang form it is more dynamic, suggesting brainstorming, new ideas and snap decisions. In its yin form, often referred to as "The Penetrating", it is more intuitive. Plans are carried forward and executed, ideas turned into designs.
YIN (−) SOUTH-EAST: Design
YANG (+) EAST: Development, ideas

 **METAL:** In its yin form, Metal is known as "The Joyous". It suggests pleasure and reflection, both in its inward and outward manifestations, mirrors and shiny objects, and contemplation. In its yang form, Metal is often referred to as "The Creative" and suggests strength and immobility as represented by large manufacturing machinery.
YIN (−) WEST: Small metal objects, e.g.

knives, ornaments, finance, meditation
YANG (+) NORTH-WEST: Heavy engineering, machinery

 **EARTH:** In its yin form, Earth is often known as "The Mountain", indicating stillness. Here we sow the seeds, prepare and provide support. In its yang form, Earth is often referred to as "The Receptive" and is productive – its output is turned into goods.
YIN (−) NORTH-EAST: Plant nurseries, printing and reprographic services
YANG (+) SOUTH-WEST: Quarrying, pottery, food production

 **FIRE:** Fire is yang and does not have a yin form. It is also known as "The Clinging" and suggests activities concerned with bringing ideas and products to fruition and promoting them.
YANG (+) SOUTH: publishing, public relations, laboratories

▲ *Laboratories do well in the south, symbolized by the Fire element.*

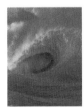 **WATER:** Water is yin and does not have a yang form. It is also known as "The Abysmal" and suggests an area where the energy is not active, but where there is a regular flow.
YIN (−) NORTH: Storage and warehousing, secret negotiations, production lines

◀ *The Metal energy of the west is an ideal location for financial markets.*

▼ *This diagram of the Bagua shows the Five Elements with their yin and yang characteristics and the directions which represent them. We can use this to arrange our workspaces to make best use of the energies of each area within them.*

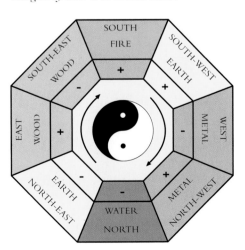

GOOD AND BAD DIRECTIONS

If you are moving office there are considerations to take into account before choosing a location, based on the directions and dates represented by the twelve Chinese animals. If we take these into account, we can plan which months to avoid moving into a new office in order to maximize the beneficial energies of the time and place.

DIRECTIONS TO AVOID EACH YEAR

Each year is represented by an animal, and the Chinese Animals Table shows the exact dates of the years ruled by each animal. Each animal governs a direction corresponding to 30° of the 360° compass. Every year, the direction opposite that of the animal which rules each year is considered to bring problems for everyone, regardless of their own animal or Magic Number. The types of problems encountered are likely to be those concerned with the breaking down of relationships, both personal and business, and of negotiations and contracts.

▲ *A pleasant human voice always gives a good impression of a company and makes clients feel comfortable.*

▼ *This South African bank is very easy to find, with its name emblazoned in large letters on all four sides of the building.*

GOOD DIRECTIONS		
MAGIC NUMBER	1ST CHOICE	2ND CHOICE
1	South-east	North
2	North-east	South-west
3	South	East
4	North	South-east
5-Male	North-east	South-west
5-Female	South-west	North-east
6	West	North-west
7	North-west	West
8	South-west	North-east
9	East	South

FIND YOUR FAVOURED DIRECTIONS

1. Check your Magic Number
2. Look at the table above to find out the first and second choices of directions for your office to face.

CHECKING THE YEARLY DIRECTIONS

1. Find the animal which rules the year when you are planning to move. Check the dates as the Chinese new year begins in January or February.
2. Locate the direction of the animal directly opposite this animal. It is not advisable to move in this direction in that year.

DIRECTIONS TO AVOID EACH MONTH

Every month there is a similar type of energy which will have a detrimental effect on an office or business. Each month is represented by one of the twelve Chinese animals and, again, it is the direction ruled by the animal which sits directly opposite ours that we should try to avoid moving towards.

CHECKING THE MONTHLY DIRECTIONS

1. Locate the animal which rules the month in which you are planning to

FAVOURED MONTHS AND TIMES

This diagram shows the element which rules the nature of each of the 12 animals and the months and times ruled by each.

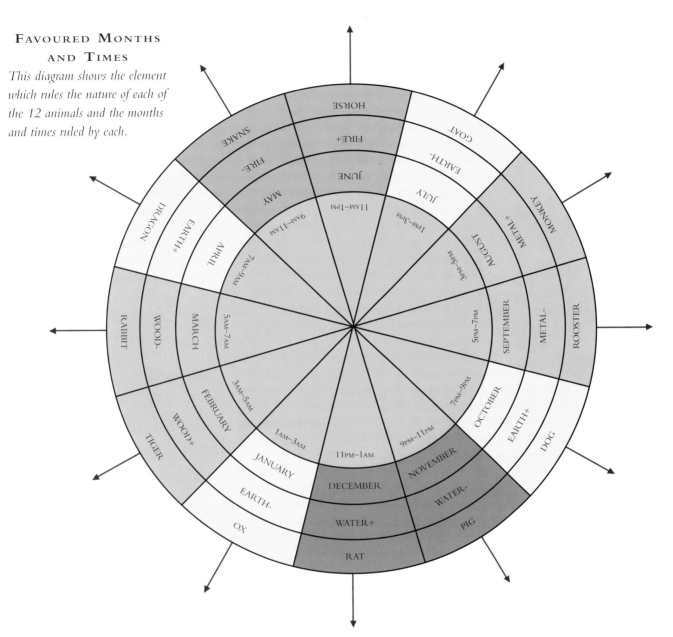

move on "The Chinese Animals Cycle" diagram (opposite).

2. Locate the direction of the animal directly opposite yours. Try to avoid moving office to this direction in that month and delay the move until the following month.

ENTRANCE DIRECTION

The direction faced by the main entrance should be in the most favourable direction for the owner of the business, as determined by his/her Magic Number.

◀▶ *Some locations are easier to take over than others, the buildings on the right would be easier to convert for a new company than a well-established, purpose-built bank.*

FIRST IMPRESSIONS

▲ *A large, clear sign, a car park and an attractive green outlook welcome visitors to this office building.*

F irst impressions of people or buildings are likely to colour our subsequent dealings with them. The ease with which we find the premises, the surrounding environment, the reception area and the greeting we receive are all indicative of the overall character and energy of a company and contribute to its success. Feng Shui can help to improve some aspects, but often it depends on the personalities involved, who will frequently determine whether we want to work with a particular organization or not.

IDENTIFICATION

On arrival at a business or office, visitors should be able to establish instantly that they have arrived in the right place. If the business occupies the whole building the company sign or logo should be prominently placed where it can be seen from the road. This may be on a signboard, but it should also be repeated on the building itself, in proportion to its size.

If the company shares a building with other businesses, a nameplate should be placed prominently outside the building and again inside to indicate which floor it is on. A notice inside the lift indicating which companies occupy each floor will make life easier for visitors, as will instructions on the wall facing the lift on each floor directing visitors to the company they are looking for or, if there is sole occupancy, to the reception desk.

COMMUNICATION

Effective communication systems are crucial to the running of a successful business. The first point of contact is usually a telephone call and this can be the first stumbling block when approaching a business.

Business cards, stationery and brochures are another point of contact which needs to be considered. Names and addresses on staionery should be clear, and if a business is in an awkward location, a small map should be included.

THE COMPANY NAME

Great importance is attached to the name of a business or retail premises. In the Chinese language, many words sound similar to others and only the intonation indicates the difference. For this reason,

▼ *A well-trained receptionist can make all the difference. There should be no conflict between telephone and visitor.*

BUSINESS STATIONERY

The first impression made by a letter is very important and business stationery should conform to the auspicious measurements. The colours used on the type should conform with the company colours and it is best if the name and address are in an easily readable font. The company logo should be featured and good-quality paper should be used to give a good impression.

▲ *This attractive reception area receives plenty of natural light, and drinking water is provided for staff and visitors.*

▼ *This powerful building is well signed. The name and the logo work well together and can be clearly seen.*

words which are similar to those that have undesirable meanings are not used for business names.

SIGNS

The importance of signs with a distinguishable company logo cannot be over-emphasized. Lettering should be legible. Colours are important and should be balanced according to the Five Elements. Three or five are the preferred number of colours; three representing growth and five, fulfilment. Signs along shopping malls and high streets which jut out at right angles to the building can be useful for drawing people in, especially if they are eye-catching. Signs should be firmly attached to a wall or other solid surface and should be in proportion to the whole of the building.

LOGOS

The images portrayed on a logo are important. Unpleasant and sharp images should be avoided. Points are normally not used, although an upward-pointing arrow symbolizes growth. Squares and circles are recommended, as well as images which denote upward energy. Again, colours should follow the Five Elements cycle and be balanced.

▼ *Vertical signs that jut out into the street are very eye-catching. Well-known companies will always dominate so you need to compete.*

THE WORKING OFFICE

—

How we function at work depends on a number of factors, some within and some beyond our control. We are usually able to organize our personal workspace so that it supports us and enables us to work efficiently. Other factors such as lighting, furnishings and layout we may not be able to change ourselves, but if we do not feel comfortable we may be able to influence the decision-making processes in order to achieve a balanced and harmonious environment to support us and ultimately benefit the company.

DRAWING THE PLAN

Having determined which directions our businesses are best suited to, we can look at the internal design and layout. The various departments in an organization should be positioned in locations where the energy supports the tasks they perform.

YOU WILL NEED

◆ A compass with the eight directions clearly marked
◆ A protractor – a circular one is best
◆ A ruler
◆ A lead pencil and five coloured pencils – green, red, yellow, black/grey, dark blue
◆ A scale plan of your office space
◆ A tracing of the Bagua with the suggested information marked on it

◀ This reception area in a restaurant enables customers to relax while they wait for their table, while being part of the atmosphere.

TAKING A COMPASS READING

◆ Remove watches, jewellery and metal objects and stand clear of cars and metal fixtures.
◆ Stand with your back parallel to the entrance and note the exact compass reading in degrees.

◆ Note the direction faced by the entrance, in this example 95° East.

NB: The coloured tip on the needle points north on the Western compass and south on a Chinese compass.

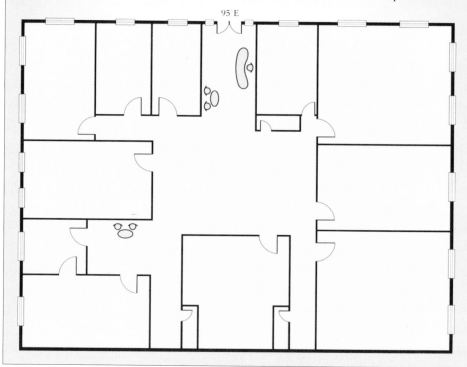

TO DRAW A PLAN

Using graph paper and a tape measure, take measurements for each of the following floor-markings:
◆ External walls
◆ Internal walls
◆ Alcoves
◆ Staircases
◆ Doors
◆ Windows
◆ Permanent fixtures

This will enable you to design the final layout using the principles discussed later to position desks, furniture and other features in positions which will benefit those working there.

TRANSFER THE COMPASS READING TO THE BAGUA

1 Place the circular protractor on the Bagua diagram so that 0° is at the bottom at the North position. Mark the eight directions.
2 Find the compass reading for your office and check you have the corresponding direction. If not, you may be reading the wrong ring.
3 Mark the position of the entrance.
4 Double-check the direction, using the table opposite.

TRANSFER THE DIRECTIONS TO THE PLAN

1 Find the centre of the plan. Match the main walls across the length of the plan and crease the paper lengthways.
2 Match the main walls across the width

and crease the paper widthways. Where the folds cross each other marks the centre of your office.

If your office is not a square or rectangle, treat a protrusion less than 50% of the width as an extension to the direction. If the protrusion is more than 50% of the width, treat the remainder as a missing part of the direction.

3 Place the centre of the Bagua on the centre point of the plan and line up the entrance position.

4 Mark the eight directions on the plan and draw in the sectors.

5 Transfer the colour markings.

▼ *Once the Bagua is in place over the plan, we can see the direction of each room and the element that represents it. The location of the rooms can now be allocated.*

▲ *In a small building this reception area would probably feel oppressive. In a large office it offers the contrast of a cosy space with access to the larger space beyond.*

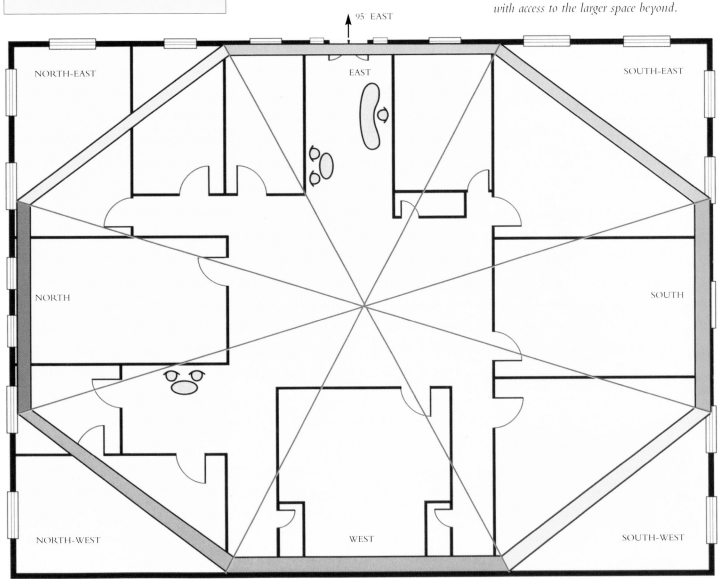

95' EAST

NORTH-EAST EAST SOUTH-EAST

NORTH SOUTH

NORTH-WEST WEST SOUTH-WEST

DESIGNING THE LAYOUT

Taking into account the types of energy associated with each of the eight major compass directions and the types of activities suited to each, we can investigate how to design our office space accordingly. Some features – toilets, car parks and eating areas – which are more suited to some directions than others can be repositioned.

It is important to give some consideration to what visitors will see when they enter the office. Ideally, they should not be able to see directly into the main working area. Every organization has times of stress, but visitors and potential clients should not be aware of the daily traumas of office life or be able to overhear any heated conversations that may be taking place. Doors should therefore be positioned out of the line of sight of visitors, who should receive an impression of calmness and efficiency in congenial surroundings.

ENTRANCES

Entrances are auspicious if they face the favourable positions of the owner of the company, as determined by his/her Magic Number. If it isn't in our power to effect

▼ *This modern office building in Singapore is distinguished by a traditional Chinese entrance, complete with guardians on either side.*

▲ *These impressive entrance doors have been carefully designed to be in proportion to the building and its surroundings.*

▶ *A loo with a view, but the large building opposite is threatening the office with a "poison arrow" of negative energy.*

this – and usually it isn't – we can place our workstations or desks in a favourable direction instead. Entrances which face east encourage the energy of growth, while west-facing entrances foster stability. The north-east, north and south-west are not considered favourable.

▲ *An attractive staff kitchen does wonders for office morale, and must be kept clean and tidy.*

BATHROOMS AND TOILETS

Always difficult to place, toilets should never face the office entrance. They should not be placed in the north, north-east, south or south-west, or face directly towards office doors. Bathroom doors should be closed at all times and should

▲ *An indoor garden gives support to the fragile staircase in this light and airy reception area.*

▶ *This model office has been designed so that all the functions are in suitable directions. Work-flow has been taken into account and the doors are positioned away from public sight, while giving the widest possible view for people entering on business.*

be designed so that even when open the toilets are not visible within. These areas should be kept clean and pleasant.

STAFF KITCHENS AND RESTAURANTS

Favourable areas for kitchens and restaurants are the east, south-east, south and south-west. Cleanliness and good ventilation are most important to ensure that the air is fresh at all times.

▲ *This entrance has a lovely view but the reception desk is cut off and has beams over it.*

STAIRCASES

Ideally staircases of any kind should not be positioned in the north, north-west or the centre of the building.

CAR PARKS

Company car parks are best situated in the east, south-east and the north-west.

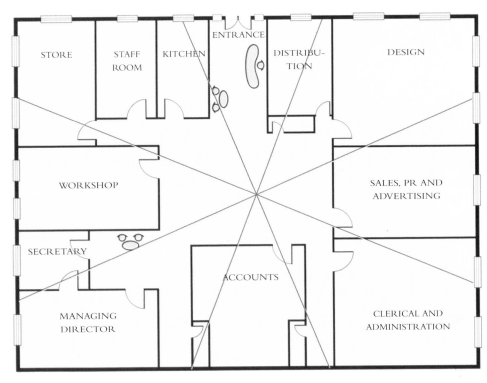

YIN AND YANG

Office activities also fall into yin and yang categories. Day-to-day administrative tasks are yin, and the yang energy is where the action is – decision-making and implementing policies. For example, a typical brainstorming session will involve several people sitting around a table in a well-lit, virtually empty room and it is almost possible to see the vibrant energy circulating around. Every now and again, a lull, a yin space, occurs when the chairman sums up the outcome before tossing another point in to build up the energy again. We can contrast this largely yang process with that of putting the ideas into practice. Programming a computer, for example, requires hours of yin time

The forces of yin and yang act together to create movement and keep a balance in the world. In the office yin and yang can relate to physical matters like layout and decor, but analysis of them also applies to the various activities which take place and to the interaction of those who work there.

Most offices tend to be more yang than yin. The straight lines of the desks, bright fluorescent lights, computer screens, shiny floor surfaces and metal cabinets, the bustle and the noise are all indicative of a yang environment. The chairman's room and the boardroom are usually remote from the hurly-burly of daily office routine and they have a more yin decor, often housing art works and other pleasing reflections of a company's wealth. In a busy office, plants can soften the harshness of the yang environment and water features can draw wealth in symbolically to the reception area, and other areas too.

▲ *This chairman's office is a yin space, decorated with paintings and with a general air of calmness.*

▼ *The straight lines and shiny surfaces of this office are yang, toned down with plants, pictures and wooden surfaces.*

▲ *This decision-making room is very functional. There are no distractions and the chairs are not too comfortable.*

compared with an occasional frustrated outburst of yang energy when things do not go according to plan. Yin is always present within yang and vice versa.

People also fall into yin and yang categories. Some people are outwardly more dynamic and energetic, but are sometimes prone to nervous disorders and illnesses caused by physical exhaustion. However, people who proceed slowly and calmly can often surprise their colleagues by giving vent to built-up frustration. An energetic, high-powered manager may need a calm and efficient assistant, and decision-makers often need people who work in a complementary way to them to put their ideas into practice.

In an office, a balance of yin and yang is necessary for the smooth running of the organization. An office atmosphere which is too yang may mean that jobs do not get done and can result in stressful

▲ *In a hectic office the constant yang energy often results in staff becoming over-stressed.*

situations. If it is too yin productivity may be low and the company could remain static, failing to move forward and keep

up with trends. As we have seen, people have either yin or yang natures and these can become evident in the workplace. Recognizing that other people work and behave differently to us is essential to a harmonious office environment.

YIN AND YANG OFFICES

YANG OFFICES CONTAIN:	YIN OFFICES CONTAIN:
Machines	Paper
Telephones and faxes	Carpets
Rectangular desks	Curtains
Blinds	Art works
Metal cabinets	Dark furniture
People traffic	One person
Conversation	Wooden cabinets
Light decor	Wallpaper
Reflective surfaces	Textured surfaces

YANG ACTIVITIES INCLUDE:	YIN ACTIVITIES INCLUDE:
Brainstorming	Administration
Deadlines	Creating
Marketing	Producing
Selling	Packaging
Promoting	Reviewing

YANG PEOPLE ARE:	YIN PEOPLE ARE:
Enthusiastic	Receptive
Energetic	Creative
Quick-thinking	Imaginative
Precise	Methodical

▶ *These two very different office spaces both show a balance of yin and yang, with straight lines and reflective surfaces softened by colours and fabrics.*

UNSEEN ENERGIES

It is now widely accepted that some buildings can create or exacerbate health problems for their occupants. Sick Building Syndrome has become a commonly accepted term for a number of problems in modern buildings which can cause minor and, occasionally, more serious illnesses or viruses. Most of these problems stem from the fact than

▲ *Office buildings with windows looking out onto green areas make better places to work.*

▼ *The air conditioning in this office is very much in evidence, and very oppressive.*

modern buildings are virtually sealed units in which air, introduced and circulated by machines, becomes stale and a breeding ground for bacteria or viruses. This stale air is continually recirculated by air conditioning units and the germs are constantly reintroduced to the atmosphere. A toxic mixture of chemicals from manufactured materials can also build up.

▲ *Modern office blocks burn huge amounts of energy to light and ventilate them.*

THE AIR WE BREATHE

Modern buildings are designed to keep the less desirable aspects of the weather out and to regulate the temperature at what is considered to be a comfortable working level. Sealed double-glazed units

▼ *We need time out from the constant pressures of modern office life to recharge our energy and also protect our health.*

keep out the damp and the cold, but at the same time they also prevent fresh air from circulating around a building. Some buildings have insulation in the walls which also prevents air from entering. In such buildings, air-conditioning keeps the air circulating. Dry air circulation can create throat irritation, respiratory problems, tiredness and headaches, with a resultant loss in working performance. Air that has been passed through cooling towers to add moisture to it can suffer from a build-up of bacteria and viruses in the water.

MATERIALS

Human beings function best when they are in the same range of vibrations as the Earth, which has a frequency of 8–12 hertz. Most large buildings have either steel frames or foundations made

▲ *In a sealed and overcrowded office the lack of fresh air can easily cause a range of illnesses, resulting in poor productivity.*

from concrete reinforced with metal rods. This metal, along with that in air-conditioning pipes and ducts, may disturb the Earth's vibrations within the building and, in consequence, have a negative effect or even harm us.

The materials which are generally used in offices are made from manufactured substances and not from natural materials. Even if the curtains are made from cotton, they are usually treated with a fire-retardant substance which releases toxic chemicals into the air. There is also an increasing incidence of allergic reactions to a variety of substances.

Where we have control over our workspaces, it is desirable to use natural materials or, if this is not possible, at least to ensure that there is a supply of fresh air. Scientists at NASA, investigating air quality inside spacecraft, discovered that some plants are useful in extracting harmful substances from the atmosphere. At the very least position one of these on your desk, especially by a computer.

STRUCTURAL DETAILS

chi of those beneath them. They are necessary to support a building, and concrete beams are often a feature in offices. Desks and seating areas should not be placed underneath beams. In open-plan offices, partitions can be placed under the beams to make the best use of the space. Otherwise, filing cabinets and bookcases should be placed there, or large plants which lift the energy.

COLUMNS

Straight-sided columns are difficult to deal with. Where the edges point at chairs, the people sitting in them will feel uncomfortable. We should take measures to disguise or soften the corners of the columns by rounding them off in some way, or by disguising them with plants and other items.

Often there is little we can do about the overall structure of an office building, and we have to work with and around the layout. Old buildings with small rooms are difficult to change, but if the building is open-plan, we can introduce screens and furniture to create our own layouts. Our working conditions make a great impact on how we feel

▲ *The barriers between these desks do not block people sitting near to them.*

about our jobs and on our performance. Being aware of problematic features enables us to design remedies to make our working lives more comfortable.

BEAMS

Beams are not recommended in Feng Shui. They can be oppressive when positioned over a desk and can suppress the

BARRIERS

Where several small rooms have been converted to one large office, there are occasionally parts of walls left for structural reasons. It is important that both eyes have the same-length view, as Feng Shui consultants recognize a pattern of illnesses which result if the view from

▼ *A staircase directly opposite the entrance will channel chi away from the office.*

▼ *The flow of chi in this room appears to have nothing to contain it.*

▲ *The chi rushes straight through these wide doors and is unchecked by anything inside.*

▼ *Patterned rugs or hanging lights would slow down the energy in this long corridor.*

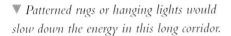

▼ *The giant curve slows down the movement of chi in this corridor.*

one eye is blocked. Barriers can create individual work-places, often leaving people's backs exposed. Facing another person can cause conflict, and facing the back of a computer can cause illness.

STAIRCASES

Staircases and escalators should not face the front entrance or the chi energy will be unable to circulate properly. Spiral staircases act as a corkscrew through a building and are not comfortable. Where they exist, place large plants at the bottom in terracotta pots to add stability.

CORRIDORS

Long, narrow corridors funnel chi very quickly. Slow it down by strategically placing mirrors or plants, or using other

▲ *A large plant at the bottom of this light, attractive spiral staircase would give it more stability and reduce the corkscrew effect.*

means to create a meandering route – for example, changes in floor covering or pattern. Hanging light-fittings are another option. Where there are many offices along a straight corridor, the occupants often feel isolated. If the doors are opposite one another there may be rivalry and bad feeling. A plant by each door may help and leaving doors open will enable people to feel part of the community. If doors are not aligned, this can also cause problems and it is recommended that mirrors or landscape views are placed to fill in the spaces on either side of the doors.

LIGHTING

▲ *These adaptable tilted reading stands are an ingenious way to get the light to fall on the page at the right angle.*

◄ *Natural daylight is the best source of light but in strong sunshine there is too much glare on these highly reflective glass surfaces.*

▼ *Coloured glass creates a wonderful energy in this entrance door, generating the feeling that this is a successful company.*

Adequate lighting is essential in the workplace for health and safety reasons and to ensure maximum efficiency. Offices should be well-lit and it may be necessary to introduce a variety of lighting to support the various functions which are carried out there.

NATURAL DAYLIGHT

By far the best form of lighting in an office is natural daylight. Our bodies rely on light not only to enable us to see but also for Vitamin D, which comes from the sun and is absorbed through the skin. In countries that receive relatively little sunlight during some parts of the year

people may suffer from SAD, or Seasonal Affective Disorder, brought about by an excess of melatonin, a hormone produced by our brains during the hours of darkness. People who work in offices that are artificially lit will almost certainly not be as healthy as those who benefit from natural light. Depression and lethargy are typical symptoms, but working in such conditions can produce a range of problems from headaches and nausea to poor eyesight, stress and fatigue, particularly where the lighting is fluorescent.

However, precautions should be taken where computer screens and desks are close to windows since the glare of the

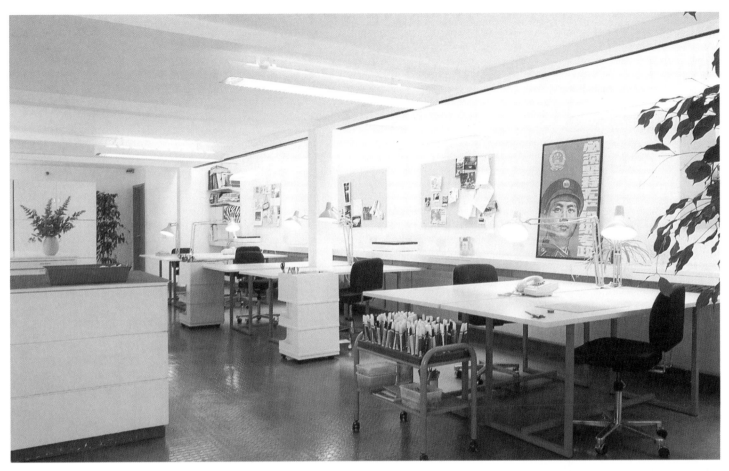

▲ *A range of different kinds of lighting are used in this studio. Shadows may fall in different areas at different times of day.*

▼ *In this colourful staff restaurant, elegant uplighters by the side of each table create the impression of individual spaces.*

sun can also create problems. Measures can be taken to filter the light through vertical blinds, plants or movable screens.

ARTIFICIAL LIGHT

The quality of light is important. Full-spectrum lighting was designed to copy natural daylight as much as possible but unfortunately contains slightly higher levels of ultraviolet radiation than ordinary light sources. Fluorescent lights are still the primary light source in offices because they are easy to install and cheap to run, but this type of lighting emits higher electromagnetic fields than other sources, which can be detrimental. The flickering from flourescent lights can cause stress and headaches and can even bring on fits in epilepsy sufferers.

Incandescent light bulbs offer a range of options, giving an even light throughout the office, and can also be used for task lighting on desks. Desk lamps should always be positioned on the opposite side to the dominant hand to prevent shadows falling across work.

▲ *Interesting lighting effects enhance this attractively-designed eating area.*

Uplighters can be useful in offices where ceilings are low and where it is not desirable to have spot lighting on desks. Reflected lighting, directed on to walls and ceilings, offers an additional lighting source; the colour of the decor will influence its effectiveness. Tungsten and halogen lamps are useful for this. Too bright to be used for task lighting and close work, they give a white light which is close to daylight and the low-voltage variety can be used for accenting. These bulbs are also energy-efficient.

DECORATION

When we use colour we are working with light, as light contains all colours, each with its own frequency. The colours we use in offices will be affected by the amount of natural daylight there and by the secondary light sources we use. The materials will also have a bearing on the overall effect of the office. Upholstered chairs and curtains in dark colours have a yin quality while smooth, hard surfaces and light and metallic surfaces have yang attributes. The materials we use in decorations and furnishings have the ability to absorb or transmit light and their colours will affect the energy in the office.

COLOUR

Colour is vibration and we each respond to it consciously and unconsciously in different ways. In our own individual offices, it is best to choose wall and floor colours that we like and feel comfortable with, but in communal offices a neutral colour to suit all tastes is preferable. Colour can be introduced in furnishings and other items – paintings, storage boxes and upholstery. The psychological effects of colour are numerous but there are some Feng Shui guidelines that we can

follow. Normally offices are yang, and yang colours (red, purple, orange and bright yellow) will add to the yang energy. Yin colours (green, blue and black) will create a less dynamic feel. The colours in public areas should be neutral, with the accent colours reflecting the nature of the company, or the colours of the logo if it is one which is well-known.

▲ *Plenty of natural daylight and lively colours make this staff dining area an energetic space.*

THE FIVE ELEMENTS

The colours associated with the Five Elements evoke the quality of the energy of each element. We can use these colours in the office to highlight the

▼ *The colours of this curved reception area suggest that the company is not dependent on quick decisions or aggressive marketing.*

▼ *In this office the use of bright but muted colours and some awkward angles give the space a disturbing feeling.*

▼ *Interesting colours and shapes have been used in this design studio, where the chi moves unimpeded round the curves.*

nature of the business or the qualities we wish to invoke there.

The colours which correspond to the Five Elements should be in balance in any office. Where one element is dominant, or lacking, then it may have an effect on the energies at work there. The table below shows the relationships of the elements and can be used to strengthen a weak energy or deplete the impact of one which is too dominant. We can use the colour, shape or material related to each element to balance an environment.

MATERIALS

If we opt for a neutral colour on office walls and floors, we can introduce the qualities of the Five Elements through the furniture and fittings, soft furnishings, pictures and plants.

Hard, shiny materials, such as metal and glass, are yang and move energy on quickly. The use of these materials in staff canteens and meeting rooms will ensure that the activities there do not go on too long. Denser materials such as non-shiny metals, dark wood and upholstered chairs are more containing and the energy associated with them is slower.

Synthetic materials are not really

▲ *The green tree balances this atrium coffee bar in the centre of the building. Colourful pictures and furnishings on each level offset the white background.*

◀ *Bright Fire colours in shades of red and orange are very appropriate for a dynamic business such as this advertising agency.*

recommended because of the associated health risks and although it is inevitable that we have these materials in the office, on computer casings, furniture trims and other office items, it is preferable for them to be kept to a minimum, particularly on desks at which people spend considerable amounts of time.

If we decide to decorate our office walls in strong colours, it is usually best to choose neutral colours for furnishings or to blend the colours. However, sometimes a clash of colours is a way of moving energy, especially useful in a company where rapid decisions are called for.

THE RELATIONSHIPS OF THE FIVE ELEMENTS

ELEMENT	HELPED BY	HARMED BY	WEAKENED BY	WEAKENS
Wood	Water	Metal	Fire	Earth
Fire	Wood	Water	Earth	Metal
Earth	Fire	Wood	Metal	Water
Metal	Earth	Fire	Water	Wood
Water	Metal	Earth	Wood	Fire

ELECTRICAL EQUIPMENT

Another potential hazard in the workplace is the electromagnetic radiation from electrical equipment, particularly computers. Electromagnetic fields, or EMFs, from high-voltage power lines and electrical appliances, are thought to be injurious to health. It is believed that they impair the cell regeneration process and could be responsible for the increasing numbers of people with impaired immune systems. It is wise to sit as far as possible away from equipment and not to surround ourselves with wires. A particularly bad spot for a desk to be situated is where the mains power enters a building – desks should be moved away from that area.

▲ *Computers are an essential part of office life but it is essential to take regular breaks if our health is not to suffer.*

◀ *The impact of electromagnetic radiation on people working in this office block will be harmful.*

▼ *In such a hi-tech environment a Cereus peruvanius* cactus *might help.*

COMPUTERS

Computers are virtually indispensable in the office, yet we place ourselves at risk from a number of illnesses, ranging from eye problems to repetitive strain injury, if we spend too long in front of them. Many countries now have legislation

▼ *Wherever possible, use a laptop in preference to another computer.*

▲ This office should be rearranged so that no-one sits behind a colleague's computer monitor.

◄ Shield the back of the monitor if people are sitting behind it.

shield us to some extent, particularly the cactus, *Cereus peruvianus*, which was adopted for that purpose by the New York Stock Exchange.

PHOTOCOPIERS AND DUPLICATING MACHINES

Photocopying and duplicating machines give off chemical emissions – the duplicating machine from the ink, and the photocopier from the toner – which are known to be carcinogenic. These machines should not be located in offices where people work all day, particularly if they are in constant use. Ideally, they should be located in a separate, well-ventilated room. Certainly, no one should sit close to a photocopier.

MOBILE PHONES

Ear and brain tumours have been attributed to the use of mobile phones. The US Food and Drug Administration advises that they should be used only when absolutely necessary and that calls should be kept short. Where it is essential to use them, ensure that the antennae do not touch the head. The use of mobile phones in cars may increase the danger, particularly hand-held models.

▼ Mobile phones have serious health implications – use a conventional telephone whenever possible.

which limits the number of hours each day which can safely be spent in front of a screen. In some American states, pregnant women are not allowed to operate computers since prolonged exposure may lead to miscarriage. Screen filters help to some extent, and laptop machines do not have cathode-ray tubes which are a major cause of such problems. Wearing natural fibres also helps because they do not create static electricity.

Most of the electromagnetic radiation comes from the back of the computer monitor and when designing offices this should be taken into consideration so that no-one is sitting facing, or with their backs towards, the rear of a monitor. It is thought that some plants can help to

CLUTTER IN THE OFFICE

Office clutter accumulates rapidly and there are few people who would not benefit from discarding extraneous items from their workplace and streamlining their procedures. Office clutter is not just things left lying about, but also the paper we hoard, out-of-date journals and uncleared hard disks.

STORAGE

There is no excuse for clutter. There are many storage options, ranging from cupboards which hide computers and printers to simple cardboard storage boxes. These are widely available in the local high street, or by mail order. Before tidying everything away in boxes or files, it is worth asking the question, "Do I really need this?"

JOURNALS

Professional journals are invariably hoarded but rarely read. Many of these are now available on-line and professional organizations hold a complete set in their libraries if an article is needed. If we skim through journals when they arrive and note the issue and page numbers of interesting articles in a diary, we can file them.

DESKS

Desk drawers harbour a considerable amount of rubbish, but if we throw away old pens and pencils which no longer

◀ These full-length storage cupboards help to keep the office free of clutter.

▶ The top shelf of a set of shelves is rarely used and should be "weeded out" frequently.

▲ This efficient storage system is in the centre of the office, where energy should circulate freely, so it is important to keep it tidy.

work, and have special places for rubber bands and paper clips, we will feel more efficient and save time spent searching for things. It is advisable only to have a single-tier in-tray, otherwise the temptation is to categorize things into urgent and not-so-urgent, and the latter will never be dealt with. A satisfying feeling

at the end of each day is to know that the in-tray is empty and that all mail has been dealt with; it can be energy-draining to begin the morning confronted with the debris from the day before. Even if you haven't been able to finish the work, tidy your desk so that you at least give the impression that all is under control. Clearing the day's mail is an excellent habit to get into and if everyone dealt with bills promptly the world would be a far less stressful place.

COMPUTERS

Computers store an amazing amount of information and if we keep the hard disks clear of out-of-date files and back up our working files regularly, we will always have rapid access to the data we need.

It can take time to set up databases to print labels for a mail shot, but it is worth the initial effort for the time saved. Random thoughts as well as notes for lectures and workshops should be recorded to help us prepare well in advance and save time and anguish at the last minute. Old hard-copy files do not have to be stored in the office and are best removed to a storeroom or cupboard elsewhere to prevent a build-up of stagnant energy.

▲ *A well-organized, uncluttered desk leads to clear thinking and reduces stress.*

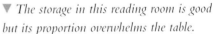

▼ *The storage in this reading room is good but its proportion overwhelms the table.*

ORGANIZERS

One of the most useful items in an office is a revolving card file by the telephone. Invaluable for instant access to addresses and telephone numbers, it can also be used to cross-reference suppliers, record birthdays and other information which, although it can now be stored on computers and electronic personal organizers, actually takes more time to access

in these formats. Personal organizers are extremely useful items for both the home and the office, but major difficulties arise if we lose them.

BOOKS

Many people find books difficult to discard, yet the speed of technological change renders information out-of-date rapidly and some books, such as directories and unread reference books, should be regarded as disposable items.

▼ *This well-designed workspace has both individual and communal storage areas.*

FURNITURE AND MEASUREMENTS

▲ *Floor-to-ceiling shelves overwhelm this already small office.*

◀ *This manager's office is ideally furnished but the glass panel allows no privacy.*

▲ *Furniture has to be the correct height in studios, where people bend and stretch.*

▼ *This efficient workshop has furniture at the right height and tools to hand.*

The importance of well-designed, ergonomically correct office furniture cannot be overstated. Life can become a struggle if we have to battle with stuck doors in confined spaces on a daily basis and we can cause ourselves physical harm if we sit on chairs with wobbly seats and no back support, or type on keyboards at the wrong height.

Office furniture is often neglected, particularly in offices not visited by outsiders. In small offices occupied by several people, it is important that procedures are streamlined so that storage cupboards and filing cabinets can be kept to a minimum. Positioning desks in accordance with the workflow can also help, by keeping the movement of people through the office to a minimum.

The corners of all furniture should be rounded to help movement through the office and so that the corners do not point at anyone working close by, which can be uncomfortable. Catching a hip on the corner of a desk every time we go to a cupboard, or being unable to open a

door without difficulty because someone's chair is in the way, will be frustrating and may lead to tensions.

HEALTH AND SAFETY

Repetitive Strain Injury (RSI) is the result of spending a long time performing the same task and can cause great discomfort for sufferers. Wrist supports and other methods of easing the condition are available. Office managers should be sympathetic to sufferers and provide suitable furniture and equipment to alleviate the problem and to prevent it occurring in the first place.

Storage units should be at a suitable height for the items contained in them so that staff do not have to bend or stretch excessively to reach them. Shelving above head height can be oppressive and create insecurity. The edges of shelves near a chair can create "poison arrows" of energy, which can cause discomfort to those sitting nearby. Where possible, cupboards are preferable to open shelves near seating and make the office look less cluttered. Floor-to-ceiling shelving is particularly overpowering in small offices, and the more shelves we have in an office, the more likely we are to fill them up with things we do not really need. Mirrors can be placed in small offices to create an illusion of space, but do not place them where people can see themselves as they work otherwise, depending on their personality, they will feel uncomfortable or be preening all day.

AUSPICIOUS MEASUREMENTS

(Yes = Auspicious, No = Inauspicious)

CMS	INCHES	
0–5.4	0–2⅛	Yes
5.4–10.7	2⅛–4¼	No
10.7–16.1	4¼–6⅜	No
16.1–21.5	6⅜–8½	Yes
21.5–26.9	8½–10⅝	Yes
26.9–32.2	10⅝–12¾	No
32.2–37.6	12¾–14⅞	No
37.6–43	14⅞–17	Yes
43–48.4	17–19⅛	Yes
48.4–53.7	19⅛–21¼	No
53.7–59.1	21¼–23⅜	No
59.1–64.5	23⅜–25½	Yes
64.5–69.9	25½–27⅝	Yes
69.9–75.2	27⅝–29¼	No
75.2–80.6	29¼–31⅞	No
80.6–86	31⅞–34	Yes
86–91.4	34–36⅛	Yes
91.4–96.7	36⅛–38¼	No
96.7–102.1	38¼–40⅜	No
102.1–107.5	40⅜–42½	Yes
107.5–112.9	42½–44⅝	Yes
112.9–118.2	44⅝–46¾	No
118.2–123.6	46¾–48⅞	No
123.6–129	48⅞–51	Yes
129–134.4	51–53⅛	Yes
134.4–139.7	53⅛–55¾	No
139.7–145.1	55¾–57⅜	No
145.1–150.5	57⅜–59½	Yes
150.5–155.9	59½–61⅝	Yes
155.9–161.2	61⅝–63¾	No
161.2–166.6	63¾–65⅞	No
166.6–172	65⅞–68	Yes

For dimensions in excess of these, the cycle repeats.

MEASUREMENTS

Furnishings are usually purchased from office suppliers. If they are specially designed, it will be advantageous to follow the preferred Feng Shui dimensions. It is felt in China that some dimensions bring good luck but others are not advantageous. By using the correct dimension for signs, windows, doors, desks, chairs, bookcases and other furnishings, we can ensure that we are in a strong position to develop our businesses successfully.

The measurements are taken from eight divisions of the diagonal, roughly 43 cm (17 in), bisecting a square based on the Chinese foot, which is virtually the same as an imperial foot. This

▼ *These modern chairs look attractive but do not offer enough support for the back.*

▲ *A round-edged table is ideal for meetings and prevents passers-by knocking into it.*

▼ *The manager's chair is larger than his visitor's, giving him the edge in negotiations.*

corresponds to the "Golden Section", "Divine Proportion" or phi in Eastern architecture, and is based on proportion in nature. It can be found in the growth patterns on shells and the markings on plants, among other phenomena.

The three main dimensions of office desks should be in accordance with the auspicious Feng Shui dimensions, as should the height and back width of the chairs, although the ergonomics of the furniture obviously has to conform to today's standards. Other furniture, such as bookcases and display cabinets, can also be designed according to these principles.

DESKS AND WORKSTATIONS

A s we spend a considerable amount
of time at work, it is important that
we position ourselves where we feel
comfortable and where we can tap into
the beneficial energies of a supportive
direction. This is easier to achieve if we
are the sole occupant of an office, but

▲ *Both desks have a view of the door, with
plenty of time to see someone approaching.*

▶ *Low barriers give a view of the office and
do not hem people into their own space.*

even where an office is shared with other
people it should be possible to find a supportive space.

The most important rule in Feng Shui
is to feel comfortable and this cannot be
achieved if we sit with our backs to a
window or door, since we will feel
uneasy and nervous. The glare of the sun
through a window onto computer screens
can cause headaches. A useful remedy is
to place plants on the windowsill, or
position a piece of furniture there, as long
as this will not restrict our space.

The best place for a desk is diagonally

◀ *This desk would be better placed sideways
to avoid having one's back to the window.*

opposite the door so that we can see anyone entering the room. This is certainly
the place for the most senior person in
the room if it is occupied by several
people, as they will be bothered less by
day-to-day tasks than those closer to the
door. Those who sit facing the door will

DESK POSITIONS

Most of us spend a considerable amount of time at our desks so it is important to feel comfortable and well supported. This will be affected by the position of the desk in the room. Try sitting in a position that allows a view of the room while being removed from the bustle at the door, and compare it to the way you feel when you are sitting in a vulnerable position next to the door.

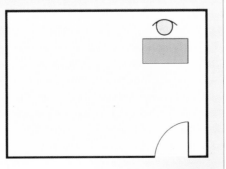

3. This position for a desk will make the occupant feel directly in the firing line.

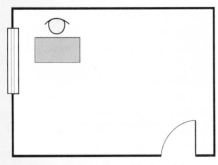

1. This is the best Feng Shui position, facing but not in front of the door..

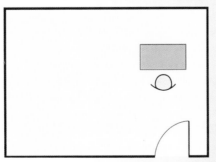

4. This is the worst position in which one could feel comfortable.

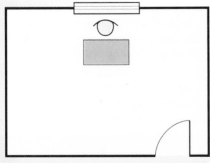

2. This is disconcerting; some plants on the windowsill as a barrier would help.

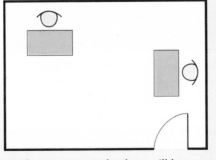

5. The person near the door will be disturbed more than the person opposite.

▲ *This is a lovely desk but the chair is not supported behind. A large plant or low screen would help.*

be in the firing line for anyone entering and those closest to it will have less job satisfaction than those further away because they will be constantly interrupted in their work by people coming in and out. People who sit in these positions rarely stay long in a job. It is their pens and equipment that visitors borrow and their papers which get knocked off the desk.

OPEN-PLAN OFFICES

In open-plan offices, desks and workstations are often in small booths and the occupants' backs face into the room. In this position, there is an element of surprise when someone approaches from behind and it is not a comfortable position in which to work. The remedy is to place a mirror on the wall.

The size of our desk should be in proportion to our position in the company. It is usual for the chairman to have a large desk and he/she would not retain much credibility if it was the smallest desk in the office.

In Feng Shui, desk shapes are important. Square and rectangular desks are considered suitable but are best if the corners are rounded so that they do not point at anyone or catch them as they pass by. L-shaped desks are perceived to resemble meat cleavers, with the shorter side being reminiscent of the blade, which will cut off communications and authority. If possible, separate the two parts of the desk and use the smaller one for a computer. Round desks will not encourage anyone to sit and work at them for long, but are ideal for meetings, which should be kept short.

Workstations can be a problem in that they come with trailing wires. These should be secured in some way or run in channels for safety reasons. It is detrimental to health to sit facing the back of a computer monitor and every attempt should be made to design the office so that this does not occur.

▼ *Wide desks ensure that people are not sitting too close to the computer screens.*

RECEPTION AREAS

The entrance to a building sets the tone for the whole company and its importance cannot be overstated. A clean, bright, welcoming entrance area will encourage clients to think well of an organization and will create a positive atmosphere for employees. A dark and scruffy area, on the other hand, will indicate a failing or shoddy company to clients and deplete the energy of employees before they start the day.

ENTRANCES
The main entrance door or doors should be in proportion to the building. If there are double doors, both should be open or the flow of chi into the building will be restricted, resulting in a dark and stale area behind the closed door. Revolving doors help to circulate energy at the entrance but are only suited to large office buildings.

Doors should open easily and not be too heavy or they will deplete personal

energy. If a company takes deliveries, or if clients bring portfolios or large sample cases, there should be some means of propping the door open to enable easy access otherwise the whole entry process will symbolize a struggle, which may continue throughout the visit. If there are windows immediately opposite the door, plants should be placed in front to prevent the chi from passing straight through without circulating around the building.

THE RECEPTION DESK
Visitors should be able to see the reception desk from the entrance but it should not be too close to it, or opposite, or the receptionist will be exhausted by the activity there. It is important that the receptionist has a comfortable chair and is backed by a solid wall so as not to be startled from behind. Receptionists should be occupied with work that will not clutter the desk and should be trained to put visitors' needs before those of

▼ *This well-designed desk enables the receptionist to keep in contact with colleagues as well as greeting clients.*

▲ *An impressive entrance, but the second door symbolizes chi escaping. It would be better turned into a window.*

▼ *This amazing sculpture is out of proportion to the entrance and exerts great pressure on it.*

tank – eight gold ones and a single black one to soak up any negative energy. Tiny darting fish create an active energy useful in commercial companies, whilst larger, slower-moving species create a calm atmosphere, which can be useful in health practices. Aquariums should be large enough to enable the fish to move freely and should recreate as natural an environment as possible.

▲ *The glass wall of this reception area acts as a barrier in what would otherwise have been a vulnerable position.*

◄ *The stained glass doors in this comfortable reception area add interest. Each door can be recognized by a different design.*

▼ *Care has been taken over the design of this reception area, decorated with a vase of fresh flowers.*

other employees and the demands of the telephone. Procedures should be in place to remove all deliveries from the reception area as soon as possible after arrival so that the area will not be cluttered.

RECEPTION AREAS

Chi flow in reception areas is important and employees should be able to move quickly through to their work areas via lifts and staircases. It is important that reception areas are fresh and that the air is circulated, so fans, plants and water features can play a useful role. Any water features outside the building can be reflected by mirrors in the reception area. Mirrors should be positioned to one side of the entrance so that the chi will not be reflected back through the door.

Fish tanks are often placed in reception areas. In China, fish symbolize wealth and often there are nine fish in the

THE IDEAL RECEPTION

This reception area contains various features to help the flow of chi:

1. A water feature with a fountain and plants lifts the chi in the reception area.

2. A well-designed reception desk supports the receptionist and is positioned so that he/she is in contact with employees and visitors.

3. Plants help to keep the air fresh and add to the Wood energy, symbolizing growth.

4. The round table indicates that energy will spin around this area quickly, suggesting that visitors will not be kept waiting long.

5. The company logo opposite the entrance adds prestige to the reception area.

6. Employees pass through this pleasant, energized area on their way to the lifts.

7. The delivery area is located close to the lifts for convenience and so that the reception area is kept clear.

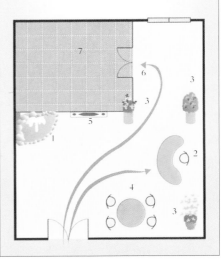

COMMUNAL AREAS

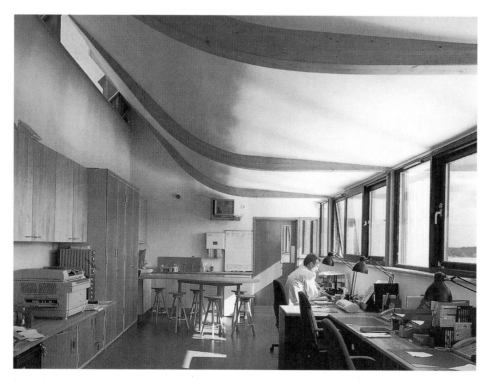

◀ *Everything is incorporated in this cleverly designed office – individual spaces, meeting and eating areas, kitchen and training – and it works quite well.*

positive images on the walls, suggest to employees that they are valued.

OFFICES

Cramped working conditions lead to cramped minds. We feel resentful if we constantly knock ourselves on colleagues' desks and cupboards. Mirrors can create an illusion of space and have a positive impact provided they do not reflect a cluttered environment. Open-plan offices can leave people feeling vulnerable so it is important that they personalize their spaces and are not surprised from behind. Strategically placed mirrors will deal with this but make sure that they are not positioned so that members of staff can see their reflections from their desk.

STAFF ROOMS

Staff rooms are where employees meet, discuss work and air grievances and the Feng Shui of these rooms is important if

The communal areas of the office are important not just for visitors but also for staff morale. It is false economy to neglect staff areas since a contented staff that feels valued and appreciated will produce more, represent the company better and feel happier at work. Consequently there will be less absenteeism. Office and desk conditions are important but refreshment, washroom and rest room facilities are equally so.

STAIRS AND CORRIDORS

Poor decoration and maintenance within the building are depressing. Shadowy corners and ill-lit passageways will not encourage staff to linger in the evening, or stay late to finish projects. Fresh paintwork and clean flooring help to create an air of efficiency and, together with

THE ENTRANCE

Even if an office building does not have visitors on a regular basis, it is important that the entrance is to the office is clearly marked and well maintained for the sake of the people who work there.

What the staff see as they arrive each day is important. Waste bins should not be placed by the entrance and deliveries should be put away immediately as they arrive. Uncollected mail and any other clutter should not be allowed to accumulate. Make sure there is someone responsible for this area. Positive images encourage staff as they arrive each day and are a "feel good" factor as they leave.

▼ *In this typical meeting room the round table encourages the circulation of ideas.*

▼ *A grand boardroom; the chairman sits at the head of the oval table and takes charge.*

staff are to be positive, though they should not be too comfortable or breaks will be extended. If the staff room has a kitchen area, it should be clean and conform to health and safety standards and provision should be made for clearing up at busy times. Notice boards are important and act as a communication medium between staff and employer. Notices should be up-to-date and changed regularly, and there should be a balance between work and social information.

MEETING ROOMS

Meeting rooms range from a small area where two or more people can meet to

▲ *There are only two safe spaces at this table, and all will feel very vulnerable in this glass box exposed to everyone in the office.*

▼ *This office design allows for invidual work spaces and the opportunity for people to come together for discussions.*

discuss a specific issue to large boardrooms. Where "Hot Desking" is practised, meetings take place standing up at hard shiny, yang tables set at "learning height", so employees do not get too comfortable and quick decisions are made. In more conventional meetings everyone should sit facing their best direction where possible. Table shapes can affect meetings. Boardroom tables are best if they are oval. Round tables are useful for brainstorming sessions and rectangular shapes for meetings with a leader who sits at the head. Boardrooms should be well furnished and the chairperson's seat should be larger than the rest, backed by a wall with a view of the door.

▲ *A staff dining room with a pleasant view will help to recharge energies for the afternoon session.*

▼ *A well-designed kitchen area, however small, will boost staff morale and make them feel valued.*

OFFICE ENERGIES AND PERSONALITIES

—

Feng Shui considers the movement of chi through a building and how it effects the working environment. It also takes into consideration the personal energies of the individuals who work there. In this section we investigate different approaches used in office communication systems, and observe how our personalities determine the way we react in certain situations, and how we respond to our colleagues. We also look at how Feng Shui can help us at interviews and on business trips, and how our home and office are linked.

OFFICE ENERGIES

▲ *A happy office is a productive one. Staff need time out in a congenial space to unwind and interact with colleagues.*

THE COLLABORATIVE OFFICE

"Hot Desking" is an office design revolution that originated in architectural colleges. It is based on the idea of an open-plan office and its purpose is to encourage people to be more creative by interacting and networking in order to foster the exchange of ideas. The characteristics of this approach are:

◆ No personal space
◆ Communal desks and equipment
◆ A variety of work spaces – communal and intimate around a central hub
◆ No internal telephone calls or memos
◆ Stand-up meetings which reduces their length
◆ No departments
◆ No clutter – anything lying around is thrown out; staff have personal lockers
◆ No receptionists or secretaries
◆ All staff can do all jobs

This system has already been adopted by several companies working mainly in the area of PR and advertising. The work ethic of these types of companies is already yang and staff tend to be young and dynamic, and work under pressure.

▼ *In this typical "Hot Desking" office, the layout does not encourage people to stay long in one place.*

As we have seen, Feng Shui is largely about ensuring that there is a free flow of movement around a building and arranging the space accordingly to ensure that the energy, or chi, flow does not become blocked, get stuck or stagnate. Moving furniture and redesigning space is comparatively easy and when the benefits are pointed out, there are few who cannot see the advantages, but a crucial factor that is overlooked in most organizations is the mental energy of the people who work there.

Where psychology is employed in a business, it is usually intended to bring advantages to the organization and to increase levels of production. While this is understandable, production will always automatically increase where staff are happy and one aspect which is generally overlooked is the fact that not everyone is the same, nor do they work in the same way. If we can accommodate a variety of working styles, then we will create a contented work force and thus generate greater productivity.

▲ *A central place for meetings and discussions ensures that ideas come from all directions.*

Such organizations need some yin in their furnishings but their efficient, clean lines suggest this is not happening, in which case the staff may feel even more pressured and eventually burn out.

At the same time as "Hot Desking" was being introduced and companies were reporting profits up by two-thirds, a report published in the *British Journal of*

Psychology of a research project at Reading University suggested that open-plan offices are bad for business since their noise can effect staff, reducing their performance by 60%. It is probable that the type of people who are attracted to fast-pace media-type jobs are those who are also attracted to "Hot Desking", but it is a hard way to live for very long.

▼ *In a "Hot Desking" office different activities, such as working on a computer and discussion, are conducted side-by-side.*

THE PERSONALIZED OFFICE

In contrast to "Hot Desking", it is known that enclosed offices with no natural light will inhibit creativity. In this type of environment, false windows, landscape pictures, mirrors and bright colours should be used to give the illusion of spaciousness.

Marking territory lies deep in the evolutionary past of all living things. Animals scent their space to lay claim to it and repel invaders. Similarly, office workers personalize their space in some way with photographs, ornaments and other items. As a result they feel more stable and committed. Research has shown that those who do not do this tend not to stay long in any organization.

A business that takes all working styles into account and provides space for different approaches and activities will have a happier, less stressed and more stable work force.

▲ *Many people in traditional offices personalize their desks with a photograph or ornament.*

▼ *A bunch of flowers is a distinctive way of making an office desk look individual as well as attractive.*

CHI FLOW

How the energy circulates in an office is important for the smooth running of the organization and also in encouraging job satisfaction and harmonious working relationships. Chi energy moves in the physical environment but its effects are subtle and affect us psychologically. Where movement, either around the building or in our dealings with colleagues, is slow or becomes stuck, this can greatly affect our performance and sense of well-being.

CHI AND POSITIONING

If we consider the model office in the diagram opposite we can see that the departments likely to import and export bulky goods are placed near the entrance. The workshops are next to the store so that products do not have to be trans-

▲ *Chi flows around each floor of these open-plan offices. The sculpture in the centre also creates energy.*

ported through the public areas and the administrative offices, accounts, sales, PR and advertising areas are all in close proximity for convenience. The managing director's office is removed from the hub of activity but is near enough to be in contact. It is linked to his/her secretary's office for speedy communication and there is a small separate reception area here for important visitors, to remove them from the busy reception area.

Difficulties often arise in rooms occupied by several people and a lot of office equipment. Inevitably, some people are better positioned than others and tensions may arise. The top diagram opposite shows a badly designed office in a large

◄ *Cramming desks and people into an awkward space restricts the flow of chi.*

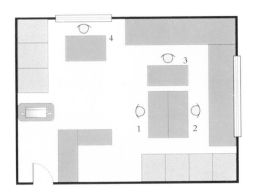

▲ *In this office layout the flow of chi is blocked, affecting working relationships and preventing harmony.*

▼ *The same office has been redesigned with a few simple features to give a more efficient work flow.*

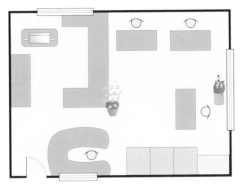

organization. The occupants were irritable and visiting staff needing stationery, photocopies or advice also became irritable because the entrance was restricted and there was always a queue for the copier. If they needed stationery they had to make their way through the office and thus the occupants there had constant disruptions. The staff were often ill; the employee who sat at desk 4 suffered from headaches from the sun glaring on her computer screen as well as the fumes from the photocopier. The occupants of desks 1 and 2 faced the backs of each other's VDUs. The employee seated at desk 1 was always short-tempered as she was also in charge of the reception area and was constantly having to get up.

The next diagram shows how a few simple adjustments can make life easier and healthier. A glass screen isolated the copier, which was repositioned near the window for ventilation and reduced

congestion in the door area. All the stationery required by those not working in the office was placed near the copier so the office staff were no longer interrupted.

A reception window was cut into the wall which reduced the number of people coming into the room and the reception desk was made into a working area for the receptionist, who no longer had to keep moving from one position to another. Clutter was removed from the office and this reduced the amount of storage required, enabling the staff to have a small kitchen area with a refrigerator and a kettle. With the desks facing into the room and an empty central area, the office felt larger and less restricted and the staff were much happier.

COMMUNICATION
Day-to-day communication among staff members is of paramount importance in a successful organization. Bulletin boards in communal areas may be useful as a reinforcement, but face-to-face communication is preferable, and a short briefing meeting during the day enables staff to be informed and to air their views. These are best not held first thing in the morning. People's internal clocks vary and many take time to adjust to the working day, particularly after a bad journey. Last

▲ *Chi cannot flow properly on a narrow desk where you have to sit too close to the computer screen.*

thing in the afternoon is equally bad as staff will be anxious to get away and may already be planning the evening's activities in their minds. By around 11am most people will be settled, attentive and willing to communicate. An informed workforce which feels that its views are valued will be a productive one.

▼ *Choosing the right time of day is important if staff communication is to be meaningful for everyone concerned.*

OFFICE PERSONALITIES

We all know individuals who greet us with a smile, radiate enthusiasm for the task in hand and volunteer their services unsolicited. Conversely, there are those who never volunteer and always find a reason why an idea will not work. Personal chi, or karma, is nothing to do with Feng Shui yet it has a great impact on the office environment.

COMPATIBILITY

Our personalities are partly determined by the year in which we were born, and Chinese astrology indicates that we are compatible with some people and not others. We can use this information to maintain harmony in the workplace.

People often become unhappy at work because they are affected by the people around them. With some knowledge of the characteristics belonging to each animal sign, it is possible to arrange the workplace so that individuals working in close proximity are compatible.

STRENGTHS AND WEAKNESSES

Each of us has characteristics that lend themselves to performing certain tasks. If we can harness particular strengths and

avoid placing people in areas of work which they are not suited to we can generate a happy and fulfilled workforce. The following pages describe the characteristics of each animal, and which kind of activity they do best.

▶ *Each coloured triangle links animals with harmonious relationships. Those immediately opposite each other are antagonistic and should be kept apart.*

▲ *An office meeting will include people of very different dispositions.*

COMPATIBILITY TABLE

	RAT	OX	TIGER	RABBIT	DRAGON	SNAKE	HORSE	GOAT	MONKEY	ROOSTER	DOG	PIG
RAT	+	=	+	−	★	=	−	−	★	−	+	+
OX	=	+	−	=	+	★	−	−	+	★	−	+
TIGER	+	−	+	−	+	−	★	+	−	=	★	=
RABBIT	+	+	−	+	=	+	−	★	−	−	=	★
DRAGON	★	−	+	=	−	+	−	+	★	+	−	=
SNAKE	+	★	−	+	=	+	+	=	−	★	+	−
HORSE	−	−	★	−	=	+	+	=	+	+	★	+
GOAT	−	−	=	★	+	+	=	+	+	−	−	★
MONKEY	★	+	−	−	★	−	−	+	=	+	+	=
ROOSTER	−	★	+	−	=	★	+	=	−	−	+	+
DOG	+	−	★	=	−	+	★	−	+	−	=	+
PIG	=	+	=	★	+	−	−	−	★	−	+	+

Key: ★ Excellent   = Good   + Workable   − Difficult

THE RAT AT WORK

Rats make good bosses, team builders and leaders. Their quick minds enable them to weigh up situations at a glance and home in on important points. They do not respond well to a "nine to five" approach and work best in flexible situations.

WOOD RAT

POSITIVE: Energetic. Full of ideas. Inspirational, Popular.
NEGATIVE: Inflexible.

FIRE RAT

POSITIVE: Competitive. Flexible.
NEGATIVE: Dislikes routine. Lack of diplomacy. Low boredom threshold.

EARTH RAT

POSITIVE: Stability. Loyalty. Even temper.
NEGATIVE: Resistant to change. Intolerant.

METAL RAT

POSITIVE: High standards. Money-handling skills.
NEGATIVE: Stubborn.

WATER RAT

POSITIVE: Sociable. Shrewd. Knowledgeable.
NEGATIVE: Conservative. Indiscreet.

THE OX AT WORK

Loyal, hardworking and honest, Oxen systematically undertake any task, often working beyond the call of duty to complete it. They do not easily tolerate what they perceive to be slacking in others.

THE TIGER AT WORK

Tigers are dynamic and can carry others along by sheer enthusiasm. They are always very eager to launch themselves into new ventures. On the other hand, they often make rash decisions and can be very critical of the others. They enjoy a challenge and have good leadership skills.

WOOD OX

POSITIVE: Leader. Spokesperson. Confident. Hard-working.
NEGATIVE: Quick-tempered

FIRE OX

POSITIVE: Determined. Honest. Protects staff. Perceptive.
NEGATIVE: Outspoken. Inconsiderate.

EARTH OX

POSITIVE: Loyal. Accurate. Shrewd.
NEGATIVE: Slow. Uninspiring.

METAL OX

POSITIVE: Energetic. Reliable.
NEGATIVE: Outspoken. Selfish.

WATER OX

POSITIVE: Integrity. Persistent. Respects the views of others.
NEGATIVE: Sensitive.

WOOD TIGER

POSITIVE: Team player. Positive. Tolerant. Innovative.
NEGATIVE: Short attention span. Aloof. Temper. Ego.

FIRE TIGER

POSITIVE: Popular. Resourceful. Optimistic.
NEGATIVE: Restless. Loner.

EARTH TIGER

POSITIVE: Analytical. Practical. Objective.
NEGATIVE: Lacks humour. Insensitive. Pushy.

METAL TIGER

POSITIVE: Assertive. Competitive. Risk taker. Staying Power.
NEGATIVE: Aggressive. Headstrong. Self-centred.

WATER TIGER

POSITIVE: Intuitive. Objective. Understanding.
NEGATIVE: Vengeful. Procrastinator.

THE RABBIT AT WORK

Rabbits are polite, considerate and dislike conflict of any sort. They wilt under criticism and dislike being backed into a corner and will always find a means of escape. Flexible, they refuse to panic. Artistic and intuitive, rabbits never miss anything. They keep close counsel and advance by weighing up situations and methodically taking advantage of them until they achieve their goals, often to the surprise of others. Rabbits have strong wills and an inbuilt sense of self worth.

WOOD RABBIT

POSITIVE: Generous. Accommodating. Flexible.
NEGATIVE: Indecisive. Lenient. Impersonal. Vain.

FIRE RABBIT

POSITIVE: Fun-loving. Progressive. Intuitive. Diplomatic.
NEGATIVE: Temperamental. Outspoken. Neurotic.

EARTH RABBIT

POSITIVE: Persistent. Trustworthy. Rational. Prudent.
NEGATIVE: Calculating. Materialistic. Introverted.

METAL RABBIT:

POSITIVE: Intuitive. Dedicated. Thorough. Ambitious.
NEGATIVE: Moody. Cunning. Intolerant.

WATER RABBIT

POSITIVE: Supportive. Good memory. Friendly.
NEGATIVE: Over-sensitive. Emotional. Indecisive.

THE DRAGON AT WORK

Dragons are entrepreneurs and leaders. They have an irrepressible energy and an unswerving confidence in their abilities. Dragons find it difficult to keep secrets and will not accept criticism, and a crossed dragon is a sight to behold.

WOOD DRAGON

POSITIVE: Innovative. Generous.
NEGATIVE: Proud. Condescending.
Outspoken. Pushy.

FIRE DRAGON

POSITIVE: Objective. Competitive.
Inspirational. Enthusiastic
NEGATIVE: Demanding. Inconsiderate.
Aggressive. Impetuous.

METAL DRAGON

POSITIVE: Honest. Charismatic.
NEGATIVE: Intolerant. Inflexible.
Ruthless. Critical.

WATER DRAGON

POSITIVE: Methodical. Resourceful.
NEGATIVE: Autocratic. Impersonal.
Pragmatic.

EARTH DRAGON

POSITIVE: Sociable. Fair. Initiator.
NEGATIVE: Bossy. Distant.

WOOD SNAKE

POSITIVE: Intuitive. Far-sighted.
Logical. Staying power.
NEGATIVE: Vain. Aloof. Big spender.

FIRE SNAKE

POSITIVE: Confident. Perseverance.
Charismatic. Ambitious.
NEGATIVE: Self-centred. Suspicious.
Jealous. Uncompromising.

EARTH SNAKE

POSITIVE: Trusting. Calm. Reliable.
Shrewd.
NEGATIVE: Conservative. Frugal.

METAL SNAKE

POSITIVE: Generous. Co-operative.
Self-sufficient. Opportunistic.
NEGATIVE: Suspicious. Scheming.
Uncommunicative. Domineering.

WATER SNAKE

POSITIVE: Intuitive. Practical.
Organized. Determined.
NEGATIVE: Secretive. Vindictive.
Calculating.

THE SNAKE AT WORK

 Snakes have an inner wisdom which, combined with intelligence, make them formidable. They usually follow their own path and leave the mundane tasks to others. If attacked they find subtle ways of revenge. Snakes are intuitive and are not easily fooled; they have a dry sense of humour.

THE HORSE AT WORK

 Horses have low boredom thresholds and attention spans. They like action and short, to-the-point instructions. Capable of work-ing tirelessly to meet a deadline, they adhere to their own timetables and like flexibility. They are perceptive and have lightning brains and can come to conclusions in an instant, although they may occasionally come to the wrong one. They work on hunches and are great improvisers. Their tempers are quick to flash, but they soon forget the cause.

WOOD HORSE

POSITIVE: Logical. Inspirational.
Intelligent. Friendly.
NEGATIVE: Restless. Highly strung.
Lacks discernment.

FIRE HORSE

POSITIVE: Intellectual. Flamboyant.
Passionate.
NEGATIVE: Volatile. Troublesome.
Inconsistent.

EARTH HORSE

POSITIVE: Methodical. Adaptable.
Logical. Amiable.
NEGATIVE: Indecisive. Overstretches.

METAL HORSE

POSITIVE: Intellectual. Intuitive.
Logical. Enthusiastic.
NEGATIVE: Headstrong. Unfinished
tasks. Foolhardy.

WATER HORSE

POSITIVE: Adaptable. Spontaneous.
Cheerful. Energetic.
NEGATIVE: Indecisive. Inconsiderate.

WOOD GOAT

POSITIVE: Compassionate. Peace-loving. Trusting. Helpful.
NEGATIVE: Clinging. Resistant to change.

FIRE GOAT

POSITIVE: Courageous. Intuitive.
Understanding.
NEGATIVE: Spendthrift. Volatile.
Impatient.

EARTH GOAT

POSITIVE: Sociable. Caring.
Optimistic. Industrious.
NEGATIVE: Sensitive. Conservative.
Self-indulgent.

METAL GOAT

POSITIVE: Artistic. Adventurous.
Self-confident.
NEGATIVE: Possessive. Moody.
Vulnerable.

WATER GOAT

POSITIVE: Articulate. Friendly.
Popular. Opportunistic.
NEGATIVE: Silky. Dislikes change.
Impressionable. Emotional.

THE GOAT AT WORK

 Goats get on well with everyone. They cannot bear confrontation and wither when disciplined. Schedules and dead-lines are not for Goats, who thrive when allowed complete freedom. Goats are idealistic and often impractical and yet they usually seem to bring others to their way of thinking by their charm and persistence. When it doesn't happen, they will sulk. Survivors, Goats worry a lot and need approval to function effectively.

THE MONKEY AT WORK

 Naturally sociable, the monkey will always have a following. His quick wit and leadership skills ensure he is never isolated. Monkeys are capable of great achievement and know it. They do not suffer from false modesty, neither do they

WOOD MONKEY

POSITIVE: Intuitive. Resourceful. Persistent. Inventive.
NEGATIVE: Restless. Dissatisfied. Rash.

FIRE MONKEY

POSITIVE: Self-confident. Truthful. Self-motivating.
NEGATIVE: Domineering. Mistrustful. Jealous. Confrontational.

EARTH MONKEY

POSITIVE: Reliable. Generous. Scholarly. Honest.
NEGATIVE: Moody. Rude. Unlawful.

METAL MONKEY

POSITIVE: Self-reliant. Loving. Creative. Hard-working.
NEGATIVE: Proud. Uncommunicative. Inflexible.

WATER MONKEY

POSITIVE: Kind. Flexible. Persuasive.
NEGATIVE: Touchy. Secretive. Evasive.

WOOD ROOSTER

POSITIVE: Enthusiastic. Reliable.
NEGATIVE: Easily confused. Regimental. Blunt

FIRE ROOSTER

POSITIVE: Independent. Organized. Dynamic.
NEGATIVE: Fanatical. Inflexible. Temperamental.

EARTH ROOSTER

POSITIVE: Hard-working. Efficient. Careful.
NEGATIVE: Critical. Dogmatic.

METAL ROOSTER

POSITIVE: Industrious. Reforming.
NEGATIVE: Opinionated. Uncompromising. Inhibited.

WATER ROOSTER

POSITIVE: Persuasive. Energetic. Practical.
NEGATIVE: Fussy. Bureaucratic.

boast. Monkeys are problem-solvers. Entirely flexible, they manipulate situations to achieve their goals. They learn quickly and their fine memories mean that no one gets the better of them. On the rare occasion that this happens, monkeys will bounce back.

THE ROOSTER AT WORK

 Roosters are proud and opinionated and are prone to offering unsolicited advice. They are however, on their good days, outgoing and amusing and make good company. They never miss anything and are real sticklers for detail, Roosters exel at accounts and will not miss even the smallest error. If the mistake is yours you will never hear the end of it.

THE DOG AT WORK

 Dogs are sociable and fair, they are also reliable. If there is a cause to fight for, or if someone they know needs some help and support, the Dog will be there. Dogs

WOOD DOG

POSITIVE: Likeable. Calm. Honest.
NEGATIVE: Hesitant. Ingratiating.

FIRE DOG

POSITIVE: Leader. Innovator. Honest.
NEGATIVE: Rebellious. Strong-tempered.

EARTH DOG

POSITIVE: Fair. Efficient. Stable. Kind-hearted.
NEGATIVE: Secretive. Demanding. Show-off.

METAL DOG

POSITIVE: Dedicated. Decisive. Charitable.
NEGATIVE: Secretive. Demanding. Extreme.

WATER DOG

POSITIVE: Sympathetic. Fair. Calm. Democratic.
NEGATIVE: Distant. Indulgent.

WOOD PIG

POSITIVE: Organising. Promoter. Orator.
NEGATIVE: Manipulating. Gullible.

FIRE PIG

POSITIVE: Optimistic. Risk taker. Determined.
NEGATIVE: Bullying. Underhand.

EARTH PIG

POSITIVE: Patient. Reliable. Diligent.
NEGATIVE: Unyielding.

METAL PIG

POSITIVE: Sociable. Direct. Enduring.
NEGATIVE: Domineering. Tactless. Resentful.

WATER PIG

POSITIVE: Persevering. Diplomatic. Honest.
NEGATIVE: Over-indulgent. Slapdash. Gullible.

work well with those they like but can ignore or dismiss those they don't get on with. If crossed, their tempers are quick, though they do not bear grudges. They will reluctantly accept, but are not really happy in, the limelight. Dogs keep a clear head in a crisis and inspire confidence in others. Their preference for a quiet life can give the impression of moodiness.

THE PIG AT WORK

 Pigs are the stabilizing force in an office. Amiable and always willing, pigs rarely attract dissent, although they can waste time in pursuing unlikely schemes. Pigs are never crafty and have an endearing innocence which attracts others to them. Competitive is not a word known to pigs who may occasionally be ridiculed for their slow reactions. Pigs are responsible and accurate workers. If there are any problems, pigs will take up the cause and carry others with them. Rarely do they flare up but when they do it will only be fleeting, then all will be forgotten.

HOME-OFFICE LINKS AND THE BAGUA

When there are problems with no obvious cause in the home, a Feng Shui consultant will often look to the office, and vice versa. However good the Feng Shui of the home and the office, karma is paramount, as of course is destiny. There are steps that can be taken to improve life, even where the odds appear to be stacked against us. Healthy lifestyles and positive attitudes help and Feng Shui can tip the balance.

A POSITIVE ATTITUDE

Negative attitudes are self-destructive and a sure way of provoking a negative reaction from others. Negative people are far less likely to get a contract or promotion than those who are always willing to try something and appear enthusiastic. Being positive is easier if we are fit and healthy and if our lives outside the office environment are happy and fulfilled. Using Feng Shui is just part of the package that will enable us to achieve what we want in life. If we live in a chemical and electromagnetic soup, eat food that is contaminated by chemicals and spend our leisure time slouched behind closed curtains in front of a TV screen, we will

▼ *We should only use the Bagua for ourselves. It would be difficult to use on this shared desk without affecting other people.*

▲ *Supple, healthy bodies enables the chi to flow unobstructed through them.*

◄ *If we spend our days like this, then our leisure activities should offer exercise and time away from electrical equipment.*

not be as healthy or able to cope with our increasingly complex society as someone who eats fresh food, exercises the body and the mind and is open to a wide range of people and experiences.

SLEEP AND HEALTH

We can use Feng Shui to make sure we are sleeping in a direction that supports us. The best direction – the one in which it is best to site our doors, desks and beds – is the one to use if all is well. There is another direction, known as the Celestial Doctor, which is useful if we are ill. It is used to tap into the energies of the universe and aid recovery. Refer to the table to the right.

USING THE BAGUA

The Bagua is a tool we can use to focus on various aspects of our lives. We can

align it to the compass directions and position it on a plan of our homes and offices, or on our desks. We can also use it to represent a symbolic journey of our lives by aligning it to where we sit at our

BED DIRECTIONS		
MAGIC NUMBER	BEST DIRECTION	CELESTIAL DOCTOR
1	South-east	East
2	North-east	West
3	South	North
4	North	South
5 (Male)	North-east	West
5 (Female)	South-west	North-west
6	West	North-east
7	North-west	South-west
8	South-west	North-west
9	East	South-east

(NB: These are the directions of the bedroom in the house and are also to be faced by the top of the head when lying down.)

desks or to the front of our houses. Most people want to focus on two areas – the Career path and Wealth. Equally as important are the Helpful People who will make success possible.

THE CAREER AREA

This area represents the start of our journey. It sits in the north direction, represented by the Water element. A water feature here will support the energy of the area and Metal will give it a boost so a wind chime or other metal object here would be helpful. A black-and-white picture representing both Water and Metal would also be useful. If we are using the Bagua symbolically, we will need to check that anything we place will not clash with the elemental energy there. We may prefer to use a brochure of the organization we wish to gain employment in or the business card of the company whose account we are hoping to take on. We can enhance the Career area in our homes, but we would need to have a private office to do this at work or we will be taking responsibility for the careers of colleagues as well.

THE HELPFUL PEOPLE AREA

By stimulating the Helpful People areas in our homes or in our offices, we

▼ *The Bagua can be positioned on to your workstation or desk, just as you would place it over a plan of your house.*

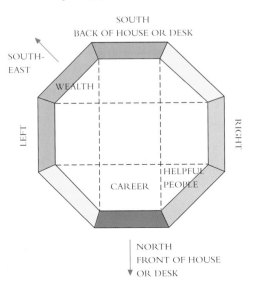

```
                    SOUTH
            BACK OF HOUSE OR DESK
                      ↑

  SOUTH-
  EAST

         WEALTH


  LEFT                              RIGHT


                          HELPFUL
                          PEOPLE
         CAREER


                      ↓
                    NORTH
               FRONT OF HOUSE
                 OR DESK
```

▲ *Using the principles of Feng Shui in the home will have the combined effect of improving life at work, the two worlds are inextricably linked.*

encourage the support of others. This is a Metal are and Metal is supported by Earth. Therefore a rock, terracotta pot or crystal here will stimulate the energy. Again, if using the Bagua symbolically, the element of the direction should be checked and the elements should be balanced. Be careful when hanging crystals; anything harmful reflected in them will be magnified by their many faces and break up rather than encourage beneficial energies.

WEALTH

Many people are attracted to Feng Shui by the promise of wealth, as represented by the Wealth corner of the Bagua. If only it were that simple! We have seen that Feng Shui is only part of the picture and that other forces such as destiny and personality come into play. If there is no demand for your services, Feng Shui cannot help. The Wealth area is a Wood area and a plant will support the energy. Other options are an empty pot placed ready for the wealth to pour in, some coins in a dish or a bowl of spring water that has been placed in moonlight and is changed every day.

▼ *We can align the Bagua to our desks and activate an area. This desk is well organized but cluttered. A small trolley to hold equipment would be useful.*

INTERVIEWS

Interviews are often gruelling and many factors besides professional competence play a part in the selection procedure. There is nothing we can do about our compatibility with members of the selection panel, but we can make use of some Feng Shui techniques to give us the best possible chance of acquiring a job. Other factors which will play a part are punctuality, awareness of the impact of our body language and maintaining eye contact.

▼ *Gestures and facial expressions tell us a lot about other people.*

CLOTHES

Research has shown that given the choice of three women candidates, one in a business suit, one in a suit but with the addition of a scarf or a piece of jewellery, and one in floral dress, most interviewers opt for the candidate in the business suit (a yang outfit) with some (yin) additions on the grounds that it looks professional but not as if the woman is trying to emulate a man. Obviously it is not always necessary to wear such an outfit and a business suit might even be inappropriate in some areas of employment. Feng Shui can help by suggesting which colours suit us and the jobs we are seeking so that we can use them either in accessories or in the outfit we wear. This does not just apply to women; men can use their suitable colours in ties, shirt patterns and socks.

Women in a predominantly male profession may feel more confident if they introduce some yang colours into their clothing – reds, purples and oranges. If a

▲ *Faced with a panel like this, you can at least move your chair to face a good direction.*

▼ *Body language plays an important part in communicating with other people.*

man wishes to be employed in an occupation that is usually the domain of females, then some yin colours – blues and greens – will be appropriate.

Each of the Five Elements is associated with different types of professions. It may be useful to introduce something of the energy of the business into clothing or even into any files or pens we carry to the interview. The table below indicates the elements associated with some of the most common businesses.

WHICH DIRECTION

Sometimes we will have the opportunity to choose where to sit. Many large organizations' selection processes now

▼ Each of the Five Elements is particularly relevant to different types of business. These are some of the most common.

▲ If you need to give a presentation, it is important to face a direction that is auspicious for you.

WOOD	FIRE	METAL	EARTH	WATER
Green/Jade	*Red/Purple*	*White/Grey*	*Yellow/Brown*	*Dark Blue/Black*
Horticulture	Marketing	Accountancy	Agriculture	Communication
Floristry	PR	Banking	Building	Electrical
Forestry	Advertising	Mining	Food	Fishing
Wood crafts	Fashion	Jewellery	Pottery	Transport
Publishing	Law	Engineering	Personnel	Travel
Media	Chemicals	Appliances	Clothing	Health

require candidates to mingle and dine with executives prior to formal interviews. If we take a small compass with us and familiarize ourselves with the orientation of the building, we may be able to sit in our best direction. If we have to give a presentation, we should aim to orientate ourselves to face one of our best directions. Even during a formal interview, it may be possible to move the chair slightly so we can gain the advantage of facing an auspicious direction. The table below is a reminder of our best direction based on our magic numbers.

◄ In an interview, Feng Shui can give us that "extra something".

▼ When you go into an interview, always remember your best direction.

MAGIC NUMBER	
1	South-east
2	North-east
3	South
4	North
5 (Male)	North-east
5 (Female)	South-west
6	West
7	North-west
8	South-west
9	East

BUSINESS TRIPS

We should follow the same procedures on business trips as we do in our homes and offices. If the trip is important and much rests on the outcome, then it is worth requesting a room in one of our best directions when we book the hotel. When packing for a business trip, always remember the compass. This will enable us to position ourselves in an auspicious direction when we are negotiating, and to align our beds to beneficial energies as we sleep.

TRAVEL ARRANGEMENTS

The energy of certain months suggests that we should not move towards a certain direction. In the "Favoured Months and Times" diagram, we can see which of the twelve Chinese animals rules each month. It is inadvisable to move towards the direction opposite the animal which rules each month, during that month. For example, in November, which is ruled by the Pig, it would not be wise to travel in the south–south-east direction. The consequences of travelling in this direction may be misunderstandings and

▼ *If you are in charge of a group, keep their instructions clear and precise.*

▲ *Business trips can be tiring and frustrating. It helps if you can arrange to travel in an auspicious direction.*

▼ *Laptops enable us to make use of travelling time. If possible, place them so that they face an auspicious direction.*

the break-up of negotiations. Although the indications are that this will only be of a temporary nature, it is obviously best to try and avoid such complications. If it is possible to alter the route of your journey so that you travel towards your destination from another direction, this will reduce the impact.

THE MEETING

Whether we meet clients or colleagues in a public place or in their offices, we can attempt to gain some advantage for ourselves if we pay attention to where we sit. We should always try to be supported by a wall behind us and never sit with our backs to a door, or at a window. In addition, if we can manoeuvre ourselves so that we face our best direction then we will be in an advantageous position.

THE HOTEL ROOM

It will benefit us if our head faces one of our auspicious directions as we sleep. The position of the bed is important and we should attempt to ensure that we are supported by a wall behind and that we do not face the en-suite bathroom since negative energy will emanate from it. If the bed does face the bathroom, make

PACKING TIPS

A compass

Details of your best directions

Something to cover a mirror

Incense or oils and a burner

A water spray

The name of a good restaurant to
    celebrate success

▲ When you want to dominate, choose the prime position for yourself and the vulnerable one for your client.

sure that the door is closed at all times. A mirror facing the bed is not considered to be good Feng Shui and we will have a disturbed sleep if we do not cover it. Many hotel beds are surrounded by electrical cables for bedside lamps, telephones and radios. Some are even built into the headboard and there is little we can do about them. Switch off and unplug all appliances and move the bed away from them if possible.

Hotel rooms will have accumulated the chi energy from all those who have been there before us. It is obviously better for us if we can remove this energy and create a pleasant environment for ourselves. Opening windows to let in fresh air is an obvious starting point. It may be difficult, because of the noise involved, to raise the sound vibrations in the room by clapping, ringing bells and

▲▼ Unplug appliances before you fall asleep. Cover a mirror or television screen as they will both reflect the bed.

making other noises to perk up the energy, but we can silently improve the air quality by burning incense or aromatic oils and spraying water around the room to increase the negative ions.

Having created a as much of a temporary home-from-home for ourselves as is possible, and tapped into our beneficial energies, we should place ourselves in the most advantageous position possible for our business discussions.

ENTERTAINING

When we take clients out to a restaurant, we can place ourselves in suitable positions to make the negotiation process work to our advantage. We can ensure that those we wish to score points against are placed in a vulnerable position – for example, with their backs to the door or in the path of cutting chi from the corner of a pillar. If, on the other hand, we want to win someone over, it may be worth allowing them the supported position while we sit in our best direction.

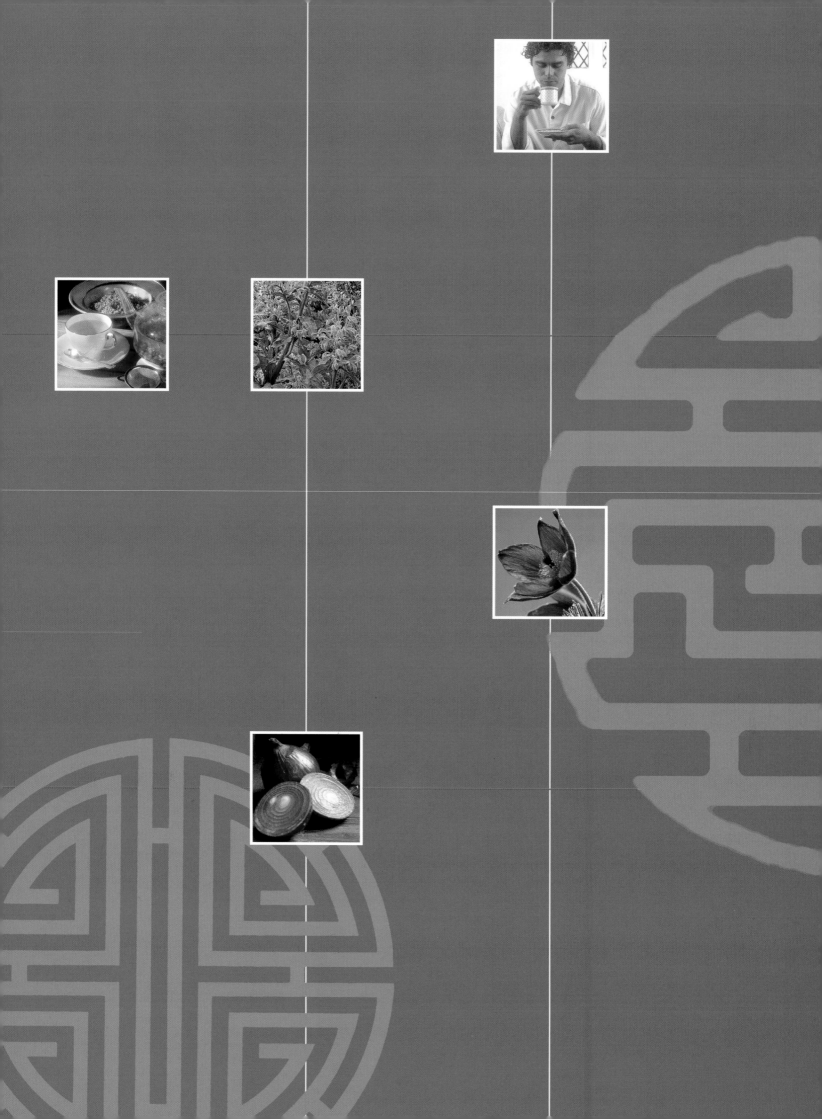

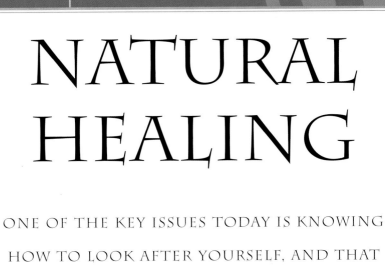

NATURAL HEALING

ONE OF THE KEY ISSUES TODAY IS KNOWING HOW TO LOOK AFTER YOURSELF, AND THAT DOES NOT JUST MEAN STEERING CLEAR OF COFFEE, ALCOHOL AND STRESS. IT MEANS KNOWING THE MANY SUBTLE AND SOPHISTICATED WAYS IN WHICH THE BODY WORKS. KNOWING, FOR EXAMPLE, HOW THE USE OF HERBS CAN QUICKLY HELP YOU REVIVE AFTER A DIFFICULT DAY, HOW USING HOMEOPATHY CAN BOLSTER YOUR BODY'S WELL-BEING, AND HOW AYURVEDA CAN HELP TACKLE ILLNESSES HOLISTICALLY.

HERBALISM

———

From the earliest times people have recognized the value of plants not only as food, but also as medicines, and over the centuries herbalists have become very skilled in matching the health-giving properties of plants to our needs. Many helpful herbs are quite familiar plants and are easy to buy or, even better, to grow in your own garden. Simple remedies can be made from dried or fresh herbs, and substituting an excellent herb tea for stimulating drinks such as tea, coffee and soft drinks will help you to relax and reduce your tension levels. Every person is unique, and just as we all have favourite foods, each of us responds best to particular herbs. Use this chapter to help you explore the ways in which gentle herbal remedies can benefit you.

THE HERB GARDEN

Herb gardens are easy to make and quickly stocked. Get a catalogue from a specialist seed supplier and you will probably find that they have eight or so different kinds of Basil from Europe and the Far East, with herbs like Coriander and Cumin. Growing them is incredibly easy. In most cases, pick regularly to encourage plenty of fresh, new tasty shoots. You will quickly see the benefits in the kitchen and your health.

PLANTING HERBS

You do not need very much space to grow herbs: a small border, or even a collection of containers, will provide a perfectly good supply. But if you do have the room, a large herb garden offers the chance to try fun designs like a circle of triangular beds pointing in to a focal point such as a small statue or painted urn.

SOIL AND SITE

Most herbs are undemanding and quick to grow. They are essentially wild plants, and do not require rich, highly cultivated soil. Many of the most useful herbs, such as Sage, Thyme, Rosemary and Lavender, are natives of southern Europe and will not survive heavy clay soils or water-logged conditions. Many moisture-loving plants, such as Lemon Balm, Mint and Valerian, will grow happily in a light soil, though not in conditions of total drought. A sunny, sheltered position protected from strong biting winds will suit all the plants, though some, such as the more tender Lemon Verbena and Bay, will need protecting in bad winters.

DESIGN

A formal layout of small beds dissected by paths provides a satisfying framework for the lax, untidy growth of many herbs. It also makes sure that you can easily tend and pick when necessary. A single species to each bed can look highly effective, evoking the magical, atmospheric style of medieval herb gardens. In contrast, an informal cottage garden provides plenty of scope for imaginative, exuberant planting with herbs cleverly mixed in with flowers. Raised beds or a lively collection of attractive containers make easy-to-control, self-contained areas.

▲ *A perfect example of a well-tended herb garden, with symmetrical beds and wide paths for easy access. The plants thrive in this warm, sheltered corner of the garden.*

EXPERIENCING HERBS

Identifying, growing and harvesting herbs can be a marvellous, healing experience itself. Handling herbs brings you closer to nature and increases your appreciation of the vitality of plants.

GROWING

The quickest way to acquire herbs that will help you stay healthy is to grow them yourself. You can easily grow most from seed. This means that you will be sure what they are, and that they will have been grown safely and organically, without the use of any chemical sprays. Most of the herbs used in the remedies on the following pages will grow extremely well in temperate climates. In fact many are often regarded as weeds, and actually thrive on patches of spare ground despite getting no care and attention whatsoever.

▲ *Many of the culinary herbs we use today were distributed throughout Europe by the Roman army.*

GATHERING

The aerial parts of herbs (the flowers, stems and leaves) should be gathered for use or for drying when the plants are in bud and totally dry. That means early morning when the sun has dried the dew. Roots should be dug in the autumn, cleaned and roughly chopped into very small pieces.

If you harvest from the wild, make quite sure that you have identified the plant correctly (use a good wild flower book) and that it has not been polluted by fertilizers, pesticides or car fumes. Never pick so much that you reduce next year's growth.

DRYING

Spread out your herbs on a rack to dry naturally in an airy position, out of direct sunlight. Alternatively, tie them in loose bundles and hang them from a beam, or dry them in an oven at a very low heat.

STORING

Always make sure that you store dried herbs in airtight containers, kept well away from the light, and do not forget to label and date them. They will keep for up to six months, but the sooner they are used the better and fresher the flavor. (When they are kept for too long they look dull and taste of sawdust.) If you are in any way worried about over-drying your herbs, try storing them in a freezer instead. This is a particularly good technique for herbs such as Lemon Balm and Parsley, which quickly lose their flavour when they are dried.

BUYING

Many shops stock dried herbs. Buy these only if they seem fresh – they should be brightly coloured and strongly aromatic.

Some herbal remedies are now readily available over the counter in the form of capsules, tablets or tinctures. These are usually of good quality. Choose the simpler ones that tell you exactly the type and quantity of herb involved.

▼ *Lime Blossom is abundant for easy picking in both the countryside and urban areas during early summer.*

HERBAL PREPARATIONS

Herbs are multi-talented. They can be used in the kitchen, fresh or dried, and to tackle a wide range of ailments from hyperactivity to insomnia. They even provide a refreshing tonic when you are feeling down-and-out. In fact, you can take herbal remedies internally as teas, decoctions and tinctures, or applied externally as soothing, relaxing oils and conditioners. Best of all, they guarantee gorgeous perfumes.

MAKING TEAS

Herbal teas are also called infusions or tisanes. They are a simple and delicious way of extracting the goodness and flavour from the aerial parts of herbs. You can use either fresh or dried herbs to make such teas; note you need to use twice as much fresh plant material as dried. If you find the taste of some herb teas rather bitter, then try sweetening them with a little honey. Alternatively, try adding extra flavour by stirring the tea with a Licorice stick, or adding ginger.

1 Put your herb(s) into a pot. Standard-strength tea is made with 1 tsp dried or 2 tsp fresh herbs to 1 cup of water.

2 Strain and drink as required. Teas can be drunk cold as well as hot. Cold teas are thoroughly invigorating.

MAKING DECOCTIONS

Infusing in boiling water is not enough to extract the constituents from roots or bark. This much tougher, harder, inflexible plant material needs to be broken up into far smaller pieces by chopping or crushing with a sharp knife.

Next, place every tiny scrap of this rough-cut material into a stainless steel, glass or enamelled pan, but absolutely not aluminium. Fill up with cold water, and gradually bring to the boil. Finally cover and simmer for about 15 minutes. The resulting liquid is what is called a decoction. Strain it and flavour, if necessary, and drink while it is still warm.

1 Harvest root and bark in the colder months. Trim the aerial parts of the plant away from the root.

2 Wash the roots thoroughly in cold water, ensuring they are perfectly clean, then chop into small pieces.

NERVINE DECOCTIONS

- Cramp Bark
- Licorice
- Valerian

Avoid using Licorice if you suffer from high blood pressure.

3 Fill a pan with cold water and add 1 tsp of the chopped herb per cup. Boil and simmer for 10–15 minutes.

4 Strain and cool before drinking. Decoctions can be kept for 24 hours in the fridge. Drink reheated or cold.

MAKING TINCTURES

Sometimes it is more convenient to take a spoonful of medicine than make a tea or decoction. Tinctures are made by steeping herbs in a mixture of alcohol and water. The alcohol extracts the medicinal constituents, and it also acts as an excellent preservative.

Herb syrups make good remedies for giving to children. They also improve the taste of herbs that might be bitter, such as Motherwort and Vervain.

MAKING SYRUPS

1 Place 500g/1¼lb sugar/honey in a pan; add 1 litre/1¾ pints/4 cups water.
2 Heat gently, stirring to dissolve,
3 Add 150g/5oz plant material and heat gently for 5 minutes.
4 Turn off the heat; steep overnight.
5 Strain and store in an airtight container for future use. Since the sugar acts as a preservative, a herb syrup will keep for 18 months.

1 Place 100 g/3½ oz dried herbs or 300g/11 oz fresh herbs in a jar.

2 Add 250ml/8fl oz/1 cup vodka and 250ml/8fl oz/1 cup water.

3 Leave the herbs to steep in the liquid for a month, preferably on a sunny windowsill. Gently shake the jar daily.

4 Strain and store the tincture in a dark glass bottle where it will keep well for approximately 18 months.

COLD INFUSED OILS

Herbal oils are suitable for external use when having a massage, or as bath oils or hair and skin conditioners. Cold infused oils are quite simple to prepare. Macerate freshly cut herbs in vegetable oil for up to two weeks, but no more. Give the jar a daily shake. Finally drain off the oil, and squeeze the excess liquid out of the herbs. You will find that chamomile invariably gives excellent results.

HERB OIL INFUSIONS

- Chamomile
- Lavender
- Marjoram
- Rosemary
- St John's Wort

Do not put St John's Wort oil on the skin before going into bright sunshine for fear of an adverse reaction.

1 Fill a glass storage jar with the flowers or leaves of your chosen dried herb.

2 Pour in a vegetable oil to cover the herbs; try sunflower or grape seed oil.

3 Stand the jar for two weeks on a windowsill to steep. Shake daily.

4 Strain. For a stronger infusion, renew the herbs in the oil every two weeks.

herbal recipes

herbal recipes

herbal recipes

In today's high-tech, high-speed world it is virtually impossible not to encounter stress, and stress at even alarmingly high levels. It can strike going to work when you get stuck in a gridlock traffic jam, at work with faxes, e-mails and meetings, and when you get back home and suddenly have to cope with meals and children. In fact, many people find that getting quality, quiet time for themselves is becoming increasingly difficult, if not impossible. But while you cannot always avoid stress, there are plenty of things you can do to help yourself cope better when life suddenly presents a barrage of testing, difficult challenges.

A good, healthy diet really does make a significant difference. It is therefore absolutely essential that you eat proper, healthy meals packed with vitamin-rich fruit and vegetables, and totally avoid artificial additives. If you miss these extra flavours, you will find that you get a far greater range using fresh or dried herbs, and of course they offer plenty of extra goodness.

Also, try as hard as you can to reduce your intake of such stimulants as tea, coffee, alcohol and cola. Instead, drink plenty of water and invigorating herbal teas. All kinds of flavours are becoming increasingly available. You simply choose what you like, and that can include Anise, Chamomile, Lemon Verbena, Lime Blossom, Mint, and Sage. They are all incredibly refreshing. Even better, you can grow these herbs in pots or in the garden, where you know they have been organically raised.

Exercise is equally important for all kinds of reasons. It dispels excess adrenaline and improves relaxation and sleep. Swimming prevents your joints from becoming stiff and gives the body a marvellous feeling of freedom. Exercise also tones up your muscles, keeps you in shape, and helps shed excess weight. In short, it keeps you feeling alert, well and able.

One of the biggest problems of stress is that it can all too easily disrupt your appetite and your ability to rest. In turn, such disruption makes you even less able to cope with any setbacks and problems. You get pulled into a depressing, downward spiral. One of the best ways to break out of this pattern is to use herbal remedies to improve your digestion, to help you relax, and to improve your adaptability.

The recipes that follow are designed to help you through difficult times. As long as you do not exceed the doses stated, and are sure that you are using the right plant, it is safe to experiment with these suggestions. But do seek professional help if a problem persists.

KEY STRESS SYMPTOMS

While some degree of stress is an inevitable part of modern life, there are fortunately several significant ways of tackling it. They should help make sure that your day is not ruined by a tense neck or a nervous stomach. In fact some ways, such as using using excellent massage oils, are so incredibly relaxing, refreshing and enjoyable that they could well become part of your daily routine.

CALMING ANXIETY

Everyone knows exactly what it feels like to be excited, but inappropriate or excessive excitement, often combined with frustration, creates anxiety. In this state, the body produces too much adrenaline. It is primed for "fight or flight" but neither is possible. The heart races, muscles tense and the chest expands. Anxiety can cause many symptoms, including palpitations, sweating, irritability and sleeplessness. In these situations, Rescue Remedy, which is bought ready-made, is useful.

▶ *Two drops of Rescue Remedy on the tongue can help prevent a panic attack, and give you ease of mind.*

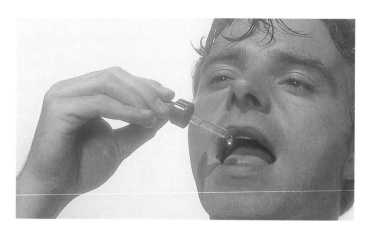

RELAXING TENSE MUSCLES

Muscles can tense as a result of anxiety which often causes slightly raised shoulders or contracted back muscles. The effort of maintaining your muscles in this semi-contracted state is tiring, possibly causing spasms and bad postural habits. The neck stiffens and the back may ache. Tight neck muscles can also hinder blood flowing to the head, creating tension headaches. Moving frequently will release the muscles. Rotate your head or stand and stretch, and take breaks from working or driving. Gently massaging the neck with oil can help.

◀ *Tension can build up in the neck and shoulders, causing stiffness.*

COLD INFUSED OIL OF LAVENDER

Fill a glass jar with lavender heads and cover with clear vegetable oil. Allow to steep on a windowsill, shaking the jar every day. Strain and bottle.

The oil can be used for massaging into a stiff neck or back. It can also be added to the bath to keep your skin soft and perfumed, while also encouraging relaxation.

Lavender is an extremely talented herb. It has traditionally been used as a sedative helping combat anxiety and tension. A few drops of infused oil added to your favourite massage oil will also help relax your over-tense muscles. Similar oils can be made from Marjoram (which is anti-spasmodic) and Rosemary.

HERBAL REMEDIES

To help your nervous system readjust and adapt, consider the value of:

- Skullcap
- St John's Wort
- Vervain
- Wild Oats
- Wood Betony

Choose whichever one suits you best and combine it with a specific remedy for the symptom that is causing you most problems.

- To ease palpitations: Motherwort or Passion Flower.
- To reduce sweating: Motherwort or Valerian.
- To help you sleep: Passion Flower.

▲ *Chamomile tea makes an ideal after-dinner drink.*

DIGESTIVES

Many people suffer from digestive upsets when they are stressed. This is because the "fight or flight" activity of the sympathetic nervous system tends to suppress digestive processes. The result may be indigestion, loss of appetite, wind, diarrhoea or even an irritable bowel.

The three recipes below have all been specially designed to help relax the nervous system, encouraging parasympathetic activity and reducing any signs of spasm in the gut.

To Calm Butterflies

Nervous stomachs can be quickly settled by Chamomile, Hops and Lemon Balm combined in a tea, or simply select the best combination for you. Lemon Balm and Chamomile can be taken as frequently as you like.

Put 1 tsp each Lemon Balm, dried Chamomile flowers and Peppermint into a small tea pot or cafetière. Fill with boiling water and allow to steep for at least 10 minutes. Strain and drink at least three times a day or after meals.

HERBAL REMEDIES

- Chamomile
- Cramp Bark
- Cumin
- Fennel, Caraway, Dill
- Hops
- Lemon Balm
- Licorice
- Peppermint

To Relieve Wind and Colic

In a small saucepan, boil 1 tsp each Fennel seeds and Cramp Bark with about 300ml/½ pint/1¼ cups water. Add 1 tsp dried Peppermint. Allow to steep for 10 minutes. Strain and drink.

To Ease Constipation

Make a decoction of Cramp Bark and Fennel as above, but add 1 tsp Licorice root. If the constipation is proving to be an unpleasant, recurrent condition, 1 tsp Linseeds added daily to your breakfast cereal can be very helpful.

The same amount can also be soaked in hot water for about two hours, and drunk before going to bed and again, if necessary, early the next morning when you wake. If the problem is not eased or solved then it is important that you consult your doctor at the first opportunity. Generally, the best way to avoid an attack of constipation is to make sure that you are regularly having a balanced, healthy diet which includes plenty of fresh fruit, vegetables and roughage on a daily basis.

CONTRAINDICATIONS

Some herbs should only be used at certain times and not if you are suffering certain other symptoms. For example, since Hops are a sedative, they should only be taken at night, and are not suitable if you are depressed or lacking in sexual energy. Likewise, Licorice should be avoided if you have high blood pressure or oedema. Always consult a medical doctor if in any doubt.

REVITALIZING RECIPES

You do not have to be so ill that you are completely confined to bed to take some of the excellent revitalizing herbal remedies now available. Many are purpose designed as a refreshing pick-me-up or tonic to get you through testing emotional and physical times – the bad, dark days – when the mind and body might otherwise become tired and sluggish. Such recipes are nature's way of keeping you healthy.

NERVOUS EXHAUSTION

It is much more likely that you will get ill or depressed after or during a long period of hard work, or from a whole battery of emotional demands. This can easily happen to teachers, for example, at the end of term, or to those who have to care for disabled or sick relations on a long-term basis. You will find that herbal remedies help to give your nervous system plenty of vital support at such testing, difficult times. To make a revitalizing tea, mix equal portions of all the dried herbs listed. Put 3–4 tsp of the mixture into a pot with a lid. Add 600ml/1 pint/2½ cups boiling water. Steep for 10 minutes, strain, and drink 3–4 cups a day.

▲ *Make a relaxing herbal tea from a blend of supportive herbs whenever you are feeling exhausted and too tired to cope.*

HERBAL REMEDIES

- Borage
- Licorice
- Skullcap
- St John's Wort
- Wild Oats
- Wood Betony

Borage, like Licorice, restores the adrenal glands.

TONICS FOR CONVALESCENCE

Remember that even if your symptoms have gone, your body needs time to recover after an illness. A tonic is extremely useful. Wild Oats and St John's Wort support the nervous system, Vervain promotes relaxation and digestion, and Licorice restores the adrenal glands. Vitamin C supplements should be continued for several weeks after an illness. Alfalfa sprouts are also high in vitamins and minerals. Also note that rest is very important.

TONIC TEA

Put ½ tsp of each of one of the dried herbs listed below into a small pot. Add boiling water. Flavour with Peppermint to taste. (Avoid Licorice if you suffer from high blood pressure or oedema.) Allow to steep for 10 minutes. Strain. Drink three or four cups, warm, each day for at least three weeks.

HERBAL REMEDIES

- Borage
- Licorice
- St John's Wort
- Vervain
- Wild Oats

▲ *St John's Wort thrives in a bright, open sunny position.*

RELIEVING WINTER BLUES

The old herbalists thought that the appearance of a plant held a clue to its healing action. For instance, Pilewort (Lesser Celandine) has roots that resemble haemorrhoids, and it does indeed make an effective ointment for piles. The flowers of St John's Wort resemble nothing so much as the sun. The plant thrives in sunlight and is known to have anti-depressant effects. There is no better herb than this to take if you are depressed in the winter, when sunlight is in short supply.

Wild Oats also help by strengthening the nervous system and keeping you warm. Rosemary, an evergreen plant, will improve circulation to the head and keep the mind clear. Also, Ginseng capsules can be taken for a month in the early autumn to help you adapt to the difficult transition between seasons.

WINTER BRIGHTENER

Combine 2 tsp dried St John's Wort with 1 tsp dried Rosemary. Add 250ml/8fl oz/1 cup boiling water. Allow to steep for 10 minutes and then strain. One cup alone is not enough. Drink three times a day throughout the winter.

HERBAL REMEDIES

- Ginseng
- Rosemary
- St John's Wort
- Wild Oats

LIFTING DEPRESSION

Depression is a very good illustration of the close connection that exists between the body and mind: physical and emotional energy are both depleted when you are in a depressed state. Both will benefit from a healthy diet that includes plenty of raw, vital foods, nuts, seeds and B vitamins. A multi-vitamin and mineral supplement is an effective kick-start that will give you an excellent lift. But do not undermine its effect by indulging in stimulants, such as caffeine, because they tend to exhaust both the body and mind.

The refreshing, restorative tea described below is a marvellous, tasty way of restoring the health of your nervous system. It has a slight, barely noticeable, stimulating effect.

RESTORATIVE TEA

Mix equal parts of each of the dried herbs listed in the box below. Put 2 tsp of the mixture into a pot. Add 600ml/1 pint/2½ cups boiling water. Allow to steep for 10 minutes and then strain. Drink one cup of this excellent tea three times a day.

HERBAL REMEDIES

- Damiana
- St John's Wort
- Wild Oats

▲ *There are many tasty ways of incorporating the goodness of Oats in your diet, including home-made snacks such as biscuits.*

HEADACHE AND NIGHT-TIME REMEDIES

From time to time everyone suffers from headaches and bad sleepless nights. Occasional attacks are just about bearable, but when they become a regular feature and interrupt your life, especially your sex life, it is clearly time to act. All these herbal solutions, ranging from baths and teas to massages, have one aim: to give you back your healthy life as quickly as possible.

RELIEVING TENSION HEADACHES

Headaches are a common symptom of stress. Often they are caused by tension in the neck and upper back muscles. This can prevent adequate blood supply to the head and thus lead to pain. Both massage and exercise can ease this kind of headache.

SCENTED BATHS

Pour a few drops of essential oil or infused oil into a hot bath, lie back and relax. Better, tie a bunch of herbs under the hot tap as you fill the bath. Rub two drops of essential oil of Lavender mixed with 1 tsp water on the head when stressed.

SOOTHING TEA

Put 1 tsp dried Wood Betony and ½ tsp dried Lavender or Rosemary into a cup. Top up with boiling water and leave for 10 minutes, before straining and drinking. Repeat hourly.

> ### HERBAL REMEDIES
> - Lavender
> - Rosemary

▲ *Hang a muslin bag of fresh or dried herbs under the hot tap.*

▲ *Help yourself beat a hangover by taking a herbal remedy.*

HANGOVER REMEDIES

Most people know what a hangover feels like – a combination of headache, nausea, fuzzy head and depression. Most of these symptoms are connected with the liver being overloaded. Bitter herbs stimulate the liver and speed up its ability to detoxify. Vervain is bitter and Lavender aids digestion; both herbs also lift the spirits. If you have a hangover it is also advisable to drink plenty of water and take extra vitamin C.

MORNING-AFTER TEA

Put 1 tsp dried Vervain and ½ tsp Lavender flowers into a pot. Add 600ml/1 pint/2½ cups boiling water and cover to keep in the volatile oils. Steep for 10 minutes. Strain and sweeten with a little honey. Sip through the day until you start to feel better.

> ### HERBAL REMEDIES
> - Lavender
> - Vervain

REVITALIZING THE LIBIDO

Depression or anxiety can all too easily hinder and interrupt your sex life. This may be because your energy is too low, or it may in fact be connected with a hormone imbalance. Damiana stimulates both the nervous and hormonal systems, and it has vital constituents which convert to hormones in the body. Vervain is good at releasing tension and stress, and it was traditionally used as an aphrodisiac. Wild Oats and Ginger root are both considered stimulating too.

ENERGIZING TEA

Put 1 tsp dried Damiana and 1 tsp dried Vervain into a pot. Add 600ml/1 pint/2½ cups of boiling water. Leave to steep for 10 minutes. Strain and flavour with Licorice, Ginger or honey, as you prefer. Drink two cups a day.

HERBAL REMEDIES
- Damiana
- Ginger
- Vervain
- Wild Oats

▲ *Teas or decoctions made with the right herbs can help restore energy of all kinds, including sexual energy.*

ENHANCING SLEEP

There are many different types of insomnia, and the causes are varied. If you really cannot sleep then it is best to experiment with the remedies below to find the one herb or combination of herbs that suits you best. If the problem is long term and you have not been sleeping well for a period of time, then take a nervous system tonic to improve your well being.

In the evenings, drink teas that have been made from relaxing herbs. Lavender oil in a hot bath before bed and on the pillow will also help. You could even try using a Hop pillow. Furthermore, it is important to give yourself plenty of time at the end of the day to relax and wind down. Exercise, meditation and yoga are all good at helping you fall asleep.

▲ *You can make or buy a herb pillow to encourage sound sleep.*

SLEEPY TEA

Put 1 tsp each dried Chamomile, Vervain and Lemon Balm into a pot. Add about 600ml/1 pint/2½ cups boiling water. Leave to steep for 10 minutes. Strain and drink one cup after supper. Warm the rest and drink before going to bed.

If you continue to have problems sleeping, add a decoction of 1 tsp Valerian root or ½ tsp dried Hops or Californian Poppy to this blend of herbs.

HERBAL REMEDIES
- Californian Poppy
- Chamomile
- Hops
- Lemon Balm
- Passion Flower
- Valerian
- Vervain

▲ *Chamomile tea is not only beneficial but extremely refreshing.*

GUIDE TO HERBS AND THEIR USES

It has long been known that herbs are an essential part of the kitchen, adding all kinds of flavours, and for helping to relieve and cure a range of problems from migraines to wind (gas). The early physic gardens in monasteries were really basic pharmacies stocking many of these essential plants. Do not try and compete. Just grow those herbs that you know will help you feel much better.

USING HERBS

The herbs described on the following pages are a particularly useful group for helping tackle stress and various other common conditions. Reading the notes and studying the pictures will help you decide which would be most beneficial for you and your garden. After all, they should also help make a special relaxing feature. If planting them in groups, remember to put the tallest in the centre and the smaller ones around.

You may well want to try several as remedies before deciding which you find most helpful. Note that herbs do not usually work instantly, so do not be impatient and give them at least two weeks to take effect. If you do not feel better in three weeks, seek the help of a qualified practitioner. Herbs can also be used in various combinations, and you will find suggestions for putting them together to give additional benefits.

Since most of us would benefit from a nerve tonic during stressful times, choose the herbal remedy best suited to you.

For example, if when stressed you start to feel depressed, then look for a stimulating herbal tonic such as Wild Oats. If, however, stress makes you feel anxious and you start developing symptoms such as palpitations, sweating and sleeplessness, then turn to those herbs that have a relaxing effect.

Rescue Remedy, because it is not strictly herbal, but a Bach Flower remedy is not included in this directory, but it is readily available over the counter.

It is quite clear that some herbs are multi-talented. Borage gives a marvellous show of flowers and adds to the cottage garden, attracting plenty of bees. The leaves add a cucumber flavour to drinks, the flowers can garnish salads, and the oil lowers blood pressure. Lavender is another all-purpose herb, essential for pot-pourris and for a range of soothing treatments. If you find some plants do not succeed in certain parts of the garden, move them around until you find a more suitables place and you may well find that they perk up.

LADY'S MANTLE
Alchemilla xanthochlora syn.
A. vulgaris, Virgin's Cape

The unusual leaves of this plant resemble a cloak, hence its common names. The name Alchemilla derives from the Arabic word for alchemy, signifying its power to help make a change. A larger species, Alchemilla mollis, is grown as a foliage plant. Lady's Mantle is a women's herb and helps balance menstrual cycles. As a douche or wash, an infusion helps sooth any itching or inflammation.

n o t e s • Parts used: Leaves and flowers.
• Dose: I tsp dried/2 tsp fresh to a cup of boiling water three times a day.

PASQUE FLOWER
Anemone pulsatilla, Wind Flower

One of the most beautiful medicinal herbs with purple spring flowers. The common name comes from *Pasch* meaning Easter. Pasque Flower is a sedative, bactericidal, anti-spasmodic painkiller used to treat the reproductive organs. It is used against all types of pain affecting male and female genital organs.

n o t e s • Parts used: Dried leaves and flowers.
• Dose: A very low dose is needed – it is advisable to consult a herbalist.
c a u t i o n : Do not use the fresh plant.

MUGWORT
Artemisia vulgaris

The "mother of herbs" grows robustly along roadsides and is said to protect the traveller. It is best described as a tonic with particular application to the digestive and nervous systems; it reduces nervous indigestion, nausea and irritability. As a womb tonic it helps regulate the menstrual cycle, reduces any associated period pain and PMS. It is also used to repel insects, including moths.

n o t e s • Parts used: Flowers and leaves.
• Dose: ¼–½ tsp three times a day.
c a u t i o n : Avoid in pregnancy.

WILD OATS
Avena sativa

Oats are an excellent tonic to the nervous system. They slightly stimulate and are a long-term remedy for nervous exhaustion. They also help cope with shingles and herpes. Oats contain vitamin E, iron, zinc, manganese and protein and help reduce cholesterol.

n o t e s • Parts used: Seeds and stalks.
• Dose: There are many ways to take oats – in gruel, porridge, flapjacks, oatcakes and other dishes, as well as tea.
c a u t i o n : Oats are not suitable for those who are sensitive to gluten.

BORAGE
Borago officinalis

A strapping plant with lovely, luminous blue flowers. They make an attractive garnish to ice cream and cold summer puddings. Borage boosts the production of adrenaline and is useful in times of stress. It is also very nutritious, and helps to treat skin diseases and rheumatism.

n o t e s • Parts used: The leaves, flowers and seeds. The leaves need to be dried quite quickly and are best heated very gently in a cool oven until they are crisp.
• Dose: 1 tsp dried/2 tsp fresh to one cup of boiling water.

CALIFORNIAN POPPY
Eschscholzia californica

The beautiful, delicate flowers last for one day and are then replaced by long pointed seed pods. The stunning hot orange, yellow and pinkish colours of the blooms might account for its French name, *globe de soleil*. Californian Poppy is a gentle painkiller and sedative which reduces spasms and over-excitability.

n o t e s • Parts used: The whole plant
• Dose: 1 tsp dried herb to a cup of boiling water.
c a u t i o n: It is important to avoid this herb if you suffer from glaucoma.

CHAMOMILE
Chamomilla recutita or
Chamaemelum nobile

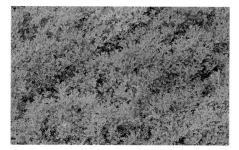

This pretty daisy is one of the better known herbs, possibly because it is so useful. Use the flowerheads alone in a tea or tincture to relax both the digestive function and those gut feelings that may sometimes disturb you. It makes a very suitable tea to drink late in the day because it has quite the opposite effect to that of coffee, which actually exacerbates tension and anxiety.

n o t e s • Parts used: Flower heads.
• Dose: 1 tsp dried/2 tsp fresh to a cup of boiling water.

LICORICE
Glycyrrhiza glabra

A highly useful herb which has been cultivated since the Middle Ages for its sweet, aromatic roots. It aids digestion and reduces inflammation along the gut, loosening the bowels. Licorice heated in honey makes a soothing syrup, helping to soothe attacks of bronchitis and asthma.

n o t e s • Parts used: The root (Licorice sticks) or solidified juice in the form of black bars.
• Dose: 1 tsp to a cup of boiling water.
c a u t i o n: Not recommended for those with high blood pressure or oedema.

HOP
Humulus lupulus

The name Hop comes from the Anglo-Saxon *hoppen*, "to climb": the twining fibrous stems may top 4.5m/15ft. Hops are taken as a bitter tonic helping both to improve digestion and to reduce any restlessness. It also has a sedative effect and will provoke deep sleep. The action is partly due to its volatile oils.

n o t e s • Parts used: Dried flowers from the female plant, called "strobiles".
• Dose: Not more than 1 tsp a day.
c a u t i o n: Avoid the use of Hops during any depressive illness.

ST JOHN'S WORT
Hypericum perforatum

Celebrated for some time for its anti-depressant action, it has now been discovered that St John's Wort can interact adversely with a long list of prescription medicines. It should never be taken internally without first consulting a qualified medical practitioner.

n o t e s • Parts used: Flowering tops.
• Dose: 1 tsp dried/2 tsp fresh to a cup of boiling water, three times a day.
c a u t i o n: Never take this herb while on any kind of medication. Always consult a doctor before taking internally.

GINSENG
Korean Ginseng, Panax spp.

By improving the production of adrenal hormones, Korean Ginseng helps the body to adapt to stress and resist disease. It should only be taken for short periods though. It benefits ME sufferers.

n o t e s • Parts used: Dried root.
• Dose: 1g per day.
c a u t i o n : Avoid the use of Ginseng during pregnancy or when taking other stimulants. Do not take high doses for more than six weeks without seeking expert advice. Stop taking Ginseng if it makes you feel agitated or if you develop a headache.

LAVENDER
Lavandula spp.

Everybody knows this fragrant plant. Herbalists call it a thymoleptic, which means it raises the spirits. This, combined with its anti-infective action and relaxing properties, makes Lavender a powerful remedy. The essential oil is used externally for relaxation and to heal sores and burns. Lavender can also be taken internally in a tea or tincture. It is also an ideal remedy for irritation, indigestion and for the onset of a migraine attack.

n o t e s • Parts used: Dried root.
• Dose: 1g per day.

MOTHERWORT
Leonurus cardiaca

The Latin name refers to the leaves shaped like a lion's tail. It is a great calmer if tension is causing palpitations or sweats. It improves the circulatory system and is also used to relieve any menstrual and menopausal problems. Motherwort can also help to lower blood pressure.

n o t e s • Parts used: Leaves and flowers.
• Dose: 1 tsp dried/2 tsp fresh to a cup of boiling water three times a day, or 2 tsp syrup.
c a u t i o n : It is important that it is avoided in the first trimester of pregnancy.

LEMON BALM
Melissa officinalis, Bee Balm

This plant has so much vitality that it can spread all over the garden. It makes a suitable drink for every day; hot in winter and iced in summer. Lemon Balm aids digestion and relaxation, and sensitive digestive systems. It is much used for irritable bowels, nervous indigestion, anxiety and depression. It makes a good bedtime drink, promoting peaceful sleep and a sense of relaxation.

n o t e s • Parts used: Leaves and flowers.
• Dose: 1 tsp to a cup of boiling water, taken up to three or four times a day.

MINT
Mentha spp.

Peppermint (Mentha piperita) is a hybrid between Spearmint and Watermint. It is antiseptic and anti-parasitic, and will reduce itching. It has a temporary anaesthetic effect on the skin and gives the impression of cooling. It is included in lotions for massaging aching muscles, and makes an effective footbath.

n o t e s • Parts used: Leaves and flowers.
• Dose: 1 tsp dried/2 tsp fresh to a cup of boiling water.
c a u t i o n : It is important that it is avoided in the first trimester of pregnancy.

EVENING PRIMROSE
Oenothera biennis

A beautiful plant, luminous in the twilight, which freely self-seeds in the garden. It is used externally for eczema and other dry skin conditions. Taken internally, Evening Primrose oil reduces cholesterol levels and benefits the circulation. It has a decent success rate on women with PMS, and can help calm hyperactive children. It also helps regenerate livers which have been damaged by alcohol.

n o t e s • Parts used: Oil from seeds.
• Dose: Capsules as directed.
c a u t i o n : Avoid in cases of epilepsy.

MARJORAM
Origanum vulgare

There are many species of Marjoram, and they are used in potpourris and cooking. Medicinally, Marjoram reduces depression and helps tackle nervous headaches. It contains volatile oils which are antispasmodic, making it useful when soothing digestive upsets. The infused oil can be used in the bath to relieve stiffness, or rubbed on to soothe sore and aching joints or muscles.

n o t e s • Parts used: Leaves.
• Dose: 1 tsp dried/2 tsp fresh to a cup of boiling water, taken twice a day.

PASSION FLOWER
Passiflora incarnata, Maypop

This is a climbing plant which produces spectacular flowers. It is often included in sleeping mixes, and is very helpful when tackling restlessness and insomnia. It counteracts the effects of adrenaline, which may cause anxiety, palpitations or nervous tremors. It is used to ease the pain of neuralgia.

n o t e s • Parts used: Dried leaves and flowers.
• Dose: ¼-½ tsp dried herb twice a day, or 1 tsp at night, or take an over-the-counter preparation as directed.

ROSEMARY
Rosmarinus officinalis

A familiar plant containing several active, aromatic oils. Like Lavender, it can be used both externally, in the form of an essential or infused oil, and internally as a flavouring, tea or tincture. The actions of Rosemary are centred on the head and womb. It increases the supply of blood to both. In the head it helps tackle cold headaches and in the gut eases spasms due to poor circulation.

n o t e s • Parts used: Leaves and flowers.
• Dose: 1 tsp to a cup of boiling water taken up to three times a day.

SAGE
Salvia officinalis

A beautiful, evergreen plant with fine purple flowers in early summer. Like many culinary herbs, it aids digestion. It has antiseptic properties and can be used as a compress on wounds that are slow to heal, or as a gargle or for infections of the mouth or throat. It is also said that it will help reduce night sweats and menopausal hot flushes, and can darken greyish hair.

n o t e s • Parts used: Leaves.
• Dose: 1 tsp dried per cup of boiling water.
c a u t i o n : Avoid during pregnancy.

SKULLCAP
Scutellaria lateriflora

This herb is another nervous tonic. It was traditionally associated with the head, because it produces skull-like seed pods. It is very calming. Skullcap can help reduce anxiety and restlessness. Its bitter taste encourages the liver to remove toxins from the body, as well as excess hormones which can cause degrees of premenstrual tension.

n o t e s • Parts used: Aerial parts, which are harvested after flowering.
• Dose: 1 tsp dried/2 tsp fresh to a cup of boiling water.

WOOD BETONY
Stachys betonica syn. S. officinalis, Betonica officinalis, Bishop's Weed

An attractive plant with purple flowers. Wood Betony aids the nervous system, especially if sick headaches and poor memory are a problem. It also encourages blood flow to the head. Always a popular remedy throughout Europe, it is certainly well worth trying if you get headaches or migraines.

n o t e s • Parts used: Aerial parts.
• Dose: 1 tsp dried/2 tsp fresh herb to a cup of boiling water.
c a u t i o n : It is important that you avoid high doses during pregnancy.

LIME BLOSSOM
Tilia x europaea, Linden Blossom

The tall upstanding Lime tree has honey-scented blossom. Medicinally it is relaxing and cleansing. It makes a helpful tea for fevers and flu, especially if combined with Yarrow and Peppermint. It encourages sweating and aids the body through fevers. It is also used to reduce hardening of the arteries and high blood pressure, and to relieve migraines.

n o t e s • Parts used: Flowers, including the pale yellowish bracts.
• Dose: 1 tsp dried/2 tsp fresh to a cup of boiling water taken three times a day.

DAMIANA
Turnera diffusa

Damiana grows in South America and the West Indies. It was previously called Turnera aphrodisiaca and is a tonic to the nervous and reproductive systems. It is useful if the sexual function is impaired. It is taken as a remedy by men, but the stimulant and tonic work equally well for women. Damiana is harvested when in flower, and is dried for use as an anti-depressant, and to relieve anxiety.

n o t e s • Parts used: Leaves and stem.
• Dose: 2 tsp to a cup of boiling water, which can be taken twice a day.

VALERIAN
Valeriana officinalis, All Heal

This is a tall herb with whitish-pink flowers which grows in damp places. The root has a powerful sedative effect on the nervous system, and effectively reduces tension. It can be used to reduce period pains, spasms, palpitations, and hyperactivity. It is good if anxiety makes sleep difficult.

n o t e s • Parts used: Dried root.
• Dose: 1 tsp to a cup of boiling water at bedtime.
c a u t i o n : High doses taken over a long period may cause headaches.

CRAMP BARK
Viburnum opulus, Guelder Rose

A decorative wild bush which produces glorious white and pale pink spring flowers, followed by autumn red berries. Writer Geoffrey Grigson said it had a smell like crisply fried, well-peppered trout. Therapeutically, the use of Cramp Bark is a good illustration of the connection between body and mind. It reduces spasms whatever the cause and helps tackle constipation, period pains, and high blood pressure.

n o t e s • Parts used: Dried bark.
• Dose: 1 tsp to a cup of boiling water.

CHASTE TREE
Vitex agnus-castus, Monk's Pepper

The common name reflects a slight anti-oestrogen effect which can cool passion: perhaps this property may account for its other common name, Monk's Pepper. Small doses of this herb can re-balance the hormones and reduce some of the symptoms of PMS, menopausal change, infertility, post-natal depression and irregular periods. It also increases milk production after birth.

n o t e s • Parts used: Dried ripe fruits.
• Dose: 10–20 drops of tincture which are taken first thing in the morning.

VERVAIN
Verbena officinalis, Herb of Grace

An unassuming plant with tiny flowers. Vervain is a nervous tonic with a slightly sedative action. It is useful for treating nervous exhaustion and symptoms of tension which include headaches, nausea and migraine. It has a bitter taste and has been used for gall bladder problems. It is quite often recommended for anyone who has depression, and works well with Wild Oats.

n o t e s • Parts used: Leaves and flowers.
• Dose: 1 tsp dried/2 tsp fresh to a cup of boiling water.

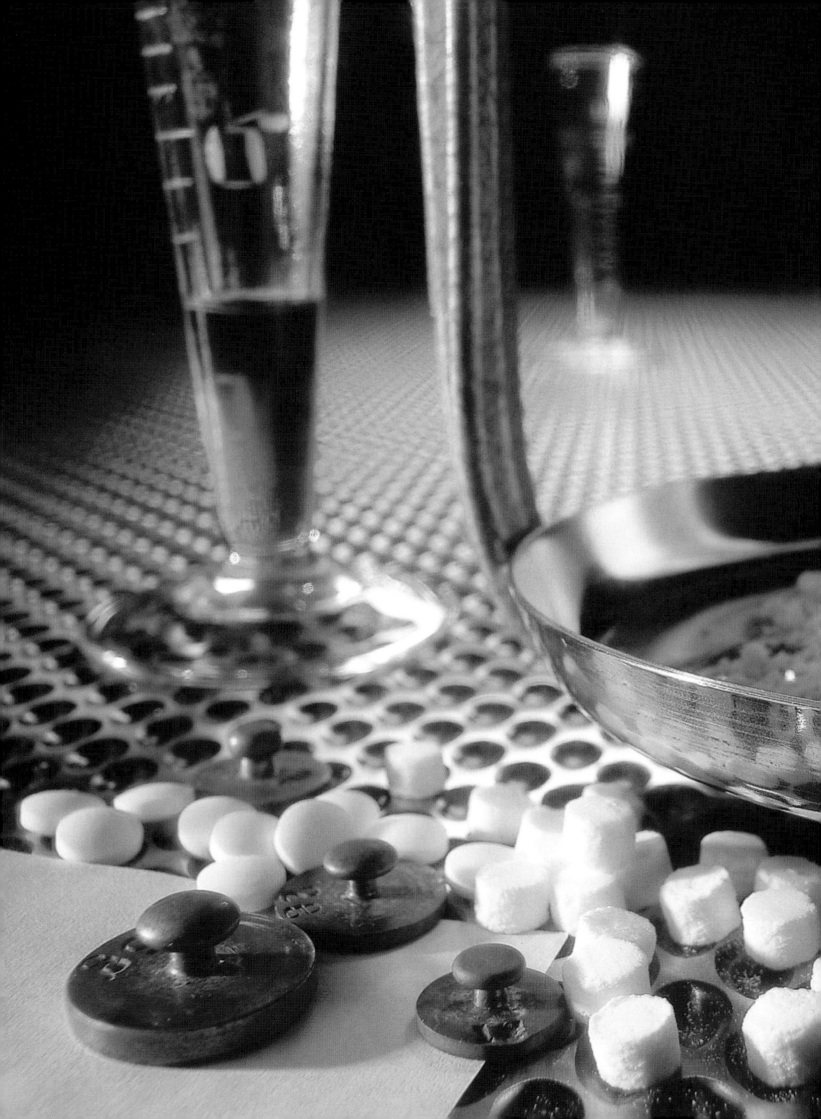

HOMEOPATHY

The name "homeopathy" was coined by Samuel Hahnemann from two Greek words meaning "similar suffering", or "like cures like". Appalled by the savage medical practices of the day, Hahnemann, a German doctor and chemist, started on a course of study that led to the development of homeopathy. His philosophy of disease and its cure through natural processes has changed very little from that day to this. The traditional approach is today's approach. The doses used in homeopathy are so minute that they cannot be acting directly on the physical body. Hahnemann considered that they act dynamically: in other words, the energy of the remedy stimulated the natural healing energy of the body. If it had been in a state of disharmony, then it would be propelled back to its former, healthy state.

HOMEOPATHY AND HEALTH

Homeopathy is not only an energy medicine, it is also holistic. Homeopaths convincingly argue that the body is much more than the sum of its various parts, and that the mind, the emotions and indeed the organs are somehow intricately interconnected. Consequently, the treatments they give are more "rounded" than those found in traditional medicine. They are not just aimed at the symptom, but at the whole person.

ENERGY WITHIN

The mechanics of this interconnection are elaborate and hard to explain, but it is clear that the process really does work. The key point is that underlying the physical and mental systems of the body is a refined system of energy which is self-regulating. It generally works extremely well. You sense it in action when you become ill. We usually get better even without taking a medicine. The body heals itself though it might need support when its own natural energy is low.

TREATMENT

The healing process is like running a car. Modern cars are so efficient that, provided you maintain them properly, give them the right fuel and drive them sensibly, problems seldom arise. Then one night you forget to turn off the lights and the next morning the battery is flat and your car incapacitated. The only way to get it moving again – the only cure – is to get a transfer of energy, in the form of a jump start from another battery. Homeopathy is in many ways just like getting an energizing jump start.

Homeopathy is becoming increasingly popular because of the serious concerns about drugs-based orthodox medicine. Many drugs are toxic and the side-effects in susceptible people can actually be quite unpleasant. Even if the side-effects are not observable, the long-term consequences from the excessive use of drugs are not always fully appreciated. In fact modern medicine seldom cures, and it does not even pretend to. What it does do is alleviate and palliate the symptoms, and manage the illness, but since it addresses the symptoms and rarely the cause, the results are not entirely satisfactory.

Homeopathy is different because it is safe and it does not treat the removal of symptoms as an end in itself. Symptoms are considered as signs of distress or adjustment. The correct remedy removes the cause of the problem; the symptoms will then fade away. Homeopathy is highly rated because it takes into account the nature of the person. It knows that when two people have been diagnosed as having the same illness, they can actually become ill in quite different ways and will require different remedies to effect a satisfactory cure.

▲ *Sometimes our bodies just do not seem to be firing on all cyclinders, and we need a carefully chosen homeopathic boost to revive them.*

DEFINING DISEASE

We become ill when our energy is depleted or when we are out of harmony. In fact the word "disease" could be more accurately written "dis-ease", indicating that we are definitely not at ease, and for a disease to be cured it is not necessary to give it a name. To cure homeopathically depends on a sensitive, accurate analysis of the symptoms. There is usually no need for a diagnosis, for it is widely said that there are no diseases, only what might be called people who are "dis-eased".

SYMPTOMS

Except for any life-threatening situations, symptoms are not the primary problem. They reflect a picture which shows how the system is making adjustments to heal itself. For example, both diarrhoea and vomiting are the body's way of ridding itself of unwanted "material", and the intolerable itching of eczema does not specifically mean that you have a skin disease. Rather it means that there is an imbalance in your whole system, and that your body is pushing the problem to the safest possible place, well away from the essential organs. The skin becomes an organ of elimination.

TREATING THE WHOLE PERSON

Some people are very robust and seldom become ill, others are over-sensitive and become run-down and sick after a slight chill or an emotional upset. For some, the chest is the greatest weakness: winter colds quickly turn to bronchitis. With others digestion is the problem: the slightest unusual change to their diet causes an immediate upset. Homeopathy acknowledges these many differences and adjusts all treatments accordingly. The professional homeopath will always prescribe "constitutionally" to try to strengthen the weak areas, as well as the whole system.

CAUSES OF ILLNESS

There are many causes of disease. Some are obvious, such as being run-down and poor nutrition, but illness might have an emotional cause. Stress creates disharmony which manifests itself in physical ailments. Homeopathy takes such factors into account and, if possible, tries to mitigate them and strengthen the sufferer.

▲ *Mental and emotional stress, often at work, can surprisingly quickly lead to a range of physical problems.*

CHRONIC DISEASES

With so much battering from within and without, it may seem a wonder that we are not all permanently ill. Of course, many people are. Although many of the acute infectious diseases of the past have ceased to be a serious problem, their places have now been taken by today's chronic diseases. Never has there been so much cancer and heart disease, eczema and asthma, or even digestive problems such as irritable bowels. Our immune systems are overstretched in combating these problems.

THE IMMUNE SYSTEM

It is all too easy to ignore the incredible adaptability and intelligence of the immune system, which appears to make heroic efforts to keep us up and running despite considerable adversity. One writer shrewdly called this intelligence the "vital force". He described it as "the spirit-like force which rules in supreme sovereignty". It has also been well described as "the invisible driver", overseeing the checks and balances that are needed to keep us in the best possible health.

THE VITAL FORCE AT WORK

Most of the time we are completely and utterly unaware of this sophisticated balancing process which is entirely automatic and pre-programmed through our genetic make-up. We can certainly observe it in action when we contract an acute illness (i.e. one that arises suddenly) such as a fever or a cough. What we may not always realize is that the fever is really a necessary, natural function and that it actually "burns up" the infection, and that the cough exists to prevent any active accumulation of mucus in the lungs. The body is extremely resourceful. However, chronic diseases (i.e. those that develop slowly, or are of long duration) might well need outside help, and a consultation with an experienced, professional practitioner.

READING THE SYMPTOMS

When trying to cure a disease, the vital force causes the body to produce symptoms. Homeopaths call this "the symptom picture". These symptoms accurately reflect exactly what is happening inside, and they also indicate what outside help or extra energy is therefore now required.

For example, during a flu epidemic two children in the same family become ill. The first child catches the flu very suddenly, overnight, and develops a high fever with a red face and a dry burning heat all over the body. The second child's symptoms might be very different, appearing quite slowly over several days. This child's fever is much lower, but he is shaky and shivery and his muscles ache all over. Both children have the same flu, but the vital force has produced completely different symptoms. Each child therefore needs to be treated in quite a different way. The homeopath will certainly understand this and give the first child the remedy Belladonna, while the second child receives quantities of Gelsemium. Homeopathy is well known for excelling at individualizing such treatments.

While it is quite true to say that in homeopathy we do not treat symptoms but the individual sufferer, we are still extremely interested in the symptoms. For it is through careful observation of the complete symptom picture that we can discover which remedy is required. In acute ailments the vital force will eventually effect a cure, given sufficient time, but by giving a helping hand from an accurate reading of the symptoms, that is by giving the body an "energy fix", the process can in fact be speeded up considerably.

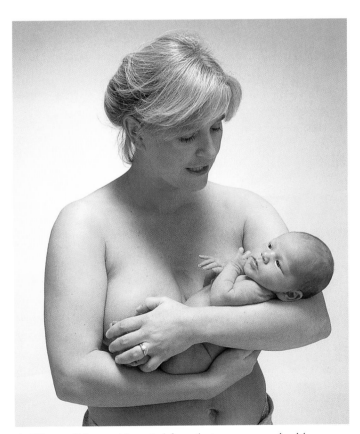

▲ *We are all born with a vital force that oversees our health.*

USING REMEDIES

When first taking a homeopathic remedy, you might well be totally bewildered how anyone could possibly know that a certain recipe of mixed ingredients is the one that is best for you. In fact there is no guesswork. The exact remedies for all kinds of problems have been known and listed for hundreds of years. The technique is precise and proven, and the beauty of it is that remedies can be subtly fine-tuned to suit your particular ailment.

REMEDY SOURCES

The remedies used in homeopathy are derived from many sources. The majority are prepared from plants, but many minerals are also used and a few remedies are even prepared from insect and snake poisons and other toxic substances. Do not be alarmed about the toxins because they have been diluted so that no danger remains. The Law of Similars shows that the most powerful poisons can be turned into equally strong remedies. In fact about 2,000 have now been described and documented, but in practice most professional homeopaths use only a fraction of that surprisingly high number.

▲ *In homeopathy every symptom is fully taken into account when trying to apply the right remedy.*

The process that turns a substance into a remedy is called "potentization", and consists of two main procedures, dilution and succussion (or vigorous shaking). When you buy a remedy note a number after its name, usually 6, but also other numbers rising in a scale: 30, 200, IM (1,000). Sometimes a "c", standing for centesimal (one hundredth) appears after the number. It shows how often the remedy has been diluted and succussed.

A remedy is prepared by dissolving a tincture of the original material, usually in alcohol. On the centesimal scale, the 6th potency means that the original substance has been diluted six times, each time using a dilution of one part in a hundred. This results in a remedy that contains only one part in a million million of the source material. Yet the greater the potency (number of dilutions), the greater the remedy's power.

Between each dilution, the remedy is succussed. When the potentization is complete the remedy is preserved in alcohol, and a few drops can be added to a bottle of milk-sugar pills or a cream. The remedy is now ready to use.

PROVINGS

Almost all homeopathic remedies have been "proved", or tested, although practitioners gain additional knowledge of them from clinical experience. In a proving, a remedy is tested on a group of healthy people over a period of time, until they develop symptoms. Neither the supervisor nor the group should know what remedy they are proving. This is a double blind test, conducted on sound, regulated principles. The symptoms that the provers develop are accurately collated until a complete symptom picture has been obtained. Consequently, we know exactly what the remedy can cure.

Once proved, remedies can be used for all time. Hundreds of original remedies are still in use today. The remedy pictures are described in great detail in volumes called *Materia Medica*. Because thousands of symptoms for thousands of remedies have been proved over the last 200 years or so, no one homeopath could possibly remember them all. They are therefore listed in another impressively detailed book called *The Homeopathic Repertory*. It is, in effect, an index to the *Materia Medica*. Between them, these two astonishing books cover most symptoms.

▼ *In homeopathy, physical examinations are seldom necessary, but bright, sparkling eyes are a sign of good health.*

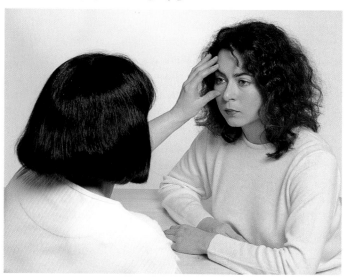

TISSUE SALTS

The 19th-century German doctor Wilhelm Schussler identified 12 vital minerals, or "tissue salts", essential to health. According to his theory, many diseases are associated with a deficiency of one or more of these substances, but they can be cured by taking the tissue salts in minute doses, singly or in all kinds of different combinations.

▲ *Even members of the same family will have different*
susceptibilities to illness and react differently.

CHOOSING THE CORRECT REMEDY

With a copy of the *Materia Medica*, the homeopath is now well equipped to match the symptoms with the symptom picture. This is usually known as finding the similimum (or similar).

THE SYMPTOM PICTURE

Finding the correct remedy is like trying to arrange a perfect marriage. If the two partners are compatible, success is almost certain. If the remedy is a good match to the symptoms, the patient is going to feel a good deal better, the natural way. The words "I feel better in myself" are like music to the ears of the prescribing homeopath, because it means that the natural healing processes have been stimulated successfully, even if some of the physical symptoms remain. It should be only a short time before they too disappear.

The prescriber is like a detective looking for clues. Apart from the obvious general symptoms, such as fever, headache or a cough, you should note what are called the "modalities" – that is, what aggravates or alleviates the symptoms, or makes the person feel generally better or worse. They might include the need for warmth, or cool air, sitting up or lying down. Notice whether the person is thirsty or sweaty; whether the tongue is coated, and the state of the breath. What kind of pain is it: throbbing, stitching or sudden stabs of intense agony?

It is also important to note if the symptoms have an obvious cause? Did they arise after an emotional shock, or after catching a chill in a cold wind? Did they arise dramatically and suddenly in the middle of the night, or have they developed in rather a nondescript way over a number of days?

It is also very important to note the person's state of mind. For example, irritable people who just want to be left alone may need quite different remedies from those who want to be comforted and are easily consoled. The homeopath has to be sensitive in all kinds of ways.

HOW TO USE REMEDIES

Many minor and self-limiting acute problems can be treated safely at home with a basic first-aid kit. However, for more serious long-term ailments, or if you feel out of your depth and really worried – especially if young children or old people are ill – seek help from your own homeopath or doctor. Access to professional homeopaths is now much easier, and they can often do wonderful things for persistent and chronic disease. Be assured that qualified practitioners will have completed three or four years' training.

What the given remedy is doing is helping your body to help itself. Sometimes there may not be a great deal you can do – a well-established cold is going to mean several days of suffering whether you intervene or not. In other cases, the sooner you act, the better: for instance, if you take Arnica (either in pill form, or rubbed-in cream if appropriate) immediately after a bad fall for the bruising and shock, the results will be very impressive with the healing time being be much shorter.

You can often limit the duration or intensity of suffering, as in fever, sepsis (pus-forming bacteria), pain, indigestion and many other conditions. Moreover, there will be many satisfying times when the problem is aborted or cured altogether.

Once you are confident of an improvement then the vital force needs no further help, and you can stop taking the remedy. You will do no harm if you do in fact carry on, but there is really no point in trying to aquire far more energy than your mind and body actually require. In homeopathy it is perfectly true to say that less is actually more.

▼ *You may feel rather hesitant and uncertain about treating very*
young children, but it is known that homeopathy usually works
extremely well on them, and can be safely used from birth.

remedies for common ailments

Many straightforward problems can be treated at home using homeopathy. For each one, the following pages list a number of remedies that are likely to be the most helpful in the situation. Read the remedy picture carefully and choose the one that best seems to match the symptoms that you have observed. Then, when you have selected your own particular remedy, double-check it very carefully with the more detailed description which you will find listed in the Materia Medica section. Rescue Remedy is often used by homeopaths, though it is not strictly homeopathic, for that reason it has not been included in the Materia Medica.

HOW TO TAKE THE REMEDY

Carefully empty one pill into the cap of the bottle. If more than one tumbles into the cap, tip the others back into the bottle without touching them. This is quite important. If you are shaky, use a folded piece of paper to help if necessary.

Next, drop the pill on to a clean tongue – that is, you should take the remedy at least ten minutes before or after eating, drinking or cleaning your teeth. The pill should be sucked for about thirty seconds before being crunched and swallowed. Remedies for babies can be crushed to a powder in an envelope and given on a teaspoon.

GIVING THE REMEDY

The 6th and 30th potencies are most useful for home use. As a rough rule of thumb, use a 6c three or four times a day, or a 30c once or twice daily until symptoms improve. One pill at a time is all that is necessary; there is no need to reduce the dosage for children.

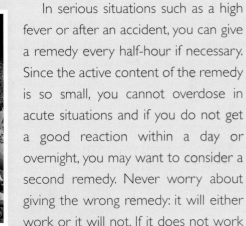

In serious situations such as a high fever or after an accident, you can give a remedy every half-hour if necessary. Since the active content of the remedy is so small, you cannot overdose in acute situations and if you do not get a good reaction within a day or overnight, you may want to consider a second remedy. Never worry about giving the wrong remedy: it will either work or it will not. If it does not work you will have done no harm to the patient.

Sometimes the symptoms may change after giving a remedy, so that a new picture emerges. You then need to find a new remedy to fit the new picture. If the situation improves, or the picture is unclear, watch and wait. Only intervene if you feel you need to.

Until you get used to the method of diagnosis, you may find it helpful to consult a practitioner on the first few occasions, this is also a good idea if symptoms persist. The Homeopath will also be able to give other effective advice.

COLDS, FLU AND TOOTHACHE

Most colds, unless nipped in the bud, take their natural course and they should clear up in about week. Even so, they can make life pretty uncomfortable, as can a throbbing toothache. Flu, however, can be much more debilitating, though a good remedy can often help ameliorate the symptoms, soon reducing the effects of aching bones, weak legs, headaches, high temperatures, shivering and even dizziness.

COLDS AND FLU

If flu comes on suddenly, often at night and perhaps after catching a chill, with symptoms of high fever and profuse sweating, Aconite is a perfectly good remedy. If the symptoms are similarly sudden and with a high temperature, but accompanied by redness, burning heat and a headache, then the remedy is much more likely to be Belladonna.

For flu that appears more slowly, accompanied by extreme thirst, irritability and the desire to be left alone, Bryonia will be very useful. Probably the most widely used remedy in flu, though, is Gelsemium. The most pronounced symptoms are shivering, aching muscles and general weakness. Where aching bones are prominent, use Eupatorium.

For head colds with sneezing and an acrid nasal discharge, Allium cepa or Arsenicum should be very helpful. If the sinuses are also affected and there is a lot of yellow-green mucus which appears in globules, or if it looks sticky and stringy, then use quantities of Kali bich.

For a general tonic, both during and after the flu, when your symptoms are not very well defined and there is a general feeling of malaise, try using Ferrum phos.

▼ *Kali bich can be a good remedy for blocked sinuses where there is pain and a green stringy discharge.*

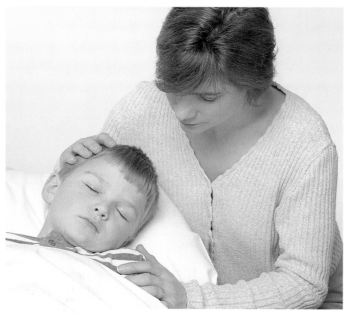

▲ *The most useful remedies at the start of a high fever in children are Aconite and Belladonna.*

FEVERS

Fevers, particularly in children, whose temperatures may be quite high, may seem alarming, but it should be remembered that they are the body's own efficient, natural response to dealing with and burning up infection.

The two main remedies for high fevers that appear suddenly are Aconite and Belladonna. Thirst and sweat characterize the Aconite picture, while Belladonna cases will reveal a dry skin, redness, and a throbbing pain in the affected area. If the fever appears more slowly and the person is irritable, wants to be left alone and is very thirsty for cold water, try Bryonia. For flu-like fevers, with shivering, weakness and aching muscles, use Gelsemium. Ferrum phos can be used in milder fevers, with no particularly distinctive symptoms. Pulsatilla is really useful in children's fevers, where the child soon becomes very emotional, clingy and weepy, and wants to be comforted.

If the period of fever is made more uncomfortable by poor circulation and chilblains, the former can be helped by herbs that stimulate the circulatory system. Angelica and Ginger have a good track record, taken with the likes of Yarrow. The latter is best treated by a tincture of Arnica.

▲ *At the first sign of a head cold, try Arsenicum or Allium cepa.*

COUGHS AND CROUP

For very harsh, dry, violent coughs, which may appear suddenly and may be worse at night, use Aconite. For a hard, dry painful cough, which seems to be helped by holding the chest very tightly and also by long drinks of cold water, use Bryonia.

For deep-seated, dry, spasmodic coughs that may end in retching or even vomiting, use Drosera. Painful, barking coughs, which produce thick yellow-green mucus, may be helped by Hepar sulph. For coughs that are really quite suffocating, and which sound sharp and rasping, like a saw going through wood, try Spongia. Where there is a lot of mucus seemingly trapped in the chest, try Ant tart.

Croup is a horrible sounding dry cough that affects small children. The main remedies are Aconite, Hepar sulph and Spongia. Try each one of these remedies in turn if it is in any way difficult to differentiate between the symptoms.

SORE THROATS

If a sore throat starts suddenly, often during the night, perhaps following a chill and accompanied by a high temperature, try Aconite. If the throat burns and throbs painfully and looks very red, it may be eased by Belladonna.

For a sore throat that looks very swollen and puffy, with a stinging pain, try Apis. Hepar sulph can be used for an extremely painful throat that feels as if there is a fish bone stuck in it, making it very difficult to try and swallow.

If the sore throat feels worse on the left side and swallowing liquids is particularly painful, use Lachesis. Use Lycopodium if the throat is worse on the right side or the pain moves from right to left; warm drinks may be comforting.

For a sore throat which is accompanied by offensive breath and saliva, with a degree of sweatiness and thirst, then you should try Mercurius. For throats that appear dark, raw and red, and feel as if a highly uncomfortable, unpleasant hot lump has got stuck inside, try taking quantities of Phytolacca. That usually proves quite effective.

RELIEVING TOOTHACHE

There is probably no worse agony than the pain of toothache, as the area is so sensitive. In most cases, a visit to the dentist will be essential, but the following remedies may well help you cope with the pain in the meantime.

For sudden and violent pains, perhaps precipitated by a cold, Aconite may be helpful. If the area looks very red and throbs violently, Belladonna should be used. For abscesses, where pus is obviously present and the saliva tastes and smells foul, the best remedy is likely to be Mercurius. If you are prone to abscesses and your teeth are generally not very strong, Silica should be used to strengthen the system.

For pain that lingers after a visit to the dentist, take Arnica or Hypericum. If the pain is in any way accompanied by extreme irritability, Chamomilla should be used.

Hepar sulph is a suitable remedy for extreme septic states (infected areas), where bad temper is a prominent symptom. Another remedy for toothache where there are spasmodic shooting pains is Mag phos.

▶ *Though there are several remedies that can help with toothache, you will still need to visit the dentist.*

EYES AND EARS

Any problems with the eyes and ears can be immediately quite distresssing, especially for young children who do not appreciate what is happening. Their world can suddenly be turned upside down. Fortunately, there is a wide range of proven remedies for helping ease such discomfort, for example reducing puffy, swollen eyes, styes, burning sensations, and even the debilitating effects of a sudden, throbbing ear infection.

SOOTHING THE EYES

Overwork, pollutants, viral and bacterial infections can all affect the delicate tissues in and around the eyes. Stress and fatigue tend to aggravate these problems by weakening the immune system's ability to fight off infection.

Aconite helps when the eye feels hot and dry, perhaps after catching a cold. The eye may feel irritated, as if it has got a piece of grit. Apis is a good remedy to use when the eyelids look puffy and swollen; the discomfort can be reduced and relieved by applying a cold compress.

Belladonna is a very good remedy for eyes that look in any way red and bloodshot, and which are over-sensitive to light. Euphrasia is one of the very best remedies for sore and burning eyes, and it can also be used in an eyebath because it can be obtained in a diluted tincture.

One of the best remedies for styes is Pulsatilla, which should be used when the eye has an infection which results in what is best described as a sticky yellow discharge. When treating eye injuries, Symphytum can be used where there has been a blow to the eyeball. For general eye injuries, Arnica will ease the bruising. Ledum helps when the eye is cold and puffy.

▲ *Eye irritants cause a lot of discomfort and need tackling quickly.*

▲ *An effective cure for children's earaches is Verbascum oil.*

EAR INFECTIONS

Acute earaches are most common in young children. They need to be treated quickly, as an infection within the middle ear can be both painful and damaging. Speedy home help can be very useful, but you must get professional medical help if the earache worsens or if it in any way persists.

One of the most soothing remedies is Verbascum oil. Pour a few drops into a spoon that has been pleasantly warmed, and drip gently into the child's ear.

For sudden and violent pains, accompanied by fever which usually start at night, use Aconite. Where there is a fever with a sudden and violent appearance, and the ear throbs and looks very red, Belladonna will effect a cure.

For earaches where there is great pain and the child is exceptionally irritable, use Chamomilla. Ferrum phos is required where the pain comes on slowly and there are no other significant distinguishing symptoms. For very painful, sore earaches with some discharge of yellow-green mucus, when the child is also clearly chilly and irritable, use Hepar sulph.

ALLERGIES

Over the last 20 or 30 years there has been a highly significant increase in all kinds of allergies, which might be better described as the body's sensitivity to an excess of substances that cannot be easily assimilated. Sadly, many such substances are the product of our time. Hay fever, eczema, asthma, irritable bowel disease and other chronic diseases have now reached almost epidemic proportions. Fortunately, homeopathy can offer you essential help.

HAY FEVER

Hay fever is rather a misnomer, for there are many other substances apart from hay which can trigger the well-known symptoms of watering eyes and runny nose, itchiness and sneezing. The problem may last for a few weeks, a few months or even all year, depending on the cause.

Euphrasia and Allium cepa are two of the most effective acute remedies. If the problem is centred in the eyes, with even the tears burning, Euphrasia is the remedy to use. However, if the nasal symptoms are worse, with constant streaming and an acrid discharge, then try Allium cepa. Another remedy that is sometimes useful when there are constant burning secretions from the mucous membranes is Arsenicum.

To build up your immune system, it is best to act about two to three months before the time when hay fever usually begins. There are plenty of tasty aids. Garlic, in pill form or meals when it can even be eaten whole if roasted in the oven, imparting a new, sweetish flavour, works well. So too do regular applications of honey. Inhaling over a steam bath using lemon balm reduces the chances of an allergic attack.

▲ *Red onion, the source of the remedy,* Allium cepa.

CHRONIC DISEASES

No one knows precisely what causes these problems. Further research is required. Quite clearly there are many different reasons. Toxicity overload is almost certainly one. The body simply cannot cope with the increasingly large number of chemicals and drugs that it was never designed to absorb. Another likely reason is deficient nutrition. Many of our foods are now so over-processed (apart from being sprayed with all kinds of chemicals) that they do not contain sufficient minerals and vitamins to allow the body to function efficiently.

Homeopathy can often work wonders in correcting the many weaknesses that result from such causes. Obviously, you should also take care to avoid toxic substances wherever possible, and eat a healthy, varied diet. The homeopathy that is needed to cure chronic ailments is complex and beyond the scope of this book; seek advice from a professional homeopath.

◄ *Allergies, or over-sensitivity to certain foods, are becoming increasingly common. Research shows that dairy products and wheat-based foods seem to cause the most problems.*

ACUTE ILLNESSES AND UPSETS

There is nothing quite as frustratingly disabling as a sudden upset stomach, whether it be diarrhoea, lingering indigestion, niggling cramps or even quite painful bouts of trapped wind. However, with the use of homeopathy you do not have to keep on suffering. It actually offers several well-proven ways of helping you tackle such problems, so that you can resume a normal life, quickly getting out and about.

SETTLING GASTRIC UPSETS

The main symptoms of stomach and intestinal infections are pain, wind (gas), nausea, vomiting and diarrhoea. Bear in mind that vomiting and diarrhoea are actually natural processes by which the body rids itself quickly of any unwanted material. Consequently these symptoms need to be treated only if they are persistent. Such problems can arise at any time and may be due to food poisoning or just a sudden reaction to unfamiliar food; this invariably seems to happen on vacation.

UPSET STOMACH

The great standby remedy is Arsenicum. Other symptoms which may accompany diarrhoea or vomiting are excessive weakness, coldness and restlessness. Mag phos is an excellent remedy for general abdominal cramps which are soothed by doubling up and making sure that you keep warm.

For constant nausea which is unrelieved by vomiting, use Ipecac. Nux vomica is a very good remedy for gastric upsets where nothing really seems to happen. The undigested food lies like a horrible dead weight in the stomach and refuses to move or be expelled, causing plenty of discomfort.

Phosphorus can be a useful remedy for diarrhoea, and it is particularly effective if attacks are accompanied by a sensation of burning in the stomach. While you may crave a cold drink, it is actually vomited as soon as it warms up in the stomach.

▲ *A piece of Arsenopyrite used in the remedy Arsenicum.*

INDIGESTION

The symptoms of indigestion are heartburn, wind (gas) and cramping pains. They are usually caused by eating too much or in fact eating too quickly. The symptoms are usually much more marked when you are eating very rich food and drinking large quantities of alcohol. The most useful remedy is Nux vomica. The digestive system seems heavy and sluggish and the feeling is that you would be much better if the undigested food would move. Another good remedy that can help is Lycopodium.

CALMING BOILS AND ABSCESSES

Sometimes, an area of skin becomes inflamed and gathers pus. This usually happens around a hair follicle. The build-up of pus can cause acute pain before it comes to a head as a boil or abscess, or until the pus is absorbed by the body.

In the early stages of a boil or abscess, when it looks red and angry and throbs painfully, Belladonna is often the best remedy. Later when it starts becoming septic (infected) and even more painful as the pus increases, use Hepar sulph. If the boil seems very slow in coming to a head, Silica should be used to speed up the process. This remedy is also helpful as a daily tissue salt for unhealthy skin that keeps producing boils. The nails may also be unhealthy, breaking and peeling too easily.

◀ *Belladonna is highly effective against a wide range of complaints.*

EMOTIONAL ISSUES

We underrate at surprisingly great risk the incredible part that our emotions can play in our health. Diseases can easily arise from any disharmony in our lives. This is even more likely if we are repressed, and unable to express and articulate our more difficult, upsetting emotions, with feelings staying trapped and locked within us. Just as joy can bolster and keep us in good health, a big build-up of grief can result in all kinds of illness.

EMOTIONAL TURMOIL

It is not unusual for a homeopathic practitioner to hear words like "I've never really got over my father's death," or "I've never properly felt well since my divorce." It is important for good health not to allow such wounds to fester. Homeopathy can often help chronic and acute conditions when needed.

In any emotional situation where you feel that you really cannot cope, the Bach Flower Rescue Remedy is useful. Although it is not strictly homeopathic, it works well with homeopathic remedies, and can be taken as often as you wish.

GRIEF AND FRIGHT

Ignatia is the number-one remedy for acute feelings of sadness and loss. It can calm both the hysterical and over-sensitive and those who tend to keep their grief bottled up. Children and emotionally dependent people can be helped by Pulsatilla. Aconite is considered the major remedy for helping people who need to get over a shock or a terrifying experience.

ANTICIPATION

The worry brought on by a forthcoming event such as an exam, appearing on the stage or meeting someone new can severely affect some people. Fortunately, there are a number of remedies that can help ease any anxiety and panic.

▲ *The most useful remedy for dealing with emotional upsets is Pulsatilla, combined with plenty of security and love.*

Gelsemium is best used when you start trembling with nerves and literally go weak at the knees. Arg nit is a good all-round anxiety remedy, where there are symptoms of great restlessness. It also has a claustrophobic picture and could help those who suffer from a fear of flying or even travelling on underground trains. The panic often causes diarrhoea, and another anxiety remedy that can help the bowels is called Lycopodium. Strangely, people who need Lycopodium are often found to excel at the ordeals that they have been worrying about, once they have overcome the panic barrier.

INSOMNIA

There can be many causes of sleeplessness including worry, habit, and bad eating. For the "hamster on the wheel" syndrome, where your mind is rushing around in never-ending circles, Valerian can be a magical aid helping you quickly fall asleep. For those sufferers who constantly wake too early, especially if they are people who live too much on their nerves and eat large quantities of rich food, try Nux vomica.

▲ *A Pasque flower, used in Pulsatilla.*

WOMEN'S HEALTH

Two of the greatest concerns to most women are their reproductive systems and the effects of their associated hormones, but many find they are treated in quite a heavy-handed way by traditional modern medicine. Fortunately, homeopathy offers another route and a range of different treatments which can include important aspects of your diet. Homeopathic self-help can ease the distress for various non-persistent conditions.

ANAEMIA

Anaemia is usually caused by an iron deficiency and manifests itself through weakness, pallor and lack of stamina. The most vulnerable times are during pregnancy or after excessive blood loss due to heavy periods. Since iron pills supplied by your doctor can often severely upset the bowels, gentler methods are actually preferable. Eat foods rich in iron and try organic iron preparations which can be obtained from health food shops. Ferrum phos should also be used on a daily basis.

CYSTITIS

Many women are familiar with the burning agony of urinating when they have a bladder infection. Cranberry juice or sodium bicarbonate can often help. Two of the most useful remedies are Cantharis and Apis. Use Cantharis as a general remedy. Apis can be helpful when the last drops in urination hurt the most.

MASTITIS

Mastitis means an inflammation of the breast and it occurs commonly during breast-feeding. It can be painful but is not normally serious. Fortunately, breast-feeding does not have to stop because of it. Homeopathy is usually very successful in curing the inflammation. Phytolacca is the most important remedy aiding breasts that may feel lumpy and swollen.

▲ *PMT mood swings are not uncommon and should not alarm you. Check your symptoms to find a remedy that might help.*

PRE-MENSTRUAL SYNDROME (PMS)

Most women are familiar with the mood changes that arise just before an oncoming period. For an unfortunate few, more extreme symptoms of depression, anger and weepiness can appear, sometimes as much as a week or more before the flow begins. A visit to a professional homeopath can certainly be of great benefit, but there are several remedies that you might like to try yourself at home in order to alleviate some of these sudden, extreme symptoms.

Pulsatilla is an excellent remedy if weeping and the feeling of neediness is prominent. Sepia should be used where there is anger and exhaustion, and even in cases of indifference towards your family. Lachesis is very helpful in minimizing the more extreme symptoms of violent anger, jealousy and suspicion.

PERIOD PAINS

If your period pains are consistently bad, you will need to consult a homeopath. For occasional pains, there are a number of self-help remedies from which you can choose. The three PMS remedies mentioned above, Pulsatilla, Sepia and Lachesis, should be considered when applicable, and if your symptoms seem significant and over-riding. All three might also be of some help during a difficult menopause.

▲ *A good diet is essential for good health. Fresh organic apples and other fruit are especially good for you.*

CHILDREN'S HEALTH

Children tend to respond very well and quickly to all kinds of homeopathic treatments, and they are a joy to treat. However, while there is actually no substitute for constitutional treatment from a professional homeopath who will try to boost the immune system as much as possible, there is no reason why you should not keep a good stock of remedies at home in case of a sudden, acute situation. You too can do a lot to help.

CHILDREN AND HOMEOPATHY

The best start you can possibly give a child is plenty of confidence, with love and security, breast milk for as long as is practical, a healthy, varied diet, as few drugs as possible, and homeopathy. Young children invariably have rather dramatic, acute conditions, such as fevers. Usually there is nothing for you to worry about if you are well informed, have professional support and have access to remedies. The dosage is the same as for adults, but remember to crush the pills first for babies.

TEETHING

The most widely used remedies for teething pains are Chamomilla and Pulsatilla. Chamomilla is an "angry" remedy and suits bad-tempered babies best. These are the ones that drain you of sympathy because you have had so many sleepless nights making you feel irritable and guilty for becoming bad tempered, and helpless. Only constant attention, picking them up and carrying them round, soothes them in any way. Pulsatilla children respond differently – they are softer, weepy and are constantly in need of your sympathy. They feel better and are significantly soothed by being given plenty of cuddles.

▲ *Give your child the right start with love and a healthy diet.*

▼ *For babies, it is essential to crush the tablet first.*

FEVERS

Many small children get fevers with very high temperatures, as they burn up infection in the most efficient way. Seek help if the fever goes on for more than 24 hours, especially if there are any signs at all of a violent headache or drowsiness. Aconite and Belladonna are the best, general high-fever remedies.

CROUP

This harsh, dry cough is very disturbing in small children, but usually sounds far worse than it really is. There are three main remedies for croup. Aconite can be used for particularly violent and sudden coughs, which are often worse at night. For harsh coughs that sound like sawing through wood, Spongia is the remedy. For a rattly chest with thick yellow-green mucus, possibly marked by irritability and chilliness, use Hepar sulph.

COLIC

Trapped wind can be very upsetting for a baby. It comes without warning, and for no apparent reason the baby will cry. Sometimes babies try to curl up to ease the pain, and warmth and a gentle massage should help. Mag phos is a useful remedy to try.

FIRST AID

Homeopathic remedies are extremely useful as first-aid treatments in all kinds of situations, but dangerous, serious injuries should always receive immediate, expert medical attention. If you are in any way alarmed or concerned, you must first call for help, at which point it might just be possible to start giving an appropriate remedy. In more minor cases, such as bruising, cuts and sprains, homeopathy can certainly make quite a difference.

BRUISES

The very first remedy to think of after any injury or accident is Arnica. For local bruising, where the skin is unbroken, apply Arnica cream, and whether you use the cream or not you can give an Arnica pill as often as you think necessary, until such time as the bruising starts to go down.

Arnica is also wonderful in cases of shock. If the person is dozy or woozy, or in fact unconscious, crush the remedy first and place the powder directly on to the lips.

Where there is serious shock, or in any real emergency, use Rescue Remedy. This can be used either alone or with Arnica in cases of physical trauma. Place a few drops of the Rescue Remedy straight on to the lips or tongue, every few minutes if considered necessary. If the injury results in pains shooting up the arms or legs, try using Hypericum.

This remedy is also very useful where sensitive areas have been injured and hurt, such as the toes, fingers, lips and ears. If the joints or bones have been hurt, Ruta may be more effective than Arnica, which is more of a soft tissue remedy.

▲ *Calendula cream is a widely available, excellent remedy to use if you have got any open cuts and sores.*

CUTS, SORES AND OPEN WOUNDS

Clean the area thoroughly to remove all dirt. If the wound is deep, it may need stitches and you must seek instant medical help. Once the wound is clean, apply some Calendula cream.

▲ *For bites that come up as any kind of bruise, small or dramatic, apply Arnica cream. For many it is very effective.*

PUNCTURE WOUNDS

Such injuries can easily occur in all kinds of ways: from animal or insect bites, pins, needles and nails, and even from standing on a sharp instrument such as a garden fork or rake.

If the wound becomes puffy and purple and feels cold, with the pain being eased by a cold compress, Ledum is the best remedy. If there are shooting pains, which travel up the limbs along the tracks of the nerves, then Hypericum should be used.

SPRAINS, STRAINS AND FRACTURES

For general muscle strains, resulting from lifting heavy weights or excessive physical exercise such as aerobics or long hikes over hilly countryside, Arnica will almost always be extremely effective. For deeper injuries where the joints are affected, as a result of a heavy fall or a strong football tackle, use Ruta.

For even more severe sprains, especially to the ankles or wrists, where the pain is agony on first moving the joint but eases with gentle limbering up, Rhus tox should be very helpful. For injuries where the slightest movement is extremely painful and hard pressure eases the pain, Bryonia will provide relief.

Once a broken bone has been set, use Symphytum daily, night and morning, for at least three weeks. This will not only ease the pain but speed up the healing of the bones.

▲ *The herb St John's Wort, used in the remedy Hypericum.*

BURNS

Severe burns need urgent medical assistance: do not delay, especially in the case of children and babies. For minor burns and scalds, Calendula or Hypercal cream can be very soothing, especially if applied straight away. If the pain remains, or the burn is severe, take one pill of the remedy Cantharis every few hours until the pain eases. In the case of shock or a hysterical child, also use Arnica (in pill form) and/or Rescue Remedy.

BITES AND STINGS

For minor injuries, you can apply Calendula or Hypercal cream. If the wound looks in any way bruised, use Arnica, either as a cream or in pill form. However, if the wound becomes dramatically swollen and starts looking red and puffy, then use Apis. For any injuries to quite sensitive areas, such as the fingers, especially when shooting pains can be felt, Hypericum is a useful remedy. Ledum is preferable if the wound looks puffy and feels cold to the touch, and is helped by the application of a cold compress.

TRAVEL SICKNESS

Many people end up getting seasick even when the waves are not too rough, and some, especially children, are also air-sick or car-sick. The symptoms are eased by the remedy Cocculus.

FEAR OF FLYING

Use Aconite and/or Rescue Remedy before you go to the airport and then as often as you need during the flight. If you actually find yourself shaking with anxiety, try Gelsemium. If the problem is more a question of claustrophobia, the fear of being trapped in a narrow space, Arg nit should be very useful.

VISITS TO THE DOCTOR OR DENTIST

For any pre-visit nerves, to which we are all prone at some time, take Arg nit. For surgery or dental work where bruising and shock to the system might well have been involved, you cannot go wrong with Arnica. Take one pill before the treatment, and one pill three times a day for as long as you actively need it.

THE HOMEOPATHIC FIRST-AID KIT

It is a good idea to keep a basic first-aid kit in the house so that you are well prepared for any sudden emergency. Many remedies are now available from health food shops and even some chemists, but for many of us there might not be a nearby source, and it is amazing how many emergencies arise outside shop-opening hours. Stock up and be safe.

A FIRST-AID KIT SHOULD INCLUDE:

Arnica cream – for bruises
Calendula cream – for cuts and sores
Echinacea tincture – for the immune system
Rescue Remedy tincture – for major emergencies

PLUS THESE BOTTLES OF PILLS:

Aconite – for fevers, coughs and colds
Apis – for bites and stings
Arnica – for bruising or shock following accidents
Arsenicum – for digestive upsets and food poisoning
Belladonna – for high fever and headaches
Bryonia – for dry coughs and fevers
Chamomilla – for teething and colic
Ferrum phos – for colds, flu and anaemia
Gelsemium – for flu and anxiety
Hepar sulph – for sore throats and infected wounds
Hypericum – for injuries

Although not strictly a homeopathic treatment, Rescue Remedy is one of Dr Edward Bach's Flower Remedies. These flower essences are a series of gentle plant remedies which are intended to treat various emotional states, regardless of the physical disorder.

Ignatia – for grief and emotional upsets
Ledum – for puncture wounds, bites and stings
Lycopodium – for anxiety and digestive problems
Mercurius – for sepsis
Nux vomica – for hangovers, nausea and indigestion
Phosphorus – for digestive problems and nosebleeds
Pulsatilla – for ear infections, fevers and eye problems
Rhus tox – for sprains, strains and rashes
Ruta – for injuries to tendons and bones

THE MATERIA MEDICA

There are something like 2,000 remedies in the homeopathic Materia Medica, though most of them are actually best left to the professional practitioner. However, there are a surprising number of remedies that can safely be used by the lay person in low potencies for acute and first-aid cases. These remedies cover a wide range of not too serious, non-persistent problems. It is well worth seeing just how much you can achieve.

HOMEOPATHIC CURES

Use this section to back up and confirm your choice from the remedies that were recommended for ailments earlier in the chapter on herbs. If your choice still looks good, then you are almost certainly on the right track. However, if it does not, then consider trying one of the other remedies which are described for the ailment. Do note, though, that not every particular symptom of the remedy has to be present. Homeopaths use the expression "a three-legged stool"; if the remedy covers three symptoms of the condition, then it is more than likely to be well indicated.

Note that you must always keep your supply of remedies in a cool, dark place or cupboard. Also do keep them well away from any strong, pervasive smells and young children. Fortunately, homeopathic remedies are known to be extremely safe, so even if a child does actually swallow a number of pills, even as much as a whole bottle, you need not be unduly alarmed or concerned.

ACONITE
Aconitum napellus

Monkshood, a beautiful yet poisonous plant with blue flowers, is native to mountainous areas of Europe and Asia. It is widely cultivated as a garden plant.

n o t e s • Symptoms appear suddenly and violently, often at night. • They may appear after catching a chill or after a fright. • Fear or extreme anxiety may accompany symptoms. • An important remedy for high fevers with extreme thirst and sweat. • Major remedy for violent, dry croupy coughs. • It is most effective when used at the beginning of an illness.

ALLIUM CEPA
Allium cepa

The remedy comes from the onion, whose characteristics are perfectly well known and obvious to anyone who has ever had to peel a strong one: it directly affects the mucous membranes of the nose, the eyes and throat.

n o t e s • Sneezing, often repeatedly, accompanied by a streaming nose. • The nose and eyes begin to burn and become irritated. • Nasal discharge is acrid while the tears are bland. • Major remedy for hay fever (when the nose is affected more than the eyes) and also for colds.

ANT TART
Antimonium tartaricum

Ant tart is prepared from the chemical substance antimony potassium tartrate, and is traditionally referred to as tartar emetic. Ant tart affects the mucous membranes of the lungs.

n o t e s • A wet, rattling cough from deep in the lungs, with shortness of breath and wheezing. • Helps to bring up mucus from the lungs.

APIS
Apis mellifica

The remedy is prepared from the honey bee. The well-known effects of its sting describe the remedy picture very well.

n o t e s • A useful remedy after injuries, especially from bites or stings where there is subsequent swelling, puffiness and redness. • The affected area feels like a water bag. • A fever appears quickly and without any thirst. • The person appears restless and irritable. • The symptoms are often relieved by the application of a cold compress, or exposure to cold air.

ARG NIT
Argentum nitricum

Silver nitrate, from which this remedy is derived, is one of the silver compounds that are used during the photographic process. It is good at helping to soothe an agitated nervous system.

n o t e s • Panic, nervousness and anxiety. • Feeling worried, hurried and without emotional and practical support. • Fears of anticipation which might include stage fright, exams, visiting the dentist, flying, and many others. • The nervousness may cause diarrhoea and wind (gas).

ARNICA
Arnica montana

Arnica is a well-known herb with yellow, daisy-like flowers. Its native habitat is mountainous areas. It has a special affinity with soft tissue and muscles, and is usually the first remedy to consider after any accident. Where there is bruising but the skin is not broken, use Arnica cream. (When the skin is broken, use Calendula or Hypercal cream.)

n o t e s • The most important remedy for bruising. • Shock following an accident. • Muscle strains after strenuous or extreme exertion.

ARSENICUM
Arsenicum album

Arsenic oxide is a well-known poison. However, when used as a homeopathic remedy it is extremely safe and works especially well on the gastro-intestinal and respiratory systems.

n o t e s • Vomiting, diarrhoea, abdominal and stomach cramps. • Often the first remedy in cases of food poisoning. • Asthmatic, wheezy breathing, often worse at night. Head colds with a runny nose. • Chilliness, restlessness, anxiety and weakness. • Warmth gives great relief.

BELLADONNA
Atropa belladonna

The valuable remedy Belladonna must be prepared from deadly nightshade, whose poisonous berries are best avoided. However, they produce a medicine which is one of the most important fever and headache remedies.

n o t e s • Violent and intense symptoms appearing suddenly. • Fever with high temperature, little thirst and burning, dry skin. • The face or the affected part is usually bright red. •Throbbing pains, especially in the head. •The pupils may be sensitive to light.

BRYONIA
Bryonia alba

Bryonia is prepared from the roots of white bryony, a climbing plant which is found in hedgerows right across Europe. The roots are surprisingly large and store a great deal of water. Bryonia patients often seem to lack "lubrication".

n o t e s • The symptoms tend to develop slowly. • Dryness marks all symptoms: in the mouth, membranes and joints. • Extreme thirst. • The condition feels worse with the slightest motion.• Bryonia coughs are dry and very painful. • The person is irritable.

CALENDULA
Calendula officinalis

Calendula has long been known to herbalists as a major first-aid remedy for injuries. It is prepared from the common marigold, and the simplest way to use it is as a cream. When combined with Hypericum it is known as Hypercal.

n o t e s • Use this cream on all cuts, sores and open wounds. (For bruises where the skin is not broken, use Arnica cream.) • Calendula is a natural antiseptic and keeps the injury free of infection, as well as helping to speed up the healing process.

IPECAC
Cephaelis ipecacuanha

Ipecacuanha is a seemingly small, insignificant South American shrub. The remedy works mainly on the digestive and respiratory tracts, and the most important symptom it treats is nausea, no matter what the ailment.

n o t e s • Persistent nausea, not helped by vomiting. • Coughs that are accompanied by feelings of nausea. • Outbreaks of morning sickness during pregnancy. • Asthma or wheeziness accompanied by degrees of nausea. • Development of "sick" headaches.

COCCULUS
Cocculus orbiculatus

The remedy is prepared from the Indian cockle, a plant that grows along the coasts of India. It profoundly affects the nervous system and can strengthen a weakened and exhausted system. Because it can also cure nausea and dizziness, it is considered an important remedy for all kinds of travel sickness, whether on a boat, plane or in a car.

n o t e s • Nausea, vomiting, and dizziness, as in travel sickness.
• Exhaustion and nervous stress, perhaps due to lack of sleep.

DROSERA
Drosera rotundifolia

Drosera is a remedy prepared from an extraordinary insectivorous plant, the round-leaved sundew. The plants are often called "flypapers" because the leaves are tipped with sticky glands. The insect prey gets more embroiled the more it struggles, and is finally dissolved. Drosera affects the respiratory system and is an important cough remedy.

n o t e s • Deep, barking coughs.
• Prolonged and incessant coughs returning in periodic fits or spasms.
• The cough may result in retching.

EUPATORIUM
Eupatorium perfoliatum

Eupatorium is a North American herb found growing in marshy places. It is used as a herb as a flu remedy, to lower fevers and even relieve congestion and constipation, as well as boosting the immune system. Its common name, boneset, gives a clue to its homeopathic use. Whatever the other symptoms, the bones usually do ache.

n o t e s • Flu-like symptoms, with aching all over, but pains that seem to have lodged deep in the bones.
• There may be a painful cough.

EUPHRASIA
Euphrasia officinalis

Also known as eyebright, Euphrasia has long been known as a remedy with a specific application to the eyes. It is a very pretty little meadow plant, much used in wild flower plantings, with colourful flowers that open wide only when there is direct sunshine.

n o t e s • Eyes that are sore, red and inflamed. • The eyes water with burning tears. • In cases of hay fever, the symptoms are sneezing, itching and a runny nose, but for most the eyes are most usually affected.

FERRUM PHOS
Ferrum phosphoricum

Iron phosphate, from which Ferrum phos is prepared, is a highly valued mineral that manages to balance the iron and oxygen in the blood. It is also a tissue salt and can be used actively as a tonic for anaemic patients who are beginning to feel rather weak and feeble.

n o t e s • Flu and cold symptoms that are not well defined.
• Weakness and tiredness. • General anaemia: the remedy can be very useful for women with heavy periods or during pregnancy.

GELSEMIUM
Gelsemium sempervirens

The remedy is prepared from a North American plant known as yellow jasmine. It acts specifically on the muscles, the motor nerves and the nervous system. It is also quite probably the most important acute remedy for helping to treat an attack of flu.

n o t e s • Aching, heavy muscles which will not obey the will.
• Tiredness, weakness, shivering and trembling. • Fever with sweating but little thirst. • Headaches concentrated at the back of the head.

HEPAR SULPH
Hepar sulphuris calcareum

The remedy was developed by Samuel Hahnemann, the first homeopath, from calcium sulphide, which is made by heating flowers of sulphur and the lime of oyster shells together. It strongly affects the nervous system and is good in acute septic states (infected areas) and in respiratory system problems.

n o t e s • Extreme irritability and over-sensitivity. • Coldness, especially around the head. • Hoarse, dry coughs with yellow mucus, croup. • Evidence of unusually heavy sweating.

HYPERICUM
Hypericum perforatum

Prepared from the herb St John's Wort, Hypericum is primarily an injury remedy. It is particularly effective on any areas that have an abundant supply of sensitive nerves. They include the fingers, toes, lips, ears, eyes, and the coccyx at the base of the spine. Apply Hypericum instead of Arnica for bruising in such sensitive areas, although Arnica may work perfectly well if Hypericum is not available.

n o t e s • Pains are often felt suddenly shooting up the limbs, travelling along the tracks of the nerves.

IGNATIA
Ignatia amara

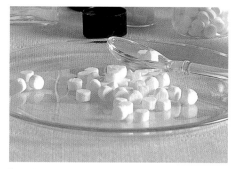

Ignatia is prepared from the seeds of a tree, the St Ignatius bean, which grows in South-east Asia. It is well known as a major "grief" remedy, and it can strongly affect the emotions.

n o t e s • Sadness and grief following emotional loss. • Sudden changeable moods: tears following laughter, or hysteria. • Suppressed emotions, when the tears will not flow. • Pronounced bouts of sighing following a period of emotional unhappiness, particularly anxiety, fear or grief.

KALI BICH
Kali bichromicum

The source of Kali bichromicum, potassium dichromate, is a chemical compound involved in many industrial processes which include dyeing, printing and photography. It especially affects the mucous membranes of the air passages, and is an important sinusitis remedy.

n o t e s • Highly unpleasant thick, strong, lumpy green discharges from the nasal passages or mouth. • Headaches in small spots as a result of catarrh. • Dry cough accompanied by sticky, yellow-green mucus.

LACHESIS
Lachesis muta

Lachesis is prepared from the venom of the bushmaster snake which is native to South America. It is a chronic remedy best left to expert, professional homeopaths, but it does have an acute use when treating sore throats and also various menstrual problems.

n o t e s • Sore throats, much worse on the left side. • Painful throats where liquids are more difficult to swallow than solids. • Menstrual pains and tension improve when the flow starts. • Hot flushes around the menopause.

LEDUM
Ledum palustre

The small shrub known as marsh tea, from which Ledum is derived, grows in boggy places across the cold wastes of the Northern Hemisphere. It is primarily a first-aid injury remedy when cold rather than warmth soon brings welcome, soothing relief.

n o t e s • Puncture wounds from nails or splinters, bites and stings, when pain is eased by cold compresses. • Wounds that look puffy and feel cold. • Injuries to the eye which looks cold, puffy and bloodshot.

LYCOPODIUM
Lycopodium clavatum

This remedy is prepared from the spores of club moss, a strange prostrate plant which likes to grow on heaths. It is generally prescribed constitutionally for aiding chronic conditions but it can also be very helpful for digestive problems and sometimes even acute sore throats.

n o t e s • Conditions which are worse on the right side, or move from the right to the left side of the body.
• Flatulence and pain in the abdomen or stomach. • Problem is aggravated by gassy foods such as beans.

CANTHARIS
Lytta vesicatoria

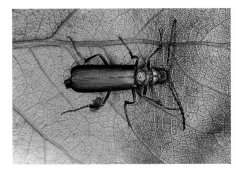

Cantharis is one of a few homeopathic remedies prepared from insects. It is derived from an iridescent green beetle which is commonly called Spanish fly. It is also known as the blister beetle because it is actually a major irritant if handled. It has an affinity with the urinary tract.

n o t e s • Cystitis – where there are highly uncomfortable, intense, burning-pains on urinating. • Evidence of burns or burning pains generally, as you would normally expect to get following sunburn, or burns from a hot pan.

MAG PHOS
Magnesia phosphorica

Magnesia phosphorica is one of the 12 tissue salts, as well as being a proven remedy. It is well known that it works directly in helping to ease tension in the nerves as well as in the muscles. It can therefore be considered as a very effective painkiller.

n o t e s • Violent, cramping and spasmodic pains, often in the abdominal area. • Pains better for warmth, gentle massage and doubling up.
• Can help with colic, period pains, sciatica, toothache and earache.

CHAMOMILLA
Matricaria chamomilla

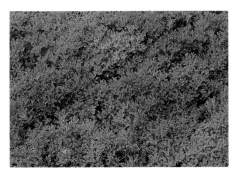

Chamomile is a member of the daisy family. It strongly affects the nervous system. It is one of the most important medicines for the treatment of children: Aconite, Belladonna and Chamomilla are together known as the "ABC" remedies.

n o t e s • Bad temper and irritability.
• Teething problems in angry babies.
• In cases of colic, the stools are usually offensive, slimy and green.
• Extreme sensitivity to pain.
• The child's temper is considerably improved on being rocked or carried.

MERCURIUS
Mercurius solubilis

The name of this remedy is sometimes abbreviated to Merc sol. It is prepared from the liquid metal mercury. It is used in acute septic states (infected areas) where the glands and their secretions are particularly affected.

n o t e s • Swollen and tender glands.
• Profuse sweating and increased thirst. • Breath, sweat and secretions can be offensive. • The tongue looks flabby, yellow and coated.
• Fevers blow hot and cold.
• Irritability and restlessness.

PHOSPHORUS
Phosphorus

Phosphorus is an important constituent of the body, particularly of the bones. It can be useful in acute situations. These include digestive problems, with immediate vomiting once the food is warmed in the stomach, and constant diarrhoea. Phosphorus can also help aid minor haemorrhages (i.e. nosebleeds). It also relieves the "spacey" feeling that lingers too long after an anaesthetic.

n o t e s • Suits people who are lively, open and friendly, but who are also occasionally nervous and anxious.

PHYTOLACCA
Phytolacca decandra

Phytolacca or poke-root is a well-known erect, unpleasant smelling plant that grows across the Northern Hemisphere, and also in South America. It is a glandular remedy that particularly affects the tonsils, and also the mammary glands. It is reckoned that Phytolacca is probably the most important remedy for helping in the treatment of mastitis.

n o t e s • Sore throats that look dark and angry. • Sore throats in which the pain feels like a hot ball. • Swollen, tender breasts with cracked nipples.

PULSATILLA
Pulsatilla nigricans

Pulsatilla is one of the most useful of acute remedies, as well as being a very important constitutional one. The remedy comes from the pasque flower and is also known as the weathercock remedy because it suits people whose moods and symptoms are constantly changing. For this reason, it is considered a wonderful remedy for small children.

n o t e s • Tendency to be weepy and clingy. • Suits people with gentle, sympathetic natures.• Yellow-green discharge from the eyes or nose.

RHUS TOX
Rhus toxicodendron

The remedy is prepared from poison ivy, native to North America. Its main use is in sprains, strains and swollen joints, but because of its itchy, rashy picture it can be a good remedy for illnesses such as chickenpox or shingles. It is also a useful remedy for acute rheumatism.

n o t e s • Extreme restlessness with a red, itchy rash. • Stiffness in the joints, which is eased by gentle motion. • The symptoms are far better for warmth, and considerably worse with cold, damp and over-exertion.

RUTA
Ruta graveolens

Ruta, or rue, is a much valued, highly attractive garden plant with blue-green leaves. It is also an ancient herbal remedy that has been often called the herb of grace. It acts particularly well on the joints, tendons, cartilages and periosteum (the membrane that covers the bones). It also has an affinity with the eyes.

n o t e s • Bruises to the bones. • Strains to the joints and connecting tissue, especially to the ankles and wrists. • The symptoms are worse for cold and damp and better for warmth.

SEPIA
Sepia officinalis

Sepia is a remedy prepared from the ink of the squid or cuttlefish. Normally its use should be left to the professional homeopath as it has a "big" picture (i.e. it can be used in many circumstances), but because of its affinity with the female reproductive system it can be helpful in some menstrual problems.

n o t e s • Suits tired, depressed, emotionally withdrawn people. • Morning sickness in pregnancy, which is worse for the smell of food. • Hot flushes during the menopause.

SILICA
Silicea

Silica is a mineral derived from flint. It is one of the 12 tissue salts, and its presence in the body aids the vital elimination of toxins. It can be used acutely in septic (infected) conditions to strengthen the body's resistance to continual infection, and also to help expel any foreign bodies such as splinters.

n o t e s • Suitable for symptoms that are slow to heal, or for people who feel the cold, or who lack stamina or vitality. • Small-scale infections that seem to be turning septic rather than healing.

SPONGIA
Spongia tosta

Spongia, as its name clearly indicates, is a remedy which is prepared from the lightly roasted skeleton part of the marine sponge. It actually works very well on the respiratory tract, and it is now generally considered to be one of homeopathy's major cough remedies. It is actually a significant and indeed important aid or remedy when it comes to treating croup in young children.

n o t e s • Dry spasmodic cough.
• The cough sounds like a saw being pulled through wood.

NUX VOMICA
Strychnos nux vomica

Nux vomica is prepared from the seeds of the poison nut tree of South-east Asia. It is a remedy that has many uses in both chronic and acute situations, and it is known to be very useful when the digestive system is involved.

n o t e s • Nausea or vomiting after a rich meal, when the food remains undigested like a load in the stomach.
• A feeling that if only you could vomit you would feel better. • An urge to pass a stool, but with unsatisfactory results. • Heartburn.

SYMPHYTUM
Symphytum officinale

The remedy is easily prepared from the common herb comfrey. It is also called knitbone, which indicates its main use in promoting the healing of broken bones. Use the remedy daily for several weeks after the bone has been set. Symphytum can also be used for many injuries to the eyeball such as, for example, getting a tennis ball directly in the eye.

n o t e s • Speeds up the knitting or fusing together of broken bones.
• Injuries to the eyeball, such as being hit by a hard object.

VALERIAN
Valeriana officinalis

Valerian is a well-known herb whose overuse in the 19th century caused insomnia and over-taxation of the nervous system to the point of hysteria. Because of the principle "like cures like", very tiny doses such as those used in homeopathy can cure these very same problems. Valerian is an important remedy for sleeplessness. Take one pill about one hour before bedtime. You should soon notice the improvement.

n o t e s • Especially useful when the mind feels like a "hamster on a wheel".

VERBASCUM
Verbascum thapsus

Verbascum is prepared from the great mullein, a common wayside herb. It is a highly regarded garden plant sending up marvellous stems. Homeopathically it is associated with earaches, and it is best used as an oil. The remedy is especially helpful for children, who tend to suffer from ear infections more often than adults. Place a few drops of the oil on a warmed teaspoon and gently insert into the ear, with the child lying on one side.

n o t e s • Earaches of all kinds, both in children and adults.

VIBURNUM OPULUS
Viburnum opulus

The guelder rose is widely distributed in woods and damp places throughout northern Europe and the US. It is a valued garden plant, especially in the form 'Roseum' which has large white flowers, giving rise to its common name, the snowball tree. It is also known as cramp bark and the homeopathic remedy, which is prepared from the bark, can be very helpful for period pains as well as for spasmodic cramps.

n o t e s • For aiding the treatment of severe cramping and muscle spasms.

AYURVEDA

Thousands of years old, Ayurveda is acknowledged as the traditional healing system of India, and has influenced many other healing systems around the world. There are many different branches to Ayurveda because it covers so many aspects of health and healing, but the main emphasis in the following pages is on diet and lifestyle, specifically tailored to modern life. This basic approach will help you to develop some simple ways to keep yourself balanced. Identify and learn how to live in accordance with your true nature, and discover how you can begin to heal your vikruti (your current emotional, physical and mental state of health) using the ancient principles of Ayurvedic healing.

WHAT IS AYURVEDA?

It may be little known – and remarkably few people seem to have heard of it – but Ayurveda is a highly respected, highly revered ancient form of learning which has an amazing amount to teach us. It brings peace of body and mind, important ways of seeing the world and your own place in the scheme of things, and highly practical, sensible ideas when it comes to medicine, diet and ways of staying calm and relaxed.

THE ORIGINS OF AYURVEDA

The origins of Ayurveda are uncertain. It is recounted that thousands of years ago, men of wisdom or rishis (meaning seers) as they are known in India, were saddened by the suffering of humanity. They knew that ill health and short lives allowed man little time to consider his spirituality and to commune with the divine – with God.

▲ Indian sadhus, like the one shown here, tend to live a nomadic life, renouncing worldly goods, and devoting themselves to prayer.

In the Himalayan mountains they prayed hard and meditated together, calling upon God to help them to relieve the plight of man, and God felt moved by compassion and gave them the essential teachings that would enlighten them in the ways of healing illness, and thereby alleviate and remove all suffering on the earth.

It is believed that these teachings are the Vedas, although this cannot be proven, due to the lack of historical records. A book called the *Atharva Veda* was one of the first detailed accounts of the system. From this, and perhaps other ancient writings, came the beginnings of Ayurvedic medicine, which has developed, changed and absorbed many other influences over hundreds of years to become what it is today. Due to the invasions of India over the years, and the subsequent suppression of many original Indian ways of life, several ancient texts have been lost or even destroyed, but enough have survived to ensure the active continuation of these highly valued, greatly respected teachings.

Ayurveda is now acknowledged as the traditional healing system of India. It comes from two Sanskrit words, *ayur*, meaning "life", and *veda*, meaning "knowing", and can be interpreted as meaning the "science of life". The oldest healing system to remain intact, it is very comprehensive and has influenced many healing systems around the world.

▼ Ayurveda travelled out of India and influenced many other countries with its ageless wisdom about living in the light of truth.

▲ *The influence of Ayurveda has spread far and wide. This is reflected in the different oils that are used. Many are made from plants that are found all over the world, not just India.*

THE INFLUENCE OF AYURVEDA

For centuries after the end of the Vedic era, Ayurvedic medicine developed into a comprehensive healing system. Its philosophy and techniques soon spread far and wide to China, Arabia, Persia and Greece, gradually influencing Middle Eastern, Greek and Chinese methods of healing. It is well known that Ayurvedic practitioners reached the ancient city of Athens, and it can be noted that the traditional Greek folk medicine, based upon the bodily humours (characteristics), is significantly similar to Ayurveda. In turn, Greek medicine strongly influenced the subsequent development of what we call traditional or orthodox Western medicine. However, it is much too difficult to say exactly how much or to what degree the medical philosophy of Ayurveda was indeed influential, or even how much Ayurveda influenced current techniques.

GREEK AND EUROPEAN MEDICINE

The five elements in Chinese medicine appear to have come from Ayurveda. It is documented that the Indian medical system was brought to China by Indian Buddhist missionaries, many of whom were skilled Ayurvedic practitioners. The missionaries also travelled to South-east Asia and Tibet, influencing the people of these lands. Tibetan medicine, for example, is an intricate mix of Ayurvedic practices and philosophy with Tibetan Buddhist and shamanic influences.

WHAT IS AYURVEDIC MEDICINE?

The main aim of Ayurvedic medicine (which is only one branch of Ayurveda) is to improve health and longevity, leaving the individual free to contemplate matters of the spirit and to follow a spiritual path. This does not mean that you have to be spiritual or religious to benefit from Ayurvedic medicine; the system is very practical in its applications and deals with all kinds of health problems, without spirituality ever being mentioned. Its main focus is nutrition, supported primarily by the use of herbs, massage and aromatic oils, but there are many complementary branches as well.

Ayurvedic philosophy encourages those who practise it to eat the fruits and seeds of the earth, rather than take the life of animals. Since some animal products have in fact been included in this introductory guide, they should only ever be used in strict moderation. Let common sense and sensitivity be your guide.

The branches of Ayurvedic medicine include specific diets, surgery, jyotish (Vedic astrology), psychiatry and pancha karma (cleansing and detoxifying techniques). Yoga is not a branch of Ayurveda, but since it shares the same roots you will find that the two are often practised together. Yoga includes meditation, mantras (prayer chants), yantras (contemplation of geometric visual patterns) and hatha yoga (practices for bringing great harmony to the spirit, mind and body).

If you are actually much more interested in the many spiritual aspects of Ayurvedic teachings, then it is strongly recommended that you think very seriously about taking up yoga so that it becomes a regular part of your life.

▼ *Most people clearly benefit from meditation or yoga, which can help to illuminate the pathway to inner relaxation and peace.*

THE DOSHAS

Instead of using modern psychology to group people into types, try using the ancient doshas. They pinpoint and identify three basic types of people, which in turn helps you to a greater self-awareness and to an appreciation of others. The doshas are also excellent ways of helping you to fine-tune and regulate your lifestyle, bringing greater peace and well-being. The doshas are not just terms, they are ways of actively improving your life.

THE SEASONS

There are three doshas (basic types of people, in terms of constitution) – vata, pitta and kapha. They are influenced by the rhythms of nature, seasonal change and the time of year. Autumn is a time of change when leaves turn brown and dry; vata is highest in the autumn and early winter, and at times of dry, cold and windy weather. Pitta is highest in late spring, throughout the summer and during times of heat and humidity. Kapha is highest in the winter months and during early spring, when the weather is frequently still cold and damp.

In Ayurvedic theory, the progress of a disease goes through several stages. There is accumulation (when it is increasing), followed by aggravation (when it is at its highest point and can cause problems). There is also decrease (when it is lessening) and a neutral time when it is passive (neither decreasing nor increasing). Use the questionnaire later in this chapter to discover your dosha, and see whether it is vata, pitta or kapha. People who are single types can refer to the dosha that scores the highest points on their questionnaire. Dual doshic types should vary their lifestyle to suit the seasonal changes, as shown in the dual doshas section.

▲ *Yoga can be a very helpful way of balancing both the body and mind. After a few classes you are free to practise by yourself.*

YOUR BODY TYPE

This section clearly outlines how you can identify your dosha or body type. Dosha means "that which tends to go out of balance easily." Your dosha is in fact your bio-type or prakruti ("nature"). You are made up of a mixture of the five elements – ether, wind, fire, water and earth, and will display certain recognizable characteristics depending on your personality and nature.

As well as your prakruti, you may also have a vikruti, which is your current state of mental or physical health. This develops throughout your life and may actually differ from your prakruti. It is important that you treat your vikruti first (how you are now), then go back to living with your prakruti. For example, you may have developed arthritis or back trouble over a long period, or you may be suffering from a cold or skin rash which lasts a few days. Once you have have cleared your condition, maintain your prakruti using a preventative treatment, such as diet, massage, oils, colours and scents.

▼ *Levels of vata increase in the autumn when the weather is changeable. Surrounding yourself with flowers helps you relax.*

WARMING UP/SPRING
pitta accumulating, kapha aggravated, vata neutral

HOT/SUMMER
vata accumulating, pitta aggravated, kapha decreasing

COOLING/AUTUMN
vata aggravated, pitta decreasing, kapha neutral

COLD/WINTER
vata decreasing, pitta neutral, kapha accumulating

Apart from the three single doshas, there are four combinations, making a total of seven differing constitutional types: vata, pitta, kapha, vata/pitta (or pitta/vata), pitta/kapha (or kapha/pitta), kapha/vata (or vata/kapha), and vata/pitta/kapha. These may be either out of balance or in a state of balance.

To discover your prakruti and vikruti, answer the questionnaire twice. Also ask other people who know you well to fill out the questionnaire for you, to give you as clear a picture of yourself as possible. The first time you fill out the questionnaire, you should concentrate upon your current condition – your vikruti – recording your answers based upon your present and recent health history.

You can discover your prakruti by answering the questionnaire a second time, this time with answers based upon your entire lifetime. Fill out the questionnaire with your complete history in mind. This will give you a better idea about the difference between your vikruti and your prakruti. Once the answers to the questionnaire have revealed both your vikruti and your prakruti (they may be the same, which is fine), the information here can be used to treat both. Follow whichever dosha scores most highly (vata, pitta or kapha).

ELEMENTAL ENERGIES
The elements are very important in Ayurveda. They descend from space (ether), down to air. Air descends into the fire element. Fire falls into the water element and water to earth, so that we move from the most rarefied elements (ether), to the most dense (earth). With this in mind, you will notice that the chart below follows a descending pattern of ether and air (vata), fire and water (pitta) and water and earth (kapha). Vata is a mixture of ether and air and is often translated as "wind". In the creation story of Ayurveda, vata leads the other doshas, because its combination of air and ether is actually the most rarefied. The

elements move from the most refined down to the most dense. Consequently, if a vata is out of balance, the end result will be that the others will be out of balance as well.

Your age and the season of the year will also have an influence upon your doshic type. From childhood up to the teenage years you are influenced by kapha; from your teens to the age of 50 or 60 you tend to come under the pitta influence, and from 50 to 60 onwards you enter the vata phase of life.

Each dosha has a particular energetic principle which influences responses within the body. Everyone has all three doshas to an extent, but it is the ratio between each that is important, and that creates your individuality. Each dosha plays an important role in this equation and balancing act. For example, movement (vata) without the stability of kapha would simply end up in chaos, and the inactivity of kapha without activity and movement would quickly result in stagnation.

▼ *A kapha type (water and earth) will be intuitive, sensitive and will dislike change but will be good at holding things together.*

ELEMENT	DOSHA	COSMIC LINK	PRINCIPLE	INFLUENCE
ether/air	vata	wind	change	activity/movement
fire/water	pitta	sun	conversion	metabolism/transformation
water/earth	kapha	moon	inertia	cohesion

YOU AND YOUR DOSHA

Working out exactly which dosha type you are is easily done, but before tackling the question-naire on the opposite page, read the following notes very carefully. They put this huge wealth of information, and its references to skin types, lifestyle, and speech, into an objective framework, giving you a clearer perspective, helping you understand precisely what are called your humoral factors.

WHICH TYPE ARE YOU?

The questionnaire opposite is designed to help you to assess your basic ratio of humoral factors. From this you can determine which diet, colours, exercise routines, crystals, oils and scents are most likely to suit you. By referring to the sections on which you score the most points, you will identify whether you are a vata, pitta or kapha dosha, or what is called a combination type. Read the questions and, to discover your prakruti, tick those descriptions which apply to you in general terms. Allocate two ticks to the statement that you think is most applicable to you; use one tick for a description that could also possibly apply, but if a particular description does not apply to you, then leave it unticked.

▲ *Gems are used in Ayurveda only with a prescription from a jyotish (Vedic or Hindu astrologer), or from an Ayurvedic physician.*

REVEALING YOUR VIKRUTI

As has already been explained, your current condition, or vikruti, may not be the same as your underlying constitution, or prakruti. If you wish to discover whether or not this is the case, go through the questions a second time, this time using crosses instead of ticks. To reveal your vikruti, answer the questions according to how you have been feeling in the more recent past, and how the descriptions relate to your current health or condition, including any illnesses or other changes, no matter how subtle, that you are currently experiencing.

When you are answering the questions, do make sure that you clearly focus either on your prakruti (your general state throughout life – ticks), or on your vikruti (current or recent state – crosses). To avoid any possible confusion, make sure that you finish with one set of answers before you start attempting to fill out and assess the questionnaire for a second time.

If you wish, you can answer the questionnaire a third time, separating questions about the mind from questions about the body. Use circles and squares to record your answers. This will indicate whether your body and mind are the same dosha. If they are different, follow the dietary advice for the mind. For example, if you have a kapha body and a pitta mind, follow the kapha eating and exercise plan, including the massage technique, and ensure that you have soothing colours and a calm environment.

"VATA", "PITTA", AND "KAPHA"

Following the questionnaire are three sections headed "Vata", "Pitta" and "Kapha". Having discovered your vikruti (condition) or prakruti (constitution), turn to the pages relevant to your predominant dosha for detailed advice on reducing any excess

▼ *Vatas need to learn how to be still because they tend to suffer from energy depletion, having the least amount of stamina.*

(vikruti), or to see how you can maintain your true character (prakruti). When referring to the various sections, do please read the information very carefully before you begin to put it into practice. Please also note that when using Ayurvedic medicinal herbs, you should take them only for as long as you are experiencing any obvious symptoms. You must check that the herbs are suited to your basic doshic needs; do this quite frequently, monitoring yourself even on a weekly basis.

When you begin to use any of the Ayurvedic prescriptions and techniques, do not be tempted to try and elaborate on them. This will do far more harm than good. The effect of the prescriptions lies in the ratio of the individual ingredients. Change this even in the subtlest way and all the good work may well be undone. Ayurveda is extremely complex and precise. For example, there are lengthy guidelines about the specific crystals that may be used to make a crystal infusion for each individual dosha. It is advisable that you do not make other infusions unless you are qualified or highly experienced; since crystals and gems can have a very powerful effect.

▲ *Choose foods and herbs according to your doshic condition.*

DISCOVER YOUR DOSHA

Mark the questionnaire with either a √ (= your general constitution – prakruti) or x (= your current or recent state – vikruti).

	VATA	PITTA	KAPHA
HEIGHT	Very short, or tall and thin	Medium	Tall or short and sturdy
MUSCULATURE	Thin, prominent tendons	Medium/firm	Plentiful/solid
BODILY FRAME	Light, narrow	Medium frame	Large/broad
WEIGHT	Light, hard to gain	Medium weight	Heavy, gains easily
SWEAT	Minimal	Profuse, especially when hot	Moderate
SKIN	Dry, cold	Soft, warm	Moist, cool, possibly oily
COMPLEXION	Darkish	Fair, pink, red, freckles	Pale, white
HAIR AMOUNT	Average amount	Early thinning and greying	Plentiful
TYPE OF HAIR	Dry, thin, dark, coarse	Fine, soft, red, fair	Thick, lustrous, brown
SIZE OF EYES	Small, narrow or sunken	Average	Large, prominent
TYPE OF EYES	Dark brown or grey, dull	Blue/grey/hazel, intense	Blue, brown, attractive
TEETH AND GUMS	Protruding, receding gums	Yellowish, gums bleed	White teeth, strong gums
SIZE OF TEETH	Small or large, irregular	Average	Large
PHYSICAL ACTIVITY	Moves quickly, active	Moderate pace, average	Slow pace, steady
ENDURANCE	Low	Good	Very good
STRENGTH	Poor	Good	Very good
TEMPERATURE	Dislikes cold, likes warmth	Likes coolness	Aversion to cool and damp
STOOLS	Tendency to constipation	Tendency to loose stools	Plentiful, slow elimination
LIFESTYLE	Variable, erratic	Busy, tends to achieve a lot	Steady, can skip meals
SLEEP	Light, interrupted, fitful	Sound, short	Deep, likes plenty
EMOTIONAL TENDENCY	Fearful, anxious, insecure	Fiery, angry, judgemental	Greedy, possessive
MENTAL ACTIVITY	Restless, lots of ideas	Sharp, precise, logical	Calm, steady, stable
MEMORY	Good recent memory	Sharp, generally good	Good long term
REACTION TO STRESS	Excites very easily	Quick temper	Not easily irritated
WORK	Creative	Intellectual	Caring
MOODS	Change quickly	Change slowly	Generally steady
SPEECH	Fast	Clear, sharp, precise	Deep, slow
RESTING PULSE			
WOMEN	Above 80	70-80	Below 70
MEN	Above 70	60-70	Below 60
Totals: *Please add up*	**Vata**	**Pitta**	**Kapha**

VATA

Vata types are known to be rather restless, cool people, who certainly notice the cold. When you have excess levels of vata, fear, depression and nervousness become quite marked, significant traits, and with repressed emotions comes a definite weakening of the immune system. However, by adopting the appropriate lifestyle, and making one or two changes, you will create a better balance within yourself, and find that you achieve much more.

The vata body type is usually thin and narrow. Vatas do not gain weight easily and are often restless by nature, especially when they are busy and active. They have dry hair and cool skin and a tendency to feel the cold. Their levels of energy are erratic, and they have to be very careful not to exhaust themselves, leading to inconsistency. They may find it quite hard to relax, which can lead to an overactive mind and insomnia.

Vata symptoms will be changeable, being cold by nature and therefore worse in cold weather. Any pain will worsen during change. Vata people can suffer from wind, low back pain, arthritis and nerve disorders. Vata types, because of their individual restless nature, certainly require a regular intake of nourishment, and they should sit down to eat or drink at regular times. Careful exercise should always be taken in moderation, clearly maintaining a gentle, regular, well-worked out routine that will help to keep the mind focused, and in perfect harmony with the body.

▲ *Vata people should try to eat warming foods which are earthy and sweet, with the emphasis upon cooked foods, such as a bowl of dhal, rather than salads.*

Elements: ether and air.
Climate: dry and cold.
Principle: movement.
Emotions: fearful, anxious, apprehensive, sensitive, timid, lacking confidence, slightly nervous, changeable.
Systems most affected by excess vata: the nervous system and also the colon.
Symptoms of excess vata: flatulence, back pain, problems with circulation, dry skin, outbreaks of arthritis, constipation, and nerve disorders.

▼ *In summer the vata quickly begins to accumulate as the heat of the sun begins to dry everything out. The best way to stop your skin from drying out too, so keeping it gently moist, is to use a top quality natural cream.*

DIETARY TIPS

Vata people must always be quite careful, but not to the point that cooking suddenly becomes something of a difficult problem. The easy-to-follow, basic guidelines are as follows.

You must avoid all kinds of fried foods, no matter how tempting, and you should eat at regular intervals. Irregular huge meals are to be avoided at all costs. To reduce any excess vata, then follow the vata diet and recommendations in your eating and living plan. Always attempt to avoid any foods and other items that are not listed, as far as is possible. If animal products are a part of your diet, they should be used strictly in moderation.

HERBS AND SPICES

Almond essence, asafoetida (hing), basil leaves, bay leaves, cardamom pods, coriander (cilantro), fennel, fresh ginger, marjoram, mint, nutmeg, oregano, paprika, parsley, peppermint, spearmint, tarragon, thyme, turmeric and vanilla.

GRAINS AND SEEDS

Oats (cooked), pumpkin seeds, quinoa, rice (this includes all kinds and varieties), sesame seeds, sprouted wheat bread, sunflower seeds and wheat.

NUTS, MEAT & FISH

Almonds, brazil nuts, cashews, hazelnuts, macadamias, pecans, pine nuts, pistachios and walnuts. Beef, chicken, duck, eggs, sea fish, shrimps and turkey.

VEGETABLES

Artichokes, asparagus, beetroot, carrots, courgettes (zucchini), cucumber, daikon radish, green beans, leeks, okra, olives, onions (cooked), parsnips, pumpkins, radishes, spinach (cooked), swede (rutabagas), sweet potatoes, tomatoes (cooked), and fresh watercress.

FRUIT

Apricots, avocados, bananas, berries, cherries, fresh coconuts, dates, fresh figs, grapefruit, grapes, lemons, limes, mangoes, melons, oranges, peaches, pineapples, rhubarb and strawberries.

DAIRY PRODUCTS

Cow's milk, cottage cheese, goat's milk, goat's' cheese and soft cheese – all are to be taken sensibly, in moderation.

COOKING OILS

Unrefined sesame oil.

DRINKS

Apricot juice, carrot juice, ginger tea, grape juice, grapefruit juice, orange juice, hot dairy drinks, lemon balm tea, lemonade and peach juice.

AROMAS AND MASSAGE OILS

Vata people are unusual because they tend to benefit much more than either of the other two doshas from having a massage. Consequently they should consider massaging their feet, hands and head every morning, and have a regular massage at least once a week. The massage should become a regular, greatly appreciated part of your lifestyle.

Vata aromas are warm and sweet, and the most appropriate massage oil for the vata personality is gently warmed sesame oil. Bottles of sesame oil are widely available, and are generally of a high, well-perfumed standard. If that is impossible to obtain, any other oil (preferably virgin olive) will suffice. It can be perfumed by the addition of your favourite herb. Oil is good for vata types, and if your vata is seriously out of balance, increase the number of massages you have a week from one to as many as three. You will soon notice the enormous improvement.

When using essential oils, note they must be diluted. Do not put them directly on your skin or take them internally. In fact it is not advisable to use the same essential oil for more than two weeks; interchange your essential oils so that you do not create a toxic build-up, or overload of one fragrance. If you are pregnant or have a diagnosed medical condition, do not use any essential oil without consulting a qualified practitioner.

Warm, calming or earthy essential oils are the most suitable for vata. These include camphor (which can be an irritant, so do test yourself for sensitivity first), eucalyptus, ginger, sandalwood and jatamansi (a spikenard species from India).

VATA MASSAGE

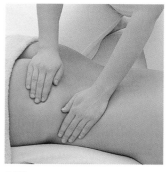

1 The correct vata massage should always be gentle.

2 Keep the actions firm, regular, soothing and relaxing.

3 Use flowing, continuous stroking movements.

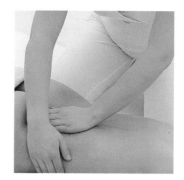

4 Oil and ease any areas displaying dry, tight skin.

COLOURS

Vata individuals generally benefit from most of the pastel colours, and from earthy colours that are gentle and warm to look at. They include ochres, browns and yellows.

OCHRE

A warm, friendly and relaxing colour, ochre is good at drawing the energy down, right through the system, helping the vata individual to feel much more solid and steady.

BROWN

A solid, reliable colour, brown helps to ground the vata type, stabilizing any tendency to flightiness. It is also good at holding the emotions in place; it consolidates and aids concentration.

YELLOW

A warming, enlivening colour, yellow is linked to the mind and intellect. It helps to keep the vata mentality alert by focusing the mind, and calming any rising emotions.

MAKING A COLOUR INFUSION

Begin by taking a piece of thin cotton or silk. The fabric should be warm yellow in colour, and sufficiently thin to allow the light through. Next, wrap it around a small transparent (not coloured) jar filled with spring water and leave it outside in the sunlight for four hours. Finally, remove the fabric. Note, vata infusions should not be stored in the fridge, but kept at room temperature.

◄ *This infusion will encourage a sense of warmth and well-being.*

GEMS AND CRYSTALS

Gems and crystals have subtle healing qualities that can be utilized in Ayurvedic medicine. Their curious, well-known powers are taken seriously by the jyotish (Vedic astrologer), who can determine which gems or crystals you will need to use, depending on the circumstances of your life chart.

Topaz is a warm stone that traditionally dispels fear, making it an ideal stone for vata because it calms high emotions and anxiety. Wear topaz whenever you want to feel confident and in control. Amethyst is an appropriate crystal to wear when you want to balance vata. It soon promotes a fine clarity of mind and thought, and will help you to radiate harmony.

There may be times when it is advisable to remove all crystals – when you find circumstances in your life are changing for the worse. This indicates that your birth chart or constitution does not require the healing qualities of a particular crystal, or that it is highlighting an area of your birth chart in a negative way. Seek expert advice on replacements.

CLEANING CRYSTALS AND CRYSTAL INFUSIONS

Before making a crystal infusion, it is best to cleanse your crystal. In fact, crystals that are used for infusions should ideally be cleansed before and after each use. Once you have filled a bowl with spring water, dissolve a teaspoon of sea salt in it. The crystal sits in for up to about eight hours before being rinsed.

1 Place the crystal in the water and leave to stand for about four hours, or leave it overnight in the dark.

2 Rinse it in spring water, visualizing any residues that were being held in the crystal being washed away.

To make a crystal infusion, take the cleansed crystal and hold it in your hands, imagining that the crystal is full of peace and calm. Place the crystal in a clear glass bowl, cover it with spring water, and leave it in the sunlight for about four hours. Remove the crystal and bottle the spring water. You can now drink the infusion prior to any mentally demanding tasks. It will aid clarity of mind and help reduce any stress that might arise as a result of pressure. You can keep the infusion for just 24 hours, after which it should be discarded. Make sure you store the infusion away from domestic appliances and electrical equipment.

EXERCISE AND TONIC

Since vata is cold in nature it benefits from warmth and comfort. Make your own warming tonic drinks for cold windy days by combining ingredients from the vata eating plan. Be aware though that sugar weakens the immune system and vatas, with their tendency to stress (another immune suppressor), need to be particularly wary of sugary and refined foods, choosing naturally sweet-tasting foods, such as fruit, instead.

Vata people benefit from gentle, relaxing forms of exercise. Being the most easily exhausted of the various categories, they should be careful not to overdo things. Examples of suitable exercise include walking, yoga and slow swimming. In essence, it is not so much the form of exercise that you take, but rather the way in which you take it. With vata, the exercise routine should always be on the gentle side; with this in mind, vata types can undertake most sports and activities.

Yoga stretches will gradually and gently lengthen your muscles, and increase your flexibility. It has enormous all-round benefits. If you do not actively practise yoga as a form of exercise, you may well find that achieving a full or even half lotus for meditation is much too strenuous and difficult. If this is the case, do not try and force yourself. Instead, use a specifically designed meditation stool, or place some firm cushions on the floor beneath you. Push your bent knees on to the floor, then tuck your feet in towards you on the floor, forming a solid triangular base with your legs.

FRESH GINGER AND LEMON TEA

This tea is remarkably quick and easy to make, and tastes absolutely delicious. It is also a marvellous tonic for a vata.

1 lemon	*Spring water*
A small slice of fresh ginger	*Raw honey or fructose*

1 Wash the lemon and then cut it into thin slices, leaving the peel on. Peel the piece of fresh ginger and slice it finely.
2 Place the lemon and ginger slices in a small teapot.
3 Add boiling spring water, then stir. Finally sweeten with honey or fructose, drink and enjoy.

PITTA

Pitta people are generally quite well-balanced, well-proportioned, rounded types, admired by all, but they can suddenly become passionately focused and intense. At its most extreme this tendency leads to a high degree of intolerance and irritability. Consequently pitta types should keep well away from any foods that are known to be hot and spicy, and which might inflame them, and concentrate on meals that promote their more soothing side.

The pitta body type is usually of average build and nicely proportioned. Pittas like food and have a healthy appetite. The hair is usually straight, fine and fair, though dark-haired people can also be pitta types. People with red hair will automatically have some level of pitta within their nature. Like the fire element, their temperament can be quite intense, and when it manifests itself in excess this can lead to marked intolerance.

Pitta skin will have a tendency to be sensitive to the sun, and pitta types will need to be very careful how much time they spend in direct sunlight. The fiery nature of the sun will sometimes inflame the pitta person, leading to skin rashes, freckles and sunburn. Cool showers, cool environments and plenty of long cooling drinks (but not ice-cold ones) will help to alleviate any high temperatures and calm down pitta types.

People of this nature can be impatient, having highly active and alert minds. However, pitta people can also have a very good sense of humour and a warm personality.

▲ *Pitta people should always aim to eat food that is rather soothing. What they must do is avoid any foods that are considered hot and spicy. Ingredients such as fiery chillies are definitely off the menu.*

Elements: fire and water.
Climate: hot and moist.
Principle: transformation.
Emotions: hate, anger, resentment, intolerance, impatience, irritability, indignation, jealousy, good humour, intelligence, alertness, open warm-heartedness.
Systems most affected by excess pitta: skin, metabolism, small intestines, eyes, liver, hair on the head.
Symptoms of excess pitta: skin disorders, acidity, sun-sensitivity, premature degrees of hair loss or loss of hair colour, outbreaks of diarrhoea.

▼ *Pitta types generally benefit from spending time away from fast, noisy, chaotic urban environments. They should seek out quiet, peaceful, well-shaded, naturally calming surroundings.*

DIETARY TIPS

The pitta person should avoid all hot, spicy and sour foods, as they will aggravate this dosha; they should also avoid all fried foods. Since heated food will increase pitta within the system, pitta types should eat more raw than cooked foods. As a primarily vegetarian system, Ayurveda does not advocate the eating of animal products, especially for the pitta dosha, so although some meats and other animal products have been included in the following list, they should really be used in the strictest moderation. Let common sense always prevail.

HERBS AND SPICES

Aloe vera juice (totally avoid during a pregnancy), basil leaves, cinnamon, coriander (cilantro), cumin, dill, fennel, fresh ginger, hijiki, mint leaves, spearmint.

GRAINS AND SEEDS

Barley, basmati rice, flax seeds, psyllium seeds, rice cakes, sunflower seeds, wheat, wheat bran, white rice.

PROTEINS

Aduki beans, black beans, black-eyed beans, chick peas (garbanzos), kidney beans, lentils (red and brown), lima beans, mung beans, pinto beans, soya beans, split peas, tempeh and tofu. Chicken, freshwater fish, rabbit, turkey.

VEGETABLES

Artichokes, asparagus, broccoli, Brussels sprouts, butternut squash, cabbages, courgettes (zucchini), celery, cucumber, fennel, green beans and green peppers, Jerusalem artichokes, kale, leafy greens, leeks, lettuces, mushrooms, onions (cooked), parsnips, spinach (cooked). Eat most vegetables raw instead of cooked.

FRUIT

Apples, apricots, avocados, berries, cherries, dates, figs, mangoes, melons, oranges, pears, pineapples, plums, pomegranates, prunes, quinces, raisins, red grapes and watermelons. Always make sure that the fruits have fully ripened, and are very sweet and fresh.

DAIRY PRODUCTS

Cottage cheese, cow's milk, diluted yoghurt, ghee (clarified butter), goat's milk, mild soft cheeses and unsalted butter may all be taken but with a reasonable degree of moderation.

COOKING OILS

Olive oil, sunflower oil, soya and walnut oil. As with all dairy products, these oils should be used in moderation.

DRINKS

Apple juice, apricot juice, cool dairy drinks, grape juice, mango juice, mixed vegetable juice, soya milk, vegetable bouillon, elderflower tea, jasmine tea, spearmint tea and strawberry tea.

AROMAS AND MASSAGE OILS

Essential oils for pitta include honeysuckle, jasmine, sandalwood and vetiver. They must be diluted and should never be taken internally. Avoid a toxic build-up by interchanging the oils every two weeks. If you are pregnant or have a diagnosed medical condition, you must consult a qualified practitioner before attempting to use essential oils.

If possible go to an experienced masseur. They understand exactly how a massage should be given. In time you will pick up the basics and may be able to start giving others a gentle massage. The key to success is to take your time, and make sure that your partner is fully relaxed. There is no point in attempting a soft massage when they are in an agitated state, and are incapable of lying still for a couple of minutes, let alone 20. When applying the essential oils, it is important that you work with firm, consistent hand movements, totally avoiding any sudden changes of direction. Think of your hands as waves, sweeping in one long curving movement over a smooth beach. That said, do not go to the opposite extreme and be so frightened of touching or hurting the skin that you barely make any contact. The right degree of pressure is about the same as for a firm hairwash.

After the massage, do not expect to get up and rush out. That would immediately undermine all the good work. Instead, take your time, possibly even have a cat-nap, and only step back into everyday life when you are feeling absolutely ready. That way you will feel refreshed, calm and clear-headed. It also helps if you have a massage on a day that you know will be stress-free.

PITTA MASSAGE

1 Start the massage in the middle of the back.

2 Use continuous, relaxing, deep, varied movements.

3 Be gentle on any areas of stiffness or soreness.

4 Continue with sweeping, slow movements.

COLOURS

If you are experiencing symptoms of excess pitta, such as irritability or impatience, or on occasions when you know that you are going to have a busy and active day ahead of you, balance your system by wearing natural fibres in cooling and calming colours, such as green, blue, violet or any quiet pastel shade.

BLUE

Blue is a soothing, healing colour which is ideal for the active pitta type. It is linked to spiritual consciousness and helps the pitta to remain open and calm without being over-stimulated.

GREEN

Green, an integral colour of the natural world, brings harmonious feelings to the pitta personality, having the ability to soothe emotions and calm passionate feelings.

VIOLET

Violet is a refined colour that soothes and opens the mind, and increases awareness of spiritual issues.

MAKING A COLOUR INFUSION

Take a piece of thin, translucent cotton or silk in violet or light blue. Wrap it around a small transparent (not coloured) bottle or jar filled with spring water. Leave it outside in dappled sunlight, not in direct sun, for approximately six hours. Finally, remove the fabric, and drink the infusion to encourage the wonderful sensation of inner peace and harmony.

◄ *A blue colour infusion will help to clear the system of a build-up of pressure.*

GEMS AND CRYSTALS

When you want to reduce excess pitta, wear pearls or a mother-of-pearl ring set in silver upon the ring finger of your right hand. Pearls have the ability to reduce inflammatory conditions, including sudden passionate, heated emotions. Ideally, natural pearls should be worn, although cultured pearls are actually quite acceptable. The most harmonious day to put on your pearls is a Monday (the moon's day) during a new moon. However, do not wear pearls when you have a kapha condition, such as a cold. The moonstone has the ability to calm emotions and is soft and cooling, being feminine in orientation. It can certainly help to pacify the pitta personality.

You can also use stones, as shown right, to make a special infusion. It involves no more than placing the stone in a glass bowl that has been topped up with spring water. The key part of the process is standing the bowl and stone outside, preferably on a night when there is a full moon and a cloudless sky. The longer you can leave it standing out the better, three hours being about the minimum period for successful results.

When you bring in the bowl, pour the special water into a clean glass and drink before breakfast. If you can make standing this bowl outside at night a regular part of your routine, then you will soon notice the difference that drinking moonstone water makes. You will feel increasingly calm, relaxed, clear-headed, stable, grounded, and above all inwardly strong. Your confidence grows and grows. You will find that other people definitely notice, and become increasingly attracted towards you. Feeling more attractive actually gives you a new lease of life.

MAKING A MOONSTONE INFUSION

1 Take a stone specimen that has already been cleansed.

2 Leave the bowl outside to stand under a full moon.

3 Remove the moonstone, and pour out the liquid.

4 Drink the moonstone infusion when you wake.

ORANGE AND ELDERFLOWER INFUSION

This infusion makes a light refreshing drink, ideal in summer.

I large sweet orange
2 heads fresh elderflower
Fresh spearmint

300ml/½ pint spring water
Fructose to taste

1 Wash the orange in spring water. Slice and put in a jug.
2 Add elderflower heads and spearmint; pour in spring water.
3 Leave for one hour, add fructose to taste, and drink.

EXERCISE AND TONIC

Cooling drinks made from fresh fruit and vegetable juices are ideal tonics for the pitta constitution.

Pittas require a moderate amount of exercise, which should involve some element of vigour and challenge – jogging, team sports and some of the gentler martial arts which do not stress sudden, fierce, aggressive movements. Pitta exercise should not overstimulate the body, and any exercise should be kept in line with an average amount of effort and challenge. You should avoid going to such extremes that your pitta nature gets carried away and you end up overdoing it. So, for example, doubles tennis is much better for you than singles, swimming is better than squash, and gentle jogging is much better for you than sudden sprinting. In the end, though, it is not so much what you do but how you do it that is deemed important.

This orange and elderflower infusion, left, is a light and delicate alternative to a cordial. Cordials are made by boiling all the ingredients together, which is not appropriate for pitta types because of the heat required in the cooking process. In fact, a general awareness of such techniques will help you make the right decisions in all aspects of your diet. Note that drinks are just as important as anything else you might have. They contribute greatly to our overall wellbeing.

KAPHA

Kapha types are restless, complex, interesting contradictions. You will also find that despite being quite athletic, they actually need plenty of motivation, without which they can easily become overweight. On the plus side, they are certainly highly sensitive, but in return they do need quite a lot of sensitive handling. All in all they are thoroughly reliable, methodical people, and with that extra energy input will always stay one step ahead.

The kapha body type is well built, with a tendency to weight problems, especially if an exercise programme is not followed to keep the kapha active and moving. Kapha people are naturally athletic but they do need motivation. They are generally very sensitive and emotional, and they do require understanding otherwise they tend to turn to food as an emotional support and stabilizer. They should always ensure that what they eat is suitable for their body type. Their hair will be thick, fine and wavy, their skin soft, smooth and sensuous, and their eyes large, trusting and attractive.

Kapha people are inclined to be slow and steady, methodical and pragmatic, with a real dislike of change. They make good managers though, because they like to be reliable and available. They act like an anchor in a business because they have an innate organizing ability. Note that bright, strong, striking colours will greatly help to reduce any excess kapha, and stimulate those who are feeling slow, sluggish and dull.

▲ *Kapha food should be light, dry, hot and stimulating. Always opt for cooked foods, such as hot and spicy vegetable curries, in preference to any kind of fresh salad.*

Elements: water and earth.
Climate: cold and damp.
Principle: cohesion.
Emotions: stubbornness, greed, jealousy, possessiveness, lethargy, reliability and methodical behaviour, kindliness, motherliness.
Systems most affected by excess kapha: joints, lymphatics, body fluids and mucous membranes throughout the body.
Symptoms of excess kapha: congestion, bronchial/nasal discharge, sluggish digestion, nausea, slow mental responses, idleness, desire for sleep, excess weight, fluid retention.

▼ *Because kapha individuals have a tendency towards inertia, they need plenty of motivation. A good kick-start to the day is regular, early morning outdoor exercise, such as a brisk walk or a jog.*

DIETARY TIPS

Kapha people should focus upon cooked food, but can have some salads occasionally. They should avoid fats and oils unless they are hot and spicy. Dairy products, sweet, sour and salty tastes and a high intake of wheat will also aggravate kapha. Although some meats and animal products have been included, they should always be used in moderation.

To reduce any excess levels of kapha (vikruti), or to maintain the right balance because you are a kapha dosha (prakruti), include the following items in your eating plan and try to avoid any foods that are not listed here.

HERBS AND SPICES

Asafoetida (hing), black or Indian pepper, chilli pepper, coriander leaves (cilantro), dry ginger, garlic, horseradish, mint leaves, mustard, parsley or any other hot spices.

GRAINS AND SEEDS

Barley, buckwheat, corn, couscous, oat bran, polenta, popcorn (plain), rye, sprouted wheat bread, toasted pumpkin seeds and occasional small quantities of toasted sunflower seeds.

BEANS AND PULSES

Aduki beans, black-eyed beans, chick peas (garbanzos), lima beans, pinto beans, red lentils, split peas and tempeh.

MEAT AND FISH

Eggs, freshwater fish, turkey, rabbit, shrimps and venison.

VEGETABLES

Artichokes, broccoli, Brussels sprouts, cabbage, carrots, cauliflower, celery, daikon radish, fennel, green beans, kale, leeks, lettuce, mushrooms, okra, onions, peas, peppers, radishes, spinach. Kapha vegetables should be cooked.

FRUITS

Apples, apricots, berries, cherries, peaches, pears, pomegranates and prunes.

COOKING OILS

Corn, almond or sunflower oil may be used in small quantities.

DRINKS

Fruit drinks should not contain sugar or additives. Recommended hot drinks include black tea, nettle tea, passion flower tea, raspberry tea. Cold drinks include carrot juice, cranberry juice, grape juice, mango juice, and occasional wine .

AROMAS AND MASSAGE OILS

Kapha individuals require minimal oil or none at all with massage, using instead a natural, unscented talcum powder which can be purchased from most health food stores. If an essential oil is used at all, the best ones for kapha individuals include eucalyptus, cinnamon, orange peel (since this can cause sun sensitivity, avoid strong sunlight after a massage with orange peel), ginger and myrrh. All of these oils are stimulating and it would be well advisable, after diluting approximately 7–10 drops of essential oil in 25ml/1 fl oz carrier oil, to test an area of skin first to check for any possible sensitive reaction.

Unlike the sensitive gentleness of the pitta massage with its sweeping regular movements designed to relax, the kapha is actually quite fast and vigorous. You will notice that when having a massage the hands sweep over you firmly and energetically, keeping to a constant rhythm. If giving such a massage to a friend or partner, be aware that it can surprisingly be quite tiring. The aim is to kick-start and stimulate the metabolism that tends towards the sluggish.

Concentrate on the hip and groin areas to encourage lymphatic drainage, and also around the armpits to release any congestion. Finally, note as always that essential oils must be diluted and should not be taken internally. Do not to use the same essential oil for more than two weeks. If you are pregnant or have a diagnosed medical condition, do not use any essential oil without consulting a qualified practitioner. The risks are not worth taking.

KAPHA MASSAGE

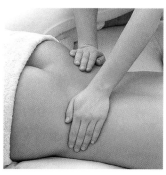

1 Kapha massage needs to fairly vigorous and stimulating.

2 Use fast movements, using talcum powder.

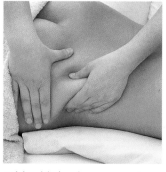

3 Use hip/groin massage to assist lymphatic drainage.

4 Another major lymph gland area is around the armpits.

COLOURS

Kapha individuals benefit from the warm and stimulating colours of the spectrum. Whenever you experience symptoms such as lethargy and sluggishness, which suggest excess kapha, or if you need to be particularly active, wear bright, invigorating, stimulating colours. You will quickly notice how effective they are, inspiring a change in your temperament.

RED

Red is the colour of blood and will increase circulation as well as being energizing and positive. It should be used sparingly to avoid over-stimulation of kapha, creating excess pitta.

ORANGE

Orange is a warming, nourishing colour which feeds the sexual organs, and its glowing colour helps to remove congestion.

PINK

Warm, comforting pinks gently stimulate kapha into activity. Being a softer colour than red, pink may be worn without ill-effects for significantly longer periods. A highly useful colour.

MAKING A COLOUR INFUSION

Take a piece of thin cotton or silk. The fabric should be a warm pink and sufficiently translucent to allow the light to penetrate. Wrap it around a transparent (not coloured) small bottle containing spring water. Stand it in full sunlight or upon a windowsill with the window open so that the light can fall naturally upon the bottle. Leave it for about four hours. Remove the fabric and drink the contents of the bottle within 24 hours.

◄ *If possible, choose a fabric which has been dyed with natural dyes.*

GEMS AND CRYSTALS

Lapis lazuli is a reliably suitable, highly useful crystal with which to reduce any excess levels of kapha. Known as the heavenly stone it will quickly help kapha individuals to increase their bodily vibrations, raising them from the level of the dense and slow to a much more refined and spiritual resonance. Lapis lazuli is a quite remarkable crystal, one that is well worth seeking out.

CRYSTAL INFUSION

Cleanse your lapis lazuli prior to making an infusion. Hold the lapis in your hands for a few moments, visualizing clarity and inspiration. Take your time to get this right. The crystal should now be ready for use. Place it in a clear glass bowl and cover it with spring water. Leave it outside in the sunlight for about four hours. The brighter and sunnier the sky, the better. Next, remove the crystal, and bottle the infused spring water. You can regularly drink small amounts of it throughout the day, as required, and this will certainly ensure a continued rising of your spirits towards inspired, enlivened action.

▲ *Make a lapis infusion to reduce excess kapha.*

EXERCISE AND TONIC

Kapha types may well avoid this page because it suggests exercise! However, kapha people must address their natural aversion to physical activity. Exercise will make an amazing difference, cleansing excess kapha, and making valuable room for their inner beauty and radiance to shine right through.

Since kapha individuals will tend to shy away from any vigorous exercise, a certain amount of self-discipline is required. Once a regular exercise routine is established, however, the kapha type will enjoy and benefit from the enlivened and energetic feeling that all activity and exercise brings. Examples of fairly vigorous exercise well suited to the kapha type include running, fast swimming, aerobics and even fitness training. If at all unused to such exercise, start with a gentle routine, and seek guidance from an expert, qualified trainer.

It is advisable to increase the exercise level during colder spells of weather when extra stimulation is required. If this becomes a regular routine it will really push the kapha type. The benefits will soon be obvious.

◄ *Kapha people need to ensure that they have vigorous exercise, such as aerobics.*

SPICED YOGI TEA

Spiced yogi tea is a delicious, warming drink which will soon help to reduce any excess kapha and is perfect for warming up cold bones on a chilly winter's day.

2.5ml/½ tsp dry ginger	1 large cinnamon stick
4 whole cardamom pods	600ml/1 pint/2½ cups spring
5 cloves	water
A pinch of black pepper or	30ml/2tbsp goat's milk or
pippali (Indian long pepper)	organic soya milk

1 Mix the spices together in a saucepan.
2 Add the spring water and boil off half the liquid.
3 Turn off the heat and add the goat's milk or soya milk.
4 Stir and strain the liquid. Serve hot.

DUAL DOSHAS

In all relationships, at home and work, it will make a great difference if you can try to adopt the approaches recommended for your own particular dosha. The vata dosha may well need to work at being much more reliably consistent, with the pitta dosha aiming at far greater tolerance and patience. The rather possessive kapha dosha, on the other hand, should always put extra trust and flexibility right at the top of the list.

VATA/PITTA – PITTA/VATA

If, when you answered the questionnaire in the introduction, you found that you scored twice as many points on any one type as on the other two, this means that you will predominantly be that type. For example, a score of 30 points on kapha and 5 or 10 on the others would indicate that you are a kapha type. However, if there is a closer gap with perhaps 30 points for kapha and 20 for pitta then you are classified as a kapha/pitta type. If you are such a dual type, read the following essential information.

Vata/pitta is a combination of ether/air and fire/water elements. If you belong to this dual type, refer to both the vata and the pitta eating and living plans. Choose items from the pitta plan during the spring and summer months, and during outbreaks of hot, humid weather. Follow the vata plan during the autumn and winter months, and during any cold, dry spells. For example, pungent foods aggravate pitta but can actually help to calm vata (because vata is cold), which is why the plans need to be changed in accordance with the weather, your health and a wide range of other factors. It is really quite important that you keep

▲ *Vata/pitta – pitta/vata herbs include the different kinds of basil, coriander (cilantro), cumin seeds, fennel, mint, turmeric and vanilla pods.*

a regular, accurate check on such factors, and modify your approach accordingly.

Eat your vegetables in season, and mostly cooked and flavoured with appropriate vata spices to minimize aggravation of vata and pitta. Only small amounts of bitter vegetables should be used. Among foods suitable for the vata/pitta type are broccoli, cauliflower, cucumber, endive, kale, onion (cooked), plantain, coconut, sweet oranges, apricots and other sweet fruits. Teas that are beneficial include elderflower, fennel, lemon balm and rosehip teas. Appropriate herbs and spices for vata/pitta – pitta/vata include fresh basil, caraway, cardamom, cumin, fennel, garam masala, spearmint and vanilla.

The nature of vata is change and when you are more familiar with the doshic influences that the climate has on you, you may be more flexible with the doshic recommendations. Remember, though, that you are influenced by everything touching your life.

▼ *Your lifestyle can be affected by your health. Pitta or vata doshas should find time to create a calming and restful ambience in which to relax and wind down.*

▲ *If you belong to the vata/pitta type, eat plenty of sweet, ripe fruits, such as melons and oranges, when they are in season.*

PITTA/KAPHA – KAPHA/PITTA

This is a combination of the fire, water and earth elements. If you belong to this dual type, follow the kapha eating and living plan during the winter months and during spells of cold, damp weather, and take note of the pitta plan during the summer months, and during hot, humid weather.

You should always choose foods that are pungent and astringent, such as onions, celery, lemons, dandelion, mustard greens and watercress, and eat fresh fruit and vegetables. All fruit juices should be diluted with water or milk. Suitable teas for the pitta/kapha – kapha/pitta type include bancha twig, blackberry, dandelion, jasmine, licorice (not to be used if you suffer from high blood pressure or oedema) and spearmint. The herbs, spices and flavourings that apply to the pitta/kapha type include coriander, dill leaves, fennel, kudzu, orange peel, parsley, rosewater, and sprigs of refreshing spearmint.

VATA/KAPHA – KAPHA/VATA

Vata/kapha is a combination of ether, air, water and earth. You should follow the kapha eating and living plan during the winter and spring months, and during cold, damp weather. You should stick to the vata plan during the autumn and summer months, and during any cold, dry windy spells.

Since the vata/kapha type is cold, you should therefore be encouraged to have plenty of pungent, hot and spicy foods. Chinese and Eastern cuisine is a "must". Good examples of suitable foods include artichokes, asparagus, mustard greens, parsnips, summer and winter squashes and watercress. Vegetables with seeds should be well cooked with the appropriate vata spices to minimize any possible aggravation.

It is equally important to eat plenty of fresh seasonal fruits, and they include apricots, berries, cherries, lemons, mangoes, peaches and strawberries. The vata/kapha type should be very careful to avoid a mono-diet of brown rice.

The herbs and spices for this particular type include allspice, anise, asafoetida (hing), basil, black pepper, basil, cinnamon, coriander, cumin, curry powder, garlic, nutmeg, poppy seeds, saffron and vanilla.

TRIDOSHA

In very rare instances a person may score more or less equally for all three doshas, revealing themselves to be all three types, or what is known as "tridosha" (literally, three-doshas). If you are this interesting combination of three doshas you will require a specially formulated tridoshic diet and living plan. Since your make-up is more elaborate than for single types, your plan is accordingly more interesting and varied. The onus is on you, however, to closely follow the seasonal changes and modify the agenda as appropriate, making sensible, sensitive modifications. Being a tridosha involves quite a degree of self-discipline, and a clever ability to switch promptly between all three lifestyle plans.

Always eat according to the weather and to your personal circumstances. For example, on hot days, and during the spring and summer months, follow the pitta plan; on cold days and during the winter months, follow the kapha plan; and during the late summer and autumn, or on windy days or during spells of cold dry weather, follow the vata plan.

If you find that you fall into this highly unusual, remarkable category, it will certainly be worthwhile seeking out and consulting an Ayurvedic practitioner to find out more about what being a tridosha entails.

▼ *Pitta/kapha – kapha/pitta foods include curry leaves or powder, garam masala, mint, orange peel oil and rosewater.*

ayurvedic treatments
ayurvedic treatments

ayurvedic treatments

The entire basis and the whole concept of Ayurvedic treatment is dietary; put bluntly, diet is exactly what it all leads back to – the tried and tested use and combination of specific foods. Fortunately, several excellent, imaginative Ayurvedic cookbooks with a wide range of tasty recipes have been published, and they are definitely well worth tracking down, collecting and studying if you want to learn more about Ayurvedic nutrition. They will make a great difference at meal times.

The following pages have been divided into several sections with the express purpose of outlining the basic characteristics of each type. This includes a wealth of vital information which forms the backbone, the foundation, and the essential core of the Ayurvedic approach. It deals with all kinds of related emotions, and the treatment systems closely associated with and most pertinent to each dosha. It also describes and explains the many symptoms of excess, together with a huge wealth of detail about what you should and should not be eating, which colours you really ought to be wearing, the scents and oils you should be using, the herbs and spices most beneficial to you, and the tonic recipes for each type, whether vata, pitta, or kapha.

In addition, there are key massage techniques, for example showing you how to follow the direction of the colon when massaging the stomach with brahmi oil, and which gem and crystal you should be working with in order to help you to reduce any excess levels in your dosha(s), thereby making sure they have a balanced, healthy relationship.

To the novice some of these ideas might seem slightly daunting, especially if you come from a background in which traditional forms of Western medicine have a stranglehold, but once they and the language in which they are expressed become familiar, you will see that the principles are actually very simple; they spell out some highly relevant advice. All you then have to do is to follow the right plan, whether you are trying to reduce an excess, or wish to build up and maintain the right balance in your system.

Once you become familiar with the many excellent Ayurvedic treatments, you can become slightly more adventurous. There is absolutely no reason why you should not start making up your own tonic recipes for your own body type. This is easily done by combining ingredients from the appropriate eating plan, and using recommended herbs and spices to enhance the healing.

THE DIGESTIVE SYSTEM

One of the main cornerstones of Ayurvedic theory and medicine is that the gastro-intestinal tract (GI) is by far the most important and crucial part of the body because it is considered to be the focal point, or the principal seat, of the doshas. Vata is formed inside the colon, pitta in the small intestine, and kapha inside the stomach. In other words, this tract has extra dimensions not recognized by traditional medicine.

CONSTIPATION

Drink warm liquids; hot water is acceptable, but not chilled water. The best herbs for constipation are triphala and satisabgol (psyllium husks). (Do not use triphala if you are pregnant or suffering from ulcers of the GI.) Triphala is a combination of three herbal fruits, each of which has a rejuvenating effect in relation to one of the doshas. Satisabgol is a demulcent laxative. It is gentle and soothing and holds moisture in the colon, thus helping vata, which is known to be quite dry and cold. Use satisabgol with triphala; they complement each other well.

GAS, BLOATING, COLIC

These symptoms are usually related to constipation. Ideally food should pass through the system in 24 hours. If it is left for much longer the process of fermentation begins, which causes a build-up of gas. The traditional herbal remedy for this is hingvastak, a mix of asafoetida, pippali, ginger, black pepper, cumin, wild celery seeds and rock salt. Another traditional remedy is a massage with brahmi oil. It restores and relaxes the nervous system.

▲ *Eating a healthy vata diet can aid many vata problems associated with the gastro-intestinal tract.*

ACIDITY/HEARTBURN

Sip aloe vera juice (without any citric acid added). Add fresh and dried coriander (cilantro), turmeric, saffron, coconut, fennel or peppermint to your diet. Shatavari (Asparagus racemosus), licorice (not to be used with high blood pressure or oedema) and amalaki are all used in traditional Ayurveda medicine in order to balance unwelcome levels of acidity.

DIARRHOEA

Pitta diarrhoea is generally hot, and often yellowish and foul-smelling. Diarrhoea is mainly related to pitta but can sometimes be caused by other factors, such as high toxicity (ama), stress or emotional factors. Persistent symptoms must always be dealt with by an experienced, professional physician. If you have diarrhoea, avoid eating hot spices and carefully follow the pitta plan. Eat abstemiously if at all, drinking plenty of fluids. A simple straightforward diet of rice, split mung dhal and vegetables is most suitable for the pitta dosha, taken while symptoms last.

PERSISTENT HUNGER/INCREASED APPETITE

In general, follow the pitta plan as outlined and use aloe vera juice as above. Increase relaxation, meditation and yoga. Also, have a long massage with brahmi oil. If strong symptoms persist, do please promptly consult your physician.

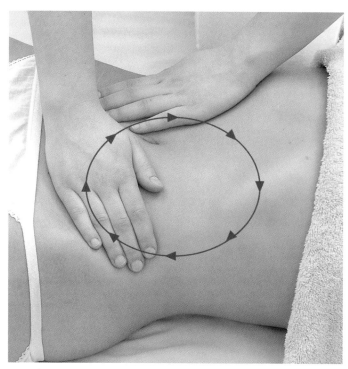

▲ *When massaging, follow the direction of the colon – from lower left, across the abdomen, up to the right and across to the left.*

▲ *Nettle tea is very good at balancing the digestive system and can help to alleviate pitta conditions such as diarrhoea.*

NAUSEA

Nausea can quite simply be defined as the strong sensation of needing to vomit. It might not actually result in vomiting, but produces a queasy, lingering feeling that needs to be quickly relieved. It certainly is not pleasant.

Ginger and cardamom tea is often very good at calming nausea. To make it, peel and thinly slice a piece of fresh ginger, add five cardamom pods and pour boiled spring water over them. Leave to stand for about five minutes, and then stir and drink while still refreshing and hot.

Ginger is also what is known as a carminative and a stimulant. This means that it has two key abilities, first to combat any intestinal bloating, and second to speed up processes in the GI so that balance is soon restored.

During the winter and spring seasons when kapha is seasonally high, dried ginger can be blended with some boiled spring water and a little fresh honey to help keep the digestive system active and moving. This also has the excellent effect of helping to reduce the possible risk of colds, coughs and flu, and any other winter bugs that might otherwise keep you confined to the bed or house for a number of days.

Cardamom (common in southern India as well as other tropical areas, and now freely available in supermarkets) can be used for kapha and vata digestive conditions. However, it can only be used in small amounts because it can quickly aggravate pitta, or bring about a high level of pitta excess.

As with all the recommended foods, herbs and spices, the purer the quality, the more beneficial they will be. Therefore, try to buy top quality, fresh organic herbs and spices whenever it is possible. You will immediately appreciate the difference.

THE DOSHAS AND THE GASTRO-INTESTINAL TRACT

Kapha

Typical kapha conditions of the GI include poor appetite – kapha tends to be low in agni (digestive fire), which can create a slow metabolism and weight gain; nausea; a build-up of mucus, leading to colds, sinus problems, coughs and flu; and poor circulation, resulting in a build-up of toxicity (ama). Follow the kapha plan and eat plenty of hot spices, such as chilli peppers, garlic, ginger and black pepper, until the condition clears, after which you should reduce your intake of hot spices. Herbs for kapha conditions of the GI include trikatu ("three hot things"), to be taken or added to meals. This contains pippali, ginger and black pepper. You should also have plenty of vigorous exercise.

Vata

Regular daily bowel movements are a sign of a healthy GI. Typical vata conditions of the GI include constipation, gas/ flatulence, and tension – cramps or spasms, such as irritable bowel syndrome.

Pitta

Pitta digestion tends to be fast and "burns" food. This is made worse by anger or frustration. Begin a pitta-reducing diet and eat in a calm and relaxed way. Typical pitta conditions of the gastro-intestinal tract include acidity and heartburn, symptomized by belching and acid indigestion; diarrhoea or frequent loose bowel movements, and constant hunger, accompanied by consequent irritability.

▲ *Hot kapha dietary spices.*

COMMON PROBLEMS

It is quite clear that the forms taken by various commonly occurring illnesses, and the appropriate remedies, will vary according to whether you have a vata, pitta or kapha dosha. The following sections therefore aim to give you individually a plan of action, setting out all the do's and do not's. Note that in the case of any persistent, or indeed serious illness, you must immediately contact a qualified professional expert.

INSOMNIA

Any vata-increasing influence can contribute to your insomnia, including regular travel, stress, an irregular lifestyle, and the excessive use of stimulants such as tea and coffee. The herbs used to treat vata-based insomnia are brahmi (Centella), jatamansi, ashwagandha (Withania somnifera) and nutmeg. Any good massage using brahmi oil will also produce considerable, quickly noticed benefits.

Insomnia in the pitta dosha is brought on by anger, jealousy, frustration, fever, excess sun or heat. Follow the pitta plan, which is cooling, and take brahmi, jatamansi, bhringaraj (Eclipta alba), shatavari and aloe vera juice. Massage brahmi oil into the head and feet. Again, this is marvellously refreshing.

As kapha types like to sleep and tend to be rather sleepy and sluggish, they rarely suffer from attacks of insomnia.

HEADACHE/MIGRAINE

Vata headaches cause extreme pain and are related to anxiety and tension. Relevant treatments include triphala to clear any congestion, jatamansi, brahmi and calamus.

Pitta headaches are associated with heat or burning sensations, flushed skin and a visual sensitivity to light. They are related to anger, frustration or irritability, and will be connected to the liver and gall bladder. Treatments are brahmi, turmeric and aloe vera juice. Kapha headaches are dull and heavy and can cause nausea. There may also be congestion, such as catarrh. Have a stimulating massage with minimal oil.

▲ *Juice from aloe vera plants can be used to combat sleeplessness.*

COLDS

A tendency to mucus production or catarrh/phlegm is unpleasant for the sufferer, and is usually the result of poor digestion of foods in the stomach which increases ama (toxicity) and kapha. In general, kapha is generally considered the most highly effective dosha.

Vata-type colds involve dry symptoms, such as a dry cough or dry throat. Herbs for vata coughs and colds are ginger, cumin, pippali, tulsi (holy basil, Ocimum sanctum), cloves and peppermint, licorice (not to be used with high blood pressure or oedema), shatavari and ashwagandha. Put one or two drops of sesame oil up each nostril, and then follow the vata plan until all the symptoms are seen to subside.

Pitta-type colds involve more heat, the face is usually red and there may even be a fever. The mucus is often yellow and can actually contain traces of blood. Herbs for tackling pitta coughs and colds include peppermint and various other mints, sandalwood, chrysanthemum and small quantities of tulsi (holy basil). Follow the pitta plan until your symptoms begin to subside.

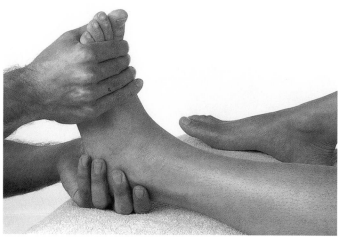

▲ *A foot massage with brahmi oil will often relieve insomnia.*

▲ *Cardamom pods are beneficial to vata-type coughs.*

Kapha colds are thick and mucusy, with a feeling of heaviness in the head and/or body. Avoid cold, damp weather and exposure to cold and damp conditions. Eliminate sugar, refined foods, meat and nuts, dairy products, bread, fats and oils from the diet and use plenty of hot spices. Drink a spiced tea of hot lemon, ginger and cinnamon with cloves or tulsi, sweetened with a little raw honey. Herbs for kapha colds are ginger, cinnamon, pippali, tulsi (holy basil), cloves and peppermint. Saunas and hot baths will help to increase the heat of the kapha person, but they should not be used in excess as this would actually increase the pitta too much. Follow the kapha plan until the symptoms subside.

COUGHS

Vata coughs are dry and irritated with very little mucus, the chief symptom being a painful cough often accompanied by a dry mouth. Herbs and spices for the vata cough include licorice (do not use this if you have high blood pressure or oedema), shatavari, ashwagandha and cardamom. Follow the vata plan until the symptoms subside.

Pitta coughs are usually associated with a lot of phlegm. The chest is congested and very uncomfortable, but the mucus cannot be brought up properly. There is often fever or heat, combined with a burning sensation in the chest or throat. High fevers should be treated by a physician, and people suffering with asthma should consult their doctor immediately if a cough or cold leads to wheezing and difficult breathing. The best herbs for pitta coughs include peppermint, tulsi (holy basil) and sandalwood. Follow the pitta plan until the symptoms have completely subsided.

With kapha coughs, the patient usually brings up lots of phlegm, and suffers a loss of appetite combined with nausea. The chest is loaded with mucus, but this may not be coughed up because the kapha individual is likely to feel tired. Treatments for kapha coughs are raw honey, lemon, cloves and chyawanprash (a herbal jam). Follow the kapha plan until the symptoms subside, increasing your intake of hot spices, and do try to use trikatu powder. Also keep warm.

SKIN PROBLEMS

These are often caused by internal conditions of toxicity (ama) and are mainly related to the pitta dosha. Vata skin problems will be dry and rough. Avoid letting the skin dry out. Herbal remedies for vata skin are triphala and satisabgol. Pitta skin problems will be red and swollen, often with a yellow head. Avoid sun, heat or hot baths, and increase your intake of salads. Follow the pitta plan and add turmeric, coriander and saffron to your diet. The remedies are manjishta (Rubia cordifolia), kutki (Picrohiza kurroa), turmeric and aloe vera juice. Kapha skin problems involve blood congestion which can cause the skin to form thick and mucusy whiteheads. Increase your level of exercise, and follow the kapha plan. Treatments should always include a small amount of calamus with some dry ginger and quantities of turmeric.

URINARY INFECTIONS

Excess cold water, tea, coffee, and alcoholic drinks will weaken the kidneys. Salt, sugar or foods that are rich in calcium, such as dairy products or spinach, will similarly tend to weaken and toxify the kidneys. The best kidney tonic to use in Ayurveda is shilajit, a mineral-rich compound from the Himalayan mountains, but avoid it if you suffer from kidney stones. Pregnant women, children or those on medication should consult an Ayurvedic practitioner before treatment.

CYSTITIS

In vata people, cystitis will tend to be less intense. Remedies are shilajit (to be avoided if you suffer from kidney stones) with bala (Sida cordifolia), ashwagandha and shatavari.

Cystitis is mainly a pitta condition because it burns and is hot. Follow the pitta plan, using plenty of coriander (cilantro) and avoiding hot spices. Remedies include aloe vera juice (not to be used in pregnancy), lime juice, coconut and sandalwood. Kapha-type cystitis is accompanied by congestion and mucus in the urinary tract. The treatments are cinnamon, trikatu combined with shilajit, gokshura and gokshurdi guggul.

▼ *It is worth having a supply of fresh mint and other herbs to hand for many of the common Ayurvedic treatments.*

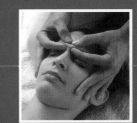

THE POWER OF TOUCH

HERE ARE FOUR TECHNIQUES THAT
DEMONSTRATE HOW TOUCH THERAPIES CAN
HELP TO CURE MANY KINDS OF AILMENTS, AND
BEST OF ALL, KEEP YOUR BODY SUPPLE AND
HEALTHY. MASSAGE, AROMATHERAPY, SHIATSU
AND REFLEXOLOGY ARE ALL BASED ON OUR
AMAZING ABILITY TO READ THE BODY'S
SIGNALS, AND, USING TOUCH, CONVERT
POOR HEALTH INTO GOOD.

MASSAGE

Do you come home at the end of the day with your neck and shoulders feeling as if they were set in concrete? Most of us almost unconsciously rub such tense, aching spots to get some instant relief: correctly performed, massage can have a wonderful effect, not just on the muscles themselves but on our whole sense of well-being. Touch is one of the most crucial, and yet often neglected, senses, and the need for human touch remains constant throughout life. Caring touch through massage has been shown to encourage the release of endorphins – chemicals that affect development in children, as well as emotional and physical well-being in adults. In addition, a massage can be an effective treatment for a range of physical problems and is a wonderfully relaxing experience.

PREPARING FOR MASSAGE

It is quite possible to give a highly effective, spontaneous massage, but generally it is far better to prepare well in advance. This will certainly give you all the time you need to create the right atmosphere, and to check that you have exactly the right ingredients, everything from towels to oils. A really good massage should be a special occasion, and one that leaves you feeling relaxed, calm, gentle and well.

CREATING THE MOOD

Creating the right environment and space for treatment will definitely help make the massage an even more quietly relaxing and beneficial experience. Before you start, though, make sure that the room is pleasantly warm and that the massage room is sufficiently furnished for your partner to be completely comfortable. Make sure you have plenty of towels or a sheet handy to cover areas not being worked on – remember that if you are working on the floor, draughts can give exposed flesh some very unrelaxing goose-pimples. If you are using oil, place it in a convenient spot where you can reach it easily without the risk of knocking it over.

Preparing yourself is important too; physically this means removing watches and jewellery, trimming nails and wearing loose, comfortable clothing, ideally short-sleeved. Try to do a few stretches and take a few deep breaths to help you to feel calm; if you give a massage when you are tense yourself, this may be transmitted to your massage partner. This can work the other way round too, so feel prepared mentally to let go of any tensions that you feel coming from the other person's body, and avoid absorbing his or her stresses.

When using oil, pour it on to your own hands first to warm it up, never directly on to your partner. Cold oil will be extremely unsettling. The oil may be placed in a bowl, glass bottle or even a squeezy bottle for ease of use. Spread the oil slowly on to the body, and gradually begin.

▲ *Gently scented oils have long been a massage favourite.*

MASSAGE OILS

The worldwide preference is for locally available oils, usually vegetable oils, to help the hands flow and glide over the skin. Olive oil, goose grease, goat butter and other ingredients have all been used successfully at various times; in parts of Africa a handful of oily dough is actually used to absorb dirt and toxins from the skin as the massage soothes and relaxes the muscles.

Some oils are far more pleasant and versatile than others, and have a beneficial effect on the skin in themselves. Probably the most useful oil, and the one most widely used in professional massage, is that of Sweet Almond. It is light, non-greasy and easily absorbed by the skin. Grapeseed oil seems to suit oily skins quite well; it is reasonably priced and probably more widely available.

Rather thicker, but still useful, is Soya oil. For dry skins a little Wheatgerm oil (but not if the person has a wheat allergy) or Avocado oil may be added. Nut oils such as Walnut are also rich but a bit sticky, and do not smell too good on the skin. Sunflower oil may be used for massage if nothing else is available, though it may give a slight hint of salad dressing! Olive oil can be used though that largely depends on how heavily flavoured it is; it is certainly a traditional favourite in Mediterranean countries. Finally, do not use mineral oils because they sit on the surface of the skin and tend to feel very greasy.

▼ *When giving a massage you can choose from a wide range of oils.*

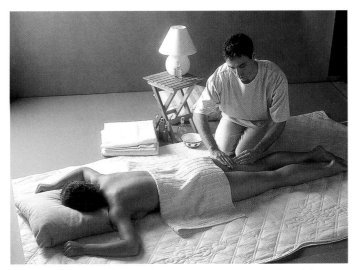

▲ *When giving a massage, always stay calm and relaxed because tense vibrations will promptly be picked up by your partner.*

ESSENTIAL OILS

As an alternative, try using essential oils which can be added to these base oils for two reasons – to add fragrance and to give extra therapeutic effects. These oils are highly concentrated and should always be treated with great respect. However, if you are in any doubt whatsoever, do not use them, and if any skin irritation does occur, wash off the offending oil immediately.

Most essential oils are now conveniently sold in dropper bottles, and it is absolutely imperative that they are only used in a diluted form on the skin. A generally safe level is considered to be 1 per cent, which is the equivalent of using just one drop of essential oil to 5ml/1 tsp of base oil. Never be tempted to try and use more than the recommended amount – this is actually counter-productive, doing more harm than good.

Adding essential oils to vegetable oils invariably works well because the latter can contribute their own health-giving properties. The best vegetable oils include Almond, which is high in vitamin D. Borage is an incredibly good source of GLA, and is frequently used to tackle eczema and psoriasis. If you need vitamin E, look no further than Jojoba oil, which has the added benefit of containing anti-bacterial agents which can help cure acne. Peachnut oil is also a good provider of vitamin E, and has the added bonus of toning up the skin, making it more elastic and supple. Try it as a facial massage.

All-purpose vegetable oils that are also worth using include Grapeseed. It suits all skin types, but being refined is best mixed with an enriching agent such as Almond oil. Safflower oil has the twin advantage of being inexpensive to buy and widely available, and it makes a very good base. So too does Sunflower oil, which is rich in vitamins and minerals.

As you get more skilled in the art of mixing oils, you will find that you can blend different essential oils together. When they are blended a particular chemical reaction occurs, creating a new compound. For example, by adding quantities of Lavender to Bergamot you can actually increase the sedative effect. However, if you add Lemon to Bergamot you increase its power to enhance and uplift. Mixing two essential oils in this way to alter effects subtly is known as synergy. It is an extremely useful means of letting you tackle several conditions simultaneously, especially your emotional and physical needs. With a bit of practice you will gradually learn exactly what ratio of oils you need, depending on your mood swings and current condition.

Getting the right scent is equally important. At first it seems quite bewildering. Will Almond oil or Sesame oil alone provide the best results, or should they be mixed, and in what quantities? By following established "recipes", you will gradually learn which oils mix best, and once you are confident at handling them you can start altering the quantities to suit your own specific needs. It is worth noting, though, that essential oils have been divided into three separate sections or "notes" to help you achieve the right balance when creating a scent. The three notes are called the top, middle and base, and theoretically a fine blend will contain one oil from each note.

The top notes are best described as fresh and immediately detectable because the oil evaporates at such a fast rate. The scent is immediately present. The core of the mix, the middle note, provides a deeper scent that wafts through, following the top note, and the base note adds a final, marvellous rich perfume. Be aware that you will need a higher quantity of top notes because the oils do evaporate so quickly. A sensible, general ratio would be 3 (top) – 2 (middle) – 2 (base).

For a generally relaxing massage blend, try essential oils of Lavender and Marjoram in equal amounts in a base vegetable oil. Both of these will help to release those tense, tired, over-stressed muscles, and will induce a general sense of well-being, followed by a warm, relaxed glow. They are highly effective. For a slightly more invigorating, uplifting blend, try essential oils of Bergamot and Geranium in your massage oil. Both have a refreshing effect on the whole system. To release tensions, and also to help increase the libido, try a dilution of an exotic, luxurious blend of essential oils of Rose and Sandalwood.

▲ *Use Bergamot oil with care – it can cause sensitivity to sunlight.*

BASIC STROKES

There are dozens of kinds of massage movements, each having a specific effect on the body. However, the pattern of each massage invariably follows certain fundamental principles. This crucially always begins with the initial contact; the confident, unhurried, relaxed way that you first touch your massage partner which lays the foundation for a long, soothing experience. It is well worth taking time to make sure you get this right.

1 Gliding strokes involves the use of the whole hand in smooth movements.

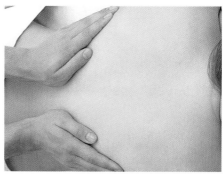

2 Apply even pressure as you move over the skin. Use plenty of oil.

GLIDING

A massage usually starts with slow, broad, relatively superficial movements, leading to deeper and perhaps more specific techniques on smaller areas of spasm or tension. If the person needs invigorating or toning up, then faster movements may be used, and finally more stretching or stroking movements to finish the massage session in a relaxed way. The first and last massage movements often consist of these gliding strokes.

CIRCLING

An allied form of movement is circling, where the hands move over large areas of muscle in a circular motion. Since tension within muscles can produce knotted areas which may need working along or across the length of the fibres, this circular action releases the knots before deeper movements are used.

Circling may be carried out with just one hand, or both hands can be used, one on top of the other, for greater depth and stability of action. Like the gliding motions, circling is essentially a slow, relaxing type of movement and should not be rushed.

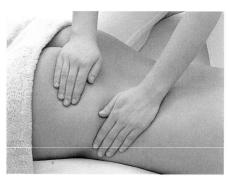

1 A variation on simple circling uses both hands. As with all massage strokes, keep your own body comfortable and avoid tensing your hands or arms.

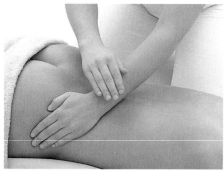

2 Take one hand around in a circle, then the other. This gradually builds up its own momentum and energy, and can be extremely calming and soothing.

Caution

Do not attempt deep work if at all unsure of the effect, or if pain occurs. Underdo rather than overdo massage – effleurage and petrissage movements can make a complete and thoroughly relaxing massage.

3 The key to success is overlapping the hands so that they follow one another smoothly. Make this action as unforced and flowing as you can.

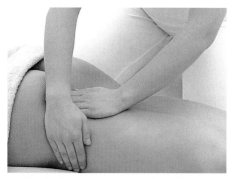

4 Gradually move the small and large circling movements of your hands up and down the back, from the base of the spine to near the neck.

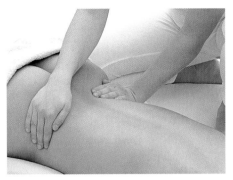

Gradually push one hand against the other in a wringing movement.

WRINGING

Another important type of movement is wringing, where the action of one hand against the other creates a powerful squeezing action. When performed on the back, for example, the person's own spine acts as a kind of block against which the muscles can be wrung. This highly useful technique enables the speedy removal of any waste matter from muscles which are much too stiff and tense.

Do not be at all surprised by the mention of waste matter. All muscular activity actually produces potentially toxic waste materials, notably lactic acid. If the person also gets tense and stiff, these wastes are quickly trapped within the muscles, making them even stiffer with far more aching. Wringing is an extremely effective way of encouraging the removal of lactic acid and any other waste matter, which in turn allows new blood to flood in, bringing oxygen and fresh nutrients to individual cells.

PRESSURE TECHNIQUES

As a massage treatment progresses, general techniques such as gliding and circling often change into more detailed and specific work on smaller areas of spasm. Professional massage therapists may move to even deeper work with firm pressure, using thumbs and fingers. Pressure is achieved by steadily leaning into the movement with the whole body, not by tensing your hands. Thinner people usually need lighter pressure.

1 The flat heel of the hand gives a broad, firm, no-nonsense effect.

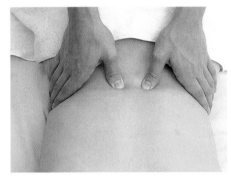

2 The thumbs can be used to exert the most precise kinds of pressure.

Light hacking movements are excellent for stimulating the circulation.

PERCUSSION

If someone has a generally sluggish system, or needs invigorating, then faster techniques can be useful. The term for these strokes is percussion, or tapotement. Unlike the other strokes that are described here, they need to be performed quickly, to stimulate the circulation under the skin, and to tone the associated muscles (pummelling with loose fists is excellent at toning larger muscles). One of the best known of these movements is hacking, in which the sides of the fingers are used to flick rhythmically up and down to create a slightly stinging sensation. Despite being the movement that most people think typifies a massage, it is not a major part of massage, but does have good results. Cupping is a similar stroke which helps bring blood to the area being massaged. It is used when treating medical conditions such as cystic fibrosis when a lot of thick, sticky mucus can build up in the lungs. Cupping on the back helps loosen this mucus.

KNEADING

After the recipient has been relaxed by steady stroking or gliding movements and any tense muscles start to release, a professional therapist may well begin to use deeper techniques to soften the knotted areas. The general term for many of these movements is petrissage, and they involve a firm, squeezing action to encourage all waste matter to be pumped out of the muscles, so allowing fresh, oxygenated blood to flow in.

1 Kneading with alternate hands helps to loosen any tense, knotted muscles.

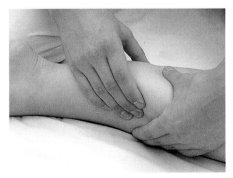

2 On smaller areas like the calves, use less pressure to avoid discomfort.

massage sequences
massage sequences

massage sequences

Probably the best way to improve and deepen a relationship is to increase caring physical contact, and massage is an ideal approach. The ability to ease tensions and deeply relax during a massage is very satisfying both for the giver and the receiver.

You can give massage to another person, or just to yourself, but whichever you choose, both are very valuable in therapeutic and emotional terms. Massage can help soothe aching and tired muscles, or it can help in releasing anxiety and tension stored in muscles.

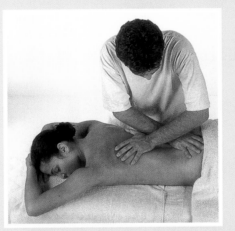

Massage does not have to be limited to yourself or your life partner; there are other members of the family, friends or colleagues who can all be helped in this way, and a better rapport will be developed with them too.

Being massaged by someone else does mean that you can let go of your muscles more completely, than if you are massaging yourself. Being massaged by another person does require a certain amount of trust, and if you are massaging a person you do not know too well, do be sensitive to this. Massage practitioners are well aware that they are being given permission to make a deep contact with their clients, which is quite a privilege.

When preparing for a massage, take a few moments to make sure that you have created the right environment. Check that the person is warm and comfortable, and that you have easy access to the part of the body needing massage. You can make a room more comfortable and relaxing by ensuring that no-one can see in from the outside, by darkening the room and by playing some gentle music. When giving a massage, remember to place everything that you might need close at hand, such as oils, talcum powder. cushions and extra towels.

Be aware that what is comfortable pressure for one person may feel like tickling or painful to another. So take care and tailor your massage to each person.

TENSE NECK EASER

Aching, tense, tired muscles are undoubtedly most usually experienced in the neck and shoulders. What is more, as you begin to get tired, your posture tends to sag and droop and the rounded shape makes your shoulders ache even more. Although it is actually most relaxing to lie down and have a long, deep massage, a self-massage can easily be done. It is extremely effective, does not take long, and leaves you feeling fine.

I A simple movement is to shrug your shoulders, exaggerating the movement by lifting them up as far as possible and then letting them drop right down, and relaxing completely. This form of massage does not even involve using your hands.

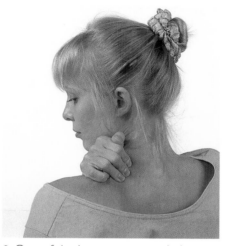

2 One of the best massage techniques for removing any waste matter from tired muscles and getting fresh, oxygenated blood into them, is kneading. You can do this to yourself by firmly gripping your opposite shoulder with your hand and using a squeezing motion.

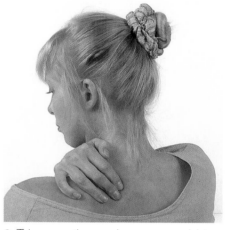

3 Take your time and move your right hand quite slowly along the top and back of the left shoulder, squeezing firmly several times. Now repeat the exercise exactly on the other shoulder, this time using your left hand.

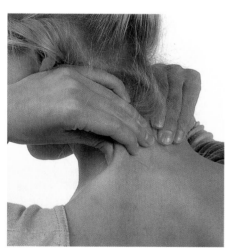

4 Next with the fingers of both hands, grip the back of your neck and squeeze slowly or rapidly in a circular motion. This very helpful technique will help you to relax all those muscles that lead up either side of the neck.

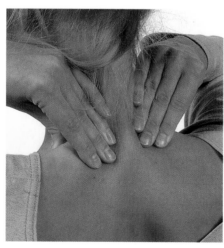

5 Slowly work up as far as the base of the skull, and then work right down again towards the shoulders.

6 To work more deeply into the neck, move the thumbs in a circular movement across the back of the neck, and then right up into the base of the skull. You will soon feel the bone as you start applying quite moderate pressure.

HEAD REVITALIZER

Almost everyone at some time or another suffers from headaches. They can have a multitude of causes, such as spending too much time in front of a VDU, anxiety, insomnia, fatigue or sinus congestion. However, the most common cause is from tension after periods of stress. Use this simple self-massage sequence to help ease headaches, whatever their cause, and to increase vitality. It will also help you to focus your mind.

1 Use small, circling movements with the fingers, working steadily down from the forehead, then down around the temples and over your cheeks.

2 Use firm pressure and work slowly to ease tensions out of the facial muscles.

3 You can also use your fingers to gently and firmly press the area just under the eye socket, by your nose. Build up a satisfying regular rhythm.

4 Next, smooth firmly and satisfyingly around the arc of your eye socket immediately beneath your brow bone.

5 Work across the cheeks and along each side of the nose, then move on to the jaw line which is often tense. Try not to pull downwards on the skin. Instead, let the circling movements smooth away the stresses, and gently lift the face as you work. All these techniques can be used at any time of day.

KEY TIPS
• Headaches are very rarely symptoms of serious disorders. The pain comes from the membranes surrounding the brain, the scalp and the blood vessels.
• There are almost as many types as causes. The causes include a tension-tightening of the muscles from the neck up. This can stay localized or set up a chain reaction, with the pain passing into the head.
• Typical causes include hangovers, bad posture, excessive noise, too much sleep and lack of fresh air. It is also vital to have a regular intake of food.
• Some people might find that certain foods, such as red wine, can trigger attacks. The moment you feel the first signs of a headache, stop what you are doing and relax. The pain is better tackled now than later.

INSTANT REVITALIZER

Do you find that you always run out of steam by eleven o'clock, or four o'clock? Have you got to be bright and alert for an early morning meeting, a long drive, picking up the kids or going out to a party where you need to impress? At any time of the day your energy can suddenly flag, without any warning. One moment you are fine, the next you are struggling. Give yourself an instant "wake-up" with this effective routine.

1 Do a kneading action on the arms, from the wrist to the shoulder and back again using a firm squeezing movement.

2 Knead more quickly than is normal in a massage. This technique will invigorate each arm and shoulder in turn.

3 Then rub firmly and swiftly up the outside of each arm which will gradually stimulate and improve your circulation.

4 Repeat in an upwards direction each time, which is good at encouraging the blood to flow back to the heart.

5 With the fingers and thumb of one hand, firmly squeeze the neck muscles using a relaxing, circular motion.

6 With the outside edge of the hands lightly hack on the front of each thigh, using a non-stop, rapid motion.

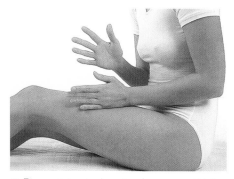

7 Do not try to karate-chop your thighs. Instead, you want the hands to spring up lightly from the muscles.

8 Next, rub the calves vigorously to loosen them and to get the blood moving. Do this with the leg bent.

9 Always work from the ankles to the knee, using alternate hands. Finally, stand and shake your whole body.

TONIC FOR ACHING LEGS

Many people, such as sales assistants and indeed shoppers, teachers and hotel receptionists, spend far too long each day standing still, or barely moving. Such occupations create real problems for circulation in our legs, which can lead to tired, aching limbs, swollen ankles or even cramp. However, a quick self-massage at the end of the day can help reduce stiffness and sluggish blood flow. It is a wonderful, instant reviver.

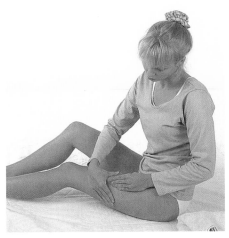

1 Using both hands, knead one thigh at a time by squeezing between the fingers and thumb. Squeeze with each hand alternately for the best effect, working from the knee to the hip and back. Repeat on the other thigh.

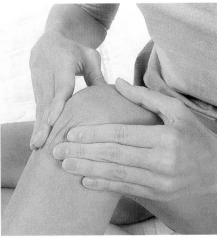

2 Right round the knees commence a similar kind of kneading action, but now use the fingers for a much lighter overall effect. Work in smaller circles.

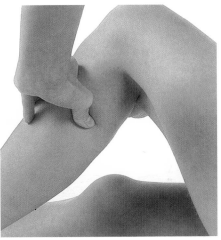

3 Bend your leg, and if possible raise the foot on to a chair or ledge. With your thumbs, work on the back of each calf with a circular, kneading action.

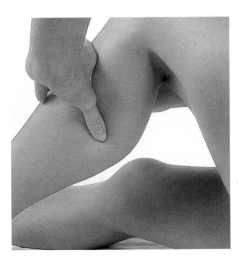

4 Repeat a few times, each time working from the ankle up the leg to the knee.

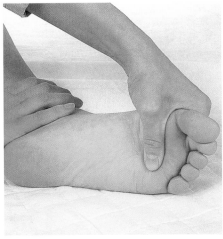

5 Squeeze the foot, loosening the muscles and then gently stretch your arch.

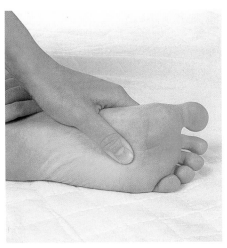

6 Use firm pressure with your thumb to stretch the foot. Repeat on the other foot.

HEADACHE AND TENSION RELIEVER

What is called the tension headache is probably the commonest result of getting stressed. Unfortunately, for some, this can become a daily occurrence and might lead to a migraine. But all this pain can be avoided by just a few minutes of soothing massage strokes which will eliminate the muscle spasms that lie behind such discomfort. It is even more relaxing if done by a partner.

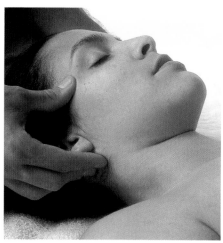

1 Gently using your fingertips, make a sequence of small alternating circles on the muscles to either side of the neck.

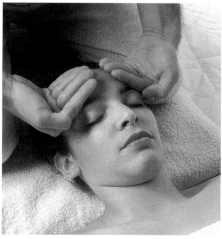

2 Continue circling, this time with both hands working around the side of the head and behind the ears.

3 Smooth tension away from the temples with the backs or sides of your hands, in a gentle, stroking motion.

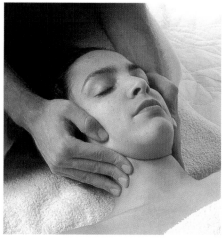

4 Gently pinch, and keep squeezing right along the line of the eyebrows, reducing pressure as you work outwards.

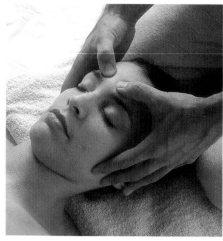

5 With your thumbs, use steady but firm pressure on the lower forehead, gradually working out from between the eyebrows.

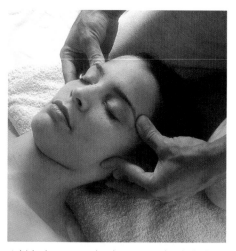

6 Work across the brow to the hair line. This also covers many acupressure points, and will release any blocked energy in the area. It can also help to relieve sinus congestion.

ARM AND HAND TONIC

There is no doubt, the most over-worked, hard-pressed parts of the body are your hands and arms. No matter what your job, they simply do not stop – turning over pages, typing, holding, reaching, pointing, you name it. Consequently, they quite often end up feeling rather stiff and tense, yet a few deft massage techniques can easily reduce these uncomfortable feelings, leaving you feeling fresh again.

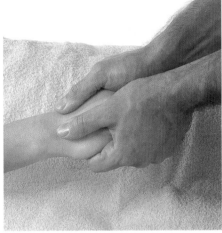

1 Kneel by your partner, who is lying face up. Hold your partner's hand, palm down, in both your hands and with your thumbs start to apply a steady stretching motion across the back of the hand.

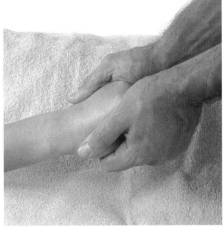

2 Repeat a few times, with a firm but comfortable pressure. Then turn the hand over and now, using your thumbs, begin smoothing and stretching the palm using a similar technique and action.

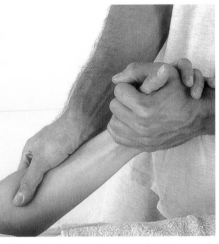

3 Next, begin gently squeezing the forearm. This too can get tense. Use your hand and thumb in order to work gradually down from the wrist, moving slowly on towards the elbow.

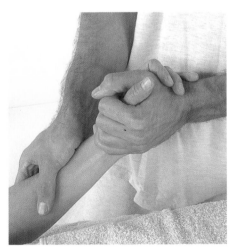

4 Repeat the motion. Move your hands quickly around the arm, not missing any area, making sure that you squeeze all the muscles that might be stiff.

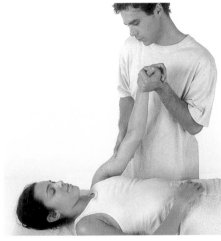

5 Lift the arm right up, not in any way forcefully, and then use a similar squeezing movement to work down the upper arm, from elbow to shoulder.

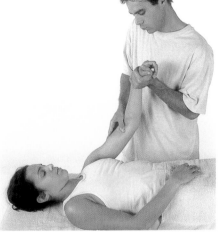

6 Repeat, working all around the arm. Swap hands if you find it necessary for a more comfortable action. Repeat all these movements on the other arm.

SHOULDER AND NECK RELIEVER

The muscle that takes the main brunt of tension in the shoulder is the trapezius; it stands out on either side when you shrug your shoulders, and connects to the neck. Lifting heavy weights, excessive gardening and bending, for example, will tighten it, and when that happens you need help. Gentle kneading is one of the very best ways of relaxing it. This quick, effective massage will soon revive you.

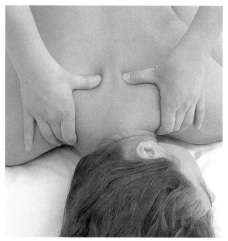

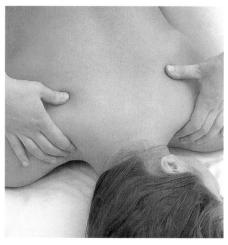

1 This technique takes a little time to master but is well worth the effort. Place both hands on the far shoulder, and with alternate hands squeeze your fingers and thumb together. Do not pinch, but roll the fingers over the thumb. Repeat by moving to the other side, again working on the shoulder away from your body.

2 Having worked on each shoulder in turn, now work on both together. Place your thumbs on either side of the spine on the upper back, with the rest of each hand over each shoulder. Squeeze your fingers and thumbs together, rolling the flesh between them.

3 Let your thumbs move out smoothly across the shoulder muscles.

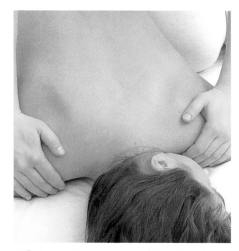

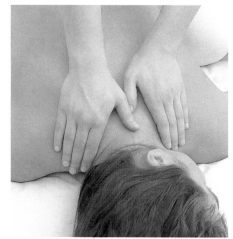

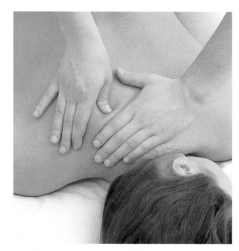

4 Release the pressure of the thumbs, and stretch the blades outwards using both your hands simultaneously.

5 Now return both hands to the centre, and get the thumbs well in position to repeat this exercise.

6 If the neck is very stiff, repeat the kneading exercise, applying slightly firmer pressure with the thumbs.

TENSION AND BACKACHE RELIEVER

The back is where most of our physical aches and pains are generally located; in fact more days are lost from work each year through back problems than from all other parts of the body combined. That is why it is a good place to massage, using broad, relaxing movements. Make sure that you keep your back in the best possible condition, treating it on a regular basis, not just when things go wrong.

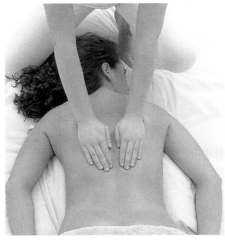

1 The best initial movement is called an effleurage. You begin by either sitting or kneeling at the head end; then place your hands on the back, with the thumbs close to, but not actually on, the spine. It is a comfortable position to find.

2 Steadily lean forward and glide your hands down the back, keeping a steady pressure all the way down.

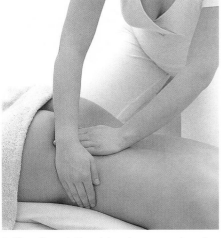

3 Kneeling at the side, place your hands on the other side of the back and move them steadily in a circular motion, using overlapping circles to work up and down the back. Move to the other side and repeat the circling technique.

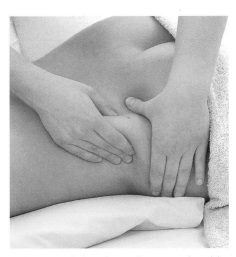

4 Place both hands on the opposite side of the back and use a firm squeezing motion with alternate hands, thereby creating a kneading effect.

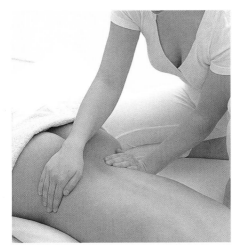

5 With one hand on the side of the back nearest you, and the other hand on the opposite side, push the hands towards and then past each other to reverse their position. Move up and down the back slowly and firmly, repeating this technique.

6 Place your hands centrally on the back and then push them away from each other, leaning forward to maintain an even pressure during this stretch.

LOWER BACK RELAXER

One of the worst possible areas for tension is the lumbar part of the back, where it curves towards the pelvis. Continuous incorrect posture and lifting things without care – you should always bend from the knees and keep your back straight – are some of the causes that can aggravate lower back discomfort. If your partner suffers in any way from such twinges, a massage will stretch and relax the body.

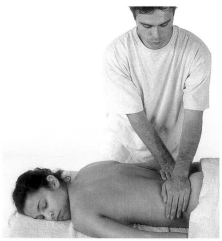

1 Standing or kneeling to the side, place your hands on the opposite side of your partner's back and pull them up towards you firmly; repeat on the other side.

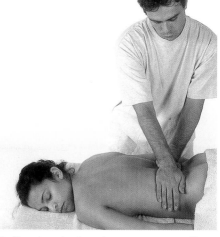

2 Overlap the hands to create an effect like bandaging, but much more soothing.

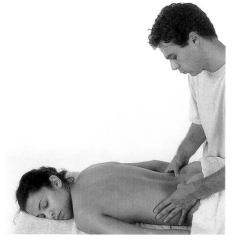

3 Using your thumbs, make circling movements over the lower back. Use a steady, even pressure, leaning with your body, but do not press on the spine.

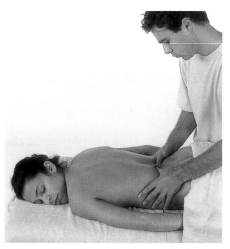

4 Stretch the lower back muscles by gliding the thumbs firmly up either side several times. Press in steadily with both thumbs just to either side of the spine, working gradually up it.

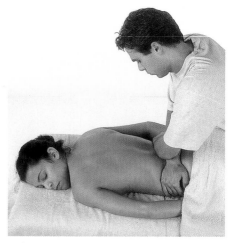

5 Stretch across the lower back with crossed hands moving away from each other to try and ease, and relax, any tense, taut muscles.

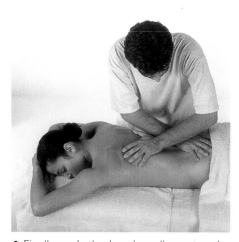

6 Finally, push the hands well apart and stretch the whole back.

Caution

Do not put pressure on the spine, and ease off if it feels at all uncomfortable.

INSTANT FOOT REVITALIZER

With really very little complaint, your feet carry you around all day, sometimes for hours on end in the most dreadful heat. When you compare the size of your feet with the rest of you, it is not surprising that they sometimes rebel and feel sore. In fact the best way to relieve tired, aching feet is with a quick, ten-minute massage. It is amazing how quickly it can revive them, letting you get on with your life again.

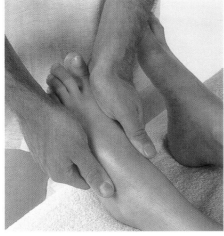

1 Hold the foot in your hands, with your thumbs on top and fingers underneath. Gently stretch across the top of the foot, trying to keep your fingers quite still while you keep moving your thumbs.

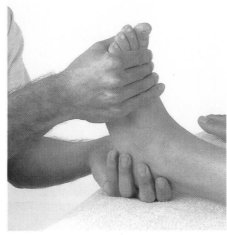

2 Flex the foot, pushing against the resistance to loosen the whole foot and ankle a little. Then gently extend the foot, stretching it as far as is comfortable.

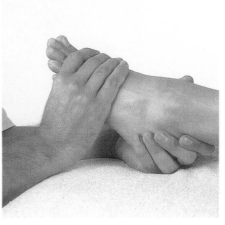

3 Now, twist the foot using a gentle wringing motion in both directions to stretch all the small muscles.

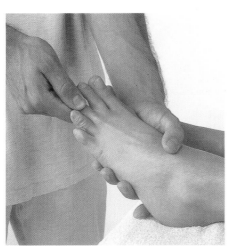

4 Firmly hold one of the toes, and then squeeze and pull it. Now repeat with every single toe.

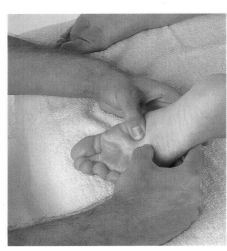

5 Circle over the sole firmly with your fingers, or thumbs if that feels much easier; make sure that you do not end up tickling your partner.

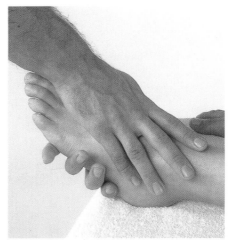

6 Support the foot with one hand, and stroke the upper side with the other hand. Smoothly stroke all the way from the toes up to the ankle. Repeat all the actions on the other foot.

TENSE ABDOMEN RELIEVER

Tension in the abdomen may reflect a degree of physical discomfort, such as indigestion, constipation or even menstrual cramp. However, the cause is just as likely to be emotional because many people hold their inner fears in this particular area. If you bottle up and cannot release or express your feelings, then abdominal spasms may occur. The following movements should ensure that such tensions soon go away.

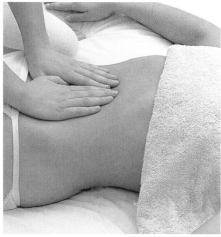

1 Begin by placing your hands gently on the abdomen. At this stage simply focus all your thoughts and energy on trying to pass good vibrations into your partner's body. You will be surprised by the results.

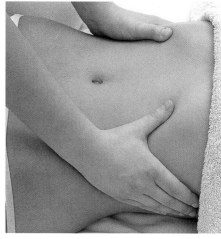

2 Next, spread each hand open, and slowly and gradually move each to the side of the abdomen. Repeat this two or three times, building up a slow, regular, soothing rhythm.

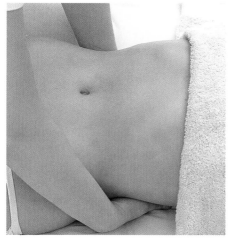

3 Kneeling by the side, now slide your hands under the back to meet at the spine. Lift the body gently to arch and stretch the back before pulling your hands out towards the hips.

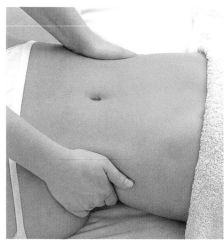

4 Firmly draw your hands out over the waist, and then gently glide them back to their original position to repeat the stroke a few times.

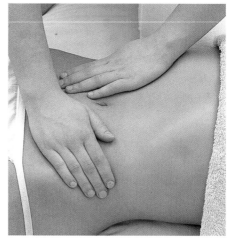

5 Placing your hands on the abdomen, move them around steadily in a clockwise direction (this follows the way in which the colon functions).

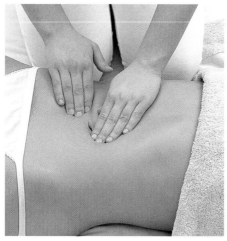

6 Finally, repeat the action, but this time working a little deeper by using your fingers, provided that there are no signs of any discomfort.

DE-STRESS YOUR COLLEAGUES

Massage is a highly versatile skill, and can be applied in many different situations, not least the office. How often have you heard one of your work colleagues complain of terrible tense, aching shoulders preventing them from doing any work? Now you can step in and do something about it. A five-minute massage is all it takes. It can be wonderfully effective, revitalizing and refreshing them.

1 Standing behind your seated colleague, place both your hands gently on the shoulders, thumbs towards you and fingers in the front.

2 Using your fingers, knead in small circles up and down the back of the neck. Support the head with your other hand while you are working on the neck.

3 Place your forearms over the shoulders, and then gradually press down with your body weight in order to squeeze and stretch the trapezius.

4 Move the forearms gradually outwards to cover the shoulders, maintaining a firm pressure all the time.

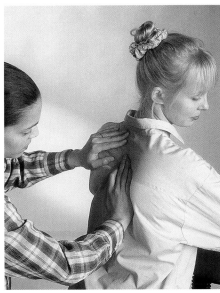

5 Allow your fingers to sink into the muscles around the shoulder blade. Repeat on the other side.

6 Place your hands on your partner's shoulder joints, and press back towards yourself to stretch the upper chest.

SENSUAL MASSAGE

As well as releasing stresses and tensions from the muscles, massage is a wonderful way to enhance a relationship by increasing caring, sharing touch. If your relationship seems to have got into a rut, and sexual energy is low, why not revitalize yourselves with deep soothing massage strokes. To make the whole experience a real treat, make the room extra warm, and play some of your favourite, soothing music.

1 Place your hands to either side of the spine and glide them down the back, move out to the side, and then back again. Repeat several times.

2 With a gentle motion, stroke down the centre of the back with one hand following the other smoothly, as if you were stroking a cat.

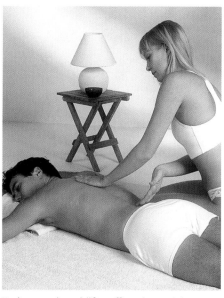

3 As one hand lifts off at the pelvis, start again with the other hand at the neck.

4 Place both your hands on the upper back and stroke outwards in a fan shape.

5 Work down the back, including the buttocks, using a fanning action.

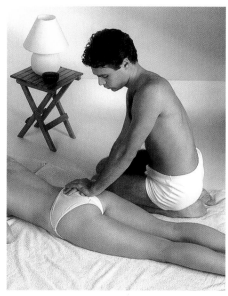

6 Use a firm, steady circling action on the buttocks.

7 Stroke up the back of the legs, with one hand after the other building up a smooth, continuous flowing motion.

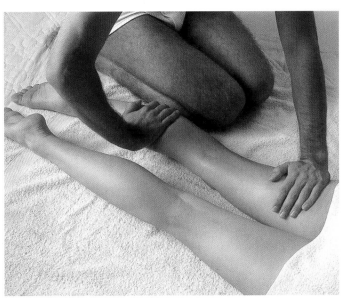

8 As one hand reaches the buttocks, start on the calf with the other hand to keep up that continuous steady rhythm.

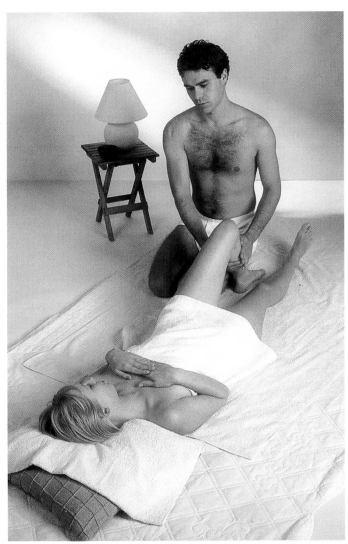

9 Turn your partner over and stroke up the front of the legs; having the leg bent greatly helps the muscles to relax.

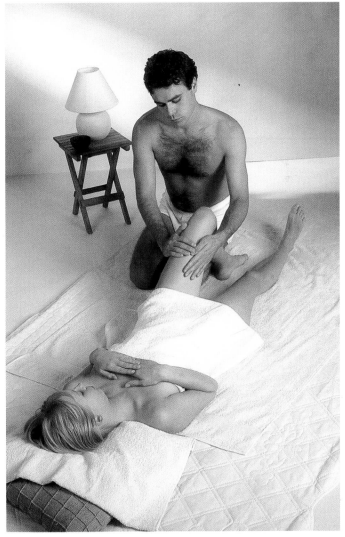

10 Continue the movement, using both hands to make stroking movements from the knees right up the thighs.

AROMATHERAPY

—

Smell is perhaps the most underrated of the senses, yet it has the most subtle significance in our lives. It arouses a very primitive area of the brain, below the level of conscious thought, and even a few atoms of scent can have an immediate effect on the body's systems, triggering changes in our physical state as well as our emotional reactions. In the early years of the 20th century, the French chemist René-Maurice Gattefosse investigated the precise therapeutic properties of essential oils and discovered that they were often more effective than isolated or synthetic compounds. The art of aromatherapy uses these precious and complex plant distillations in many ways, including massage, bath oils, steam inhalations and room scents, to bring about gentle, beneficial change.

USING OILS

If you have never quite understood the art of aromatherapy, and are afraid that it involves all kinds of strange pieces of equipment, then you could not be more wrong. It actually involves a collection of small, highly attractive bottles that can be quite a feature, and maybe even a candle burner. That is all that it takes to become an aficionado. Once hooked, you will certainly never look back, and those oils will start improving your health.

BUYING AND KEEPING OILS

Aromatic essential oils can be used in various ways to restore good health. However, the oils are in fact concentrated substances, and need to be diluted for safety. A test massage with a weak dose will quickly reveal potential skin reactions. Also, seek medical advice before massaging a pregnant woman.

You will find that many companies now sell essential oils, and when buying them always make sure that they are pure and of a high quality (you get what you pay for in general). If possible, try to smell the sample bottle of the oil that you are buying, and make sure that it has a good, clean, non-synthetic perfume. Since essential oils are liable to deteriorate quite quickly as a direct result of sunlight, they should always be stored in a dark glass jar in a cool, dark place. Keep the lid firmly closed to prevent any evaporation. One good tip is always to buy small quantities, especially of citrus oil which deteriorates quickly.

▲ *Aromas are always tempered by an emotional reaction – a lasting memory of them from the past.*

CREATING SCENTS

When using essential oils at home, it is very helpful to have some basic equipment. A burner is an excellent way of vaporizing oils into the atmosphere. It consists of a candle in a simple, small, invariably terracotta, open-top container, and a bowl for the oil, which sits on top. When you want to simmer pot-pourri in a bowl, again all you need is a candle. Place it under the bowl and gently warm it until you can detect a delicious scent. This is an an excellent way of making a room much more fragrant. If you want a long-term scent, albeit one that is slightly fainter, use a ready-prepared commercial mix of dry pot-pourri. Place the bowls strategically round the house. They come in different perfumes and strengths.

▼ *Rose oil is a favourite for massage as it has such pleasant connotations. It will help even the most tense person relax.*

HOW IT ALL BEGAN

When you take up aromatherapy, it is worth noting that it has a highly impressive history. People have been using scented products for thousands of years. Ancient written records dating back 3,000 years, in the case of the Indian Verdic manuscripts, describe in marvellous detail the use of aromatic oils. Egyptian papyri from 1500 BC, and biblical stories of the Jewish exodus from Egypt about 300 years later, also describe the widespread use of aromatic oils. Many were used in religious ceremonies and in rituals, but many were also used when having a massage, taking a bath, and for scenting the body and hair. To that extent, little has changed. Scented products have long been justifiably popular.

AROMATIC OILS

These oils were probably first made by Arabic physicians in the 10th century AD. That much is definite, though it is now strongly argued by some that they were also used in the Indus valley, in the foothills of the Himalayas 5,000 years ago. Certainly, the Arabic use of concentrated, distilled oils – widely famed in the West as the "perfumes of Arabia" – did lead to a renaissance in the use of aromatic plants.

As distillation was taken up in the West, many more oils were extracted. There was also a gradual separation of the perfume side and more medical applications. Ironically, the former was the one that really provided the impetus for the development of aromatherapy. Today, it is enjoying a worldwide popularity rarely seen before. While aromatherapists now use specific essential oils for their physiological effects, there is no reason why they may not also be used for their relaxing properties. In fact, in today's turbulent, demanding world, that often seems to be their chief attraction. A calming, soothing, marvellously scented way of getting the body and mind back on track. Aromatherapy, with its long history, is guaranteed a long future.

▲ *A collection of oils quickly becomes an attractive feature.*

MIXING ESSENTIAL OILS FOR MASSAGE

1 Before you begin, wash and dry your hands and make sure that all the utensils are clean and dry. Measure out about 10ml /2 tsp of your chosen vegetable oil. Next, carefully pour the vegetable oil into the blending bowl.

2 Add the essential oil, never rushing things, always with great care, one drop at a time. Mix gently using a clean, dry cocktail stick or perhaps even a toothpick. Make sure that the children are well away before doing this.

HOW AROMATHERAPY CAN BE USED

Aromatherapy is surprisingly varied in its uses. It can help with all kinds of problems, and what can make it such a regular part of your life is that it can also tackle everyday aches and pains. It is also marvellous for coping with poor circulation and headaches, and those long, hard days at work which result in a tired, sore back. Treat oils with respect, and they will soon perk you up.

MASSAGE

Massage is a wonderful way to use essential oils, suitably diluted in a good base oil, for your partner or family. Always try to use soft, thick towels to cover any areas of the body that you are not massaging, and make sure that the room is kept warm, perhaps with an additional portable heater. Do not undermine the effect of the massage by draughty, cold conditions.

Also note that while essential oils are wonderful natural remedies they are highly concentrated and must therefore be used with care and caution. You should consequently only take essential oils internally if they have been professionally prescribed for you, and always use essential oils in a diluted form – normally I per cent for massage and just 5 drops in a bath or for a steam inhalation. You should also be extra careful with anyone who has asthma or epilepsy, and if anyone does experience any kind of adverse reaction, use common sense and stop using the oils immediately. A quick test beforehand will usually reveal possible problems.

▲ *Gently rubbing the body all over with a loofa greatly increases the effect of an aromatherapy bath.*

BATHS

Imagine soaking in a hot bath, enveloped in a delicious scent of exotic flowers, feeling all the day's tensions drop away . . . well, that can easily become a reality with aromatherapy. The oils seem to capture the essence of the plant, and can effortlessly transport you to pine-scented forests, refreshing orange groves or even magical, oriental spice markets.

When using oils in the bath, pour in 5 drops just before you get in. The oils form a thin film on the surface of the water which, aided by the relaxing warmth of the water, will be partly absorbed by your skin as you breathe in the scent, producing an immediate psychological and physiological effect.

MORNING AND EVENING BATHS

For a refreshing, uplifting bath in the mornings, try a blend of 3 drops Bergamot and 2 drops Geranium essential oils. To relax and unwind after a long day, make a blend of 3 drops Lavender and 2 drops Ylang Ylang. For tired, tense muscles when you have been overdoing it, have a long soak in a deep, warm bath to which you have added approximately 3 drops Marjoram and 2 drops Chamomile essential oils.

HAND AND FOOTBATHS

The circulation to our extremities can be greatly affected by levels of tension and stress, among other factors, and the warmth of the water quickly helps the blood vessels to dilate. This can be very helpful when treating tension headaches and even painful migraines, when the blood vessels in the head are frequently engorged with blood. When you are using essential oils to make a hand or even a footbath, you should two-thirds fill a large bowl with warm, but not too hot, water and then carefully add and stir in 3–4 drops of your favourite oil.

EXCESS HEAT WHEN HOT AND TIRED

For hot, aching feet or hands, use a mixture of 2 drops peppermint and 2 drops lemon. To boost your circulation try the following: add 2 drops Lavender and 2 drops Marjoram oils. This is also extremely good for those who suffer from poor circulation and tense, cold extremities.

▲ *A relaxing bath in the evening promotes enhanced sleep.*

STEAM INHALATIONS

Colds and sinus problems may all too easily cause congestion, but we can also feel blocked up and unable to breathe freely as a result of all kinds of tension levels. Using a steam inhalation warms and moistens the membranes, and the use of essential oils also helps to open and relax the airways. Just boil a kettle, pour the water into a bowl, add the oils and inhale deeply. It makes a simple but highly effective cure.

If you suffer from nasal congestion, and have that extremely irritating, stuffed-up feeling, possibly combined with tiredness, do try using 3 drops Eucalyptus and 2 drops Peppermint. Just mix them in a large bowl filled with steaming water; it should make a marvellous remedy. For those who have that tight, tense feeling in their chest which makes breathing rather uncomfortable, try to relax your airways using just 4 drops Lavender, and 3 drops Frankincense.

▲ *For respiratory complaints in particular, steam inhalations have long been considered very helpful remedies.*

SCENTED ROOMS

Aromatherapy has many applications in the home or office including the creation of an aromatic environment which has wide-ranging beneficial effects.

POT-POURRI

It is possible to scent a room by making a simmering pot-pourri. Place a mixture of scented flowers and leaves (without any fixatives or additives) in a bowl of water and heat gently from below – a candle may well be sufficient. Unlike dry pot-pourri, the simmering variety does not last for long but gives off a much stronger aroma. Try making your own blends; add about 1 cupful of dried material to 1.2 litres/2 pints/5 cups water.

For a sleep-enhancing pot-pourri use ½ cup Lime flowers, ¼ cup Chamomile flowers, 1 tbsp Sweet Marjoram and 1 tbsp Lavender flowers. For a more refreshing, uplifting blend try ½ cup Lemon Verbena leaves, ¼ cup Jasmine flowers, 2 tbsp Lemon peel and 1 tsp Coriander seeds.

▲ *A wonderfully fragrant bowl of potpourri.*

ESSENTIAL OIL BURNERS

Most oils can be used with a burner. The basic principle is very simple: a small dish to hold a few drops of essential oil, with some type of gentle heat underneath, often in the form of a candle. The heat needs to be fairly low in order to allow slow evaporation of the oil and a longer-lasting scent.

If you want to fumigate a room, then try adding 3–4 drops of oils such as Pine, Eucalyptus or Juniper to a burner. In order to help you keep really sharp and alert, a couple of drops of Peppermint or Rosemary may work wonders, while 2–3 drops of Ylang Ylang or Lavender will have the opposite effect and soon help you to wind down at the end of a long, tiring, difficult day.

It is well worth visiting a specialist shop with a wide range of such burners. Chose an attractive one that makes an interesting feature; the Oriental kind often have interesting ornamental styles. They also make good presents – the whole kit, with oils, makes a marvellous surprise Christmas present, one that will get someone quickly hooked on the subject.

BOWL OF HOT WATER

Adding a couple of drops of an essential oil to a bowl of hot water is a pleasant way to give fragrance to a room or office. Try to use an attractive bowl and make sure that it is placed well out of reach of any children. Use an oil that is a big favourite, as it will release its scent for some time when used in this way. For mornings, Bergamot, Mandarin or Lemon would be uplifting. Later in the day you may wish to use Rose or Jasmine.

OTHER SCENTED PRODUCTS

Essential oils are quite often included in a wide variety of excellent gift items. They range from candles to incense sticks and cones. It is quite important, though, that you check the natural essential oil that is being used to scent these products. You may well find that they actually repeat scents that you are already using, which can produce an excessively strong aroma.

therapeutic recipes
therapeutic recipes

therapeutic recipes

One of the great delights of taking up the ancient art of aromatherapy is discovering the many exciting ways in which oils can be blended to create a wide range of enhanced therapeutic effects, with new fragrances to soothe the senses at the same time.

On the following pages you will find scores of all kinds of ideas for using different combinations of oils; they have been specially selected for their healing properties, and also because they provide an array of exquisite aromas. However, since the sense of smell is very individual and highly subjective, do not feel that you  have to like certain aromas. Above all, do not feel that the not-so-good has to be enjoyed. It does not. If you find that you dislike a particular combination then feel free to make your own blends, bearing in mind the actions of the oils and the dilution rates that were described earlier.

The key to success is quite simple. Always try to ensure that you buy good quality essential oils, with a pure scent that comes from the natural, unadulterated extract. There are no rules about what you should like. The best way to proceed is by trusting your nose. If something has what might be called the ooh-ah factor, an aroma that is totally arresting rather than subtle almost to the point of not being present, but without being fiercely competitive and dominating your senses, then feel free to enjoy it.

For each of the blends suggested in this section, the number of drops of oils given should be diluted for massage purposes in 20ml/4 tsp of a base vegetable oil such as sweet Almond oil. When creating a steam inhalation, use the number of drops given in a large bowl holding about 1 litre/1¾ pints/4 cups hot water, and for a compress add the specified number of oil drops to a bowl holding 250ml/8fl oz/1 cup hot water. Also remember that when creating a mix about which you are slightly unsure, make a tiny dose to check that it is what you want. It is prudent to proceed by caution.

STRESS SOOTHERS

Sadly, stress is now playing far too large a part in all our lives, and while we cannot always avoid the causes, we can at least dispel its effects on us. All you need to do is set aside just a few minutes at the end of the day when you can be quiet and relax. Then, using a variety of soothing, relaxing therapeutic measures, such as a marvellous, long, slow rhythmic massage, you will end up feeling totally invigorated and refreshed.

STRESS RELIEVERS

Stress, or rather our inability to cope with an excess amount of it, is one of the biggest health problems today. Lifestyles seem to include so many varied and often conflicting demands that it is not surprising that most of us feel stressed at times, sometimes constantly. We all react to excess stress in different ways, perhaps through anxiety, depression or exhaustion, but we can all certainly benefit from the wonderfully balancing and stress-calming effects provided by aromatic oils.

Our bodies are geared to cope with a stressful situation by producing various hormones that trigger off a series of physiological actions in the body; they are known collectively as the "fight or flight" syndrome, and serve to place the body in a state of alert in a potentially dangerous situation. Extra blood is shunted to the muscles, and the heart rate speeds up while the digestion slows down. These responses are appropriate when we are faced with a physical threat, but can nowadays be triggered by quite different kinds of stress and end up placing a strain on our bodies without fulfilling any useful need.

In order to help reduce the impact of stress on the whole system, it is necessary to find ways both to avoid getting over-stressed in the first instance, and of letting go of the changes that occur internally under stress. Aromatherapy can be a great help in each case, especially during and immediately after a long relaxing massage, because the oils will help to keep you calm.

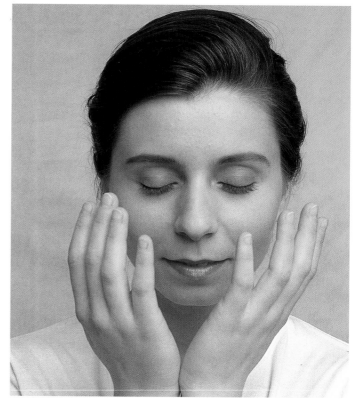

▲ *It should not take you long to discover which particular essential oils work best for you as an individual.*

1 Ideally have the person lying down with the head in your lap or on a cushion. With your fingertips, gently begin smoothing the essential oil into the face.

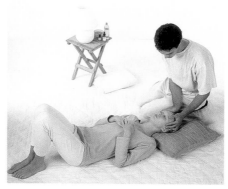

2 Using your thumbs, one after the other, stroke tension gently and carefully away from the centre of the forehead.

ANXIETY CALMERS

When people are described as being "uptight", that is often exactly what they are: tense muscles in the face and neck are a sure sign of anxiety. You can release that tension with a face massage, using gentle, soothing strokes on the temples and forehead especially. This is very good as an evening treat, calming away the day's cares and worries.

Use just a few drops of oil because most people do not like having a greasy feeling on the face. Make up a blend of 4 drops Lavender and 2 drops Ylang Ylang in a light oil such as Sweet Almond.

MUSCULAR ACHES

When you are under any kind of difficult stress for any length of time, your body promptly reacts by becoming and staying permanently tense. Clearly this is not good for you. It can make quite specific muscles, or indeed all of your muscles, ache and feel overwhelmingly tired and sluggish, leaden and heavy.

In order to relieve this all too familiar list of thoroughly unwanted symptoms, and also to start releasing the underlying tension, use essential oils in what is called a massage blend.

As the massage movements begin to work on the aching muscles at surface and deeper levels, the oils begin to be absorbed. In time they too get to work and start tackling the inner tension. Such treatment is in itself quite refreshing.

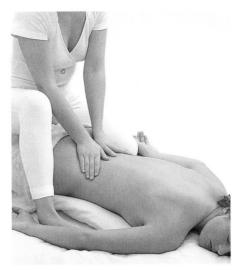

1 Rest your hands on the lower back to either side of the spine. Lean your weight into your hands and stroke up the back towards the head. Mould your hands to the body as they glide firmly along.

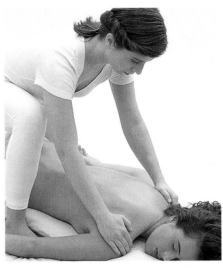

2 As your hands reach the top of the back, fan them out towards the shoulders in a long, smooth, flowing, ceaseless motion.

BLOOD PRESSURE

It should be emphasized that anyone with very high blood pressure should first seek expert medical (or professional) treatment. You should not even think about trying to tackle such a condition yourself without accurate guidance. However, in much milder, far less dangerous or acute cases, which are almost entirely related to anxiety and tension, you can help get temporary relief by using essential oils.

Begin by giving yourself or your partner a special treat – a marvellous soothing footbath. For such a bath you should fill a large bowl three-quarters full with hot water. Then carefully add 2 drops Rose, 2 drops Ylang Ylang and 3 drops Lavender. Using a clean, new wooden kitchen spoon, specially reserved for the job, mix everything in, and let stand for a couple of minutes. Then let the feet sink into the water and soak for at least five well-earned, relaxing minutes.

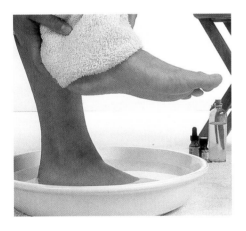

COLIC

Colic is the term that is used to describe spasmodic bouts of cramping pain, building up in intensity until it finally reaches a peak, before abating and returning a short while later.

The causes can range from an obstructing stone, for which professional medical treatment is required, to intestinal gas. The latter is extremely common in babies, and it may strike adults as a result of high tension levels. Fortunately, you can easily aid the adult condition by having a short gentle massage that will also leave you feeling calm and gently relaxed. It only takes about ten minutes.

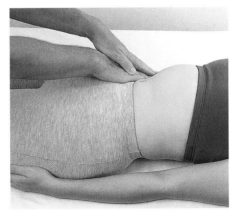

1 Starting in the lower right-hand corner, steadily and firmly press in using both your hands, but taking care not to cause any discomfort.

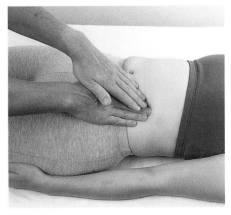

2 Slowly move the hands in a clockwise direction around the abdomen. Keep making continuous small circles to massage the colon.

REDUCING ANXIETY

One of the worst problems of anxiety is that it can end up causing headaches. To some people they are but a mild inconvenience, others might find that they slow them down, but in severe cases they can be totally debilitating. The sooner you act, especially if you tend to have major attacks, the more likely you are to be fine. One of the best remedies is a soothing head massage – it can work wonders in reducing the pain.

HEADACHE EASERS

Tension headaches are quite a common feature in most people's lives. In fact they are often completely unavoidable, caused by anything from long tedious slavish hours on a computer to bringing up unruly small children.

Whatever the cause, try and stop what you are doing at the first available opportunity, and take a break. Impractical though it sounds, it is the only way to stop the massive build-up of a nasty headache.

Try to draw the curtains, and to create a deep, dark relaxing astmosphere shut off from the outside world. Besides the massage described on the right, see if you can find time to make yourself a wonderful warm compress. If the head feels at all hot, then try using an oil infused with 4 drops of Peppermint. Another option is 4 drops of Chamomile.

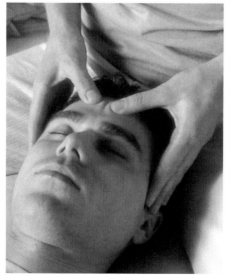

I Ease tension headaches by massaging oils gently into the forehead. With your thumbs, use steady but gentle pressure to stroke the forehead. Repeat this technique for several minutes.

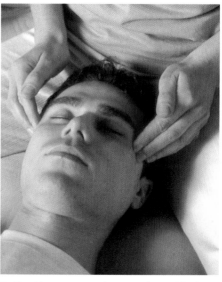

2 Gently massage the temples with the fingers to release tension and stress.

I Use small circling movements just under the bony edge of the skull.

2 Now gently squeeze the neck muscles in a slow, rhythmic way.

MIGRAINE EASERS

One of the most complex of health problems, migraines are nature's way of shutting us down when life has been too demanding. The triggers that spark off a migraine attack are highly individual, and professional treatment is really needed to try to understand the causes for each person. Since many migraine sufferers have a heightened sense of smell at the onset of the attack they may find any aroma intolerable, so do use oils sparingly and sensitively.

At the earliest stage of a migraine attack, try using a blend of 2 drops Rosemary, I drop Marjoram and I drop Clary Sage, diluted in a massage oil and very gently massaged into the temples and forehead.

BREATHING ENHANCERS

"Breathe" . . . how often have we said this to ourselves when we are tense and stressed? Although breathing occurs without our conscious control, it can be affected to quite a considerable extent as we start to tense up, with a tightening of the chest muscles, which restricts any lung expansion.

The tightening feeling in the chest can be extremely uncomfortable, and you should most certainly seek expert medical advice at the first onset if it appears on the left-hand side of the body. Assuming that it is nothing too serious, though, your first consideration is to make sure that you start to relax, and begin breathing deeply and regularly. Take your time, and do not rush this. It is important that you regulate your controlled breathing sensibly.

Once you are happy that you have taken every step to calm down, shutting out whatever the cause might be, you can try the following steam inhalation. The key to success is making an aromatic blend. This is best done by taking a bowl of steaming water and adding 3 drops Benzoin, 2 drops Marjoram and 2 drops Eucalyptus. Mix them all together, leave to stand for a couple of minutes, and then with a covering towel placed over your head, begin inhaling deeply. You will soon notice the beneficial effects.

▶ *As the oils vaporize, inhale the steam deeply. If you hold a towel over your head this will slow down the evaporation.*

MILD SHOCK SOOTHERS

You bump your head, trip over the cat, fall down the stairs, or stand on the upturned end of a garden rake so that it suddenly smacks you viciously on the head. In fact garden injuries are among the commonest, and most dangerous kind. As in the case of the rake, they can leave you absolutely taken aback, shocked and stunned. You might well feel a little weak and giddy, and need to sit down for a few minutes. At these times, essential oils can be a remarkably useful first-aid help, quickly bringing us right back to our senses.

The quickest, and by far the simplest way to benefit from aromatherapy in instances of mild shock, is to put an open bottle of either Lavender or Clary Sage oil under the injured person's nose and let them sniff the aroma directly. Of course you cannot always have such an oil on the spot, and it is therefore well worth having the pre-made "Rescue Remedy" ready to hand for such an occasion. Another extremely good remedy involves putting a couple of oil drops on a tissue, holding it under the nose and inhaling deeply for just a few minutes.

If, however, you suspect that the injured person is in severe shock, then do not try to treat them at home. Seek medical advice immediately. Such shock is caused by a sudden reduction in blood flow which, in extreme cases, can lead to collapse. The symptoms to look out for include fast, shallow intakes of breath, cold damp skin, a weak pulse, dizziness and even fainting.

TUMMY PROBLEMS

Stomach problems might sound slight and comical, but they certainly are not when you are the sufferer. They can be completely debilitating, easily ruin a night out, make a long journey impossible, or disrupt that highly crucial meeting at work. Knowing how to deal with them promptly, however, can quickly revolutionize your life. Take any of the measures described and explained below, and you will find that you never look back.

DIGESTIVE SETTLERS

Nervousness often shows itself in an upset stomach, or abdominal spasm. It has been said that our digestive organs also digest stress, and too often they end up storing emotions, causing all manner of discomfort and indigestion.

The key is to teach our bodies to let go of any such worries, and aromatherapy can help a great deal. One of the easiest ways to use oils in this context is to make a hot compress and then place it over the abdomen, keeping the area warm for about ten minutes. Begin by filling a bowl of hot water with either 2 drops Orange and 3 drops Peppermint, or 3 drops Chamomile and 2 drops Orange. Then soak a flannel in the hot water. Place the compress over the abdomen and relax.

TRAVEL CALMERS

They say that travel broadens the mind; unfortunately, for some people it does quite the opposite. It contracts the mind and condenses it into a compact series of dark, inescapable worries – will the car break down? Is this plane safe? Will I be sick? Will I come though this in one piece, and alive? Once you are on the conveyer belt of anxiety and possible problems, it simply does not stop.

If you are indeed such a poor traveller, try using one of the following essential oils to calm the mind and stomach. They will let you enjoy the delights of new horizons freely without being stressed by how to reach them. The simplest way to use essential oils is to put a couple of drops on to a tissue or handkerchief, and smell them frequently. Useful oils are Peppermint, Mandarin or Neroli.

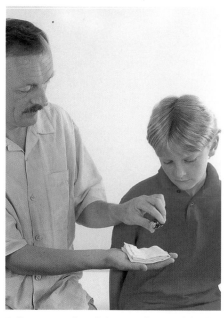

1 Put a couple of drops of essential oil on a tissue, and keep it freely available so that you can reach for it when you wish.

2 To use, hold the tissue under the nose and lean the head slightly forward. Inhale two or three times.

WOMEN'S HEALTH

While for many it used to be a case of grin and bear any problems, and suffer in silence, widespread help is fortunately now available. In extreme cases you should, of course, always consult your doctor, but for more minor conditions there are all kinds of different, soothing massages you can have. They should certainly reduce the impact of too much discomfort, and make sure that normal life is not too greatly disrupted.

PMT SOOTHERS

For many women the days leading up to a period can be fraught with mood swings, irritability and other symptoms. Sometimes they feel guilty that they are snapping, and this adds to the general sense of irritability. One feeds upon the other. While in particularly difficult cases professional help can be sought, in more low level cases there is much that you can do to help yourself.

Try this satisfying blend of oils using 3 drops Rose, 3 drops Jasmine and 2 drops Clary Sage to a bath. Then get in and lie back, allowing the tension to soak away. Alternatively use this mixture to make a massage oil, and rub it gently into the abdomen for a relaxing, soothing, long-lasting effect. In fact you may find this so comforting it becomes a habit.

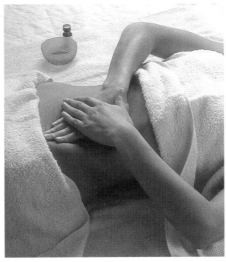

I Slowly and firmly massage the abdomen with your hands. Rub in increasing and then decreasing circles, so that you can actually feel the discomfort slowly diminish and then vanish.

2 You can try moving your hands first in a clockwise, then anti-clockwise direction. It may be more beneficial if your partner helps give the massage. This should help make him more understanding.

MENSTRUAL PAIN RELIEVERS

Painful periods can be due to a number of reasons, but tension will certainly add to muscle spasm and cramping pains. There is nothing more infuriating and frustrating than having a gnawing, cramping painful period just when you have reached a crucially important stage at work, or are planning a major day out.

If there is no organic or structural cause of the discomfort, try using essential oils as part of your routine. They can be applied in one of two key ways, either as a hot compress over the lower abdomen, or while having a deliciously long and soothing bath. Some oils actually have a reputation for improving the menstrual cycle in other ways; seek advice from a professional aromatherapist if you would like to find out more about such long-term treatments.

To make a compress, use 1 drop of Rose, Geranium and Clary Sage oils. Alternatively, a fairly hot bath with 3 drops Rose, 3 drops Geranium and 2 drops Clary Sage will relax cramped muscles.

◄ A long bath with a few drops of oil will help you to relax and soon soothe away any discomfort.

MOOD CHANGING RECIPES

It is all too easy to get dragged down by the ever-increasing, remorseless demands made on you. There never seems to be a moment when you can be quiet and alone, and recharge your batteries. Everything seems stacked against you. But just take a little time out with these oils and you can quickly change your mood, getting rid of the blues and giving yourself a wonderful, refreshing pick-me-up.

UPLIFTING OILS

There are unfortunately times in all our lives when we get depressed to some extent, whether due to a specific event or an accumulation of chronic tiredness. As part of a programme of recuperation and restoring your vitality, aromatherapy can certainly be very effective in lifting the mood and giving a boost to your overall energy levels.

For a strong, but relatively short-lived effect, try 4 drops Bergamot and 2 drops Neroli in the bath, ideally first thing in the morning when you are still feeling quite well and relaxed. Do not leave it until too late in the day when the effects of tiredness and stress have taken a strong hold. Aromatherapy stands a far better chance right now of working, and what is more, when it does work it will set you up for the day, giving you renewed confidence. Incidentally, after the bath, gently pat the skin with a soft towel. Do not rub yourself too vigorously.

A gentler effect, which should also pervade the atmosphere all day long, involves using Bergamot or Neroli oils in an essential oil burner. You will probably only need just one drop of each oil at a time, repeating the process as many times as you like.

REVITALIZING OILS

In today's high pressure world, "high pressure" is exactly what it is all about. We are all expected to pack two lifestyles into one. Mother and worker, father and possibly chief provider. Nobody gets the right amount of time to themselves to boost their energy levels, or become quietly absorbed in reading or listening to music, etc. The end result of trying to juggle too many demands is that nearly all of us reach a state of "brain fag", when mental fatigue and exhaustion grind us to a halt.

Rather than reach for the coffee, or worse still alcohol, which far from being a relaxant is actually well known for depressing the central nervous system, try using these revitalizing oils. They will give you an instant, revitalizing pick-me-up and make you feel wonderfully more alert.

You can use 1–2 drops of Rosemary or Peppermint oil in a burner. Alternatively, add 3 drops Rosemary and 2 drops Peppermint to a bowl of steaming water, or use 4 drops of either oils on their own. Give the oils plenty of time to evaporate into the room, and breathe freely. Make sure you then spend some time quietly relaxing, taking in the full benefits of these oils.

INVIGORATING OILS

Chronic tension all too often leads to a feeling of inescapable exhaustion, when we just totally run out of steam. At these demoralizing, difficult times we need a sudden boost, and many oils have a tremendous tonic effect, restoring vitality but without in any way over-stimulating. As a group, the citrus oils are excellent for this purpose, ranging from the more soothing Mandarin to the highly refreshing Lemon oil.

Have a warm, but not too hot bath, with 4 drops Mandarin and 2 drops Orange or 4 drops Neroli and 2 drops Lemon. Alternatively, just add a couple of drops of any of these oils to a bowl full of steaming water. Then sit down calmly, and gently begin inhaling. This will soon help you clear away the tiredness and lift your spirits again.

This kind of steam inhalation is a valuable and simple way to receive the benefits of essential oils when either time or circumstance prevents a massage or indeed a bath.

SENSUAL OILS

Tension, anxiety, worry, depression, and loss of confidence and self-belief – these are just some of the many factors that can adversely affect your sexual energy and performance. Sometimes this leads into a no-escape negative spiral of anxiety about sex, leading to less enjoyment, and so on.

The best answer is not to get dragged down, feeling ever more anxious and depressed, until the problem becomes seemingly insurmountable, but to take a little time out of your hectic life. Be together with your partner and have fun; add to your sensual pleasure with an intimate massage session, using one of these excellent blends to release tensions and allow your natural sexual energy to respond freely.

Use whichever of these blends – 5 drops Rose and 5 drops Sandalwood or 4 drops Jasmine and 4 drops Ylang Ylang – appeals to you both, and include in a massage oil. Use gentle, stroking movements all over the back, buttocks, legs and front.

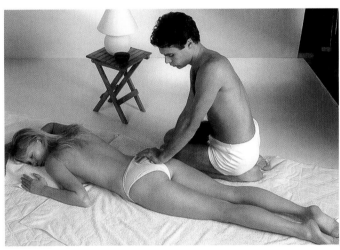

▲ *Massage gently all over the body with a light, caring touch. The secret is taking your time, getting the atmosphere right and making sure you choose the right moment.*

SLEEP ENHANCERS

Worries can go round and round inside our heads, usually just as we are trying to get to sleep. Worse, they strike in the middle of the night and get blown out of all proportion. The resulting disturbed and restless night leaves us more prone to stress and anxiety, and a vicious cycle can be created. Help break into this cycle with a pleasantly hot and relaxing evening bath. Many oils can be useful – just having a fragrance that you enjoy will help you to unwind after a long day.

Add oils to an evening bath to aid relaxation and sleep. A couple of blends that relax without over-sedating are 4 drops Rose and 3 drops Sandalwood or 5 drops Lavender and 3 drops Ylang Ylang. Incorporate aromatherapy preparations into your daily bathing routine.

THE OILS

The more you study and learn about oils, the better you will be at making up your own mixtures or recipes to tackle your own highly individual needs. It is not as difficult and demanding as you might think. Just take your time and quietly browse through the following descriptions, and you will quickly see how oils are capable of overcoming a wide range of problems. They will make a wonderful addition to your lifestyle.

THE KEY PLANTS

Essential oils may be extracted from exotic plants such as Sandalwood or Ylang Ylang, or from the more common plants such as Lavender and Chamomile, but each one has its own characteristics and properties. Try to get used to a few oils at first, understand their different effects, and enjoy their fragrance!

Essential oils are in fact concentrated substances; while the skin of citrus fruits such as Lemon or Orange may yield a fair amount of oil, flowers such as roses only contain tiny amounts of the precious essence – about 5,000 roses may be needed to obtain 5ml/1 tsp of what is called a pure essential oil. Such a concentration really emphasizes the importance of only using drop doses of the oils in a suitable dilution, because a little goes a long way.

Oils are extracted from many different plant parts. Each contains powerful healing properties, Nature provides an abundance of therapeutic compounds to help us regain our health.

SANDALWOOD
Santalum album

Probably the oldest perfume in history, known to have been used for over 4,000 years. Sandalwood has a heavy scent, and often appeals to men as much as to women. It has a relaxing, antidepressant effect on the nervous system, and where depression causes sexual inhibitions and problems, Sandalwood can be the answer – a genuine aphrodisiac.

CHAMOMILE
Matricaria recutita [German] or Chamaemelum nobile [Roman]

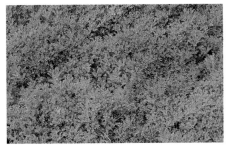

Roman and German Chamomile are both used to obtain essential oils with very similar properties. Chamomile is relaxing and antispasmodic, helping to relieve tension headaches, nervous digestive problems or insomnia, for instance.

BENZOIN
Styrax benzoin

This Asiatic tree produces a gum which is usually dissolved in a solvent to produce the "oil". It has a wonderful fragrance of vanilla, and is widely used in various kinds of inhalation mixtures. It is good at relaxing the airways, and it can be used whenever tension levels lead to an uncomfortable tight chest or cause restricted breathing.

GERANIUM
Pelargonium graveolens

The Rose-scented Geranium has very useful properties, not least being its ability to bring a blend together, to make a more harmonious scent. Geranium has a refreshing, antidepressant quality, good for nervous tension and exhaustion.

YLANG YLANG
Cananga odorata var. genuina

This tropical tree, native to Indonesia, produces an intensely sweet essential oil that has a sedative yet antidepressant action. It is very good for a range of symptoms such as excessive tension, insomnia, panic attacks, anxiety and depression. It also has a good reputation as an aphrodisiac, through its ability to reduce stress levels.

PEPPERMINT
Mentha piperita

This oil is another classic ingredient in inhalations for relieving catarrh, although commercial menthol (a major part of the oil) may be used with good results. Peppermint's many known analgesic and antispasmodic effects make it very useful for rubbing on the temples in order to ease any tension headaches; ideally dilute a drop in a little base cream or oil before you begin applying.

JASMINE
Jasminum officinale

One of the most wonderful aromas, Jasmine has a relaxing, euphoric effect, and can greatly lift the mood when there is debility, depression and listlessness. Use in the bath or in massage oils, or use Jasmine flower water for oily skin.

EUCALYPTUS
Eucalyptus globulus

One of the finest oils for respiratory complaints, found in most commercial inhalants. Well diluted (never use more than 1 per cent) in a base vegetable oil, it can be applied to the forehead to help relieve a hot, tense headache.

LAVENDER
Lavandula angustifolia

One of the most well-known scents, Lavender has been used for centuries to refresh and add fragrance to the home, and as a remedy for many stress-related ailments. It is especially useful for helping to relieve tension headaches, or for nervous digestive upsets; use in a massage oil or in the bath for a deeply relaxing and calming experience. The finest oil is produced from the true Lavender (Lavandula angustifolia), and is one of the most versatile of all oils. Its uses range from first-aid treatment of burns, to stress reduction.

ROSEMARY
Rosmarinus officinalis

With its highly penetrating, stimulating aroma, Rosemary has been used for many centuries to help relieve nervous exhaustion, various tension headaches and migraines. It is also known to improve the circulation to the brain, and is an excellent oil for overcoming mental fatigue and debility. **Caution** Do not use in pregnancy without seeking professional advice.

MARJORAM
Origanum marjorana

Marjoram has a calming and warming effect, and is good for both cold, tight muscles and for cold, tense people who might suffer from headaches, migraines and insomnia. Use in massage blends for rubbing into tired and aching muscles, or in the bath, especially in the evening to help obtain a good night's sleep. **Caution** Do not use in pregnancy without seeking professional advice.

PINE
Pinus sylvestris

There are a few species of Pine that produce oils, notably the American Longleaf Pine which is a commercial source of oil of turpentine. However, the Pine oil used in aromatherapy generally comes from the Scots Pine. It helps to clear the air passages when used as an inhalation, and is also good for relieving fatigue. Tired, aching muscles can be eased with massage using diluted Pine oil.

CLARY SAGE
Salvia sclarea

This oil gives a definite euphoric uplift to the brain; do not use too much, however, as you can be left feeling very spacey! Like Ylang Ylang and Jasmine, its antidepressant and relaxing qualities have contributed to its reputation as an aphrodisiac. **Caution** Do not use in pregnancy without seeking professional advice.

ROSE
Rosa x damascena, centifolia

Rose is probably the most famous of all oils. There is probably more symbolism attached to roses than any other flower. Several kinds have been used to extract the oil, notably the Damask Rose and the Cabbage Rose. Each one is slightly different, but the overall actions are sedating, calming and anti-inflammatory. Not surprisingly, Rose oil has a wide reputation as an aphrodisiac, and where anxiety is a factor, it may be very beneficial. Use in the bath for a sensual, unwinding experience, or add to a base massage oil to soothe muscular and nervous tension.

BERGAMOT
Citrus bergamia

The peel of the ripe fruit yields an oil that is mild and gentle. It is the most effective antidepressant oil of all, best used at the start of the day. Its leaves give the distinctive aroma and flavour to Earl Grey tea. The oil can be used on a burner for generally lifting the atmosphere. Do not use on the skin in bright sunlight, as it increases photosensitivity.

LEMON
Citrus limon

Possibly the most cleansing and antiseptic of the citrus oils, useful for boosting the immune system and in skin care. It is also very good at helping to refresh and clarify the thinking process.

GRAPEFRUIT
Citrus x paradisi

Oil of Grapefruit is very helpful in the digestion of fatty foods and helps to combat cellulite and congested pores. It has an uplifting effect and will soothe headaches and nervous exhaustion.

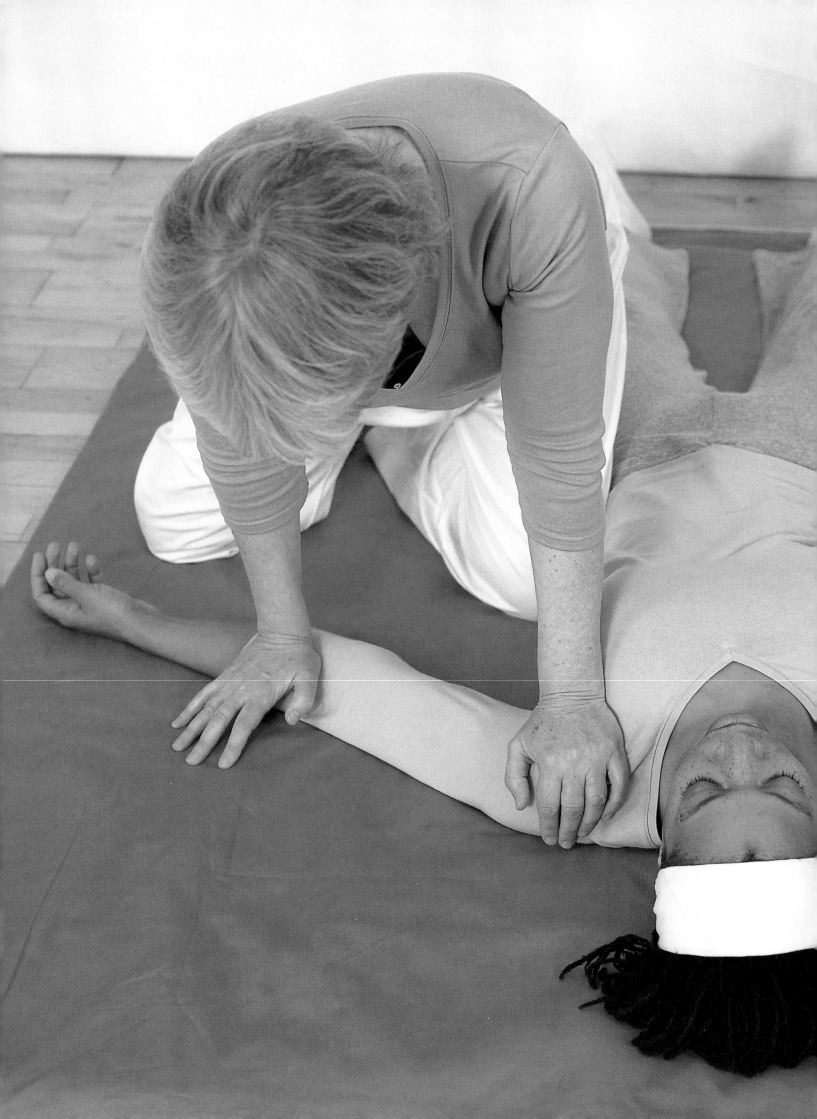

SHIATSU

—

Based on the Eastern concept of energy flow, Shiatsu is a traditional Japanese touch therapy that can be used to relax and balance the body. It is an effective treatment for many common ailments, particularly back pain, headaches and other symptoms of stress, as well as helping to restore mobility in the joints due to inactivity or injury. Freeing blocked energy is the essence of shiatsu, and a session often results in a sense of increased well-being and vitality as the vital self-healing process is triggered. It is easy to learn the basic principles of the technique, which is enjoyable both to give and to receive. The following pages include a self-massage routine as well as sequences to follow with a partner.

MERIDIAN HEALTH

It is always very exciting to hear and learn about radically different interpretations of how the body and mind work. While you may not agree with every last precise detail, they do, as in the case of shiatsu, provide a large number of marvellous insights into how we can manage and regulate our lives. One really beneficial result is knowing how to eliminate stress, enabling you to stay young, vibrant and healthy.

COPING WITH STRESS

Stress upsets both your mental and physical well-being, and every one of us has felt its grasp at one time or another. Stress is well known to all shiatsu practitioners and is recognized as one of the major factors affecting health in our modern society. It is a normal part of life; in fact, a certain level of stress is actually considered quite good for us. Some people seem to be able to thrive on it, yet for others the same degree of pressure can quite simply be too much.

The increasing, cumulative impact of events sometimes means that, eventually, we can not cope. The pressure becomes overpowering and we begin to react to the stress in different ways. These reactions will affect our health and well-being and may interfere with our jobs and social lives in a significant, negative way. The body reacts to a stressor with first a diminished, then an increased, level of resistance. This is usually

▲ *A well-balanced diet, with plenty of daily fruit and vegetables, is essential for excellent health.*

called the "fight or flight" reaction, which means that the body is instinctively ready to stand and confront, or escape. But stress, with all its different symptoms, is a sure sign that we have lost the wonderful sense of balance in our lives. Human beings have a marvellous natural system for maintaining balance, and the body is always striving to achieve this state of inner harmony. It is this balancing adaptive energy that is tested by stress, and which is constantly under challenge.

Coping with stress can be made easier by asking for help and support from family and friends. Talking to someone helps you to see a problem more clearly. It puts it into a sharper, wider perspective. Far better than just talking, however, having someone give you a long and gentle shiatsu treatment will relax your body and mind, and bring back a marvellous sense of general well-being. It is the ultimate experience when it comes to winding down.

A BALANCED LIFESTYLE

You can improve your general health and well-being, and your battery of defences, by understanding exactly what causes you stress, and by learning how to avoid it or even how to adapt to it. There are basically two key aspects to stress reduction: lifestyle modification and relaxation.

Lifestyle modification could mean changing your job and reassessing your goals in life, or simply adapting a more open attitude to what you are doing. Having a sense of control over events lessens their stressful impact. There is no point in trying to over-reach yourself. Ambition is good, but not when it leaves you constantly floundering with a marked sense of failure and desperation. Give yourself a chance.

Daily relaxation represents the most important element of maintaining health and vitality. Deep relaxation is not the same as sleep, and to gain full benefit from it, it is important not to fall asleep while you are relaxing. Giving or receiving a shiatsu treatment will relax your whole body and mind, and you will feel totally refreshed and energized afterwards.

The back-up treatment involves eating a well-balanced diet rich in fibres, grains and fresh vegetables. Cut down on sugar and

salt as well as coffee, tea and carbonated soft drinks. Water and quality fruit juice are so much better for you. A certain amount of physical exercise is also necessary if you want to maintain your health and vitality. A pleasant, brisk 20-minute walk in the fresh air every day will stimulate and balance the energy within. Never attempt any kind of exercise that is too difficult or demanding.

FIGHT OR FLIGHT RESPONSE

• The brain registers danger and sends messages along the nerves to different muscles and organs to react accordingly (nervous/muscular system).
• The heart beats faster, pumping out blood to muscles and areas in need and you start to sweat (circulatory system).
• The breathing rhythm changes; you start to breathe faster due to more air being drawn in through the bronchial tubes as they expand (respiratory system).
• The digestion slows down (digestive system).
• Increased production of certain hormones, such as adrenaline and noradrenaline (hormonal system).

ORGANS - MERIDIANS

The balanced functioning of our body is controlled by 12 vital internal organs. In Oriental medicine the organs have a wider meaning than in the West, based on their physiological and energetic function. Each has a different quality of energetic movement and responsibility and is linked to a meridian, or energy channel, named according to the internal organ it affects. The meridians run in pairs either side of the body, and they ensure the successful nurturing of energy, known as Chi.

TSUBO — PRESSURE POINTS

Along each meridian are a varying number of tsubo, or pressure points. They are points along the meridian where the energy is thought to be flowing near the surface of the body and therefore more accessible for treatment. There are more than 700 tsubo in your body, and they are numbered in sequence according to which meridian they are on. The first point on the kidney meridian, for example, will be Kidney 1 (KID 1). The points reflect the internal functioning of the body.

Lungs (LU):
- Take in air and vital Chi during respiration to refine and distribute it around the body. A fundamental process for building up resistance against external intrusions.
- Elimination of gases through exhalation.
- Openness, emotional stability, enthusiasm and a fulsome positive approach.

Large Intestine (LI):
- Helps the function of the lungs. Processes food substances and eliminates what is unnecessary.
- The ability to "let go". Elimination.

Spleen (SP):
- Corresponds to the function of the pancreas in Western terms and governs all organs secreting digestive enzymes. It also relates to reproductive glands in women and is a controlling factor in the immune system.
- Maintains the health of the flesh, the connective soft tissue and the muscle tissue.
- Self-image is strongly affected by the spleen function, as is the desire to help others. Self-confidence.

Stomach (ST):
- It is responsible for "receiving and ripening" ingested food and all fluids.
- Information for mental and physical nourishment.
- Groundedness, centredness, self-confidence and reliability.

Heart (HT):
- It governs blood and blood vessels as well as the circulatory system.
- Houses the mind and our emotions.
- Joy, calmness and communication.

Small Intestine (SI):
- The quality of the blood and tissue reflects the condition of the small intestine, and anxiety, emotional excitement or nervous shock can adversely affect the small intestine energy.
- Emotional stability and calmness.

Kidneys (KID):
- The kidneys include the function of the adrenals, controlling the whole of the hormonal system.
- Provides and stores essential Chi for all other organs and governs birth, growth, reproduction and development; the reproductive system.
- Nourishes the spine, bones and the brain; the nervous system.
- Vitality, direction, courage and will power.

Bladder (BL):
- Purification and regulation.
- Nourishes the spine.
- Courage and the ability to move forward confidently in life.

Heart Governor (HG):
- Protector of the heart and closely related to emotional responses.
- Related to central circulation.
- Relationships with others; protection of others.

Triple Heater (TH):
- Transports energy, blood and heat to the peripheral parts of the body; circulatory system.
- Helpfulness and emotional interaction.

Liver (LIV):
- Stores blood and nutrients which are subsequently distributed throughout the body. Ensures free flow of Chi throughout the body.
- Governs the muscular and digestive systems.
- Creativity and ideas; good planning and organization.

Gall Bladder (GB):
- Stores bile produced by the liver and distributes it in the small intestine; digestive system.
- Practical application of ideas and decision-making.

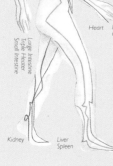

treatments
treatments

treatments

Giving and receiving shiatsu is both extremely enjoyable and relaxing, and a wonderful way of spending time with another person. Before you begin, however, you must consider a few key points. First, consider your own health and condition. How are you feeling? Never try to give a shiatsu treatment if you are feeling in any way tired or depressed, or even intoxicated, have a contagious disease, or for any reason do not feel quite up to the task in hand. You must be fully alert, and able to concentrate. Your partner will quickly pick up the fact that your heart is not in it.

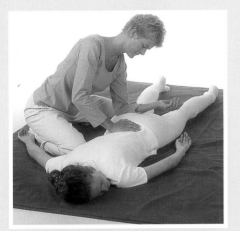

Before giving treatment you must also check that the environment is clean, warm and totally comforting. In fact it is well worth spending quite a bit of time getting this side of the treatment right. You do not want the excellent effects of shiatsu being undermined by the likes of a small, hot, airless room with the radio playing pop music. What you do want is calm, relaxing music, perhaps even a tape of bird song or early morning church bells, and soft muted lighting instead of a fierce glare. As for clothes, wear a loose fitting, airy, comfortable garment, possibly one made of cotton, and avoid eating any heavy meals for two hours before giving the treatment. Such detailed consideration is essential for a good session.

The next crucial step involves taking just a few moments to prepare yourself and your partner. Sitting in the Seiza position (that is, on your knees), to your partner's right-hand side, place your hand on the sacrum, as shown. Sit quietly, gradually begin to regulate your breathing, empty your mind until you feel totally quiet and at one with your partner, and focus on how they feel right now. Shiatsu practitioners always have excellent empathy.

The final point to note is that when giving treatment, sometimes your touch needs to be very light, and at other times it should be firm for deep tissue work. Try using your hands as an extension of your heart, and remember to be sensitive to your partner's needs at all times.

DOLN EXERCISES

The term "Doln" literally means self-massage, and involves a combination of different techniques to improve the circulation and flow of Chi throughout the whole body. The following exercises can be used not only to revitalize your tired muscles and low spirits, but also to relieve a stiff, tense body and a stressed mind. Starting your day with a Doln session will quickly awaken your body and mind. You will soon notice the benefits.

THE PREPARATION

Prepare yourself by gently shaking all your limbs, and body. Shake your arms and hands to help release any tension in your upper body. Now gently shake your legs and feet as well. Place your feet shoulder-width apart and unlock your knees. Straighten your back to allow a better energy flow, relax your shoulders and then close your eyes. Take a minute to focus internally, and get in touch with how you and your body are feeling before starting the Doln routine.

Note that when doing this exercise it is vitally important that you become aware of any areas that might be in any discomfort, and that you try completely to empty your mind of any disturbing or distracting thoughts. It takes time to learn how to do the latter, and you will eventually succeed. What counts in the end is that you do not let tension ruin the effects of the Doln.

THE BEST WAY TO COMPLETE

After having worked through your whole body as described in the following pages, stand up and gently shake out again. Now place your feet shoulder-width apart and bend your knees slightly. Imagine a string passing through your spine, from the tail bone to the top of your head. Stretch the string and feel your spine straighten up to allow for better Chi flow. Close your eyes for a moment and see how you feel after your Doln session. Try to remember how you felt at the beginning and compare that with the sensation you have now. Open your eyes again and to complete your session, practise breathing deeply.

You can do this Doln exercise as often as time permits. Ideally it should become a part of your daily routine, being practised early in the morning and again perhaps later in the evening. You will quickly notice and appreciate the benefits.

NECK

1 Using one hand, place the palm across the back of your neck and firmly massage in a squeezing motion. This will increase the flow of blood and Chi to the area, release stagnation, and remove waste products such as lactic acid.

2 With your thumbs, gently apply pressure to the point at the base of the skull, directing the pressure upwards against the skull.

3 Use your fingers and rub across the muscle fibres at the base of the skull. This technique will release the muscles and tendons in the area, and also help to relieve headaches and any level of pain in the shoulder.

HEAD AND FACE

1 Open your eyes and make a loose fist with both hands. Keep your wrists relaxed and tap the top of your head.

2 Slowly work your way all around the head, covering the sides, front and back. This exercise will wake up your brain and stimulate blood circulation.

3 Pull your fingers through your hair, stimulating the bladder and gall bladder meridians on the top and side.

4 Place your fingers on your forehead, and apply a little pressure and stroke out from the centre to the temples.

5 Bring your fingers up to your temples. Drop your elbows, and massage your temples, using circular movements.

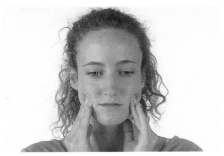

6 Massage down the sides of your face until you reach your jaw.

7 Squeeze along the jawbone, working outwards from the centre. This is a very good technique for trying to relax.

8 Using your index finger and thumb, squeeze your eyebrows starting from the centre line and move slowly and laterally.

9 Bring your thumbs to the inside of the eyebrows (point BL2). Allow the weight of your head to rest on your thumbs.

10 With your index finger and thumb, pinch the bridge of your nose and the corners of your eyes.

11 Apply your thumbs to the sides of your nose. Breathe in as you stroke down the side of your nose.

KEY TIPS

The above routine is particularly good if you feel a cold coming on, or have one already. Although Doln exercises are specifically designed for self-help, they can just as easily be carried out by another person, particularly if you are feeling too lethargic to do it yourself. The above routine will ease discomfort and speed recovery.

SHOULDERS, ARMS AND HANDS

1 Lift up your shoulders up and breathe in. Breathe out, letting your shoulders drop and relax. Repeat.

2 Support your left elbow and with a loose fist you can begin tapping across your shoulder.

3 Press your middle finger into the shoulder's highest point, known as point GBL21, the "Shoulder Well". **Caution** Sometimes used in childbirth to speed up labour; do not use during pregnancy.

4 Straighten your arm, open your palm and tap down the inside of your arm from the shoulder to the open hand. Good for the heart meridians.

5 Turn your arm over and tap up the back of your arm, from the hand to the shoulders. This technique stimulates the meridians for the intestines. Repeat three times.

6 Use your left thumb to work through your right hand, gently massaging the centre of your palm to relieve general tension and revitalize you spiritually.

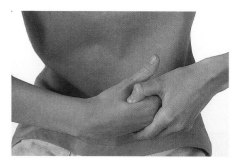

7 Stimulate the "Great Eliminator" on the large intestine meridian, in the web between the index finger and the thumb. **Caution** Sometimes used in childbirth to speed up labour; do not use during pregnancy.

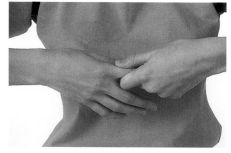

8 Carefully squeeze and massage the joints of each finger using your index finger and thumb. Repeat as often as you find it necessary.

9 Pulling out the fingers will stimulate the starting and end points of all the meridians. This is a great way to release any stress and tension in your hands.

CHEST, ABDOMEN AND LOWER BACK

1 Open up your chest, and using either a loose fist or flat hands for comfort, tap across your chest, above and around the breasts. This will stimulate your lungs and strengthen your respiratory system.

2 Take a deep breath in as you open your chest again; then on the out breath tap your chest and make a deep resounding "Ahhh…" sound.

3 Proceed down towards your abdomen, and with open hands tap round your abdomen, clockwise, for about a minute.

4 Place one hand on top of the other, and then make exactly the same circular motion around your abdomen for about another minute.

5 Place your hands on your back, just below your ribcage. Start to rub the area until you feel some warmth. This will stimulate your kidney energy.

6 Place one hand on your knee. Using the back of your other hand, tap across your sacrum bone at the base of the spine. It activates the nervous system.

LEGS AND FEET

1 Tap down the backs of your legs from your buttocks to your heels, following the flow of energy. Tap up the inside of your legs, stimulating your liver.

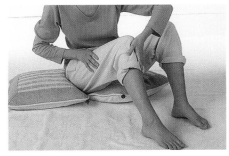

2 Sit down on the floor, and measure four finger widths down from the knee-cap on the outside of your leg. Place your thumb on the point ST36 and press. Good for tired legs.

3 On the dorsal part of your foot, between the big toe and the second toe is LIV3, "Big Rush". Good against cramp. **Caution** Do not use this particular point during pregnancy.

SYSTEM CALMERS WITH A PARTNER

If you notice that your partner looks listless, is feeling at all tired and stressed, is experiencing any tension in the upper body, or suffers from shallow, rapid breathing, the following treatment will be very beneficial. It will aid relaxation and promote much deeper breathing, facilitating a more efficient energy distribution to all parts of the body. The treatment is quickly and easily given.

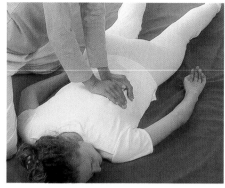

1 To prepare for treatment, kneel by your partner's side and place your hand at the base of the spine. Concentrate on how your partner feels. Then place your palms on either side of your partner's spine. Crouch down if it feels easier.

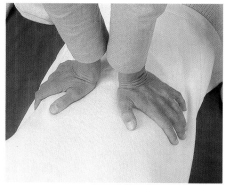

2 Ask your partner to breathe in; on the out-breath lean into your hands and apply pressure to your partner's back. Ease the pressure to allow your partner to breathe in again. Move your hands down and press on the next exhalation.

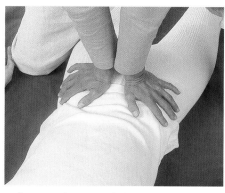

3 Start at the top of the back between the shoulder blades. Work your way down towards the sacrum. Repeat three times. Always keep your elbows straight, and use your body weight as you work.

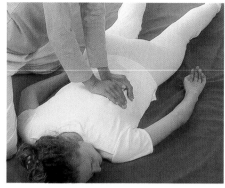

4 Kneel at 90 degrees to your partner, place your palms in the valley (on the opposite side of the spine) formed by the spinous processes (spinal bumps) and the broad muscles running on either side of the spine. Rock the body with the heels of your hands. As you rock, you can move your hands down the back, one following the other. The rocking should be continuous and rhythmic. Repeat three times. Do both sides, working from the opposite side of the body.

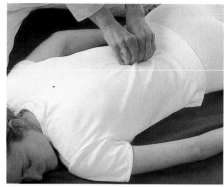

5 This technique allows you to focus specifically upon the spinal column. You still need to rock; however, this time the spinous processes are gripped between the fingers and the thumbs. Applying a positive (firm) contact, gradually work the hands along the full length of the spine, moving it from side to side. This action is good for loosening the muscles and stimulating the nervous system.

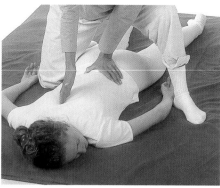

6 Place your left hand on your partner's sacrum. Using the edge of your right hand like a knife, perform a sawing action down either side of the spine. Work both sides alternately, repeating the sequence three times.

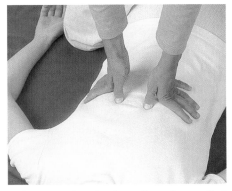

7 Run your hands along the spine to feel the undulations of the spinous processes. Bring your thumbs sideways, two fingers' breadth from the dip between the two spinous processes. Apply perpendicular pressure.

8 Put one hand on top of the other and place your hands on your partner's sacrum. Apply pressure to the sacrum, focusing all your energy into the base of the spine.

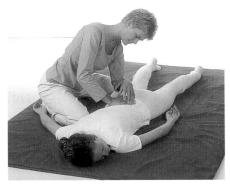

9 Turn around to face your partner, spread your knees and, using the fleshy part of your forearm in a penetrating and rolling action, apply pressure across the buttocks. Stay on the same side to work both buttocks.

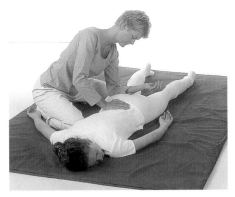

10 Note the position of the "mother hand", and keep the hands relaxed as you roll your forearm right across the surface of the buttocks.

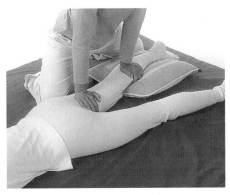

11 Adjust your position so that you can move down the leg. One hand remains on the sacrum or is placed on the back of the thigh. Starting from the back of the thigh, gradually work down the leg, applying pressure with your thumb. Support your partner's lower leg with a cushion beneath the shin.

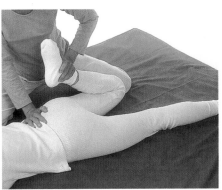

12 Take hold of your partner's ankle and bend the leg towards the buttock. Adjust your position to allow you to use your body weight to achieve the stretch. Now move yourself all the way down to the feet. With both hands, take a firm hold of the ankle, lean back and stretch out the leg to its full length.

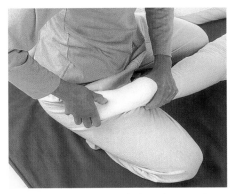

13 Place your partner's foot in your lap and using your thumb apply pressure to Kid 1, "Gushing Spring", one-third of the distance from the base of the second toe to the base of the heel.

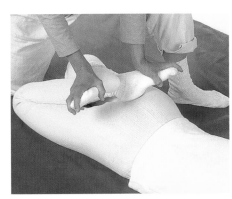

14 Cross your partner's ankles and bring them slowly towards the buttocks. Do this stretch twice, the first time placing the more flexible leg in front (nearest to the buttocks), then reverse the position.

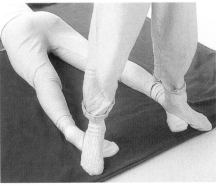

15 Stand up and walk on the soles of your partner's feet using your heels. Have the feet turned inwards and apply pressure to the soles but with no weight at all on the toes.

NERVOUS SYSTEM CALMERS: SELF-HELP

Stress can have quite a significant and dramatic effect on the nervous system, and badly affect a wide range of functions, including breathing. One excellent way to get you back on track is to balance the energy in the bladder channel through the following exercises and the shiatsu treatment of the back. Both techniques are tailor-made to calm your nervous system.

1 Stand with your feet shoulder-width apart and knees bent. Keep your back straight. Let your arms hang loose at your sides. Swing them from side to side.

2 Swinging your arms will create a twist in your spine, gradually loosening up the joints between the lumbar vertebrae and allowing for better flexible movement.

3 Bring your arms a bit higher up so that you now feel the twist in the middle part of your back. This will loosen up the thoracic vertebrae and the diaphragm.

4 With your feet wider than shoulder-width apart place your hands on your legs, above your knees, and straighten your back. Sway back and look up.

5 Bend your arms and slowly bring your upper body down towards the floor. Keep looking at the ceiling until you no longer see it. Relax the head downwards.

6 Pull your abdominal muscles in and slowly roll up your spine allowing the head to come up last. Lift your head and straighten your spine. Return to the sway back and repeat the whole movement about ten times.

7 Stay in the same position as for the last step of the previous sequence.

8 Breathe in and, on the exhalation, drop the left shoulder down as shown. Keep your elbows gently locked and look up to the ceiling over your right shoulder. Feel the twist in your spine.

9 Take another deep breath in, return to the starting position and drop your right shoulder down as you exhale. Repeat another three or four times on each side. Finish by coming back to the starting position. Relax your upper body forward. Move your feet closer together and slowly roll up your spine, until you come to a relaxed standing position.

10 To treat your back further in case of pain and tension, or whenever you feel in need of general relaxation, try using tennis balls as extra help. Put two tennis balls into a sock and knot the top. Lower yourself on to the tennis balls, which should be placed on either side of the spine. This is where your bladder meridian is located. Start from the area between your shoulders, or anywhere where you feel any pain and discomfort.

11 Breathe deeply and allow your back to sink on to the balls. The balls will mould themselves to the contours of your back and stimulate your bladder energy. Keep the balls in one place until you feel the muscles relax and then slowly roll the balls to the next area "in need". Work this area in the same way, using your breath to enhance the relaxation. Give yourself 10–15 minutes, working down the whole spine. Afterwards your spine will feel open and relaxed against the floor. You will have a sensation of warmth down your back.

12 When you have finished these spinal exercises it is good to lie down on the floor and relax with your lower legs resting on a chair. This relaxes the lumbar area of your back and realigns the whole spine. Close your eyes, allow your breathing to slow down and feel the energy moving from the top of your spine down to the sacrum like a wave. Stay in this position for 10–15 minutes.

This relaxation exercise works directly on the nervous system, calming it down, and you can use the exercise at any time when you feel stressed.

BREATHING ENHANCERS WITH PARTNER

Correct breathing is the first, fundamental technique that keeps us going. Surprisingly, when things get stressful we do not always breathe as we should. Deep, relaxing inhaling is replaced by short shallow gasps for air, and the whole body quickly suffers. The following techniques are aimed at the upper part of the body, helping you feel calm, relaxed and well in control again.

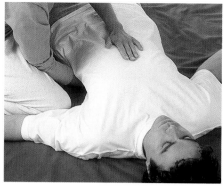

1 Place one hand underneath your partner's back in the area opposite the solar plexus and the other hand on top covering the area just below the sternum (breastbone). Focus into the area between your hands and encourage your partner to do the same. Feel the Chi from the breath of your partner reach this space, slowly allowing it to open and expand. You will gradually feel the tension go and the muscles relax to allow a deeper and more relaxed breathing.

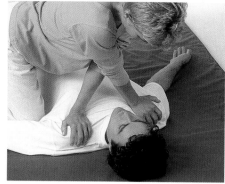

2 Cross your arms over and place the palms of your hands on your partner's shoulders. Ask your partner to breathe in and on the out-breath bring your body weight over your hands, stimulating the first point of the lung meridian and gently opening the chest. Repeat this three times.

3 Keep your left hand on the shoulder and take a firm hold of your partner's hand with your right hand. Lift the arm from the floor, shake it out, and then finally allow it to relax again.

4 Firmly hold on to the thumb and give the arm and the lung meridian a good revitalizing stretch. You can repeat this technique several times.

5 Place your partner's arm at a 45-degree angle to the body. Use one of your hands to support the shoulder while the other hand palms along the arm to the hand. Stay on the thumb side of the arm to activate the energy in the lung meridian.

6 Continue all the way down to the thumb (end point of the lung channel). Avoid applying any direct heavy pressure over the elbow joint.

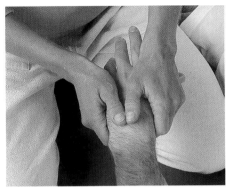

7 Using your thumbs, massage the whole of the dorsal side of your partner's hand.

8 Loosen up the wrist joint by slowly rotating the hand.

9 Open up the palm of the hand and gently massage. Apply pressure to the point in the centre of the palm, called "Palace of Anxiety". A very good point for calming and releasing tension.

10 Find point LI4 which is located in the web between the index finger and thumb. Stimulating this point with gentle pressure from your thumb will relieve headaches and help clear any mucous congestion taking place in the lungs.

11 Hold your partner's arm by the wrist and support the shoulder with your other hand. Step forward and rotate the arm into an overhead stretch. Before you step forward, you need to apply pressure to the supporting hand at the shoulder. Maintaining this pressure ensures a strong stretch. Step back, allowing the arm to return to the starting position.

12 Place both hands on top of your knees and stretch the arms by leaning backwards. Let go of the arm you have treated and move over to the other side. Repeat the whole sequence working on the other arm.

13 Stand behind your partner. Take hold of the hands, gripping around the thumbs, and as you both exhale, lift up from your knees and lean backwards until your partner feels the stretch.

14 Kneel down behind your partner and ask them to clasp the hands behind the neck. Bring your arms in front of your partner's arms, and on the out-breath gently open up the elbows to the sides.

15 Bring one knee up to support your partner's lower back. Take hold of the lower arms, and on the out-breath bring the elbows towards each other behind your partner's back.

SELF-HELP BREATHING ENHANCERS

The lung energy controls our intake of fresh air and Chi from the external environment. However, when your stress levels are high for a period the bronchial tubes expand to let in more air and the end result is that we tend to "over-breathe", or hyperventilate. By working on the lung meridian and practising these breathing exercises, you will facilitate deeper, more satisfying breathing.

1 Link your index finger and thumb on both hands. Step forward with your right foot and reach to the ceiling. Step back, relax the arms and repeat with your left foot. Repeat 3 or 4 times on each side.

2 Stand with your feet apart. Lift your arms to the sides with elbows bent, and make loose fists. Take a deep breath in, opening your chest by bringing your arms back as far as is possible.

3 On the exhalation, cross your arms over in front of you and relax your head down. Keep your knees bent, press back the area in between your shoulder blades. Repeat four or five times.

4 Stand with your feet shoulder-width apart and knees bent, and spread your feet slightly apart so that your toes point out. Hook your thumbs together behind your back, and inhale as you look up.

5 On the exhalation, bend forward and stretch your arms over your head. Breath in and feel the stretch along the back of your legs, back and arms, Slowly exhale. Stay down and repeat twice more.

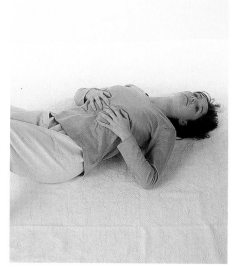

6 Lie down with a rolled-up towel along your spine, allowing the head to drop back on to the floor or a pillow. Place your fingers along your ribs, gently pressing as you breathe out.

IMMUNE SYSTEM REVIVERS

The immune system includes your spleen, thymus gland and lymph nodes. It is responsible for moving proteins and fats around the body, and is also responsible for filtering body fluids, producing white blood cells and immunity. However, periods of stress will weaken your immune system and leave you prone to infections. These simple shiatsu techniques will help awaken your immune and lymphatic systems.

1 Ask your partner to lie down on the back with legs straight. Place your palms over the soles of your partner's feet. Intermittently rock the feet towards the head in a rhythmic motion of about two movements per second for 3-4 minutes.

2 Bend your partner's leg and move yourself up to the side. Hold the leg just below the knee. Slowly rotate the hip joint, moving from the centre of yourself. Keep a fixed distance between your chest and your partner's knee.

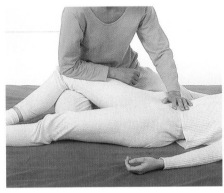

3 Place your partner's foot against the opposite inside ankle so that the leg is bent, exposing the inside leg. Ask your partner to inhale and gently use your forearm to stretch open the spleen meridian on the out-breath.

4 Support the lower leg with a cushion and, starting from the inside of your partner's big toe, use your thumb to apply perpendicular pressure along the medial part of the foot.

5 At the top of the shin bone on the medial side of the leg is SP9, another powerful point on the spleen meridian. Press this point to treat abdominal and menstrual pain, or local pain in the knee.

6 Rotate the leg you have worked on and then bend the other leg as well. Come to a standing position, bring your feet close to your partner's hips for support and gently bring the knees to the chest. Ease up on the stretch and rotate both legs. Move over to the other side, stretch out the treated leg and repeat the sequence for the other leg.

WORKING ON THE DIGESTIVE SYSTEM

The stomach and spleen energy channels are associated with the highly important functions of ingestion and digestion of food. In traditional Chinese medicine, the stomach corresponds to the entire digestive tract, from the mouth to the small intestine, and it creates Chi energy. The following exercises are aimed at fine-tuning and improving the health of your digestive system.

1 Sit in the Seiza position at your partner's side. Take a few moments of stillness to "tune in" and observe. Be aware of any tension and note the breathing rate: fast and shallow indicates tension; slow and deep shows relaxation.

Trace the borderlines of your partner's *Hara* (vital body centre). Start at the ribcage just below the breastbone and move slowly out to the pelvis.

2 Using two hands, one on top of the other, apply finger-pad pressure in a clockwise movement around the Hara, as shown. Where you find tension, apply gradually deeper pressure to dissolve it.

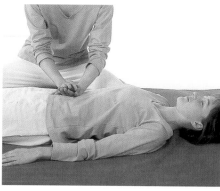

3 With one hand on top of the other, make a rocking and pushing type motion like rolling dough, from one side to the other, and pull back using the heel of the hand. Repeat for relaxation.

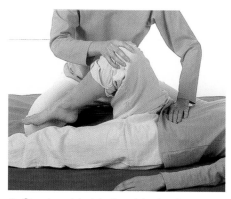

4 One hand holds the right leg just below the knee. Move from your centre, using your whole body, not just your arm muscles, to rotate your partner's leg. Keep a fixed distance between your chest and your partner's knee to ensure a balanced rotation of the hip.

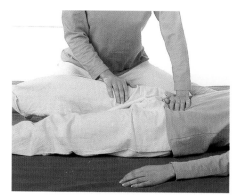

5 Stretch your partner's leg out, and place your knee underneath your partner's knee for support or use a pillow. Apply palm pressure along the outside frontal edge of the leg following the stomach meridian. Start from the top of the thigh and work to the foot. Repeat three or four times.

6 Stimulate ST36, "Leg Three Miles", using thumb pressure. The point is located four fingers' width below the knee-cap on the outside of the shin-bone. The name refers to this point's remarkable effect. It has been used since ancient times to build up endurance.

CIRCULATORY SYSTEM ENHANCERS

The heart organ, the heart and heart governor channels are the central focuses for regulating circulation, according to traditional Chinese medicine. However, heart energy can be surprisingly weakened in several circumstances. One excellent way of tackling the problem is by using wonderfully specialized shiatsu techniques. Dual functional, they will help calm the mind and cure such problems.

1 To expose the energy channel, place your partner's arm with the hand above the head, palm facing upwards. Support your partner's elbow with a cushion, and kneel in an open Seiza position. To improve the blood circulation to the skin generally and to the peripheries in particular, give yourself a daily body scrub. Use a dry loofah, skin brush, rough face cloth or even a towel.

2 To balance the energy in the heart meridian, sit on the floor, bend your knees and bring the soles of your feet together in front of you. Hold on to your ankles and straighten your spine. Inhale and lean forwards, keeping your back as straight as possible. Breathe out as you bring your head towards your feet and your elbows in front of your legs. Open up the axilla (armpit) and relax.

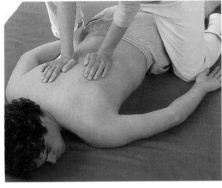

3 Use both palms in a technique known as palm rubbing to apply pressure quite firmly and rub down either side of the spine.

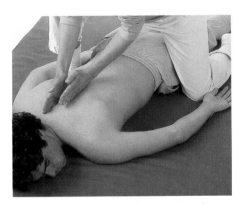

4 To rub, use the little finger side of your hands and vigorously rub down either side of the spine a few times until the area begins to redden.

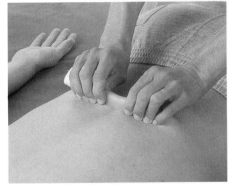

5 Rolling the skin involves pinching and taking hold of the skin on the lower part of the spine (lumbar area). Lift the tissue and gradually "roll" it up the spine. Repeat three or four times. Then roll the skin from the spine, the centre line, out towards the sides to the back.

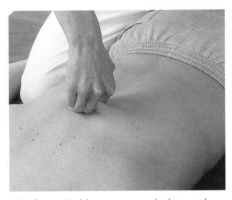

6 When pinching, use your index and middle fingers to pinch and take hold of the tissue. Twist and lift the skin at the same time. Work within your partner's pain threshold. Cover the whole back using this technique. You will see the area redden as the circulation improves.

TENSION RELIEVERS

Surprising though it may sound, when you are under stress your centre of gravity tends to lurch and shift from the abdominal area up to the chest, causing tension levels in the neck, shoulders and face. It often also results in a feeling of great heaviness on your shoulders. Imagine how wonderful it would be to have someone who could touch these tender areas sympathetically, providing instant, soothing, long-lasting relief.

1 Sit down in the Seiza position at your partner's head. Place your hands on the shoulders and tune in. Be aware of the breathing and state of relaxation before you start. Ask your partner to breathe in, and on the exhalation apply a bit of pressure to the shoulders by leaning into your arms. Repeat a few times. This encourages relaxation.

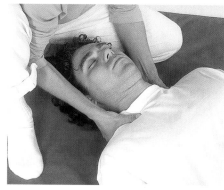

2 With your fingers underneath and thumbs on top, gently and firmly massage the shoulders using a kneading action. Feel the tension in the muscles relaxing and the tissue gradually softening up.

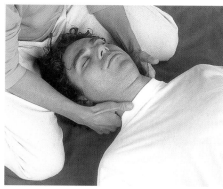

3 Move your hands to the neck. With your thumbs on the side and fingers underneath, stretch out the neck by gently pulling away. Repeat a few times until you feel the neck muscles relax.

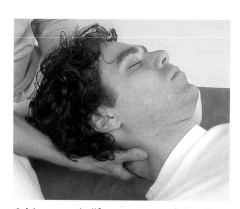

4 Now, gently lift your partner's head off the floor and firmly squeeze the muscles of the neck. Do be careful not to squeeze too hard, causing possible discomfort.

5 Turn the head to one side and support it with one hand. Use the finger pads of your other hand to "rub" across the muscle fibres. Treat the other side of the head in the same way.

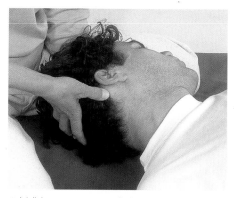

6 With your partner's head turned to the side, press the points along the base of the skull. Start at the ear and work towards the spine. Turn the head and treat the other side in the same way.

7 Rub the scalp using your fingertips, and then run your fingers firmly through the hair. Repeat several times.

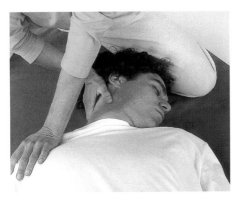

8 Turn your partner's head to one side and support it by placing one hand under the skull. Tell your partner to breathe deeply.

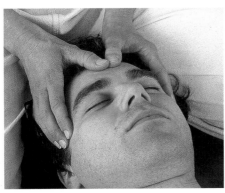

9 Start treating the face by placing your thumbs gently on the midline of your partner's forehead, with your fingertips to the side.

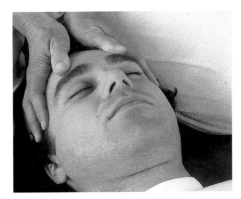

10 Apply a bit of pressure and stroke your thumbs out towards the temples. Repeat three or four times. This will ease tension in the head.

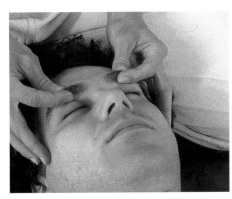

11 Use your index finger and thumb to squeeze your partner's eyebrows. Work from the centre out to the sides. Repeat a few times to clear sinus problems.

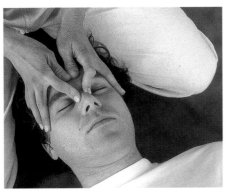

12 Using your index fingers, stroke along the side of the nose to help clear nasal congestion. Come all the way up to the bridge of the nose.

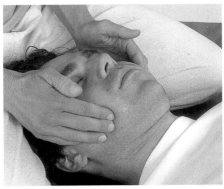

13 Massage the side of your partner's face, moving down to the jaw. This treatment will relax the whole body.

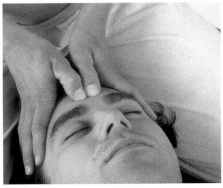

14 Come back to the starting point at your partner's forehead. Apply some pressure and stroke out to the sides.

KEY TIPS

When giving tension relievers, try to take a little time fully relaxing yourselves. Commence the techniques from a position of well-being and strength. Listen to some calming music, make sure that the room is warm and dry, and when you are feeling entirely comfortable, begin. Since this is an intimate kind of massage, it is also important that the subject feels completely at ease with you. A little deep breathing before the first exercise will help induce a marvellous, soothing feeling of harmony. It will certainly make all the difference. Afterwards, you may begin.

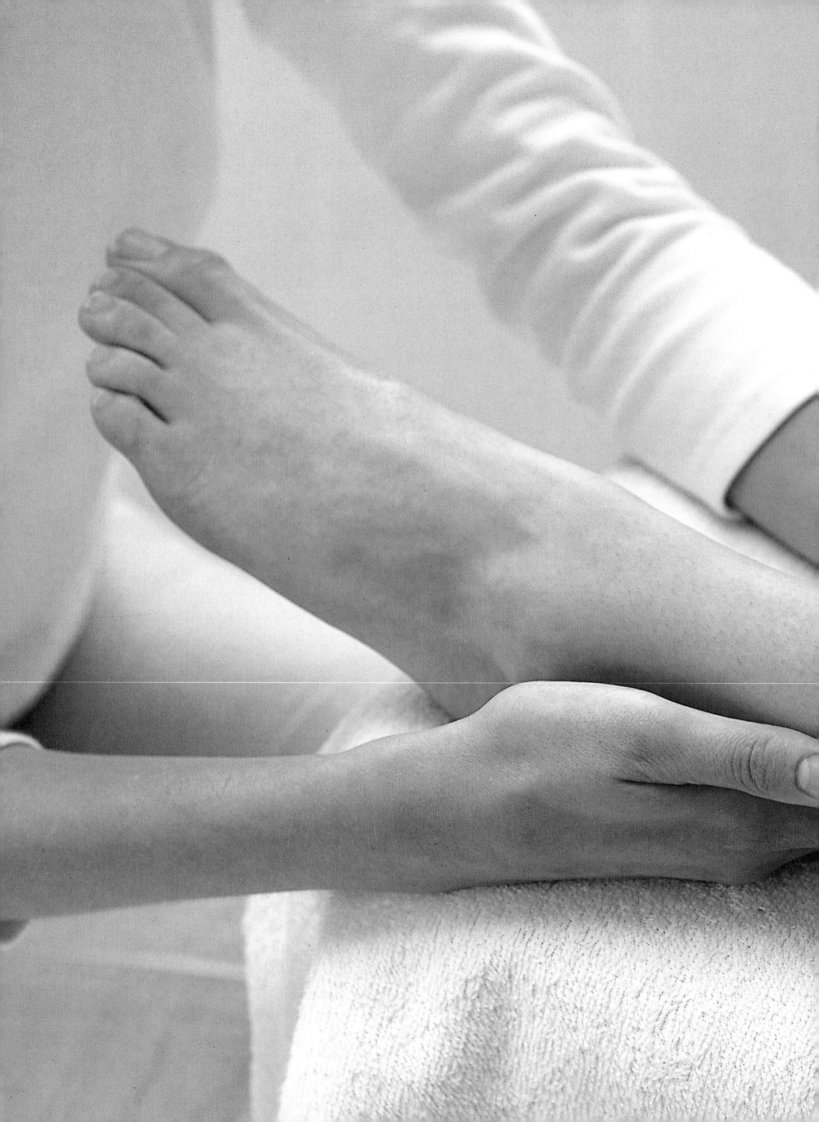

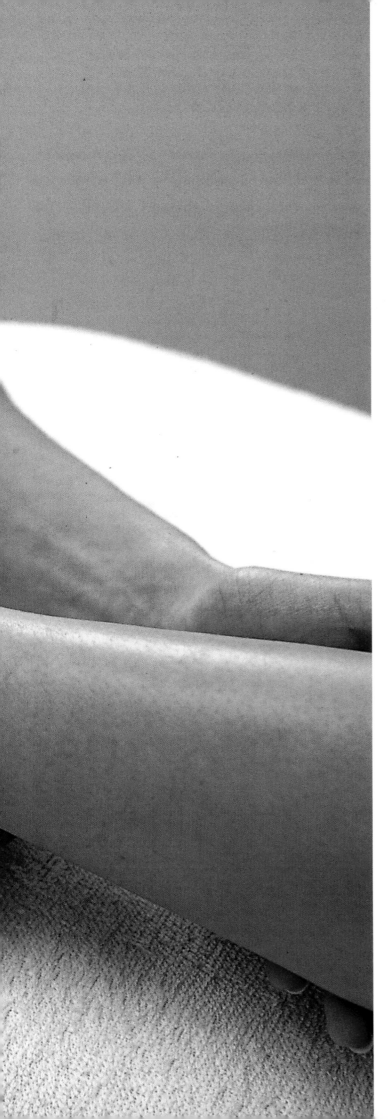

REFLEXOLOGY

—

In reflexology the hands, specifically the fingers and thumbs, are used to apply pressure to key points, usually on the feet, although often on the hands. Pressure points on the feet and hands reflect all the other parts of the body, both external and internal, so that this treatment can be used to correct problems associated with the organs and glands as well as the limbs, torso and head. The treatment is not just a foot massage, although massage can be used first to release tension and aid relaxation.

This chapter shows a full reflexology routine, which works on the reflexes of the whole body. It should always be practised before treating specific problem areas, for which suggestions are also given.

HOW REFLEXOLOGY WORKS

Reflexology acts on parts of the body by stimulating the corresponding reflexes with compression techniques applied with the fingers. Where there is inhibited functioning we find congestion in the form of deposits that have not been cleared away by the venous circulation and the lymph. Both feet together hold the reflexes to the whole body. The part that corresponds to the spine runs along the instep of each foot.

HEAD AND NECK
Your head is represented on the toes; to be more precise, the right side of your head lies on the right big toe and the left side on the left big toe. In addition to the whole head being fully represented on the two big toes, the eight other toes hold the reflexes to specific parts of your head for fine tuning.

Your neck reflex is actually found in the "necks" of all the toes: if you find tension in one area of your neck, you will find tension or discomfort, or be able to feel congestion, in the corresponding areas of your toes. The correspondence between the head and toes may be initially difficult to understand because you have only one head while you have ten toes (or two sides to your head and five toes on either side). However, reflexology is a long-lived, well-known art, and you will quickly come to appreciate these close connections.

▲ *Gently working on the spinal reflex which in fact runs right along the instep of each foot.*

PELVIS
The whole of your heel all around your foot contains the reflexes to your pelvic area: they lie on the sole and the sides of your heel and also across the top of your ankle.

LIMBS
The limbs are clearly represented on the outer edge of your foot but also, and most particularly, on the corresponding upper or lower limb. There is no part of the foot that actually resembles the limbs. The arms and legs, however, follow the same basic structure, and as such each limb holds and contains the reflexes to the other limb on the same side. Shoulders reflect hips and vice versa. Elbows and knees, wrists and ankles and hands and feet are related in the same way. These are known to practising, experienced reflexologists as the cross reflexes.

TORSO AND SPINE
It is much easier to comprehend how the torso is reflected in or fits on to the body of the feet once you have grasped the concept of your two feet together representing your whole body. The key to such understanding lies in the fact that the spinal line runs right down and along the insteps of your feet, where they finally meet if you put them firmly together. In your feet the whole of you comes together.

CHEST
The ball of each foot represents one side of your chest. So in the balls of your feet, and on the same area on the top of your feet, lie the reflexes to your lungs, air passages, heart, thymus gland, breast, shoulders and everything contained in your chest. The whole area is bounded by your diaphragm, the important reflex that lies across the base of the ball of each foot.

ABDOMEN
In your instep, where your feet are not weight-bearing and are therefore not padded like the ball, you will find contained all the reflexes to your abdominal organs – those concerned with digestion and those dealing with the maintenance and well-being of life. This crucial area is clearly bounded by the diaphragm line above, and also by the heel line that lies below.

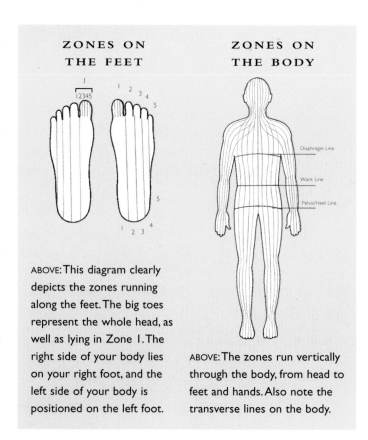

ABOVE: This diagram clearly depicts the zones running along the feet. The big toes represent the whole head, as well as lying in Zone 1. The right side of your body lies on your right foot, and the left side of your body is positioned on the left foot.

ABOVE: The zones run vertically through the body, from head to feet and hands. Also note the transverse lines on the body.

THE BENEFITS OF REFLEXOLOGY

Reflexology works quite simply, and in a highly effective, efficient way. It manages to relax and overcome any build up of excess tension in the muscles. Consequently, during a treatment, all parts of the feet will be stimulated and the significant dual effect is to relax your muscles and also to increase the efficiency of the circulation to all parts of the body. You will quickly notice the effects.

REFLEXOLOGY AND YOU

Working along holistic principles, reflexology takes into account body, mind and spirit as they are all interrelated. Whatever happens to you will affect all levels of your being, whether you notice or not. If you feel under pressure or are stressed, the effect on your body will be detrimental, as your muscles remain tense and taut, constricting the circulation and nerves, and compromising their functioning. Similarly, if you have a physical mishap, your feelings will be affected by the degree of pain you experience, the way in which the accident happened, and the effect it has on you afterwards.

▲ *Through working the hands (or feet) you are working the whole body.*

Although you are working mostly on the feet in reflexology, you are affecting the whole of the body, both inside and out, through the treatment. This is achieved by working the reflexes to the internal organs and glands as well as to the surface of the body. It appears that you can have a more far-reaching effect by working the reflexes than by working directly on the corresponding body part. Such referral treatment, as it is sometimes called, is highly effective.

Pain in the back, for instance, may be due to the onset of structural problems in which the bones are actually out of place and misaligned, and should be checked by an osteopath, cranial osteopath or chiropractor. If the pain results from muscular problems, or if manipulation has already been done but muscular strain remains, the next step is to identify the muscles involved and then begin work to relieve the situation with massage and reflexology. As a follow-up treatment it is highly effective.

Massage has an immediate and profoundly relieving effect, but the pain and discomfort is likely to recur when the effects of the massage have worn off. Benefits resulting from working the reflexes to the relevant area of the back will be more long term than those produced by working directly on the muscles them-selves. This is because through the reflexes you are stimulating the body from within, rather than exercising and soothing the muscles from without. Stimulating the reflex to a troubled area will promote healing. Reflexology uses both massage and specific stimulation of the reflexes to gain lasting relief.

▶ *Always wash your feet before any treatment to refresh the skin.*

WHAT TREATMENTS INVOLVE

Reflexology is not just a foot massage, but this technique is certainly incorporated. Sweeping whole hand movements on the whole foot will relax the entire person and prepare the feet for reflex work. During the working of the reflexes, massage soothes and relaxes the area where congestion or discomfort is to be found. It actively links the treatment together into a continuous, flowing whole, and manages to relax and stimulate the whole of the body while various individual parts are being treated specifically. Equally beneficial is the use of whole hand massage movements which is used to complete a reflexology treatment, and to give a feeling of well-being to the entire person before ending the session.

A reflexology session can be both relaxing and stimulating for the patient. As muscle tensions are relaxed, and the nerve supply freed from constriction, the body slips into a deep state of relaxation. At the same time, the circulation is being stimulated to bring nutrients to all parts of the body, and to remove waste products that interfere with the healthy functioning of the parts and the whole. Energy is able to flow more freely around the body, and feelings of total well-being result.

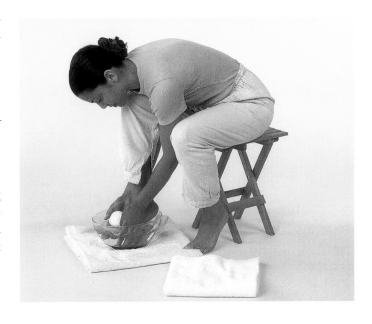

GIVING REFLEXOLOGY

Anyone new to reflexology will immediately notice a marvellous difference in the way treatment is given. Instead of being seen as an assembly of parts with one or two needing a quick over-haul, the whole body is considered, and the whole is carefully fine-tuned to get you back into shape. It is the recognition of the way in which every part of the body interacts with another that makes reflexology such a success.

THE HOLISTIC APPROACH

Reflexology works on the whole of the body, stimulating the reflexes to the internal organs, glands and body parts, as well as massaging the outside of the body. Through working on your feet as a whole, healing is stimulated throughout the body rather than just in one part that may well be influenced, or have influence on, other parts or systems. This is what makes the holistic approach of natural medicine so completely effective.

When you have a problem, natural therapies do not address you as a machine - repairing or replacing the part that does not work, but treat you in your entirety to deal with the cause of the problem, rather than merely alleviating the symptoms locally. If you have a raging toothache you may be able to relieve it by taking painkillers, but you will not make the abscess to go away unless you deal with the poison that gave rise to it in the first place.

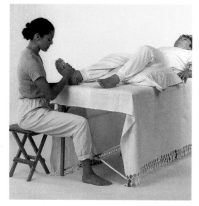

▲ *Make sure that your partner is comfortable, with pillows under their head, neck and knees for support.*

LOCATING THE PROBLEM

If you develop a headache you may or may not know its cause. Where in your body is the trouble seated? Does it come from tension in your neck or lower down your spine, from digestive disturbance, or even from held-in tension in your legs? Many headaches have such roots even though we do not notice the beginning of the trouble until the pounding in our head attracts our attention. Recurrent headaches happen because their causes have not been recognized and dealt with.

If you massage the reflexes to the head you might give temporary relief, but you will probably not cure the headache. Stimulating a related reflex, however, is effective. You will only find it if you work the whole foot, and do not spot-work for one symptom.

▼ *The feet must be where you can comfortably reach them.*

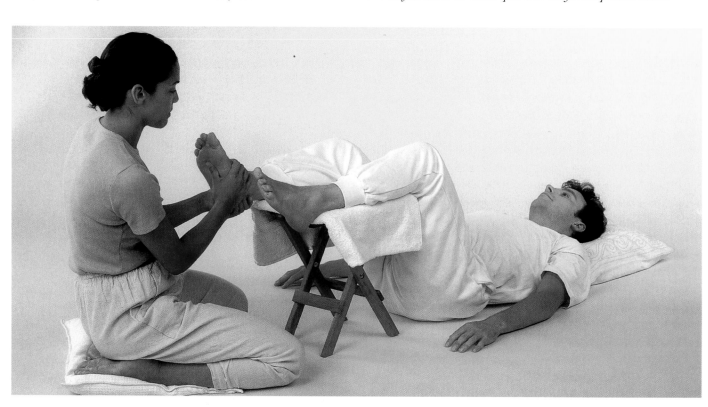

BASIC TECHNIQUES

Make sure that the room you are going to use is warm and quiet without any interruptions from telephones, faxes, pagers or people coming and going. Once you have created the right conditions you can proceed with the basic techniques for the hands and feet. They make an excellent introduction. Once mastered you will quickly pick up reflexology's movements. They are straightforward and highly effective.

HAND AND FOOT TREATMENTS

1 To thumbwalk, hold your two thumbs straight up and bend one at a time at the first joint. Repeat several times.

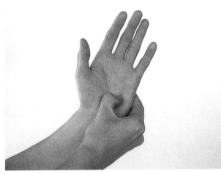

2 The therapeutic movement is on the firm downward press with your thumb bent. Use one hand only.

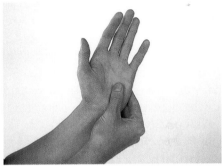

3 Slide forward as you straighten your thumb. The technique is sometimes called caterpillar walking.

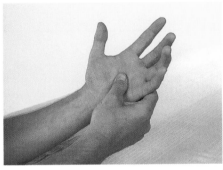

4 To rotate, place your thumb on part of your hand and gently rotate it on the spot. Try exerting a little more pressure.

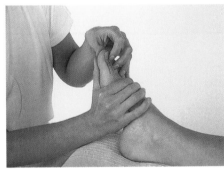

5 To fingerwalk, use the index finger. The technique is as for thumbwalking but using one or more fingers.

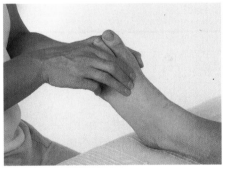

6 Continue the fingerwalking exercise, but this time keep the three middle fingers together.

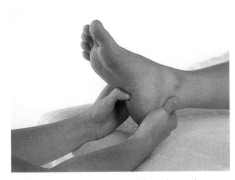

7 To pinpoint, use your thumb and fingers. Move them together and apart, like a pincer, then press in the thumb.

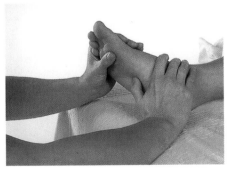

8 To hold and support, use one hand to hold the foot securely. This will help you give more sensitive treatment.

GETTING RELAXED
Make sure that you find a comfortable position for the person whose feet you are going to treat. They may be lying on a sofa, with cushions to support their back, head and neck in one corner, and their feet at the opposite end so that you can reach them easily. If they are sitting in an armchair, find an upright chair or stool of a suitable height and support their legs with a cushion. Be sure you sit comfortably too.

WARM-UP FOOT MASSAGE

It is always of great benefit to the patient if their feet are massaged right at the beginning of a reflexology treatment. This gives them time to get used to your touch, and to leave behind the cares of the day. Their overall mood is extremely important, and you should do your best to make sure that they are feeling relaxed. Give another massage at the end of the reflex work, and then at the end of the session.

THE FIRST STEPS

Massage prepares the feet for reflex work: it warms and relaxes the tissues, accustoms the receiver to your touch and soothes and relaxes the whole body. Massage will also loosen tensions in the muscles and stimulate the blood supply to and around the feet. Consequently, when the reflex points are worked the tissues will not be strained, and they will respond fully. Do not miss out this stage, as it is extremely important.

During treatment use plenty of massage to link the movement from one reflex area to the next, to soothe and relax the foot in between working the reflex points, which may produce sensations of tenderness, and use it where any tenderness or discomfort is found.

OIL AND MASSAGE TREATMENTS

When you have covered all the reflex points, end with a massage on both feet to instil a sense of deep relaxation. Use 2–3 drops of essential oils mixed in with some almond oil. Do not use the oil beforehand because once on your hands it will counter any accurate hand reflexology movements.

When it comes to massage movements, note that there is no one set sequence. The prime object is to fit movements together in a way that is customized to your individual needs. They should feel good to you and to the person you are working on. The first few movements are good as an introduction, and you should always rotate the ankles as this frees up the blood and nerve supply through the ankle to the foot.

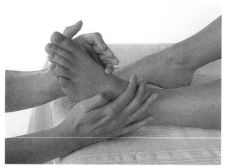

1 Stroking movements, or effleurage, are just as they sound, sweeping and soothing, and are good all over the foot. Add wherever appropriate.

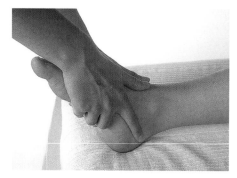

2 To make spreading movements on the top of the foot, draw your thumbs off sideways, keeping your fingers still.

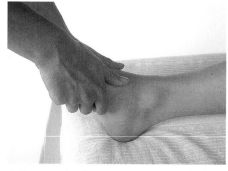

3 Repeat the first movement, gradually working your way down the foot with each subsequent repetition.

4 To cover the sole of the foot, start in the same position as before, but this time draw your fingers off sideways, keeping your thumbs still.

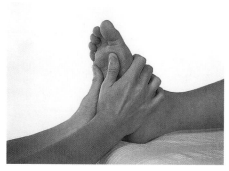

5 Finally, massage into the ball of the foot with your thumbs.

6 To knead, use a movement like kneading dough and work into the sole of the foot using the lower section of your fingers.

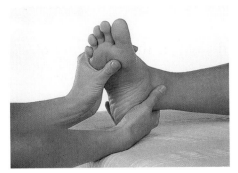

7 To rotate the ankle, rotate the foot clockwise several times, feeling gently as you proceed so that you do not force stiff ankles, but you do manage to exercise the joint.

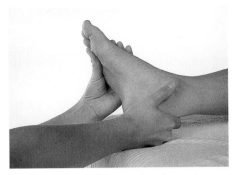

8 Repeat the ankle rotation, but this time in an anti-clockwise direction.

9 To make vigorous, fast movements, massage both sides of the foot, running your hands freely up and down the whole length of the foot. Repeat this technique several times.

10 With your hands in the same starting position, this time move them alternately up and down from the top to the sole of the foot so that the foot tips from side to side. Do take great care not to twist the ankle.

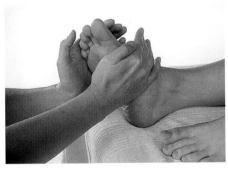

11 With your hands palms up on either side of the foot, move them quickly to and fro, to exercise and loosen the ankle. When this movement is done correctly, the foot will waggle around.

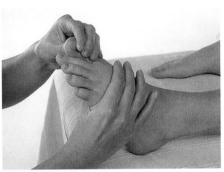

12 To rotate the toes, begin with the big toe, holding it securely but not too tightly and gently rotate. Repeat this movement carefully with each toe.

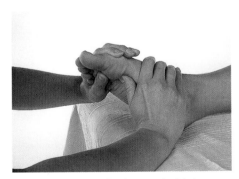

13 To relax the diaphragm, hold the foot and bring it down on to the thumb of your other hand, and lift it off again. Next, move your thumb one step to the side and repeat the movement.

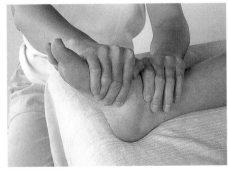

14 To make a spinal twist, the hand on the ankle remains still while the other, lower hand moves to and fro across the top of the foot, round the instep and finally back again. Repeat several times.

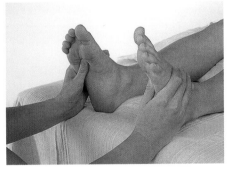

15 For good breathing and to relax the solar plexus reflex, place your thumbs in the natural dent. As your partner breathes in, press in with your thumbs and as they breathe out, release them.

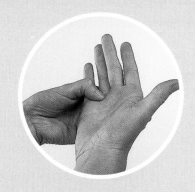

reflexology routines
reflexology routines

reflexology routines

The following pages are a clear step-by-step illustration of the full reflexology routine, which should be performed on your partner before you begin treating specific problems. In fact, the full routine covers most key parts of the body, and includes the spine, toes, chest, abdomen, pelvis and limbs. Depending on how it is given, it can be an invigorating or relaxing beginning to a treatment.

To see how all these parts of the body are reflected and simultaneously contained in your hands and feet, look at the detailed charts shown at the end of this chapter. It is immediately clear that both hands and feet are much more than themselves; they have become highly detailed referral points, in essence being like blueprints to all parts of the body. It obviously takes time to remember the exact wherabouts of all these areas, and to feel confident that you are treating the lungs alone and not, say, the adjacent stomach or even the spleen. Part of the art of reflexology is sensitivity and pinpoint accuracy.

In order to guarantee such accuracy it is important that your hands are not covered with any essential oils or they will glide and slide everywhere, which is not what you want. Also note that though this routine runs before more detailed work, it is not something that can or should be rushed. Besides fully toning up your partner, and making sure that their body is fully tuned in and responsive to what is happening, the routine is an excellent way of helping them relax. It gears up the body for what is to come. Interestingly, many patients claim that this is the high point of the treatment; and it can certainly be highly effective.

When you start giving such treatment there is invariably a stop-start feel to it as you have to remember precisely what to do next. The joy of working with an experienced practitioner is that one routine seamlessly and effortlessly flows into the next, and your body quickly learns to yield itself up to the continuous waves of well-being that the routine soon imparts.

THE FULL REFLEXOLOGY ROUTINE

The following step-by-step illustration of the full reflexology routine should be performed on your partner before moving to treat specific problem areas. Always try to treat the areas of the body in exactly the same order as outlined here, from the spine to the limbs. Just occasionally, as a guide, fine lines have been drawn on the feet in the photographs to highlight the position of the important reflex points.

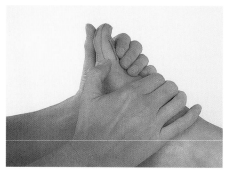

1 To treat the spine, thumbwalk up and down the spinal lline as shown here. Repeat several times.

2 Use the three middle fingers to fingerwalk across the spine/instep in stages, from big toe to heel.

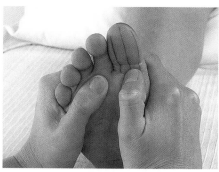

3 To treat the head and neck, work up the back of the big toe, thumbwalking in three lines to cover the whole area.

4 Use your index finger to fingerwalk down the front of the big toe again in three lines. Next, work up the side of the big toe with your thumb.

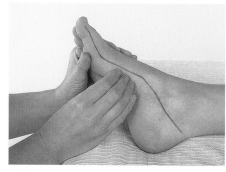

5 For the other side of the toe, approach from the back and tuck your thumb between this toe and the second one. Now thumbwalk the side of neck.

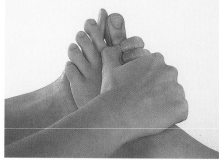

6 Change hands and, using your other thumb, approach from the front and tuck it in between the big toe and second toe again. Work up this side to the top.

7 Find the centre of the whorls of the big toe print and position your hand for pinpointing the pituitary reflex. Press gently at first, as it can be tender.

8 Work around the neck of the big toe in two semi-circles: thumbwalk the back part first of all.

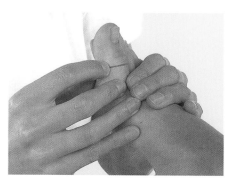

9 Fingerwalk right around the front of the big toe, but this time using your index finger.

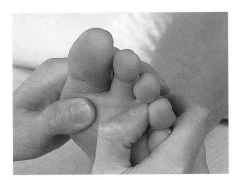

10 For the smaller toes, follow exactly the same routine as for the big toe. These toes can be covered in one line to each surface. Thumbwalk up the back. Fingerwalk down the front.

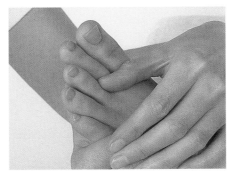

11 Thumbwalk up one side of the toe. Always approach the side from the front. Next, change hands and then gradually work up the other side of the same toe.

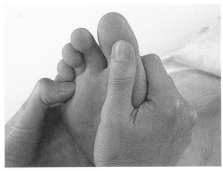

12 Finally, commence thumbwalking the ridge under the little toes. Repeat several times, then culminate this routine.

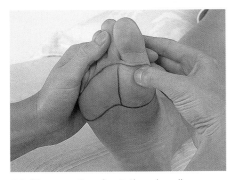

13 To treat the chest, thumbwalk horizontally in from the instep under the big toe, starting just next to the neck. Repeat just below the first line, bordering on it. Continue thumbwalking lines like this until you have covered the ball under the big toe down to the diaphragm line.

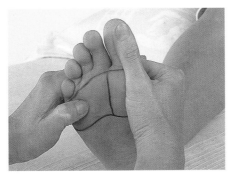

14 Thumbwalk horizontally in from the outside of the foot under the little toes, starting just below the ridge. Cover the whole of this area in the same way as described in step 13.

15 Next, work carefully along the diaphragm line under the big toe, and follow the natural line up between the big and second toes to the actual base of the toes.

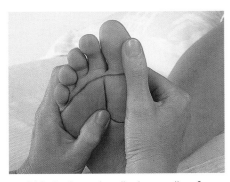

16 Work along the diaphragm line from the outside of the foot, and when you finally meet the line between the big and the second toes you can continue up this line to the base of the toes.

17 Starting from just under the big toe, thumbwalk the whole diaphragm line.

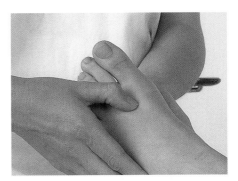

18 When on the top of the foot, you may now commence thumbwalking right along each individual channel that exists between the bones which lead up to the toes.

19 The last step involves using the three middle fingers together to fingerwalk the whole of the top of the foot. You should work from the base of the toes right up the foot.

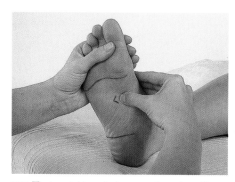

20 To treat the abdomen, thumbwalk from the medial edge, under the big toe, to the outer edge in horizontal lines as you did for the chest, each line bordering the previous one.

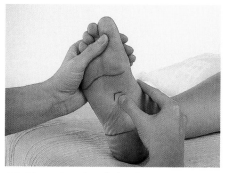

21 Next thumbwalk in diagonal lines covering the same area, as described in the previous step.

22 Now swiftly change hands and thumbwalk in horizontal lines. You should now be working from the outside of the foot towards the inner (medial) edge, as previously shown.

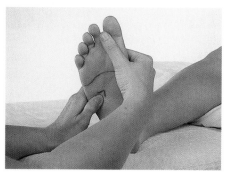

23 Employing the same thumb, begin thumbwalking in diagonal lines and gradually work from the outside towards the inner edge, covering the whole area, as before.

24 While referring to the foot chart, gently begin rotating the reflex to the adrenal glands, pushing in under the tendon running down from the big toe.

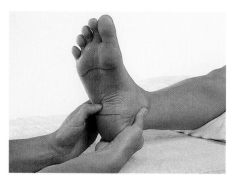

25 Work along what is called the ileo-caecal valve reflex, using the inner corner of your thumb to pinpoint it.

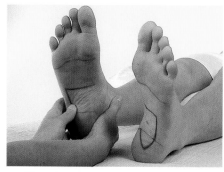

26 Thumbwalk the path of the colon, starting on the right foot at the bottom of the colon line.

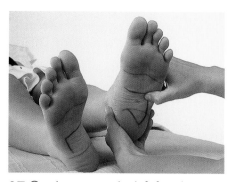

27 Continue on to the left foot, but change from the left hand to right hand at the point above.

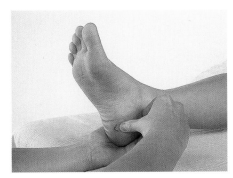

28 To treat the pelvis, begin by thumbwalking the heel across the sole in horizontal, overlapping lines. Note that this can actually be quite hard work.

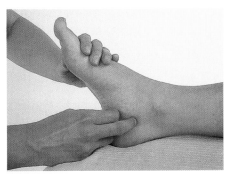

29 Find the little hollow halfway along a diagonal line between the centre of the ankle bone and the right angle of the heel on the inside of the foot, and rotate this point with your middle fingertip. Do not apply too much pressure.

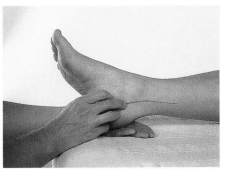

30 From this point, begin the fingerwalking movement using the same finger, going up the line running behind the ankle and up the leg.

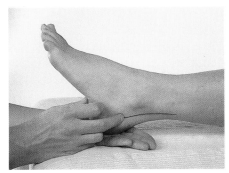

31 Now find the point described in step 2, but on the outside of the foot. Rotate it with the middle finger of your other hand and then fingerwalk up the outside of the ankle and leg, just as you did on the inside.

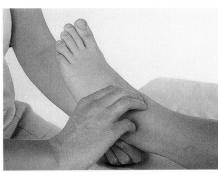

32 Now begin using the three middle fingers, and start fingerwalking right across the top of the ankle.

33 Continue the fingerwalking movement, going right round the ankle bone, using the same fingertips.

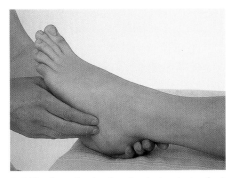

34 Finally, refer to the foot charts to find the hip/knee reflex, and work it by fingerwalking two fingers together.

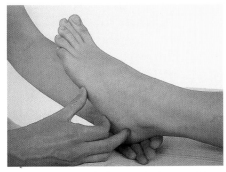

35 To treat the limbs, work the outside of the foot, then begin massaging the relevant cross reflex.

KEY TIPS

Although the routine is described for one foot only. Remember to treat the other foot too. Start with the right foot, as here, then when you have completed the routine, move to the left foot and duplicate what you have done (reversing hands and movements as appropriate to the shape of the left foot). It is always a good idea to start with general foot massage and to incorporate some soothing massage movements into the routine.

TENSION RELEASERS

We collect far too much tension in our necks. If you are not aware of how much neck tension can accumulate, put your hands to either side of your neck and begin to massage gently. If it feels in any way tight or uncomfortable you may benefit from this sequence as your partner carefully works your feet. When the neck muscles are tense and tight they may lead to pain, noises in the ears, and tired eyes. These releasers will cure that.

NECK AND SHOULDER TENSION

1 Treat neck tension by thumbwalking up and round the side of the big toe, then up the necks of all toes.

2 Thumbwalk right along the ridge immediately under the toes. Make sure that you are right on top of this ridge.

SELF-HELP

Thumbwalk along the base of your fingers, and repeat several times.

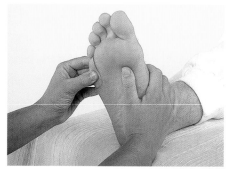

3 Ease shoulder tension by thumbwalking along the line of the shoulders in horizontal, overlapping lines.

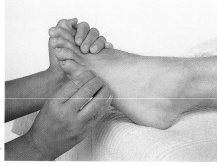

4 Fingerwalk across the same area on the top of the foot with three fingers. Fingerwalk around the mid-back (from the little toe to halfway down the foot).

5 To relax the diaphragm, position your thumb on the diaphragm line. Hold the foot, bring it down on to the thumb and lift it off again. Repeat across the foot.

6 Ease whiplash injuries by thumbwalking between the big and second toes.

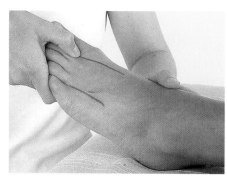

7 Work the same area on the top of the feet with your thumb.

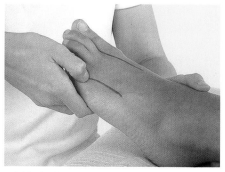

8 Work the shoulder reflex on the top and the bottom of the feet.

BACKACHE RELIEVERS

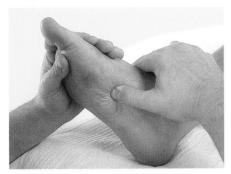

1 Thumbwalk up and down the spine, gently supporting the outer edge of the foot as you work.

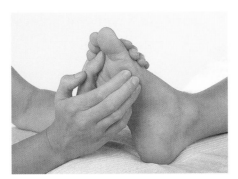

2 Fingerwalk across the spinal reflex with three fingers together, right down the instep in stripes.

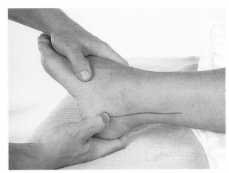

3 Thumbwalk up the helper reflexes for the lower back, behind the ankle bones on either side.

RELIEVING REPETITIVE STRAIN

1 Thumbwalk up the back and sides of the second and third toes for the eye reflex. This will also relieve neck tension.

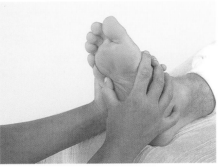

2 Work the shoulder reflexes thoroughly by using the thumbwalking technique. Then fingerwalk across the same area on the top of the foot, with the three middle fingers together.

3 Rotate the ankles to ease any aching wrists and to stimulate the healing process within the joints.

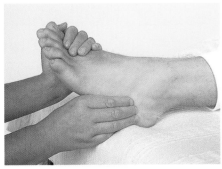

4 For the penultimate step, work across and down the outer foot on both feet to relax shoulders, arms, legs and knees.

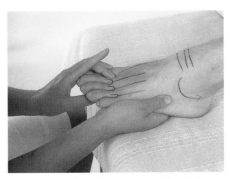

5 Work the lymph system on both feet. Fingerwalk down the lines from the toes to the ankle. Then work round the ankle.

SELF-HELP

Use the detailed hand chart on page 175 when trying to locate the relevant reflex on your hands to give temporary, quick relief for your particular problem. The key point to remember at all times when dealing with repetitive strain is that there is no one particular sequence of movements that guarantees special help. It is completely up to you to work out exactly which part of your body is suffering from the strain. You must then set about locating the relevant reflex on the charts. Then proceed with the treatment.

STRESS AND PAIN RELIEVERS

Excessive stress lies somewhere behind most troubles and illness. If your adrenalin runs at a high level for long periods, with little chance of appropriate action, your adrenal glands will become depleted. Your breathing will also become too rapid or will be restricted and shallow, and your digestion will be upset or strained in some way. When this happens, you know it is time to act and start curing yourself.

RELIEVING GENERAL STRESS

1 Relax the diaphragm by bringing the foot down on to the thumb of your other hand, and then lifting off again. Repeat, moving your thumb to the outside.

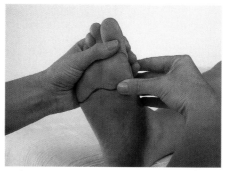

2 Thumbwalk along the diaphragm line. Tension collects in the diaphragm, causing tightness. When the diaphragm is relaxed the abdominal organs are stimulated.

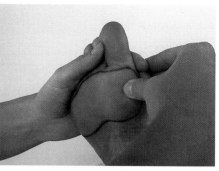

3 Work the lung reflexes on the chest area so that once the diaphragm is relaxed, breathing can be increased. This will help with relaxation.

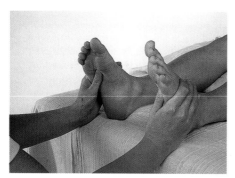

4 With both feet together put your thumbs in the diaphragm line. Press in on the in-breath, and release on the out.

5 Thumbwalk the stomach area and the whole of the instep, which is the abdominal area. This will help digestion.

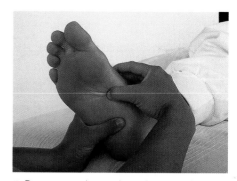

6 Rotate gently on the adrenal reflex.

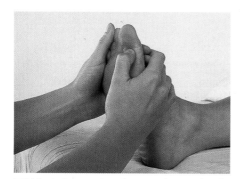

7 Work the neck reflex on the neck of the toes where tension collects.

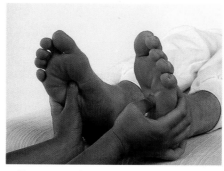

8 Ease stress from anger by working the solar plexus reflexes on both feet.

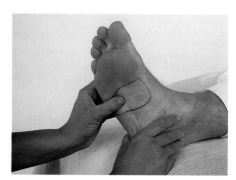

9 Work the liver area.

BACK PAIN

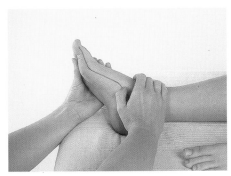

1 Work along the spine and find the tender parts. Work these to try to disperse some of the congestion.

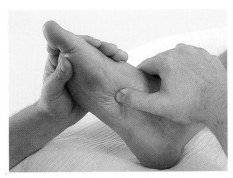

2 Work the adrenal gland reflexes on both feet. These glands deal with inflammation and aid good muscle tone when working effectively.

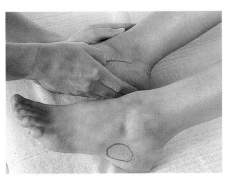

3 For lower back trouble, work the helper area by carefully rotating with your thumb.

NERVE PAIN

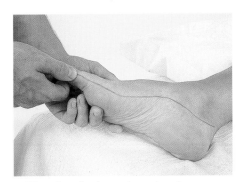

1 Thumbwalk along the spine for the central nervous system in the spinal cord.

2 Find the local area, for example, for the neck, work the cervical vertebrae and find the part of the neck of the toes that is tender.

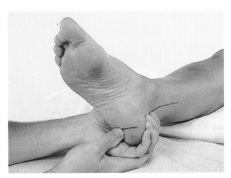

3 To treat sciatic pain, begin working the sciatic reflex as clearly shown in the foot chart.

CRAMP

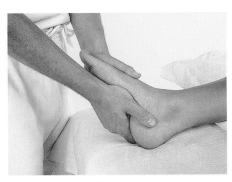

1 Hold the area and massage the appropriate cross reflex. For example, for cramp in the calf, massage the cross reflex on the lower arm.

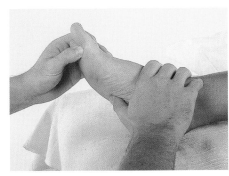

2 Work the parathyroid reflexes round the neck of the big toe.

TOOTHACHE

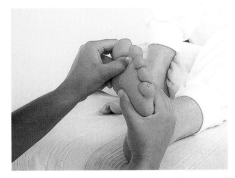

1 Find the toe or finger that has much tenderness, and work that area carefully but thoroughly.

HEADACHES, BREATHING AND SLEEPING

The three key elements to our continued health and well-being are breathing and sleeping, and a clear head. Poor breathing, possibly caused by too much tension, can easily result in headaches though. A bad night's sleep can also have unpleasant side effects, leading to a heavy head the next day. The following techniques are all excellent ways of helping overcome such problems.

1 Ease headaches by working the hypothalamus reflex, which controls the release of endorphins for pain relief.

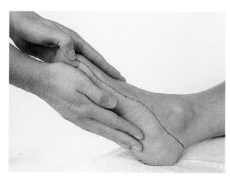

2 Work down the spine to take pressure away from the head. This will draw energy down the body.

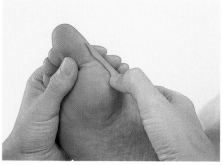

3 Work the cervical spine on the big toe. Work the neck of all the toes to relieve any tension.

4 Aid efficient breathing by working the whole chest area on the bottom of the feet to relieve the chest and lungs.

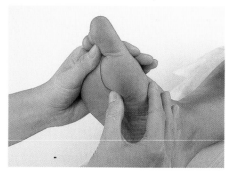

5 Work the air passages. This prompts them to clear themselves.

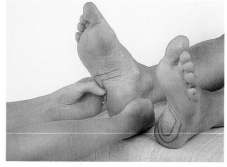

6 Work the ileo-caecal valve and the whole of the colon because this will help balance mucus levels.

7 For a good night's sleep hold the foot with your outside hand and bring it down on to the thumb of your other hand and lift off. Move your thumb one step to the side and repeat.

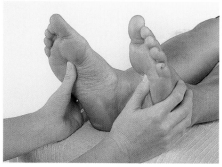

8 Do the solar plexus breathing exercise: take both feet together and position your thumbs in the centre of the diaphragm line. Press in on the in-breath, and release on the out.

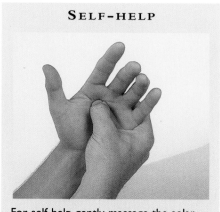

SELF-HELP

For self-help gently massage the solar plexus reflex in the palms of your hands.

REPRODUCTIVE PROBLEMS

Reflexology is an excellent way of keeping your reproductive side in good working order. Surprisingly, it is far too often ignored, yet there are simple but highly effective techniques that will cover a wide range of problems including menstrual cramps, painful breasts, and even attacks of nausea. Note that all these reflexology movements concentrate on the feet, particularly on the area around the ankle.

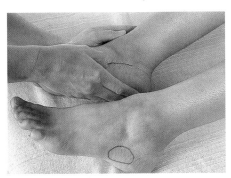

1 Work the ovaries or testes on the outside of the feet.

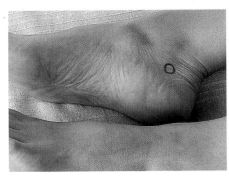

2 Work the uterus or prostate gland on the inside of the feet.

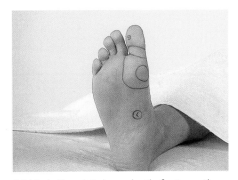

3 Work the fallopian tubes or vas deferens across the top of the ankle.

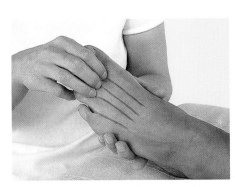

4 Ease menstrual cramps by working the lower spine for nerves to the uterus.

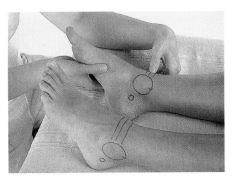

5 Work the uterus reflex area on the inside of the feet.

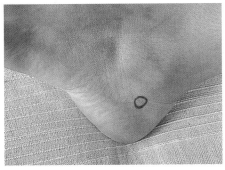

6 Work the glands on both feet, on the areas marked above.

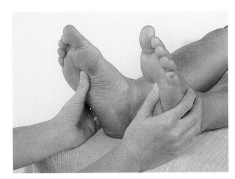

7 Ease painful breasts by fingerwalking up the chest area on top of the foot with three fingers together.

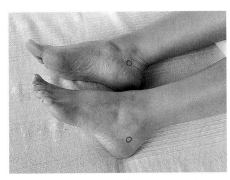

8 Relieve nausea by working the whole abdomen, especially where it seems tender. Do this gently and with care.

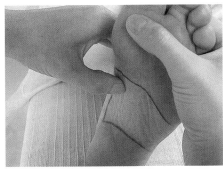

9 Do the solar plexus breathing exercise: press in with your thumbs, and release on the out.

COLDS, THROATS AND SINUSES

It is virtually impossible to avoid minor colds and the whole battery of side effects that go with them. Suddenly you are laid low by relentless outbreaks of sneezing and then sore throats and sinus problems. Fortunately, you do not have to grin and bear it. There are some excellent reflexology techniques that will help you overcome all these nasty extras. They will soon have you on the road to recovery.

1 Ease colds by working the chest area fully to encourage clear breathing.

2 Begin with the big toe and work the toe tops to clear the sinuses. Pinpoint the pituitary gland in the centre of the big toes for the endocrine system.

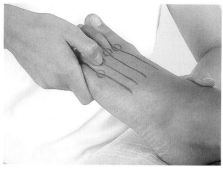

3 Work the upper lymph system to stimulate the immune system.

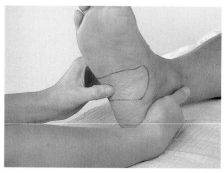

4 Work the small intestines to aid elimination of toxins and uptake of nutrients. Then work on the colon to aid elimination.

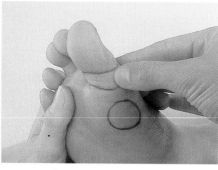

5 Help sore throats by working the upper lymph system, the throat by working the neck, and the thymus gland for the immune system.

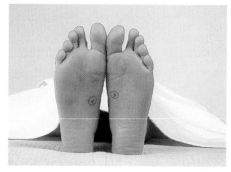

6 Rotate the adrenal reflex in the direction of the arrow.

7 Work the trachea and the larynx to stimulate them. Work the thyroid area in the area of the chest under the big toe.

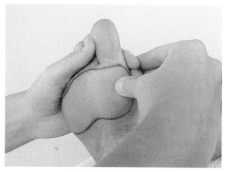

8 Ease sinus problems by working the whole chest area in order to aid good respiration.

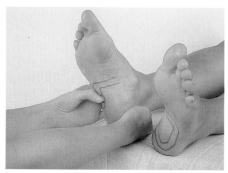

9 Pinpoint the ileo-caecal valve to balance mucus levels. Work the whole chest and rotate the adrenal reflex.

IMPROVING THE DIGESTION

The digestive system is all too frequently overlooked, yet it is vital that it is operating in a smooth and efficient way. To avoid any irritating problems, try carrying out the following quick and easy routines, and make them part of your daily or weekly reflexology session. One of the extra benefits is that they will help fine-tune the rest of you, leaving you feeling wonderfully calm, refreshed and invigorated.

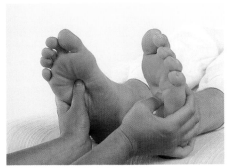

1 Aid any indigestion by working the solar plexus to relax the nerves to the stomach area.

2 Work the stomach, where digestion really begins. Then work the duodenum, the first section of the small intestines.

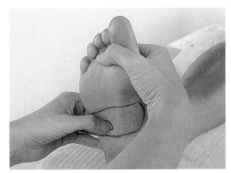

3 Work the liver and the gall bladder: the liver area is shown above, with the thumb rotating on the gall bladder reflex. These deal with digestion of fats.

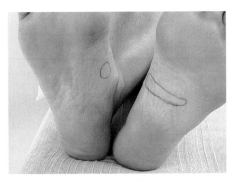

4 Work the pancreas which regulates the blood sugar levels and also helps aid digestion.

5 Ease constipation by working the diaphragm area in order to relax the abdomen.

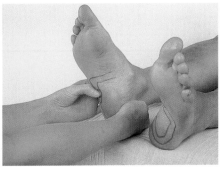

6 Pinpoint the ileo-caecal valve, which links small and large intestines. Work the colon or large intestine.

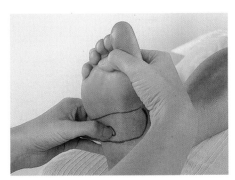

7 Work the liver and gall bladder: the liver area is shown above, with the thumb rotating on the gall bladder.

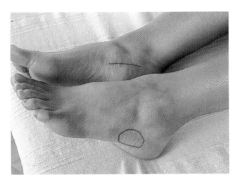

8 Work the lower spine and its helper areas for the crucial nerve supply to the colon.

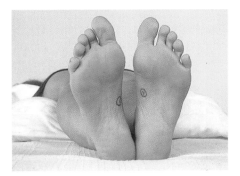

9 Work the adrenals for muscle tone. Rotate the reflex with your thumb in the direction of the arrows.

CHARTS

The foot charts are marvellous guidelines for interpretation. When you find a tender part of the foot you can look for that part on the charts and see approximately which reflex the tenderness lies on. Do bear in mind though, that every pair of feet is different and will not be the same shape as your chart. Also, the charts are two-dimensional and your body is three-dimensional. Nonetheless, the charts are every reflexologer's means to success.

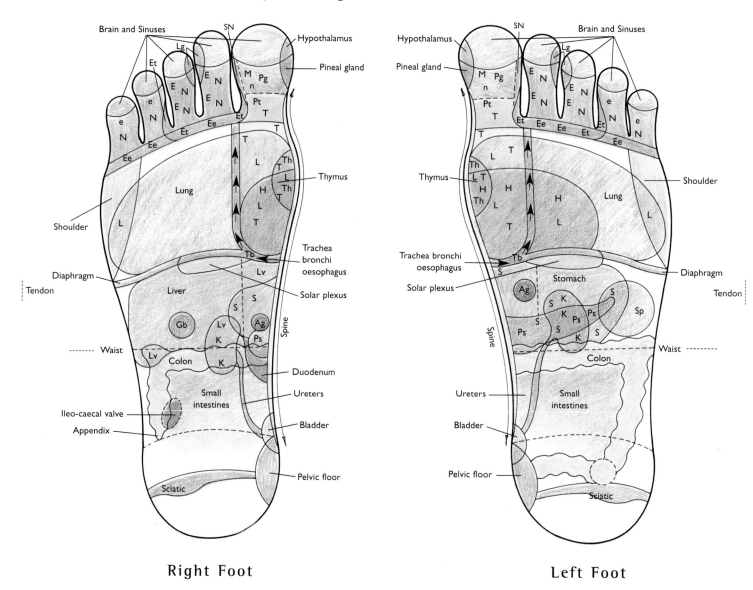

Right Foot   **Left Foot**

KEY			
Ag Adrenal glands	**H** Heart	**N** Neck	**Sp** Spleen
e Ears	**K** Kidneys	**n** Nose	**S** Stomach
Et Eustachian tubes	**Lg** Lachrymal glands	**Ps** Pancreas	**Tb** Trachea bronchi oesophagus
Ee Eye/Ear helper	**Lv** Liver	**Pt** Para-thyroid	**Th** Thymus
E Eyes	**L** Lungs	**Pg** Pituitary glands	**T** Thyroid
Gb Gall bladder	**M** Mouth	**SN** Side of neck	

TOP AND SIDES OF FOOT

The spinal reflex (bottom) is especially important and should always be massaged, and the reflex worked thoroughly. Not only is our spinal column our main boney support but it also contains the spinal cord, and through the central nervous system the whole body may be treated on the spinal reflex.

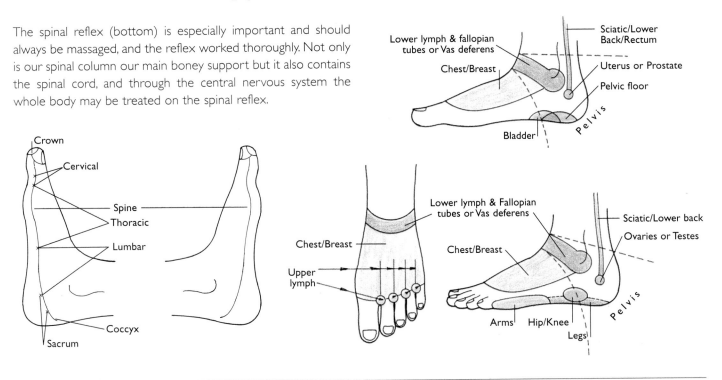

HAND CHART

The hands reflect all the body, as do the feet. They are a very different shape to feet, but once you have adjusted to that and learnt the basic layout, the location of reflexes is quite straightforward. Use the reflexes on the hand when it is impossible to work the feet, such as when only the hands are accessible or when the feet are damaged or diseased.

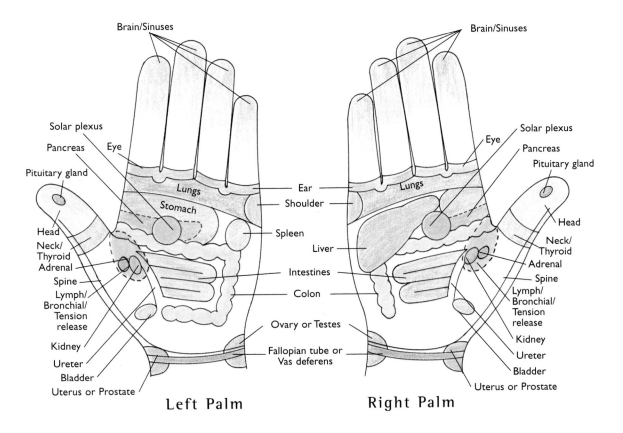

Left Palm   Right Palm

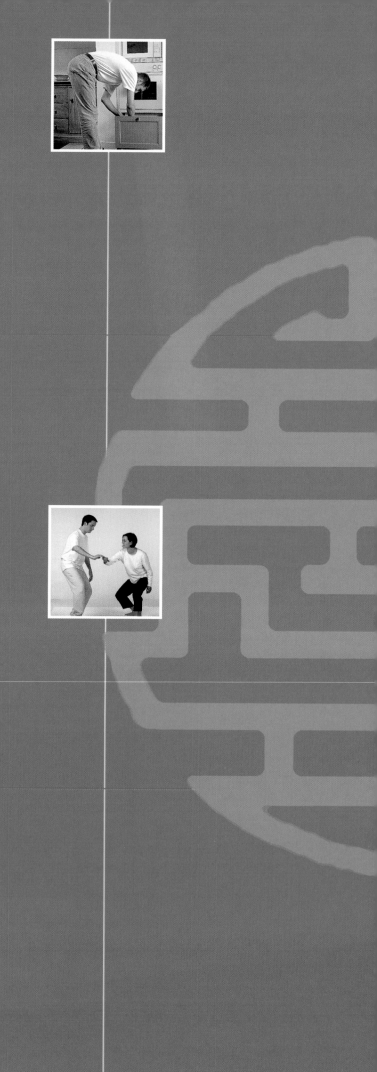

THE PATH TO INNER HARMONY

EVERYDAY LIFE BRINGS PLENTY OF
CHALLENGES, BUT KNOWING WHEN TO TAKE
A BREAK AND ENTER AN INNER WORLD OF
HARMONY CAN RENEW YOUR ENERGY AND
STRENGTH, HELPING YOU TO STAY CALM AND
SAIL CONFIDENTLY THROUGH TRYING TIMES.
ALL THE DISCIPLINES ON THE FOLLOWING
PAGES EMPHASIZE THE UNITY OF BODY, MIND
AND SPIRIT, AND DAILY PRACTICE WILL
ENHANCE YOUR POISE AND VITALITY.

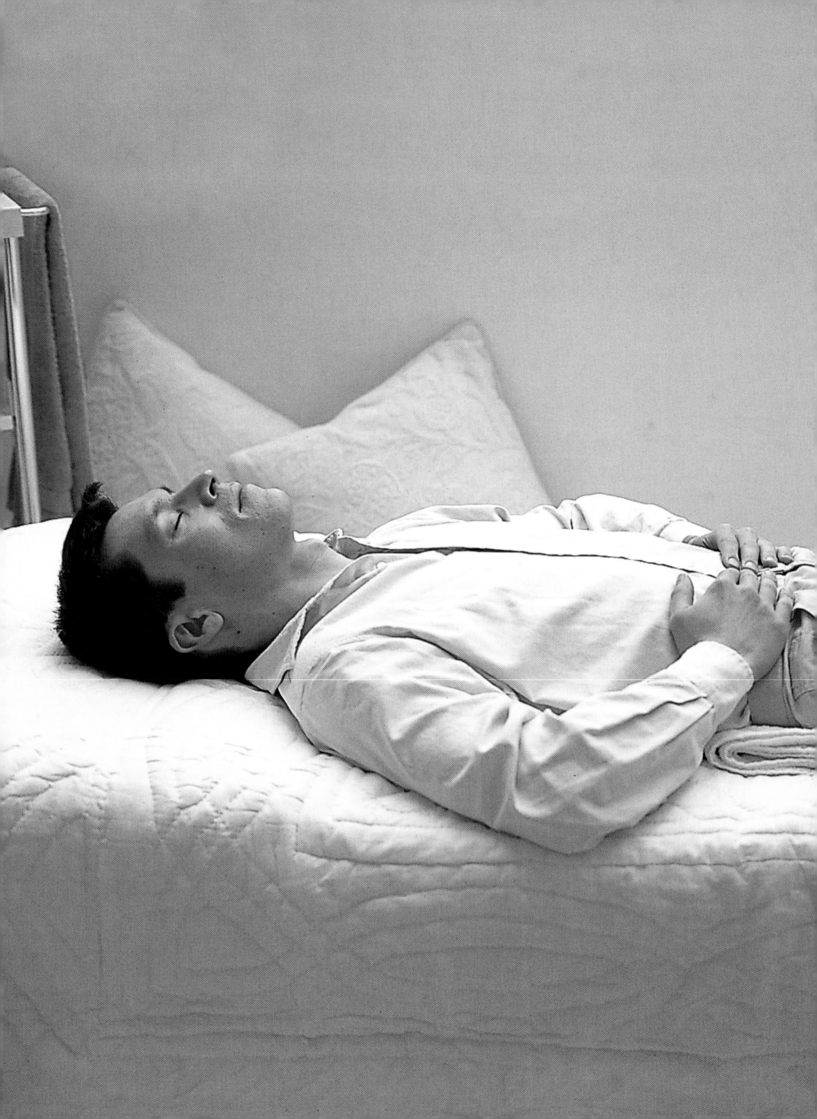

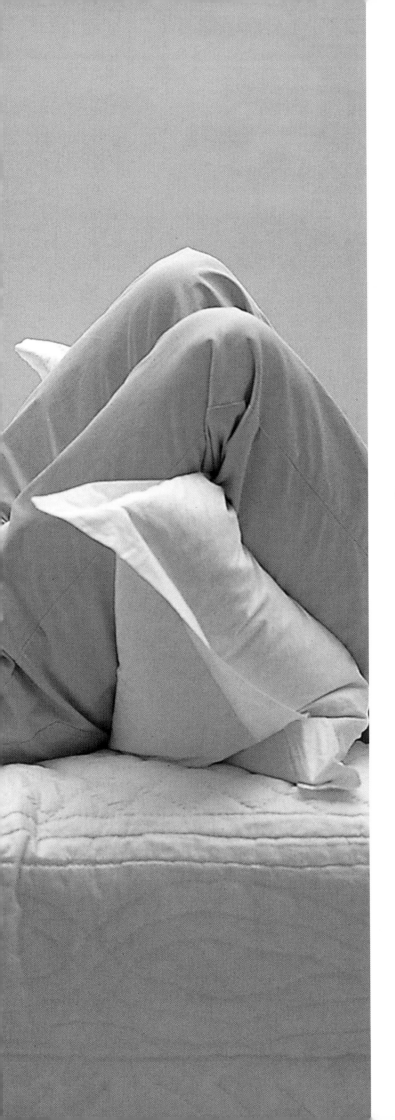

ALEXANDER TECHNIQUE

Exponents of the Alexander technique believe in the indivisibility of mind and body, and in their psycho-physical unity. The main objective of the practice is to encourage people to use their bodies and minds more effectively in their day-to-day lives. It emphasizes the development of correct posture and natural alignment as a means of enhancing energy and relieving pain. Used as a preventive therapy, the Alexander technique maintains tone and general well-being, but it can also assist people with stress-related illnesses such as respiratory and gastro-intestinal problems, psychosomatic conditions, psychological distress and depression, as well as facilitating recovery from accidents and injuries.

THE ALEXANDER TECHNIQUE PRINCIPLES

Once you start studying the technique, it quickly becomes clear that it helps you in all kinds of ways that other alternative remedies do not. That is not because it is superior, but because of its key agenda. As shown here, it helps us focus on our minds and bodies in new ways, and on aspects of our being that we might take for granted. The technique gets us back to basics.

PRIMARY CONTROL

"Misuse" occurs by contracting the muscles of the neck and pulling the head back and down into the shoulders. This has the twin effect of actually compressing the spine and narrowing and shortening the stature, creating tensions throughout the body. It is definitely something to be avoided.

Frederick Matthias Alexander discovered that the relationship between the head, the neck and the back, or "primary control", mechanically controlled movement and co-ordination in the whole body. To make ourselves aware of this consciously in our daily activities is the basis of good use.

▲ *See how this model is misusing himself. He is leaning over to the right, shortening and creating an imbalance in his body.*

INHIBITION

In its psychological-physiological sense, inhibition means a fast-moving yet natural control of your reactions, suppressing and smothering any possible spontaneity.

However, Alexander discovered that if he managed to stop himself from behaving in his habitual way, he could choose how he wished to respond to a stimulus. If someone rings the doorbell, your immediate response may be to go straight to the door. In doing so, you will be responding habitually. If you stop yourself from responding automatically, you then choose exactly how you will approach the door with the minimum effort.

CONCEPTS

The concept of end-gaining is extremely important in the work of Alexander technique teachers. Alexander realized that the habits he was encountering were far more deep-rooted and powerful than he had at first thought. The most serious of these was the tendency to try to react impulsively – end-gaining. End-gaining means reacting immediately and too quickly to a stimulus, without thinking. You respond by wanting something to happen, and become interested in the end result instead of being in the present. A typical example is if you are going to be late for an appointment and start to worry about the consequences. You get worked up during this process, forgetting that you might be sitting on a train, and that things are happening around you. In effect you are letting your thoughts take the situation into the future, instead of being in the "here and now", in the present.

Cutting yourself off from your environment has inevitable consequences for body positioning. It tends to lead to a pulling back of the head, a rounding of the back, a tightening of the legs and a loss of connection between the arms and the back. The gaze becomes fixed, the breath held. Essentially, the whole person is affected, both in mind and in body.

Alexander suggests you should use your "means-whereby". To put Alexander's conclusion into context, if we accept that we cannot change circumstances, we can change our approach to our bodies and allow ourselves to experience the new. It is then possible to learn to be in the moment rather than the past or the future, and to maintain a sense of inner balance and unity.

DIRECTION

Directions are signals given by the brain to parts of the body prior to or during physical action. It is possible to alter these signals to promote a positive change. You will find that the combination of direction and inhibition enables one to transform habitual ways of moving and eliminate old patterns of misuse.

▲ *Note how this model is walking. Her head, neck and back are all correctly aligned. Her arms are free to move in a relaxed way.*

NATURAL POISE

Nothing is more elegant and enviable than someone with perfect poise. It is something most of us have when young, but sadly it can be quickly lost to laziness and bad postural habits. In fact, it is quite easy to be totally unaware just how bad our posture is. At various times during the day it is worth freezing your movements, and taking a good look at yourself. You will be surprised at how often you fall well short of the ideal. Sitting at work is probably the one situation when your back is almost always wrongly positioned, becoming increasingly hunched, tense and stiff. Once you have ascertained exactly when and how you are going wrong, you can start putting matters right. If in any doubt, just look at young children. They instinctively know how to move gracefully and effortlessly without strain. That is something we should all try to emulate.

▲ *This child carries his toy close to his body., allowing it to lengthen and relax. This ensures good nervous energy and blood flow and allows full expansion of the lungs for breathing.*

THE HUMAN SKELETON

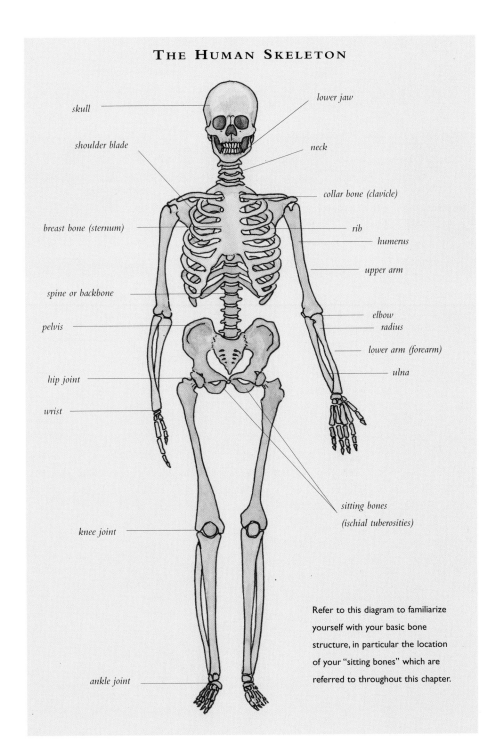

skull

lower jaw

shoulder blade

neck

collar bone (clavicle)

breast bone (sternum)

rib

humerus

upper arm

spine or backbone

elbow

radius

pelvis

lower arm (forearm)

ulna

hip joint

wrist

sitting bones
(ischial tuberosities)

knee joint

ankle joint

Refer to this diagram to familiarize yourself with your basic bone structure, in particular the location of your "sitting bones" which are referred to throughout this chapter.

PRIMARY DIRECTIONS
- Think of freeing the neck.
- Let the head go forward and up.
- Let the back lengthen and widen.

▲ *Note how this child is using his joints to squat, and how he simultaneously holds the plastic bag quite effortlessly.*

"Possession of property ... a means to happiness not an end."
Thomas Jefferson

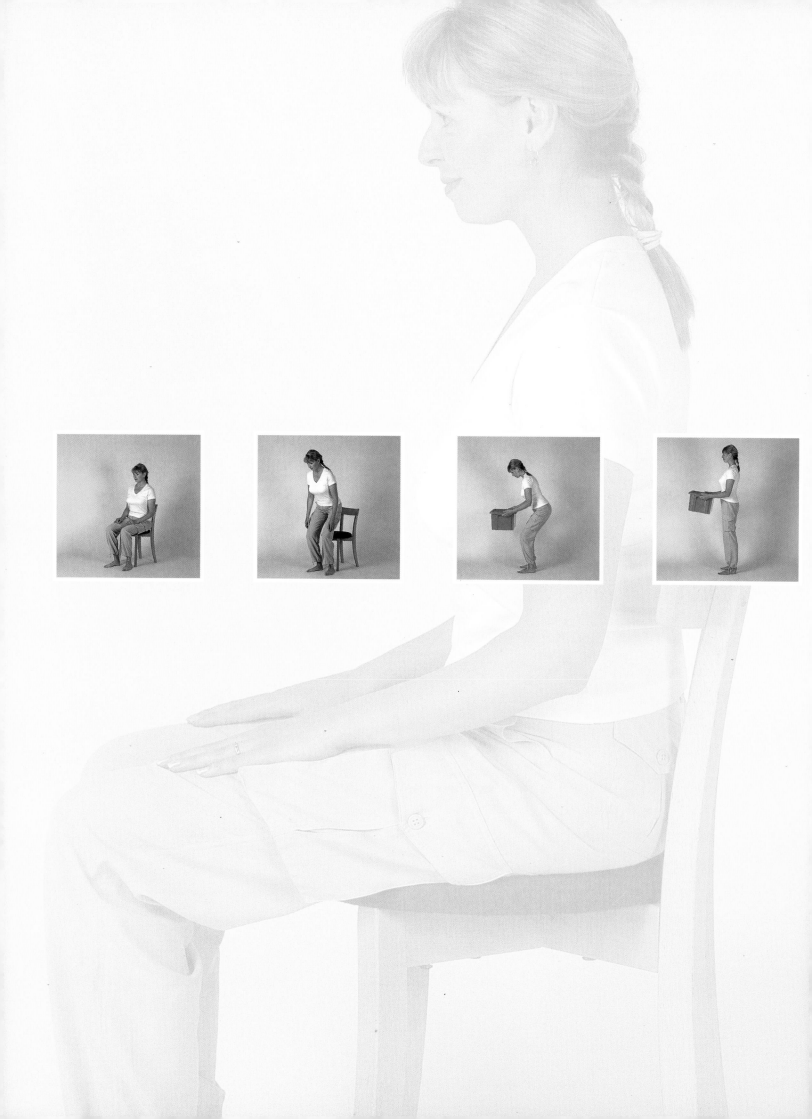

putting the alexander technique into practice

A certain, rightful degree of commitment is paramount during a course of lessons because the older and more set in your ways you are, the longer it can take to change, to release unnecessary muscular tension, and to re-educate the system. Success, however, is not hard to achieve but note that it will not happen overnight, and that some slight pitfalls are always going to be inevitable, so do not be put off.

For example, you may well find yourself trying to do the directions as a routine mechanical exercise when in reality success lies in the power of the body and mind uniting as one, and in the power to think about what you are doing. Do not imagine there are any short cuts, there are not. There is also the distinct possibility that you might be tempted to give up out of sheer frustration because your time scale is too unrealistically short and limiting, and you have not allowed sufficient time for a significant, quantifiable improvement. Do not be hard on yourself, and do not imagine that you can become an expert in a ridiculously short space of time. The technique deserves more respect.

What therefore follows is the identification of the main procedures that we use most often in daily life, the areas that most concern us. In fact, the use of the word "procedure" is quite deliberate because it totally avoids the suggestion of a mind-body split and maintains a sense of psycho-physical unity. The emphasis throughout is on the means of achieving these procedures, but with the minimum of muscular tension and effort. Many students have said that a course of lessons in the technique could be compared to learning to drive or learning a new language. Dedication and determination are a sure basis for total success.

USE OF THE EYES

If you want to know something about someone, just look straight into their eyes. They reveal an amazing amount about their current frame of mind. You can easily spot the depressed, dull and lifeless by their deadpan, almost one-dimensional eyes; the totally alert looking for a lively reply; the sad; the plaintive; the cheeky; and the happy. The technique reminds you how to stay lively and alert, and in touch with the rest of the world.

STAYING ALERT

If you observe people when they are either standing or walking, they often seem to be completely locked in a private world of their own, totally unaware of their own surroundings. They have stopped communicating with that is out there. When the gaze is fixed, the breathing also tends to suffer. It becomes rather restricted and there is less freedom in the body. The gaze should therefore be directed towards the outside world, taking in information so that you are not exclusively concentrating on what is happening within.

One of the strongest habits that a teacher perceives is the tendency of certain pupils to look down, not with their eyes, but by a general collapsing motion from the neck. This is the result of a fundamental misunderstanding of the alignment of the head, the neck and the back, and the position of the joints in the body.

Note how the models in this sequence of photographs (*below*) are using their eyes. Which do you think is the correct position? Can there be any doubt?.

▲ *Here children are using their eyes to look at their toys. They have not disturbed the alignment between their heads, their necks and their backs, thus maintaining their good use.*

"It's no good shutting your eyes if you're crossing a busy road."
F. M. Alexander

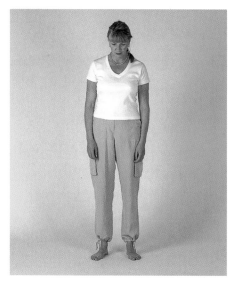

▲ *In this position, the model is breaking the alignment between her head, her neck and her back as she looks down, thus using her neck inappropriately.*

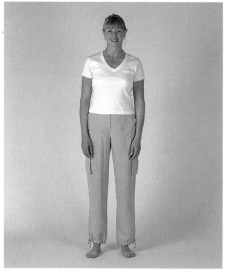

▲ *Note how the model is correctly aligned. She is maintaining her length and her width. Her eyes are alert and taking in her surroundings.*

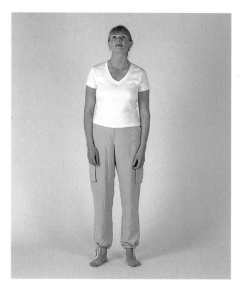

▲ *Here the model is breaking at the neckline and pulling her head back to look up, disturbing the alignment between her head, neck and back.*

THE SEMI-SUPINE POSITION

Standing for long periods easily compresses the spine. Lying down in a semi-supine position is a way of alleviating unnecessary tensions in the muscles and joints, and should be practised every day for at least 20 minutes. It encourages a better awareness of the head-neck-back relationship. This position does not necessarily need monitoring by a teacher, and it also gives you much needed time for yourself.

THE POSITION

Try to keep your eyes alert and open. It is preferable to avoid closing them because you will probably find it quite difficult not to fall asleep, which is definitely not the point of the exercise!

During your daily 20-minute session try and give yourself the time to practise some sharp, well directed thoughts to avoid your mind from wandering and spreading out, covering other possible important issues. This session can also encourage you to put into practice your excellent skills of observation. A good practice is to go over the primary directions, and to notice if you are aware of any tension in your body and to address it without trying to correct it. That is the secret of success.

▲ *Books support the head here. If you have too many, however, your chin will drop and you will feel pressure on your throat.*

▲ *Correspondingly, if you do not have enough books your head will tilt back and will not be properly supported.*

MOVING INTO THE SEMI-SUPINE

It is preferable to lie down on a hard, carpeted surface or alternatively on a rug on the floor. Avoid beds as they will not offer you adequate support. The number of books you need will depend on their thickness, and will also vary from person to person.

To lie down on the floor, place the books far enough behind you to give enough space for the whole of your torso and your bottom. When sitting, you can place your hands palms down on the floor behind you to help you lower your back. Take care not to stiffen the arms or to hold your breath in the process. To get up, it is preferable to roll over to one side, leading with your eyes rather than your head, and following with your torso and legs. Then place the free hand flat on the floor and go on to all fours. Be careful to maintain the alignment between your head, your neck and your back and not to hold your breath. Walk your hands back so that you move your bottom back towards your heels.

▲ *Make sure that your legs are about hip-width apart and that your knees are directed towards the ceiling.*

▲ *If your knees are falling out, you will probably lose the contact between the inner side of your foot and the floor.*

SITTING AND STANDING

Correct posture is as much about what is right as what is wrong. It is vital that you know what to do, and what not to do. It is easy to start out with correct posture, but fall into bad habits. You must know when to correct yourself. Remember to keep a straight alignment between head, neck and back, and to keep your legs hip-width apart with knees pointing forward, in the same direction as your feet.

SITTING

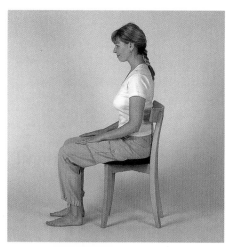

▲ *Correct: think of the shoulders going away from each other.*

▲ *Incorrect: rounded shoulders and feet wrapped around chair legs.*

▲ *Incorrect: arching the back, folding legs and leaning to one side.*

FROM SITTING TO STANDING

It is well worth practising this basic technique several times to perfect it. You will be surprised how ingrained bad habits are. Start by placing your legs about hip-width apart. Avoid pushing firmly up with them; that is not the object. Also, make sure that your feet are flat and are not placed so far forwards that coming up to stand is in any way difficult. Finally, remember to lead with the head; that is the key to getting this technique right.

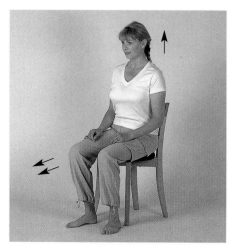

1 Here the model is relaxed, feet apart, hands resting comfortably, ready to go into the standing position.

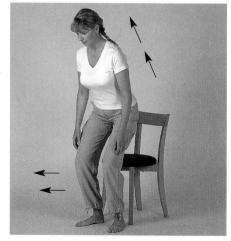

2 As she stands she has managed to keep the correct alignment between her head, neck and back.

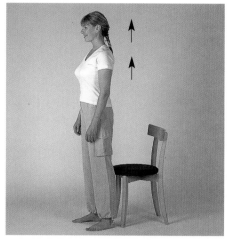

3 Having hinged from the hip, sending her knees forwards and away over her feet, she is now properly upright.

REACHING AND HANDLING

It is impossible to avoid two basic movements, reaching and handling. Yet how many of us know how to do them properly, according to the Alexander technique? Reaching means keeping the alignment between the head, neck and back, whether you are low down or standing up. If you are indeed squatting, it is important that you allow your hand to lead your movement. Let everything else follow behind.

HANDLING

▲ *See how the model's weight is balanced over the feet, and how she is allowing her hand to lead her wrist and arm.*

▲ *Here, the legs are straight and the head is pulled back, causing a lot of strain on the neck, and the shoulders are tense.*

▲ *See how the arms remain well connected to the shoulder blades and back, with no tension in the arms and wrists.*

GOING UP ON TIPTOES

When going on tiptoes correctly, the weight that is placed on the middle of the feet when standing is placed on the balls of the feet, as the head leads the body forwards and upwards. It is important to maintain the alignment between the head, the neck and the back. The breath is not held, and the eyes are alert.

▲ *Look at how this model is going on tiptoes to enable her hand to lead her arm to close the window.*

▲ *Note how the model is well poised and correctly aligned. There is no undue stress on the body.*

▲ *Here the head contraction is severe. The model is holding his breath, causing unnecessary tension in the body.*

"MONKEY" OR BENDING

The position known as the "monkey" enables us to move with more flexibility in our daily activities. It is a useful means of moving from standing to sitting or squatting, as well as helping with lifting, picking things up, working at a desk, washing, ironing, and participating in sports such as skiing and golf. The "monkey" respects the relationship between the head, neck and back.

THE POSITION

The "monkey" position might sound tricky, but it really is not. Try it slowly, see how it works, then try it again at a more natural speed. It basically involves the head moving forwards and up, and then the knees moving forwards and away over the feet to counterbalance the bottom going back over the heels, enabling the arms to move freely. It is also important to remember that when you go into "monkey" you must review your primary directions. What is more, stay alert at all times, and avoid fixing your gaze or holding your breath. Such moves will quickly undermine the marvellous effects of the "monkey".

To be more precise then, stand with your legs hip-width apart, with the feet slightly turned outwards. Your weight should be evenly distributed, neither too far forwards nor too far back on your feet. To start going into the "monkey", allow the knees to bend slightly over your feet as you tilt forwards from your hip joints, making sure your head, your neck and your back are aligned. Avoid collapsing over yourself!

One final point is to make sure you think of widening and lengthening your back as you widen across the shoulder girdle, to allow free movement and your arms to hang freely. This extra tip will ensure you enjoy the full effect of "the monkey".

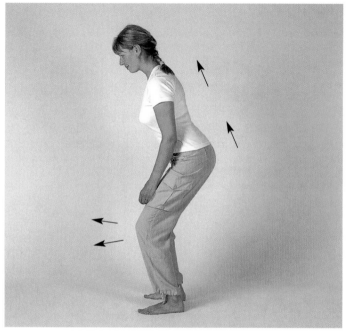

▲ *This model is in the correct "monkey" position. Her head, her neck and her back are aligned. Her knees are bent forward and away from her hips.*

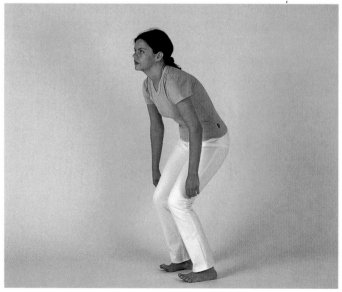

▲ *When going into the "monkey" avoid retracting the head back and down into the spine. Note how the model has rounded her shoulders and pulled in her knees.*

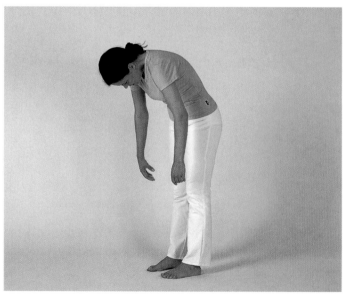

▲ *Here the model is not bending her knees as she bends forwards. Her back is collapsed over her body, and her legs are straight and braced.*

EVERYDAY SITUATIONS

In everyday situations it is important to pause before reacting, to make sure you are so positioned that you do not misuse yourself. The more aware you are, the more likely you will encourage muscular release through your whole system. Equally, the more at peace you are, the easier it is to apply the principles of the Alexander technique. The following excellent examples show how the "monkey" can keep you healthy.

▲ *Note how the model's back is correctly aligned, keeping to the head-neck-back principle. See how she is using her joints and allowing her widening arms to handle the dish.*

▲ *How things can go wrong. Here the model has started pulling her head back. Also, her back is rounded, her legs are braced and her arms have become much too tense.*

▲ *In this highly incorrect stance, the man is collapsing from his waist down as he begins works in the garden. His shoulders are far too rounded, and his head is being pulled back.*

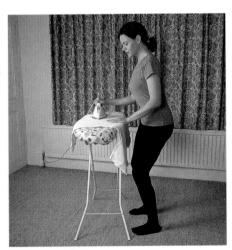

▲ *In this correct procedure, the model is neatly poised and balanced, and she is well aligned to begin her ironing. Her hand, wrist and arm are also free as she holds the iron. The other crucial point to note is how she is widening across her upper arms. It is clear that she looks balanced and feels alert.*

▲ *See how the model is using the whole of his back quite correctly. He is sensibly allowing his weight to come back on to his heels, and his knees go forwards and away over his feet.*

▲ *An example of how not to do it. Here he is completely out of alignment. You can sense it is not right, but why? He is actually pulling his head back, rounding the back, and holding in the arms. This position is entirely the result of bad habits. Without the Alexander technique, he would never know how to right this.*

"LUNGE MONKEY"

The "lunge monkey" is similar to the "monkey" because the knees go forwards and away, and the torso tilts slightly forwards from the hip joints. Also, one foot is placed behind the other, and the legs are placed hip-width apart, enabling you to balance the upper part of your body on to the forward or the back leg whenever the need arises. In this way, your weight is placed forwards or backwards according to your activity.

BENDING

The "lunge monkey" is extremely useful when you need to lift something heavy from the floor; when you need to move an object from one side of a surface to another, for example during cooking; or when you need to push or pull something rather heavy into place.

When you adapt the "lunge monkey" it is important to remember to keep your head, your neck and your back correctly aligned. The legs must be hip-width apart, with the arms hanging freely on either side of your torso.

Also, allow your weight to move to the right on to the right foot (or to the left, as the situation demands). If moving to the left, reverse the instructions.

▲ *See how the model has collapsed badly from the waist down. Her shoulders are rounded, the legs are straight and the knees are braced, causing tension.*

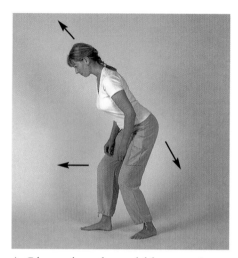

▲ *Observe how the model has gone into the "lunge monkey". Her head, neck and back are neatly aligned, and her knees are going forward away from her hips.*

▲ *Note how the model has completely lost the correct alignment with her back as she squats. Her head has dropped, and her shoulders are hunched and rounded. Furthermore, she looks ill at ease and uncomfortable. There is no poise or grace. This position is definitely one to avoid.*

▲ *In this correct procedure, observe how the model's head, neck and back are correctly aligned. Her shoulders are widening across her upper arms. She looks well balanced, and fully in control of her movements. Also note how her heels are tucked in under the bottom. The position is also easy to get into.*

SQUATTING

In Western societies most people find it difficult to squat in their everyday lives. Young children have very little difficulty in doing so, but as we grow older we lose the necessary flexibility to squat as our joints become less mobile.

A low "monkey" or semi-squat is the best way that an Alexander teacher can re-introduce a student to squatting over a series of lessons. To squat, follow the same guidelines as for the "monkey", but with a wider stance. Remember to maintain the alignment between the head, the neck and the back, and to allow the joints in the hips, the knees and the ankles to be free. As you go into a deeper squat you might find that your heels come off the ground. This does not present a problem as far as the technique is concerned, so long as you keep your balance. As a general rule, go only as far as you feel comfortable.

THE TECHNIQUE IN THE HOME

The key point to note about the Alexander technique is that it is not an abstract theory that you can apply when the mood takes you. It is a specific, practical everyday guide that will help you enormously whether you are bending, squatting, lifting or carrying. It gives you terrific control whatever you are doing, injecting extra confidence that will keep you alert and relaxed.

BENDING

▲ *Note how the model is tilted forwards to get a greater range of movement. His arms are free, supported by his back.*

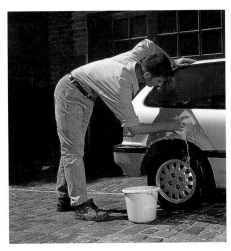

▲ *Now he is incorrectly bending forwards from the waist. His legs are braced, and his head is pulled back.*

▲ *Here the model has aligned herself nicely to make the bed. Her legs are bent, creating a greater range of movement.*

SQUATTING

▲ *This model is lunge squatting to brush up dirt from the floor. She has maintained her good use, giving herself a maximum range of movement. She looks good and feels good.*

▲ *Here, in an incorrect example of how you should sweep the floor, the model is badly restricting his range of movement. He is quite clearly unbalanced, and feels totally uncomfortable.*

▲ *Note how this man is squatting sensibly to plant a rose bush in his garden. By placing himself at the same level as the rose, he is allowing himself a greater range of movement.*

LIFTING AND CARRYING

A lot of back pain is the result of lifting heavy weights. To avoid back strain, stand near to the load by placing your feet either side of it, and maintain the alignment between head, neck and back. Go into the "monkey" or "lunge monkey" and squat. Then bend your arms so that your elbows are close to your body. Make sure that you widen out across the upper arms, and avoid tension in the arms and wrists.

LIFTING

1 Once you are holding the load as closely to your body as you can, come out of a squat or lunge squat into a "monkey" before standing.

2 Lift the weight in a flowing action, that does not jar or suddenly pull against the back. If the weight proves too heavy, it is easy to bend and put it down.

3 To place the load back on the ground, reverse the process and apply the same principles, making sure that your head, neck and back are aligned.

CARRYING

▲ *Here the model is carrying all her shopping bags in one hand, creating an imbalance as she is pulled down to the left. She is raising her right shoulder in an attempt to support her handbag.*

▲ *This model is carrying her shopping bags sensibly and correctly so that they are evenly distributed on both sides. She is well balanced and able to walk freely. She looks content.*

▲ *Look at the excellent way this mother is carrying her child. Her weight is evenly distributed and she is holding the child close to her body, firmly supporting his upper and lower body.*

DAILY ROUTINES

The most surprising point about the Alexander technique is that it is not just for big, set piece movements such as lifting heavy weights, when doing it incorrectly can obviously lead to back problems. The technique even extends to the minutiae of life, routines that we completely take for granted, such as eating, drinking, and driving. If you had always wondered how they should be done, read on. These tips will make all the difference.

EATING AND DRINKING

If you are standing upright while you are drinking remember that you still need to be fully alert at all times. Therefore, make sure that you do not fix your gaze rigidly and thereby lose all communication and contact with the outside world. You also need to ensure that your head leads you away from your heels (see the section on Standing for further guidance). You will find that your shoulder girdle brings mobility to your arms, and that the pelvis provides stability which simultaneously facilitates mobility in your legs.

The very same principles also apply to eating. Whether you are going to eat something from your hand or use a fork, it is all too easy to forget your posture completely. Remember that you should not totally focus on the matter in hand, but that you must also consider your stance, alertness and poise.

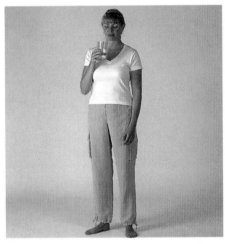

▲ *Avoid gripping or clutching your glass. Be aware of the connection with your arm, which links to your back and then into your heels. As you raise the cup to your lips, bring your weight back on to the heels, so as not to pull in your lower back. Also, bring the glass to the lips, rather than leaning down into it.*

▲ *Take some time to consider how you are seated at the table and then bring the food up to your mouth, rather than the reverse. Your feet should be correctly positioned on the floor. You should also be aware of both your sitting bones, and how your back should be lengthening and widening. This position also aids digestion.*

DRIVING

Most of the problems experienced by drivers are due to fixed postures, long journeys and poor seating support.

Too many people who spend huge amounts of time driving find themselves constricted by the position of the steering wheel and the pedals. Such a cramped environment is bound to lead to stress and strain on the back, and equally on the arms and legs.

When choosing a car take time to see whether the seat is firm and supportive. If you already own a car and it does not have a lumbar support adjustment, you can use a wedge-shaped cushion to give you adequate support in the lumbar area and the pelvis. It makes a vital difference.

▲ *You should be able to reach the pedals quite easily. A wedge-shaped cushion is extremely useful to avoid a poor, slumping position.*

▲ *See how the model is badly collapsing forward, how the neck is being strained and the arms are rigidly tense. Such a position will cause lots of discomfort.*

OFFICE WORK

Before reading it is important to spend some time considering exactly how you are going to sit in order to avoid badly slumping, which is very easy to do, especially in a big old comfortable armchair. Once you get drawn into what you are reading it is virtually certain that you will completely forget about your posture. It is vitally important that you do not end up creating all kinds of stresses and strains in your body.

READING AND WRITING

When you are sitting at your desk or at a table, it is important that you adjust your chair in such a way that your lower arms and hands can be placed on the surface of your table or desk at a right angle. If your chair is too close you are likely to end up lifting your shoulders to adjust your arms. If your chair is too high, you will probably find that you start slumping. You must also avoid crossing your legs, and do make sure that your feet remain comfortably flat on the floor.

▲ *A useful trick when reading is to use a sloping board to avoid slumping over your desk or table.*

▲ *Note how the model is holding her body badly with her arm, and how her legs are folded, offering no support.*

▲ *Keep the alignment between your head, your neck and your back.*

▲ *This model is firmly gripping the pen, causing tension in her wrist and hand.*

▲ *Here the model is tensing her wrist, hand and arm, restricting her movement.*

DESKWORK

An increasing number of people are complaining of neck and shoulder tension, wrist problems and back pain resulting from their working environment. Some cases are directly linked to badly designed furniture, awkward or unfavourable sitting positions and immobility. In other instances, although chairs and work surfaces are good, the posture is poor. You must therefore remember your primary directions: the head, neck and back should be aligned, and the head should be lengthening away from the sitting bones.

▲ *How not to do it. See how the model is slumping badly, causing unnecessary tension in the spine, so weakening the muscles surrounding the torso.*

▲ *Here the spine is correctly aligned, and the head is poised gracefully above the neck. The feet are well placed on the floor, nicely apart.*

OFFICE EQUIPMENT

The office is not what it used to be. It now offers amazing improvements in high-tech equipment, but also plenty of opportunities for repetitive strain injury, aching backs and tense necks. The temptation is to spend far too long in one awkward position. So always be aware of what you are doing, how long it will take, and the best position you need to adopt. Such awareness makes all the difference between a good and bad day.

MOBILE PHONE USE

OBSERVE YOURSELF WHEN THE TELEPHONE RINGS
Do you snatch and grab it? Or do you try to give yourself some time before you pick up the receiver? Next time the telephone rings, stop and go over your primary directions. Make sure that you bring the receiver up to your ear rather than suddenly leaning down towards it, thus compromising your position.

▲ *Here the model is pulling her head down wrongly towards her mobile phone to talk, and slouching.*

▲ *In this example the model has maintained her balance throughout her body. She looks poised and relaxed.*

WORKING AT A COMPUTER

▲ *If you are working at a computer or portable computer, use your eyes to look down towards it. Avoid lurching at the neck as you will lose the correct alignment with your back.*

▲ *Here the model badly collapses over her computer. She has lost the correct alignment between her hands, her wrists and her lower arms. Her shoulders are far too hunched.*

▲ *Here the model is incorrectly holding in her wrist, arms and shoulders, causing unnecessary strain and discomfort. She will soon feel very uncomfortable, and have to adopt a new position.*

T'AI CHI

Originating in China, t'ai chi has its roots in Taoist philosophy. Its movements gently tone and strengthen the organs and muscles, improve circulation and posture, and relax both mind and body. Its name translates as "supreme ultimate fist", but this is not its true meaning. "Strength within softness" and "moving harmony" come closer to expressing the spirit of t'ai chi. Unlike the hard martial arts, which rely on force and speed, t'ai chi is soft or internal. Its emphasis lies in using the yielding aspect of nature to overcome obstacles – like the waterfall that eventually wears away the hard rock beneath. T'ai chi teaches patience and relaxation, and fosters an understanding of the co-ordination of mind, body and spirit. It is the perfect antidote to the stresses and strains of today's modern lifestyle.

T'AI CHI FOR HEALTH OR SELF DEFENCE

If you simply want to go out and strike a pose, jumping about like Bruce Lee, t'ai chi is not for you. It is a very serious, highly regarded ancient technique that has two major qualities. It improves your health, and teaches you how to overcome stronger hostile forces when you are under attack. The most amazing part of t'ai chi is the way its movements are almost balletic.

THE BENEFITS OF T'AI CHI

Although t'ai chi can eventually be used in self-defence, and most classes do incorporate some of its practical applications, it is initially practised mainly for its health-giving benefits. It is particularly useful for increasing alertness and body awareness, and for developing concentration and sensitivity. It helps with balance and posture, and enhances a sense of "groundedness". However, all the postures can also be used when defending yourself against an attack by an opponent. Its gentleness and subtlety do not preclude its use as a very effective form of self-defence.

It is not easy to separate the physical and mental aspects of t'ai chi, as they are closely interrelated. In Chinese medicine, the interdependence of mind, body and spirit is seen as integral to well-being.

▲ *The ancient art of t'ai chi instills enormous grace and confidence.*

THE THEORY OF T'AI CHI

Like music, t'ai chi cannot be appreciated purely on an intellectual level. It also has an enormous spiritual side, and when you watch any highly experienced t'ai chi practitioners you will see how they are almost in a kind of trance, in a separate world where they cannot be touched. Correctly done, it is quite hypnotic.

For now, we must look at some of the concepts that are fundamental to the martial arts, as well as to medicine and philosophy. Although these disciplines are all treated quite separately by those in the West, they are all inseparable in the Eastern view. From thousands of years of close observation of patterns of energy, the Chinese successfully evolved a way of life that actually ropes all three ingredients together.

CHI

Chi is the prime driving force of human life, the spark behind thought, creativity and growth which maintains and nurtures us. It can be felt as movement of energy in the body, like the ceaseless flow of an electrical current. Chi flows through the body along channels called meridians.

THE TAN TIEN

The Chi is stored in the Tan Tien. This is an area about the size of a golf ball, located four finger-widths below the navel, and about one-third of the way from the front to the back of the body. It is the centre of gravity of the body, and in t'ai chi all movement emanates from it. Try to let the breath and the mind sink to the Tan Tien.

YIN AND YANG

Yin and Yang describe the complementary yet opposing forces of nature. Their relationship has a harmony and balance: both Yin and Yang are necessary, are constantly moving and balancing each other, and this interaction creates Chi. The Chinese observed that when the balance of Yin and Yang is disrupted so too will be the body's Chi, leading to ill health.

◀ *One of the key requirements for t'ai chi is excellent balance.*

WARM-UP EXERCISES

Perform these exercises slowly and gently, with the mind and the breath focused in the Tan Tien. Notice any differences between the right and left sides of your body, and between the upper and lower parts. The object is gradually to enter the world of t'ai chi, and to warm up all your muscles so that you do not get any strains. The more you warm up, the better your technique will be. The movements will flow like a stream.

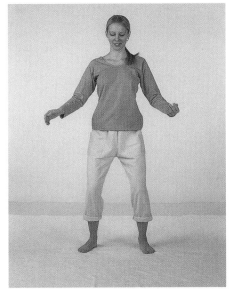

1 Gently shake out any tension in your wrists and hands. Gradually work up to include your shoulders. This is especially useful after long periods at work.

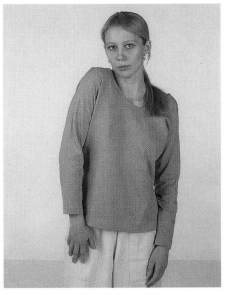

2 Make increasing circles with one shoulder. Change direction and decrease the size of the circles. Repeat for the other shoulder. Rotate both shoulders.

3 Place both hands lightly on your hips. Keeping your head up, begin by spiralling your hips slowly outwards, feeling for any restriction, tightness or lack of ease.

4 Place your palms lightly on your upper kneecaps. Feel the Chi from your palms radiating deep into your knee joints. Circle your knees clockwise.

5 Turn out your left foot and step forward with your right. Raise your toes. Drop forward, keeping your right leg straight. Hold then repeat on the left.

6 Stand on one leg while gently shaking tension from the other leg. Do this for 10–15 seconds and then repeat with the other leg. Repeat several times.

yang-style short form

yang-style short form

After completing all the warm-up exercises, and having a moment or so quietly standing to see if you can find a point of equilibrium, a few minutes of t'ai chi walking may now follow. This is known as walking with an "empty step", rather in the manner of a cat tentatively putting out its paw before committing its full weight on to the front leg.

In fact, it is well worth studying an adult cat that is gracefully walking, or gliding forwards when it has spotted its prey. Its whole movement is one of ceaseless flow, of elegant, unforced movement when every part of its body seems to be an extension of another part, and nothing is hurried or rushed.

As you progress through the form, use the following pages as an aide-mémoire for your practice, especially for the transitions from one posture to the next. Remember to keep your movements slow and smooth, like clouds drifting gently by on a summer's day, and relax. If you worry about this new exercise, you will not succeed.

In many ways that is the key problem for the new Western practitioner. Doing these exercises initially means that you will be highly self-conscious because there is nothing like it in our culture. Yet gradually, after a few lessons, and above all after watching expert t'ai chi practitioners, it becomes clear that this is something which you can do successfully, and without having to worry about what you look like.

Once you launch into the first few movements, the rest follow, and you find that an awkward state of self-consciousness is quickly replaced by an inner calm as you become less aware of the outside world, and more aware of inner ones. The key to t'ai chi is being able to make seamless flowing moves, with the emphasis not so much on specific poses as on the linking means of getting there. Ultimately, you too may be able to go into a park in the early morning, as they do in the East, and carry out t'ai chi utterly unselfconsciously, gaining spiritual refreshment.

ATTENTION, PREPARATION AND BEGINNING

1 Stand in a relaxed and upright posture, feet pointing diagonally outwards, making a right angle. Distribute your weight evenly through your body.

2 Bend your right knee and sink all your weight down through your right leg into the foot, without leaning across. Then move the "empty" left leg a shoulder-width away, with the toes pointing straight ahead.

3 Transfer 70% of your weight to your left leg, simultaneously turning your waist and therefore your whole body diagonally to the right.

4 Keeping 70% of your weight in your left leg, turn your whole body back to face the front. Bring your right foot around to the front as your waist moves. Your feet should be shoulder-width apart and parallel. Your hands also move with your body, the palms facing the ground as if resting on a cushion of air.

5 Relax your wrists and let your arms float up and away from your body. When your hands reach shoulder height, gently extend the fingertips.

6 Draw your hands back in towards your body by dropping the elbows. This penultimate posture is one of relaxed, graceful ease.

WARD OFF LEFT

7 In the final position, relax your wrists and let your hands float down the front of your body, just in front of and below the waist. The bulk of your weight is in your left leg.

1 Sink all your weight on to your left leg, and turn your body to the right, pivoting on your right heel. Imagine you are holding a large ball, with the right hand in front of the chest.

2 Sink all your weight on to your right leg, as if carrying the ball forward. Pick up your "empty" (weightless) left leg and step forwards, toes pointing to the front.

WARD OFF RIGHT

3 Turn the waist to the left, facing the front. Your left hand comes up, palm facing the chest, and the right floats down with 70% of your weight now on your left leg, as your right moves around.

1 Sink all your weight into your left leg. Turn to the right: the left palm turns face down, the right palm turns up as if both hands are again holding the large ball. The heels should be slightly apart.

2 Turn your waist to face the right-hand side and shift 70% of your weight on to your right foot, and turn your left foot to 45°. Raise your right arm so that the palm faces your chest.

ROLL BACK, PRESS AND PUSH

This posture, together with the one that follows it, "Single Whip", is also known as "Grasping the Sparrow's Tail".

1 Turn your body to the right. Point the fingertips of your right hand to the sky in a relaxed way. Your left arm moves horizontally with the fingertips almost touching the right elbow, palm facing the body. Your weight remains 70% on the right leg, 30% on the left.

2 As you turn your waist to the left, begin to shift weight to your left leg. Follow the movement of the body with your arms until your right hand is horizontal. Your left hand begins to flow down with the movement of your waist. Your weight settles on your left leg.

3 Turn your waist back to the right and let your left arm follow this movement. All your weight remains in the left leg. Bring your palm gradually across to rest against your right wrist, opposite the centre of your chest.

4 Press forward, keeping the hands in full contact. Shift 70% of your weight into your front (right) leg. Ensure that your heels are still shoulder-width apart, and that the right foot is pointing forward, and the left foot at 45°.

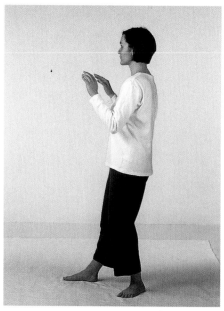

5 Separate your hands and sink all your weight back into your left foot. Your fingertips are now shoulder-width apart at shoulder height.

6 Move your weight forward 70% into your right leg. Your arms and hands keep the same position.

SINGLE WHIP

1 As your weight shifts back into the left leg, leave your fingers where they are in space, effectively straightening – but not locking – your arms. The palms now face down towards the ground.

2 Turn your whole body to the left and shift all your weight into your left leg. Your right heel remains on the ground while your toes turn through 120°, following the body round.

3 Sink your weight back into your right leg. Bring your left hand under the right to hold the imaginary ball in front of your body. Then form a "hook" with the fingers and thumb of your right hand.

LIFTING HANDS

4 Ensure all your weight is in your right leg. Bend the right knee and turn your body to the left, sending out the hook in line with, and at the same height as, your shoulder. Take an "empty" (weightless) shoulder-width step with your left foot.

5 Shift 70% of your weight on to your left leg, adjusting your right foot to 45°. Ensure that your heels are shoulder-width apart, your left hand in line with your left shoulder and your right hand hook at 90° to the rest of your body.

1 Place your weight on the left leg, open your hands and palms inwards, the left palm facing the right elbow. Pick up your empty right foot and place down the heel without weight, directly in front of the left heel.

2 Turn your waist to the left, your hands following the movement of your waist. Bring your right toe by your left heel, touching the ground but weightless.

3 Take an "empty" step to the right, and transfer 70% of the weight to the right foot. The left palm ends up opposite your inner right elbow. Your right arm is curved, guarding the groin, and your feet are at right angles to each other.

1 Drop all your weight into your right leg. Turn your waist to the left. As your right hand begins to rise, your left hand sweeps down in front of your left thigh.

2 Pick up your "empty" left leg and touch the toe on the ground but without shifting your weight. Bring your right hand up to guard your temple, turning to face diagonally outwards as it moves up. Your left hand floats down.

3 As you turn your waist to the left, your right hand follows and sweeps down; your left palm opens outwards.

4 As you turn your waist to the right, your right hand continues in a circle. Your left hand follows the move of your waist and faces down in front of your chest. As your waist returns to the centre, the right hand is level with the shoulder.

PLAY GUITAR. BRUSH LEFT KNEE AND PUSH

This posture is also known as "Strumming the Lute".

5 Take a shoulder-width step with your left foot, heel first. Move 70% of your weight into your left leg as your left hand brushes down across it. Meanwhile, your right hand follows a concave curve into the centre to finish by the mouth.

1 As all your weight sinks into your left leg, adjust the "empty" right foot by drawing it slightly nearer the left foot, toe first. Bring your weight into the right foot. Your left leg and arm float up simultaneously — imagine a thread connecting them.

2 Turn to the right, dropping your right hand down while your left hand follows the movement of your waist to the centre of your chest, palm facing down. As your waist returns to the front, your right hand comes to shoulder height.

STEP FORWARD, DEFLECT, INTERCEPT AND PUNCH

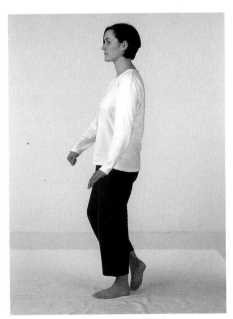

3 Take a shoulder-width step with your left foot, heel first. Move 70% of your weight into your left leg as your left hand brushes down across it. Your right hand follows a curve ending by your mouth.

1 Turn your waist 45° to the left and sink all your weight into your right foot. As the weight shifts back, lift the toes of your left foot and pivot 45° on the heel. Bring your hands down by your left leg.

2 Shift all your weight into your left leg. Form a loose fist with your right hand, but check that the fingers are not wrapped around the thumb. The right toes are behind the left heel.

3 Arc both of your hands and your right foot simultaneously towards the centre line, as your waist turns around to the right. The right foot now lands "empty", in line with the left instep. Check that your position is correct. Note that your left thumb should roughly be in line with your left eye.

4 Continue to turn your waist to the right, bringing the right fist palm upwards to rest on the right hip. You should now commence transferring all your weight on to your right foot. Your eyes should skim across the tops of your left fingers.

5 Place your left foot a shoulder width from the right foot. Shift 70% of your weight to your left leg and bring your right fist forward as if to punch, rotating it through a quarter turn in a corkscrew motion. Then bring your left arm across your body, with the palm facing your inner right elbow.

WITHDRAW AND PUSH. CROSSING HANDS

1 As you turn your waist to the left, your right arm follows your body to an angle of 45° and the fist opens up. Meanwhile, cup your left hand gracefully a couple of inches under your right elbow, as if supporting it.

2 Draw your right arm across your left palm as your weight sinks into your right foot, and your waist turns to the right.

3 Bring your waist back to the centre and turn both palms to face the front.

4 Move your weight forward 70% on to your left leg. Your hands remain at shoulder width and shoulder height.

5 Turn your waist to the right and simultaneously sink all your weight into your left leg. Draw your hands in towards your chest in a softly inverted "V" shape, as if holding the top of a ball.

6 As your whole weight shifts into your right leg, turn your waist to the right. Your left toes turn with your waist and your right hand travels out both diagonally and upwards.

EMBRACE TIGER, RETURN TO MOUNTAIN

7 Sink all your weight back into your left leg. Your left hand now travels out diagonally. Though the position might seem slightly awkward and lopsided, it actually flows naturally into the final step.

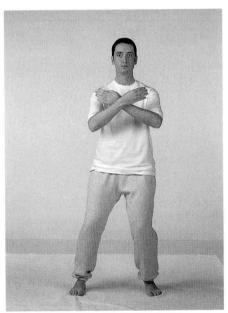

8 Finally, bring your right foot shoulder-width away from and parallel to the left, but maintain your weight 70% in the left leg. Both hands circle down and up, stopping opposite your chest, palms facing the body. The wrists are touching, with the right wrist outside the left one. Hold this stance for a few seconds.

1 Keeping all your weight in your left leg, turn your waist to the right. Open your hands outwards. Step diagonally back with your right foot. Move your weight 70% on to your right foot. As your waist completes its turn, move your left hand so that the fingertips are in line with your left shoulder, palm facing forward.

ROLL BACK, PRESS AND PUSH: SINGLE WHIP

PUNCH UNDER ELBOW

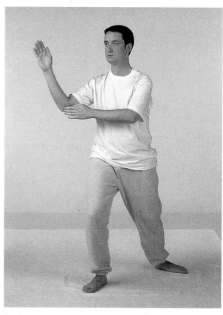

2 As you turn your waist slightly to the right, allow your left hand to come across so that the fingertips point to your right elbow. Meanwhile, your right hand travels upwards so that the fingertips point heavenward.

I Now repeat the sequence in "Roll Back, Press and Push". This time, perform this section from one diagonal corner to the other rather than from one side to the other. This picture shows your position at the end of the sequence.

I Sink all your weight back on to your right foot. Turn your waist 45° to the left, lifting the left toes and letting your left foot and both arms pivot 45° to the left.

2 Lower your left foot, gradually shifting your weight forward into it. When all your weight is on your left foot, step forward with your right foot so that the heel is in line with your left instep.

3 Rotate your upper body 90° to the left. Your arms follow this waist movement, so that the hook (your right hand) is now out in front level with your right shoulder, and your left hand is level with your face at 90° to the front. Your weight is in your left leg.

4 Transfer all your weight to your right leg, turning your waist to the right and letting your left hand move down, then up, until the fingers are in line with your left shoulder. Your left arm and leg move around simultaneously. Rest your left heel on the ground without any weight.

STEP BACK TO REPULSE THE MONKEY

1 As you turn your waist further to the right, your right hand opens and moves down by your hip, then floats up to shoulder height. The palm of your left hand turns over to face down.

2 Step back with your left foot as your waist turns to the left. Your right hand travels forward, palm facing down, while your left hand travels down towards the left hip with the palm facing up.

3 The right toes also straighten as the waist turns. As you continue to turn to the left, your left hand floats up to shoulder height, while your right hand comes forward, palm facing down.

STEP BACK TO REPULSE THE MONKEY (RIGHT). DIAGONAL FLYING

1 Turn your waist to the right, step back with your right foot and let your left hand travel forward, palm down. Your right hand moves down to rest on your hip, palm up. Your left foot turns to face the front as the waist moves. Your right hand now comes up to shoulder height.

2 With your weight on your left foot, turn your waist to the left. Turn your right hand palm upwards as it travels round in front of your waist, while your left hand, palm downwards, comes in front of your chest. Your hands are now holding an imaginary ball in front of you.

3 Turn your waist 90° to the right, maintaining the position of your arms and hands in front of your chest, as if carrying the ball.

WAVING HANDS IN CLOUDS (RIGHT, LEFT, RIGHT)

4 Stepping with your right foot, turn a further 135° to the right, and then transfer 70% of your weight into the right foot. Your waist also turns to the right and your right hand moves with it, travelling to shoulder height, arm extended and facing diagonally upwards. Your left hand moves simultaneously to just outside your left thigh, palm facing down.

1 Bring all your weight on to your right foot. Turn your waist to the right and move your left hand across near your right hip. At the same time, your right hand turns palm downwards at shoulder height. Raise your left foot and move it forward until the left heel is now level and in line with the right.

2 As your waist turns to the front, move your right hand to face it and your left hand to face your chest. The right toes swivel round to face forwards so that your feet are now shoulder-width apart.

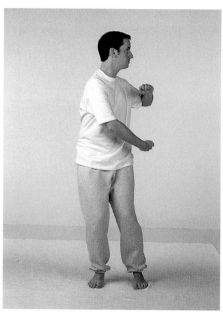

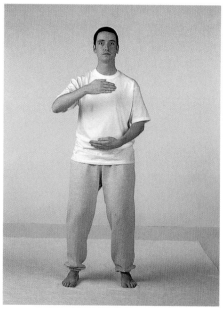

3 As your waist turns to the left, turn your palms towards each other, as if holding a large ball to the left of your body. All your weight is in your left leg and your right foot steps in to about half shoulder width.

4 Turn your waist back to the centre. Your hands again change position, the left hand descending to be opposite and facing your waist, and the right hand opposite and facing your chest.

5 Turn your waist to the right, your hands holding the imaginary ball, with the right hand uppermost, palm facing down, and the left hand below it, palm facing up. When all your weight is on your right foot, step back to shoulder-width apart.

WAVING HANDS IN CLOUDS (LEFT, RIGHT, LEFT). THE WHIP

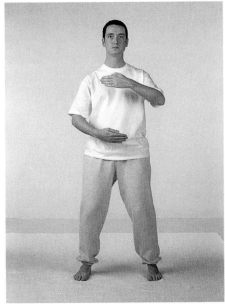

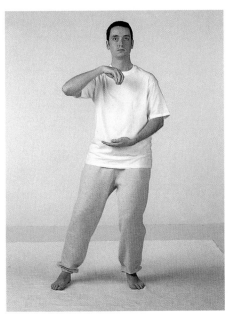

1 Turn your waist back to the centre, bringing your right hand down to face your waist and your left hand up to face your chest. Repeat Steps 3, 4 and 5, then Steps 2 and 3 from "Waving Hands in Clouds, Right, Left, Right".

2 Turn your waist back to the centre and form a hook with your right hand, as it moves in level with your chest, directly above your left hand. It is located in front of your waist, palm upwards.

3 Step forward with your right foot. Turn your waist to the right, then to the left as you transfer your weight to your right foot, sending out the hook at 90° to the front of your body.

GOLDEN ROOSTER STANDS ON ONE LEG (LEFT). SQUATTING SINGLE WHIP

4 Continue turning your waist around towards the left, and then step with your left foot to about shoulder-width apart, with your left palm now facing your left shoulder.

5 Shift your weight 70% on to your left foot, turning away your left palm at shoulder height, and turning the right toes to 45°.

1 Sink all your weight into your left leg, turning your left hand over so that the palm faces upwards. Simultaneously turn out the right toes. This is a nicely balanced, elegant position.

2 Move your weight across into your right leg, bringing your left palm in towards your chest. The left toes turn 45° to the right.

3 Sink down into your right leg, keeping your back straight. Move your waist to the left, brush open your left knee with your left arm and turn your left toes out 90° to the left.

4 Transfer all your weight into your left leg. Open the right hand hook, lower the hand then bring it up in front of your chest. Raise your right leg as your weight shifts forward into your left leg, so that your right thigh becomes parallel with the ground. Bend your left knee.

GOLDEN ROOSTER STANDS ON ONE LEG (RIGHT). SEPARATE RIGHT FOOT

1 Place your right foot down and move all your weight on to it. As your weight sinks into your right leg, your right hand descends to rest on a cushion of air by your right thigh. Your left arm and left leg simultaneously move up to form a mirror image of the previous posture.

2 Step out with your "empty" left foot diagonally to the left, and form a ward-off position with your left arm horizontally positioned across your body, opposite your chest.

3 Shift all your weight into your left leg, bringing your right arm up to cross in front of your left arm, with the wrists touching. Bring your right toe to your left heel. Turn your wrists, maintaining skin contact as you do so, so that your left arm now crosses your right.

SEPARATE LEFT FOOT.
BRUSH LEFT KNEE
AND PUSH

4 Then turn your hands away from your body, and open them out in a fan-like action. Your eyes should be level with the tips of your fingers.

5 Keep your left hand level with your left ear, palm facing away. Open out your right hand to the corner, below shoulder height, and simultaneously kick gently with your right leg, to knee height. You should be so balanced that you do not fall over.

1 Keeping all your weight in your left leg, turn to the left-hand corner, forming a ward-off position with your right arm.

2 Turn your waist to the right and step to the right with your right leg. As you transfer weight into it, bring your left hand up outside the right so that the wrists meet. The left toes come up to meet the right heel.

3 Open out your hands, the right hand this time remaining level with the head and the left hand travelling to below shoulder height. The left foot follows, kicking gently to the corner.

4 Turn your waist and left knee to the front again. Take a shoulder-width "empty" step with your left leg, toes pointing in the forward direction.

NEEDLES AT SEA BOTTOM

5 Brush your left hand across and above the front of your left leg, to just outside your left thigh. Your right hand curves in, fingertips forward, to finish with the fingers in line with your mouth.

1 Move all your weight into your left leg. Pick up your empty right foot and make a small adjustment step forward.

2 Place your right toes down, then bring your left hand across your body so that the left palm rests above your right wrist. At the same time, pick up your left leg and place the toes down.

IRON FAN PENETRATES BACK. TURN BODY, CHOP AND PUSH

3 Move your right arm forwards and diagonally downwards with your body, then vertically downwards. The arm remains in line with your right leg, and all your weight remains in your right leg.

1 Your weight remains in your right leg and both hands assume a ward-off position. Take a shoulder-width step with the left foot. Shift your weight 70% into your left leg and turn your hands outwards, the left hand by your chest, the right guarding your temple.

2 Turn your waist to the right and sink all your weight back into your right leg, bringing your left toes round. Bring your left hand up, turning the palm diagonally outwards to guard the temple. At the same time, form a loose fist with your right hand, palm facing downwards.

3 Sink all your weight back on to your left leg. As you transfer the weight back, the fist descends in front of your groin.

4 Step to shoulder width with your right foot. Your right arm pivots at the elbow and your left arm folds across so that the left hand faces the right inner elbow. All your weight remains on your left leg. You are nicely balanced as shown above.

5 Transfer your weight forward 70% into your right leg. Your left arm pushes forward, fingertips in line with your left shoulder, and your right fist descends to your right hip, palm upwards. The left toes are at 45°.

STEP FORWARD, DEFLECT DOWNWARDS, INTERCEPT AND PUNCH, KICK WITH HEEL

1 Sink all your weight into the left leg as your waist turns to the left. Bring the right toe to the left heel. The right hand comes across the body, and the palm faces down by the left hip. The left hand is below the right hand, palm up. Go to "Step Forward, Deflect, Intercept and Punch" and repeat Steps 3, 4 and 5.

2 Sink your weight into your left leg, turning your waist to the right. Cross your wrists, the right outside the left. Sink the weight back into your right leg. Your waist turns left and your left foot pivots on the heel 45° to the left. Shift all your weight forward into your left leg, turning your hands palms outwards.

3 Open your hands out gracefully like a fan, the right hand to below shoulder height, the left hand at head height, palms facing away. Your right foot now comes up from the ground, and the heel kicks diagonally away.

BRUSH RIGHT KNEE AND PUSH. BRUSH LEFT KNEE AND PUNCH DOWN

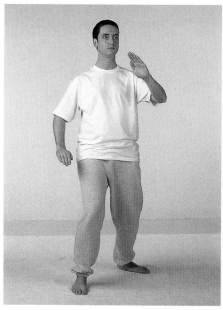

❙ Place your "empty" right foot on the ground, toes forward. Your right hand curves down to rest on a cushion of air outside your right thigh. Your left hand curves forward to push to the centre, fingertips in line with your mouth.

2 Sink back into your left leg, turning your waist to the right, with the palm of your left hand facing towards your body in the Yang-style ward-off position.

3 Transfer your weight forward into your right foot, with your left palm turning so that it faces downwards.

WARD OFF RIGHT. ROLL BACK, PRESS AND PUSH

4 Take a shoulder-width step with your left foot and bring 70% of your weight onto it. Your right hand forms a loose fist, which comes over your hip and punches down the centre. Your left hand brushes your left leg and rests by the left knee.

❙ Sink back into your right leg. Your left hand now assumes a ward-off position, the fingertips of your right hand pointing towards the centre of the left palm. Your right palm faces downwards. Gaze steadily and confidently forwards.

2 Turn your body 45° to the left, pivoting neatly on the left heel. Shift all your weight forward into your left leg. Your left arm should remain in this position, while your right hand now presses smartly down.

FAIR LADY WEAVES SHUTTLES (RIGHT AND LEFT)

3 Step through at shoulder width with your "empty" right foot. As you transfer 70% of your weight into it, your right hand comes up into a ward-off position opposite your chest, with the left fingertips now pointing towards the right palm, left palm downwards. Repeat "Roll Back, Press and Push" and "Single Whip".

1 Transfer your weight to your right leg as you turn your waist to the right, and turn the "empty" left toes through 90°. Bring your left hand across your body and under your elbow. Open the hook of your right hand and lower the right arm, palm turning to face upwards.

2 Sink your weight back into your left leg, turn your waist further to the right and turn out your right foot so the heel is in line with the left instep.

3 Sink your weight into your right leg, drawing your left arm across your right palm, and step at shoulder width to the left corner with your left foot. As you shift your weight forward into your left leg, turn both palms outwards.

4 Transfer your weight into your right foot and turn your waist and left foot to the right as far as possible (135°). Turn your palms to face your body, the right palm by the left elbow.

5 Sink your weight back into your left leg and draw your left arm across your right palm.

FAIR LADY WEAVES SHUTTLES (RIGHT AND LEFT)

6 Turn a further 135° right, to the corner. Step to shoulder width with your right foot, and shift 70% of your weight into it, pushing towards the centre of your mouth with your left hand. Bring the right hand up to guard your forehead, palm facing diagonally.

I Turn to the left, sinking all your weight into your left leg. Pick up your right foot and draw it in. Transfer all your weight to your right foot, then step to the left (45°) with your left foot. Turn your palms in and draw your right arm across the left palm, left arm in a ward-off position.

2 Your left hand then moves up and turns outwards by your head, while the fingers of your right hand come into the centre in line with your mouth. Now repeat the postures described in Steps 4, 5 and 6 of the previous exercise.

WARD OFF LEFT. WARD OFF RIGHT. ROLL BACK, PRESS AND PUSH. SINGLE WHIP

I Sink your weight into your left leg as your waist turns to the left. Both arms come round with the movement of your waist, the left hand lower than the right. The right toes come round to the front.

2 Sink your weight into your right leg as your left hand presses down, palm facing downwards. Take a shoulder-width step with your left foot.

3 Transfer your weight 70% into your left foot. Your left hand comes up in front of your chest. Your right hand floats outside your right thigh. Repeat as in above heading, from "Ward Off Right".

SQUATTING SINGLE WHIP. STEP FORWARD FOR SEVEN STARS RIDE TIGER

1 Repeat the postures described in Steps 1, 2 and 3 of "Golden Rooster Stands on One Leg (Left). Squatting Single Whip", ending by brushing open the left knee.

2 Transfer all your weight into your left leg. The right hand hook opens and the hand descends, then comes up in front of your neck, where it forms a loose fist. At the same time, your left hand rises up to form a loose fist, and connects at the wrist inside your right hand. Move your right toes forward to touch the ground without any weight whatsoever.

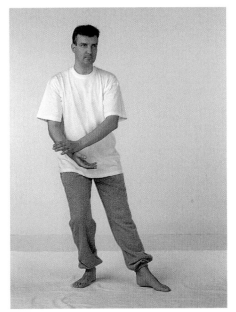

1 Keep your weight in your left leg and step back with your right foot, toes touching the ground first. Sink your weight into it and turn your waist to the right. The fists open and then move down by your right hip, with the wrists still connected.

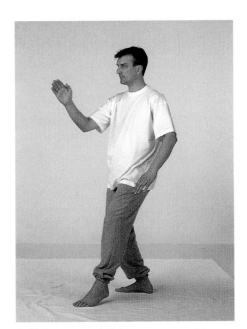

2 Pick up your left leg as your waist turns right, then place your toes down as your waist turns back to the left. Your right hand comes round to the front, fingertips level with your right ear, and your left hand rests by your left thigh.

3 Pick up your left toes, turn your waist to the left corner and place the toes down empty of any weight. Your right palm faces your inner left elbow. Your left hand is at the height of your left shoulder, elbow relaxed.

4 Lift your left toes and swing your waist clockwise, pivoting on the ball of your right foot. Your arms swing to the right with the movement of your waist.

5 Drop your left foot and transfer all your weight into it straight away. Look closely at the photograph above to check how you should be standing.

6 When your arms and waist reach the front (the arms at shoulder height and shoulder width with the palms facing downwards), your right foot lifts up and circles clockwise.

7 After circling, your right leg comes to rest with the upper leg parallel to the ground and the foot comfortably relaxed. Your left leg is bent while the arms are still pointing ahead.

BEND BOW TO SHOOT TIGER. STEP FORWARD, DEFLECT DOWN, INTERCEPT AND PUNCH

1 Turn your waist to the right. Your arms follow your waist, dropping down parallel, and your right foot is placed facing the right corner.

2 As your waist turns to the right, shift the weight into your right leg and circle your arms round to the right. As your waist turns back to the left, raise your arms and circle round with the waist. Form loose fists. Bring the right hand up to the right of your forehead, knuckles facing the right eyebrow. The left hand is at shoulder height.

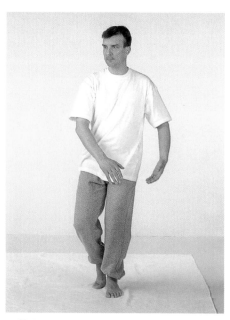

3 Sink your weight into your left leg and pick up your right foot, placing the toes by your left heel. Open the left fist as your arms move across your body following the waist movement.

4 Both hands and your right foot simultaneously arc in towards the centre line, as your waist turns to the right. The right foot lands "empty", completely in line with the left instep.

5 Continue to turn your waist, bringing the right fist palm upwards to rest on your right hip and shifting your weight to the right foot. Step through at shoulder width with your left foot. Shift 70% of your weight to the left and bring your right fist forward to punch in a corkscrew. Your left arm comes across your body.

I Repeat the postures described in "Withdraw and Push. Crossing Hands". Ensure your weight is 70% in your left leg when crossing hands.

2 From crossing the hands, turn both palms down to face the ground as your body now rises up.

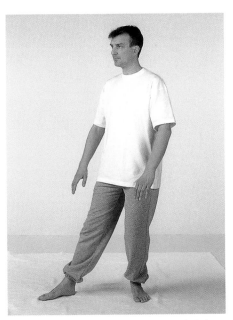

3 Bring all your weight into your left leg, turn your waist to the right and pivot on your left heel, turning the foot out to an angle of 45°.

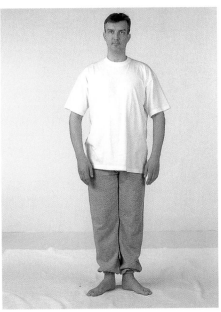

4 Move all your weight into your right leg. Step in with your left foot so that the feet make a right angle. Bring half your weight to the left foot. Rest your arms and hands by your side with shoulders relaxed. You may now begin again.

YOGA STRETCHES

———

Most of us tend to hold in patterns of tension arising from everyday cares and worries, bad posture, lack of exercise and so on. These patterns make us feel stiff and unbending, and directly interfere with our movements. Inflexibility within our bodies can in turn affect mental flexibility, and we can become stuck in thought as well as in action. Regular stretching exercises not only free our bodies, allowing us to move easily, but can also help us to think and act without being so restricted. They are excellent improvers. By stretching muscles, ligaments and tendons, we make them much more efficient and stronger. The joints are better supported and are more able to go through their full range of movements, while the muscles are better nourished from the increased blood supply. The stretches in the following pages give you that extra edge.

WARM-UP EXERCISES

As any athlete will tell you, before starting to do any serious stretching or exercise, such as tennis, it is important that you first do some gentle warm-up exercises. They ensure that your muscles are nicely warmed and loosened, and will help to prevent any sudden strain or injury. The best thing is they only take a few minutes, and they can also be practised at any time if you are feeling stiff and need to loosen up.

SHRUGGING SHOULDERS

ARM CIRCLING

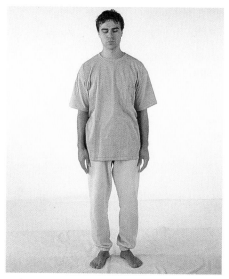

1 Stand upright with your feet slightly apart and your shoulders relaxed.

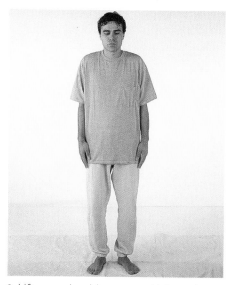

2 Lift your shoulders up as high as they will go, then let them fall down again. Stay relaxed and repeat a few times.

1 Wheel your arms around from the shoulders in slow, large circles.

SQUATS

2 Do this a few times going backwards, then repeat circling your arms forwards.

1 Stand with your feet slightly apart, hands on hips. Go slowly into a squat.

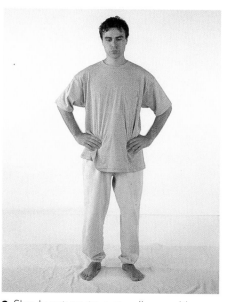

2 Slowly return to a standing position, then repeat. Your back should be upright.

LOOSE TWISTS

▌ In a standing position with feet comfortably apart and knees relaxed, swing your arms loosely backwards and forwards around your body. Keep your head and body facing forward all the time, and keep your feet and pelvis still. Repeat a few times to loosen your arms and shoulders.

ARM STRETCHING

▌ Stand with your arms straight out in front of you, at chest height. Take in a deep breath and exhale.

SIDEWAYS BEND

▌ Stand with your feet at least shoulder-width apart and your arms hanging down at your sides. Bend down to one side, trying not to twist. Slowly return to the upright and then bend to the other side. Straighten up and now repeat.

SHAKE

▌ Try to relax and let your whole body go completely floppy. Shake your limbs to release any tension. Continue for as long as you feel comfortable. If you prefer, shake each limb in sequence, starting with your right arm.

CAT STRETCH

▌ Kneel on all fours, with your hands and knees shoulder-width apart. As you start to inhale, bring your head forward and slightly hollow your back.

2 Now breathe out and, as you do so, arch the back upwards like a cat, allowing your head to drop down. Repeat a few times.

therapeutic movements
therapeutic movements

therapeutic movements

One of the best things about stretches is that you can do some simple, straightforward exercises anywhere, at any time: at home, in the office, standing in a queue or even sitting in the car; there are no restrictions. However, in order to get the most benefit from regular stretching, and particularly from doing yoga practice, it is important to create a quiet, comfortable space and to give yourself plenty of time to do the movements without any pressure or interruptions from the telephone or colleagues. In fact, making this space is in itself a relaxing, unwinding step, and will enhance the effectiveness of the actual exercises.

Ideally, make an area that feels quiet and calming to you, perhaps with softer lighting if it is needed, maybe with a thick, soft mat for the floor-based stretches. If you have any back discomfort, or just need extra support when lying down, then a couple of cushions may be extremely useful. It is helpful to wear loose fitting, airy clothing so that you can move freely and easily. If the weather permits try to let in some fresh air, but do not risk getting cold. These exercises are not intended to work up a good sweat or strain the heart, but to make you feel altogether less stiff and tense, and generally much more flexible. They are great for loosening you up, releasing tensions, improving circulation, toning the body, and generally making you feel much freer and more confident with your own body. They can really perk you up. After each exercise you will also need time to relax quietly, before you plunge back into everyday life

If you find them an enormous benefit and become inspired, and want to try out more exercises, then do find a good, local class. Yoga exercises are generally best learnt in such a class, with a skilled, experienced teacher for maximum benefit. Alternatively you could create your own class at home, inviting friends and family on a regular basis.

TENSION AND BACKACHE RELIEVERS

In the great majority of cases back trouble is the result of chronic tensions which can build up around the spine. Tired, tight muscles are also much more prone to strain or injury. The stretches that are shown here are intended to aid flexibility of the spine, and to make you feel much more supple, but if you already suffer from back pain or an injury then you must seek professional advice.

COBRA

1 Lie on your front, with your arms bent and your hands under your shoulders.

2 Slowly lift your head and push down on your arms to help raise your trunk.

3 If you can, tilt your head backwards and stretch up and back, then relax.

SIMPLE TWIST

1 Sit on the floor with your legs stetched straight out in front of you.

2 Bend one leg and place the foot on the floor across the other knee.

3 With your opposite arm, reach around the bent leg to catch hold of your foot.

FULL TWIST

1 Bend one leg so that the foot rests on the inner thigh of the other leg.

2 Bring this leg over the first one, then grasp your foot with the other arm.

3 Twist as far around as you can, hold, then relax. Swap over your legs. Repeat.

TRIANGLE

1 Stand with your feet shoulder-width apart and your arms straight out to the sides. This should be a well-balanced, easily held position. Your head should feel like a ball balancing on your neck. Stare straight ahead.

2 Bend down to one side without twisting your body, letting the opposite arm rise in the air. If you find this awkward or uncomfortable, do not strain yourself. The object is to loosen the body, not injure it.

3 Stretch the raised arm, look up and hold. Slowly straighten and repeat on the other side. If you can, repeat several times, but be careful to move slowly into position to avoid a strain.

BENDING TWIST

SLOUCH STRESS

1 Stand with your feet shoulder-width apart and your arms straight out to the sides. Bending forward, try to touch your foot, or the floor in front of it if you can, with your opposite hand. Slowly uncurl and return to the starting position. Repeat on the other side.

1 Sit on a tall stool so that your feet are just off the floor. With your hands behind your back, slouch so that your back is rounded, with your head now lowered down towards your chest.

2 Flex one foot, and lift the leg to straighten it if possible. Release the leg, relax, then repeat a few times. Repeat with the other leg. Note that the object is to build up a slow pace, not to go fast.

SOOTHING AND REMOVING TENSION

Many of us suffer at some time from tension headaches and know that they begin with a gradual feeling of pressure in the head or neck, or a taut sensation in the facial muscles. Once you are aware of such tension, tackle it immediately. A few simple stretches can help to relieve these muscular spasms and prevent them leading to a severe headache. They can be done almost anywhere.

SIDEWAYS NECK STRETCH

1 Slowly stretch your head down to one side, feeling the pull in the neck muscles. Return the head to the upright position and repeat on the other side.

2 To make this stretch of the neck muscles more effective, use your hands to give extra leverage. Place one hand under your chin and the other on top of your head; repeat the other side.

HEAD TO CHEST

1 Lower your head towards your chest, feeling the pull on the back of the neck. Hold at your furthest stretch before slowly raising the head again. Repeat two or three times.

LION POSTURE

1 To stretch the facial muscles and release tension, open your mouth as wide as possible and push out your tongue. At the same time, open your eyes into as wide a stare as you can manage. Repeat a couple of times.

SEMICIRCLE ROTATION

1 Turn the head to one side, then steadily rotate it in a semicircular movement, letting the chin drop down across the chest.

2 Dropping the head backwards compresses the neck, so it is best not to make this a full circle rotation. Repeat, going back in the opposite direction.

POSTURE ENHANCERS

One of the great benefits of an exercise system such as yoga is the fact that it gradually and increasingly gives you considerable grace and poise. In addition it will make a huge difference to your overall posture. If it was previously a bit lax, and you ended up slouching, you will really notice the difference. In fact, learning to hold yourself properly can help you to look and feel much younger, and reduce muscle strain.

1 Stand with feet slightly apart and arms raised in front. Slowly twist to one side. Repeat on the other side.

2 Stand with your feet apart, and hold your arms out. Bend over, sliding one hand down the inside of the same leg.

3 Reach as far as is comfortable, then slowly return to the upright and repeat on the other side.

4 For the tree routine, stand on one leg and bend the other knee, as shown.

5 Either place your palms together above your head, or raise the hands.

6 For the arm and leg stance, stand on one leg and hold the other foot behind.

TIRED AND ACHING LEG REVIVERS

Most of us spend too long each day with our legs stuck in fixed positions, and stiffness of the lower limbs from inactivity or tension can make you feel quite tired. Legs benefit from being stretched, keeping them toned and supple. These exercises prevent the legs, thighs and lower back from getting too tense. Since some of these positions are quite difficult, do beware of straining yourself.

ALTERNATE LEG PULLS

1 Sit on the floor, with one leg out straight and the other bent so that the foot rests on the inner thigh of your extended leg. Do it with care.

2 Lean forward and clasp the straight leg as far down as is comfortable; pull your chest down a little further and hold for a moment. Change legs and repeat.

FULL LEG PULLS

1 The previous stretch can be extended by starting with both legs straight out in front of you. Repeat as described.

SIDE LEG RAISE

2 Lean forward and hold the legs with both hands; pull yourself down a little further and hold for a moment. If this is difficult, bend the legs slightly.

1 Lie on your side with your legs and body in a straight line. Support your head with one hand and place your free hand on the floor for balance.

2 Without twisting your hips, steadily raise the upper leg as far as is comfortable. Hold, then lower slowly. Repeat with the other leg.

CAT STRETCH

I Kneel on all fours with your hands and knees shoulder-width apart. Raise your head and look straight ahead.

2 Breathe in, and as you exhale lift and arch your back. Hold for a moment before relaxing back into the original position. Inhale, then repeat.

BACK PUSH-UP

I Lie on your back with your knees bent and your feet on the floor, hip-width apart. Now place your hands on the floor by your shoulders.

SIT UP/LIE DOWN

2 Push up with your hands and feet, arching your back at the same time. Hold for a moment, then lower your body back to the floor. Do not strain yourself with this movement – it works on lots of muscles at the same time.

I Sit on the floor with both legs straight out in front of you. Your torso should be at right angles to your legs, with your eyes looking forward.

2 Slowly lower your back to the floor, then start to bend the legs and raise them off the floor.

3 As you raise the legs, slowly start to straighten them until they are as close to the vertical as you can manage. Again, take care not to strain yourself.

4 Keeping the legs straight, slowly lower them to the floor.

5 Continue the movement by sitting up and clasping your legs with your hands to bend forwards. Slowly return to the original sitting position.

ABDOMINAL TENSION RELIEVERS

We tend to hold and lock up too much tension in our abdomen, especially if we are the kind of people who always bottle up our feelings. Even simple muscular tension can leave us feeling stiff and rather uncomfortable, and much less flexible around the waist. Consequently exercises aimed at reducing stiffness and increasing flexibility in the abdominal region are extremely useful.

LOTUS

ABDOMINAL MOVEMENTS

1 Sit with one leg bent so that the foot rests on the inner thigh of the other leg. Bend the second leg and place the foot on top of the opposite thigh. Keep the spine upright to avoid straining.

2 For the full lotus, the first leg should be bent with the foot on top of the other thigh, and the second leg bent so that the foot goes over the other leg on to the opposite thigh. Hold if possible.

1 Either sit cross-legged or kneel, and place your hands on your waist or thighs. Breathe out completely.

LEG OVER

2 Without inhaling, pull in your abdomen as far as you can, then "snap" it in and out up to five times before taking a breath. Relax for a few moments, breathing freely, before repeating.

1 Lie on your back, with your legs out straight. Raise one leg as close to the vertical as is comfortable, then move it across the body, keeping your hips in contact with the floor.

2 Push the leg as far over as possible, then slowly return to the original position. Repeat with the other leg.

LYING TWISTS

I Lie on your back, hands behind your head and legs together, knees bent.

2 Twist the legs from side to side, keeping the back and hips on the floor.

SIDE BENDS

I Stand with feet apart and hands on hips. Bend down to one side.

ROLL TWIST

2 Slowly return to the upright position and bend to the other side. Repeat.

I Keeping the legs and hips still, roll your upper body around in a clockwise circle.

2 Move slowly and carefully, and bend only as far as is comfortable.

SIT UP/LIE DOWN

I Sit on the floor with both legs straight out in front of you.

2 Slowly lie back, then start to bend the legs and raise them off the floor.

3 Sit up, bend forwards, clasp your legs and slowly return to the sitting position.

OFFICE TENSIONS AND STIFF MUSCLES

For people who spend their working day sitting at a desk it is very easy to get stiff, aching muscles. Badly designed chairs do not help, and as you get tired, so posture suffers and you can end up getting round-shouldered. It is therefore absolutely essential that every now and again you get up and walk around, relax your body, and try some of these excellent loosening-up exercises.

SEATED CAT STRETCH

I Pull the chair back from the desk slightly to give yourself more room, then bend forward and clasp your ankles.

2 Carefully arch your back to stretch, then relax back and repeat.

CALF STRETCH

I Sit fairly upright, then lift and straighten each leg alternately. Repeat a few times.

2 Flex the foot to stretch the calf muscle. Repeat a few times.

NECK TWISTS

I Turn your head to one side, feeling the extension in the neck muscles.

2 Repeat, turning the head from side to side. Do both steps quite slowly.

ARM AND CHEST STRETCH

▌ Sitting upright, link your hands together, palms away from your body, and push your arms straight out in front of you. Hold for a couple of seconds, relax and then repeat.

ARM AND BACK STRETCH

▌ Link your hands together behind your back, over the top of the chair, and lift your arms slightly. Do not strain yourself. Push away from your body, hold, then repeat the exercise.

FOREARM STRETCH

▌ Hold your arms straight out to the sides and stretch them. Alternately flex and extend your hands. Feel the pull on the upper and lower sides of your forearms as you do so.

BACK/SHOULDER STRETCH

▌ Stretch your arms up in the air over your head. As you breathe in, arch your back ever so slightly. Relax with the exhalation and repeat the exercise a couple of times.

POSTURE CLASP

▌ Put one arm behind your back and bend it up, with the hand reaching the other shoulder. With your other arm raised and bent down over your shoulder, try to clasp your fingers.

SHOULDER RELEASE

▌ Finally, link your fingers together and stretch your arms high above your head. Repeat several times.

MEDITATION

—

Many people find that their lives are so full of the demands of work, family, friends and organized leisure pursuits that they have no time to "stand and stare". Many are so caught up in planning and working towards the future that they take little pleasure from the here and now. In the bustle they miss out on the beauty and joy to be seen and experienced all around them. Meditation creates the quiet space needed to do just this, and its benefits come from regular use. If you are under stress, you may find that daily meditation will restore your composure. Make a time and space you can call your own, and use breathing and relaxation exercises to ease yourself into the meditative state. Some guided meditations are suggested in this chapter.

THE BENEFITS OF MEDITATION

Human beings were never designed to cope with the high-pressure demands of life in the 21st century, when you are constantly in demand, having to make vital decisions at breakneck speed right through the day, and even during the night. You might say it cannot be done, but it can, with help. Knowing how as well as when to switch off makes all the difference, and even scientists agree.

PSYCHO-PHYSICAL LINKS

A period of meditation can often lead to a feeling of being refreshed, with a more positive attitude and a general feeling of well-being. Things that had been bothering you may now be seen in a new and more helpful way. You gain a different, wider perspective on things and feel very much more in control.

These beneficial reactions have been well known for years, but only in recent times has anyone found a physiological explanation. Detailed, extensive knowledge of brain scans and even brain wave patterns has given extraordinary new information about what is commonly called the "alpha state".

▲ *Mind and body work together in meditation to promote health and well-being in the whole person.*

MEDITATION AND WORK

The tensions of modern working practices often mean that people are so bound up in meeting all the vigorous demands placed upon them that they maintain a high level of mental and physical activity right through the day. This frequently means that they are not only cutting off their extremely important emotional responses and their enjoyment of the simple things in life, but they are also pushing their physical and mental health right to the very limit. Much has now been written about the management of stress, and the significant need for periods of mental and physical relaxation during the working day.

ENDORPHIN RELEASE

When we are truly relaxed, both mentally and physically, there are changes in the brain wave pattern until it is predominantly located and fixed within the alpha state. Within this particular state the brain triggers chemicals known as endorphins. It is in fact this chemical trigger that has the benefits that are experienced as a feeling of well-being. Indeed, endorphins have frequently been called "nature's very own special opiates". Meditation is one of the easiest ways to achieve this, and these good feelings can easily linger for some time after the meditation has ended, the length of time varying considerably. There is also a real physical benefit, as these endorphins boost and recharge the immune system, helping you to fight off all kinds of infections.

THE 20-MINUTE RULE

One writer, Ernest Rossi, has formulated the 20-minute rule which is based on the theory of ultradian rhythms. Ultradian rhythms are biorhythms that the body works through during each day – a little like hyperbolic curves of energy which repeat every 90 to 120 minutes. Naturally, it would be best to work only at peak performance times, but this is just not possible. However, timing work breaks to coincide with the mind/body slow-down pattern every 90 minutes does ensure maximum productivity and restricts the potential build-up of stress.

Rossi suggested the pattern of working for 90 minutes and then taking a brief 20-minute break. He himself usually lies down and meditates during this period because it is the best form of total mental and physical relaxation, and is good preparation for returning to optimum mental processing.

It is important that these breaks take place every 90 minutes or so, and in such a way as to completely change the mind/body state. Ideally, you should stop all work activity and experience a change of physical status (standing rather than sitting, looking into the distance rather than close up, for example) and mental focus. A 20-minute meditation is ideal and the benefits will be felt immediately. On returning to work after the 20 minutes, you will see things afresh and deal with them more efficiently, as you are ready to climb to peak performance on the biorhythmic curve. The feeling of well-being lasts into the next 90-minute period.

◄ *To be at your best for meetings ensure you take regular breaks.*

GAINING THE MEDITATIVE STATE

Many religious groups, as well as adherents of Transcendental Meditation, talk of using a sound, or "mantra", to help with meditation. The constant repetition of a phrase, word or sound ("aum" is commonly used in Hinduism) creates the alpha state by an almost hypnotic focus of attention upon that particular sound. In fact chants repeated again and again can lead to its members reaching a "high".

SOUND

An effortless sound, repeated with the natural regular rhythm of breathing, can have the same soothing, liberating effect as the constant natural sound of running water, rustling leaves or a beating heart. The single sound, or mantra as it is known, is used to blot out the "chatter" of intrusive thoughts, allowing the mind to find deep repose. Speaking or chanting a mantra as a flowing stream of endless sound is a very old method of heightening a person's awareness by concentrating the senses. The simple gentle sound "om", or "aum", is sometimes known as the first mantra, which is literally an instrument of thought. The curving Sanskrit (the ancient language of Hindus in India) symbol for this primordial word represents the various states of consciousness: waking, dreaming, deep sleep and the transcendental state.

However, the actual sound need not be a special word or incantation; something simple and meaningful will be as effective. The sound of the word "calm" spoken or thought with each exhalation can be very effective, especially while imagining tension leaving your body. Any word that appeals to you will do.

▲ *Make sure that you are sitting quite comfortably and then start breathing in the colour of your choice.*

TOUCH

You can use your sense of touch in a lulling, soothing way to induce a state of meditation at times of stress. Young children do this when they adopt a satisfyingly smooth ribbon or piece of fabric to hold and manipulate when they are feeling tense. The same technique is seen all over the Middle East, where strings of worry beads are rhythmically passed through the fingers at difficult moments to focus the mind and calm anxiety. Their uniform size, gentle round shapes, smooth surfaces and rhythmic, orderly clicking as they are passed along their string all assist the meditative state. Use one or two smooth, rounded stones in the same way, passing them slowly from hand to hand.

COLOURS

Some colours are associated with relaxation and can be a helpful way to clear the mind of tension and allow meditation to start. Sit with your eyes closed, and be aware of the colour that comes into your mind: it may be any colour of the rainbow – red or purple are common. Then slowly and gradually allow that colour to change to a blue or green colour, allowing it to fill the whole of your mind's eye and replacing all other colours. The colour pink is also recommended by colour therapists and this may prove helpful. You will find a feeling of relaxation growing as the new colour builds in your mind, and when the relaxed colour is complete, you will experience feelings of inner peace.

Establish a comfortable rhythm of breathing and then focus on it until your mind is completely still, relaxed and clear. Colours are associated with all kinds of qualities, so choose the best for your own particular moods and needs. Red: vitality, energy, strength and willpower (complementary colour turquoise). Orange: happiness and laughter (complementary colour blue). Yellow: intellect and objectivity (complementary colour violet). Green: cleansing and harmony (complementary colour magenta). Turquoise: boosts and strengthens the immune system, counteracts disease (complementary colour red). Blue: peace and relaxation, restful sleep (complementary colour orange). Violet: beauty, dignity, assured self-respect (complementary colour yellow). Magenta: the liberating release of all obsessional thoughts and memories (complementary colour green).

▲ *Repeating a mantra takes you into a world of peace and harmony.*

how to use meditation
how to use meditation

how to use meditation

The key to using meditation lies in recognizing that you actually need it. Once you get into the whirlpool of work and stress, they can both all too easily become an integral part of your lifestyle. In fact, they can be such a formidable cornerstone that you cannot imagine what life could possibly be like without them. But once you stand back and see clearly and exactly what is happening to you, what your life has become, then suddenly you see you actually need a way out. One of the best ways involves deep meditation.

Meditation needs to be done like regular exercise. In fact you might say you are exercising the ways in which you relax. The very first step involves switching off, like switching off a light in a room, and concentrating on what could be called the "Inner Other", that is to say the marvellous, relaxed, empty inner spaces inside your head and body. This stage, put crudely, means sweeping out all the noise and mayhem and chaos of everyday life and getting ready to enter another world.

The second stage involves being carried along what one expert teacher calls "a moving but going nowhere sound that coils round and even through itself in a perpetual state of being". Perhaps the best way of evaluating it is by hearing what people have to say after meditation. "As good as a holiday" or "like a wonderful deep refreshing sleep" is what most people say. If you are to get its full, continuous benefits then you really must make sure that meditation is something that you do regularly every day, at certain times, because like almost all forms of exercise the more often you do it, the better you are at it; the quicker you can switch off and tune in, and enter that fantastic deep state of total energizing, refreshing relaxation.

You must use meditation with care though. It is not like switching on and off a tap. It needs to be respected. Few people who meditate try, even if they could, to describe its ultimate power. That would be like divulging a wonderful private secret; to have it is quite enough.

SIMPLE MEDITATION TECHIQUES

While meditating might sound like something that everyone can do in just a few minutes, when you start learning to meditate you need an experienced teacher to help you understand what you have got to do. There is no point in sitting there and closing your eyes and hoping. Nothing will happen. The following techniques give a great understanding of exactly what happens. Try them and see.

▲ *Introduce a child to meditation by using the Numbers Game.*

THE NUMBERS GAME

This is a very simple form of meditation using a blackboard, real or imaginary. It is a good "game" to use with children (or adults), giving them a taste of meditation, and they really enjoy it. It is described here as if you are leading a group, but it can be easily used on one person, and provides an excellent way to clear the mind through concentration, imagination and patterns: all wonderful ways of gaining a real experience of deep meditation.

What you must do is this ...

I Get the children to sit or lie comfortably. Once they have found a really comfortable position ask them to remember it.
2 With chalk on the blackboard, draw a diagram of numbers, making sure that there are no mathematical links, like this:

$$3 \quad 1 \quad 5$$
$$8 \quad 6 \quad 9$$
$$4 \quad 7 \quad 2$$

3 Give the children one minute to memorize this sequence.
4 Ask them to return to their relaxed position, eyes closed, and concentrate on the numbers alone.
5 Rub out the numbers, telling them to do the same in their minds. Do this slowly saying "That leaves just four numbers", etc.
6 Then rub out the last number, saying "Now concentrate on what is left" ... Let them remain in silence until you notice a restlessness – this is often three or more minutes.
7 Wake them gently with an instruction to "Sit up". Ask them what the last number was and for their reactions.

THE HAVEN

Once you have managed to achieve complete physical relaxation and calm, gradually allow your mind to enter a place, whether real or imaginary, that is quite special to you. Now you can allow your mind to drift ... drift to a pleasant, peaceful place. A place that you know and where you always feel able to relax ... completely. A safe ... secure ... place ... where no one ... and nothing can ever bother you.

It may be a place you have visited on holiday, a beach or a place in the countryside. Or it may be a room ... a room you have had ... a room you do have ... or a room you would like to have ... an imaginary place. But it is a place where you can always feel able to let go ... completely ... a haven, a haven of tranquillity, unique and special to you.

In order to help you imagine this place ... notice first the light: is it bright, natural or dim ... is there any particular source of light ... natural or man-made? Notice also the temperature level ... hot, warm or cool ... and any particular source of heat. Be aware of the colours that surround you ... shapes ... and textures ... the familiar objects that make that place special. Begin to see it in all its detail. You can just be there ... whether sitting, lying or reclining, enjoying the sounds ... the smells ... the atmosphere ... with nobody wanting anything, nobody needing anything and no one demanding anything from you. Relax.

▲ *Everyone has their own haven, a quiet magical place like this.*

▲ *Try to imagine your perfect country house.*

A GUIDED VISIT TO A COUNTRY HOUSE

Imagine that you are visiting a beautiful country house … a really beautiful old country house or a stately home with magnificent sweeping lawns on a warm, sunny, summer's afternoon. You are standing on the staircase that leads into the entrance hall, one of those wide ceremonial types of staircase. And as you look down across the entrance hall you can just glimpse, through the open doors opposite, a gravel drive, and the sunlight on the gravel. It is a beautiful, sunny, summer's afternoon and there is no one around to trouble or bother you as you stand alone on that staircase …

Now you are moving down the last ten steps to the hallway, relaxing more and more with each step down.

10 Taking one step down, relaxing and letting go …

9 Taking another step down, feeling at ease …

8 Becoming more relaxed, letting go even more …

7 Just drifting deeper … and deeper … everything is getting darker and darker, and even deeper down still …

6 Becoming calmer … and calmer … even calmer still …

5 Continuing to relax, continuing to let go and feeling good …

4 Relaxing even more … letting go even more …

3 Sinking deeper … drifting even further into this welcoming, relaxed state …

2 Enjoying those good feelings, all those feelings of inner peace and relaxation …

1 Nearly all the way down now, feeling very good … beautifully relaxed … and **0**.

You are wandering across that hallway now, towards the open doors and the gardens beyond, soaking up the atmosphere of peace and permanence in that lovely old building. You wander out through the doors and down the stone steps outside … and find yourself standing on the gravel drive outside, a wide gravel drive that leads down to the entrance gates.

As you stand there you notice the lush green lawns, so flat and well-clipped … and there are shrubs and trees, different shades of green and brown against a clear, blue sky … and you can feel the warmth of the sun on your head and shoulders as you enjoy this beautiful summer's afternoon in this lovely old garden … There are flowerbeds with their splashes of colour so carefully arranged and neatly tended. And there's no one else about … nobody needing anything, nobody wanting anything and nobody expecting anything from you, so you can enjoy the peace and serenity and solitude of this afternoon in this beautiful garden that's been so well looked after for so many, many years.

A little way down on the right-hand side of the driveway, you notice an ornamental fish pond. So you decide to wander down and have a look at those fish. Sometimes they seem almost to disappear behind the weed and shadows, but always they reappear, with their scales catching the sunlight, red, gold, silver or black. And as you watch those fish your mind becomes even more deeply relaxed …

THE WELL

This continues from the previous visualization of the beautiful country house and is intended to take you to even deeper levels of meditation.

… As you watch those fish you notice that the centre of the pond is very deep. It could be the top of a disused well. You take from your pocket a silver-coloured coin, and toss that coin so that it lands over the centre of the pond, and then you watch as it swings down through the water. The ripples drift to the edges of the pond, but you just watch that coin as it sinks deeper and deeper through that clear water, sometimes it seems to disappear as it turns on edge, at other times a face of the coin catches the sunlight and it flashes through the water … sinking, drifting deeper and deeper, twisting and turning as it makes its way down … Finally it rests at the bottom lying on a cushion of soft brown mud, a silver coin in that still, clean water on its own cushion of mud … And you feel as still as that coin, as still and cool and motionless as that water, enjoying that feeling of inner peace and stillness.

▲ *Watch the ripples as the coin lands in the very centre of the pond. Look even more closely as it tumbles down through the water …*

PERSONAL DEVELOPMENT

Affirmations are a deceptively simple device that can be used by anyone and they are remarkably effective. Try to use this method while in the meditative state, having planned and memorized the affirmations involved. These powerful, positive phrases will improve communication with all parts of your mind. All you need is a simple phrase summing up how you want to be.

THE POWER OF WORDS

To make affirmations effective, they should

- be made in the present tense
- be positively phrased
- have an emotional reward.

Now contrast the power of such phrases with what happens if you are asked not to do or think of something. The words "no", "not", "never" and so on generally have the opposite effect to that intended, and why? Yours is the most influential voice in your life because you believe it. It comes live, straight out of the personality and intellect, and is fuelled by your dreams and language. The power you have over yourself is extraordinary. That is precisely why you must be careful to avoid any negative or demeaning statements you regularly make about yourself, either to others or to yourself – "I am shy", "I lack confidence", "I cannot", "I get nervous when" and so on – they are self-limiting beliefs that you are reinforcing each time they slip into your conversation or mind. You become what you say.

The point about affirmations is that instead of running yourself down, albeit in a subtle, insidious way, you actually start building yourself up. You start creating the inner psychological scaffolding to support the new you. Such affirmations are best used while in a wonderful state of meditation.

▲ *Thinking through what you want to be is the big key to success.*

IMPROVED SELF-WORTH

We all have attributes and qualities in which we can take pride and pleasure. This exercise is about emphasizing these positive aspects to allay the doubts that only serve to limit our potential.

- I like my [physical attribute].
- I am proud of my [attitude or achievement].
- I love meeting people – they are fascinating.
- My contribution is valuable to [name person].
- I am lovable and can give love.
- Others appreciate my [opinions, assistance, a personal quality].
- I enjoy being a unique combination of mind and body.

Now imagine yourself speaking to colleagues, boss, employees or friends ... See yourself behaving and looking confident, standing and looking a confident person ... Notice how you stand ... your facial expression ... hear the way that you speak ... slowly, calmly, quietly, clearly and with confidence. You are communicating your needs ... ideas ... opinions in a positive way. Notice how your words flow easily, and how others are listening attentively to you ... valuing what you have to say. Now "climb aboard" ... be there – know how it feels to stand like that ... to speak like that ... and to have that positive reception from others. Get in touch with the stance ... expression ... and feelings ... and know that you can use these any time in the future to gain those same feelings or that inner strength in everything you do. See yourself in different situations: at home, in a social setting, in all the parts of your life, confident and assured, going from strength to strength.

▲ *The difference affirmations can make is extraordinary. From shy and introverted to open, confident and winning.*

▲ *If you want to be No. 1, then take time to concentrate on seeing yourself as the best. Give yourself the power to come out top.*

VISUALIZATION

In the same way that you can utilize your voice, so, perhaps more powerfully, you can use your imagination. The imagination can stimulate emotions, and they can register new attitudes in the mind. It can be a direct communication with the deeper levels of the mind, providing a powerful influence for improvements in your attitudes, behaviour patterns and overall confidence.

Visualization requires that you imagine yourself in a situation, behaving, reacting and looking as you would wish to do at an interview, an important meeting, a social gathering, a one-to-one situation, or perhaps a sporting event. Imagine what that will mean for you, your reactions, the reactions of those around you and, importantly, feel all the good feelings that will be there when this happens in reality.

It is like playing a video of the event, on that screen on the inside of the forehead, the mind's eye, from the beginning of the situation through to the perfect outcome. Should any doubts or negative images creep into your "video", push them away and replace them with positive ones. Keep this realistic, and base it upon real information from your past.

CONFIDENCE IN FUTURE SITUATIONS

The meditative state, affirmations and visualization can be a valuable rehearsal and preparation for a future event. Athletes and other sportsmen have proved that it actually does work. We can all use these extraordinary techniques to achieve our own optimum performance during any situation. Now consider the following phrases, and how they relate to you …

- I am quietly confident in meetings.
- I speak slowly, quietly and confidently so that others listen.
- My contribution is wanted and valued by others.
- I enjoy meetings, as they bring forth new ideas and help to renew my enthusiasm.

Imagine an important meeting that is about to happen, and see yourself there, filling in all the details that you know, and the people too; imagine yourself there looking confident and relaxed, concentrating on what is happening. Be aware of the acute interest you are giving to what is happening with complete, concentrated attention, and then imagine yourself speaking, to give information or to ask a question: hear yourself speaking quietly, slowly and calmly …

Notice people listening to what you are saying; they wish you well and support you, as you are expressing your viewpoint or raising a question they may well have wanted to ask, too. Notice how you are sitting or standing, how you lean slightly forward when speaking, that expression of calm confidence on your face. When this is clear in your mind, just like a film playing in your mind's eye, play it back and forth. When you are feeling comfortable with it, get into that imaginary you, "climb aboard" and be there in your mind, seeing things from that perspective, hearing things from that point in the meeting. As you speak, get in touch with those calm feelings, and the attitudes that allow you to feel calm, in control, and quietly confident … It is like a rehearsal; the more you manage to rehearse the better the final performance will be. You will acquire the right attitudes, stance and tone of voice, so that when you are in that situation all of these will be available to you, and it will be just as you imagined, as if you had done it all, successfully, before.

In short, what this technique does is take you step by step through a rehearsal. Imagine every possible scenario, and how you will deal with it. That is the key to a successful outcome.

▲ *The preparation was worth it; you went into a meeting knowing you could do it, and that is exactly what happened.*

ENJOYMENT AND ACHIEVEMENT

The mind and the body are so completely interlinked that if we keep physically fit we are also mentally alert. The one boosts the other, but it also works the other way around. If we really utilize our mental capacities we can affect and improve our physical health and performance. So it is up to you to make sure that these twin forces keep functioning at full power. Do not let either slip.

▲ *A well-tuned lively body keeps you feeling well and alert.*

THE BODY/MIND LINK

Regularly say to yourself …
* I feel safe, happy and content in the knowledge that my body is constantly renewing itself. It is alive and well.
* It feels marvellous to know that every damaged cell is replaced by a healthy one.
* My immune system is strong and fights off any infections easily.
* My mind and my body are working in harmony to keep me healthy, well and alert.

Now, imagine yourself lying or sitting comfortably. As you see yourself there you notice a healing glow of coloured light surrounding your body, but not touching it. Let that colour become stronger, until it has a very clear pure colour, which is the colour of healing for you.

Now, as you watch, that healing, coloured light begins to flow into the top of your head. You can see it slowly draining into all parts of the head, face, ears, and starts its journey down through the neck and shoulders, into the tops of the arms … It continues to flow down through the arms and the chest area, that healing, coloured light, penetrating all the muscles and organs … even as you watch you can also feel a healing warmth coming into your body … NOW … as it flows down into the stomach area, the back, right the way down to the base of the spine. Then you can allow the light to disperse again and gradually return to your normal wakeful state, knowing that in those areas that need it, the healing process will continue.

STRESS REDUCTION

Stress is a factor in everyone's life and can even be a major motivator in some circumstances. Meditation can be a great help in coping with it, and combined with visualization, it can change your whole response to stressful demands. Keep saying …
* I enjoy solving problems.
* I work well under pressure.
* I am a calm, methodical and efficient worker.
* I love that feeling of having achieved so much in a day.
* I enjoy being calm when others around me are not.

Imagine yourself in a situation that has in the past caused stress. Picture the situation, and the other people involved … See yourself there … and notice a slight shimmer of light between yourself and those other people … a sort of bubble around you … a protective bubble that reflects any negative feelings back to them … leaving you able to get on with your tasks … your life, with an inner strength and calmness that surprises even you. A protective, invisible bubble surrounds you at all times. It will only allow those feelings that are positive and helpful to you to pass through for you to enjoy and build upon. Others may catch stress from each other … negativity, too, can be infectious … but you are protected … you continue to keep things in perspective … and to deal with things calmly and methodically. You are able to see the way forward clearly … solve problems … find ways around difficulties … by using your own inner resources and strengths, born of experience. In you alone lies the secret of success. You can and you will succeed.

▲ *Imagine yourself leading a healthy lifestyle and it will happen.*

LIVING NOW

Although we cannot change the past, we can learn from it and build up a range of skills and useful insights from it. The future is that unknown world of possibilities and opportunities before us – but all that we can truly have any effect upon is the present. Keep saying to yourself …

- I have learned a great deal from the past.
- The future is an exciting range of opportunities.
- I enjoy laying good foundations NOW on which to build a better future.

Imagine yourself standing on a pathway. As you look around the left, right and above is brilliantly illuminated, and sounds are amazingly clear. As you check over your shoulder you notice the path behind is unclear. You hear a clock chime in the distance and take a step forward. You notice the slightest of noises, movements or shifts of light, and take pleasure even in the pure sound of silence, too. You can hear that same clock ticking now, and with each tick you can take a small step forward, effortlessly, along the path, and that illumination and awareness moves with you. At any fork in the path you can make decisions easily as you are truly involved in the moment, rather than looking over your shoulder at what might have been, or staring blindly into the future at what might happen. You enjoy being in the brilliantly illuminated, acute awareness of sound, hearing, feeling, taste and smell that is NOW.

▲ *For a complete experience, be more acutely aware of shapes and textures as well as sounds, colours and scents.*

GOAL ACHIEVEMENT

A goal, in all areas of life, is vitally important in order to focus your attention and inner resources. A goal provides a sense of direction and ultimately the joy of achievement. Without it you might flounder, so keep saying to yourself …

- I direct my energies to achieve my goals.
- I enjoy directing my energies positively.
- I know where I am going and how I am getting there.
- Step by step I am moving in the right direction.
- I have the ability, I have the determination, I shall succeed.

▲ *Keep your eyes firmly fixed on your goal and you will achieve it.*

Be aware of the different areas of your life: work, social, leisure activities, emotional and spiritual. Select one of these for this exercise … and be aware of what you want to happen in that area of your life, what you want to achieve … Make it realistic and clear in your mind. It may be useful to write it down and describe it fully before beginning this visualization.

While in the meditative state, imagine yourself having achieved that goal, imagine yourself there, in that situation. Surround yourself with all the things or people that indicate that you have achieved that goal. Be as specific as you can … be aware of all the senses … what are you seeing … hearing … touching or sensing … smelling … tasting. Be there … make it real … be specific … about colours … temperatures … lighting, to make it more and more real in your mind.

Now, from where you are at that moment of achieving that goal … look back … as if along a path, a pathway of time … to where you were … and notice the different stages of change … of movement towards achieving that goal … along the way … along that path … the different actions you have taken … the contacts you have made … and the people involved. Be aware of all the stages along the way … and as you return to the here and now … you remain in touch with the feelings that will make it all worthwhile … and you feel more and more determined to take one step at a time … make one change at a time … along that path to the successful achievement of your goal. And as you return from the meditative state so you are more determined to be success-ful in the achievement of your goal.

USEFUL ADDRESSES

Feng Shui

UK
The Feng Shui Association
31 Woburn Place
Brighton BN1 9GA

The Feng Shui Society
277 Edgware Road
London W2 1BT

USA
American Feng Shui Institute
108 North Ynez
Suite 202
Monterey Park CA91754

The Feng Shui Guild
PO Box 766
Boulder, CO80306

AUSTRALIA
Feng Shui Society of Australia
PO Box 1566
Rozelle NSW 2039

Herbalism

UK
National Institute of Medical
Herbalists
56 Longbrook Street
Exeter
DevonEX4 6AH

The Herb Society
134 Buckingham Palace Road
London
SW1W 9SA

The School of
Phytotherapy/Herbal Medicine
Buckstreep Manor
Bodle Street Green
Hailsham
East Sussex
BN27 4RJ

US
The Herb Research Foundation
1007 Pearl Street, Suite 200
Boulder
CO 80302

American Botanical Council
PO Box 144345
Austin
TX 78714

Blazing Star Herb School
PO Box 6
Shelburne Falls
MA 01370

Outlets for Herbs
Cameron Park Botanicals
Highway 64 East
Raleigh
NC 27610

Caprilands Herb Farm
Silver Street
North Coventry
CT 06238

Seeds Blum
Idaho City State
Boise
ID 83706

AUSTRALIA
National Herbalist Association
PO Box 61
Broadway
NSW 2066

Homeopathy

UK
The Homeopathic Society
2 Powis Place
Great Ormond Street
London
WC1N 3HT
The Society of Homeopaths
2 Artizan Road
Northampton
NN1 4HU

**Outlets for Homeopathic
Remedies**
*Most chemists and health food shops
will stock a limited supply of
homeopathic remedies. The list below
will stock a complete range.*

Buxton and Grant
176 Whiteladies Road
Bristol
BS8 2XU

Freeman's Pharmacy
7 Eaglesham Road
Clarkston
Glasgow
G76 7BU

Goulds the Chemist
14 Crowndale Road
London
NW1 1TT

Helios Pharmacy
97 Camden Road
Tunbridge Wells
Kent
TN1 2QR

USA
Homeopathic Educational Services
2124 Kittredge Street
Berkeley
CA 94704

National Center for Homeopathy
801 N Fairfax No 306
Alexandria
VA 22314

AUSTRALIA
Australian Institute of
Homeopathy
PO Box 122
Roseville
NSW 2069

Massage

UK
The Massage Training Institute/
The Academy of On-site Massage
24 Brunswick Square
Hove BN13 1EH

London College of Massage
5 Newman Passage
London
W1P 3PF

Clare Maxwell-Hudson Massage
Training Centre
PO Box 457
London
NW2 4BR

The School of Holistic Massage
c/o Nitya Lacroix
75 Dresden Road
London
N19 3BG

USA
American Massage Therapy
Association
820 Davies Street, Suite 100
Evanston
IL 60201

Pacific School of Massage and
Healing Arts
44800 Fish Rock Road
Gualala
CA 95445

Body Therapy Center
368 California Avenue
Palo Alto.
CA 94306

AUSTRALIA
Association of Massage Therapists
3/33 Denham Street
Bondi
New South Wales

Aromatherapy

UK
International Society of
Professional Aromatherapists
The Hinckley and District
Hospital
Mount Road
Hinckley
Leicestershire
LE10 1AG

International Federation of
Aromatherapists
4 Eastmearn Road
Dulwich
London
SE21 8HA

USA
Institute of Aromatherapy
3108 Route 10
West Denville
NJ 07834

Aromatherapy School and Herbal
Studies
219 Carl Street
San Fransisco
CA 94117

AUSTRALIA
Australian School of Awareness
251 Dorset Road
Croydon
Victoria 3136

International Federation of
Aromatherapists
83 Riversdale Road
Hawthorn
Victoria 3122

Shiatsu

UK
The British School of
Shiatsu-Do
3rd Floor
130-132 Tooley Street
London
SE1 2TU

The Shiatsu Society
Interchange Studios
Dalby Street
London
NW5 3NQ

The European Shiatsu School
Central Administration
Highbanks
Lockeridge
Marlborough
Wiltshire
SN8 4EQ

USA
International School of Shiatsu
10 South Clinton Street, Suite 300
Doylestown
PA 18901

School of Shiatsu and Massage at
Harbin Hot Springs
PO Box 889
Middletown
CA 95461

AUSTRALIA
The Shiatsu Therapy Association
of Australia
2 Caminoley Wynd
Templestowe
Victoria 3106

Australian Natural Therapies
Association Ltd.
Suite 1, 2nd Floor
468-472 George Street
(PO Box A964)
Sydney
New South Wales 2000

Reflexology

UK
Association of Reflexologists
27 Old Gloucester Street
London
WIN 3XX

Holistic Association of
Reflexologists
92 Sheering Road
Old Harrow
Essex
CM17 0JW

The British Reflexology
Association
12 Pond Road
London
SE3 6JL

USA
International Institute of
Reflexology
PO Box 12462
St Petersburg.
FL 33733

Reflexology Center
Scarborough Professional Center
136 Route One
Scarborough
ME 04074

AUSTRALIA
Reflexology Association of
Australia
15 Kedumba Crescent
Turramurra
New South Wales 2074

RASA (Australia)
73 Illawong Way
Karand Downs
Brisbane
Queensland 4306

Australian School of Reflexology
and Relaxation
165 Progress Road
Eltham North
Victoria 3095

Tai Chi

UK
Tai Chi Union of Great Britain
69 Kilpatrick Gardens
Clarkston
Glasgow
Scotland
G76 7RF

Golden Rooster Tai Chi School
19 Albany Road
London
N4 4RR

Rainbow Tai Chi Kung Centre
Creek Farm
Pitley Hill
Woodland Ashburton
Devon
PQ13 7JY

British Tai Chi Chuan & Kung Fu
Association
28 Linden Farm Drive
Countesthorpe
Leicestershire
LE8 5SX

USA
Mind, Body, Spirit Academy
PO Box 415
Chadsford
PA 19317

Tai Chi Cultural Centre
PO Box 8885
Stanford
CA 94309

Sarasota Shaolia Academy
4655 Flatbush Avenue
Sarasota
Florida
FL 34233-1920

AUSTRALASIA
Australian Academy of Tai Chi
686 Parrametta Road
Croydon
NSW 2132

Shaolin Wahnan Tai Chi
RSD Strathfelsaye Road
Victoria 3551

Yoga

UK
Iyengar Yoga Institute
223a Randolph Avenue
London
W9 1NL

Manchester & District Institute of
Iyengar Yoga
134 King Street
Dukinfield
Tameside
Greater Manchester
M60 8HG

Edinburgh Iyengar Yoga Centre
195 Bruntsfield Place
Edinburgh
EH10 4DQ
The British Wheel of Yoga
1 Hamilton Place
Boston Road
Sleaford
Lincolnshire
NG24 7EI

USA
Satchidananda Ashram - Yogaville
Buckingham
VA 23921

International Yoga Association
92 Main Street
Warrenton
VA 20186

BKS Iyengar Yoga National
Association of the United States
Inc.
8223 West Third Street
Los Angeles
CA 90038

Sivanda Yoga Vedanta Center
1246 Bryn Mawr
Chicago
IL 60660

AUSTRALASIA
BKS Iyengar Association of
Australasia
1 Rickman Avenue
Mosman
NSW 2088

Sivananda Yoga Vedanta Centre
409th Avenue
Katoomba
NSW 2780

Meditation

UK
Gateway Books
The Hollies
Wellow
Bath
Somerset, BA2 8QJ

Western Zen Retreats
Winterhead Hill Farm
Shipham
Winscombe
Somerset
BS25 1RS

Transcendental Meditation
Freepost
London SW1P 4YY

The Community Health
Foundation 188 Old Street
London
EC1V 9FR

USA

Greater Washington DC
Association of Professionals
Practising the Transcendental
Meditation Program
4818 Montgomery Lane
Bethesda
MD 20814
Institute of Noetic Sciences
PO Box 909
Sausalito
CA 94966

First Zen Institute of America
113E 30th Street
New York
NY 10016

American Buddhist Association
1151 West Leland Avenue
Chicago
IL 60640

AUSTRALASIA
Transcendental Meditation Centre
68 Wood Street
Manly
Sydney
NSW 2095

The Barry Long Centre
Box 5277
Gold Coast MC
Queensland 4217

Transcendental Meditation Centre
5 Adam Street
Green Lane
Auckland 5
New Zealand

GLOSSARY

Adaptogen
A herbal remedy, such as ginseng, that helps the body adapt to stress; it is suitable for short-term use only.

Affirmation
A simple, positive statement about a situation used in meditation to reinforce feelings of self-worth and confidence.

Alpha state
A pattern of brain waves that can be identified when an individual achieves a state of complete mental and physical relaxation, leading to the release of endorphins.

Bagua mirror
A circular mirror used in Feng Shui; framed by the symbols of the Bagua, it is intended to be hung on the outside of a building to deflect negative energy.

Bagua or Pa Gua
The representation of the energies associated with the eight cardinal directions; it takes the form of the eight trigrams arranged around the points of the compass.

Biorhythms
Any of the body's natural patterns, such as rhythms of sleep and wakefulness or periodic rises and falls in levels of energy.

Brahmi oil
An Ayurvedic blend of brahmi and other Indian herbs with coconut oil, used in massage; it is soothing to the pitta dosha.

Carrier oil
Light vegetable oil, such as almond or grapeseed, used to dilute essential oils for aromatherapy massage.

Chi
The life force or energy that flows throughout the universe, including the human body; the principles of Feng Shui are partly concerned with regulating its healthy flow in the environment.

Chi kung
Chinese energy work.

Decoction
A herbal remedy prepared by boiling the hard parts of a plant, such as roots or bark, in water.

Doln exercise
Shiatsu self-massage routine.

Dosha
In Ayurveda, an individual's nature or body type, defined as vata, pitta, kapha or any combination of two or three.

Dragon position
In Landform Feng Shui, the side boundary of a building.

Empty step
In T'ai Chi, a step taken before putting any weight on the foot.

End-gaining
In Alexander technique, reacting impulsively and too quickly to a stimulus.

Endorphins
A group of hormones produced by the body to cope with acute stress and mediate the perception of pain; their effect is similar to that of opiate drugs.

Enhancer or enhancement
An object, such as a mirror or wind chime, used in Feng Shui to focus the mind and nurture supportive energy.

Essential oils
Aromatic oils extracted from various parts of plants, such as flowers or leaves, by a process of distillation, used in aromatherapy.

Fight or flight response
The body's natural response to stress, involving the release of hormones such as adrenaline and noradrenaline, the acceleration of the circulatory and respiratory systems and the slowing of the digestive system.

Fingerwalking
In reflexology, the technique of exerting rhythmic pressure with the finger while moving it across the foot.

Five Elements
Representations of different manifestations of chi, all of which need to be in a balanced relationship with each other to create a comfortable, supportive environment.

Form
A complete sequence of moves in T'ai Chi; long and short forms may be practised.

Geomancy
The practice of identifying subtle energies in the Earth and correcting disruptive imbalances.

Geopathic stress
Naturally occurring energetic imbalances in the Earth that may result in ill-health and other problems.

Guided meditation
A meditation on a given theme that takes a previously dictated course.

Hatha yoga
Physical and breathing exercises designed as a preparation for the spiritual path of yoga.

Hexagram
One of the 64 six-line figures that form the basis of the I Ching, made by combining the trigrams of the Bagua.

Holistic therapy
Any treatment that observes the principle of psycho-physical unity, regarding physical, mental and emotional states as interdependent, and treats the whole person.

I Ching
The Book of Changes, an ancient Taoist interpretation of universal energies based on the 64 hexagrams, formed from the eight trigrams of the Bagua; it is the basis of a method of divination.

Immune system
The system of the body, including the spleen, thymus gland and lymph nodes, that is responsible for filtering body fluids, producing white blood cells and immunity to invading organisms; it may be weakened by disease or by prolonged periods of stress.

Infusion
A herbal remedy prepared by steeping leaves or flowers in boiling water.

Internal martial arts
Chi kung disciplines such as T'ai Chi that emphasize the internal workings of the body and the flow of chi.

Kapha
One of the three doshas, or body types, in Ayurveda.

Landform or Form School
The earliest and most traditional branch of Feng Shui, concerned with the propitious siting of buildings and the growing of crops.

Law of Similars
The homeopathic principle that like cures like, by stimulating the body's natural response to a harmful substance.

Leys or ley lines
Lines of energy running along the Earth's surface.

Lunge monkey
A method of movement used in Alexander Technique for activities that involve bending combined with forward movement.

Luo pan
A compass-like instrument used by geomancers and Feng Shui consultants to indicate the energy of a particular direction.

Magic Square
A symbol representing the universe that forms the basis of Feng Shui.

Mantra
A repeated syllable or series of sounds used to focus the mind in meditation.

Materia Medica
A list of homeopathic remedies.

Meridians
The body's energy channels along which chi flows.

Monkey
A style of bending movement used in Alexander technique.

Moon gate
An opening in a solid wall giving a view to the outside.

Nervine
A herbal remedy that supports the nervous system.

Phoenix position
In Landform Feng Shui, the boundary in front of a building.

Pitta
One of the three doshas, or body types, in Ayurveda.

Poison arrow
Harmful chi directed by, for instance, the sharp corner of a building or spiky leaves on a plant.

Potentization
The process of dilution and shaking used to make homeopathic remedies.

Primary control
In Alexander technique, the relationship between the head, neck and back that controls movement and co-ordination in the whole body.

Proving
The testing process for a new homeopathic remedy.

Seiza
The kneeling position used by a practitioner performing shiatsu.

Succussion
The shaking process used to make homeopathic remedies.

T'ai Chi symbol
The circular symbol representing the interdependence of yin and yang.

Tan Tien
In Chinese energy work, the body's centre of gravity, four finger-widths below the navel and one-third of the way from front to back; all movement in T'ai Chi Chuan emanates from this point.

Tao
Literally the "Way": the spiritual path of Taoism.

Taoism
The Chinese philosophy underlying practices such as Feng Shui, T'ai Chi and other forms of energy work, Chinese medicine and astrology.

Thumbwalking
In reflexology, the technique of

exerting rhythmic pressure with the thumb while moving it across the foot.

Tiger position
In Landform Feng Shui, the side boundary of a building.

Tincture
A herbal remedy prepared by steeping herbs in alcohol.

Tortoise position
In Landform Feng Shui, the protective position behind a building.

Transcendental Meditation (TM)
The style of meditation taught by the Maharishi Mahesh Yogi, which focuses on a secret mantra that is given to each adherent for their individual use.

Tridosha
In Ayurveda, a person who exhibits the characteristics of all doshas.

Trigram
A symbol representing the changing proportions of yin and yang energy.

Tsubo
Pressure points on the body used in acupressure and shiatsu.

Ultradian rhythms
Biorhythms that repeat every 90–120 minutes.

Vata
One of the three doshas, or body types, in Ayurveda.

Vedas
The ancient sacred texts of India.

Vikruti
In Ayurveda, a person's current physical, mental or spiritual state.

Visualization
An imagined scene used in meditation to reinforce feelings of self-worth and confidence.

Yin and yang
Two opposing interdependent forces whose changing strengths give rise to the energy of the universe.

INDEX

A

abdomen 402
  massage 354
  shiatsu 387
  yoga 484-5
abscesses 292
access 206-7
achievement 498-9
aching leg revivers 482-3
acidity 330
aconite 299
acupressure 32
acupuncture 19, 32
affirmations 496
air 119, 131, 222-3
alcohol 259
  hangovers 272
Alexander technique 425, 427, 428-9
  applications 431, 432-43
Alexander, Frederick Matthias 428
allergies 176
  homeopathy 291
allium cepa 299
allopathic medicine 10
aloe vera 332
alternate leg pulls 482
anaemia 294
Animals
  astrology 22-9
  Chinese Animals Table 23
  Directions 210
  Four Animals Formation 16, 17, 143, 206
  Nature of the Animals 22, 131
  office personalities 248-9
  Symbolic Chinese Animals 133
ant tart 299
anticipation 293
anxiety 268
  aromatherapy 366, 368-9
apis 299
appetite 330
arg nit 299
arms 386
  arm and back stretch 487
  arm and chest stretch 487
  arm and hand tonic 349
  arm circling 474
  arm stretching 475
  forearm stretch 487
arnica 300
aromatherapy 8, 335, 359, 360-3
  recipes 365, 366-73
arsenicum 300
Assessing a Location 41
astrology 14-15, 22-9
  compatibility 28, 248
Auspicious Measurements 235

B

Ayurveda 259, 307, 308-9
  doshas 310-27
  treatments 329-33

babies
  health 295
  homeopathy 285
  nurseries 110-11
Bach, Dr Edward 297
back 428-9
  back exercises 387
  back push-up 483
  back relaxer 352
  back stretch 487
backache 417
  backache relievers 351, 415, 478-9
Bagua 30, 32-3, 209
  Bagua and Desks 127
  Bagua and Family Seating 101
  home offices 127
  mirrors 67
  planning gardens 155, 158-9
  planning homes 57, 252-3
  planning offices 209, 216-17, 252-3
  Symbolic Bagua 32-3, 84-5
  Three Gates Bagua 33
balanced lifestyle 380
balconies 122-3
bamboo 65
barbecues 168
barriers 224-5

basement gardens 190, 191
bathing 272, 362
bathrooms 116-19, 219
beams 60-1, 224
Bed Directions 250
bedrooms 11, 106-9
  children 110-11
  en suite bathrooms 118
  hotels 256-7
  teenagers 114-15
beds 106-7, 110
  Bed Directions 250
belladonna 300
Bend Bow to Shoot Tiger, Step Forward, Deflect Down, Intercept and Punch 470-1
bending 436-7, 438, 439
bending twist 479
bends
  bending twist 479
  side bends 485
  sideways bend 475
beneficial locations 46
beneficial positions 54-5
benzoin 375
bergamot 377
Best and Worst Directions 55, 209, 255
bites 297
black 81, 229
bladder 381
bloating 330
blood pressure 367
blue 81, 187, 320

body and mind link 490, 498
body types 310-11, 312-13
boils 292
books 82-3, 233
borage 276
boundaries 164-5, 194
Boundaries and the Five Elements 49
breathing 119, 222-3, 418
  breathing enhancers 369, 394
  breathing enhancers with a partner 392-3
bridges 147

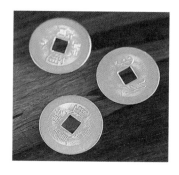

Bright Hall 153
brown 81, 229, 316
bruises 296
Brush Right Knee and Push, Brush Left Knee and Punch Down 466
bryonia 300
Building Positions 17
Buildings and the Five Elements 255
burns 297
business trips 256-7
Businesses and the Five Elements 255
butterflies in the stomach 269

C

cabinets 118
calendar 22
calendula 300
calf stretch 486
Californian poppy 276
candles 98
cantharis 303
cardamom 333
Career 84, 253
carrying 440
cars 130-1
  car parks 219-20
Cat stretch 475, 483
cats 132
ceramics 65
chairs 90-1, 99, 168
chamomile 276, 375
chamomilla 303
chaste tree 279

chemicals in the home 64
chest 402
  chest exercises 347
chi 19, 446 see also energy
  Chi Kung 30
  gardens 146-7
  kitchens 103-4
  living rooms 59
  offices 242, 246-7
  roads 45
children 89
  health 295
  rooms 110-11, 112-13,
    114-15
  Symbolic Bagua 84
China 6, 10, 445
Chinese Animals Table 23
Chinese astrology see astrology
Chinese gardens 140-1, 146-7
chronic disease 283, 291
circling 340
circulatory system enhancers
  397
cities 42-3
clary sage 377
clay in the home 65
clearing unseen energies 43
clothes 108
  interviews 254-5
clutter 82-3
  bathrooms 118
  bedrooms 109
  cars 131
  children 112
  gardens 181
  living rooms 96
  offices 232-3
  studies 129
  teenagers 114
coastal areas 47, 196-7
Cobra 478
cocculus 301
coffee 259
coir matting 65
cold infused oils 265
  lavender 268
colds
  Ayurveda 332-3
  homeopathy 288
  reflexology 420
colic
  aromatherapy 367
  Ayurveda 330, 367
  herbalism 269
  homeopathy 295
coloured glass 75
colours 28, 248, 491
  bathrooms 119
  black 81, 229
  blue 81, 187, 320
  brown 81, 229, 316
  cars 131
  clothes 254-5
  gardens 184-7

  green 81, 186-7, 229, 320
  homes 8, 80-1
  infusions 316, 320, 324
  kapha 324
  ochre 316
  offices 228-9
  orange 81, 187, 324
  pink 81, 187, 324
  pitta 320
  purple 81, 187
  red 81, 186, 229, 324
  Useful Shapes and Colours
    for Cornerstones 169
  vata 316
  violet 320
  white 81, 186, 229
  yellow 81, 186, 229, 316
columns 224
companion planting 176-7
compasses 16, 30, 33
  planning gardens 154-5
  planning homes 56-7, 252-3
  planning offices 216-17
compatibility 28, 242
computers 72, 129, 230-1, 233,
  443
confidence in future situations
  497
conservatories 120-1
  kitchens 120
constipation
  Ayurveda 330
  herbalism 269
containers 170, 171
convalescence 270
corners 58
cornerstones 169

corridors 225, 240
coughs
  Ayurveda 333
  homeopathy 289
courtyard gardens 188-9
cramp 417
cramp bark 279
croup 289, 295
crystals 75
  infusions 317, 321, 325
curtains 95
cuts 296
cystitis
  Ayurveda 333
  homeopathy 294, 333

D
damiana 279
decoctions 264
dentists 289, 297
depression 271
desks
  Bagua and Desks 127
  home offices 126-7
  offices 232-3, 236-7
  posture 442
  reception areas 238-9
  studies 128-9
diarrhoea 330
digestive system 396, 421
digestives 269, 292, 370
dining rooms 98-101, 120-1
dinner parties 101
direction (Alexander
  technique) 428
Directions 54, 56, 155, 210-11,
  252

Bed Directions 250
Best and Worst Directions
  55, 209, 255
East and West groups 57
Favored Months and
Directions 211
  gardens 155
  interviews 255
  offices 206-11
disease 73, 282-3
doctors 297
Dog 22-3, 27, 28, 29
  office personalities 248
dogs 132
doln exercises 384-7
doors 62-3
  front doors 51, 90
  offices 238
doshas 310-11
  assessing 312-13
  dual 326-7
  kapha 311, 312-13, 322-5,
    331
  pitta 312-13, 318-21, 331
  triple 327
  vata 310, 312-13, 314-17, 331
  dowsing 43
Dragon 22-3, 25, 28, 29
  Four Animal Formation 16,
    17, 143, 206
  office personalities 248, 250
drinking (Alexander technique)
  441
driving 441
drosera 301

E
ear infections 290
Earth 20-21
  buildings 205
  earth grids 43
  gardens 149
  interviews 255
  office personalities 249-51
  offices 209
East Group 31, 57
eating (Alexander technique)
  441
edges 58
effleurage 340
electrical equipment 72-3,
  108-9, 230-1

electromagnetic radiation 72-3, 109, 230-1
elements 20-1, 33 see also Five Elements
  Ayurveda 311
  balancing 48
  boundaries 165
  buildings 49, 205
  correcting imbalances 49
  gardens 148-9
  interviews 255
  materials in the home 65
  office personalities 249-51
  offices 208-9, 228-9
  plants 69
  tastes 100
  transformation 149
Embrace Tiger, Return to Mountain 457-8
emotional problems 293
en suite bathrooms 118
endorphins 490
energy 19, 20-1 see also chi
  Energy of Numbers 31
  homeopathy 282-3
  homes 83
  offices 244-7
  unseen energies 42-3, 150-1, 222-3
enhancements in gardens 158-9
enjoyment 498-9
entrances 50
  offices 211, 218, 238, 240
environment 6, 16-17, 35, 40-1
  environmental issues 8-9
  urban environment 44-5
essential oils 11, 339, 361, 363, 372-3, 374-7
euaptorium 301
eucalyptus 376
euphrasia 301
evening primrose 277
exercise
  back 387
  bends 475, 479, 485
  chest 347
  face 385
  feet 387
  head 385
  kapha 325
  pitta 321
  revitalizers 345, 346, 353
  shiatsu 384-7
  stretches 475, 480, 483, 486, 487
  twists 475, 478, 479, 485, 486
  vata 317
eyes 290
  use of the eyes 432

F
fabrics in the home 65
Fair Lady Weaves Shuttles (Left and Right) 468

Fair Lady Weaves Shuttles (Right and Left) 467-8
Fame 85
Family 84
Favored Months and Directions 211
feet 362, 403, 404
  feet exercises 387
  foot charts 422-3
  foot massage 332
  foot revitalizer 353
  hand and foot treatments 405
  warm-up foot massage 406-7
fences 165
Feng Shui 6-10, 12-15
  gardens 134-9, 142-3, 160-1, 174-5
  health 32
  homes 36-9, 52-3, 88-9
  modern world 34-5
  offices 198-203, 214-15, 242-3
  theories 16-19
ferrum phos 301
fevers 288, 295
fight or flight response 380
Fire 20-1
  buildings 205
  gardens 148-9
  interviews 255
  office personalities 249-251
  offices 209
fireplaces 94
first aid 296-7
fish 76, 239
Five Elements 31, 255 see also Elements
  Boundaries and the Five Elements 49
  Buildings and the Five Elements 255

Businesses and the Five Elements 255
Five Elements Features in the Garden 149
Materials and the Five Elements 65
Plants that Represent the Five Elements 69
Qualities of the Five Elements 229
Relationships of the Five Elements 20, 48, 229
Tastes and the Elements 100
flowers 69
flu 288
flying, fear of 297
forearm stretch 487
Form School 16
Four Animals Formation 16, 17, 143, 206
fractures 296
fresh ginger and lemon tea 317
fright 293
frogs 132
front gardens
  boundaries 164
  paths 162
full leg pulls 482
full twist 478
furniture
  beds 106-7, 110
  cabinets 118
  chairs 90-1, 99, 168
  gardens 147, 168
  offices 234-7
  sofas 90-1
  tables 99-100, 168, 241
  wardrobes 108

G
Gaia 35
gall bladder 381

gardens 10, 134-9, 142-3, 160-1, 174-5
  basement gardens 190, 191
  boundaries 164-5
  Chinese gardens 140-1, 146-7
  choosing plants 178-9
  colours 184-7
  courtyard gardens 188-9
  Five Elements 148-9
  furniture 147, 168
  healthy gardens 176-7
  herb gardens 262-3
  lighting 173
  ornaments 170-1
  paths 162-3
  patios 192-3
  plans 154-7, 158-9
  Planting Times 151
  Plants that Represent the Five Elements 69
  pots 170-1
  roof gardens 190-1
  rural 194-5
  senses 180-3
  shapes 152-3
  statues 172
  structures 147, 169
  Symbolic Bagua 158-9
  terraces 192-3
  Unseen Energies 150-1
  Useful Shapes and Colours for Cornerstones 169
  water 166-7, 196-7
  Yin and Yang 144-5
gas see wind
gastric upsets 292
Gattefosse, René-Maurice 359
gelsemium 301
gems 312, 317, 321, 325
geopathic stress 42, 43
geranium 375

ginger and lemon tea 317
ginseng 277
glass 65
   coloured 75
gliding 340
goal achievement 499
Goat 22-3, 26, 28, 29
   office personalities 248, 251
Golden Rooster Stands on One
   Leg (Left), Squatting Single
   Whip 461-2
Golden Rooster Stands on One
   Leg (Right), Separate Right
   Foot 462-3
grapefruit 377

Greece 309
green 81, 186-7, 229, 320
grief 293
Guided Visit to a Country
House 495

H
Hahnemann, Samuel 281
halls 90
handling 435
hands 362, 386
   arm and hand tonic 349
   hand and foot treatments
      405
   hand charts 423
hangovers 272
Haven 494
hay fever 291
head 402
   head and face exercises 385
   head revitalizer 345
   head to chest 480
headaches
   aromatherapy 368
   Ayurveda 332
   head revitalizer 345
   headache and tension
      reliever 348
   herbalism 272
   reflexology 418
health 6, 10-11
   children 295
   Feng Shui 32
   meridians 380-1
   pets 133
   T'ai Chi 446

women 294, 371, 419
heart 381
heart governor 381
heartburn 330
hedges 164-5
Helpful People 84, 253
hepar sulph 302
herbalism 10, 259, 261, 274-5
   contraindications 269
   herbal preparations 264-5
   herbal recipes 267, 268-73
herbs 177, 275-9
   herb gardens 262-3
holism 6, 10-11, 34, 404
homeopathy 259, 281, 292-3
   Materia Medica 298-305
   remedies 284-5, 287,
      288-97, 299
homes 10, 36-9, 52-3, 88-9
   assessing 86-7
   beneficial positions 54-5
   home offices 126-7
   home study or studio 128-9
   house styles 48-9
   location 40-1
   materials 64-5
   plans 56-7, 252-3
   rural 46-7
   structural details 58-63
   unseen energies 42-3
   urban 44-5
Hong Kong and Shanghai Bank
   201
hop 276
Horse 22-3, 26, 28, 29
   office personalities 248, 251
Hot Desking 241
hotels 256-7
houseplants 68-9
houses
   house styles 48-9
   selling houses 41
   shapes 49
Hoyle, Fred 35
hunger 330
hypericum 276, 302

I
I Ching 16
ignatia 302
immune system 283
   immune system revivers 395
improved self-worth 496
India 10, 307, 308, 309
indigestion 292
infusions
   colours 316, 320, 324
   crystals 317, 321, 325
   oils 265
   orange and elderflower
      infusion 321
inhibition 429
insects 177
insomnia 250

aromatherapy 373
   Ayurveda 332
   herbalism 273
   homeopathy 293
   reflexology 418
instant foot revitalizer 353
instant revitalizer 346
interviews 254-5
intestines 381
intuition 16-17, 35
Inuit 35
investigating your home 86-7
invigorating oils 373
ipecac 300
Iron Fan Penetrates Back, Turn
Body, Chop and Push 464-5
Island of the Immortals 145

J
jasmine 376
jyotishes 312

K
kali bich 302
kidneys 381
kitchens 102-5
   conservatories 120
   offices 219
kneading 341
Knowledge 85

L
lachesis 302
lady's mantle 275
lakes 46-7
Landform School 16
lapis 325

lavender 277, 376
   cold infused oil 268
ledum 302
legs 347, 387
   leg massage 347
   leg over 484
   leg pulls 482
   leg raise 482
   leg revivers 482-3
lemon 377
lemon balm 277
ley lines 42
libido 273
licorice 276
lie down/sit up 483, 485
life force see chi
lifting 440
lighting 70-1
   dining rooms 98
   gardens 173
   living rooms 94
   offices 226-7
limbs 402
lime blossom 279
Lion posture 480
liver 381
living now 499
living rooms 82-7, 121
   lighting 94
lobbies 91
location
   homes 40-9
   offices 204-7
   rural locations 46-7, 194-5
   urban locations 44-5
logos 213
loose twists 475

Lotus 484
Lovelock, James 35
lower back exercises 387
lower back relaxer 352
lunge monkey 438
lungs 381
luo pan 16, 22, 30, 33
lycopodium 303
lying twists 485
Lyme disease 35

M
mag phos 303
Magic Numbers 31, 255
Magic Square 30, 33, 142
Maoris 35
marble 65
Margulis, Lynne 35
marjoram 278, 376
massage 10, 11, 335-7
    abdominal 330, 354, 387
    aromatherapy 362
    basic strokes 340-1
    colleagues 355
    feet 332
    kapha 324
    oils 338, 339
    pitta 320
    preparation 338-9
    sensual 356-7
    sequences 343, 344-57
    vata 316
mastitis 294
Materia Medica 298-305
materials 64-5
    boundaries 164
    courtyard gardens 189
    Materials and the Five
        Elements 65
    offices 223, 229
    paths 163
measurements 235
meditation 10, 30, 32, 119, 425,
    489, 491, 493
    benefits 490
    techniques 494-5
mercurius 303
meridian health 380-1
Metal 20-1
    buildings 205
    gardens 149
    homes 65

interviews 255
    office personalities 249-251
    offices 209
microwaves 73
migraine 332, 368
mint 277, 333
mirrors 9, 66-7
    bathrooms 117-18
    bedrooms 107-8
mobile phones 72, 231, 443
money plant 69
monkey (Alexander technique)
    436-7, 438
Monkey 22-3, 26, 28, 29
    office personalities 248, 251
mood changing recipes 372-3
moonstones 321
motherwort 277
mountains 16-17, 33, 140, 143
mugwort 275
muscular aches 367
muscular tension 268
    abdominal tension relievers
        484-5
    lower back relaxer 352
    neck easer 344
    offices 486-7
    shoulder and neck reliever
        350
    soothing and removing
        tension 480
    tension and backache
relievers 351, 415, 478-9
    tension releasers 414-15

N

natural poise 429
natural world 6, 9, 34, 35
Nature of the Animals 22, 131
nausea 330
neck 384, 402
    neck and shoulder reliever
        350
    neck and shoulder tension
        414
    neck easer 344
    neck twists 486
Needles at Sea Bottom 464
negative attitudes 252
nerve pain 417
nervous exhaustion 270
nervous system calmers
    self-help 390-1
nettle tea 331
numbers
    cars 131
    Energy of Numbers 31
    Magic Numbers 31, 255
    Magic Square 30, 33, 142
    Numbers Game 494
nurseries 110-11
nutrition 32, 78, 100
    Ayurveda 313, 315, 319, 323
nux vomica 305

O
oaks 35
ochre 316
offices 10, 198-203, 214-15,
    242-3
    access 206-7
    Alexander technique 442,

443
    clutter 232-3
    communal areas 240-1
    decoration 228-9
    desks 232-3, 236-7
    Directions 208-11
    electrical equipment 230-1
    energies 244-7
    first impressions 212-13
    furniture 234-5
    home offices 126-7
    Hot Desking 241
    kitchens 219
    layouts 218-19
    lighting 226-7
    location 204-7
    measurements 235
    office personalities 248-51
    open-plan 237, 244, 245
    plans 209, 216-17, 252-3
    reception areas 238-9
    structural details 224-5
    unseen energies 222-3
    Yin and Yang 220-1
    yoga 486-7
oils 309
    aromatherapy 360-1
    burners 363
    essential oils 339, 361, 363,
        372-3, 374-7
    infusions 265
    kapha 324
    massage oils 338
    pitta 320
    vata 316
open wounds 296
orange 81, 187, 324
orange and elderflower infusion
    321
organizers 233
orientation 49
    homes 54
ornaments
    cars 130
    dining rooms 98-9
    gardens 170-1
    living rooms 96-7
Ox 22-3, 24, 28, 29
    office personalities 248, 249

P
Pa Kua see Bagua
paintings 96, 98-9
parks 44
Pasque flower 275
passion flower 278
paths 50-1, 147, 162-3, 194-5
patios 192-3
pelvis 402
peppermint 376
percussion 341
period pains 294, 371
personal development 496-7
personalities in the office

248-51
perspective 145
pests 177
petrissage 340
pets 132-3
Phoenix 16, 17, 143, 206
phosphorus 303
photocopiers 231
phytolacca 304
pictures 96, 98-9
Pig 22-3, 27, 28, 29
    office personalities 248
pine 377
pink 81, 187, 324
Placing Pots and Ornaments
    171
plans
    gardens 154-7, 158-9
    homes 56-7, 252-3
    offices 209, 216-17, 252-3
plants 188-91, 193, 195, 197
    air cleaning 223
    choosing plants 178-9
    colours 184-7
    conservatories 120
    essential oils 375
    healthy gardens 176-7
    homes 64, 68-9
    meanings 141
    moon 151
    offices 231
    Planting Times 151
    Plants that Represent the
Five Elements 69
    scented plants 183
    Yin and Yang 145
plastics 65
Play Guitar, Brush Left Knee
    and Push 455
poison arrows 51, 93, 104, 166,
    201, 234
poisonous plants 176
ponds 166
positive attitudes 252
posture 428-9
    posture clasp 487
    posture enhancers 481
pot-pourri 363
pots 170, 171
pre-menstrual syndrome (PMS)
    294, 371
pregnancy 387
pressure points 381
pressure techniques 341
primary control 428
psycho-physical links 490, 498
pulsatilla 304
Punch Under Elbow 458
puncture wounds 296

Q
Qualities of the Five Elements
    229

R
Rabbit 22-3, 25, 28, 29
    office personalities 248, 250
radiation 43, 72-3, 230-1
radon 43
railways 45
Rat 22-3, 24, 28, 29
rattan 65
reaching 435
reading 442
red 81, 186, 229, 324
reflexology 335, 401, 402
    addresses 501
    basic techniques 405
    benefits 403
    routines 409, 410-21
    treatment 404

warm-up foot massage 406-7
Relationships 84
Relationships of the Five
Elements 20, 48, 229
removing and soothing tension
    480
repetitive strain 415
reproductive problems 419
Rescue Remedy 297
restaurants 219, 257
revitalizers
    foot revitalizer 353
    head revitalizer 345
    instant revitalizer 346
    revitalizing oils 372
rhus tox 304
Ride Tiger 469-70
right time 85
rivers 16-17, 46-7, 197
roads 45, 47, 206-7
rocks in gardens 146, 166
Roll Back, Press and Push 452
Roll Back, Press and Push:
    Single Whip 458
roll twist 485
roof gardens 190-1
rooms, position 54-5
Rooster 22-3, 27, 28, 29
    office personalities 248
rose oil 360, 377
rosemary 278, 376
Ross, Ernest 420
rural locations 46-7, 194-5
ruta 304

S
SAD (Seasonal Affective
    Disorder) 70
safety 340, 387
sage 278
sandalwood 375
scent 360
    scented plants 183
    scented rooms 363
Schussler, Wilhelm 284
seasonal plants 178, 179
seasons 310, 311
seated Cat stretch 486
seating
    dining rooms 101
    living rooms 92-3
self-defence 446
self-worth 496
selling houses 41
semi-supine position 433
semicircle rotation 480
senses 74-9, 180-3
    cars 131
    nurseries 110-11
sensual massage 356-7
sensual oils 373
Separate Left Foot, Brush Left
    Knee and Push 463-4
sepia 304
shade plants 188
shake 475
shapes
    gardens 150-1
    houses 49
shiatsu 8, 335, 379, 380-1
    treatments 383, 384-99

shock 369
shoulders 386
    shoulder and neck reliever
        350
    shoulder and neck tension
        414
    shoulder release 487
    shoulder stretch 487
    shrugging shoulders 474
Sick Building Syndrome 222
side bends 485
side leg raise 482
sideways bend 475
sideways neck stretch 480
sight 74, 131, 180
signs, offices 213
silica 304
silver 186
simple twist 478
Single Whip 453-4
sinuses 420
sisal matting 65
sit up/lie down 483, 485
sitting 434
skin problems 333
skullcap 278
slanting walls 59
sleep 250
    aromatherapy 373
    Ayurveda 332
    herbalism 273
    homeopathy 293
    reflexology 418
slouch stress 479
smell 79, 183
Snake 22-3, 25, 28, 29

office personalities 248, 250-1
sofas 90-1
soil 150-1
solar year dates 31
soothing and removing tension 480
sore throats 289, 420
sores 296
sounds 76, 111, 181, 491
spiced yogi tea 325
spine 402
spirit of place 151
spleen 381
spongia 305
sprains 296
squats 474
squatting 438, 439
Squatting Single Whip Step Forward for Seven Stars 469
St John's wort 276, 302
staff rooms 240-1
staircases 91, 219, 225, 240
standing 434
stationery 212
steam inhalations 363
Step Back to Repulse the Monkey (Right) Diagonal Flying 459-60
Step Back to Repulse the Monkey 459
Step Forward, Deflect Downwards, Intercept and Punch, Kick with Heel 465
Step Forward, Deflect, Intercept and Punch 455-6
stereos 95

stings 297
stomach 381
stomach upsets 292
stone 65
storage in offices 232, 234-5
stoves 102
strains 296
streams 42, 150
stress 10, 11, 133
stress 259, 359
    aromatherapy 366
    massage 355
    relieving general stress 416
    shiatsu 380
    stress reduction 498
    system calmers 388-9, 390-1
stretches
    arm and back stretch 487
    arm and chest stretch 487
    arm stretching 475
    back stretch 487
    calf stretch 486
    Cat stretch 475, 483
    forearm stretch 487
    seated Cat stretch 486
    shoulder stretch 497
    sideways neck stretch 480
studies 128-9
studios 128-9
suburbs 44
sun 151
swimming pools 124-5
Symbolic Bagua 32-3, 84-5
Symbolic Chinese Animals 133
symphytum 305
syrups 265
system calmers self-help 390-1

system calmers with a partner 388-9

T
T'ai Chi 19, 29, 70, 425, 445, 446
    addresses 501
    attention, preparation and beginning 450
    sequences 449-71
    warm-ups 447
tables
    dining rooms 99-100
    gardens 168
    meeting rooms 241
Tan Tien 446
Taoism 6, 18, 30, 35, 445
taste 78, 100, 182-3
Tastes and the Elements 100
teas 264, 270, 271, 272, 273, 331
    fresh ginger and lemon 317
    spiced yogi tea 325
teenagers 114-15
teething 295
telephones 72, 109, 212, 231
television 72, 95, 112
templates, Bagua 32-3
tension
    abdominal tension relievers 484-5
    lower back relaxer 352
    neck easer 344
    offices 486-7
    shoulder and neck reliever 350
    soothing and removing tension 480
    tense abdomen reliever 354
    tense neck easer 344
    tension and backache relievers 351, 478-9
    tension releasers 414-15
    tension relievers 398-9
terraces 192-3
Three Gates Bagua 33
Tiger 22-3, 24, 28, 29
    Four Animal Formation 16, 17, 143, 206
    office personalities 248, 249-50
tinctures 265

tiptoes 435
tired leg revivers 482-3
tissue salts 284
toilets 116-17, 219
tonics
    aching legs 347
    kapha 325
    pitta 321
    vata 317
toothache 289, 417
torso 402
Tortoise 16, 17, 143, 206
touch 77, 111, 182, 491
Transcendental Meditation 491
transport networks 206-7
travel 256-7
travel sickness 297, 370
trees 35, 141, 147, 179
triangle 479
triple heater 381
tsubo 381
twenty-minute rule 420
twists
    bending twist 479
    full twist 478
    loose twists 475
    lying twists 485
    neck twists 486
    roll twist 485
    simple twist 478

U
underground water 42, 152
unseen energies 42-3, 150-1, 222-3
uplifting oils 372
urban environment 44-5
urinary infections 333
use of the eyes 432
Useful Shapes and Colours for Cornerstones 169

V
valerian 279, 305
vegetable gardens 195
verbascum 305
vervain 279
vibrations 20, 83, 223
viburnum opulus 305
vikruti 307, 312
violet 320
vision 74, 131, 180
Visit to a Country House 495
    visualization 497

W
walls
    plants 188
    slanting 59
Ward Off Left 451
Ward Off Left, Ward Off Right, Roll Back, Press and Push, Single Whip 468
Ward Off Right 451

Ward Off Right, Roll back, Press and Push 466-7
warm-up foot massage 406-7
Water 20-1
  bathrooms 116
  buildings 205
  gardens 146, 149, 195, 166-7 196-7
  interviews 255
  office personalities 249-51
  offices 209
  rivers and lakes 46-7, 197
  swimming pools 124-5
  underground 42, 150
  Water Dragon Classic 17, 167
Waving Hands in Clouds (Left, Right, Left), the Whip 461
Waving Hands in Clouds (Right, Left, Right) 460
Wealth 84, 253
  wealth and frogs 132
West Group 31, 57
Where to Sit 156
white 81, 186, 229
White Crane Sreads Wings and Push 454-5
wildlife in gardens 166
wind 269, 330
wind chimes 10, 76
window-boxes 122-3
windows 63
Withdraw and Push, Crossing Hands 456-7
Withdraw and Push, Crossing Hands 471
women's health 294, 371, 419
Wood 20-1
  buildings 205
  gardens 148, 149
  homes 65
  interviews 255
  office personalities 249-51
  offices 209
wood betony 278
Worst and Best Directions 55, 209, 255

Y
years
  Animal rulers 29
  Directions 210
yellow 81, 186, 229, 316

Yin and Yang 7, 18-19, 70, 144-5, 208, 220-1
  T'ai Chi 446
  Yin and Yang Offices 221
ylang ylang 375
yoga 309, 310, 425, 473
  addresses 501
  movements 477-87
  warm-ups 474-5
yogi tea 325

Z
Zodiac see astrology

INDEX OF TABLES

A
Animals
  Chinese Animals Table 23
  Four Animals Formation 16, 17, 143, 206
  Nature of the Animals 22, 131
  Symbolic Chinese Animals 133
Assessing a Location 41
Auspicious Measurements 235

B
Bagua 30, 209
  Bagua and Desks 127
  Bagua and Family Seating 101
  Three Gates Bagua 33
Bed Directions 250
Best and Worst Directions 55, 209, 255
Boundaries and the Five Elements 49
Building Positions 17
Buildings and the Five Elements 255
Businesses and the Five Elements 255

C
Chinese Animals Table 23
Colours 28, 248
  Useful Shapes and Colours for Cornerstones 169

D
Directions 56, 155
  Bed Directions 250
  Best and Worst Directions 55, 209, 255
  Favored Months and Directions 211
E
Energy of Numbers 31

F
Favored Months and Directions 211
Five Elements 31, 255
  Boundaries and the Five Elements 49

  Buildings and the Five Elements 255
  Businesses and the Five Elements 255
  Five Elements Features in the Garden 149
  Materials and the Five Elements 65
  Plants that Represent the Five Elements 69
  Qualities of the Five Elements 229
  Relationships of the Five Elements 20, 48, 229
  Tastes and the Elements 100
Four Animals Formation 16, 17, 143, 206

M
Magic Numbers 31, 255
Magic Square 30
Materials and the Five Elements 65

N
Nature of the Animals 22, 131
Numbers
  Energy of Numbers 31
  Magic Numbers 31, 255

P
Pa Kua see Bagua
Placing Pots and Ornaments 171
Planting Times 151
Plants that Represent the Five Elements 69

Q
Qualities of the Five Elements 229

R
Relationships of the Five Elements 20, 48, 229

S
Symbolic Chinese Animals 133

T
Tastes and the Elements 100
Three Gates Bagua 33

U
Useful Shapes and Colours for Cornerstones 169
W
Where to Sit 156

Y
Yin and Yang 19, 145
Yin and Yang Offices 221

PICTURE ACKNOWLEDGEMENTS

The publishers would like to thank the following picture libraries for the use of their pictures.

Abode UK: 107br; 114t; 115tl. A-Z Botanical Collection ltd.: 47br(Mike Vardy); 140tr(Jean Deval), br(Robert Murray); 152t (Bjorn Svensson); 166br(Margaret Higginson); 188tr(J. Whitworth); 197tr(A. Stenning), b(J. Whitworth). 275bl; 287tr; 292 bl; 300bl; 301 bl, br; 302br; 303tl; 305tm; 492ml. Bruce Coleman: 133m(Werner Layer); 135bl; 136r(Paul van Gaalen), m (Stefano Amantini); 141r; 147bl(Dr.Stephen Coyne), Bruce Coleman Collection: 302bm; 303TM; 304bm.

Frank Lane Photographic Agency: 279bm.

The Garden Picture Library: 47bl(Morley Read); 138-9(Ron Sutherland); 141tl(Erika Craddock); 143tr(Erika Craddock), bl(Juliette Wade), br(Erika Craddock); 144tr (Ron Sutherland), bl(Ron Sutherland); 145tr; 146tr(John Glover); 156tr(Eric Crichton); 160-61; 164bl; 167br(Steven Wooster); 173tl(Ron Sutherland), bl(Sunniva Harte), br(John Glover); 184bl(Jaqui Hurst); 190tl(Ron Sutherland), r(Linda Burgess); 191tr(Linda Burgess), m(Vaughan Fleming); 196tr(Steven Wooster), 276bl, tr; 278tm; 279br; 303bl; 375bm, br, tr; 376tr, tm.

Garden & Wildlife Matters: 278tl; 299bm 376tl, tm, bm, br; 499tr.

Robert Harding Picture Library: 111tl(IPC Magazines); 113tl(IPC Magazines); 114b(IPD Magazines); 115bl(IPC Magazines). Holt Studios Int.: 135bl; 141br(Willem Harinck); 147tr(MichaelMayer); 164tr(Alan & Linda Detrick); 166bl(Primrose Peacock); 167tl(Bob Gibbons). Houses and Interiors: 46tr(Roger Brooks); 54bl(Roger Brooks), tr (Roger Brooks); 58tr(Mark Bolton); 59bl(Mark Bolton); 62tr(Roger Brooks); 91l(Verne); 94bl(Mark Bolton); 96tr; 120tr(Mark Bolton), bl(Mark Bolton); 92tr(Roger Brooks), bl(Roger Brooks); 193tr(Roger Brooks); 253tr(Mark Bolton).

The Hutchinson Library: 14br (Robert Francis); 16tr(Merilyn Thorold); 19tr(Melanie Friend); 32bl(T. Moser), br(Lesley Nelson); 33tl(F. Horner); 34t(Edward Parker), bl (Sarah Errington), r(John G Egan); 35bl(Tony Souter); 40tr (Pern.), r(P. W. Rippon), bl(Robert Francis); 41tl(Tony Souter), bl (Carlos Freire), tr(G. Griffiths- Jones); 48t; 49tl (Phillip Wolmuth), t (L.Taylor), t, m, br(Andrew Sole); 94b(Sarah Murray); 75tl(Lesley Nelson); 77t(N. Durrell McKenna); 126bl(Nancy Durrell); 130tl(Tony Souter), br(Robert Francis); 131bl (Robert Francis); 142br(Hatt); 150bl (Tony souter); 101tr(Christine Pemberton); 204tr(Robert Aberman); 206(Leslie Woodhead)t; 207tl(Sarah Murray), m(Robert Francis), b(Tim Motion); 210bl (Robert Aberman); 211bl(Sarah Murray), br(Robert Francis); 212tl (Tim Motion); 213br(Robert Francis); 212bl(Juliet Highet); 224l (Robert Francis); 232m(Jeremy A. Horner).

Images Colour Library: 17b; 18b; 19bl, bl; 20tr; 21 no. 2, no. 5; 31br; 35tr; 140bl; 142t; 149; 160r; 151bl; 209; 254t, bl, br, 314b

The Interior Archive: 14tl (Schulenburg); 15tr(Schulenburg); 60tr(Schulenburg); 54r(C. Simon Sykes); 62bl(Schulenburg); 61t (Schulenburg); 73tr (Henry Wilson); 80 (Schulenburg); 82tr (Schulenburg); 83tl (Schulenburg); 86bl (Schulenburg), t(Simon Upton); 90bl (Schulenburg); 92b (Schulenburg); 93tr (Schulenburg); 95bl (Schulenburg); 96br(Henry Wilson); 98t(Tim Beddow); 100bl (Schulenburg); 103r (Schulenburg); 106tr(Schulenburg),b(Schulenburg); 108l (Schulen-burg); 111tr

(Schulenburg);112bl (Schulenburg); 116tr(Henry Wilson), bl (Schulenburg); 117bl(Schulenburg), br (Schulenburg); 119tl (Schulen-burg), br(Schulenburg); 125tl; 128br (Schulenburg); 129tr(Schulenburg); 235tr (Schulenburg).

Peter McHoy: 165tl; 172tr; 180bl; 181tl; 186tl; 191tl.

Don Morley: 130tr, bl; 131bl, tr.

The Stock Market: 20br; 121no. 1(K. Biggs); 42tr, bl, br; 43b, t; 44tl, m; 45tl; 72t(David Lawrence); 72br; 73tl, tr; 74t; 121b; 149; 150tr; 151bl; 198bl; 199br; 200bl; 207tr; 209bl(B. Simmons); 210t; 212r; 221tr; 223tr; 235r; 245br; 247br(Jon Feingersh); 252m; 255bl; 256br.

Tony Stone: 72b(Angus M. Mackillop); 231br(Laurence Monneret); 233tr(Tim Flach); 237br (Robert Mort); 245r(Bruce Ayres); 247tr(Tim Flach); 252tr(Jon Gray); 255tr(Dan Bosler); 256tr(Peter Correz), bl(David Hanover); 257t (Christopher Bissell). Jessica Strang: 126r; 129bl; 218br; 219tl, bl; 220r; 223l; 226br; 234tl, tr, br; 239l; 241tr, bl, br; 253br; 275bl; 308t, b, 311b; 312b; 318b; 322b; 490bl; 491bl; 493tr; 494tl, br; 495tl, br; 496bl; 497t; 499bl.

Harry Smith Collection: 293bl; 301tm; 304tl, tr; 305bm.

Superstock: 28tr, m; 29br.

View: 15m(Phillip Bier); 21no.1 (Dennis Gilbert); 49tr(Phillip Bier); 51l(Chris Gascoigne); 60tr(Phillip Bier), br(Phillip Bier); 61bl(Phillip Bier); 71tr(Peter Cook); 94tr(Phillip Bier); 100bl(Peter Cook); 102tr (Chris Gascoigne); 105tl(Phillip Bier); 121tl(PhillipBier); 126t(Chris Gascoigne); 127l(Peter Cook); 149; 198m; 199bl, tl); 200t(Chris Gascoigne), r(Chris Gascoigne); 200-201(Peter Cook); 204b(Dennis Gilbert); 205tr(Peter Cook), br (Chris Gascoigne); 206b(Dennis Gilbert); 208t, b(Peter Cook); 209tr (Chris Gascoigne); 213m(Dennis Gilbert),bl(Dennis Gilbert); 216bl (Chris Gascoigne); 217tr(Peter Cook);218tr(Dennis Gilbert); 220br (Chris Gascoigne); 221r(Peter Cook), br(Peter Romaniuk); 222tr (Chris Gascoigne), tl(Peter Cook), b(Dennis Gilbert); 224tl(Chris Gascoigne), bl(Peter Cook), br(Dennis Gilbert); 225tl(Dennis Gilbert), l(Chris Gascoigne), bl(Chris Gascoigne), tr(Chris Gascoigne); 226tl(Nick Hufton), tr(Peter Cook); 227r(Chris Gascoigne), bl(Chris Gascoigne); 228tr(Chris Gascoigne), br(Chris Gascoigne); 229bl(Nick Hufton), tr(Chris Gascoigne); 230tr(Chris Gascoigne), bl(Dennis Gilbert), br(Peter Cook); 231t(Nick Hufton), l(Chris Gascoigne); 232t(Nick Hufton), bl(Nick Hufton), br(Peter Cook); 233r(Chris Gascoigne), bl(Peter Cook); 234tl(Chris Gascoigne); 235b(Peter Cook); 236t(Nick Hufton), bl(Peter Cook), br(Chris Gascoigne); 237tr(Chris Gascoigne); 238t(Chris Gascoigne); 239tl(Chris Gascoigne); 240tl(Dennis Gilbert), m(Chris Gascoigne), br(Chris Gascoigne); 241l(Chris Gascoigne); 242-43; 244tl(Chris Gascoigne), br(Chris Gascoigne); 245tl(Peter Cook), bl(Chris Gascoigne); 246t(Peter Cook), b(Dennis Gilbert); 252bl(Chris Gascoigne); 257m(Peter Cook), b(Peter Cook); 260t. Elizabeth Whiting Associates: 48m; 49m, tr; 50br; 54r; 66tr, bl; 67tr; 70bl; 75r, br; 76bl, l; 83tr; 90t; 95t; 96tr; 99tl; 108br; 122tr; 123r, bl; 124t; 125tr, bl; 198t; 214-15; 219tr; 220tl; 227t; 228bl, b; 238bl, br; 239b.